International Law and Economics

The world has been experiencing a long period of globalization. At the same time, ever more international law has been created to deal with the many consequences of globalization such as problems of coordination, spillover effects across countries, the protection of foreign direct investment or the prosecution of crimes against humanity. To date, the economic analysis of international law has been lagging behind this development. This series aims at changing this by contributing to the understanding of international law. It strives to be a forum for contributions on all aspects of the economic analysis of international law ranging from the analysis of the genesis of international law, its ratification, its effects on government behavior, the means to monitor compliance to sanctions against actors not complying with the law.

Sergio Mittlaender

Equity, Efficiency, and Ethics in Remedies for Breach of Contract

Theory and Experimental Evidence

Springer

Sergio Mittlaender
Fundação Getulio Vargas Law School
in São Paulo (FGV Direito SP)
São Paulo, Brazil

Max Planck Institute for Social Law
and Social Policy
Munich, Germany

ISSN 2364-1851 ISSN 2364-186X (electronic)
International Law and Economics
ISBN 978-3-031-10803-7 ISBN 978-3-031-10804-4 (eBook)
https://doi.org/10.1007/978-3-031-10804-4

This Springer imprint is published by the registered company Springer Nature Switzerland AG
The registered company address is: Gewerbestrasse 11, 6330 Cham, Switzerland

To my parents,
for everything.

Foreword

Do the Victims of Breach of Contract Want Vengeance?

Should a court punish someone for choosing to break a contract? After centuries of legal development and decades of scholarship on the subject, one would think that this fundamental question about contract law had been answered. And yet, scholars continue to struggle to identify the appropriate remedy for breach of contract. On one side of the debate, scholars like Charles Fried and Seana Shiffrin assert that a contractual obligation carries with it a moral promise that one will perform.[1] Intentional torts produce punitive damages, so why should the intentional breach of contract be any different? On the other side stand the law-and-economics scholars, who worry that punitive measures would discourage parties from efficiently re-allocating rights when events develop in a way different than parties expect, from breaching whenever breach is socially efficient, or even discourage parties from entering into contracts in the first place.

Despite the scholarly debate, the law on the subject is completely clear. Except for acts of fraud and a few other isolated exceptions, parties are not penalized with punitive damages for breach of contract. Over a century ago, Oliver Wendel Holmes stated that "the duty to keep a contract at common law means a prediction that you must pay damages if you do not keep it,—and nothing else."[2] His assertion accurately describes the state of the law then and the state of the law today.

Legal realities, however, have not stopped academic debate. And for good reason. Those who argue that contract has a moral dimension have two points in their favor. First, many contracting parties behave as if their contractual promise has a moral dimension. Parties frequently honor their contractual obligations even though they might be better off breaching and paying damages. Furthermore, these scholars have intuition on their side. Extensive research by Tess Wilkinson-Ryan and David

---

[1] Charles Fried, Contract as Promise: A Theory of Contractual Obligation (1981); Seana Shiffrin, The Divergence between Contract and Promise, 120 Harv. L. Rev. 708 (2007).

[2] Oliver W. Holmes, The Path of the Law, 10 Harv. L. Rev. 457, 462 (1897), reprinted in 110 Harv. L. Rev. 991, 996 (1996–1997).

Hoffman shows that people treat breaches of contracts as immoral.[3] For example, people who are the victims of breach see themselves as "suckers" who foolishly trusted another party. This reaction is hard to explain if performing a contract is simply an economic choice. Furthermore, victims of breach assess the context surrounding a breach in ways that an economic approach cannot easily explain. For example, people are more apt to breach to avoid incurring a loss than to obtain an extraordinary gain. They also perceive breach to avoid incurring a loss as less morally reprehensible than breach to obtain higher profits,[4] and react accordingly.[5] To many parties, contracts feel like a moral obligation. For those who argue that contracts have a moral component, the law is simply deficient.

Enter Sergio Mittlaender into the debate. Mittlaender's perspective is clearly rooted in economics. His analysis of appropriate contract remedies is relentlessly utilitarian. He does not, however, cling to the conventional approach. One of the primary contributions of this book is his blending of behavioral economics—primarily behavioral game theory—into the economic analysis of remedies. As he properly notes, one of the core findings of behavioral game theory is that people punish deviations from prosocial norms. For example, in ultimatum games, in which one party may propose a split of a sum of money in a take-it-or-leave it fashion to a partner, the partner will commonly reject any proposal that offers them less than half of the value of the good.[6] They do this even though rejecting a proposal means they sacrifice their own offer. Similarly, in stylized behavioral economics games, people are willing to incur costs to themselves to reduce the gains that other players obtain by defecting from a cooperative norm.[7] Behavioral economists have concluded that people actually enjoy punishing wrongdoers.

This observation would seem to support the scholars who argue that breach of contract has a moral component. After all, when someone fails to perform a contract, they have defected from a norm of cooperating with their contracting partner. The research from behavioral economic demonstrates that people want to punish such defections. People's intuitions thus seem to be in line with the arguments Charles Fried and Seana Shiffrin make about the morality of contracts.

Sergio Mittlaender, however, stands this argument on its head. He argues that the desire of victims of breach to punish those who breach contracts is inefficient, or at least socially costly. In contrast, conventional, expectancy damages for breach of contract are efficient in two different dimensions. Mittlaender contends that contract damages not only incentivize promisors to perform if and only if performance is

---

[3] Tess Wilkinson-Ryan & David Hoffman, Breach is for Suckers, 63 Vand. L. Rev. 1003 (2010).

[4] Tess Wilkinson-Ryan & Jonathan Baron, Moral Judgment and Moral Heuristics in Breach of Contract, 6 J. Empirical Legal Stud. 405 (2009); Sergio Mittlaender, Morality, Compensation, and the Contractual Obligation, 16 J. Empirical Legal Stud. 119 (2019).

[5] Sergio Mittlaender & Vincent Buskens, Retaliation, Remedies, and Contracts, 21 Am. Law & Econ. Rev. 280 (2019).

[6] Werner Güth, Rolf Schmittberger & Bernd Schwarze, An Experimental Analysis of Ultimatum Bargaining, 3 J. Econ. Behav. & Organ. 367 (1982).

[7] Ernst Fehr & Simon Gächter, Cooperation and Punishment in Public Goods Experiments, 90 Am. Econ. Rev. 980 (2000).

socially efficient, but they can also satisfy the victim's desire to punish. He argues that legal remedies can displace, or "crowd out" the desire to extract revenge on the breaching party.

Although it is possible that Mittlaender is right, the victims might correctly perceive the conventional contract remedy as no punishment at all. As the proponents of the moral theory of contracting argue, conventional damages sometimes reward breaching parties. When a party refuses to deliver a good or service to someone it was promised to, they are free to sell it to someone else at a higher price, pay the damages, and be better off. Why should the victim of breach be satisfied with simply being compensated? And yet, as Mittlaender shows in a series of experiments, the conventional remedy appears to assuage the victims of breach. People who find themselves the victims of breach in Mittlaender's experiments decline to punish when a conventional, compensatory remedy is available.

Sergio Mittlaender's theory and data thus show that both sides of the debate have it right. The moral theorists correctly identify a strong component of morality in contractual obligation. In Mittlaender's theory, victims feel aggrieved because, among other reasons he identifies in this book, they often perceive the act of breach as morally reprehensible, and retaliate against the wrongdoer accordingly. But the economics theorists also have it right that the conventional remedy is an adequate response in the face of breach. As Mittlaender shows, not only does the remedy deter inefficient breaches, but it also avoids a loss of welfare by reducing costly forms of retaliation by victims. Although there is much to be said for the moralists' theories, victims of breach seem satisfied with compensation and do not harbor further latent desires for vengeance. To paraphrase the classic film, "The Godfather," contract is not "personal," it is "just business" after all.

Jeffrey J. Rachlinski
Henry Allen Mark Professor of Law
Cornell Law School
Ithaca, US

Acknowledgements

First and foremost, I want to express my since gratitude to my promoters Vincent Buskens and Jeffrey Rachlinski, as well as to Ann-Sophie Vandenberghe. I have been amazingly fortunate to have promoters who gave me the freedom to explore on my own and at the same time the guidance to recover when my steps faltered. During the most difficult times when writing this thesis, they gave me the moral support and the freedom I needed to move on.

I am very thankful to Vincent for encouraging the use of correct grammar and consistent notation in my writings and for carefully reading and commenting on countless revisions of this manuscript. Independent of whether the subject matter was moral philosophy, jurisprudence, contract law, neurocognitive psychology, game theory, experimental economics, econometrics, or comparative law, Vincent was always there to read lengthy texts and to provide precise suggestions for improvements.

I am especially thankful to Jeff for advocating the use of straightforward syntax and simple language in my texts and for ingeniously bringing whole arguments and sections back on track when they seemed not to advance the thesis. In any of the subjects mentioned above, Jeff was always there to listen patiently to my ideas and thoughts, and to grasp the whole picture that I was so often unable to see.

Moreover, I am thankful to Ann-Sophie for defending existing theories against any accusation of incompleteness and thereby reminding me that different explanations exist and must be confronted, independent of how unpersuasive or implausible they may sound to the lawyer or economist. Our meetings often ended in long checklists of points to be tackled in my writings, and from which this thesis benefited.

The road to my graduate degree has been long and winding, so I would also like to thank some people from the early days in Brazil and Germany. My former promoters of my bachelor thesis in law, Celso Campilongo, and in economics, Zilton Macedo, guided my first investigations in law and economics and taught me how to develop independent research. My former promoters of my master thesis in law, Joseph Drexl, and in economics, Ekkerhart Schlicht, advised me in my supervening theses and taught me how to produce more mature research.

Paulo Arvate has been an instructor, mentor, friend, and co-author since my first courses in Macroeconomics and Economics of the Public Sector. Paola Bertoli has supported me and listened about my research in all these years. Marianne Breijer has promptly helped me whenever I needed. Without their support, encouragement, and solicitude, this thesis would not have benefited from the fresh air and open mindedness I needed for its writing.

I would also like to thank those who contributed to this project in the European Doctorate in Law and Economics, and in the several conferences, summer schools, and seminars I participated.

There is no point in trying to express gratitude to my mother and my father for their role in every step I take, for I am not a poet. It is not about reciprocity, morality, or fairness, but rather something else I cannot explain. And expressing what cannot be explained is outside the scope of this book.

List of Legal Materials Cited

Institutes of Gaius (*Gaii Institutiones*) (ca. 170 A.D.)
Corpus Iuris Civilis (Institutiones Iustiniani, Digesta Iustiniani) (529–534)
Restatement (First) of Contracts (1932)
Uniform Commercial Code (1952) [UCC]
Restatement (Second) of Agency (1958)
Restatement (Second) of Torts (1965–1979)
Restatement (Second) of Contracts (1981)
German Constitution (*Grundgesetz*) (1949) [GG]
German Civil Code (*Bürgerliches Gesetzbuch*) (1900) [BGB]
German Code of Civil Procedure (*Zivilprozessordnung*) (2005) [ZPO]
French Civil Code (*Code Civil*) (1804)
Law n. 91–650 of 9 July 1991
Decree n. 92–755 of 31 July 1992
Law n. 92–644 of 13 July 1992
Italian Civil Code (*Codice Civile*) (1942)
Dutch Civil Code (*Burgerlijk Wetboek*) (1838/1992)

American Case Law

Kirksey v. Kirksey, 8 Ala. 131 (1845)
Jaquith v. Hudson, 5 Mich. 123 (1858)
Ricketts v. Scothorn, 57 Neb. 51, 77 N.W. 365 (1898)
Hotchkiss v. National City Bank, 200 F. 287 (S.D.N.Y. 1911)
Shubert Theatrical Co. v. Rath, 271 F. 827 (2d. Cir. 1921)
Hawkins v. McGee, 84 N.H. 114, 146 A. 641 (1929)
Mission Indep. School Dist. v. Diserens, 188 S.W. 2d 568 (Tex. 1945)
Johnson & Johnson v. Charmley Drug Co., 95 A.2d 391 (N.J. 1953)
Hoffman v. Red Owl Stores, 26 Wis.2d 683, 133 N.W.2d. 267 (1965)
Snepp v. United States, 445 U.S. 507 (1980)
United States Naval Inst. v. Charter Communications, 936 F.2d 692 (2d Cir. 1991)
Gibbs v. Citicorp Mortgage, Inc., 246 Neb. 355, 518 N.W.2d 910 (Neb. 1994)
Perkins v. Regional Transp. Dist., 907 P.2d 672 (Colo. App. 1995)
S.A. Healy Co. v. Milwaukee Metropolitan Sewage District, 50 F.3d 476 (7th Cir. 1995)
Haslund v. Simon Property Group, Inc., 378 F.3d 653 (7th Cir. 2004)
Petruska v. Gannon University, 462 F.3d 294 (3d Cir. 2006)

British Case Law

Robinson v. Harman 1 Exch. 850, per Baron Parke (1848)
Lumley v. Wagner, 42 Eng. Rep. 687 (Chap. 1852)
Wertheim (Sally) v. Chicoutimi Pulp Co. A.C. 301, per Lord Atkinson (P.C.) (1911)
Wrotham Park Estate Co Ltd v. Parkside Homes Ltd, 1 W.L.R. 798 (CH) (1974)
Sotiros Shipping Inc. v. Samiet Solhot (The Solhot), 1 Lloyd's Rep. 605 (CA) (1983)
Attorney General v. Blake, UKHL 45 (2000), 1 A.C. 268 (2001)
Experience Hendrix LLC v. PPX Enterprise Inc., EWCA Civ 323 (2003), 1 All E.R. (Comm) 830 (CA)
WWF v. World Wrestling Federation Entertainment Inc., EWCA Civ 286 (2007), 1. W.L.R. 445 (2008)
Pell Frischmann Engineering Ltd v. Bow Valley Iran Ltd., UKPC 45 (2009), B.L.R. 73 (2010)
Giedo van der Garde BV v. Force India Formula One Team Ltd., EWHC 2373 (QB) (2010)
Abbar v. Saudi Economic & Development Co. (SEDCO) Real Estate Ltd., EWHC 1414 (CH) (2013)

Contents

Chapter 1
Introduction

> "There is more than one purpose underlying the rules of law that provide for the giving of damages for breach of contract. One of the ends to be obtained is, without doubt, the keeping of the peace. The party injured by the breach has a sense of grievance. In the absence of a public remedy, he would do his best to redress his own wrong. This means private war, with all of the resulting harm that it entails to the interest of other people. A second purpose in the giving of damages, however, one that is equally important as the first, is the prevention of similar harms in the future. The fact that damages must be paid tends directly to the prevention of breaches of contract." (Arthur L. Corbin)[1]

Compensation is the fundamental principle in the law of remedies for breach of contract, providing the normative basis for the key doctrines that specify the legal consequences of breach.[2] Accordingly, expectation damages and specific performance are the default remedies for breach of contract in common law and

---

[1] 5 ARTHUR L. CORBIN, A COMPREHENSIVE TREATISE ON THE RULES OF CONTRACT LAW 30–31 § 1002 (1st ed. 1951).

[2] *See* 1 WILLIAM BLACKSTONE, COMMENTARIES ON THE LAWS OF ENGLAND IN FOUR BOOKS, book 2, ch. 23, 226–227 (George Sharswood ed., Philadelphia, J. B. Lippincott 1893) (1765–1769) ("upon all contracts or promises, … just as for all infringements of the natural or relative rights of another, the law gives redress by action against the wrongdoer by an action to recover the damage sustained."); 1 THEODORE SEDGWICK, A TREATISE ON THE MEASURE OF DAMAGES 34 (1847) (Arthur Sedgwick & G. Willet van Nest eds., 7th ed. New York, Baker, Voorhuis & Co. 1880) ("in all cases of civil injury, or breach of contract … the declared object is to give compensation to the party injured", and cmt. a: "[t]he general principle undoubtedly at common law, both in actions for breach of contract and (…), is to give compensation for pecuniary injury"); WILLIAM ANSTON, PRINCIPLES OF THE ENGLISH LAW OF CONTRACTS AND OF AGENCY IN ITS RELATION TO CONTRACT 377 § 3 (Ernst W. Huffcut editor, 8th ed., New York, Banks Law Publishing 1899) ("Damages for breach of contract are by way of compensation"); 3 SAMUEL WILLISTON, THE LAW OF CONTRACTS 2392–2393 (1st ed. New York, Baker, Voorhuis & Co. 1920) ("§1338. Compensation is the fundamental principle. In fixing the amount of these damages [for breach of contract], the general purpose of the law is, *and should be*, to give compensation") (own emphasis); Max Radin, *Fundamental Concepts of the Roman Law*, 12 CALIFORNIA LAW REVIEW 481, 485 (1924) ("At the Common law, the nature of the obligation created by a wrongful act is in general undisputed. The purpose is compensation. The victim is to be made whole. Since this is also the theory of damages in breach of contract…"); E. Allan Farnsworth, *Legal Remedies for Breach of Contract*, 70 COLUMBIA LAW REVIEW 1145, 1147 (1970); E. ALLAN FARNSWORTH, CONTRACTS 757 § 12.8 (4th ed. New York, Aspen 2004) ("The basic principle for the measurement of those damages [for breach of contract] is that of compensation based on the injured party's expectation") [hereinafter FARNSWORTH ON CONTRACTS].

S. Mittlaender, *Equity, Efficiency, and Ethics in Remedies for Breach of Contract*, International Law and Economics, https://doi.org/10.1007/978-3-031-10804-4_1

civil law systems, ensuring that parties to a contract receive the benefit of their bargain (the value of the promised thing or act) or performance as promised (the promised thing or act), respectively.[3] In both cases, the promisee is put in a position as good as the one in which she would have been had the promisor performed by

---

The centrality of the principle of compensation in the law of remedies for breach of contract has been widely recognized in the Economic Analysis of Law. *Cf.* Charles Goetz & Robert Scott, *Liquidated Damages, Penalties and the Just Compensation Principle: Some Notes on an Enforcement Model and a Theory of Efficient Breach,* 77 COLUMBIA LAW REVIEW 554, 558 (1977) ("it is clear that the central purpose of contract damages is compensatory and not punitive"); Charles Goetz, *Enforcing Promises: An Examination of the Basis of Contract,* 89 YALE LAW JOURNAL 1261, 1297 (1980) ("Full enforcement compensation is the standard recovery for breach of reciprocal-bargain promises, whenever such an award can be determined accurately."); Robert Cooter & Melvin Eisenberg, *Damages for Breach of Contract,* 73 CALIFORNIA LAW REVIEW 1434, 1434 (1985) ("the goal, compensation, and the means, expectation damages, are so ingrained in contract law as to seem self-evident."); Melvin Eisenberg, *Actual and Virtual Specific Performance, the Theory of Efficient Breach, and the Indifference Principle in Contract Law,* 93 CALIFORNIA LAW REVIEW 975, 979 (2005) ("The traditional objective of remedies in most areas of private law is to compensate a wrongfully injured party for the effects of the injury by restoring him to the position he was in before he interacted with the wrongdoer.").

[3] At the common law, the default remedy for breach of contract is a monetary award, or *substitutive relief*, and its explicit purpose is to compensate the promisee by putting her in the position she would have been in if the promisor had performed. This is achieved by measuring damages according to the expectation measure, and thereby ensuring promisees the benefit of the bargain. *See* RESTATEMENT (SECOND) OF CONTRACTS, introductory note to chapter 16, at 100 (1981) ("The traditional goal of the law of contract remedies has not been compulsion of the promisor to perform his promise but compensation of the promisee for the loss resulting from breach.") and § 344 (a) cmt. a (courts protect the expectation interest "by attempting to put him [the promisee] in as good a position as he would have been in had the contract been performed, that is, had there been no breach."); UNIFORM COMMERCIAL CODE [hereinafter U.C.C.] § 1–305 (a) ("The remedies provided by this Act must be liberally administered to the end that the aggrieved party may be put in as good a position as if the other party had fully performed") and cmt. 1 (explaining that the central purpose of contract damages is to provide compensation for disappointed promisees).

Historically, the principle of compensation shaped the legal rule according to which damages must put the promisee in the position she would have been in if the contract had been performed, being thereby measured by the expectation measurement. *Cf*. Robinson v. Harman 1 Exch. 850, 855 (1848), per Baron Parke ("what damages is the plaintiff entitled to recover? The rule of the common law is, that where a party sustains a loss by reason of a breach of contract, he is, so far as money can do it, to be placed in the same situation, with respect to damages, as if the contract had been performed."); Wertheim (Sally) v. Chicoutimi Pulp Co. A.C. 301, 307 (1911), per Lord Atkinson (P.C.) ("And it is the general intention of the law that, in giving damages for breach of contract, the party complaining should, so far as it can be done by money, be placed in the same position as he would have been in if the contract had been performed. ... That is a ruling principle. It is a just principle.").

The principle and the legal rule it defines are equally found in the American law of contracts. *Cf*. Jaquith v. Hudson, 5 Mich. 123, 133–134 (1858) ("The law, following the dictates of equity and natural justice ... adopts the principle of just compensation for the loss or injury actually sustained"); Hawkins v. McGee, 84 N.H. 114, 146 A. 641 (1929) ("By 'damages,' as that term is used in the law of contracts, is intended compensation for a breach."); United States Naval Inst. v. Charter Communications, 936 F.2d 692, 696 (2d Cir. 1991) ("the purpose of damages for breach of contract is to compensate the injured party for the loss caused by breach.").

In civil law systems, specific performance, or *injunctive relief* consisting in a court order for the promisor in breach to perform and to undertake the contracted action is the default remedy for breach the agreed-upon time. Both types of remedies are hence well suited to compensate the victim of breach for loss sustained and to undo harm from breach deliberately created by the promisor and incurred by the promisee.[4]

Although compensation is the fundamental principle in the law of remedies for breach of contract, it lacks a theoretical justification, in terms of social welfare, capable of explaining such a prominent function.[5] Compensation is ex post redistribution, a monetary transfer from the promisor in breach to the disappointed promisee, being thus, at first sight, incapable of increasing social welfare in traditional economic models.[6] It fulfills no instrumental function, since undoing a harm or loss, ex post,

---

of contract. *See* the discussion *infra* in Chaps. 2 and 6 and, e.g., RUDOLF SCHLESINGER ET AL., COMPARATIVE LAW 740 (6th ed. 1998) ("performance in accordance with the terms of the contract is the normal, primary remedy for non performance in most civil-law countries."). This does not mean that monetary damages are not regularly awarded. For some, damages for breach have in the praxis a central function while specific performance has arguably a complementary function. *Cf.* Ulrich Huber, *Schadensersatz statt der Leistung,* 210 ARCHIV FÜR DIE ZIVILISTISCHE PRAXIS 319, 322 (2010) (*"Für die Praxis steht der Schadensersatzanspruch statt der Leistung ganz im Vordergrund, und der Anspruch auf Erfüllung in Natur hat eher ergänzende Bedeutung."*) *See infra* Chap. 2.

[4] *Cf.* FARNSWORTH ON CONTRACTS 739 § 12.4 ("specific relief is plainly better suited to the objective of putting the promisee in the position in which it would have been had the promise been performed") (since the promisee often cannot accurately demonstrate the losses resulting from breach); Farnsworth, *Legal Remedies for Breach of Contract, op. cit. supra,* at 1145, 1150 (similar, also discussing civil law systems and their logic).

[5] *Cf.* Louis Kaplow & Steven Shavell, *Fairness versus Welfare,* 114 HARVARD LAW REVIEW 961, 1103 n.321 (2001) ("conventional syntheses of contract law say little about the purpose of contract remedies," then criticizing Corbin for "referring to the objective of putting an injured party in as good a position as would have resulted from performance, but not addressing why this should be the purpose of contract remedies," Williston for "insisting that the purpose of damages is to compensate plaintiffs by putting them in as good a position as if their contracts had been performed, but not stating why this is the case," and the *Restatement* for "listing various abstract 'interests' (...) but not explaining why protecting these interests is desirable.").

The authors, however, do make one late addend to these criticisms ("Corbin does, however, suggest that awarding compensatory damages serves to keep the peace and also to deter future harm arising from breaches of contract, thereby encouraging business transactions, both purposes obviously related to individuals' well-being.") *Id. See also* Goetz & Scott, *Liquidated Damages, Penalties and the Just Compensation Principle, op. cit supra,* at 558 n.19 ("the economic bases of the compensation principle have not been fully articulated.").

[6] *Cf.* Kaplow & Shavell, *Fairness versus Welfare, op. cit. supra,* at 998 n.73 ("the bare fact that money may change hands in a lawsuit in certain circumstances, thereby changing how a loss is divided between the two parties, is of no consequence under welfare economics" unless parties are risk-averse or compensation can affect the *overall* distribution of income in a society).

With respect to the first exception, the social function of compensation is simply "negated" whenever insurance markets work. *See* STEVEN SHAVELL, FOUNDATIONS OF ECONOMIC ANALYSIS OF LAW 311 (2004) (in the presence of functioning insurance markets, "the need for damages to compensate the victim is negated, and damages have a role mainly as an incentive device") and the discussion *infra* in Chap. 2, Sect. 2.4.

With respect to the second exception, the authors develop elsewhere in detail the argument that this should better be done through the tax system, being furthermore unachievable through the rules of contract law because parties may negotiate prices ex ante. *Cf.* Louis Kaplow & Steven Shavell, *Why the Legal System is Less Efficient than the Income Tax in Redistributing Income,* 23 JOURNAL OF by redistributing wealth from claimant to defendant does not contribute, in itself, to social welfare, and hence "compensation itself plays no independent role in economic models."[7]

Consistently, Economic Analysis of Law assigns no more than *contingent* or *external* reasons for its existence, with scholars recently making the case *against* compensation for breach. It has been argued that its profound influence in modern and contemporary contract law is no more than the result of "ill-conceived path dependence," with tenuous economic support by being "virtually ignored in the theoretical analysis of efficient contract design."[8] "In short, in economic theories the concept of compensation can be dispensed with entirely."[9]

Lawmakers and legal scholars, on the contrary, understand damages as aimed at providing compensation to victims of breach, and the concept of compensation, instead of disposable, is rather fundamental.[10] Legal enforcement of contracts is understood as providing relief for promisees to *redress* breach.[11] It is supposed to

---

LEGAL STUDIES 667, 674 (1994) ("when parties are in a contractual relationship, it is well understood that redistribution usually is not accomplished because prices generally adjust to reflect the expected costs of legal rules"); *Fairness versus Welfare, op. cit. supra*, at 1103 ("the division of gain between the parties from contracting may be relevant on distributive grounds, but, in most of the examples we study, contract law will not have any distributive effect because changes in the contract price will offset any tendency of a contract rule to favor one or another party.") In short, in the law of contracts, compensation is not a *fundamental* principle, with a very minute role, if there is one at all. *See* the complete discussion *infra* in Chap. 2, Sect. 2.4.4, also including the possible justification of compensation based on the need to give incentives for victims of breach to report breach to the state.

[7] Richard Craswell, *Instrumental Theories of Compensation: A Survey*, 40 SAN DIEGO LAW REVIEW 1135, 1138–1139 (2003) ("From the standpoint of modern economics, the analysis is instrumental all the way down, so the concept of compensation does no meaningful work.").

[8] Robert Scott & George Triantis, *Embedded Options and the Case Against Compensation in Contract Law*, 104 COLUMBIA LAW REVIEW 1428, 1429 (2004) ("As a result of an unfortunate turn in history, lawmakers view contract damages as compensation for wrongs. This has impeded both the efficient evolution of default remedies and the efficient regulation of liquidated damages.") *See* also George Triantis, *Promissory Autonomy, Imperfect Courts, and the Immorality of the Expectation Damages Default*, 45 SUFFOLK UNIVERSITY LAW REVIEW 827, 832–833 (2011) ("the endorsement of and justification for compensation provided by many scholars is partly to blame [for the stickiness of expectation damages, from which parties cannot easily opt out]. The unfortunate result is the expectation damages default can cause significant inefficiency in contracting and, from the promissory perspective, a large encumbrance on the autonomy of the promisor.").

[9] Craswell, *Instrumental Theories of Compensation, op. cit. supra*, at 178.

[10] As stated by Corbin in the passage at the beginning of this introduction, *supra* n.1. *See* further *supra* n.2 for legal scholars, including Blackstone, Sedgwick, Anston, Williston, Corbin, Radin, and Farnsworth that share the view that compensation is the fundamental principle or, at least, the goal and purpose of remedies for breach. Note, moreover, that this is the *purpose* of remedies for breach explicit mentioned by the RESTATEMENT (SECOND) OF CONTRACTS, as in n.3 *supra*.

[11] For Blackstone, "strictly speaking, the primary right to a satisfaction for injuries is given by the law of nature, and the suit is only the means of ascertaining and recovering that satisfaction." The injured party has that right given by natural law, and that right emerges in "the instant he receives an injury; the verdict of jurors, and the judgment of the court (…) do not *give*, but define the *right*." 1 BLACKSTONE, COMMENTARIES ON THE LAWS OF ENGLAND IN FOUR BOOKS, *op. cit. supra*,

provide a true *remedy* for the promisee, and existing law in fact does so by awarding either performance as promised, or its monetary equivalent *to the promisee*.

Remedies for breach have, for different legal scholars, the first goal of substituting private for public redress, thereby crowding out the human tendency that aggrieved victims have to retaliate, by their own means, if they are not entitled to a public remedy.[12] They seek to avoid what Corbin and Perillo called "private war," and to avoid the "resulting harm" that it occasions to the interest of others.[13] The basis of contract law, for the lawyer, is arguably "the desire to keep the public peace."[14]

Moreover, remedies for breach impose a cost, for the promisor, on the decision to breach and hence deter breaches of contract.[15] Fully compensatory damages (expectation damages) have an additional goal, purpose, and justification in ensuring that promisors internalize the negative externality of breach, given by the loss of expected and promised gains that the promisee foregoes because of breach.[16] Expectation damages fulfill this goal and are apt to induce performance by the promisor

---

book 2, ch. 29, at 438 (emphasis in original). *See*, more recently, FARNSWORTH ON CONTRACTS 730 § 12 ("Our system of contract remedies is not directed at *compulsion* of *promisors* to *prevent* breach; it is aimed, instead, at *relief* to *promisees* to *redress* breach.").

[12] *Cf.* RUDOLPH VON JHERING, GEIST DES RÖMISCHEN RECHTS 113 (Leipzig: Breitkopf und Härtel 1852) ("*Die ersten unausbleiblichen Regungen des verletzten Rechtsgefühls bestehen in der gewaltsamen Reaktion gegen das zugefügte Unrecht, in der Selbsthülfe und Rache; mit Selbsthülfe und Rache hat daher ein jedes Recht begonnen.*") ("The first inevitable impulses of the injured sense of justice consist in a violent reaction against the inflicted wrong, in self-help and revenge; every right thus began with self-help and revenge.") (own transl.); O. W. HOLMES, THE COMMON LAW 37 (Toronto: Typographical Society 2011) (1881) ("My aim and purpose has been to show that the various forms of liability known to modern law spring from the common ground of revenge"); MAX WEBER, WIRTSCHAFT UND GESELLSCHAFT 421 (Tübingen: Paul Siebeck 1922) ("*Die ökonomische Rationalisierung des Rechts begünstigte die Entstehung der Vorstellung, dass die Sühnehaftung nicht sowohl Abkauf der Rache (die ursprüngliche Auffassung) wie Ersatz des Schadens sei. Nichterfüllung eines Kontrakts konnte nun ebenfalls als sühnepflichtige Schädigung qualifiziert werden.*") ("The economic rationalization of the law favored the rise of the conception that liability for composition was not only buying off of vengeance (the original conception) but also compensation for harm. Nonperformance of contract could now be qualified as harm requiring compensation.") (own transl.).

[13] *See* 5 CORBIN, A COMPREHENSIVE TREATISE ON THE RULES OF CONTRACT LAW, *op. cit. supra*, at 30–31; JOSEPH PERILLO, *Misreading Oliver Wendell Holmes on Efficient Breach and Tortious Interference*, 68 FORDHAM LAW REVIEW 1085, 1092–1093 (2000) ("The legal system knows what economic science does not know: damages and other legal remedies are substitutes for private warfare.").

[14] *See* JOHN CALAMARI & JOSEPH PERILLO, CONTRACTS 6 (6th ed., St. Paul, West, 2009) ("It is well-recognized that the law of crimes and torts owe their origin to the state's desire to eliminate private vengeance and to minimize other forms of self-help. It is not as well known that contract law has the same genesis. ... Anthropology and history have proven that a basis of contract law is the desire to keep the public peace.").

[15] Note how Corbin, for example, explicitly mentions a second purpose of an award of damages for breach consisting in the prevention of breaches of contract. *See supra* n.1.

[16] Remedies for breach further provide incentives for individuals to enter into mutually profitable contracts, for parties to rely on promises and to take precautions to avoid breach, among others. *See* Steven Shavell, *Damage Measures for Breach of Contract*, 11 BELL JOURNAL OF ECONOMICS 466 (1980); Steven Shavell, *The Design of Contracts and Remedies for Breach*, 99 QUARTERLY JOURNAL OF ECONOMICS 121 (1984) (introducing incentives for reliance investments); Robert Cooter, *Unity in Torts, Contract, and Property: The Model of Precaution*, 73 CALIFORNIA LAW

if and only if performance is socially efficient in any given contingency and thereby provide a contribution to the welfare of society.[17]

Rather than conceiving damages as by way of compensation, economic analysis of contract law considers damages for breach more restrictively, providing incentives for promisors to keep contractual promises, and hence deterring breaches. And for that purpose, it is neither necessary nor fundamental that the promisee be compensated. It is only necessary that the promisor anticipate that she will have to bear a cost, given by the legal remedy, if she breaches when breach is socially inefficient. Compensation is seen as capable of contributing to social welfare only as a means to re-allocate risks between the parties if at least one of them is risk-averse, the risk to be borne is detrimental instead of beneficial or monetary instead of non-monetary, and insurance markets concomitantly fail.[18] It is not conceived as fundamental in the law of damages and, rather, is only accessory, secondary, or even, at the limit, simply disposable and replaceable by penalties for breach that do not compensate the promisee.[19]

In effect, when breach is socially efficient, there is no welfare reason to compensate the promisee, or for the promisor to bear any cost. The loss could lie where it falls, since for overall social welfare, it is irrelevant whether it is the plaintiff or the defendant who bears it *ex post*, after the occurrence of breach. However, existing legal systems do allow promisees to recover damages, or to specifically enforce the contract, both when breach is efficient and when it is inefficient.[20]

Moreover, when accounting for reliance investments by the promisee, efficient incentives require the promisor to pay an amount equivalent to expectation damages

---

REVIEW 1, 1 (1985) (introducing incentives for precautions). *See* also the detailed discussion and explanation *infra* in Chap. 2, Sect. 2.4.

[17] Incentives created by an award of a remedy for breach and the theory of efficient breach are discussed in detail in Chap. 2, Sect. 2.4 *infra*.

[18] *See* the complete discussion in Chap. 2, Sect. 4.4 *infra* (discussing the role of compensation as a mean to provide incentives for promisees to report breaches to the state with low social costs).

[19] *Cf.* Gerrit de Geest, *N Problems require N instruments*, 35 INTERNATIONAL REVIEW OF LAW AND ECONOMICS 42, 48 (2013) ("The optimal rules I will find can be summarized as follows. First, if breaching is clearly efficient, it should be allowed without compensation except for in three cases: (a) if the breacher negligently overpromised; (b) if the breach became efficient after a negligent performance; (c) if paying damages is required for optimal risk allocation. Second, if breaching is not clearly efficient (either because it is clearly inefficient or it is unclear), the breacher should be penalized.").

[20] As long as performance is not, in the realized contingency, impossible or impractical, among others. *See* chap. 6 *infra*. These defenses are not, however, defined by the efficiency of breach, and are very restrictive and do not include all cases of inefficient breach, but those such as the one where the promised ring to be delivered to a buyer falls into the bottom of the sea.

See Claus-Wilhelm Canaris, *Die Reform der Leistungsstörungsrecht*, in 3 GESAMMELTE SCHRIFTEN 451, 457–458 (Hans Grigoleit & Jörg Neuner eds. Berlin, Walter de Gruyter 2012) (2001), and the discussion *infra* in Chap. 6. Impossibility and impracticability allow the promisor to breach *without* having to pay *expectation* damages, since courts will, in those cases, normally *rescind* the contract and attempt to put parties in the position they were before the contract was made.

(as sanction or penalty) and the promisee to receive *no compensation at all*.[21] Yet again, no modern legal system known to the author adopts such a system that would, according to economic models, better provide for a maximal social welfare. Instead of penalties for breach, the law grants compensatory remedies for the victim that are actionably independent of the efficiency or inefficiency of breach.

The main reason for the difficulties that Economic Analysis of Law faces in locating the value of compensation for victims of breach lies in its disregard for how individuals' normative understandings of the wrong in breaking promises and contracts affect individual behavior, with its own consequences upon overall social welfare. Underlying most economic theories of contract law is the understanding of the contractual obligation as an obligation *either* to perform *or* to pay damages in case of breach.[22] It is an understanding that denies the normative significance of the contractual obligation, implying that breach is neither moral nor immoral, but rather an act that, when followed by the payment of compensatory damages, is

---

[21] *See* Robert Cooter & Ariel Porat, *Anti-Insurance*, 31 JOURNAL OF LEGAL STUDIES 203, 203–204 (2002) ("In standard models of contracts, efficient incentives require the promisor to pay damages for nonperformance and the promisee to receive no damages. (...) Liability for less than 100 percent of the harm caused by nonperformance erodes the promisor's incentives [to perform if and only if socially efficient], and liability for more than 0 percent erodes the promisee's incentives [for optimal levels of reliance]." The authors then "propose a novel contract requiring the promisor to pay damages for nonperformance to a third party, not to the promisee."). It is worth noting that their proposal is not to change the contract law, but a proposal for a new contractual design or type, and they inquire into the reasons why such proposed type of contract does not exist in the real world (history and the possibility of abuse). *Id.* at 227 ("perhaps the necessary institutional innovations to sustain anti-insurance markets will appear in the twenty-first century. In any case, the prospects for anti-insurance markets will improve substantially after more people appreciate the concept.").

Robert Cooter, in fact, stressed many years before how the principle of compensation has as its goal the realization of *equity*, and "that there are circumstances in which compensation is required by reasons of justice," although often conflicting with the goal of inducing efficient reliance. Robert Cooter, *Unity in Torts, Contract, and Property: The Model of Precaution, op. cit. supra.* Cooter further listed, as one among seven types of behavior that contract damages may affect, that damages influence the behavior of parties by "resolving disputes about broken promises" (closely related to one examined in the present thesis). *Id.* at 12, n.27.

The trade-off present in contract damages to provide incentives to induce performance only when socially efficient and to induce optimal levels of reliance was first analyzed by Steven Shavell, *Damage Measures for Breach of Contract, op. cit. supra.* It is resumed in his proposition 6, which is a fundamental piece in the economic analysis of contract damages: "There does not exist a damage measure which always induces Pareto efficient behavior; equivalently, any damage measure will lead either to Pareto inefficient reliance or to Pareto inefficient breach in some contractual situations." *Id.* at 483.

[22] This understanding stems from Holmes in his classical passage where he states how "the only universal consequence of a legally binding promise is, that the law makes the promisor pay damages if the promised event does not come to pass." *Cf.* OLIVER W. HOLMES, THE COMMON LAW 266 (Paulo Pereira & Diego Beltran eds., Toronto, Typographical Society 2011) (1881). *See* also Oliver W. Holmes, *The Path of the Law*, 10 HARVARD LAW REVIEW 457, 462 (1897) ("The duty to keep a contract at common law means a prediction that you must pay damages if you do not keep it,—and nothing else."). *See* the discussion *infra* in Chap. 2.

simply amoral.[23] In such a stylized and ascetic world, normative conflict does not arise since breach of contract is never wrong.[24]

While some individuals may in fact understand the contractual obligation as such, many others clearly have different *normative* understandings of promissory and contractual obligations. Some individuals understand contractual obligations as promissory obligations that morally require performance by the promisor, based in respect for the autonomy and will of the promisee.[25] Other individuals may well understand the contractual obligation as morally requiring performance by the promisor only if performance is socially efficient and capable of providing overall gains of welfare for both parties considered together.[26] Others may also perceive breach as a wrong only if breach would create an unequal and unfair distribution of gains and losses between the parties, and they may also perceive breach as not immoral when it can prevent the promisor from incurring high losses in order to perform.[27] Individuals often perceive breach as a *transgression*, perhaps depending on the circumstances under which breach is committed. They will tend to feel

---

[23] Although Posner does not explicitly say that breach, when socially efficient and followed by the payment of expectation damages is *moral*, at least the amorality of breach must be implied (unless one interprets his position as stating that the law *should* give incentives for immoral conduct, which is clearly not the case). *Cf*. RICHARD POSNER, ECONOMIC ANALYSIS OF LAW 57 (1st ed. 1972) ("In some cases a party [to a contract] would be tempted to breach the contract simply because his profit from breach would exceed his expected profit from completion of the contract. If his profit from breach would also exceed the expected profit to the other party from completion of the contract, and if damages are limited to loss of expected profit, there will be an incentive to commit a breach. There should be.").

[24] Unless of course it is not followed by the payment of compensatory damages.

[25] As defended by CHARLES FRIED, CONTRACT AS PROMISE: A THEORY OF CONTRACTUAL OBLIGATION 16–17 (1981) ("The obligation to keep a promise is grounded not in arguments of utility but in respect for individual autonomy and in trust. (…) [S]ince a contract is first of all a promise, the contract must be kept because a promise must be kept.") *See* the detailed discussion *infra* in Chap. 2, Sect. 2.2.

[26] As advanced by Steven Shavell, in *Is Breach of Contract Immoral?*, 56 EMORY LAW JOURNAL 439, 449–450 (2006) ("under the expectation measure of damages for breach, the seller will fail to perform in the same contingencies as the seller would be permitted not to perform in a complete contract. Accordingly, breach should not be characterized as immoral under our assumptions") (emphasis omitted). Shavell further assumes that under those assumptions and circumstances, breach, when observed, can be inferred to be *moral*. *Id.* ("Furthermore, we as onlookers know that when breach occurs, it must be *moral*, for we can infer that the cost of performance must have been higher than the value of performance from the willingness of the seller to commit breach.") (own emphasis).

[27] In order to see this, it is necessary to distinguish between two paradigmatic cases where breach is likely to occur, denoted the "loss-avoidance paradigm" and the "overbidder paradigm," as distinguished by Melvin Eisenberg, in *Actual and Virtual Specific Performance, the Theory of Efficient Breach, and the Indifference Principle in Contract Law*, *op. cit. supra*, at 998; Eisenberg, *The Disgorgement Interest in Contract Law*, 105 MICHIGAN LAW REVIEW 559, 567 (2006). In cases where another bidder offers a higher price for a good or service already promised to another, then breach allows the promisor in breach to achieve profits while leaving the promisee, who does not receive the promised performance, without any earning in case compensation is absent. In cases where the promisor breaches because of a spike in costs of production, then the promisor does not incur those costs, does not perform, and neither party earns anything. The result, in the last

aggrieved and tempted to retaliate and to redress their own wrong if they are not entitled to a public remedy.[28]

Retaliation is an act that imposes losses upon its victim at a cost for the person retaliating, thereby creating losses for the welfare of the society.[29] It is pervasive and widespread even in modern societies, where the law in general prohibits the use of violence by the citizens. The citizens can always tell others about an act of breach committed by the seller, thereby harming her reputation in the market, or refuse to transact with that same seller in the future, even when doing so would mutually profitable, thereby withholding cooperation.[30]

Moreover, aggrieved promisees may file frivolous suits, or shade and deliver a counter-performance of poor quality, among many other forms of retaliation mentioned by Oliver Hart and John Moore.[31] Lastly, they may name and shame the promise-breaker, perhaps ostracizing and excluding her from the industry in which she operates. At the limit, victims of breach may also recur to violent means to retaliate against a perceived wrongdoer, but acts of retaliation are not restricted to acts of violence. Retaliation is ubiquitous in commercial relationships just as it is in daily, common, and recurrent sale and service contracts. As advanced by Richard Posner, since "retaliation may sometimes operate as a constraint on market activity, even economists who take a narrow view of the proper scope of economics might include retaliation within that scope."[32]

Legal relief is apt to have a fundamental role in suppressing that behavioral tendency to react to perceived wrongful conduct by ensuring disappointed promisees access to courts and an actionable legal remedy. Legal relief, moreover, is implemented independently of the parties' individual normative understanding of the contractual obligation, or of the morality of breach, and is circumscribed to the remedy or remedies prescribed by the law. In this manner, promisors do not need to

paradigm, is an *equal* distribution. In the first one, on the contrary, it is an *unequal* distribution, and promisees are apt to perceive the second one as unfair.

[28] *See* Chap. 4 *infra* for a review of the existing empirical evidence concerning the morality of breach.

[29] Retaliation is defined and studied in Chap. 3 *infra*, where acts of retaliation based on the norm of (strong) reciprocity and those based on tit-for-tat, or grim-trigger strategies are distinguished.

[30] Similar to the forms of retaliation discussed by David Charny in commercial relationships. *Cf.* David Charny, *Nonlegal Sanctions in Commercial Relationships*, 104 HARVARD LAW REVIEW 373, 392f. (1990).

[31] *See* Oliver Hart & John Moore, *Contracts as Reference Points*, 73 QUARTERLY JOURNAL OF ECONOMICS 1 (2008) ("It may be useful to give some examples of shading. There are many ways one trading partner can hurt another. A seller can shade by cutting quality: in the wedding example, she can stint on some of the ingredients of the wedding cake. Or the seller may withhold cooperation … A third example would be 'working to rule': the seller abides by the strict terms of the contract and offers no more. Buyers can also shade. Although it is harder to imagine a buyer cutting back on quality, it is easy to think of situations where a buyer refuses to make minor concessions or to cooperate…The buyer can also make life difficult for the seller by quibbling about details of performance, by delaying payment, or by giving a bad reference.").

[32] *Retribution and Related Concepts of Punishment*, 9 JOURNAL OF LEGAL STUDIES 71, 73 n.4 (1980).

fear that promisees will recurrently resort to private acts of retaliation that accord to their own individual normative understandings, subject to the passions and emotions triggered by an act they perceive as morally wrong. Promisees, by the same token, do not need to fear that promisors, in pursuit of their own material self-interest, will decide to perform or breach without paying adequate respect for their interests, since the law ensures them compensation for their losses.

In order to understand such a function of compensatory damages to "keep the peace," there is the need to overcome and abandon the outdated and pernicious conception that individuals in a society understand promissory or contractual obligations in one specific manner, whatever it is, and to endorse the plurality of normative understandings that exist in complex societies of today. Whenever the disappointed promisee understands breach in certain circumstances as *wrong*, while the promisor perceives it as justified and *right*, then *normative conflict* emerges because multiple norms on how the promisor ought to behave coexist.[33] Absent a public remedy and some form of compensation, victims of breach may seek justice by their own means, with all the harm that this entails for society as a whole.

Once this is established, it becomes possible to develop an analysis of the impact of the fairness of the ex post remedy upon promisees' ex ante behavior, crowding out the tendency to react to perceived wrongful and unfair behavior in manners that are socially costly, and that are responsible for a deadweight loss. The legal remedy, at the same time, surely has its own ex ante effect also upon the promisor's decision to perform or breach at first place, and it is predicted to deter breach as long as the law provides a remedy that is certain and secure instead of being motivated by no more than caprice or compassion to the victim.

Remedies for breach are studied and analyzed according to their contribution to the welfare of society. The impact of the fairness of the legal remedy is considered in a very limited fashion and reduced to its adequacy to provide satisfaction for victims of breach in order to minimize social losses stemming from private forms of retaliation. This brings the analysis in line with what Kaplow and Shavell demand. For them, "notions of fairness that call for compensation to protect promisees who have been wronged by promisors' breaches are incomplete: it is necessary to go further and specify some substantive theory that explains which refusals to perform should be deemed wrongful and that provides an explicit justification for choosing a particular remedy."[34]

Its completion, in social welfare terms, may reveal that the fairness of the legal remedy is in fact as important as the incentives it creates to induce efficient levels of performance.

---

[33] *Cf*. Nikos Nikiforakis et al., *Normative Conflict & Feuds: The Limits of Self-Enforcement*, 96 Journal of Public Economics 797, 798 (2012) ("A normative conflict arises when there coexist multiple plausible rules about how one ought to behave in a given situation.").

[34] *Cf.* Kaplow & Shavell, *Fairness versus Welfare, op. cit. supra*, at 1142.

1.1 Objective

The objective of this thesis is to provide a justification, on social welfare grounds, for why compensation is fundamental in the law of remedies for breach of contract.

Following the method employed by the Economic Analysis of Law, this thesis develops firstly a *positive analysis* of the behavioral effects of remedies for breach of contract.[35] It firstly reviews the effect of the remedy to provide ex ante incentives for promisors to perform and other incentives created by remedies for the parties. Concerning the well-known function of expectation damages to induce performance if and only if performance is socially efficient, this thesis further attempts to provide empirical evidence for this theoretical prediction that still lacks empirical support in a controlled laboratory experiment.

Secondly, this thesis examines a specific effect of the legal norm that entitles promisees to seek relief to redress breach that has not received adequate attention by the theoretical and empirical economic literature. It examines the capacity and adequacy of remedies for breach to provide satisfaction for the victim and thereby to substitute private for public redress, and goes into other benefits for society that legal enforcement of contracts provide, and that have not been carefully considered in economic theories of contract. In doing so, this thesis inquires into the relevance of the moral norm of keeping promises, and of the efficiency and fairness of the outcome implemented by legal remedies to crowd out the human tendency to retaliate to perceived wrong in breach of contract.

The theoretical conjectures and predictions are *all* falsifiable and are, in fact, subject to empirical investigation in an economic experiment. They are subject to scrutiny in a controlled environment that isolates and abstracts from several different factors that may *also* affect individual's decisions in the contractual environment in order to study the precise relationship between the institutions and behavior under study *ceteris paribus*.[36] This is how knowledge can not only be produced, but also be contested, and how science can seriously inform policy recommendations.[37]

The positive analysis aims to provide an explanation for the existing law, as it is: Remedies for breach of contract provide incentives for promisors to perform while fundamentally providing compensation to the promisee. They are apt to fulfill different functions by implementing, ex post, a transfer of wealth from the wrongdoer to the victim. Remedies for breach, both at common law and civil law, do not penalize breach, nor do they solely impose a cost on breach for the promisor that induces socially efficient performance. Rather, they explicitly seek to compensate victims of

---

[35] To undertake a positive analysis in the Economic Analysis of Law is to determine the effects of a policy, institution, or legal norm upon individual behavior in order to evaluate it. *Cf.* Kaplow & Shavell, *Fairness versus Welfare, op. cit. supra*, at 977.

[36] *See* VINCENT BUSKENS, BETWEEN HOBBES' LEVIATHAN AND SMITH'S INVISIBLE HAND (2011) as well as CHRISTOPH ENGEL, LEGAL EXPERIMENTS: MISSION IMPOSSIBLE? (2013) (discussing the value of experimental studies in the Law).

[37] *Cf.* Richard Posner, *Let Us Never Blame a Contract Breaker*, 107 MICHIGAN LAW REVIEW 1349, 1349 (2009) ("contract doctrines should normally be alterable only on the basis of empirical investigations.").

breach through ex post redistribution of wealth—in fact doing so——and this thesis attempts to advance one explanation for why this is so.

This thesis, lastly, further develops a normative analysis in providing recommendations for how the law of remedies for breach of contract should be in order to maximize social welfare through both channels, effectively fulfilling both functions of an award of remedies for breach mentioned by Corbin.[38] It reduces the value and legitimacy of compensation to the same common denominator as the incentives created by remedies for behaving in socially desirable manners in order to provide a comparison of the gains of social welfare provided by those two functions of legal relief. Recommendations for changes in the law can thereby rely on the theoretical analysis concerning the behavioral impact of the remedy, translated into social welfare because of its consequences.[39]

This thesis does not develop any criticism on Richard Posner's thesis, borrowed from Holmes, "that concepts of fault or blame, at least when understood in moral terms rather than translated into economic or other practical terms, are not useful addenda to the doctrines of contract law."[40] Concepts of right or wrong are instead relevant because of their impact upon contractual behavior, and not in themselves. In their capacity to induce certain patterns of behavior, such as the tendency to retaliate to breach, they are translated into economic and practical terms, as demanded by Posner, have their own impact upon social welfare, and are therefore of economic relevance.

Recommendations for changes in the law consider existing empirical evidence as well as evidence collected in the implemented experiment. In doing so, this thesis seeks to comply with *another* of Richard Posner's demands, namely "that contract doctrines should normally be alterable only on the basis of empirical investigations."[41] The normative analysis is based on a monist theory that considers one and only one goal of the law: namely, to maximize social welfare. In this way, there is no need to balance values when they compete or to develop meta-principles or methods to achieve that balancing. The desirability of and the justifications for different remedies for breach are analyzed according to their respective contributions to social welfare.

1.2 Research Questions

Contractual behavior under investigation involves mainly the promisor's decision to perform or breach and the promisee's decision to retaliate or not to breach. The contractual relations under analysis are common, simple, and everyday *sales* and

[38] *See supra* n.1.

[39] *Cf.* Steven Burton, *Normative Legal Theories: The Case for Pluralism and Balancing*, 98 IOWA LAW REVIEW 535, 539–540 (2013) ("the ultimate goal of all normative legal theories is to justify final recommendations about what the law should be, all things considered, insofar as the state of the art permits.").

[40] Richard Posner, *Let Us Never Blame a Contract Breaker*, *op. cit. supra*, at 1349.

[41] *Id.*

service contracts.[42] Moreover, this thesis does not consider how different moral and normative understandings of contractual obligations emerged and evolved; rather, the object of study is restricted to the phenomenon as it is, in its present observable form, and the same holds true for the contract law.

Research Question 1. How does promissory commitment (the primary duty to perform) affect both parties' contractual behavior?

The first research question concerns the effect of the obligation to perform, or the primary duty to perform, upon both (i) the promisor's decision to perform and (ii) the promisee's tendency to retaliate.

The first part of the question has been studied, in theory, in more philosophical approaches to the study of the contractual obligation. Some theories hold that the contractual obligation, incurred by the giving of a promise with consideration, is a promissory obligation that carries with it normative significance. Promisors may tend to perform contracts because of the moral duty to keep promises, and the need

---

[42] This thesis does not develop the study of those functions of legal redress in relational and labor contracts. There is plenty of evidence that this is the case in employment relationships, as studied by the theory of breach of the psychological contract developed mainly by Denise Rousseau. *See, e.g.*, ROUSSEAU, PSYCHOLOGICAL CONTRACT IN ORGANIZATIONS: UNDERSTANDING WRITTEN AND UNWRITTEN AGREEMENTS (1995). With respect to those specific contracts, it is worth noting that their main distinctive note is the existence of asymmetry of power between the employer and the employee, since the employee sells her labor force and thereby does not perform her job with *autonomy*. *Cf.* OTTO KAHN-FREUND, LABOUR AND THE LAW 18 (Paul Davies and Mark Freedland eds., 3rd. ed. 1983) ("the relation between an employer and an isolated employee or worker is typically a relation between a bearer of power and one who is not a bearer of power. In its inception it is an act of submission, in its operation it is a condition of subordination, however much the submission and the subordination may be concealed by that indispensable figment of the legal mind known as the 'contract of employment.'") The employee, in sum, must obey orders, and the employer has the right to control the details of performance. *See* RESTATEMENT (SECOND) OF AGENCY, § 220 (1) (1958) ("A servant is a person employed to perform services in the affairs of another and who with respect to the physical conduct in the performance of the service is subject to the other's control or right of control"), as well as Perkins v. Regional Transp. Dist., 907 P.2d 672, 675 (Colo. App. 1995) (stressing the right to control as the element to consider, not its actual exercise).

Very similarly, and in general, the labor contract is characterized, in civil law systems, by the presence of *dependency*, in which case the employee must in the same manner obey orders. Under German law, for instance, labor relations are marked by the recognition of the presence of asymmetry of power and employees are, given the constitutional order of the welfare state (*Gebot der Sozialstaatlichkeit*, in Art. 20 I GG), subject to protection, by the labor law, from the party that can exercise that power. *Cf.* DIETER MEDICUS, SCHULDRECHT II: BESONDERER TEIL 116–117 Rn. 314–315, 321 (14th. ed, Munich, Beck 2007).

This is not the case in service contracts, where the promisee cannot demand from the promisor performance of the task in any specific manner, with no right to control, but only with the right to sue the promisor for breach of contract in case of defective or inexistent performance. The service contract is marked by *autonomy* and excludes *dependency*. This thesis thus focuses only on sales and service contracts and excludes from its object labor contracts and the impact of power in contractual relations. There is little evidence and scholarship devoted to the study of the individual propensity to retaliate to breach of sales and service contracts, and even less about the function of compensatory damages to crowd out retaliation in those contracts, differently from labor contracts, justifying the choice of the present object of study.

of remedies to provide incentives for promisors to perform depends on how far the moral norm of promise-keeping is capable to induce promisors to perform.

There is evidence that individuals often keep their promises even at a cost to themselves, but there is no precise experimental evidence that this is so when no more than the expectation interest is at stake.[43] The experiment implements a game where only the expectation interest is involved, as in wholly executory contracts (for future trade), and thereby attempts to provide evidence for whether individuals keep promises in a situation not empirically studied before, but that can justify the contract law's protection of the expectation interest.

The second part of the question, in turn, has received much less attention in the literature, from both a theoretical and empirical perspective, and is therefore the focus of the analysis.[44] The question, with respect to the behavior of victims of breach, is how breach of the contract leads to conflict between the parties, and often to acts of retaliation, and the circumstances under which this type of behavior is most likely to emerge. Promisees will tend to retaliate when they expect the promisor to perform and when they perceive breach, in the realized circumstances, as morally wrong. In case parties are unable to settle the emerging dispute privately and peacefully, something facilitated by different cognitive biases, then the conflict can escalate and parties are hypothesized to engage in acts of retaliation and private punishment.

The two effects of the primary duty to induce performance by the promisor and to trigger retaliation by the victim in case of breach are subject to empirical investigation in the experiment. The welfare contribution of the secondary duty to pay damages for breach, and of the incentives created by the legal remedy, depends on to what extent promises are sufficient for promisors to perform. On the other hand, the welfare contribution of compensation for promisees depends on to what extent breach of promise in fact induces promisees to retaliate.

Research Question 2. How does the legal remedy (the secondary duty to pay damages for breach) affect both parties' contractual behavior?

The second research question concerns the effect of the legal remedy (expectation damages in the empirical study) upon both (i) the promisor's decision to perform and (ii) the promisee's tendency to retaliate to breach.

The first part of the question has been extensively studied, in theory, by the Economic Analysis of Law. This thesis complements the analysis by introducing retaliation as a behavioral tendency that is also capable of inducing promisors to perform. Moreover, the theoretical prediction that expectation damages induce performance if performance is socially efficient, and breach if breach is socially efficient, in any possible contingency, is still missing precise empirical evidence that this thesis attempts to deliver.

The second part of the question, concerning the effect of the legal remedy upon the behavior of the disappointed promisee and its social welfare value, has received

---

[43] *See* the review of the existing empirical literature *infra* in Chaps. 4 and 5.

[44] With the above-mentioned exception of the theory of breach of the psychological contract, focusing however on labor relations marked by asymmetry of power and dependency. *See supra* n.40.

almost no attention in the economic literature that studies incentives provided by remedies for breach. Evidence that remedies can crowd out a tendency to retaliate to breach, and thereby save social resources, in common and daily, single sale or service contracts, is almost inexistent, and this thesis investigates the capacity of compensatory remedies to in effect fulfill those two roles.

The two effects of the secondary duty to pay the legal remedy are also subject to empirical investigation in the implement experiment. The welfare contribution of each function, under the parameters chosen for the implemented trade game, is all estimated *net* of the welfare contribution of promises and retaliation to breach. The behavioral tendency to retaliate to breach in certain types of contingencies provides the scope for the hypothesized function of legal remedies to crowd it out.

Research Question 3. How can remedies for breach be designed to provide optimal incentives for promisors to perform while effectively crowding out retaliation, thereby delivering a superior contribution to social welfare than the one delivered by expectation damages and specific performance?

Different remedies fulfill the functions of inducing performance and of reducing retaliation in different manners. Substitutive and injunctive relief can both put the disappointed promisee in the position she would have been in if the promisor had performed, if perfectly implemented, but they both disregard the profits that the promisor can realize by breach. Considering the remedy's capacity to provide a fairer distribution of gains and losses from breach, specific performance has disadvantages that, even when parties can renegotiate their contracts without any transaction cost, are not always fully taken into account by the existing literature. This thesis develops a study of the capacity of different legal remedies for breach to crowd out retaliation in providing fairer redress while concomitantly creating incentives for optimal levels of performance.

Redistribution of the profits from breach, when they do not belong by the contract to either of the parties, can avoid disagreement, aggrievement, and retaliation, and a fairer result is better apt to crowd out retaliation in certain types of contingencies. The profits from breach are not, however, considered in an award of either expectation damages or specific performance. The promisor is free, in the first case, to breach and profit from her own wrong as long as she compensates the promisee for the loss of expectancy. In case of specific performance, the promisor that breaches and transfers the good to a third party in good faith makes performance of the original contract legally impossible and prevents a claim of specific performance by the promisee, who must them content herself with an award of damages.[45]

Different legal systems deal with that case in different manners. The promisee is not entitled to any share of those profits in the U.S., unless the promisor concomitantly violates a fiduciary duty or a property right. In France, the expansion of the *astreinte*, especially after its codification in 1992, now allows the promisee to prevent the promisor from realizing those profits even in obligations to do, departing from the

[45] In Germany, the promisee can recover the surrogate (the *stellvertretendes commodum*) and is hence entitled to recover disgorgement damages when specific performance is unavailable. *See* the detailed discussion *infra* in Chap. 6, Sects. 6.3 and 6.4.

Roman principle that *nemo potest praecise cogi ad factum* enshrined in Art. 1142 of the *Code Civil* (every obligation to do is resolved by an award of damages), which has been recently declared "deactivated" by some scholars. The BGB entitles the promisee to a claim on the surrogate in that case (*Anspruch auf das stellvertretende commodum*), thereby allowing the promisee—and not the promisor—to appropriate those profits. English courts now allow the promisee to recover *all* or *some* of the profits from breach, according to different rationales, and only in some specific circumstances, since the decisions of the House of Lords in *Blake* and in *Hendrix Experience* in 2001 and 2003. The last question tackled in this thesis is which of these solutions and developments is better apt, considering those two functions of remedies for breach of contract, to contribute to social welfare.

1.3 Outline

The second chapter reviews the three main theories of contract and contract law, namely promissory, reliance, and economic theories. It inquires, firstly, into the nature of the contractual obligation with the aim of identifying why breach of contract is an act possibly perceived by individuals as a wrong in need of redress. Among the candidates advanced by those theories are the violation of the moral norm of keeping promises, or of *pacta sunt servanda* (as advanced by promissory or deontological theories), the loss of reliance suffered by the promisee (in reliance theories), and the loss of welfare associated with breach in certain circumstances (in consequentialist or economic theories). The chapter studies, secondly, although also from the perspective of those same theories, some of the reasons and justifications for legal enforcement of contractual promises, focusing on its contribution to the welfare of society by providing incentives for individuals to behave in socially optimal manners.

The third chapter studies how the promisor may breach in circumstances in which the promisee might expect performance, and how retaliation to breach is, in the absence of legal relief, often the expected and observed final product of the parties' unresolved dispute. It identifies different reasons for why parties might disagree on whether the promisor should have performed or breached, including the incompleteness of contracts, conflicting understandings of the morality of breach, disagreement on what consequences of breach are undesirable, and different cognitive biases. Moreover, the three theories of contract and contract law studied in the second chapter do not provide a definitive answer to the question of whether the promisor should have performed or breached. Instead, they often conflict with each other, as for example when the promisor breaches the contract because breach is socially efficient and, in doing so, violates the moral norm of keeping promises and commits a transgression. Since each party is apt to have her own understanding on the proper course of conduct, contractual disputes acquire a normative character, and the danger is that they escalate to a real conflict.

The fourth chapter identifies, in the existing empirical evidence, some of the reasons for why individuals engage in retaliation and punishment of others, while also considering why individual behavior may differ when parties are bound to each other by contract, and hence by an obligation they voluntarily and autonomously entered into. It endogenizes, in the traditional model of contractual behavior developed in the Economic Analysis of Law, the possibility of retaliation by the promisee together with the possibility to seek legal redress, and how they can both serve to induce promisors to perform, each with its own costs and benefits. It then considers some of the elements that may lead promisees to retaliate to breach of promise and that are subject to experimental scrutiny in the following chapter: the loss of expectancy endured by the promisee, the inefficiency created by breach, and the unfairness of the resulting distribution. Lastly, the chapter explains how legal remedies are superior to retaliation to induce performance of promises because instead of causing, whenever implemented, a deadweight loss, as retaliation causes, legal remedies such as damages only redistribute wealth between the parties, and social welfare is thereby not impaired.

The fifth chapter presents the implemented experiment and empirical investigation, firstly, on the behavioral impact of bargained-for promises both (i) to induce performance by the promisor and (ii) to instigate retaliation by the promisee in case of breach. Secondly, it reveals the behavioral impact of expectation damages both to (iii) induce performance by the promisor and (iv) to crowd out retaliation by the disappointed promisee. The experiment further distinguishes between different circumstances where the promisor can breach, and thereby disentangles different consequences of the act of breach, including its social efficiency or inefficiency, and the fairness or unfairness of its result. Lastly, the experiment provides estimates for the gains of social welfare achieved by expectation damages through both functions and compares them in order to assess, under the parameters and setup of the experiment, their relative contribution to the maximization of welfare.

The sixth chapter studies how expectation and disgorgement damages, as well as specific performance, perform those two functions, and their impact on social welfare. It considers both situations where the promisor can renegotiate with the promisee and where she cannot and situations where the promisor breaches to avoid incurring losses from those where she breaches to achieve higher profits from a substitutive transaction. Lastly, the chapter assesses, from a normative perspective, recent developments in American, French, German, and English law. Courts and legal scholarship have insisted on the primacy of expectation damages (U.S.), expanded the scope of specific performance under *astreintes* even upon obligations to do (France), allowed promisees to recover disgorgement damages in cases of breach to make profits, in an extensive interpretation of § 285 I BGB (Germany), and expanded the scope of an award of damages at the common law in awarding, in certain cases, total or partial disgorgement damages (U.K.).

Chapter 2
Theories of Contract and Contract Law

> "The way to gain a liberal view of your subject is … to get to the bottom of the subject itself. The means of doing that are, in the first place, to follow the existing body of dogma into its highest generalizations by the help of jurisprudence; next, to discover from history how it has come to be what it is; and, finally, so far as you can, to consider the ends which the several rules seek to accomplish, the reasons why those ends are desired, what is given up to gain them, and whether they are worth the price." (O. W. Holmes).[1]

This chapter of this thesis reviews the three main theories of contracts and contract law in order to explain, firstly, the reasons they advance for why, and under what circumstances, breach of contract is a wrong in need of redress. Promisors will tend to keep contracts in circumstances where they perceive performance as morally required, and promisees will tend to retaliate to breach when they perceive breach as morally unacceptable. The investigation on the theoretical reasons for why it is wrong to breach contracts can shed light into the motives of the parties to behave in certain manners in contractual relationships, attempting to keep promises and contracts even at a personal cost, or retaliating against its breach in socially costly manners.

Secondly, the chapter studies how, and why, the law enforces contracts from the perspective of those three theories. They advance different reasons for why there is value in legal enforcement of contracts, and how different types of remedies for breach provide different incentives for parties to behave, ex ante, in certain manners. Economic theories, in studying the incentives provided by legal relief, have not considered the incentives that compensatory remedies provide to promisees to refrain from private acts of retaliation. In order to study this function of legal relief, there is the need to overcome the conception that all individuals understand the contractual obligation in one specific manner and to consider that they often attach normative significance to that obligation. Because the contractual obligation carries, for parties themselves, normative significance, parties are apt to understand breach as morally acceptable or unacceptable depending on the reasons and motives that lead the promisor to breach, and on the consequences of the act.

[1] *The Path of the Law*, 10 Harvard Law Review 457, 476 (1887).

S. Mittlaender, *Equity, Efficiency, and Ethics in Remedies for Breach of Contract*, International Law and Economics, https://doi.org/10.1007/978-3-031-10804-4_2

The next chapter complements this study and explains how promisees might expect, in certain types of contingencies, performance of the contract, while the promisor might perceive performance as not morally required and hence decide to breach. When this type of normative conflict emerges, for any of the reasons identified in the next chapter, disagreement and contractual disputes emerge. When the parties disagree on whether the promisor ought to have performed or breached, and are unsuccessful at privately settling the issue, the conflict might escalate and the party that feels wronged from breach will tend to engage in acts of retaliation and punishment if not entitled to a public remedy.

2.1 Introduction

Contracts are agreements that create obligations enforceable by law. They therefore consist in, first of all, agreements made between two or more legally capable individuals. However, not all agreements are contracts. Individuals agree in their daily life on a variety of things, ranging from the best way to study contract law from an economic perspective to the actions that two individuals should take in order to implement a mutually desired exchange, and thereby to trade. Distinctive in contractual agreements is the fact that at least one of the parties (and often both) commits to a future course of conduct by undertaking an obligation.

The first example of an agreement mentioned above, where individuals simply agree on a matter of fact, does not include a commitment to future behavior and hence does not commit the parties to do, not to do, or the give something to each other. It is not a contract, does not create an obligation, and is hence not subject to legal enforcement. The second example of an agreement, in contrast, is apt to create legal obligations for the parties, but, without an examination of its content and nature, one cannot ascertain whether the parties incur legal liability in case of breach.

Accordingly, the first question under examination is what characterizes agreements that the law will enforce, and hence what is a contract. After discussing the legal definitions of contract in the present section, the chapter reviews the three main theories of the contractual obligation that provide different reasons for why—and when—it is wrong to breach a contract. Parties will often refer to those reasons in order to ascertain their rights and duties when the deal breaks down, and will feel aggrieved and tempted to retaliate whenever the elements that make breach morally wrong are present in the realized contingency.

The second question under examination is how the law enforces contracts, and the remedies that disappointed promisees have at their disposal in case of breach. After the discussion of the default remedy for breach in common and civil law systems in the subsequent section, the chapter reviews the theoretical justifications for legal enforcement of contracts provided by those theories, and the reasons they advance for why the law enforces contractual promises.

2.1.1 *The Legal Concept of Contract in Common and Civil Law Systems*

The French civil code defines contracts, following Domat and Pothier, as agreements in which one or more individuals commit, by undertaking an obligation, to a future course of action consisting in to give, to do, or not to do something.[2]

> Art. 1101. Contract is an agreement by which one or more persons oblige themselves, towards one or several others, to give, to do or not to do something.[3]

The contract is therefore, in French law, a particular species of agreements, namely the one that generates obligations for the parties to take a certain course of conduct. A contract generates those obligations because of the meeting of wills, i.e., the *accord des volontés*, and based on the notion that only consent obliges.[4] Individuals want to be legally obliged by consent, and the law, in respect for their individual autonomy, enforces the agreements they make. They are then a source of individual obligations enforceable by law.

Similarly, the Italian civil code defines contract as an agreement between two or more parties to create, regulate, or extinguish a pecuniary obligation (*rapporto giuridico*):

---

[2] *Cf.* 1 JEAN DOMAT, LES LOIS CIVILES DANS LEUR ORDRE NATUREL, *in* OUVRES DE JEAN DOMAT 75, 121 (Joseph Remy ed., Paris, Firmin Didot 1828) (1695) ("*les conventions sont les engagements, qui se forment par le consentement mutuel de deux ou plusieurs personnes, qui se font entre elles une loi d'exécuter ce qu'elles promettent.*"); 1 ROBERT-JOSEPH POTHIER, TRAITÉ DES OBLIGATIONS, *in* OUVRES DE R.-J. POTHIER 1, 2–3 (Ainé Dupin org., Bruxelles, J. P. Jonker 1761) (1831) ("*on doit définir [le contrat comme] une convention par laquelle les deux parties réciproquement (...) promettent et s'engagent envers l'autre à lui donner quelque chose, où à faire ou à ne pas faire quelque chose.*").

Domat and Pothier both relied on the idea that contracts are agreements formed by consent, and in which parties promise performance to each other. The element of promise was, however, omitted in the French civil code's definition of contract. For the historical development from unilaterally binding promises to the principle of consent, *see* MARC-PHILLIPPE WELLER, DIE VERTRAGSTREUE 59f. (Tübingen, Mohr Siebeck 2009). For the influence of Domat and Pothier's scholarship, especially concerning the contract law, on the *Code Civil*, *see*, e.g., Marc-Phillippe Weller, *Das Vertrags- und Konsensprinzip: Vom Naturrecht über Domat und Pothier zum Code Civil*, *in* WEITSICHT IN VERSICHERUNG UND WIRTSCHAFT—GEDÄCHTNISSCHRIFT FÜR ULRICH HÜBNER 435, 451 (Roland Beckmann et al. eds., Heidelberg, Müller 2012) ("*Domats Arbeiten waren wichtige Impulsgeber für den Civil Code. ... Gewisse Formulierungen des Code Civil selbst, besonders im Bereich der Verträge, wurden durch die Werke Domats beeinflusst oder stammen von ihnen ab.*")

[3] Own transl. In original: "*Le contrat est une convention par laquelle une ou plusieurs personnes s'obligent, envers une ou plusieurs autres, à donner, à faire ou à ne pas faire quelque chose*".

[4] *See* 2 HENRY MAZEAUD, LÉON MAZEAUD AND JEAN MAZEAUD, LEÇONS DE DROIT CIVIL 45 n. 52–53 (3rd ed., Paris, Montchrestien 1966) (1955) ("*Comment le contrat engendre-t-il un droit personnel, une obligation?... la création des obligations demeure gouvernée par la règle* 'solus consensus obligat.'").

> Art. 1321. Contract is an agreement of two or more parties to constitute, regulate or extinguish a legal relationship between them.[5]

The contract is thus also in Italian law a source of legal obligations, together with delicts and other facts foreseen by law, as advanced by Gaius, and as still explicitly foreseen by the current Italian civil code.[6] Accordingly, when the parties enter into a sales contract, they incur the obligations mentioned by the law. The principal obligation of the seller is "the one to deliver the thing to the buyer…" (art. 1476, *Obbligazioni del venditore*), and of the buyer the one to "pay the price at the time and place stipulated in the contract" (art. 1498, *Obbligazioni del compratore*).

Although the German civil code (hereinafter BGB) does not provide a definition of contract, contracts are understood as multilateral legal transactions (*mehrseitige Rechtsgeschäfte*) through which individuals create (or alter) obligations (*Schuldverhältnisse*).

> § 311 I. In order to create an obligation by legal transaction as well as to alter the contents of an obligation, a contract between the parties is necessary, unless otherwise provided by statute.[7]

By the making of a contract, parties undertake an obligation to perform, and to bring about a change in the goods world (*Güterwelt*) such as the transfer of a good or performance of a service.[8] Accordingly, through a sales contract, the debtor incurs the obligation to deliver the good and to procure ownership of the good to the debtor (BGB § 433 I 1), and the debtor the obligation to pay the agreed price and to receive the contracted good (BGB § 433 II).[9] Similarly, in a service contract, the promisor is obliged to perform the promised service, and the promisee is obliged to pay the agreed price (BGB § 611 I). These actions constitute performances

---

[5] Own transl. In original: "*Il contratto è l'accordo di due o più parti per costituire, regolare o estinguere tra loro un rapporto giuridico patrimoniale.*"

[6] *Cf*. GAIUS, INSTITUTIONES III 88 ("*Nunc transeamus ad obligationes, quarum summa divisio in duas species diducitur: omnis enim obligatio vel ex contractu nascitur vel ex delicto.*") ("Let us now move on to obligations. The principal division of these puts them into two species: for every obligation arises either from contract or from delict.") Gaius later expanded the number of species of obligations to include, thirdly, "other events foreseen by the law." *See* D.44.7.I PR. (GAIUS LIBRO SECUNDO AUREORUM) ("*Obligationes aut ex contractu nascuntur aut ex maleficio aut proprio quodam iure ex variis causarum figuris.*") ("Obligations are born either of contract or of wrongdoing or, by virtue of some particular law, from a variety of types and causes") (transl. by PETER BIRKS, THE ROMAN LAW OF OBLIGATIONS 17–18, Oxford, Oxford University 2014).

The Civil Code practically translated the division advanced by Gaius in Art. 1173. ("*Fonti delle Obbligazioni. Le obbligazioni derivano da contratto, da fatto illecito o da ogni altro atto o fatto idoneo a produrle in conformità dell'ordenamento giuridico.*")

[7] Own transl. In original: "*Zur Begründung eines Schuldverhältnisses durch Rechtsgeschäft sowie zur Änderung des Inhalts eines Schuldverhältnisses ist ein Vertrag zwischen der Beteiligten erforderlich, soweit das Gesetz ein anderes vorschreibt.*"

[8] *Cf.* DIETER MEDICUS & STEPHAN LORENZ, SCHULDRECHT I: ALLGEMEINER TEIL 2 Rn. 4,5 (18th ed. Munich, Beck 2008).

[9] *See* further MEDICUS, SCHULDRECHT II: BESONDERER TEIL *op. cit. supra*, at 7 Rn. 19 *et. seq.* (obligations of the seller), 10 Rn. 27 *et. seq.* (obligations of the buyer).

(*Leistungen*), and the obligation to undertake those actions the parties' contractual duties (*Vertragspflichten*).

Lastly, the Dutch civil code similarly defines contract in book 6 (The Law of Obligations) also as a legal transaction (*rechtshandeling*) that creates obligations (*verbintenis*). The incurred obligation can be to do, to give, or to tolerate, which constitute the performance (*prestatie*) to be delivered by the obligor.

> Art. 6:213 1. An agreement in the sense of this section [an obligatory agreement, or a contract] is a multilateral legal act under which one or more parties have subjected themselves to an obligation towards one or more other parties.[10]

Thus in all these legal systems, and in civil law systems in general, the undertaking of an obligation by agreement is fundamental in the concept of contract. Underlying such conception of contract, there is further, certainly, the old debate concerning the nature *of the acts* forming the agreement, which can be understood as promises, meeting of minds, corresponding declarations of wills, reciprocal consent, or elsewise.[11] For the purpose of the present study, the question is not what is the nature of those acts, but rather the nature *of the obligation* that can be breached or performed, and thereby influence parties' contractual behavior.

There are two understandings of legal obligations underlying European legal thinking.[12] According to *Paulus*, "the substance of obligations does not consist in that it makes some property or servitude ours, but that it binds another person to give, do or furnish something to us."[13] And as per *Justinian*, "an obligation is a legal tie

[10] Own transl. In original: "*Een overeenkomst in de zin van deze titel is een meerzijdige rechtshandeling, waarbij een of meer partijen jegens een of meer andere een verbintenis aangaan.*"

[11] Domat and Potheir still relied on the element of promises in the understanding and definition of contracts. In Germany, independent of the BGB's acceptance of Savigny's understanding of contracts as "corresponding declarations of will" (*übereinstimmende Willenserkärungen*), the undertaken commitment to future behavior is still recurrently referred to by legal scholars as a *promise to perform. Cf.* Claus-Wilhelm Canaris, *Zur Bedeutung der Kategorie der „Unmöglichkeit " für das Recht der Leistungsstörungen, in* 3 GESAMMELTE SCHRIFTEN 423, 441 (Berlin, Walter der Gruyter 2012) (2001) ("*M.E. erklärt sich die Haftung des Schuldners auf Schadensersatz wegen Nichterfüllung bei einem anfänglichen Leistungshindernis einfach daraus, dass dieser die Leistung* versprochen *hat und sie nun nicht erbringen, also sein* Versprechen *nicht erfüllen kann und dass daher folgerichtig an die Stelle der versprochenen Leistung deren Äquivalent in Geld trifft.*") (own emphasis); HORST EHMANN & HOLGER SUTSCHET, MODERNISIERTES SCHULDRECHT 125 (München: Vahlen 2012) ("*Der Schuldner haftet auf das Erfüllungsinteresse, weil er die Leistung* versprochen *hat*") (own emphasis).

In effect, the BGB itself often refers to the *promised* performance in several parts, as in title 3 of book 2 ("*Versprechen der Leistung an einen Dritten*"), §§ 340–341 ("*Strafversprechen*"), § 518 ("*Schenkungsversprechen*"), § 520 ("*Rentenversprechen*"), § 780 ("*Schuldversprechen*"), among others.

[12] *Cf.* Riccardo Fercia, *Le Obbligazzioni Naturali*, in TRATTATTO DELLE OBBLIGAZZIONI 165, 216 (Luigi Garofalo ed. Padova, Wolters Kluwer 2010).

[13] PAULUS, IUSTINIAN DIGESTA 44.7.3 pr. ("*obligationum substantia non in eo consistit, ut aliquod corpus nostrum aut servitutem nostram faciat, sed ut alium nobis obstringat ad dandum aliquid vel faciendum vel praestandum.*") (translation into English by Helge Dedek & Martin Schermaier, *Obligation (Greek and Roman), in* ENCYCLOPEDIA OF ANCIENT HISTORY, Roger Bagnall et. al. eds. Oxford, Wiley & Blackwell 2011).

which binds us to the necessity of making some performance in accordance with the laws of our state."[14]

According to both, promisor and promisee are bound to each other and required to take a certain course of action. There are two fundamental elements in those definitions. The first one is the specific and concrete relation that is formed between the parties. They are not, after entering into a contract, strangers to each other anymore. They become bound to each other by the making of the contract and have duties and rights that go beyond those that members of a state, not bound by a contract, owe to one another.

The second one is the content of that bound. The individual is obliged to "give, do or furnish something" (according to Paulus), or "to make some performance" (as per Justinian). The bound is therefore restricted to perform what was agreed, and it is extinguished with the rendering of the promised performance. Performance delineates the boundaries of the obligation, and its delivery dissolves the bound and hence also the relationship.

In common law systems, contracts are understood and defined as promises that the law will enforce. In the U.S., according to the *Restatement*, "a contract is a promise or a set of promises for the breach of which the law gives a remedy, or the performance of which the law in some way recognizes as a duty."[15] The *Restatement* then provides a definition of a promise as "a manifestation of intention to act or refrain from acting in a specified way, so made as to justify a promisee in understanding that a commitment has been made."[16] A contract is therefore an enforceable promise, or a promise that the law will enforce by an award of a remedy for breach.[17]

At the common law, this is the orthodox and traditional understanding of the contractual obligation, both in theory and in practice. The contractual obligation is created by the giving of a promise with consideration. Because of that act, parties incur a contractual obligation, and legal liability in case of breach of that obligation.

It is however not, at common law, the sole theory of contractual obligation. In several cases, the sole application of such a theory of contract led to injustice in the result, and courts developed other grounds upon which a promisor may be held liable for the consequences of her conduct.[18] Promissory estoppel became a widely recognized theory for the imposition of legal obligations upon those that, in promising, induce a change in behavior of the promisee and, in subsequently breaching it, cause

[14] IUSTINIAN INSTITUTIONES 3.13.pr ("*Obligatio est iuris vinculum, quo necessitate adstringimur alicuius rei solvendae secundum iura nostrae civitatis.*") Translation into English *in* JUSTINIAN'S INSTITUTES 105 (Peter Birks and Grant McLeod trans., Ithaca: Cornell University 1987).

[15] RESTATEMENT (SECOND) OF CONTRACTS § 1.

[16] RESTATEMENT (SECOND) OF CONTRACTS § 2.

[17] *Cf.* with the definition provided by Judge Learned Hand: "A contract is an obligation attached by the mere force of law to certain acts of the parties, usually words, which ordinarily accompany and represent a known intent." Hotchkiss v. National City Bank, 200 F. 287, 293 (S.D.N.Y. 1911).

[18] As the result reached in Kirksey v. Kirksey, 8 Ala. 131 (1845), further described in the explanatory notes of the RESTATEMENT (FIRST) OF CONTRACTS § 90 ("the injustice of the result is manifest.")

harm to the latter.[19] There are reasons for why no one can change his mind to the injury of another ("*nemo potest mutare consilium suum in alterius iniuriam*"), and for the expansion of contractual liability beyond the confines of promises with consideration.[20]

From a theoretical perspective, there is, in the American scholarship, a distinct conception of the contractual obligation that was elaborated by Holmes at the end of the nineteenth century. It holds that contractual obligations have a disjunctive structure. They are generated by acts of promising,[21] but contractual promises give rise to an obligation that is not simply to do or to give something to the other, as in civil law systems. It is rather an obligation *either* to perform *or* to pay compensation, and nothing else.[22]

Under this understanding of the contractual obligation, breach of contract does not imply breach of promise if the promisor that breaches also pays compensatory damages to the promisee. As explained by Richard Posner, "you have not *really* broken your promise, because what you promised (though that is not how the contract will have been worded) was either-or: not performance but *either* performance *or* compensation for the cost of nonperformance to the other party to the contract."[23]

For Holmes, breach followed by compensation amounts to performance and, consequently, there is nothing wrong with it because there is no breach in the first place, but rather performance of the disjunctive obligation. This is true if and only if the promisee is *compensated* for losses from non-performance.[24] Therefore, compensation was, for Holmes, fundamental in the law of remedies for breach, and breach without compensation for the victim, even when socially efficient, was a wrong in need of redress.[25]

---

[19] *See* RESTATEMENT (FIRST) OF CONTRACTS §90; RESTATEMENT (SECOND) OF CONTRACTS § 90 (1) ("a promise which the promisor should reasonably expect to induce action or forbearance on the part of the promisee or a third party and which does induce such action or forbearance is binding if injustice can be avoided only by enforcement of the promise. The remedy granted for breach may be limited as justice requires.")

[20] PAPINIANUS, in CORPUS IURIS CIVILIS, DIGEST, D.50.17.75 Pap. 3 quaest. (*De Diversis Regulis Iuris Antiqui*), (Paul Krueger et al. eds., Princeton: Princeton University), 870 (1893).

[21] *Cf.* HOLMES, THE COMMON LAW, *op. cit. supra*, at 277 ("Where parties having power to bind themselves do acts and use words which are fit to create an obligation, I take it that an obligation arises.")

[22] *See* Holmes, *The Path of the Law*, *op. cit. supra*, at 462 ("The duty to keep a contract at common law means a prediction that you must pay damages if you do not keep it—and nothing else.") *Id.* at 466 ("The only universal consequence of a legally binding promise is, that the law makes the promisor pay damages if the promised event does not come to pass.")

[23] Richard Posner, *Let us Never Blame a Contract Breaker*, *op. cit. supra*, at 1350.

[24] *Cf.* Holmes, *The Path of the Law*, *op. cit. supra*, at 462 ("If you commit a contract, you are liable to pay a compensatory sum unless the promised event comes to pass.")

[25] Holmes recognized that not all individuals understand breach of contract followed by the payment of compensation as *amoral*, and that those that believe that there is some ethics in the law do understand breach of contract differently. He famously recognized that his understanding of the contractual obligation was not universal: "such a mode of looking at the matter stinks in the nostrils of those who think it advantageous to get as much ethics into the law as they can." Holmes, *The Path of the Law*, *op. cit. supra*, at 462.

Contract law enforces, both in common and civil law systems, voluntary and autonomous commitments to undertake future actions. The commitment is undertaken, at common law, by the giving of a promise with consideration; in civil law systems, by the meeting of the minds or by corresponding declarations of will. In both cases, in committing to perform a future action, parties undertake a legal obligation and incur legal liability in case of its breach.

What is far from undisputed is what makes breach of the contractual obligation a wrong. The question is important for understanding the behavior of the parties to a contract. The promisor may tend to perform, independent of material incentives, if she perceives breach as wrong, but not when she perceives breach as morally justified. The promisee, on the other hand, will feel aggrieved and tempted to retaliate when she perceives breach as wrong, but not when she believes that the promisor was justified in breach, given the realized contingency. Disagreement between the parties on whether the promisor should have performed or breached, and the feeling of aggrievement experienced by the victim, are both founded on the perception that breach of contract was wrong.[26]

Consider the situation where a buyer and a seller enter into a sales contract. If written, the contract might specify that "the seller shall deliver the specified good to the buyer at the agreed date and place" and that "the buyer shall make the payment of the agreed price upon delivery." Before that date, the seller calls the buyer and says she will not perform, but is rather breaching the contract.

The question that emerges is simple: What is the problem with that act, if any? After all, the buyer has not yet paid for what she does not receive. What makes the seller's breach of that contract a wrong, if anything at all?

One may think that it is wrong to breach a contract because contracts ought to be kept (*pacta sunt servanda*), or because promises ought to be kept (the sanctity of promises). This answer alone, however, does not satisfy, for it does not explicate why it is wrong to violate such a legal maxim, or why it is wrong to break a promise independent of further considerations related to the realized contingency.

Alternatively, one might believe that breach is wrong because (and only when) it harms the other party. This answer is also not sufficient because it does not specify what constitutes harm from breach of contract, and what should count as such. What harm does the promisee incur in the above-mentioned example? Assuming she did not invest or rely in the contract, then she suffers no material harm, and does not make any tangible loss because of breach.

Lastly, it could be the loss of expectancy endured by the victim that makes breach wrong. The promisee does not realize her promised rent of the transaction that she would have realized if the seller had performed. This assumes, however, that the baseline for harm is the hypothetical situation where the contract would have been performed. But why that baseline? After all, if the buyer had simply asked the seller for the price of the good, and left without striking a deal, then she could well have formed an expectation that she would make certain earnings in the future. In that

[26] Cf. HOLMES, THE COMMON LAW, *op. cit. supra*, at 6–7 ("vengeance imports a feeling of blame, and an opinion, however distorted by passion, that a wrong has been done.")

case, when she comes back to the shop, and the seller refuses to sell for that very same price, rather asking for a higher price for the good, then that action is not wrong, despite the loss of expected gains endured by the buyer.

There are, moreover, other consequences of breach of contract that may be responsible for the perception that breach is wrong in certain cases. Depending on the type of contingency in which the promisor breaches, the resulting distribution of gains and losses from breach may be perceived as unfair and hence as morally undesirable. Additionally, breach will often lead to an overall loss of resources, considering the interests of both parties to the contract together, and they may also influence parties' perception that breach is morally wrong or justified.

The answer depends, ultimately, on how individuals understand the contractual obligation, from a normative point of view. Theories of contract attempt to, in specifying the content of the contractual obligation, advance reasons for why it is wrong to breach contracts. They inquire into the nature of the obligation that, when violated, may give rise to disagreement and aggrievement, and, in case the agreement is legally enforceable, also to the possibility of claiming a legal remedy. It is an analytic question about the nature of the contractual obligation.[27] The question is what sorts of acts or events give rise to the contractual obligation, and, especially important for this thesis, what are the distinctive features of that type of obligation.[28]

In this respect, legal and economic theories do not agree on a fundamental issue for the law of contracts. While legal theories, including promissory and reliance-based theories, attach *normative significance* to the contractual obligation, economic theories most often disregard it.[29] Economic theories rely on the conception of the contractual obligations as a disjunctive obligation either to perform or to pay damages, with the consequence that there is nothing wrong with breach of contract if the promisor pays damages for breach.

Individuals, however, do attach normative significance to the contractual obligation and will consider breach as justified or not independently and in accordance to

---

[27] *See* STEPHEN SMITH, CONTRACT THEORY 43–46, 54–55 (Oxford, Clarendon 2003).

[28] The answer provided by theory can at times justify the autonomy of contract law vis-à-vis other legal obligations such as those arising by tort and property law, because of the distinctive nature of the contractual obligation. Or it may point to the convergence of contract law with tort or property law, because the contractual obligation is not theoretically distinct for those other obligations. This is the conclusion reached by the "death of contract" movement, advanced, e.g., by GRANT GILMORE, THE DEATH OF CONTRACT 87 (1st ed. Columbus, Ohio State University 1974), ("we might say that what is happening is that 'contract' is being reabsorbed into the mainstream of 'tort.'") For a more recent discussion, *see* Robert Scott, *The Death of Contract Law*, 54 UNIVERSITY OF TORONTO LAW JOURNAL 369, 369 (2004) (mentioning how, for Gilmore, "the triumph of reliance over bargain was an entirely salutary development" before criticizing Gilmore's prediction that the bargain theory of contract was dying).

[29] Although it is possible to develop a moral argument in favor of efficient breach on a utilitarian basis, scholars in economic analysis of law have refrained from doing so. Perhaps the single exception is Steven Shavell's recent attempt to establish the immorality of breach in an imaginary consent, justifying efficient breach in terms of consent present in the hypothetical complete contract. *See* Shavell, *Is Breach of Contract Immoral?*, *op. cit. supra*, at 439, and *Why Breach of Contract may not be Immoral given the Incompleteness of Contracts*, 107 MICHIGAN LAW REVIEW 1569 (2009).

their own understanding of the obligation they incur when making a contract. In any contingency where parties had not reached an explicit agreement on the proper course of conduct, parties will often have *conflicting* normative understandings on what is the appropriate course of action. They will often disagree whether the promisor should perform or breach.

When a contractual dispute arises, parties will cite the other's duties established in the agreement as basis for claims of right.[30] The promisee may cite the promisor's moral duty to keep the promise and the deal, and the promisor in breach may cite some justification for breach. For example, she may advance that she has the right to breach as long as she pays damages, as per Holmes, denying that the contractual obligation includes a moral duty to perform as promised. The promisee, on the other hand, may cite the violation of the moral norm of keeping promises, or of *pacta sunt servanda*, and insist that performance is, even if socially inefficient, the right thing to do.

When the deal breaks down, parties will use those duties and rights as grounds for criticizing the other party's actions:

> "[P]arties will ordinarily view the duties (and rights) arising under a theory of obligation (…) from an internal *normative* vantage-point, rather than merely from an external *predictive* point of view (as per Holmes) in which 'the duty to keep a contract' (…) [merely] means a prediction that you must pay damages if you do not keep it.' Viewed normatively, a valid agreement is far more than a mere basis for predicting the availability of judicial remedies for breach."[31]

2.1.2 Legal Enforcement of Contracts in Common and Civil Law Systems

The theoretical disagreement on the nature of the contractual obligation, and on whether it carries normative significance, leads to opposing understandings of the functions and justifications of an award of a remedy for breach. This concerns the second main question studied by theories of contract and contract law, namely why the law enforces contractual obligations by providing a remedy for the victim. The question is studied in the chapter from the perspective of those three main theories, but it is worth specifying, before undertaking that study, how positive law enforces contractual obligations in civil and common law systems.

The traditional remedy for breach of contract, in civil law systems, is specific performance of the obligation, or injunctive relief. Although this is, in principle and in theory, correct, specific performance is not the exclusive remedy to breach for all types of contractual obligations, as explained below.[32] It is also not, arguably, the most relevant and usually sought remedy, and its primacy in principle does not do

---

[30] Robert Summers & Robert Hillman, Contract and Related Obligation: Theory, Doctrine and Practice 50 (6th. ed. St. Paul, West 2011).

[31] *Id.*

[32] *See also* the detailed discussion, and the implications for social welfare, in Chap. 6 *infra*.

justice to the importance of damages for breach, and of substitutive relief, in the praxis.

In fact, in classic Roman law the principle was *omnis condemnatio pecuniaria*, i.e., for whatever performance the promisor owed, the remedy for breach was invariably a monetary award.[33] If the promisor promised to deliver a good or tract of land, perform a service, or elsewise, and did not fulfill his obligation, then the party in breach would always be required to pay a monetary amount to the victim in compensation. It was mainly in post-classical Roman law (especially in the *Corpus Iuris Civilis*) that specific performance gained its high prominence.[34] And it was this very late remedy, developed in post-classical Roman law, that modern French scholars of the eighteenth century and the German pandectists in the nineteenth century accepted and built upon.

In France, the primacy of specific performance stems from the work of Jean Domat,who famously—and very influentially—held that "the first effect of the agreement is that each of the contracting parties can oblige the other to fulfill its commitment."[35]

Under French law, the contractual obligation can entail a commitment *to do* (or *not to do*), or *to give* something, as discussed before. The remedy for breach of a contractual obligation to do something, at least in principle,[36] is inevitably an award of damages for breach, and not of specific performance, because, as advanced by Pothier, *nemo potest praecise cogi ad factum* ("no one can be coerced to a specific act").[37] The *Code Civil* accordingly foresees:

> Art. 1142. Every obligation to do or not to do is resolved by damages [and interest] in case of non-performance by the promisor.[38]

An obligation to give does not fall within that norm because enforcement of such obligation is understood to be based on the creditor's right of ownership, and not

[33] *Cf.* REINHARD ZIMMERMANN, THE LAW OF OBLIGATIONS: ROMAN FOUNDATIONS OF THE CIVILIAN TRADITION 770–773 (Oxford, Oxford University 1990); Reinhard Zimmermann, *Roman-Dutch Jurisprudence and its Contribution to European Private Law*, 66 TULANE LAW REVIEW 1685, 1698 (1992).

[34] *Cf.* Reinhard Zimmermann, *Roman-Dutch Jurisprudence and its Contribution to European Private Law*, *op. cit. supra*, at 1698–1699.

[35] JEAN DOMAT, LES LOIX CIVILES DANS LEUR ORDRE NATUREL, *in* OUVRES DE JEAN DOMAT, *op. cit. supra*, at 134 ("*le premier effet de la convention, est que chacun des contractants peut obliger l'autre à exécuter son engagement.*") (own transl.).

[36] With the expansive use of the *astreintes*, even in the enforcement of obligations to do with a personal character. *See* the discussion *infra* in Chap. 6, Sect. 6.4.2.

[37] 1 ROBERT J. POTHIER, TRAITÉ DES OBLIGATIONS ET TRAITÉ DU CONTRAT DE VENTE, *in* OUVRES DE R.-J. POTHIER, *op. cit. supra*, at 39 n. 157 (explaining that, with respect to *obligations to do*, "*[l]orsque quelqu'un s'est obligé à faire quelque chose, cette obligation ne donne pas au créancier le droit de contraindre le débiteur précisément à faire ce qu'il est obligé de faire, mais seulement celui de le faire condamner en ses dommages et intérêts, faute d'avoir satisfait à son obligation. C'est en cette obligation de dommages et intérêts que se résolvent toutes les obligations de faire quelque chose; car* nemo potest praecise cogi ad factum.")

[38] Own transl. In original: "*Toute obligation de faire ou de ne pas faire se résout en dommages et intérêts en cas d'inexécution de la part du débiteur*".

on contract.[39] Art. 711 of the Code prescribes that "property of goods is acquired and transferred (…) because of the effect of obligations."[40] Peculiar to French law, and adopted in Belgium, Portugal, Italy, and Luxemburg, is the fact that the transfer of property results exclusively from the consent of the parties. That is, contracts in France already translate property, in contrast to several other systems where it is the physical delivery of the promised good (the *traditio*) that operates that effect.

Therefore, in case of an obligation to give something to the other, which requires only that the promisor deliver the good that is already property of the other, as in sales contracts, the remedy dispensed by the law is, and should be, specific performance. This was as advanced by Pothier.[41] In essence, his argument was that the promisor cannot oblige the promisee to receive something different than the object of the contract.[42]

Specific performance is to a great extent restricted to obligations to give and is furthermore subject to several different defenses that can be alleged by the promisor in breach. It is actionable only if performance in kind is still possible in the realized circumstances. Moreover, the promisee has the choice between insisting on receiving performance in kind or recovering its monetary equivalent.[43]

In German law, the primacy of specific performance was strongly advanced by Savigny, who defined an obligation as a relation between two specific individuals, as per *Paulus*, but where one individual submits performance of a specific act to the will of the other: "a relation between two particular individuals in which a single act of one is subjected to the will of the other is the essence of *obligatio*. *Obligatio* is a legal relation."[44]

---

[39] *See* 2 HENRY MAZEAUD, LÉON MAZEAUD & JEAN MAZEAUD, LEÇONS DE DROIT CIVIL n. 946 (3rd ed., Paris, Montchrestien 1966) (1955).

[40] *See* also Art. 1138 and Art. 1583.

[41] *Id.* ("*Les effets de l'obligation par rapport au créancier sont 1° le droit qu'elle lui donne de poursuivre en justice le débiteur, pour le paiement de ce qui est contenue dans l'obligation.*"), with the important remark that *paiement* denoted not only monetary payment but also the *traditio* (delivery of possession with the intention of passing ownership) of the promised good ("*le paiement est la donation et translation de la proprieté de cette chose.*").

[42] *Id.* ("*un débiteur ne peut obliger son créancier à recevoir en paiement autre chose que ce qu'il lui doit.*") Or, in English, "a debtor cannot oblige the creditor to receive in payment another thing than the one she owes." (own transl.).

[43] Specifically concerning sales contracts, Art. 1610 follows Pothier's understanding ("*Si le vendeur manque à faire la délivrance dans le temps convenu entre les parties, l'acquéreur pourra, à son choix, demander la résolution de la vente, ou sa mise en possession, si le retard ne vient que du fait du vendeur.*") *See* further Art. 1184, which gives the opportunity for the aggrieved party to choose between performance in specie (*exécution en nature*) or the resolution of the contract and recovery of damages for breach in bilateral, synallagmatic contracts. The promisee can demand specific performance only if performance is still possible. *Cf*. Art. 1184 ("*La condition résolutoire est toujours sous entendue dans les contrats synallagmatiques, pour le cas où l'une des deux parties ne satisfera point à son engagement. Dans ce cas, le contrat n'est point résolu de plein droit. La partie envers laquelle l'engagement n'a point été exécuté, a le choix ou de forcer l'autre à l'exécution de la convention lorsqu'elle est possible, ou d'en demander la résolution avec dommages et intérêts.*").

[44] FRIEDRICH KARL VON SAVIGNY, PANDEKTENVORLESUNG 1824/25 vol. 1, book 3, at 279 (Horst Hammen org. Frankfurt, Klostermann 1993) (1824–1825) ("*Ein Verhältnis zwischen*

The consequence of this understanding is the creditor's right to demand that the debtor perform precisely what she promised to perform, or to do or give exactly what was agreed in the contract.[45] This conception was later adopted in the BGB as the principle of natural, in-kind performance (*Grundsatz der Naturalerfüllung*).[46]

> § 241 I 1. By virtue of an obligation the promisee is entitled to demand performance from the promisor. The performance may also consist in forbearance.[47]

The fundamental principle is the *Naturalkondemnation*, which refers to the promised performance and not (as by the *condemnation pecuniaria* of Roman law) to a monetary award.[48] This is not, however, and especially after the reform of the German law of obligations of 2002, the sole remedy for breach the promisee is entitled to.[49] The promisee can, if she prefers, in case of non-performance, require an award of monetary damages instead of insisting on receiving performance as promised,

---

zwei bestimmten Individuen, worin eine einzelne Handlung des einen der Willkühr des andern unterworfen wird, ist das Wesen der Obligatio. Obligatio *ist ein Rechtsverhältnis.*") (own transl.).

Savigny argued that this subjugation to the will of another is not incompatible with individual freedom and individual rights of personality, nor does it treat persons as objects, for it is restricted to one specific action and does not extend to the whole person, and thereby does not conceive individuals as objects. *Cf.* FRIEDRICH KARL VON SAVIGNY, SYSTEM DES HEUTIGEN RÖMISCHEN RECHTS (1840), vol. 1, book 2, at 338–339 ("*Soll dieses nicht sein, wollen wir uns vielmehr ein besonderes Rechtverhältnis denken, welches in der Herrschaft über eine fremde Person, ohne Zerstörung ihrer Freiheit besteht, so dass es dem Eigentum ähnlich, und doch von ihm verschieden ist, so muss die Herrschaft nicht auf die fremde Person im Ganzen, sondern nur auf eine einzelne Handlung derselben bezogen werden; diese Handlung wird dann, als aus der Freiheit des Handelnden ausgeschieden, und unserem Willen unterworfen gedacht. Ein solches Verhältnis der Herrschaft über eine einzelne Handlung der fremden Person nennen wir Obligation.*")

[45] Similarly, in the evolution of Dutch law, specific performance acquired prominence at the detriment of the Roman principle of *omnis condemnation pecuniaria. See* Reinhard Zimmermann, *Roman-Dutch Jurisprudence and its Contribution to European Private Law, op. cit. supra*, at 1700–1701 ("Dutch legal science had conclusively abandoned the concept of a necessary *condemnatio pecuniaria* and had achieved, in theory as well as in actual practice, the uniformity on the basis of a claim to demand specific performance which is characteristic of, for example, modem German law.")

[46] *See* MARK-PHILLIPPE WELLER, DER VERTRAGSTREUE 371f. (Tübingen, Mohr Siebeck 2009); THOMAS RIEHM, DER GRUNDSATZ DER NATURALERFÜLLUNG 219f. (Tübingen, Mohr Siebeck 2015).

[47] Own transl. In original: "*Kraft des Schuldverhältnisses ist der Gläubiger berechtigt, von dem Schuldner eine Leistung zu fordern. Die Leistung kann auch in einem Unterlassen bestehen.*"

[48] *See* MEDICUS & LORENZ, SCHULDRECHT I, *op. cit. supra*, at 8 Rn 18. (For example, "the seller will be sentenced to deliver and transfer the car brand x vehicle identification number y next to the registration papers to the buyer.")

[49] With respect to the reform and its far-reaching changes in the German law of obligations, *see* Claus-Wilhem Canaris, *Die Reform des Rechts der Leistungstörungen, op. cit. supra*; Canaris, *Das allgemeine Leistungsstörungsrecht in Schuldrechtmodernisierungsgesetz*, in 3 GESAMMELTE SCHRIFTEN 541, *op. cit. supra*; Gerhard Wagner, *Das Zweite Schadensersatzrechtsänderungsgesetz*, 55 NEUE JURISTISCHE WOCHENSCHRIFT 2049 (2002); Gerhard Wagner, *Schadensersatz—Zwecke, Inhalte, Grenzen*, in 35 SCHRIFTENREIHE DER ZEITSCHRIFT VERSICHERUNGSRECHT 5 (Egon Lorenz ed. Karlsruhe, Versischerungswirtschaft 2006); REINHARD ZIMMERMANN, THE NEW GERMAN LAW OF OBLIGATIONS (Oxford, Oxford University 2005).

provided that she confers a period for the promisor to perform late (BGB § 280 I and III, 281 I).[50] If the seller, for example, delivers a defective good, § 437 BGB gives to the buyer the choice between several different remedies for breach, including (i) specific performance (*Nacherfüllung* as in § 439), (ii) rescission (*Rücktritt* according to §§ 440, 323, and 326 V), (iii) reduction of the price (*Preisminderung* as in § 411), and (iv) damages for breach (*Schadensersatz* in one of its different forms).

Moreover, even in case the buyer demands specific performance, requiring *Nacherfüllung* as per § 439, then the seller can refuse to deliver performance in kind whenever doing so would require disproportional costs (§ 439 III 1). In this case, the buyer can only choose between the other remedies and must accept substitutive relief (either through rescission, reduction of price, or damages). There are further provisions barring specific performance: § 275 I prevents it in case of impossibility of performance (*Echte Unmöglichkeit*), § 275 II in case performance would be disproportional to interest of the promisee in receiving it (*Unechte* or *Praktische Unmöglichkeit*), and § 275 III in case the promisor must perform personally and performance is unreasonable for the promisor (*persönliche Unmöglichkeit*). In any of these cases, the promisee must console herself with damages for breach.[51]

Since the promisee's entitlement to specific performance depends on no further elements, while the release of the promisor from such a remedy (and its substitution for damages for breach) requires additional conditions, the primacy of specific performance persists in theory. "The general starting point in German law remains what it has been throughout the twentieth century: the parties to a contract, as a matter of course, are entitled to demand performance of their respective obligations *in specie*."[52]

In the praxis, however, damages for breach (in the present discussion, restricted to damages for non-performance, or *Schadenserstaz statt der Leistung*) have a much higher importance than the remedy of specific performance.[53] Promisors can often refuse to deliver performance in kind and instead pay damages for breach in different types of circumstances, and these circumstances were expanded with the reform of 2002.[54] Promisees often prefer, after the deal breaks down, a monetary award than

---

[50] The promisee must, if she prefers to claim damages for breach, fix a reasonable time limit for the promisor to perform before doing so (BGB § 281 I 1, dispensable under the conditions foreseen by § 281 II, i.e., "*wenn der Schuldner die Leistung ernsthaft und endgültig verweigert oder wenn besondere Umstände vorliegen, die unter Abwägung der beiderseitigen Interessen die sofortige Geltendmachung des Schadensersatzanspruchs rechtfertigen.*" The norm respects the promisor's right to cure (*Recht zur zweiten Andienung*). *See* the discussion *infra* in Chap. 6, Sect. 6.3 *infra*.

[51] *See* the detailed discussion in Chap. 6, Sect. 6.3 *infra*.

[52] *Cf*. Reinhard Zimmerman, *Breach of Contract and Remedies under the New German Law of Obligations*, 48 SAGGI, CONFERENZE E SEMINARI 9 (2002), adapted and reproduced in *Remedies for Non-Performance*, 6 EDINBURGH LAW REVIEW 271 (2002).

[53] *Cf.* Ulrich Huber, *Schadensersatz statt der Leistung*, 210 ARCHIV FÜR DIE ZIVILISTISCHE PRAXIS 319, 322–323 (2010); ULRICH HUBER, 2 LEISTUNGSSTÖRUNGEN 138 (Tübingen, Mohr Siebeck 1999).

[54] In a nutshell, the main impact of the reform, for the questions under discussion here, is the dispensing of the requirement of fault by the promisor for her possible release from the obligation to perform, under specific conditions. *Cf*. BGB § 275 I ("*Der Anspruch auf Leistung ist ausgeschlossen,*

performance in kind. Considering those possibilities, Huber is certain to ascertain "the paramount practical importance of the damages claim."[55]

The goal of damages for breach, under German law, is the *total compensation* for all losses sustained (*Totalreparation*), as in the BGB:

> § 249 I. A person who is liable in damages must restore the position that would exist if the circumstance obliging him to pay damages had not occurred.[56]

The promisor in breach shall compensate for all losses resulting from breach of contract, and this amount is, according to the BGB, reduced only in case the victim contributed to the occurrence of the losses (§ 254).[57] The promisor must put the victim of breach in the position in which she would have been in the absence of the event that created the losses (breach), according to the principle of the natural restitution (*Naturalrestitution*).[58]

In common law systems, the primary and default remedy for breach of contract is an award of damages for breach, and injunctive relief is exceptional and restricted to cases where an award in money would be inadequate to provide satisfaction for the promisee.[59] This is the case, for example, of contracts for the sale of land, or for delivery of unique goods, which are not readily available in the market and hence cannot find a substitute through money.

There are three widely recognized interests protected by an award of damages for breach, following the categorization advanced by Fuller and Perdue and adopted in the *Restatement*.[60] They correspond to the three purposes of remedies for breach that have, as explicitly mentioned by the *Restatement*, the purpose of compensating the victim for losses sustained:

> the *restitution interest*, which is the promisee's "interest in having restored to him any benefit that he has conferred on the other party,"
> the *reliance interest*, or the "interest in being reimbursed for loss caused by reliance on the contract by being put in as good a position as he would have been in had the contract not been made," and

---

soweit diese für den Schuldner oder für jedermann unmöglich ist.") to the older version of the same article, before the reform of 2002 ("*Der Schuldner wird von der Verpflichtung zur Leistung frei, soweit die Leistung infolge eines nach der Entstehung des Schuldverhältnisses eintretenden Umstandes, den er nicht zu vertreten hat, unmöglich wird.*").

[55] Huber, *Schadensersatz statt der Leistung, op. cit. supra*, at 350 ("*die überragende praktische Bedeutung des Schadensersatzanspruchs.*") (own transl.).

[56] Own transl. In original: "*Wer zum Schadensersatz verpflichtet ist, hat den Zustand herzustellen, der bestehen würde, wenn der zum Ersatz verpflichtende Umstand nicht eingetreten wäre.*"

[57] *See* MEDICUS & LORENZ, SCHULDRECHT I, *op. cit. supra*, at 303 Rn. 624.

[58] *Id.* at 304 Rn. 625 ("*Vielmehr soll der Schädiger den Zustand herstellen, der ohne das Schadensereignis bestünde.*").

[59] *See* the discussion *infra* in Chap. 6, Sect. 6.2.

[60] *See* Lon Fuller & William Perdue, *The Reliance Interest in Contract Damages I*, 46 YALE LAW JOURNAL 52 (1936).

the *expectation interest*, or the "interest in having the benefit of his bargain by being put in as good a position as he would have been in had the contract been performed."[61]

Independent of whether the law enforces contracts through injunctive or substitutive relief, awarding monetary damages or specific performance, the promisee is under both forms of legal relief equally *compensated*. By receiving performance as promised (as under injunctive relief) or its monetary equivalent measured by the expectation measure (as under expectation damages), the promisee is put in the position she would have been in case the promisor would have performed. She is equally put, under both remedies, in a position in which she suffers no loss or harm. They are both equally well suited to compensate disappointed promisees, and to undo the injustice done by the breacher to the breachee.

While legal scholars, courts and the law itself regard remedies as aimed at providing relief for promisees to redress breach,[62] thereby in effect providing a true *remedy* to cure or repair a wrong or loss, Economic Analysis of Law approaches remedies for breach exclusively as instruments providing incentives for parties that are not aimed at curing or repairing a wrong. It has studied the incentives created by remedies for promisors to perform, for promisees to rely and make reliance investments, and for parties to take precautions and to enter into only mutually profitable transactions.[63] Once breach occurs, however, there is no value in providing relief and satisfaction for victims of breach, and remedies do not have a role as a true *remedies* for wrong or harm.[64]

This is so because economic theories do not consider the *reactions* that victims of breach undertake when they perceive breach as wrong and feel harmed by it. This type of behavior is absent in models of contractual behavior developed in the Economic Analysis of Law because breach, in those models, has no normative significance.

---

[61] RESTATEMENT (SECOND) OF CONTRACTS § 344.

[62] *See* n.12–14, chap. 1, *supra* and accompanying text, and e.g., FARNSWORTH ON CONTRACTS 730 § 12.1.

[63] *See*, e.g., the original formulation of the efficient breach theory by Robert Birmingham, *Breach of Contract, Damage Measures, and Economic Efficiency*, 24 RUTGERS LAW REVIEW 273, 284 (1969) and John Barton, *The Economic Basis of Damages for Breach of Contract*, 1 JOURNAL OF LEGAL STUDIES 277, 300 (1972) (expectation damages provide optimal incentives for breach).

Steven Shavell introduced the incentives provided by different measurements of damages for the parties to make reliance investments. *See* Shavell, *Damage Measures for Breach of Contract, op. cit. supra*; *The Design of Contracts and Remedies for Breach, op. cit. supra*.

Robert Cooter further introduced incentives for parties to take precautions. *See* Cooter, *Unity in Torts, Contracts, and Property: The Model of Precaution, op. cit. supra*. For a survey of the different incentives provided by contractual remedies and different types of decisions that can be influenced by them, *see* Craswell, *Instrumental Theories of Compensation: A Survey, op. cit. supra*, at 1135.

[64] *Cf.* Craswell, *Instrumental Theories of Compensation: A Survey, op. cit. supra*, at 1178 ("In short, in economic theories the concept of compensation can be dispensed with entirely, whereas in corrective justice theories that concept is absolutely crucial.")

Without it, there is nothing wrong with breach of contract, and no reason for aggrievement or for a change in behavior. Consequently, "the concept of compensation itself plays no independent role in economic analysis."[65]

Individuals, however, do attach normative significance to the obligation created by contract, as attested by different recent empirical studies.[66] They often feel aggrieved, wronged, and harmed by deliberate breach, and this state of affairs has its very own behavioral effects, for individuals are well known to retaliate against and punish those that have wronged and harmed them.[67] They react to what they perceive as wrong.

The study of different theories of contract sheds light on the possible reasons for why, and under what circumstances, individuals may perceive breach of the contractual obligation as wrong. They identify elements that make breach wrong and that parties themselves may rely upon to assess whether breach of contract is a wrong in need of redress. Secondly, it provides reasons for why legal enforcement of contracts is necessary and justified, and discusses the functions identified by those different theories for an award of remedies for breach.

2.2 Promissory Theories

Promissory theories depart from the examination of the nature of the contractual obligation. That is, they inquire into the essential characteristics of that obligation, its distinctive normative structure, and what distinguishes them from other legal obligations, as for example those arising from torts or unjust enrichment.[68] The answer provided by the theory tells what types of events or actions give rise to a contractual obligation, and, most importantly for the argument of this thesis, what its content is, and why it is wrong to breach contracts.

Promissory theories, in brief, hold that contractual obligations are essentially promissory obligations (contract as promise). The contractual obligation arises because of a promise freely and autonomously made to another person. Consequently, the essential characteristic of the contractual obligation, shared with promissory ones,

---

[65] *Id.* at 1138.

[66] From an empirical point of view, *see* Tess Wilkinson-Ryan & Jonathan Baron, *Moral Judgment and Moral Heuristics in Breach of Contract,* 6 JOURNAL OF EMPIRICAL LEGAL STUDIES 405, 406 (2009) ("Most people agree that breaking a promise is immoral … Our results suggest that people are quite sensitive to the moral dimensions of a breach of contract"); Tess Wilkinson-Ryan & David Hoffman, *Breach is for Suckers, op. cit. supra,* at 1004 ("ordinary people think that breach is morally wrong and believe that contract damages should reflect the ethical culpability of the breaching party."); 1011 (even in single commercial arrangements, individuals "believe that breach is immoral"); Tess Wilkinson-Ryan, *The Commonsense of Contract Formation,* STANFORD LAW REVIEW (forthcoming), at 1 ("we also document a series of situations in which misunderstandings have limited practical repercussions, because even parties who believe that legal obligation is about formalities take seriously the moral obligations associated with informal promises and exchanges.")

[67] *See* the detailed discussion *infra* in Chap. 4, Sect. 4.2.

[68] *See* SMITH, CONTRACT THEORY, *op. cit. supra,* at 43, 54, 56 *et. seq.*

is its voluntary, self-imposed character.[69] The conception of the will binding itself lies in the heart of promissory theories and is a necessary and sufficient condition for the creation of the contractual obligation.[70]

In civil law systems, promissory theories are known as *will theories of contract*, since at least the nineteenth century, because of this precise conception that the contractual obligation is voluntary and self-imposed: the contractual parties "willed" the obligation.[71] They thus share the same fundamental understanding of the contractual obligation as based on individual *autonomy* in the Kantian sense that the human will is autonomous and that a person is free only when bound by her own will and not by the will of others. Moreover, promissory theories often describe themselves as will theories.[72] The fundamental idea is always that a person is obliged by contract because she voluntarily undertakes that obligation.[73]

Promissory and contractual obligations are created by communicating an intention *to undertake an obligation*.[74] They are hence, first of all, acts of communication addressed to another person.[75] However, promises express one's intentions not only to do something, but, further, to be bound to do it, that is, to undertake that obligation. Its content is to do the very thing promised.[76] The promise not only provides a reason to do the promised thing but also excludes other reasons not to perform the promised act. Following Joseph Raz, promises preempt and exclude other considerations for action, preventing the promisor from reconsidering the promised act in providing a reason to exclude considering reasons not to do it.[77]

---

[69] *See*, e.g., Neil MacCormick, *Voluntary Obligations and Normative Powers*, 46 PROCEEDINGS OF THE ARISTOTELIAN SOCIETY supp. 59 (1972) (voluntary obligations are those that arise from promises).

[70] *See* FRIED, CONTRACT AS PROMISE, *op. cit. supra*, at 2–3 (also criticizing and rebuffing several "lines of attack" on that conception).

[71] For its historical development in civil law systems, *see* JAMES GORDLEY, THE PHILOSOPHICAL ORIGINS OF MODERN CONTRACT DOCTRINE 161–229 (Oxford: Clarendon 1991) (summarizing will theories of contract law in Europe). For its development in England, *see* PATRICK ATIYAH, THE RISE AND FALL OF FREEDOM OF CONTRACT 405–419 (Oxford, Clarendon 1979).

[72] *See* FRIED, CONTRACT AS PROMISE, *op. cit. supra*, at 2, 5–6 ("I begin with a statement of the central conception of contract as promise. This is my version of the classical of contract proposed by the will theory and implicit in the assertion that contract offers a distinct and compelling ground of obligation.")

[73] *See* Johnson & Johnson v. Charmley Drug Co., 95 A.2d 391, 397 (N.J.1953) ("A contract is a voluntary obligation proceeding from a common intention arising from an offer and acceptance"); Petruska v. Gannon University, 462 F.3d 294, 310 (3d Cir. 2006) ("contractual obligations are entirely voluntary.")

[74] *See* SMITH, CONTRACT THEORY, *op. cit. supra*, at 57.

[75] In this, promises are distinct from vows, which are also voluntary self-imposed obligations upon oneself that are not made to another person.

[76] *Cf.* JOSEPH RAZ, THE MORALITY OF FREEDOM 173 (Oxford, Clarendom 1986) ("The promising principle establishes that if we promise we are obligated to act as we promised. It also establishes a present obligation to keep our promises, i.e., we are obligated to perform action X, if we promised to perform X.")

[77] *See* Joseph Raz, *Promises in Morality and Law*, 95 HARVARD LAW REVIEW 916, 928 (1982) ("All promises communicate an intention to undertake, by that very act of communication, an

At the time of deciding whether to make a promise or not, the person legitimately considers several reasons, including its costs and benefits. In promising to perform a service for a client at a future date, the contractor will consider both its costs of performance and how much she will receive in exchange (the price to be paid for the service). Once a promise is made, however, it becomes a binding directive: It provides a reason to behave in accordance with the promise and furthermore excludes reasons for not performing (technically, promises provide a reason to perform and further reasons for not following the reason provided by the directive, and this is why promises are binding).[78]

Therefore, a promise and a contract cannot be withdrawn unless with the explicit assent of the promisee. The promise is owed to the promisee and it is not up to the promisor to consider, according to promissory theories, whether breach is acceptable or justified in the realized circumstances. The promise preempts the decision to breach because of considerations of utility or harm. The obligation remains in place even when non-performance would not bring harm to the promisee or create any gain for any of the parties.

A promissory or contractual obligation is, as any of obligation, an *ought* statement. To say that a person is obliged to do something is equivalent to saying that the person *ought to* do it. And any ought statement binds the person because of a normative fundament, that is to say, because of an existent and valid norm that prescribes that one ought to do it.

Since contractual obligations are first of all promissory obligations, the aforementioned normative fundament is not originally found in a legal norm, but in a preexisting social convention or practice. For promissory obligations, the social convention of promises provides that normative fundament. The convention, following Rawls, states that

> "if one says the words 'I promise to do X' in the appropriate circumstances, one is to do X, unless certain excusing conditions apply."[79]

For Charles Fried, the notable defender of this understanding, it is the convention of promises that permits individuals to fully exert their autonomy while respecting

---

obligation"); Joseph Raz, *Authority and Consent*, 67 VIRGINIA LAW REVIEW 103, 121 (1981) ("promises are made by acts intended to undertake obligations and confer right"); Joseph Raz, *Promises and Obligations*, *in* LAW, MORALITY AND SOCIETY: ESSAYS IN HONOUR OF H. L. A. HART 210, 225–26 (Peter Hacker & Joseph Raz eds. Oxford, Oxford University 1977).

[78] *See* Joseph Raz, *The Problem of Authority: Revising the Service Conception*, 90 MINNESOTA LAW REVIEW 1003, 1003 (2006).

[79] JOHN RAWLS, A THEORY OF JUSTICE 344–345 (1st ed. 1971). Rawls' original understanding is in his classical article *Two Concepts of Rules*, 64 THE PHILOSOPHICAL REVIEW 3 (1955). *See* also Thomas Scanlon, *Promises and Practices*, 19 PHILOSOPHY & PUBLIC AFFAIRS 199, 214 (1990) ("Saying 'I promise to… normally binds one to do the thing promised, but it does not bind unconditionally or absolutely. It does not bind unconditionally because the binding force of promises depends on the conditions under which the promise is made: a promise may not bind if it was obtained by coercion or through deceit. It does not bind absolutely because, while a promise binds one against reconsidering one's intention simply on the grounds of one's own convenience, it does not bind one to do the thing promised whatever the cost to oneself and to others.")

the autonomy of the others. The convention allows individuals to project their own intentions into the future and to engage the collaboration and cooperation of others to jointly achieve their goals. Promises make this possible since they are the instruments that moral individuals have to commit themselves to a future course of action that, absent a freely undertaken commitment, would be morally neutral.[80]

An individual is thereby *morally* bound to keep his promises "because he has intentionally invoked a convention whose function is to give grounds—moral grounds—for another to expect the promised performance."[81] Since a contract is a promise, and since a promise must be kept because it is wrong to invoke the social convention, make a promise, and then break it, it is also wrong to make a contract and then breach it.[82]

John Rawls similarly viewed promising as an act of commitment, of assuming an obligation to carry on later in the future in order to further one's own ends.[83] The moral duty is substantiated when an individual invokes the convention and accepts the benefits that it makes possible for both individuals involved.[84] Upholding the promise is similar to upholding the convention, and breach of promise is similar to free-riding behavior. To renege is a moral wrong that implies abusing the social practice to exclusively further one's own goals.

The shortcomings of promissory theories lie in the failure to specify the conditions that make breach of promise legitimate, excusable, and justified. As any proposer of promissory theories must recognize, one is not obliged to keep promises or to perform contracts under all circumstances and under any possible hardship that may materialize. Rawls explicitly mentioned the possibility that one is *not* obliged to do X, after promising it, if "certain excusing conditions apply," but never explained or described those conditions.[85] He solely noted that to be binding, the promise must be

---

[80] *Cf*. FRIED, CONTRACTS AS PROMISE, *op. cit. supra*, at 14 ("The institution of promising is a way for me to bind myself to another so that the other may expect a future performance, and binding myself in this way is something that I may want to able to do.")

[81] *Id*. As the author resumes, "there exists a convention that defines the practice of promising and its entailments. This convention provides a way that a person may create expectations in others. By virtue of the basic Kantian principles of trust and respect, it is wrong to invoke that convention in order to make a promise, and then to break it." *Id*. at 17.

[82] *Id*. ("The moralist of duty thus posits a general obligation to keep promises, of which the obligation of contract will only be a special case—that special case in which certain promises have attained legal as well as moral force.")

[83] RAWLS, A THEORY OF JUSTICE, *op. cit. supra*, at 345.

[84] *Id*. at 346 ("It is essential to distinguish (…) between the rule of promising and the principle of fidelity. The rule is simply a constitutive convention, whereas the principle of fidelity is a moral principle, a consequence of the principle of fairness.") As Thomas Scanlon notes, "Rawls invokes what he calls the Principle of Fairness: If you have voluntarily helped yourself to the benefits of a just social practice, then you are obligated to do your part in turn as the rules of that practice specify. This is a general moral principle, meant to capture the wrong involved in many forms of free-riding. (…) A person who makes a promise helps himself to the good that the practice provides. According to the Principle of Fairness, then, he is obligated to comply with the rules of the practice, hence to keep his promise." *Cf*. Thomas Scanlon, *Promises and Practices, op. cit. supra, at* 199, 199–200.

[85] RAWLS, A THEORY OF JUSTICE, *op. cit. supra*, at 345 ("unavoidably the many complications here cannot be considered.")

voluntary and deliberate. As noticed by Atiyah, "few philosophers have attempted to analyze the circumstances in which a breach of promise may be found morally justifiable. When they discuss this question at all, it is usually in terms of trivial cases such as a social promise to meet or dine with a friend, which is broken because the promisor's son is taken ill."[86]

Therefore, the question of whether breach of contract (and of promise) is morally wrong, in the realized contingency, persists, for while the violation of the moral norm of keeping promises or of the societal convention makes breach wrong, not all breaches violate the norm or the convention, and thus not all breaches are morally wrong.

As explained in the following chapter, this issue may well lead parties to a contract, even when they both understand contracts as promises, in such a deontological manner, to disagree on whether breach in a concrete case is morally wrong or rather justified and excused by convention. Parties are apt to disagree in that assessment, and any reference to the moral norm of keeping promises will not provide a definitive and univocal answer to whether the promisor shall perform or is entitled to breach in the concrete case.

Promissory theories further provide a justification for legal enforcement of promises, or reasons for why there is the need to enforce promissory obligations through the law. They attempt to provide an explanation for the existence and value of contract law and a justification for the autonomy of contract law vis-à-vis tort and property law. Breach of promise is wrong, and contracts are promises. Ergo, the result of the syllogism is clear: Breach of contract is wrong. The question that remains is why is there the need to enforce contractual promises and voluntary obligations through the law.

Contractual enforcement is justified because breach violates and infringes *individual rights*. In enforcing contracts, contract law considers, for promissory theories, only the duties that the parties owe to each other. It does not consider *social goals* such as the promotion of social welfare, redistributive concerns or the keeping of the peace.[87] Moreover, it *should not* consider those social goals in the enforcement of promises.

According to Charles Fried, these social goals all lie beneath different lines of attack in the conception that the contractual obligation is self-imposed and has independent force, and are incompatible with the concept of will binding itself. Enforcement of promises because of social goals or policies, or because of the harm suffered by the promisee, are *external* to the will of the parties, or "collectively determined

---

[86] Patrick Atiyah, Promises, Morals and Law 142 (Oxford, Oxford University 1981).

[87] *See* Stephen Smith, Contract Theory, *op. cit. supra*, at 147, arguing that existing rules of contract law are consist with the rights-based conception of legal remedies ("Consistent with a right-based account, the only interests represented before the court in a contract case are those of the parties; the court does not hear from representatives of the public or other persons whose future behavior is, according to utilitarian theories, the law's real concern") before presenting fit objections.

grounds of resolution."[88] Legal enforcement of promises can be justified, without disposing of the concept of the will binding itself, and without reference to goals that are social and hence external to the promissory principle because breach infringes individual rights.

The individual rights that breach violates are the classic individual rights to property and integrity (in the sense of the right not to be harmed by other's conduct). Breach of contract violates individual interests derived from individual rights whenever the restitution or the reliance interests are involved.

Consider the case of a half-complete exchange, or the "contractual archetype."[89] One party confers a benefit on the other in advance of performance (for example an upfront payment), and the second party breaches the contract without returning that benefit. In this case, property rights of the first party are infringed: The party in breach obtains a benefit at the expense of the other, and through appropriation of a property interest held by the breachee. The promisee only consented to exchange her property for performance, and not to give her property unconditionally to the other. Enforcing the promise and returning that benefit to the promisee protects her restitution interest, and hence individual property rights.

In case of reliance on a promise and subsequent breach of promise, the promisee most often makes a monetary loss because of breach by the promisor. Contractual protection against harm wrongfully perpetrated by breach is akin to protection provided by tort law. The loss incurred by the promisee is a loss in real, material and monetary terms, caused by the conduct of the promisor, and legal enforcement of the promise is justified in order to undo that harm.[90]

The individual interests that breach of contract violates in the above-mentioned cases of retention of benefit or loss of reliance are derived from *pre-existing rights*. They are not rights created by contract. Before one entered into a contract, one already had a right of property upon the benefit as well as a right not to suffer losses because of induced reliance. In those cases, breach of contract violates rights that are not uniquely contractual rights.

Contractual liability, however, goes well beyond the protection of those interests in further protecting parties' expectation interest, which includes something that the promisee never had and never had a right to in the absence of a contract. It protects mere promissory expectations of gain. In case the promisee never conferred a prior benefit, nor invested in the contract, there is no violation of property or tortious interest, for the promisee incurs no material loss. One does not have a property right on one's expectations of gains, or upon a promissory expectation of gain.

---

[88] FRIED, CONTRACT AS PROMISE, *op. cit. supra,* at 57–58. *Id.* at 1–6 (arguing that those grounds of resolution are incompatible with liberal individualism), 72–73 (discussing when the application of the principle of sharing does not conflict with the will, autonomy or intentions of the parties).

[89] *See* Lon Fuller, *Consideration and Form,* 41 COLUMBIA LAW REVIEW 799, 815 (1941) ("A delivers a horse to B in return for B's promise to pay him ten dollars; B defaults on his promise, and A sues for the agreed price.")

[90] *See* SAMUEL PUFENDORF, DE JURE NATURAE ET GENTIUM, book III, ch. v, sec. 11 (1688) ("If a man has suffered any damage from the non-fulfilment of a promise …, the promisor is bound by natural law to make good the matter.")

Promissory theories thus need to develop an explanation for why, in promising, one creates a right to the promisee.[91] If the promise creates a right for the promisee, then that right can be protected by an entitlement, such as one to promised gains. The content of the moral obligation is, as explained before, precisely to do what one promised. Consequently, the right created by the giving of a promise is the right to performance of the very thing promised. This points to an award of specific performance, and to a court's order for the promisor in breach to perform what she had promised to do, thereby vindicating and protecting the moral norm and societal convention of promises.[92]

The first criticism that emerges is the incompatibility of such an explanation with the content of existing law in common law systems. If promises create a right for the promisee to receive the promised performance, then the remedy provided by the law should be specific performance, and not monetary damages.[93] In reality, however, damage for breach is the default and common remedy at the common law, and promisees are entitled to injunctive relief only in exceptional circumstances.

In effect, several authors recently argued that existing contract law is at odds or is at least incompatible with the morality of promises because it fails to impose a legal duty upon promisors that would correspond to the moral duty.[94] Moreover, the

---

[91] *Cf.* H. L. A. Hart, *Are There any Natural Rights?*, 64 THE PHILOSOPHICAL REVIEW 175, 183 (1955) ("By promising to do or not to do something, we voluntarily incur obligations and *create* or confer *rights* on those to whom we promise.")

[92] In civil law systems, specific performance is in fact the default remedy for breach, and it is justified precisely on that basis, and on the vindication of the principle of *pacta sunt servanda.* The contract realizes private autonomy and imposes an obligation to do exactly what one *promised* to do, since this is what one "willed." For Canaris, "*Für Verträge führt dies folgerichtig grundsätzlich zur Haftung auf Erfüllung, weil (und sofern) diese im Vertrag versprochen wird. Demgemäss ist der Grundsatz pacta sunt servanda insoweit einer zusätzlichen Legitimation weder zugänglich noch bedürftig.*" Claus-Wilhelm Canaris, *Die Vertrauenshaftung im Lichte der Rechtsprechung des Bundesgerichtshof*, in 2 GESAMMELTE SCHRIFTEN, *op. cit. supra*, at 814. ("For contracts this leads naturally to liability for performance, because (and if) this is promised in the contract. Accordingly, an additional legitimacy of the principle *pacta sunt servanda* is so far neither accessible nor in need.") (own transl.).

Others have pointed that the remedy for breach of contract has the primary function to *sanction* violations of contractual obligations in order to realize and stabilize the principle of *pacta sunt servanda. Cf*. Huber, *Schadensersatz statt der Leistung*, *op. cit. supra*, at 320 ("*Die Rechtsbehelfe, die das Gesetz dem Gläubiger für den Fall der unterbliebenen und der mangelhaften Erfüllung zur Verfügung stellt, haben in erster Linie die Funktion, die Verletzung vertraglicher Verbindlichkeiten, vor allem von Verbindlichkeiten aus entgeltlichen Austauschverträgen, mit effektiven Sanktionen zu versehen und auf diese Weise das Prinzip 'pacta sunt servanda' zu verwirklichen und zu stabilisieren.*") Or, in English, "The remedies that the law provides to the creditor in the event of nonexistent and improper performance have in the first place the function to attach effective sanctions for breach of contractual obligations, especially obligations from monetary exchange contracts, and in this way to realize and stabilize the principle of 'pacta sunt servanda.'" (own transl.).

[93] *See* Kaplow & Shavell, *Fairness versus Welfare*, *op. cit. supra*, at 1107 ("Based on their rationales for the promise-keeping notion, one might imagine that the theory's proponents would have a preference for a remedy of specific performance—for such a remedy amounts to a requirement that the promisor keep his word.")

[94] *See* Seana Shiffrin, *The Divergence between Contract and Promise*, 120 HARVARD LAW REVIEW 708 (2007), the criticism by Shavell, *Is Breach of Contract Immoral?*, *op. cit. supra*, at 439, the

objection is wider and stronger because, as explained below, expectation damages not only allow promisors to breach whenever breach is socially efficient, but also *encourage* it. Contract law thus not only falls short in enforcing the promisor's moral duty, but affirmatively *undermines* the morality of promises.[95]

According to this objection, often called the "moral objection," from a positive perspective of explaining the law, existent contract law does not *fit* with a theory of contract as promises. Secondly, from a normative perspective, it is at odds with the morality of promises in fostering efficient breach and hence immoral conduct. There is, however, another argument against the justification of legal enforcement of promises *qua* promises that is different from the one advanced by the "moral objection."

For promissory theories, the contractual obligation arises, is valid and remains in place independent of loss of benefit or reliance. Even in case the promisee is *not* made worse off by breach, thus suffering no harm by breach, the promisor is still obliged by law to perform or, at least, to pay expectation damages. In other words, one stays bound to keep a promise, or is liable for lost expectancy, in order to merely *benefit* the promisee.

Consider the situation where a buyer reaches a deal with a seller. Seconds after a shake of hands and an exchange of promises, the buyer regrets the deal for some reason, for example because she found a better price somewhere else, or because she discovered she will have extra expenses that month and thus does not want to spend money on that deal anymore. This happens before the seller starts production of the good, and before the seller can turn down any other offer from other clients, thus incurring no loss. According to promissory theories of contract, the buyer is still obliged by the promise and cannot withdraw even in case her act would not cause any harm to the other party.

The other party does suffer a disappointment or a loss of expectancy. That type of loss is not, however, a harm or a pecuniary loss. "No definitional jugglery can actually equate the position of the party who suffers a diminution of his assets in reliance on a promise, and a person who suffers no such diminution."[96] Individuals create expectations and suffer disappointments several times a day, for example when waiting in line to buy a certain good or sitting in a restaurant waiting for a certain dish before discovering that the good or the dish is sold out. They may be disappointed, but they are not harmed.

Enforcement of promises *qua* promises is hence incompatible with the harm principle, the foundational principle of modern liberalism that holds that "the only purpose for which power can be rightfully exercised over any member of a civilized

---

reply of Seana Shiffrin, *Could Breach of Contract be Immoral?*, 107 MICHIGAN LAW REVIEW 1551 (2009), and the last comments by Shavell, *Why Breach of Contract may not be Immoral Given the Incompleteness of Contracts*, *op. cit. supra*, at 1569. See further the discussion by Jody Kraus, *The Correspondence of Contract and Promise*, 109 COLUMBIA LAW REVIEW 1603, 1606 (2009).

[95] *Cf.* Shiffrin, *The Divergence between Contract and Promise*, *op. cit. supra*, at 718–19.

[96] Patrick Atiyah, *Contracts, Promises and the Law of Obligation*, 94 LAW QUARTERLY REVIEW 193, 203.

community, against his will, is to prevent harm to others."[97] According to the harm principle, it is illegitimate for the state to interfere with an individual's liberty unless because of harm, whether imminent or already perpetrated. When breach of promise and of contract does not create harm, there is no justification for legal enforcement of the promise. Consequently, the law should enforce promises and contracts only when breach creates harm.[98]

Charles Fried's arguments present the best-known defense of enforcement of promises *qua* promises, based on the violation of the social convention of promises. As detailed above, invoking the convention of promises and then reneging is wrong because it violates the convention. Stephen Smith pointed out, however, what he considers a flaw in Fried's argument.[99] While the convention provides reasons for individuals to understand breach of promise as a moral wrong, reflecting the beliefs of the vast majority of the citizens, this fact by itself does not provide a legitimate reason for the law to enforce the convention through legal sanctions. There are several different social conventions that the law does not enforce. The law should sanction only harmful acts, and while violations of the convention can trigger moral outrage and indignation in the victim, as the author notes, they do not create, by themselves, any harm to the promisee.[100]

Stephen Smith's criticism, although correct, is however incomplete. In creating moral outrage and indignation, which are not harms in themselves, breach of promise and contract, when perceived as wrong and unjustified by the promisee, is well apt to lead aggrieved promisees to feel tempted to retaliate against the wrongdoer in manners that are harmful. Decentralized retaliation and private punishment of the perceived wrongdoer harm, firstly, its victim. Secondly, it harms society itself, since the victim punishes breach according to her own individual understanding of what is wrong in breach of contract, and not according to what the law defines as a wrong in need of redress.

Legal enforcement of bargained-for promises can be justified because of its capacity to substitute for private redress, and thus to avoid harm to the victim of private punishment, and to the interest of other members of the society. Both are subject, however, to empirical and not sole theoretical investigation. They depend, firstly, on whether promisees in fact tend to retaliate and impose a real and material harm upon the promisor in breach, in certain circumstances.

---

[97] Stuart Mill, On Liberty 21–22 (Oxford, Oxford University 1859).

[98] Smith, Contract Theory, *op. cit. supra*, at 69.

[99] *Id.* at 71–72 ("nevertheless, Fried's book, *Contract as Promise*, remains the most sophisticated and complete defence of a promissory theory to date.")

[100] *Id.* at 69.

2.3 Reliance Theories

Reliance theories hold that the contractual obligation is an obligation owed to those we induce to rely. Promises and contracts are well known to induce reliance by others, and breach of contract makes the relying party most often worse off than she would have been in the absence of contract and breach. The contractual obligation is then, in brief, an obligation not to make those who we induce to rely on us worse off because of their reliance.[101]

For Atiyah, one of main defenders of this understanding of the contractual obligation as a reliance-based obligation, promises, per se, do not create moral obligations, and thus, reliance-based theories of contract stand in contrast with promissory theories.[102] Promises are, for reliance-based theories, essentially an admission of a pre-existing obligation by those that promise: an obligation based on the harm that breach of promise imposes upon the promisee.[103]

Consider the situation where a person enters a contract to rent a salon for a wedding party. This same person, relying that the salon will be at her disposal at the agreed-upon date, enters into other contracts such as hiring catering services and perhaps a band to perform at the party. If there is breach and the person cannot find another adequate salon for the party, then she loses the value of those investments made in reliance on the promise. She loses the amount invested in catering and in hiring the band, excluding what she could still receive by selling those investments in the market.

Reliance theories do not attempt to provide a full-fledged explanation for the entirety of contract law. Despite its long history in legal scholarship,[104] a recognized theory of obligation based on the protection of the reliance interest emerged from considerations of courts that, in not protecting the reliance interest because of a strict adherence to the orthodox promissory theory, promisees would have to bear a disproportionate burden in certain cases.[105] Over time, a new theory for imposing contractual obligations, *promissory estoppel*, capable of creating a legal duty where

---

[101] The fundamental piece that stresses the importance and centrality of reliance for the contract law is Fuller & Perdue, *The Reliance Interest in Contract Damages I*, *op. cit. supra*. The authors' focus was, however, to deliver an explanation of damages and not to develop a general theory of contract. In effect, Fuller reiterated and exploited ideas associated with promissory theories later on in *Consideration and Form*, *op. cit. supra*, at 799.

The best expositions of reliance theories were developed by ATIYAH, THE RISE AND FALL OF THE FREEDOM OF CONTRACT, *op. cit. supra* and by GILMORE, THE DEATH OF CONTRACT, *op. cit. supra*. *See* also SMITH, CONTRACT THEORY, *op. cit. supra*, at 78–85, and Randy Barnett, *The Death of Reliance*, 46 JOURNAL OF LEGAL EDUCATION 518 (1996) for an analysis and review of the theory.

[102] *See* ATIYAH, PROMISES, MORALS, AND LAW, *op. cit. supra*, at 123–29.

[103] *Id*. at 184–202.

[104] *Cf*. Fuller & Perdue, *The Reliance Interest in Contract Damages*, *op. cit. supra*.

[105] *See* Kirksey v. Kirksey, 8 Ala. 131 (1845). Adopting promissory estoppel, *see* Ricketts v. Scothorn, 57 Neb. 51, 77 N.W. 365 (1898) ("Having intentionally influenced the plaintiff to alter her position for the worse on the faith of the note being paid when due, it would be grossly inequitable to permit the maker, or his executor, to resist payment on the ground that the promise was given

a simple promise with consideration would not suffice, became widely recognized with the first Restatement.[106]

Contractual liability for breach of promise, according to reliance-based theories, arises when one does not do what one promised to do, and not because of falseness of the statement or promise. That is, the obligation based on reliance is not an obligation to be sincere in promising and negotiating, akin to an obligation not to lie. The wrong committed in lying is committed at the time of the utterance and is not the result of breach of contract. Liability for fraudulent and negligent misrepresentation is quite distinct from liability for breach of contract.[107]

With respect to the *content* of the contractual obligation, there are two possible explanations under reliance theories. The first alternative, defended by Neil MacCormick, is that the content of the obligation is to do precisely what one said one intended to do in order not to create losses for the other party.[108] The second alternative, defended by Stephen Smith, is that the content of the obligation is better understood as an obligation to compensate the party who relied on the statement for losses that result from breach.[109]

In accepting the first alternative, the obligation becomes almost undistinguishable from the obligation derived by promise, or the duty to perform. However, promissory theories, as discussed above, provide a normative basis for the obligation, based on the convention of promises. There is not, on the other hand, a normative basis for holding one bound to keep a promise because of harm breach would create. There exists a normative fundament for not causing harm upon others, and for compensating others for harm, but neither of these implies a norm for keeping promises.

In effect, for Atiyah, in case there has been no reliance by the promisee, there is no immorality in withdrawing the promise.[110] With no reliance, no harm can be caused through that act, and the act is then not wrong. This understanding stands in sharp contrast with promissory theories, according to which the promise cannot be

---

without consideration."); An expansion of such theory is found in Hoffman v. Red Owl Stores, 26 Wis.2d 683, 133 N.W.2d. 267 (1965) (allowing recovery for precontractual reliance).

[106] *See* RESTATEMENT (FIRST) OF CONTRACTS § 90.

[107] Victims of negligent, even if innocent, misrepresentations are entitled to rescind the contract and to recover consequential damages due to detrimental reliance. *See* RESTATEMENT (SECOND) OF TORTS § 552C. Victims of fraudulent misrepresentations can also recover expectation damages. *See* Gibbs v. Citicorp Mortgage, Inc., 246 Neb. 355, 518 N.W.2d 910, 592 (Neb.1994) (victim can recover under a negligence or a fraud theory).

[108] *Cf.* Neil MacCormick, *Voluntary Obligations and Normative Powers*, *op. cit. supra*, at 68 ("If one persons acts in potentially detrimental way in reliance upon beliefs about another's future conduct, and if the latter person has by some act of his intentionally and knowingly induced the former to rely upon him, then the latter has an obligation *not to act in a manner which will disappoint the other's reliance*") (own emphasis stressing that the obligation is not to breach, or, conversely, to perform).

[109] *Id.* at 80 (and following pages) (noting that while Fuller and Perdue, as well as Atiyah possibly regarded the making of a promise as a precondition for a reliance-based obligation, this position is in fact difficult to defend, for "if the aim of the contract law is to protect the reliance interest, there seems to be no good reason why reliance that is induced without a promise should be ignored.")

[110] *See* ATIYAH, PROMISES, MORALS, AND LAW, *op. cit. supra*, at 202–215.

withdrawn without consent of the promisee, independent of whether the promisee has something to lose from breach or not.

The content of reliance-based obligations is hence arguably better understood as a duty to reimburse or to compensate those who relied on a promise for their losses resulting from breach.[111] The contractual obligation is then simply to compensate the other for reliance losses. It is, in brief, an obligation not to make others worse off because of one's change of mind.

The advantage of reliance theories is that they justify contractual enforcement on the basis of *harm* caused by one's conduct upon others. The harm is measurable and the obligation to compensate the other for harm suffered is based on the other's *right* not to be made worse off as a result of reliance. Legal relief aims at *undoing the harm or loss*, and not at enforcing or vindicating a moral norm or an abstract legal principle.

With that, reliance-based duties are not subject to the criticism that they violate the harm principle, as they do not impose legal obligations upon individuals in the absence of real and material harm. While promises *qua* promises do not bring any material change to the world, statements that induce reliance bring, by definition, such a change in inducing acts of reliance. Those that make them are responsible for that change because of a promise, and legal intervention is justified in order to undo the harm caused by that change.

The shortcoming of reliance theories is, on the other hand, its restrictive notion of harm. They only consider harm caused by breach of contract to the promisee and do not consider the loss that the promisor would often incur in order *not* to cause a harm to the promisee. That is, they still consider only harm to the promisee, sole individual interests, and do not consider harm to both parties considered together, nor harm to fairness in the distribution of gains and losses. Moreover, they do not consider the harm to society, in the form of retaliation by victims, that compensation for reliance losses can avoid.

2.4 Economic Theories

Economic theories are defined as those that depart from the conjunction of the axioms of methodological individualism and individual rationality.[112] Economic Analysis

[111] *See* SMITH, CONTRACT THEORY, *op. cit. supra*, at 83–85.

[112] *Cf.* Milton Friedman, *The Methodology of Positive Economics*, in ESSAYS IN POSITIVE ECONOMICS 3 (Chicago, University of Chicago Press 1966) (Economics as positive science is based on the assumption that *individuals* behave as if they were *rational*); Gary Becker, *The Economic Approach to Human Behavior* 5 (Chicago, University of Chicago Press 1976) ("The combined assumptions of maximizing behavior, market equilibrium, and stable preferences, used relentlessly and unflinchingly, form the heart of the economic approach"); James Buchanan, *The Constitution of Economic Policy*, 77 AMERICAN ECONOMIC REVIEW 243 (1987) (methodological individuals and homo economicus as the constitutive elements of that provide the foundations of choice theory—when attached to with "politics-as-exchange," then they constitute public choice theory);

of Law, accordingly, assumes that individuals respond rationally to the incentives created by the law and investigates individual behavior that is affected by those incentives established by the positive, existing law. This lies in the foundations of the application of economic method to the study of the law and is denoted positive analysis.

Economic Analysis of Law additionally applies the economic method to provide a theory of law. It goes beyond the application of economic theory to make explicit how individuals respond to legal incentives with the aim of providing an explanation for the content of existing law. For that, it relies on the additional assumption that the goal of the law *is*, or *should be*, to maximize social welfare or social wealth.

In assuming that the law's goal is to maximize social welfare, Economic Analysis of Law seeks to explain existing legal rules as establishing incentives for welfare-maximizing behavior. Furthermore, in comparing incentives created by existing legal rules with other types of incentives that would lead to behavior more apt to maximize social welfare, Economic Analysis of Law provides policy recommendations. The analysis that departs from the norm that the law ought to maximize social welfare or social wealth (and, if it already does so, ought to remain unchanged) is denoted normative analysis.

Neither positive nor normative Economic Analysis of Law can provide an explanation of the nature of the contractual obligation.[113] Most scholars, in this respect, simply depart, in approval and hail, from Holmes' famous assertion that "the duty to keep a promise at common law means a prediction that you must pay damages if do not keep it—and nothing else."[114] They do not inquire, in theory, into the normative significance of that duty and do not take into account how parties' normative understandings of the contractual obligation affect their individual behavior.

In effect, the contractual obligation has, as in Holmes, a disjunctive structure. Since breach followed by the payment of damages amounts to performance of the contract, the promisor that breaches and pays damages does not breach the contractual obligation, but rather performs it. There is nothing wrong with breach of a valid contract because if the promisor pays damages, or is forced by a court's order to pay damages, then the promisor does not breach the obligation.

The problem with that understanding is not theoretical, at least as developed in the present thesis, but empirical. In following Holmes, Economic Analysis of Law does

---

Daniel Hausman & Michael McPherson, *The Philosophical Foundations of Mainstream Normative Economics*, in THE PHILOSOPHY OF ECONOMICS 226, 235 (Daniel Hausman ed., 3rd ed. Cambridge, Cambridge University Press 1984) ("If one conjoins this basic view of human nature [that human beings are rational] with explanatory individualism, one arrives at the view that the central explanatory principles of economics should be principles of rational individual choice"); Robert Sugden, *Rational Choice: A Survey of Contributions from Economics and Philosophy*, 101 ECONOMIC JOURNAL 751 (1991), 751 ("In mainstream economics, explanations are regarded as 'economic' to the extent that they explain the relevant phenomena in terms of rational choices of individual economic agents.")

[113] *Cf.* Daniel Markovits, *Making and Keeping Contracts*, 92 VANDERBILT LAW REVIEW 1325, 1333–34 (2006) ("it is famously difficult for utilitarian and economic approaches to agreements to account for the obligations of agreement-keeping.")

[114] Holmes, *The Path of the Law*, *op. cit. supra*, at 462.

more than ostracizing moral and ethical convictions from theoretical scholarship. Economic Analysis of Law additionally disregards that not all individuals, in reality, understand contractual obligations in that manner. Whether the *option theory of contract* is theoretically sound is hardly the question. What matters for individual behavior of parties to a contract is how *parties themselves* understand the contractual obligation and perceive breach, and the relationship between such understandings and their own individual behavior.

In effect, not all individuals behave *as if* breach had no normative significance. Individuals do often feel wronged from breach of promise and aggrieved from harm wrongfully perpetrated, and this has behavioral consequences. It becomes relevant for any economic analysis when it has social welfare consequences. These are of major relevance for the Economic Analysis of Law because the law is the instrument that the modern state has to influence that type of behavior, with the goal of improving social welfare.

The result of assuming that breach is understood as utterly amoral conceals the effects of breach of promise for the behavior of parties to a contract.[115] With the payment of damages, no wrong is committed through breach, and promisees have no reasons to feel aggrieved, exploited or wronged. Economic Analysis of Law then fails to locate the beneficial social welfare effects of providing just compensation for aggrieved promisees and ultimately does not advance a reason for why the law fundamentally seeks to provide just compensation for victims of breach.[116]

This is the criticism posed upon the economic analysis of contract law in the present thesis. The analysis is all throughout hardly positive in studying the ex ante effects of breach of contract upon individual behavior of parties to a contract, and how legal remedies for breach, especially monetary compensation, can influence individual behavior. The analysis is furthermore normative in assuming that the law seeks to maximize social welfare and thus to influence individual's behavior *in order to* maximize social welfare.

Economic theories have, however, delivered several reasons for why the law should enforce contracts. It has made explicit how damages for breach affect certain types of parties' contractual behavior in providing ex ante incentives for behavior apt to contribute to social welfare. These are reviewed in the next sections.

---

[115] For a newer defense and reconstruction of the disjunctive structure of the contractual obligation, *see* Markovits & Schwartz, *The Myth of Efficient Breach: New Defenses of the Expectation Interest, op. cit. supra* (defending the "dual performance hypothesis"); Markovits & Schwartz, *The Expectation Interest and the Promissory Basis of Contract*, 45 SUFFOLK LAW REVIEW 799, 808–811 (2012).

[116] *Cf.* Craswell, *Instrumental Theories of Compensation, op cit. supra,* at 1138 ("the concept of compensation itself plays no independent role in economic analysis.")

2.4.1 Anticipation of Opportunism and the Protection of the Restitution Interest

A voluntary exchange between rational individuals is, in the absence of market failures (that is, asymmetry of information, externalities, and public goods) necessarily profitable for all involved individuals, and is therefore capable of improving overall social welfare. If a person agrees to exchange a good or service for a certain amount of money, then this act reveals that this person prefers that monetary amount to the good or service. The same holds true for the other person, who, in freely and consciously agreeing to exchange, reveals that she prefers the good or service to the monetary amount she agrees to pay for it.

The agreement, however, does not bring any gain either for the parties or for society. It is the *implementation* of the transaction desired by the parties that is apt to increase individual well-being and social welfare, making both parties and hence society itself strictly better off. Simply successfully reaching an agreement does not affect, by itself, social welfare. Contract law thus seeks, firstly, to create incentives for individuals to fulfill mutually profitable agreements, such that agreed exchanges are indeed implemented.

In any present exchange, individual self-interest alone suffices for the implementation of such an exchange, for in case both parties can execute performance at the present moment, then there is no risk of non-performance by one of the parties. When trade can be implemented simultaneously, there is no need for contracting.[117] This need emerges only when the exchange that the parties desire involves a lapse of time between each parties' performance, such as when one party performs in the present and the other party must perform in the future.[118]

---

[117] *Cf*. Benjamin Hermalin, Avery Katz & Richard Craswell, *Contract Law*, in HANDBOOK OF LAW AND ECONOMICS 3, 8 (A. Mitchell Polinsky & Steven Shavell eds. Amsterdam, North Holland 2006) ("Contracting becomes worthwhile when there is a temporal element to their exchange or one party, at least, is unsure as to what her counterparty will do. For example, when the item to be exchanged needs to produced or the service being rendered takes time. Absent a contract, the parties could be reluctant to trust each other to complete the agreed upon exchange at the called-upon time, and thus valuable exchange is forgone.")

[118] Sales contracts, for example, are necessary whenever the good requires time to be produced or when the future need cannot be met on the spot, such as when the good is not readily available in the market by the time the buyer needs it. If the good can be acquired, at that time, directly on the market, then parties can well simply implement a "simultaneous exchange" at that time, with no need for a prior contract. *See* SHAVELL, FOUNDATIONS OF ECONOMIC ANALYSIS OF LAW, *op. cit. supra*, at 296 ("it is mainly for custom or specialized goods and services, not readily available on markets, that production contracts may be necessary.")

Services contracts, differently, take time to perform, such that "an exchange of services for payment cannot be simultaneous—an extension of credit by one of the parties is inevitable." FARNSWORTH ON CONTRACTS 7 §1.3. *See also* PATRICK ATIYAH, INTRODUCTION TO THE LAW OF CONTRACTS 6 (Oxford, Clarendon 1989) ("Only the simplest of the transactions can be consummated by a simultaneous exchange, such as takes place at a supermarket check-out, where the consumer unloads his trolley and hands over his money. Most exchanges of any complexity cannot be performed simultaneously. One or both parties will have to perform in the future, which

In any future exchange, the party who performs first bears the risk of non-performance by the other.[119] In the absence of legal enforcement, the first party has no assurance that the second one will fulfill her part of the deal. In effect, rational first-movers must anticipate that the second party will *not* abide but will rather default with certainty, for the other is known to prefer both receiving performance and withholding payment, and rational individuals must anticipate that choice.

Legal contractual enforcement is hence necessary to allow individuals to implement future (deferred) exchanges, for without legal enforcement, the second-mover does not have incentives to perform her part of the deal. This account that contracts are needed only for future exchanges coincides neatly with the contract law's self-described restriction of its object to exchanges that relate to the future. The transaction of barter, or any simultaneous present exchange, is not, for the law, a contract, and is not subject to legal enforcement by contract law.[120]

When individuals are assured that their contracting parties will perform their part of the deal, they are encouraged to enter into not only present exchanges, but also future exchanges. These are needed to implement several different types of exchanges that cannot be implement simultaneously. Legal enforcement has the additional function to encourage parties to enter into mutually profitable agreements for future exchanges.

For that, contract law must firstly protect the restitution interest of parties, assuring that if one party performs first, then the other party will also have incentives to perform later, and not to renege and retain any upfront benefit. With the assurance provided by the protection of the restitution interest, the party who must perform first knows that the other party will prefer to perform instead of retaining the upfront benefit, for this benefit will be restituted to the first party in case of breach.

2.4.2 *Loss of Reliance Investments and the Protection of the Reliance Interest*

The lapse of time between parties' performances entails another risk for the parties that goes beyond the risk of non-performance by the party who must perform later. It also includes the risk that circumstances might change and that even under the protection of the restitution interest, breach by the party who must perform second may become profitable for that party. If parties plan to invest in the contract, and to make investments in reliance on the promise, then they may not enter into certain

means that the other party has to *trust* him so to perform, has to have confidence that he will perform.")

[119] *See* Hermalin, Katz & Craswell, *Contract Law*, *op. cit. supra*, at 4 ("More generally, some form of commitment is necessary in any exchange in which performance is sequential, because the party who performs first is effectively extending credit to the party who performs second.")

[120] *See* FARNSWORTH ON CONTRACTS 4.

mutually profitable contracts if the law does not offer any protection to the value of those investments.

In the period between the agreement and performance, variations in costs of performance may render performance under the terms of the original agreement individually unprofitable for one party. This party will then prefer to breach and to restitute any upfront payment rather than incurring possibly very high costs in order to perform and be able to lawfully keep the previously received benefit. If the party who must rely on the promise anticipates that she will lose the value of reliance investments with a high enough probability, then she may refrain from entering into the contract or abstain from making socially efficient reliance investments.

Consider the example described above where a party rents a salon, pays for it, and, in reliance on the promise, additionally contracts a catering service and hires a music band for the party. In a contingency where the salon catches fire one day before the party, then performance becomes prohibitively expensive, with the costs of refitting the salon on such short notice being exorbitant. The landlord will prefer to breach the contract and restitute any upfront payment to the promisee.

In anticipation of the possibility of breach with positive probability, the promisee has suboptimal incentives to make valuable investments in reliance on performance if the law does not protect the reliance interest. The promisee knows that whenever breach becomes individually profitable for the promisor, the latter will only restitute benefits and will breach the contract, in which case the promisee loses the value of her investments. She will internalize the expected losses of reliance in case of breach, and if those are not compensated, then she will underinvest ex ante.

Reliance investments, or investments that lose value in case of breach, benefit only the party who makes them, and the promisor does not internalize the loss of such investments when deciding to perform or breach. This is a negative externality of breach of contract, a market failure that requires legal protection of more than just the restitution interest in order to maximize social welfare. The protection of the reliance interest through the award of reliance damages compensates the promisee for all losses incurred in reliance on performance. The promisee is put in the position she would have been in case she had not entered the contract. She is compensated for reliance losses and has incentives to make them.

Protection of the reliance interest, however, induces promisees to take *individually* optimal levels of reliance, for they are then compensated for the whole loss of those investments. They will invest up to the point where the individual marginal benefit of reliance is equal to its marginal cost. They then do not consider the probability of breach by the promisor and do not internalize the costs of socially inefficient performance.

The problem with incentives created by reliance damages is that they do not provide incentives for *socially* optimal levels of reliance. The level of reliance is socially optimal when it maximizes its *expected* benefits, that is, when it maximizes its benefits given the probability of breach. Whenever performance is not socially optimal, reliance investments are waste. If the promisee is entitled to recover all the value lost in reliance, then she will invest without considering the social costs of performance in certain circumstances, and the result is overinvestment under full protection of the reliance interest.

The protection of the reliance interest is thus justified in order to allow individuals to make welfare-improving investments before performance of the contract, knowing that in any case of non-performance they will recover not only any previously given benefits but also the value of their lost investments. Full protection of that interest, however, induces overreliance and does not maximize overall social welfare.

2.4.3 *The Theory of Efficient Breach and the Protection of the Expectation Interest*

Contract law protects not only the restitution and reliance interests, but also the expectation interest. Promissory theories justify the protection of the former based on the dictates of corrective justice, as the legal sanction for violations of the moral norm of keeping promises or of *pacta sunt servanda*), and as a mean to protect individual rights. Reliance theories, in contrast, treat the protection of the expectation interest as either not justified or justified because, given the inherent difficulties in assessing the reliance interest, computing damages according to the expectation damages better protects the reliance interest.[121]

The *theory of efficient breach*, developed in the early 1970s,[122] and refined in the following decades,[123] attempted to provide an explanation for the contract law's protection of the expectation interest (in its positive claim), and a justification for why the law enforces promises through an award of expectation damages (in its normative claim) from an economic perspective.

The theory departs from the prediction that whenever the law measures damages by the loss of expected gains from performance incurred by the promisee, promisors will have incentives to perform whenever performance is socially efficient, and will have incentives to breach whenever breach is socially efficient. Expectation damages make the promisor internalize the negative externality of breach, given by the loss of expectancy endured by the promisee. Consequently, the promisor will breach only when gains from breach are higher than the negative externality, i.e., only when breach is socially efficient.

---

[121] As argued by Fuller and Perdue in *The Reliance Interest in Contract Damages, op. cit supra*, at 61 ("as we have suggested, the rule measuring damages by the expectancy may also be regarded as a prophylaxis against the losses resulting from detrimental reliance.")

[122] *See* Barton, *The Economic Basis of Damages for Breach of Contract, op. cit. supra*, at 277; Birmingham, *Breach of Contract, Damage Measures, and Economic Efficiency, op. cit. supra*, at 273. The term efficient breach theory was introduced by Goetz & Scott, *Liquidated Damages, Penalties and the Just Compensation Principle, op. cit. supra*, at 554.

[123] One major refinement is the introduction of reliance investments. *See* Shavell, *Damage Measures for Breach of Contract, op. cit. supra*; Shavell, *The Design of Contracts and Remedies for Breach, op. cit. supra*.

As mentioned before, Economic Analysis of Law not only analyzes individual incentives created by legal norms, but further attempts to provide an explanation for existing law. The common law establishes that the default remedy for breach of contract is expectation damages, and not specific performance. However, specific performance, the default remedy for breach in civil law countries, equally protects the expectation interest since through performance, just as through an award of its monetary equivalent in damages, the promisee is equally better off.[124] In either case, she equally receives what she expected to earn, in kind or in money.

The theory of efficient breach attempted to explain the fact that the common law protects the expectation interest through a liability rule rather than through a property rule.[125]

A *liability* rule protects the promisee's entitlement by requiring the promisor that wishes to breach a contract to pay a monetary sum determined by law to the holder of the entitlement.[126] It allows promisors to violate the entitlement at their own will and requires them only to pay an objectively determined sum to the promisee. If the promisor violates the entitlement and refuses to pay that sum, then the promisee has a claim for the amount of damages prescribed by the law, in the case of expectation damages.

A *property* rule protects the entitlement when it requires that the promisee acquiesce to its transfer. In contracts, this means that promisors cannot infringe that entitlement unless the promisee consents to it, voluntarily, either for no return benefit or by selling the entitlement to the promisor. The promisor must purchase from the promisee the permission *not* to render performance as promised. In case the promisee does not acquiesce, and the promisor still breaches the contract, then courts will impose increasing sanctions upon the promisor until she performs.[127] This is achieved by a property rule when the law allows promisees a claim for specific performance of the contract.

---

124 This surely requires the assumption that the promisee does not attach any value to performance per se, and is indifferent between receiving performance or its monetary equivalent. This assumption is made throughout the whole body of the literature on the economic analysis of law.

125 According to the distinction, or "view of the cathedral" advanced by Guido Calabresi & A. Douglas Melamed, *Property Rules, Liability Rules and Inalienability: One View of the Cathedral*, 85 HARVARD LAW REVIEW 1089 (1972).

126 An entitlement is an individual's right to a value granted by the law or by the contract itself. If parties agree on a liquidated damages clause and specify in the contract the amount of damages to be paid in case of breach, and this clause is valid (because it is not punitive, in general), then the promisee is entitled only to that amount agreed by the parties. If parties do not specify in their (incomplete) agreement how much a promisor must pay in case of breach, then it is the law, through its default rule, that defines the victim's entitlements and the available remedy.

127 Property rule protection also involves sanctions imposed by courts upon the promisor in order to encourage, "force" or "oblige" her to perform. In French law—with influence upon many other continental legal systems—this is reflected in the *astreintes*, increasing sanctions that courts may impose on the promisor until he or she performs, and that can be directed to the disappointed promisee. In Germany, *Zwangsgeld* play the same role but are directed to the state. *See* Law n. 91–650 of 9 July 1991 (abrogated) and the new regulation in art. 51–53 of Decree n. 92–755 of 31 July 1992, as well as, in Germany, §§ 888 and 890 *Zivilprozessordnung* (ZPO).

Expectation damages provide incentives for promisors to perform if and only if performance is socially efficient, and hence maximize the ex ante value of the contract. Specific performance can, as proposed by the theory, lead to performance in situations where performance, in being too costly, would be socially inefficient. Since the goal of the law is assumed to be the maximization of social welfare, the explanation for the contract law's adoption of liability rule protection is that it maximizes social welfare. This is the theory's *positive claim*, which attempts to explain why the law adopts a liability rule protection and the expectation measurement of damages for breach.

Furthermore, the theory holds that in order to maximize social welfare, promisors *should* be allowed to breach whenever breach is, in the realized contingency, socially efficient. That is, breach should be encouraged whenever joint gains from breach are larger than joint gains from performance. This is the theory's *normative claim*, based on the norm that the law ought to maximize social welfare.[128]

The theory, however, as pointed out initially by Ian Macneil, and recently reiterated by Markovits and Schwartz, is, at least with respect to its positive claim, simply vacuous.[129] The reason for this is that both liability and property rule protection equally lead, under the assumptions of the theory, to the occurrence of breach whenever breach is socially efficient. This is true for both a liability rule and a property rule whenever the assumptions of the theory hold: (i) Parties can renegotiate their agreements once economic conditions change without transaction costs and (ii) parties do not make reliance investments.[130]

Under the theory's assumptions, parties have incentives to renegotiate for the release of the promisor from her obligation to perform if and only if they can both profit from it. Ex post coasean bargaining ensures that entitlements are allocated to the party who values them the most. The promisor will have incentives to buy that entitlement (that is, the right to breach) if and only if its value for herself (equal to the gain from breach) is higher than its value for the promisee (equal to the promisee's loss of expectancy). If the entitlement is more valuable to the promisee than to the promisor—that is, if breach is socially inefficient—then the promisee has no interest in selling it and the promisor no interest in buying it, and the entitlement remains in the hands of the person who values it the most.

---

[128] *Cf.* RICHARD POSNER, ECONOMIC ANALYSIS OF LAW, *op. cit. supra*, at 57 (often a party "would be tempted to breach the contract simply because his profit from breach would exceed his expected profit from completion of the contract. If his profit from breach would also exceed the expected profit to the other party from completion of the contract, and if damages are limited to loss of expected profit, there will be an incentive to commit a breach. There should be.")

[129] *Cf.* Ian Macneil, *Efficient Breach of Contract: Circles in the Sky*, 68 VIRGINIA LAW REVIEW 947, 952 (1982) ("It is, therefore, illogical to conclude that either a right to specific performance or a right to expectation damages will lead to such a [efficient, although with a different wealth distribution] result in the real world. Whatever "direction" towards or away from efficiency either of these rules has depends entirely upon the relative transaction costs each will generate"); Markovits & Schwartz, *The Myth of Efficient Breach: New Defenses of the Expectation Interest, op. cit. supra,* at 1944 ("The theory of efficient breach is vacuous, however.")

[130] *See* Markovits & Schwartz, *The Myth of Efficient Breach, op. cit. supra,* at 1945.

Social welfare thus does not depend, firstly, under the theory's assumptions, on the type of protection dispensed by the law (liability or property rule). Secondly, it also does not depend on the *measure* of damages promisors must pay in order to breach. In order to ensure an efficient outcome, the law must only define the amount to be paid in case of a violation and clearly allocate it to one of the parties. Ex post bargaining ensures that whenever breach turns out to be socially efficient, either the promisor will renegotiate with the promisee and buy her release from the obligation to perform, or the promisee will buy performance from the promisor by paying her some extra amount.

Consider the case where the law protects only the promisee's restitution interest, allowing promisors to breach as long as they return any upfront payment previously made. If breach turns out to be, in the realized contingency, unprofitable for the promisor, then the promisee that still has an interest in receiving performance will offer a price up to her whole valuation of the desired good or service in order to buy performance from the seller, but not more. The promisor will only accept to perform for a price higher than her own gains from breach, and the promisee will offer up to her whole valuation, such that parties will successfully renegotiate whenever performance is still socially efficient.

Furthermore, the theory cannot explain why parties would prefer, ex ante, liability rule protection instead of a property rule protection. If ex post renegotiation is costless, then parties will inevitably capture any gain (or avoid any loss) that breach permits and will simply bargain for the right to breach, realizing efficiency under both rules.[131]

As Markovits and Schwartz argue, there are two potential explanations that can "rescue liability rule protection of the expectation interest from this theoretical lacuna."[132] The first one is to relax the assumption of the absence of transaction costs in order to develop an explanation for why these costs are higher under a property rule than under a liability rule. The second one is to relax the assumption that parties do not make relationship-specific investments that lose value in case the promisor does not perform. "When these assumptions hold, however, the remedy (expectation damages) is theoretically ungrounded."[133]

[131] *See* Eric Posner, *Economic Analysis of Contract Law After Three Decades: Success or Failure?*, 112 YALE LAW JOURNAL 829, 836 (2003) (going further and mentioning that the argument presented by the efficient breach theory suggests that *specific performance* would be efficient, and not expectation damages: "the argument [the theory of efficient breach] neglects the ability of the parties to design remedial provisions for their contract. If expectation damages are optimal, the parties can achieve the effect of this remedy by giving each side the option to perform or pay an amount that is the function of revealed ex post values. If expectation damages are not optimal, then the parties can choose some superior remedy that would, for example, take account of reliance incentives. These considerations suggest that specific performance of the remedial portion of the contract would be efficient, not expectation damages, which in essence convert the obligation to perform into an option to perform or pay an amount determined by a court.")

[132] Markovits & Schwartz, *The Myth of Efficient Breach*, *op. cit. supra*, at 1945.

[133] *Id.*

2.4.4 *The Role of Compensatory Remedies in Economic Theories*

In the analysis of the protection of the three contractual interests, Economic Analysis of Law never attempts to justify legal remedies for breach as providing a true *remedy* for victims of breach, but exclusively as providing incentives for individuals to behave in manners apt to maximize social welfare. It does not take into account the specifically *compensatory* form through which the law protects disappointed promisees. The role of legal relief dispensed to victims to redress breach, and its social welfare value, is absent all throughout the analysis.

This is a consequence of the fact that, from an ex post perspective, compensatory remedies have only redistributive effects, and these are not *necessary* for a system to maximize social welfare.,[134,135] The only *necessary* effects are the ex ante incentives, that is, setting a remedy that makes the promisor internalize the negative externality that breach occasions. Expectation damages achieve this goal while providing incentives for promisors to breach efficiently without the need of renegotiation and are, for this reason, under the theory, justified—not because they provide just compensation for the promisee.

The implication of the economic perspective of treating damages for breach as aiming at inducing efficient performance (or, conversely, deterring inefficient breaches) by the promisor is that "the primary purpose of remedies is not to compensate for wrongful breach but to prevent it from happening at first place."[136] "Compensation itself plays no independent role in economic models" because economic theories do not locate the effect of compensation upon parties' contractual behavior, and consequently upon overall social welfare.[137] "In short, in economic theories the concept of compensation can be dispensed with entirely."[138]

---

134 As Hermalin, Katz and Craswell put it, "larger monetary remedies increase the non-breacher's payoff (and reduce the breacher's payoff) in the event of a breach, while smaller remedies produce the opposite effect. However, this effect by itself is merely distributional, and will not by itself change the transaction's expected value. As long as both parties correctly estimate the probability of a breach, the prospect of liability for higher (or lower) damages can be offset by charging a higher (or lower) price, leaving both parties with the same expected return.") Hermalin et al., *Contract Law, op. cit. supra*, at 97.

135 The remedy of specific performance also has, ex post, its own redistributive effects, since in any obligation *to do* something, courts would transform that obligation into an obligation to pay monetary damages, and in any obligation *to give* something, courts would simply order the "redistribution" of the promised good to the promisee.

136 Kaplow & Shavell, *Fairness versus Welfare, op. cit. supra*, at 1143 (adding that "we do not mean to suggest that there never could be a compensatory function. Because breach will sometimes occur (in our example and with expectation damages, only when breach is desirable), and because promisees may be risk-averse and uninsured, awarding damages may enhance well-being.") Basing the value of compensation on parties' risk-aversion makes it at the most an accessory function and purpose of remedies for breach, disposable whenever parties are risk-neutral.

137 Craswell, *Instrumental Theories of Compensation, op. cit. supra*, at 1138.

138 *Id.* at 1178.

One reason mentioned by economic theories for why the existing positive law provides compensation for promisees is to provide an implicit form of insurance for the victim, if the victim is more risk-averse than the promisor. This reason is, however, as argued by Shavell, most often irrelevant and disposable in an award of remedies for breach. Firstly, compensation can fulfill that function of providing implicit insurance if the promisee is risk-averse, and more risk-averse than the promisor. Secondly, the prospect of payment of damages is a risk for the promisor, who may also be risk-averse, and in that case parties will want to avoid the use of damages as an incentive device altogether.[139] Thirdly, in case the risk to be borne is detrimental (such as an increase in costs of production) instead of beneficial (such as a more profitable outside offer), then an attempt to allocate of risks will not lead to lower damages for the promisor.[140] Fourthly, if the risk to be borne is non-monetary instead of monetary, then compensation through damages is not an optimal form of insurance.[141] Lastly, and perhaps most important of all, whenever insurance markets work, "then the need for damages to compensate the victim is negated, and damages have a role mainly as an incentive device."[142]

In the economy, in theory, a system of penalties for breach of contract optimally calibrated at the socially optimal level would ensure performance of promises only when doing so is socially efficient, maximizing social welfare just as a compensatory system based on an award of damages for breach. After all, sanctioning breach through penalties that do not compensate disappointed promisees, but that are set at the optimal level to induce performance only when performance is socially efficient would equally maximize social welfare, providing the same incentives for rational self-interested promisors that expectation damages provide.[143]

The sole reason for the need to compensate victims of breach boils down to the costs of monitoring: "When individuals make contracts, they know each others' identity, and when one of the parties defaults on his obligation, the other automatically knows it. Hence, society ensures that this information about breach is reported by

---

[139] *See* SHAVELL, FOUNDATIONS OF ECONOMIC ANALYSIS OF LAW, *op. cit. supra*, at 311.

[140] *Id.*

[141] *Id.*

[142] *Id.*

[143] Moreover, such a system would equally encourage entering into mutually beneficial contracts, since promisees would anticipate that while promisors would perform whenever it is still socially efficient to so (if they do not, they would have to pay the fine), thus earning the expected gains through performance that would always be realized when performance is socially efficient. In such a system, promisors would not perform only when breach is socially efficient, in which case promisors would prefer to pay the optimally defined penalty (without the compensatory character, could be directed to the state) instead of performing.

These are the cases in which any hypothetical complete contract would *not* call for performance, since inefficient, although would still entitle the promisee to compensation whenever breach occurs, independent of the social efficiency of the breach. This would not, however, discourage individuals from entering into contracts because the equivalent value of the expected compensation that promisors would receive in a system of compensation should be reflected on the price paid negotiated between the parties in a system of penalties. Both systems would however equally maximize social welfare.

allowing the victim of a breach to collect or to obtain specific performance. It would be a wasteful folly to have public enforcement agents attempt to identify those who made contracts and whether they were living up to them in a world where victims of breach were not given redress and would not be motivated to report breach (except out of irritation or anger)."[144]

Of course, the fact that the promisee must earn something in order to have incentives to report breach, except out of irritation or anger, does not explain why the law protects specifically the promisee's expectation interest. Any positive amount would suffice to incentivize the promisee to report breach, provided it is higher than the costs of doing so. The law of remedies for breach is not shaped by the need to provide incentives for promisees to report breach, but rather by the need to provide compensation.[145]

Therefore, quite explicitly, Economic Analysis of Law does not provide reasons for this fundamental principle in the law of remedies for breach of contract. It solely provides a justification for why the loss that the law imposes upon the decision to breach, or the loss that promisor must bear in case of breach, should be measured by the promisee's loss of expectancy. It does not explain why there is any value, in social welfare terms, in providing just compensation for disappointed promisees. Compensation is, for economic theories, not a goal to be pursued by legal remedies and is not understood as a fundamental principle in the law of remedies for breach.

2.5 Conclusion

The main theories of contract and contract law examine the nature of contractual obligations and the justifications for legal enforcement of such. They often conflict with each other and do not provide a definitive solution to whether breach is wrong or justified in circumstances where breach may be excused according to the convention of promises or not, may cause harm to the promisee or not, and may maximize social welfare or not. Parties themselves will often assert their rights and duties, in case of breach, based on those considerations, and will often disagree on whether the promisor should have performed or breached in the concrete case.

For promissory theories, the act that gives rise to the contractual obligation is the giving of a promise with consideration, and the fundamental characteristic of that obligation is the fact that it is voluntarily and autonomously undertaken. The parties' primary contractual duty is to perform the promised act. In promising, one invokes the social convention of promises that creates the duty to perform and that provides its normative fundament. Individuals may hence well attach normative significance to breach of the contractual obligation because it is a violation of the convention and norm of keeping promises, or of *pacta sunt servanda*. Breach is therefore, for

---

[144] *See* SHAVELL, FOUNDATIONS OF ECONOMIC ANALYSIS OF LAW, *op. cit. supra*, at 588.

[145] *See supra* chap. 1, n.2, n.3, n.6, and accompanying text.

promissory theories, a moral wrong, and individuals might perceive it as such by convention.

The criticism developed herein lies in the fact that the convention itself allows for breach under certain excusing circumstances. One is not, however, as all proposers of promissory theories will agree, bound to keep promises in all possible circumstances, and breach is, at times, justified by convention itself. Therefore, it is not enough to treat breach of promise as a wrong in need of redress independent of the examination of the circumstances under which breach occurs.

According to reliance theories, the act that creates contractual obligations is the intentional inducement of reliance by the recipient of the promise. In promising, individuals induce and invite reliance, and breach of the primary duty to perform can then be understood as consisting in a duty not to cause harm to those whom we induce to rely on us. In case of breach, the victim shall be compensated for all harm sustained from breach, so that the norm is protected.

The criticism developed above considers that there are different consequences of breach of contract that can be considered as harms and hence as undesirable. Different harms will often conflict in certain types of contingencies, as detailed in the next chapter. By breaching, the promisor may cause harm to the promisee in order to do less harm to both parties considered together. There is the need to understand harm in breach of contract more broadly, including not only individual harm caused to the promisee, but also harm to the interest of both parties considered together, and harm to a fair distribution of unforeseen gains and losses.

Economic theories most often depart from Holmes' disjunctive theory of the contractual obligation. The implication is that once the promisor breaches the contract but pays damages, the contractual obligation is actually fulfilled, and no wrong is committed by breach. In effect, there is no breach in the first place, since payment of damages amounts to performance of an obligation either to perform or to pay damages.

While some individuals may share, in reality, that specific understanding of contracts, its straightforward adoption by the theory conceals that other individuals may understand the contractual obligation differently. Economic Analysis of Law, in not considering how parties themselves can attach normative significance to the primary duty, also does not consider the correlative right to the duty to perform. This, however, hides the normative conflict that might arise when parties disagree on whether and why the promisor should have performed or breached. The ultimate consequence is that, for economic theories, there is no need for legal remedies to provide relief, redress, satisfaction, or compensation to the victim of breach, since these only redistribute money between claimant and defendant, ex post, and have therefore no effect upon overall social welfare.

Chapter 3
Disagreement, Conflict, and Retaliation in Breach of Contract

"Since … retaliation may sometimes operate as a constraint on market activity, even economists who take a narrow view of the proper scope of economics might include retaliation within that scope." (Richard Posner)[1]

The present chapter studies the reasons why promisees might expect performance of the contract while the promisor might understand she is justified to breach, and thereby inquires into the patterns and characteristics of disagreement and disputes that arise after breach of contract. It reviews different cognitive biases that facilitate disagreement between the parties and which can often hinder the private settlement of the dispute. Lastly, the chapter introduces acts of retaliation as the final product of unresolved contractual disputes that have a normative character and that can often escalate to such acts of retaliation, based on the norm of reciprocity.

Parties' possibility to resort to courts, and how legal enforcement of contracts can substitute private for public redress, is studied in the next chapter. That chapter studies firstly how both retaliation and legal remedies can induce promisors to perform, although with different social welfare consequences. Secondly, it develops the argument that legal enforcement of contracts has several other advantages that makes it, when compared to decentralized enforcement through punishment, a Pareto-superior mechanism.

3.1 Introduction

Contractual disputes are recurrently observed after breach of contract. They emerge when the promisee understands that the promisor should have performed while the promisor understands that she was not required to perform by the contract. Parties then fail to agree on a fundamental normative issue in their contractual relationship: whether breach was the right or the wrong thing to do in the realized circumstances.

[1] *Retribution and Related Concepts of Punishment*, 9 Journal of Legal Studies 71, 73 n.4 (1980).

S. Mittlaender, *Equity, Efficiency, and Ethics in Remedies for Breach of Contract*, International Law and Economics, https://doi.org/10.1007/978-3-031-10804-4_3

The final product of such disagreement, in case parties furthermore fail to settle the dispute privately, will often be an act based on the norm of reciprocity. The norm of reciprocity lies in the foundations of human sociality and is a main component of any moral code.[2] It defines how the appropriate reaction to a good act is another good act and that the victim of a wrong can retaliate against the wrongdoer. The promisee who believes that the promisor ought to have performed feels wronged in case of breach. She will tend to behave in a reciprocal manner against the promisor in breach, retaliating against perceived wrongful behavior.

There are several different reasons why a promisor might fail to perform in situations where the promisee expects performance of the contract. They present different sources of disagreement that can lead the promisee to feel wronged and harmed in not receiving the expected and promised performance, and thereby tempted to retaliate. The chapter studies those in detail and later explains how retaliation to perceived wrong in breach of contract is a recurrent final product of the parties' unresolved contractual dispute.

Firstly, contracts are always incomplete and do not condition the obligation to perform upon all different possible contingencies that can materialize. They thereby very often fail to specify the appropriate course of action for the promisor. When a non-contracted contingency materializes, then each party to the contract is apt to understand whether the promisor should have performed or breached differently.

Secondly, parties can have different understandings of the contractual obligation. In any contractual gap, each party will assess whether breach is acceptable or not, in the realized contingency, by herself. They may assess the moral value of breach according to the norm of keeping promises or of *pacta sunt servanda* if they adopt or advance a promissory theory of the contractual obligation. Alternatively, they may assess whether breach was morally acceptable or not solely because of its consequences, adopting and advancing an economic theory of that obligation. Since these theories often conflict with each other, parties will often have conflicting perceptions of the moral value of breach.

Moreover, even if the promisor and the promisee both assess the moral value of breach according to its consequences, they are still apt to have conflicting understandings of what constitutes harmful consequences of breach. A party may well consider the inequality created by breach as a negative and undesirable consequence of the act, while the other party may disregard inequality and consider solely the material consequences of breach. They will hence often disagree on whether the consequences of breach make the act morally acceptable or not.

Thirdly, there are different cognitive biases that facilitate disagreement and a difference in perspective between the promisor and the promisee. The promisor in breach may well have a prior and general understanding that breach, under certain circumstances, is wrong, but in case she falls to temptation and breaches in order to achieve a higher material gain, then she will later attempt to justify and legitimize

---

[2] *See* Alvin Gouldner, *The Norm of Reciprocity*, 25 AMERICAN SOCIOLOGICAL REVIEW 161 (1960). *See* also the detailed discussion on the distinction between strong and weak reciprocity, and positive and negative reciprocity in Sect. 3.6 *infra*.

her conduct in order to avoid *cognitive dissonance*.[3] Convinced, ex post, that her conduct was legitimate and hence not wrong, she will not be willing to apologize or to voluntarily compensate the promisee.

Parties further assess the morality of breach, ex ante and ex post, subject to the *self-serving bias*.[4] The promisor will tend to interpret the conditions that excuse and justify breach, entailed in the convention of promises, more broadly and most likely including the realized contingency. She will also tend to interpret the consequences of her action as less likely to be real harms in need of compensation. The promisee, on the other hand, will tend to do the opposite, interpreting, ex post, the realized contingency as no legitimate reason for the promisor to breach, and the consequences of the act as seriously harmful.

Lastly, in their attempt to solve the dispute privately, parties will assess the moral value of breach ex post, and thus in hindsight. The *hindsight bias* inherent to any ex post judgment can lead to misperception of facts, selective recall, and a distorted assessment of the consequences of breach.[5] The victim of breach will tend to consider, with the benefit of feedback, the promisor responsible for those consequences, convinced that the promisor knew, could know, or perhaps should have known that they would arise from breach.

For these reasons, parties will very often disagree on whether the promisor should have performed or should have breached. When both parties agree that breach should not have occurred, the promisor might well simply compensate the promise and neither disagreement nor conflict emerges. In the opposite case, when both parties agree that breach should have occurred, then the promisee is unlikely to be aggrieved and hence also unlikely to retaliate or otherwise seek compensation, and yet again neither disagreement nor conflict emerges. But when the promisor does not believe breach is immoral while the promisee believes that it is so, the result is disagreement and the emergence of a contractual dispute.

The parties themselves can often resolve contractual disputes through apologies or side-payments. These will often avoid escalation of the contractual dispute to a serious conflict. Still, they are not always capable of providing a final and commonly accepted resolution to the dispute. When the dispute acquires a strong normative character, with one party convinced she did the right thing and the other convinced the act was wrong, then the party who is convinced to be in the right is unlikely to be willing to apologize or to offer any compensation to the other.

---

[3] *See* LEON FESTINGER, A THEORY OF COGNITIVE DISSONANCE (1957); *Cognitive Dissonance*, 207 SCIENTIFIC AMERICAN 93 (1962), and Sect. 3.5 *infra*.

[4] *See* David Messick & Keith Sentis, *Fairness and Preference*, 15 JOURNAL OF EXPERIMENTAL SOCIAL PSYCHOLOGY 418 (1979); Linda Babcock et al., *Biased Judgments in Fairness Bargaining*, 85 AMERICAN ECONOMIC REVIEW 1337 (1995); Linda Babcock & George Loewenstein, *Explaining Bargaining Impasse: The Role of Self-Serving Biases*, 11 JOURNAL OF ECONOMIC PERSPECTIVES 109 (1997), and the more detailed discussion in Sect. 3.5 *infra*.

[5] *See* Scott Hawkins & Reid Hastie, *Hindsight: Biased judgments of past events after the outcomes are known*, 107 PSYCHOLOGICAL BULLETIN 311 (1990); Jay Christensen-Szalanski, *The Hindsight Bias: A Meta-Analysis*, 48 ORGANIZATIONAL BEHAVIOR AND HUMAN DECISION PROCESSES 147 (1991), and Sect. 3.6 *infra*.

The theories of contractual obligation studied in the previous chapter are often unable to solve the dispute. In fact, they often conflict with each other, such as when the promisee believes the promisor ought to have performed because performance of a promise is the moral thing to do, while the promisor believes performance is only morally required when doing so is socially efficient. Each party is apt to advance her claims and assertion of rights and duties based on theories that conflict with each other and that thereby do not provide a definite resolution to their dispute. This acquires more relevance because each party will tend to advance the theory that best serves her own interests, in a self-serving manner.

In case of failure of the private resolution of the dispute, the promisee that understands she was wronged feels aggrieved. In the absence of a public remedy, she will then tend to retaliate against the promisor in breach, reciprocating against perceived wrong in a negative fashion. The final product of unresolved contractual disputes and disagreement will therefore often be an act of private retaliation and punishment.

The present chapter attempts to establish the notion of retaliation as an important aspect of contract law and explains how it is the product of unresolved contractual dispute and disagreement. There are common patterns—studied in detail in the next three sections—responsible for contractual disagreement, which is caused by the factors described above. Section 3.2 studies how the incompleteness of contracts allows parties to disagree on whether breach should have occurred or not in any non-contracted contingency. Section 3.3 explains how parties are apt to have different individual understandings of the contractual obligation that conflict with other, and Sect. 3.4 explains how even parties that understand the moral value of breach solely according to its consequences will also often disagree on whether breach was morally acceptable or not. Section 3.5 explains how different cognitive biases that facilitate disagreement make the problem more widespread and pervasive in reality than in theory.

The final product of such unresolved disagreement will then often be retaliation to breach. It is an act that goes far beyond acts of revenge and that is not restricted to acts of physical violence that are, in general, prohibited by the law. Retaliation acquires different forms in modern societies that are lawful and common, including acts such as harming the breacher's reputation in the market, refusing to transact with the breacher in the future, shading, naming and shaming, and ostracism, among others.[6] It is therefore an important and widespread type of behavior of high relevance for the law that is studied in Sect. 3.6.

[6] Similar to the forms of retaliation discussed by David Charny in commercial relationships. *Cf.* Charny, *Nonlegal Sanctions in Commercial Relationships*, 104 HARVARD LAW REVIEW 373, 392f. (1990).

3.2 Contractual Disputes and the Incompleteness of Contracts

When parties negotiate a contract, they bargain for performance and around the actions they shall take to implement the desired transaction.[7] They normally do not bargain for a remedy and tend not to consider the different factors that might lead to the failure of the transaction.[8] There are different reasons for contracts to be incomplete.

Parties write simple contracts that do not condition the obligation to perform on all possible contingencies often in order to economize on transaction costs.[9] Bargaining under asymmetric information, and the use of markets and contracts, causes haggling and inefficient trade.[10] It will often be profitable for the parties to leave the contracts incomplete in order to economize on costs of collecting information, reaching an agreement and integrating it into a contract.

Another approach that attempts to explain why parties write incomplete contracts is bounded rationality. This approach recognizes the cost of collecting and processing information and focuses on the use of heuristics in the negotiation of the contract. Rational parties are often unable to distinguish the possible contingencies that can materialize, and often do not recognize the need to specify them in the contract.[11]

---

[7] *See* Melvin Eisenberg, *The Limits of Cognition and the Limits of Contract*, 47 STANFORD LAW REVIEW 211, 217 (1995) ("Contracting parties will normally find it relatively easy to evaluate the proposed performance terms, such as subject matter, quantity, and price. In contrast, at time the contract is made it is often impracticable, if not impossible, to imagine all the scenarios of breach.").

[8] *See* Eisenberg, *Actual and Virtual Specific Performance, the Theory of Efficient Breach, and the Indifference Principle in Contract Law*, *op. cit. supra*, at 977 ("contracting parties bargain for performance, not for legal relief.").

[9] *See* Ronald Coase, *The Nature of the Firm*, 4 ECONOMICA 386 (1937) (where transaction costs are understood as costs involved in the use of the market mechanism).

[10] For Coase, the reduction of haggling is then a major benefit of integration and a driving force for vertical mergers, and a reason for the use of other institutions different from contracts, and that can save transaction costs. Williamson developed the study on how different governance structures other than market contracts deal with the problem of economizing transaction costs. *See* OLIVER WILLIAMSON, THE ECONOMIC INSTITUTIONS OF CAPITALISM (New York, Free Press 1985); Williamson, *The New Institutional Economics: Taking Stock, Looking Ahead*, 38 JOURNAL OF ECONOMIC LITERATURE 595, 599 (2000) ("any issue that arises as or can be reformulated as a contracting issue can be examined to advantage in transaction cost economizing terms.").

[11] *See* Herbert Simon, *A Formal Theory of the Employment Relationship*, 19 ECONOMETRICA 293 (1951) (studying when an employment contract will be preferred to a sales contract); *A Behavioral Model of Rational Choice*, 69 QUARTERLY JOURNAL OF ECONOMICS 99 (1955); HERBERT SIMON, THE SCIENCES OF THE ARTIFICIAL 40–41 (Cambridge MA, MIT Press 1981) (arguing that the explanation advanced by the New Institutional Economics approach, as developed by Williamson, for the relative advantages of organizations instead of market contracts misses "essential parts of the story" because it assumes that all economic actors are motivated by selfish interest. Among those "essential parts" that are missed, Simon stresses the opportunities for decentralization of decision-making within the organization that depend on loyalty of employees and their identification with the objectives of the organization, which cannot be accounted for under the traditional assumption of self-interest). *See* Ann-Sophie Vandenberghe, *Behavioral Approaches to Contract Law*, in 6 CONTRACT LAW AND ECONOMICS 401 (Gerrit de Geest ed., Cheltenham, Edgar Elgar 2011) (summarizing evidence and applications relating to bounded rationality in contracts).

Jean Tirole attempts to combine those two approaches and develops a model where parties are rationally bound and thus unaware of the limitations of the contract, but are aware that they are unaware. That is, they know the contract can go wrong, but do not know how. Parties could then spend cognitive resources to realize what can go wrong with the transaction—since they are aware this can happen—but since doing so is costly, they will often prefer to leave the contract incomplete, and save on those resources.[12]

Parties, accordingly, will tend not to consider how circumstances may change in all possible relevant manners that would render performance unprofitable for one party, or even for both of them. They tend not to specify the appropriate actions parties shall take in case circumstances change in those manners. Lastly, they tend not to specify how gains and losses shall be distributed and allocated in case of the realization of those contingencies.

Still, parties may well agree that performance is required or excused in a contingency that would entail, most commonly, a change in the costs of performance of the promisor. Parties can condition the obligation to perform on the realization of a certain contingency. The contract may well foresee that the photographer is required to take pictures of the wedding that will be celebrated outside even if it rains, snows, or thunders, or that the photographer is not obliged to do it in some or all of those contingencies.

In that case, if parties foresaw the contingency and agreed that performance was required, then one can infer they did so because performance was valuable enough for the promisee to require a commitment from the promisor to perform even in those conditions. The promisee may want that commitment, for example, because she places an inestimable value upon the photographs of the wedding. The promisor, knowing that performance will then entail higher costs, will negotiate and require a higher price for the contract than in case she did not foresee the contingency. The promisor will consider her expected costs and will undertake the contractual obligation to perform if and only if she receives its monetary equivalent. In doing so, the promisor assumes a risk for which she is remunerated and that was voluntarily assumed because it was profitable to do so.

The promisor then cannot, afterward, and in case the contingency materializes, refer to the possibly very high losses she would have to incur in order to deliver performance, for she received its monetary equivalent ex ante. The promisor is then, unequivocally, morally, and legally obliged to perform. Breach is then never justified, and, while the promisor has no reason to understand that she is released from the obligation to perform, the promisee has every reason to understand that the promisor ought to have performed.

There is no normative conflict in those cases, for there are no reasons to understand breach as justified and as not immoral, either by the promisor or by the promisee. A normative conflict does not arise when there are no grounds to deny the obligation to

[12] *See* Jean Tirole, *Cognition and Incomplete Contracts*, 99 AMERICAN ECONOMIC REVIEW 265 (1999); Jean Tirole, *Cognitive Games and Cognitive Traps* (forthcoming) (especially the section "cognition-intensive contracting" for a more general model that encompasses the previous one).

perform. If the promisor breaches in a contingency explicitly foreseen by the contract as requiring performance, then conflict is certain to emerge without being preceded by normative conflict, or by disagreement. Breach is then certainly immoral.[13]

Parties will only agree that performance is required in a certain contingency if the value of performance for the promisee is higher than the costs of performance for the promisor. Otherwise, there are no joint gains to be achieved through performance in the contingency, and parties will not agree on it. They may, however, either explicitly agree that the promisor is excused from the obligation to perform whenever such contingencies materialize or leave the contract incomplete. In case they explicitly agree on a release clause, there is not, yet again, any ground for normative conflict in case of breach in that contingency, for there are no reasons for the promisee to understand breach as wrong, and every reason for the promisor to understand that she is not obliged to perform.[14]

Contractual disputes emerge in contingencies that were not explicitly foreseen by the parties or that were not included in the contract, thus in any situation where there was no explicit agreement on the proper course of conduct. Furthermore, in these cases, parties do not reach an agreement on what constitutes, for them, harm in their relationship, and on who should bear those harms if they materialize. These constitute the elements that parties must interpret in order to assess whether breach was justified or wrong, and thus for the emergence of a normative conflict.

It is well known that contracts are largely incomplete.[15] Common and everyday contracts, just as extremely complex business contracts, all certainly fail to condition

---

[13] *Cf.* Shavell, *Is Breach of Contract Immoral?, op. cit. supra*, at 444 ("if a person makes a promise to do something in a given contingency, he has imposed upon himself a moral obligation to do that thing if the named contingency arises"); *Why Breach of Contract May Not Be Immoral Given the Incompleteness of Contracts, op. cit. supra*, at 1570 ("Suppose that the contract specifies that if (…) theft occurs, the seller still has an obligation to clear snow (perhaps because he can readily rent snow clearing equipment). Then the seller is assumed to have a moral duty to clear snow even if his equipment is stolen.").

[14] *Cf.* Shavell, *Is Breach of Contract Immoral?, op. cit. supra*, at 443 ("if the contract says that the seller is excused from having to clear snow if his equipment is stolen, then the seller would not have a moral duty to perform if his equipment is stolen.").

[15] *Cf*. Jean Tirole, *Incomplete Contracts*, 67 ECONOMETRICA 741, 741 (1999) ("Almost every economist would agree that actual contracts are or appear quite incomplete. Many contracts are vague or silent on a number of key features"); Eric Maskin & Jean Tirole, *Unforeseen Contingencies and Incomplete Contracts*, 66 REVIEW OF ECONOMIC STUDIES 83, 83 (1999) (same), Jean Tirole, *Cognition and Incomplete Contracts, op. cit. supra*, at 265 ("Contracts are never too detailed or too long.") The seminal works of Grossman, Hart, and Moore assume the existence of contingencies that cannot be described at the time parties contract, and that parties thus cannot make the contractual clauses a function of them. They will rather have incentives to re-negotiate their contracts when they materialize. *See* Sanford Grossman & Oliver Hart, *The Costs and Benefits of Ownership: A Theory of Vertical and Lateral Integration*, 94 JOURNAL OF POLITICAL ECONOMY 691, 696 (1986) ("We have in mind a situation in which it is prohibitively difficult to think about and describe unambiguously in advance how all the potentially relevant aspects of the production allocation should be chosen as a function of the many states of the world") Oliver Hart & John Moore, *Property Rights and the Nature of the Firm*, 98 JOURNAL OF POLITICAL ECONOMY 1119, 1122 (1990) (assuming, somehow differently, "that it is costly for agents to write detailed long-term contracts that precisely specify current and future actions as a function of every possible eventuality.").

upon all possible contingencies that may materialize. As noted by Richard Posner, complete contingent contracts are simply impossible.[16] There are three main reasons advanced by the literature for this fact.

First, unforeseen contingencies cannot be discussed, by definition, by the parties at the time of negotiations (for otherwise, they would not be *unforeseen* contingencies). They are therefore absent in the parties' contract. When they materialize, the parties cannot refer to the agreement for a precise, univocal, and convergent assessment of what parties ought to do.

Second, even if the parties foresee the contingency, it may not be common knowledge (commonly observable). This type of asymmetry of information can occur between the parties, or between those and a third party. In the first case, one of the parties, most commonly the promisee, cannot observe either the realized state of the world (hidden information) or the action taken by the promisor (hidden action). In the second case, the third party (normally courts) cannot verify the realized state or the actions undertaken by the parties in the realized contingency.

If the contingency is not common knowledge to the parties, but can be foreseen by them, then parties could, in principle, agree that the promisor is or is not obliged to perform in it. Parties may, for example, know that there can be a storm, but if the promisee is out of town, then she may be unable to observe whether the storm affected the street or neighborhood of the promisor. Parties could agree, ex ante, that the promisor is released from performance in a contingency that they know that can happen with a certain probability and with certain consequences, and negotiate the contract price accordingly. If the storm can happen with probability of 0.1, entailing an increase in costs of performance of $100, then the promisor can give a discount of $10 for the promisee in exchange for the release, and both parties could be made better off. Parties could, in principle, complete their contract.

This is not, however, a real possibility for the parties, and it can be, quite on the contrary, a receipt for opportunism and for contractual inefficiency. When the promisee cannot observe the realized contingency, agreeing on a clause that releases the promisor in such contingency leaves the promisor free to breach whenever she wants and free to claim, later, that the realized contingency was exactly the one releasing her. The promisee would not be able to do anything against it since she cannot observe the realized state. If the contract releases the promisor in case of a storm, and the promisee (or anyone else) cannot observe it, then under sun, rain, snow, or storm, the promisor can always breach and later claim that there was a torrential storm.

Rational promisees will anticipate that they will not be able to discern which was the realized contingency or the action undertaken by the promisor, and will not pay a higher price to contract performance upon its realization, nor will they accept any lower price to agree on a release clause in favor of the promisor. Parties are thereby

---

[16] *Cf.* Haslund v. Simon Property Group, Inc., 378 F.3d 653 (7th Cir.2004) ("Complete contingent contracts are impossible. The future, over which contracted performance evolves, is too uncertain. We once decided a case in which the contract exceeded 2000 pages yet the dispute that gave rise to the suit had not been anticipated (or, if anticipated, provided for). *S.A. Healy Co. v. Milwaukee Metropolitan Sewage District*, 50 F.3d 476 (7th Cir.1995).").

very often prevented from completing the contract even when they can foresee the contingency, but when the contingency is not commonly observable.

Moreover, even if the contingency is foreseen and observable to both parties, it may not be verifiable before courts.[17] In this case, parties could, yet again, agree on a contractual clause addressing it, and later further observe the realized state. However, in anticipation that courts will not be able to discern the state, being thus be unable to enforce any contractual clause including it, parties are again prevented from contracting upon it.[18] The promisee knows, ex ante, that the promisor may breach in the contingency without legal consequences and will not pay a higher price for the promisor's commitment to perform under that contingency, for this commitment, in being unenforceable, is valueless for rational individuals.

Third, agreeing on all possible different contingencies that may materialize requires time and energy, as does describing them in the agreement, and parties will often find it unprofitable to do so. Although they could foresee the contingency, agree on it, include it in the contract, and later enforce the contractual clause addressing it, parties are often prevented from contracting upon it because of the resource costs of negotiating and reducing the agreed-upon allocation of risks to a written form.[19]

For any of these reasons, parties often do not reach an explicit agreement on what is the proper course of conduct under circumstances different from those in place at the time of striking the deal.[20] When a non-contracted contingency materializes, there is no straightforward answer to the question of whether breach is immoral, not immoral, or perhaps even the moral thing to do.[21] Parties must assess the moral

---

[17] It is worth noting that the fact that the contract is incomplete does not make it unenforceable for indefiniteness. *Cf. Haslund v. Simon Property Group, Inc.*, 378 F.3d 653 (7th Cir.2004) ("The fact that a contract is incomplete, presents interpretative questions, bristles with unresolved contingencies, and in short has as many holes as a Swiss cheese does not make it unenforceable for indefiniteness."). It is unenforceable for indefiniteness when there is an omission of a crucial term that courts cannot supply through interpretation, such as the price.

[18] In effect, if parties can observe the realization of the contingency, they can assess that the promisor then ought to have performed. They are able to contract upon it but must rely solely on self-enforcing mechanisms, what can be effective in relational contracts and in repeated interactions. In any single interaction, however, this is not a possibility for strict self-interested individuals, for there are no future gains from repeated interactions.

[19] These resource costs include furthermore the possibility that parties can err in expressing their mutual agreement on which of them should bear what risks in their contract. *See* Charles Goetz & Robert Scott, *The Limits of Expanded Choice: An Analysis of the Interactions Between Express and Implied Contract Terms*, 73 CALIFORNIA LAW REVIEW 261 (1985).

[20] Moreover, an incomplete contract reveals that there is no agreement regarding the consequences of breach in non-contracted contingencies. Parties not only do not reach an agreement on whether performance was required or not, but also fail to specify the actions they should take in case that contingency materializes, including the duty and extent of compensation. That is, there is no agreement on who should appropriate the gains or bear the losses resulting from breach, and on what each party is entitled to in those cases. Parties will hence often disagree also on the amount of compensation.

[21] There is also no straightforward answer to how courts should solve the dispute, letting the losses lie where they fall—thus doing nothing about it—adopting an ex ante perspective and filling in the gaps on the basis of what parties reasonably agreed to at the time of contracting, or adopting an

value of breach, given the realized circumstances, by themselves.[22] They can do so either in a deontological or consequentialist manner, something that will often cause further disagreement.

3.3 Disagreement on the Moral Value of Breach

According to a deontological assessment, an act is immoral if it violates a moral norm.[23] In case of breach of contract, the relevant moral norm is the norm of keeping promises.[24] The norm itself, however, foresees that one is not obliged to perform under all circumstances and that there are excusing conditions that, if materialized, release the promisor from the obligation to perform. As any proposer of promissory theories of contract—and any individual that understands contractual obligations in this manner—must accept, one is not obliged to keep a promise under all possible circumstances and hardships that may materialize.

---

ex post perspective by imposing an equitable adjustment to the disputed contract by taking into consideration all the information courts have at the time of adjudication.

[22] In case of a contractual gap, performance can become, for the promisor, *impossible*, in which case the promisor is clearly neither morally nor legally obliged to perform. The concept of impossibility is certainly open and subject to interpretation, for performance is almost never *really* impossible. It may be, however, *impractical*. A painter with a broken right arm can still paint, even if this would take ten times longer than in case of no broken arm, and a contractor can always clear the snow from the front of the promisee's shop, even under extreme adverse weather conditions, if she hires adequate equipment (man is able to reach the earth's pole nowadays).

In Germany, the classical case of impractical performance is the case of the lost ring, promised to somebody else, which falls into the sea. In case performance is impossible (for the promisor or for anybody), then it leads to the exclusion of the primary duty to perform (*Ausschluss des primären Leistungsanspruch*), as in BGB § 275 I. In case performance is impractical, as is the case of the ring that, as advanced by Canaris, still *can* be found, then the promisor can refuse to perform, as in BGB § 275 II, subject to several conditions. Impracticability requires that the interest of the promisee stand in great disproportion to the costs that the promisor would have to incur to find the ring with divers. *Cf*. Canaris, *Die Reform des Rechts der Leistungsstörungen, op. cit. supra*, at 499, 501–502; Canaris, *Die Behandlung nicht zu vertretender Leistungshindernisse nach § 275 Abs. 2 BGB beim Stückkauf*, 59 Nr. 5 JURISTENZEITUNG 214 (2004).

Both in case of impossibility and impracticability, even when the promisor claims she could not possibly have performed, or that performance was impractical ("*in einem groben Missverhältnis zu dem Leistungsinteresse des Gläubigers steht,*" as in BGB § 275 II), the promisee may well disagree and argue it was possible and practical, and that the promisor should bear those costs to perform as promised. There is therefore much room for disagreement, and for parties to have conflicting understandings on the moral value of breach. The promisor, in a self-serving manner, will tend to claim (and understand) performance as impossible or impractical, while the promisee will tend to do the opposite, and conflict can then escalate.

[23] *Cf.* JOHN RAWLS, A THEORY OF JUSTICE, *op. cit. supra*, at 30 (a deontological theory is "one that either does not specify the good independently from the right, or does not interpret the right as maximizing the good.").

[24] *See* the discussion *supra* in Chap. 2, Sect. 2.2.

There is not, however, any exhaustive and precise listing of those circumstances, and individuals will often disagree on whether a certain contingency amounts to an excusing condition or not. Therefore, even if both parties to a contract assess the morality of breach according to the same moral theory, in a deontological fashion, they will often have, in practice, conflicting views of the moral value of breach *in concreto*.[25]

According to a consequentialist conception, an act is moral if and only if it maximizes the "good," however defined and understood, and is immoral whenever it does not, thereby creating harm (act consequentialism).[26] It is opposed to deontology in denying that the morality of an act can depend on anything else apart from its consequences, such as whether the individual promised to take an act. Utilitarianism, the best-known form of consequentialism, assesses the morality of the act according to its overall net benefit, described in terms of well-being or welfare. An act that does not maximize a certain conception of well-being or welfare creates harm and is therefore immoral.

In theory and in practice, both scholars and individuals often disagree on what constitutes well-being and welfare, and benefits and harms. Utilitarian philosophers have different, very often conflicting notions of the "good," considering it as consisting in pleasure, happiness, satisfaction of preferences, welfare, or even wealth.[27] Moreover, this plurality of conceptions is not restricted to philosophical theories.

There is, in economic theory, a plurality of ways to rank allocations as more or less desirable, embedded in the different possible social welfare functions (utilitarian,

---

[25] From a deontological perspective, breach that is excused by convention does not violate the moral norm of keeping promises. Depending on the theory, however, this act can be either *not immoral* or perhaps even *moral*. Under some theories, if an act is not immoral, then it must be moral, with no room for acts that are morally neutral. For others theories, an act that is excused by convention is not the moral thing to do, but solely not immoral. In this thesis, it is assumed that the party that understands breach as not wrong in the realized contingency considers it is simply *moral*.

[26] The term "consequentialism" was probably first introduced by Gertrud Anscombe in *Modern Moral Philosophy*, 33 PHILOSOPHY 1, 10 (1958) (criticizing Henry Sidgwick's utilitarian philosophy). For a review of consequentialism, its nuances and the many different consequentialist theories, *see* Philip Pettit, *Consequentialism,* in A COMPANION TO ETHICS 230 (Peter Singer ed. 1991).

[27] Richard Posner famously defended the maximization of wealth as the ethical norm for social and political choice. *See* R. Posner, *Utilitarianism, Economics, and Legal Theory*, 8 JOURNAL OF LEGAL STUDIES 103 (1979); R. Posner, *Wealth Maximization Revisited*, 2 JOURNAL OF LAW, ETHICS AND PUBLIC CHOICE 85 (1985). His position is that "wealth-maximization is achieved when goods and other resources are in the hands of those who value them the most, and someone values a good more if and only if he is both willing and able to pay more in money (or in the equivalent of money) to have it." *Cf*. Ronald Dworkin, *Is Wealth a Value?*, 9 JOURNAL OF LEGAL STUDIES 191, 191 (1980), reproduced and endorsed by Richard Posner in *The Value of Wealth: A Comment on Dworkin and Kronman*, 9 JOURNAL OF LEGAL STUDIES 243, 243 (1980).

Several scholars disagreed with Posner's normative criterion, including Jules Coleman, *Efficiency, Utility and Wealth Maximization*, 8 HOFSTRA LAW REVIEW 509 (1980); Ronald Dworkin, *Is Wealth a Value?*, 9 JOURNAL OF LEGAL STUDIES 191 (1980); Anthony Kronman, *Wealth Maximization as a Normative Principle*, 9 JOURNAL OF LEGAL STUDIES 227 (1980). There is therefore no agreement that an action that maximizes wealth is the appropriate one.

Table 3.1 Moral value of breach and the emergence of normative conflict

Breach	Avoided harm	Created Harm
Excused by convention	Deontologically: moral Consequentialistic: moral *No conflict*	Deontologically: moral Consequentialistic: immoral *Conflict emerges*
Not excused by convention	Deontologically: immoral Consequentialistic: moral *Conflict emerges*	Deontologically: immoral Consequentialistic: immoral *No conflict*

generalized utilitarian, egalitarian, or Rawlsian).[28] An act that brings about a certain state and that maximizes the social welfare function under one definition of welfare may not be the one maximizing it under a different definition. An act that creates a gain of $100 for A and a loss of $90 for B, compared to another one that creates a gain of $1 for each, maximizes an utilitarian social welfare function but not an egalitarian or Rawlsian one.

Therefore, even if both parties assess the morality of breach in a consequentialist, welfarist manner, they will often disagree on which act maximizes the "good." Because of different understandings of what is the "good," different individuals that assess the morality of breach in a consequentialist manner will often have conflicting understandings of the morality of the concrete act itself.

Still, for consequentialist theories, and independent of the question of what constitutes benefits and harms (studied in brief in the next section), breach that maximizes benefits and avoids the creation of harm is the moral thing to do (for it is the act that, vis-à-vis performance, maximizes net benefits, or overall social welfare). Breach that creates harm, when performance would not, does not maximize welfare, and is finally immoral.

Table 3.1 resumes the moral value of breach according to each perspective. From a deontological perspective, breach is either moral or immoral. The table describes how different possible manners of assessing the morality of breach often conflict and stresses when normative conflict is expected to emerge.

As discussed in the last section, when the promisor breaches in a contingency explicitly foreseen by the contract as requiring performance, *normative* conflict does not emerge, and the conflict that is then certain to emerge is not preceded by conflicting normative understandings. Breach is, in that case, unequivocally immoral. In any contractual gap, in contrast, individuals can assess breach according to a deontological or consequentialist perspective, and normative conflict *can* at times emerge, depending on the combination of how each party to the contract assesses the moral value of breach, as depicted in Table 3.1.

[28] *See* ANDREU MAS-COLELL, MICHAEL WHINSTON & JERRY GREEN, MICROECONOMIC THEORY 827–829 (New York, Oxford University 1995).

3.4 Disagreement on the Harmful Consequences of Breach

Individuals that assess the morality of breach of contract according to its consequences may furthermore disagree on what constitutes *harmful consequences from breach.*[29] Breach of contract often imposes losses upon the promisee, but it may well bring about further consequences that do not constitute harms in the absence of a contract, but that can be perceived by the parties as harms when created *inside a contractual relationship.*

The contractual relation is a concrete relation where individuals are no longer strangers to each other, but are instead bound to each other by their contractual obligations.[30] Each party promises something to another in exchange for a return promise or benefit, and they can implement the contractual objective only if both perform their obligations. Parties are in a joint enterprise where their common goal requires actions from both parties, and that can only then bring about the mutual gains of trade that justify, ex ante, the making of a contract and the creation of the relation.

In such a relation, not only are individual interests present, but also the interests that appear as such when considering both parties to the contract. These social interests include the interest in maximizing aggregate gains, extensively studied by the Economic Analysis of Law, and the interest in maintaining an equitable distribution of gains and losses for the parties to the contract, as detailed below. Violations of one or both of these social interests may well be perceived by a party as a harm in their contractual relation that arises because of the other party's intentional and deliberate decision to breach.

Breach of contract can create three different *individual harms*, corresponding to violations of the classic individual interests protected by contract law.

Firstly, breach of contract creates *loss of previously conferred benefits* when the promisor in breach does not return them to the promisee. This is univocally a harm to the promisee's rights, for the promisor that does not fulfill her part of the deal has no right to retain those benefits. The promisee never agreed to give that benefit to the promisor unless in case she receives what she has bargained for.[31]

---

[29] *Harm* is defined as a setback of an interest, and an *interest* can be defined as something one has a stake in. *Cf.* JOEL FEINBERG, THE MORAL LIMITS OF THE CRIMINAL LAW VOLUME 1: HARM TO OTHERS 33–34 (1987) ("In general, a person has a stake in *X* (whether *X* be a company, a career, or some kind of "issue" of events) when he stands to gain or lose depending on the nature or condition of *X*.") X, for the present discussion, is the performance of the contract. For a broader account of harm that goes beyond a setback of interest, *see* Seana Shiffrin, *Harm and its Moral Significance*, 18 LEGAL THEORY 357 (2012).

[30] Charles Fried develops this argument that contractual parties stand closer to each other than mere members of same political community. *Cf.* FRIED, CONTRACT AS PROMISE, *op. cit. supra*, at 73 ("Those in concrete or personal relations must have a greater care for each other than those who stand to each other in the abstract relation of fellow citizens, or fellow man. (…) Making another person the object of your intention, a step along the way in your plans, particularizes that person and forms a concrete relation between you and him.").

[31] In this respect, there is the need to refer to a normative concept of harm, for according to a simple definition of harm as loss of social resources, there is no harm in taking something from another

Secondly, breach of contract creates *loss of reliance investments* whenever the promisor breaches and does not reimburse the promisee for such losses. This is not univocally understood as a harm. The promisor may well understand that it was the promisee's *own* decision to make those investments in reliance on performance, a decision not taken by the promisor, and that the promisor could not control. She may thus not feel responsible for those losses.[32]

This is the case when parties did not discuss those investments at the time of striking the deal. Without information on the consequences of her act to the promisee (such as the losses of reliance expenses), the promisor may well understand that she is not responsible for them since she could not know they would result from her decision. The buyer of a car to be delivered upon payment next week may decide, by herself, and on a whim, to buy a new custom-made radio in advance, and subsequently lose its value in case of breach by the seller. The latter may well claim she is not responsible for that loss when she could not foresee or imagine that the buyer would so hastily invest in the car she does not yet possess. Still, these are real and material losses, and when the promisor knew that the promisee would invest in the contract when the deal was struck, then the promisee has good reasons to understand her losses as a harm resulting from the promisor's decision, and to hold the promisor responsible for them.

Thirdly, breach of contract further creates an immaterial, non-monetary *loss of expectancy* when the promisee does not earn what she expected (and was promised) to earn through the performance of the contract. This harm is not a necessary consequence of breach, for the promisee may find a substitute good or another contractor in the market for the very same price. In this case, she realizes, independent of breach, the same expected gains. Moreover, even when present, loss of expectancy may well be understood as no harm because, as developed by Joseph Raz, the loss of expectation, being hypothetical and measured only against a baseline of what might have been, is not a real harm.[33]

---

person, for this does not necessarily lower overall social welfare. In effect, without reference to a norm or right, theft is efficient whenever the criminal values the good more than the owner (efficient theft). In the same manner, retention of an upfront benefit does not necessarily decrease social welfare, but is only a transfer of resources, being thus no harm in a non-normative sense. Any sane person, however, will regard that conduct as immoral as harmful, and promisees will do the same when the promisor breaches, does not deliver what she promised to deliver, and still keeps an upfront payment, claiming that that does not lower overall social welfare, creates no harm for society, and is thus not immoral.

[32] According to subjective consequentialism. According to objective consequentialism, whether an act such as breach is right or wrong depends only on the actual consequences, and not on the foreseen, foreseeable, intended, or probable consequences. *See* Frank Jackson, *Decision-theoretic Consequentialism and the Nearest and Dearest Objection*, 101 ETHICS 461 (1991), and Fred Feldman, *Actual Utility, the Objection from Impracticality, and the Move to Expected Utility*, 129 PHILOSOPHICAL STUDIES 49 (2006) for an overview.

[33] *See* Joseph Raz, *Promises in Morality and Law*, *op. cit. supra,* at 916; Liam Murphy, *The Practice of Promise and Contract*, (forthcoming in PHILOSOPHICAL FOUNDATIONS OF CONTRACT LAW, Gregory Klass, George Letsas & Prince Saprai eds. 2014).

Loss of expectancy is still, if perceived as a harm, an *individual harm* created by breach, and one that is a harm only because of breach of a prior promise. Without reference to a moral norm that one ought to keep promises, which justifies the creation of *promissory* expectations, loss of expected gains is not different from disappointments one suffers every day because of actions of others that are not morally wrong.

Consider, for example, the case where a buyer goes to a shop and inquires into the price of the good, and where the seller creates expectations in the buyer by telling her that the good costs $10. If the buyer values it at $15, then she creates expectations of earning $5. If they do not broker a deal at that time, then it is not necessarily wrong for the seller to ask for $20 tomorrow, when the buyer goes back to the shop. In this case, the buyer suffers a disappointment of $5, but will not understand the seller's action as wrong. In contrast, in case they had exchanged promises, and at the time of implementing the exchange the seller refuses to sell for the promised $10, requiring then $20, then the promisee may or may not understand the seller's breach, because of the loss of expected and promised gains she incurs, as wrong.

Breach of contract can further create *social harms*, or harms that appear as such only when the interests of both parties to the contract are concomitantly considered.

Social harms in contractual relations are defined, herein, as harms that appear as such only when considering the interests of all parties to the contract, and not only the interests of the victim of breach. They are thus defined as harms exclusively by reference to the parties' utilities, and to the agreement they make. No other variable defines them. With that, they are distinct from moral harm, harm to the moral order, and harm to the practice of promising.[34] Social harms, as understood herein, appear as harms only inside the parties' relationship and depend exclusively on the parties' gains and losses from breach of promise, and hence only by reference to the agreement parties entered into.

The first social harm is harm to the aggregate material interests of both parties. Breach of contract can either enable the promisor to achieve higher gains through breach than the losses suffered by the promisee (as in the "overbidder paradigm") or enable the promisor to incur lower losses through breach than the gains the promisee would make in receiving performance (as in the "loss paradigm"). Breach is, in both cases, the moral thing to do from the exclusive point of view of maximizing overall gains, increasing them vis-à-vis performance. In other words, efficient breaches avoid harm to social welfare, considering only material gains, and inefficient breaches create that same harm.

The second social harm is harm to the interests of both parties, to a fair distribution of gains and losses from performance or breach, or to fairness or equity. For the questions under study, what is a fair distribution is hardly the question, since what

[34] In contrast, *see* Shiffrin, *Harm and its Moral Significance*, *op. cit. supra*, at 386 ("If one's *autonomy* right is violated but one's resultant condition is not in itself a state of harm, the violation itself may still be a harm, because another's will is being imposed upon one in an arena in which one's will is supposed to be supreme.") For how legal enforcement of promises can be justified in order to prevent harm to the practice of promises, or its erosion, *see* Joseph Raz, *Promises in Morality and Law*, *op. cit. supra*, at 938 ("The distinctive mark of contract law is that the harms it protects against are harms to the practice of undertaking voluntary obligations and harms resulting from its abuse.").

matters for the emergence of disagreement and normative conflict is that parties *can* understand a certain distribution as unfair. There is no need to provide an answer as to what is fair, but rather to recognize that some individuals might consider and perceive unequal distributions inside a promissory relation, and that were created by a deliberate decision of the promisor, as unfair.

Breach of contract motivated by an absolute increase in costs of performance avoids the promisor's incurrence of costs in order to perform (the loss paradigm). Breach motivated by an absolute increase in costs of performance may be socially efficient or inefficient, depending on the magnitude of the increase in costs. With respect to fairness, breach, in this paradigm, always realizes an equal distribution where nobody earns anything. The promisor that does not perform does not incur any cost and does not deliver any gain to the promisee. In comparison with performance, breach to save costs *avoids the creation of non-contract inequality* in the outcome.[35]

Breach of contract motivated by a more tempting outside offer allows the promisor to achieve higher profits than through performance of the original contract (the over-bidder paradigm). Breach may be socially efficient or inefficient, depending on how high the outside offer is, and on how much the third party values performance. Through breach, however, the promisor always earns something, given by the price paid by the third party, and the promisee earns nothing (and may even make a loss if she considers loss of pure expectancy as a real loss). In comparison with performance, breach to profit from an outside offer *creates non-contracted inequality* in the outcome.[36]

These two social harms often present a trade-off for the promisor. She may choose to accept an outside opportunity in order to maximize overall gains, thereby creating inequality. She then creates social gains but also creates a harm in the form of inequality. On the other hand, she may choose not to take the outside opportunity and perform the original contract as promised, avoiding the creation of inequality but not maximizing overall possible gains. She then creates social losses but does not create a harm in form of inequality.

Table 3.2 presents the possible trade-off between efficiency and equity in breach of contract, depending on the magnitude of the variation in costs of performance and on the nature of the realized contingency (whether it consists in an absolute increase in costs of performance or in a more profitable outside option). Whether breach is

---

[35] It is important to note that the issue in question is inequality from breach, or the unfairness of the result from breach. This is different from inequality in performance, or inequality in the agreed distribution of the gains from the transaction, which is contracted and consented. In case of an increase in costs of production not addressed by the contract, the inequality that would arise through performance in that contingency was never contracted and the promisor was not remunerated for those unforeseen costs, because there is a contractual gap. *See* the complete discussion *infra* in Chap. 4, Sect. 4.4.

[36] Again, in a contractual gap, parties never agreed that the promisor could retain the gains from breach, and therefore the resulting inequality is not part of the contract. From the perspective of the hypothetical complete contingent contract developed by Steven Shavell, one cannot know whether parties *would have agreed* that those gains would belong to one or the other party. *See* Richard Brooks, *The Efficient Performance Hypothesis*, 116 YALE LAW JOURNAL 568 (2006), and the complete discussion *infra* in Chap. 4, Sect. 4.4.

Table 3.2 Moral value of breach, depending on the created social harms, according to a consequentialist perspective

Degree of variation in costs of performance	Nature of the contingency	
	Increase in costs	Outside offer
Low (inefficient breach)	Breach creates inefficiency but avoids inequality *Uncertain moral value*	Breach creates inefficiency and creates inequality *Breach is immoral*
High (efficient breach)	Breach avoids inefficiency and avoids inequality *Breach is moral*	Breach avoids inefficiency but creates inequality *Uncertain moral value*

morally acceptable or not will depend on whether each party considers inefficiency and inequality as harmful consequences of breach. The table thereby stresses how, even if both parties assess the morality of breach in a consequentialist manner, they can disagree on the moral value of breach.

Breach is, in some types of contingencies, and considering only social harms, always *moral* from a consequentialist perspective. In case of a very high increase in costs of production, where breach is socially efficient *and* would avoid the creation of inequality, breach is, from a consequentialist perspective, surely moral, for it can avoid both harmful consequences. On the other hand, in case the promisor breaches to profit from an outside offer that was minimally higher than the price in the original contract, then breach is socially inefficient and creates inequality, and can thereby create only harmful consequences. Breach is then surely immoral in a consequentialist perspective, for it can create only harmful consequences.

In the other two possible types of contingency, breach creates one social harm while avoiding the other one. Whether a party will consider breach moral or immoral, being capable of maximizing the "good" or not depends on what consequences of breach individuals understand as harmful. It is an empirical question, and when breach involves one harmful consequence while avoiding the other, then it is uncertain whether individuals will consider it is wrong or not. In this case, and in conclusion, even if both parties assess the morality of breach according to the same moral theory, in a consequentialist fashion, normative conflict will still, at times, emerge.

3.5 Cognitive Biases that Facilitate Disagreement

There are reasons for why normative conflict in breach of contract is much more pervasive in real life than a general incompatibility of individuals' normative understandings would imply. Individuals have, certainly, their own prior opinions on what is right or wrong in breach of contract, but when they are part of a contract, they make that assessment subject to several cognitive biases. These can create normative conflict where there was none, and further reinforce and magnify it when it is present, making it more likely to emerge and stronger in practice than in theory.

Firstly, individual will assess the morality of conduct, ex ante and ex post, subject to the self-serving bias.[37] This cognitive bias works both upon individuals assessing the morality of breach deontologically, as well as upon those doing so based on the consequences of the act.

The societal convention of promises allows for excusing conditions releasing the promisor from her moral obligation to perform. Since there is no exhausting and precise listing of those conditions, parties themselves must interpret whether the realized circumstances excuse and justify breach or not. Promisors, at the time of deciding to perform or breach, will tend to interpret them broadly and most likely including the realized one, for this serves, ex ante, to allow the promisor to realize material gains without understanding her action as wrong. Ex post, at the time of attempting to explain and justify her action, it serves the promisor to avoid feelings of guilt and cognitive dissonance (detailed below). Promisees, on the other hand, will tend to interpret those restrictively, for this reinforces, ex post, their claims and assertion of rights, and thereby their perception of blame of the promisor.

The consequences of breach must be further understood by individuals as harmful or not, and promisors will consider them, ex ante and ex post, most likely as not real and serious harms. Promisees, on the other hand, are those that experience the harm, and will tend to consider certain consequences such as loss of expectancy, creation of inequity, or loss of aggregate resources as serious and real harms when they are the ones that suffer from them.

Secondly, the promisor that decides to breach will, ex post, attempt to rationalize and justify her conduct. She will search for justifications for her wrong in an attempt to convince herself that her conduct was not, after all, and given all the realized circumstances, wrong or immoral. The individual that believes, in general, that breach is wrong in certain circumstances, and that breaches when they materialize, commits the wrong in order to achieve higher material gains. She will then experiences *cognitive dissonance*, a mental stress that is unpleasant and uncomfortable, and will strive to eliminate it.[38]

An individual experiences cognitive dissonance when confronted with information that conflicts with and contradicts her own general beliefs. When the promisee claims that the promisor behaved immorally, the promisor is then confronted with a fact that contradicts her moral values if she understands breach as wrong and may

---

[37] For the literature on the self-serving bias, *see*, e.g., David Messick & Keith Sentis, *Fairness and Preference*, 15 JOURNAL OF EXPERIMENTAL SOCIAL PSYCHOLOGY 418 (1979) (finding how fairness judgments are influenced by a bias in the direction of overpayment to oneself); Linda Babcock et al., *Biased Judgments in Fairness Bargaining*, 85 AMERICAN ECONOMIC REVIEW 1337 (1995) (predictions of judicial decisions are systematically biased in a self-serving manner); Linda Babcock & George Loewenstein, *Explaining Bargaining Impasse: The Role of Self-Serving Biases*, 11 JOURNAL OF ECONOMIC PERSPECTIVES 109 (1997) (reviewing empirical findings and their implications). There are also some economic models of the self-serving bias. *See* Matthew Rabin, *Moral Preferences, Moral Constraints, and Self-Serving Biases*, mimeo (University of California, Berkeley) (1995); Roland Benabou & Jean Tirole, *A Cognitive Theory of Identity*, mimeo (Princeton University) (2006).

[38] *See* LEON FESTINGER, A THEORY OF COGNITIVE DISSONANCE (1957); *Cognitive Dissonance*, 207 SCIENTIFIC AMERICAN 93 (1962).

realize that she, in fact, trampled her own morality for profits. The promisor will then attempt to reduce dissonance firstly by changing her own belief (in the belief disconfirmation paradigm), thereby claiming, ex post, that she does not understand breach in those circumstances as wrong.[39] If the dissonance is not reduced in this manner, it may result in misperception, rejection or even refutation of the commitment of the wrong, and the promisor will attempt to persuade the promisee that her action was not wrong.[40]

The promisee, ex post, will be met with the promisor's allegations and will uphold reasons for why breach was not, in that case, wrong. Individuals that are confronted with information that challenges their beliefs will often strengthen their own beliefs.[41] A promisee that is confronted with a justification for breach on the basis that it avoided inefficiency and an overall loss of resources, being thus the moral thing to do, may strengthen her own belief that promises are sacred and that such "cheap excuses" do not release the promisor from her moral obligation. Conflict can then easily escalate.

Thirdly, parties assess the morality of breach *ex post*, after the act has taken place, being thus furthermore subject to the *hindsight bias*.[42] It is a phenomenon that causes memory distortion and that affects how individuals recall events and facts, such as the realized circumstances that motivated breach, when given the benefit of feedback. When recalling the circumstances under which the decision to breach was taken, and

---

[39] *See* the classic work developed by LEON FESTINGER, HENRY RIECKEN & STANLEY SCHLACHTER, WHEN PROPHECY FAILS: A SOCIAL AND PSYCHOLOGICAL STUDY OF A MODERN GROUP THAT PREDICTED THE DESTRUCTION OF THE WORLD (1956) (reporting how many followers of a sect that preached that the end of the world would happen, in a flood, on December 21, 1954, did not accept that their belief was wrong after that day but rather searched—and found—reasons for why that did not happen in order to maintain their beliefs). Claude Steele, differently from Festiger, advanced that individuals strive to maintain an overall self-image of moral adequacy, being motivated to affirm the integrity of the self, and will try to change their attitude to reduce dissonance in order to maintain a positive self-image (affirmation theory). *Cf*. Claude Steele, *The psychology of self-affirmation: Sustaining the integrity of the self*, 21 ADVANCES IN EXPERIMENTAL SOCIAL PSYCHOLOGY 261 (1988). For a review of affirmation theory, *see* David Sherman & Geoffrey Cohen, *The Psychology of Self-defense: Self-affirmation theory*, 38 ADVANCES IN EXPERIMENTAL SOCIAL PSYCHOLOGY 183 (2006).

[40] *See* Eddie Harmon-Jones, *A Cognitive Dissonance Theory Perspective on Persuasion*, in THE PERSUASION HANDBOOK: DEVELOPMENTS IN THEORY AND PRACTICE 99, 101 (James Dillard & Michael Pfau eds. Thousand Oaks, Sage Publications 2002).

[41] *See* C. Daniel Batson, *Rational processing or rationalization? The effect of disconfirming information on a stated religious belief*, 32 JOURNAL OF PERSONALITY AND SOCIAL PSYCHOLOGY 176 (1975); Christopher Burris, Eddie Harmon-Jones & W. Ryan Tarpley, *"By Faith Alone": Religious Agitation and Cognitive Dissonance*, 19 BASIC AND APPLIED SOCIAL PSYCHOLOGY 17 (1997).

[42] *See* Scott Hawkins & Reid Hastie, *Hindsight: Biased judgments of past events after the outcomes are known*, 107 PSYCHOLOGICAL BULLETIN 311 (1990) (review of the literature listing four general strategies for responding to the request for a hindsight judgment); Jay Christensen-Szalanski, *The Hindsight Bias: A Meta-Analysis*, 48 ORGANIZATIONAL BEHAVIOR AND HUMAN DECISION PROCESSES 147 (1991); Ulrich Hoffrage, Ralph Hertwig & Gerd Gigerenzer, *Hindsight Bias: A By-Product of Knowledge Updating?*, 26 JOURNAL OF EXPERIMENTAL PSYCHOLOGY: LEARNING, MEMORY AND COGNITION 566 (2000) (empirical study followed by the argument that the hindsight bias can be understood the result of an adaptive process through which individuals update knowledge).

how far the promisor could foresee the negative consequences of her act, parties will reconstruct them, tending to avoid accepting blame (promisor) or reinforcing their perception of responsibility of the decision-maker for them (promisees).

Promisors will tend to forget the details of such circumstances when recalling and reconstructing them. They will recall, for example, in a distorted fashion, the promisee's warnings that the painting of the house by next Friday was necessary because the promisee would celebrate her wedding there ("-Your wedding? You told me about a party on Sunday, but not about a wedding party!"). Promisors may recall them most likely as "buyer's talk" rather than serious affirmations. The promisee, on the other hand, will put, ex post, much more weight on what she at the time of negotiation perhaps saw as no more than "seller's talk" ("-You did what you promised you would have done? You told me you would have painted the whole house perfectly by Friday, and not by next week, so what about those spots up there now?").

Furthermore, promisors will misconstruct, ex post, how far they knew, could know, or should have known, at the time of deciding, that the act would lead to the realized harms. Promisees will, in contrast, search for evidence and facts, with the benefit of feedback, that ascertain that the promisor knew, could know, or should have known that the consequences of breach would come to pass. They will judge the promisor, ex post, as most likely having been capable of preventing their occurrence, and thus as responsible for them.

All three biases work to create, reinforce, or reassure the perception in the promisor that no wrong was committed, and in the promisee that the conduct of the promisor was wrong. They are thus of vital importance for the likelihood that normative conflict may not be solved peacefully, since normative understandings of right or wrong are first elements hindering such a resolution by the parties themselves.

3.6 Retaliation to Perceived Wrong as the Product of Disagreement

When breach occurs and parties disagree whether the promisor should have performed and are unable or unsuccessful in solving their disputes privately, then normative conflict can escalate to a real, material conflict between the parties. In the absence of a public remedy, the promisee will often behave according to the norm of reciprocity and will tend to attempt to redress the wrong by her own means, in a private and decentralized manner.

Retaliation is the attempt, at some cost or risk to oneself, to punish or to impose harm upon the perceived wrongdoer. Individuals can retaliate in a variety of forms, as described below, but the act is always costly to the person engaging in it and requires that the person spend some time, energy, and resources in order to punish the other. For example, writing an online negative feedback about the seller that did not deliver a good on time (or not at all) costs some time and energy for the person. At the same time, any act of retaliation must be apt to impose a harm upon its target, be it material or solely immaterial, for example in form of a loss of potential clients, or reputational harm.

Retaliation, in this manner, does not coincide with a rational action that could further the goals and interests of the person engaging in it, but is rather understood as an act of *strong negative reciprocity*.[43] The end pursued by rational retaliation can only be material gains, and such action is rather based on *weak negative reciprocity*.[44] As a means to achieve an end such as ensuring future cooperation by the other party in an iterated social dilemma, rational acts of retaliation do equally impose a harm or loss to the other party while also being costly to the person that takes them.

However, rational acts of retaliation are not caused by the perception that a wrong has been done, or by the moral value of breach. Rational retaliation is caused by the prospective individual gains that can be achieved by a certain choice of the other (such as to cooperate) and that is not her dominant strategy, but that can be transformed into one by acts and (credible) threats of retaliation.[45] Rational retaliation is therefore different from an act pursuing the punishment of wrongdoers, which is, in turn, and from a strictly rational point of view, simply irrational.

Retaliation is also not an exclusively emotional act, nor an impulsive response against certain types of behavior, since it depends on normative understandings. The role of emotions when individuals act under a norm is to support judgments and expectations about what is the appropriate course of action in a given situation.[46] Retaliation is hence only *mediated* by emotions, since its ultimate cause is not the state of mind of outrage, anger, disappointment, or elsewise, but rather the external factors that lead one to feel that way.

Its ultimate cause, therefore, consists in the elements that can be perceived by the individual as making the act a moral wrong. In case of breach of contract, the elements needed for individuals to understand it as wrong are either the violation of

---

[43] *See* Herbert Gintis, *Strong Reciprocity and Human Sociality*, 206 Journal of Theoretical Biology 169 (2000); Ernst Fehr, Urs Fischbacher & Simon Gächter, *Strong Reciprocity, Human Cooperation and the Enforcement of Social* Norms, 13 Human Nature 1, 3 (2002) ("The essential feature of strong reciprocity is a willingness to sacrifice resources for rewarding fair and punishing unfair behavior *even if this is costly and provides neither present nor future material rewards for the reciprocator*"); Samuel Bowles & Herbert Gintis, *The Evolution of Strong Reciprocity: Cooperation in Heterogeneous Populations*, 65 Theoretical Population Biology 17 (2004); Francesco Guala, *Reciprocity: Weak or Strong? What Punishment Experiments do (and do not) Demonstrate*, 35 Behavioral and Brain Sciences 1, 1 (2012) (distinguishing between models of weak reciprocity, which "require that reciprocal strategies be profitable for the agents who play them," and model of strong reciprocity, which "allow players to choose suboptimal strategies, and thus diverge substantially from the models of self-interested behavior that are typically used by evolutionary biologists and rational choice theorists."); Herbert Gintis et al., *Strong Reciprocity and the Roots of Human Morality*, 21 Social Justice Research 241 (2008).

[44] *Cf.* Jon Elster, *Norms of Revenge*, 100 Ethics 862, 872 (1990).

[45] The adjective *strong* thus distinguishes irrational retaliation from other forms of reciprocity that exclude it, such as tit-for-tat strategies, as developed by Robert Axelrod and William Hamilton in *The Evolution of Cooperation*, 211 Science 1390 (1981), and from reciprocal altruism, as developed by Robert Trivers in *The Evolution of Reciprocal Altruism*, 46 Quarterly Review of Biology 35 (1971).

[46] *Cf.* Jon Elster, *Norms of Revenge*, 100 Ethics 862, 863 (1990).

the moral norm, or any of the harms possibly created by breach of contract. Their perpetration provides reason for individuals to understand breach as wrong and to feel aggrieved by it. The type of retaliation considered in this thesis thus consists in strong reciprocal behavior, in its negative form, that is only mediated by emotions, and that is not caused by prospective future material gains.[47]

Revenge, much similarly to retaliation, can be defined as "the attempt, at some cost or risk to oneself, to impose suffering upon those who have made one suffer, because they have made one suffer."[48] They do, as understood in here, differ in some ways. Retaliation is not necessarily caused only by the intentional imposition of harm by the other, such as revenge. Retaliation can be caused by the violation of norms different from the norm that one ought not harm other persons. For example, an individual may understand breach of contract as wrong because it violates the norm of keeping promises, independently of harm suffered, and can retaliate against breach of contract that created no harm, for example because she was able to find a substitutive good in the market for the same price.

Retaliation can therefore emerge even when the promisee does not incur any loss from breach and does not suffer from it. Revenge, in contrast, is caused by the suffering one endures, and making the other suffer is a much more straightforward harm than some of the possible consequences of breach of contract, such as a mere non-material loss of expectancy or the creation of inefficiency or inequality. Retaliation is, in brief, a broader and much more widespread phenomenon than revenge. Any act of revenge is an act of retaliation, but not any act of retaliation is an act of revenge.[49]

Moreover, retaliation to breach of contract is not restricted to the hypothetical situation where the law is absent. It is widespread and pervasive in our societies, even when the law forbids, in general, the use of force and violence by the citizens. There are uncountable manners through which a disappointed and aggrieved promisee might retaliate against a promise-breaker that are lawful and thus possible

[47] Although not confined to intentional acts, retaliation is normally a reaction to an intentional act. *See* HOLMES, THE COMMON LAW, *op. cit. supra*, at 3 ("It [revenge] can hardly go very far beyond the case of a harm intentionally inflicted: even a dog distinguishes between being stumbled over and being kicked.").

[48] *Cf*. Jon Elster, *Norms of Revenge*, *op. cit. supra*, at 862.

[49] There is wide empirical evidence that individuals are prone to retaliate against individuals that refrain from cooperating, even in the absence of a norm prescribing that behavior. *See, e.g.*, Ernst Fehr & Simon Gächter, *Cooperation and Punishment in Public Goods Experiments*, 90 AMERICAN ECONOMIC REVIEW 980 (2000); Fehr & Gächter, *Altruistic Punishment in Humans*, 415 NATURE 137 (2002). The question whether individuals would also retaliate to breach of promise, and the reasons for doing so persist, since retaliation, in the form of costly punishment, has been subject to experimental tests only in games which do not completely capture the buyer–seller contractual relationship, and that do not include prior promises to cooperate or to do something. In this sense, there is no existing evidence on the existence, causes, and consequences of retaliation to breach of contractual promises, with the exception of retaliation in organizations, and to breach of the psychological contract, which is however restricted to labor relations, and requires repeated interactions marked by the presence of the power to control. *See* n.42 *supra* in the Introduction.

without violating existing law. Still, there is always *also* the possibility that, at times, normative conflict may escalate and lead a party to retaliate in a violent manner.

The victim of breach may retaliate in the heat of the moment, in a hot mode, immediately after breach by the promisor. When the seller breaches and does not deliver the promised good or does not perform the promised service, the aggrieved buyer may first of all start a sharp discussion and argument with the seller. She may do so in the middle of the shop, airport or restaurant, creating a long line at the cashier, or disturbance and discomfort for the other clients sitting in the restaurant. The buyer, angry and upset with breach and with the explanation provided by the seller for why she did it, may furthermore threaten to call the police (or in fact do it), even without a legitimate reason.

After cooling down, the buyer can retaliate by spreading the word that seller breaches her contracts. She may do so in an attempt to discourage others from doing business with her, with a deliberate intention to impose harm upon the seller by discouraging potential clients to buy her services.[50] Alternatively, she may do so without any intention of imposing harm, but rather with the intention of helping others by informing them that the seller is simply unreliable. There is, in this respect, no need for the buyer to try to convince others (say, friends, family, and neighbors) of what is the right thing to do and that, for example, one should never breach a promise or a contract. Simply truly stating the fact that the seller breached may be enough for other persons not to engage the services of that seller in the future.

When booking an air ticket or a hotel room, or when buying goods online, individuals nowadays first observe the ratings and comments posted by other clients about the reliability of the seller or service provider. When an airline company or a hotel breaches a contract with a client, then this person might easily spend some of her time, maybe not more than a few minutes, to post a nasty review of a seller online. Such action may impose a serious cost to the former in terms of fewer future clients. Sellers that reach a low rating (that may often mean 90% of good ratings, as long as other sellers have ratings above 98%) simply go out of business. Buyers are not willing to buy from someone that is well known to fail to deliver, from an airline company that does not allow the boarding of some of her passengers, or to book hotels that do not provide their clients with the services and amenities promised in an advertisement.

At the same time, when a hotel or an airline company breaches because, for some reason beyond its control, its costs dramatically increased (such as a general strike in the whole city and a flood), then the promisee may be unable to blame the promisor for breach. She may refrain from retaliation, understanding breach in those circumstances as not wrong, but rather justified and excused. Alternatively, she may still feel aggrieved and disagree that even those events excuse and justify breach, and still provide a negative feedback. Other clients may be more understandable when reading it, and if the service provider can also react and explain, online, the reasons

[50] This may also happen unconsciously and without a clear intention to discourage others to transact with that seller, simply by chatting with neighbors and friends about people in the neighborhood.

that lead her to breach, apologizing and perhaps even compensating the buyer, then her reputation may not be harmed.

The buyer may also retaliate by refusing to transact with that seller in the future, even when doing so would be mutually profitable. One might expect that very few persons would again engage the services of a real-estate agent that some years ago promised them a house but that afterward breached because someone else offered, before the day of the delivery of the keys, a slightly higher price. Similarly, few would ever again choose to fly with the same company that refused their boarding because of overbooking, or would continue to buy from a seller that did not deliver the last birthday gift on time, but rather only after the birthday, even if that seller has the best prices in town.

Finally, the buyer may retaliate by suing the seller. Being part of a legal process demands more of the seller's time and leads to further discussions about the issue, and on whether the action was right or wrong, legal or illegal. It may also possibly impose a further harm to the reputation of the seller that breached by having her brought to court.

Underlying all these actions are costs for the person retaliating and possibly quite higher costs for the victim. All these costs are socially avoidable costs, since they are not inevitable in every case of breach. When the law provides victims of breach certain and secure legal relief, then it can also fulfill the role of crowding out such acts of retaliation by providing an alternative way for individuals to resolve their conflicts. As Joseph Perillo explains,

> In modern law, where contract law refuses to enter, vengeance and self-help fill the vacuum. On nearly a daily basis, residents of our major cities are informed by the media of a 'drug-related' murder or kidnapping. The relationship between the victim and the enforcer is usually that of debtor and creditor. Because the legal system will not aid in the collection of the debt formed by a criminal sale, vengeance and hostage-taking substitute for the law. It is not only drug-related transactions that give rise to extra-legal punishment or enforcement. Take the example a builder who went to a prospective lender for a loan. Not realizing the nature of the business of the person he was applying to, he inquired about the collateral the lender might want. He was told: 'Your body is your collateral'.[51]

Retaliatory behavior is not necessarily and is always, at first sight, undesirable, since it rather encourages promisors to perform instead of the opposite. It thus deters breaches, but only at a cost for both promisor and promisee, and these costs most often outweigh the benefits of private punishment by inducing cooperation and, in case of contract, performance.[52] Retaliation is, as argued in the next chapter, most often Pareto-inferior to legal remedies because the latter do not entail such costs

---

51 CALAMARI & PERILLO, CONTRACTS, *op. cit. supra*, at 6. The last example comes from the movie "Rocky."

52 *Cf.* Benedikt Herrmann, Christian Thöni & Simon Gächter, *Antisocial Punishment across societies*, 319 SCIENCE 1362 (2008), 1366–67 ("The detrimental effects of antisocial punishment on cooperation (and efficiency) also provide a further rationale why modern societies shun revenge and centralize punishment in the hands of the state.") *See* also Bettina Rockenbach & Manfred Milinski, *The efficient interaction of indirect reciprocity and costly punishment*, 444 NATURE 718 (2006) (finding social gains in costly punishment, but only in presence of reputation building); Anna Dreber et al., *Winners don't punish*, 452 NATURE 348 (2008), 348 ("people who gain the

for the parties. Damages for breach only redistribute wealth between the parties and thereby do not cause any loss of social welfare, as costly punishment of wrongdoers does.

There are, for sure, costs in maintaining a system of legal enforcement, but when the legal remedy is certain and secure, then the promisor will anticipate the cost of breach with certainty and will be deterred from breaching in certain cases (depending on the available remedy). Retaliation is not, on the contrary, certain and secure, for the promisor does not necessarily, if ever, know how the promisee will assess the morality of breach, especially when subject to cognitive biases. The promisor can never anticipate with certainty how disappointed promisees will react to breach. Promisors are thus unable to anticipate how high losses from retaliation will be, but can with higher certainty anticipate how much they will have to pay to the promisee through damages for breach.

Retaliation further serves, in deterring breach of (contractual) promises, to reinforce the moral norm of keeping promises, and thus perhaps morality itself. This is a function of retaliation that, in case of breach of contract, is subject to a severe criticism.

In retaliating, one may well apply his or her own understanding of what is the moral thing to do against those that break promises. This reaction is taken by the person that feels wronged and that sees herself as a victim, and is not guided by an impartial assessment, nor is she restricted by any precise and general guideline. As Atiyah pointed out, "there is therefore a greater danger that morality will overshoot the mark in encouraging too great a degree of respect for the rule that promises must be kept; the law may overshoot the mark also, but given the discretionary and mitigating techniques used by the law, this is less likely to happen."[53]

Since not all members of the society share the same moral understanding, an attempt to enforce what one perceives as the moral thing will often be no more than the sole exercise of power. The victim of retaliation, in case she holds a different moral understanding, will most often engage in counter-retaliation, and feuds and

highest total payoff tend not to use costly punishment: winners don't punish. This suggests that costly punishment behavior is maladaptive in cooperation games and might have evolved for other reasons"); Hisashi Ohtsuki, Yoh Iwasa & Martin Novak, *Indirect Reciprocity Provides a Narrow Margin of Efficiency for Costly Punishment*, 457 NATURE 79 (2009), 82 ("the evolution of improved mechanisms of indirect reciprocity leads to societies where costly punishment between individuals is not an efficient behavior for promoting cooperation.").

Differently, Simon Gächter, Elke Renner and Martin Sefton, *The Long-Run Benefits of Punishment*, 322 SCIENCE 1510 (2008) (presenting evidence that on longer repeated interactions, the costs of punishment are outweighed by the increased gains from cooperation). However, *see* evidence of spiteful punishment present in different societies in Joseph Henrich et al., *Costly Punishment Across Human Societies*, 312 SCIENCE 1767 (2006), 1770 ("costly punishment is present across a highly diverse range of human populations and emerges in a patterned fashion in each population. In every population, less-equal offers [in an ultimatum game] were punished more frequently.").

[53] ATIYAH, PROMISES, MORALS, AND LAW *op. cit. supra,* at 137.

vicious circles of retaliation are expected to emerge, as empirically attested.[54] And this is, for sure, undesirable and pernicious to any society.

Ultimately, the law allows individuals to contract in peace, knowing that, in case they commit an action that may be understood as wrong by the other, arousing in the former a feeling of aggrievement and an urge to *react*, this conflict can, if needed, be solved by courts. Individuals are not left alone to solve their conflicts by themselves, but are all entitled to legal relief to settle the dispute and conflict. Citizens have the right to a legal solution of a conflict from an independent third party that will apply the law, utopically blindly, to the concrete case, providing the same solution independent of the parties' individual perceptions of wrong, and of their levels of aggrievement.

3.7 Conclusion

Conflict is not a necessary consequence of breach of contract. There is always the chance that both parties to the contract will agree that the promisor should not have performed in the realized circumstances and that no contractual dispute or normative conflict arises in the concrete case. Alternatively, there is always the possibility that the promisor in breach may understand her own conduct as wrong, and will be willing to apologize and perhaps even voluntarily compensate the promisee for the loss sustained. There is, in effect, evidence that in economic exchange relations, compensation can restore trust and often preserves cooperation in future interactions.[55]

Often, however, the promisor herself will understand breach as right while the promisee will understand it as wrong. If the promisor is not convinced to be in the right, but understands that breach was only "not immoral," then she may still apologize and attempt to solve the dispute through apologies and side-payments. But when the promisor is convinced she did the right thing, given the incompleteness

[54] *See* Francesco Parisi, *The Genesis of Liability in Ancient* Law, 3 AMERICAN LAW AND ECONOMICS REVIEW (2001) (acts such involuntary imposition of harm on others or mistakes in blaming somebody for a transgression may be enough to induce mutual aggression) and experimental evidence from Nikiforakis et al., *Normative Conflicts and Feuds*, *op. cit. supra*, at 797 ("punishment is much more likely to trigger counter-punishment and start a feud when there is a normative conflict, than it is in a setting in which no such conflict exists. While the possibility of a feud sustains cooperation, the cost of feuding fully offsets the efficiency gains from increased cooperation.").

[55] *See* Pieter Desmet et al., *On the Psychology of Financial Compensations to Restore Fairness Transgressions: When Intentions Determine Value*, 95 JOURNAL OF BUSINESS ETHICS 105 (2010); Pieter Desmet et al., *In Money we Trust? The Use of Financial Compensations to Repair Trust in the Aftermath of Distributive Harm*, 114 ORGANIZATIONAL BEHAVIOR AND HUMAN DECISION PROCESSES 75 (2011); Pieter Desmet et al., *Trust Recovery Following Voluntary or Forced Financial Compensations in the Trust Game: The Role of Trait Forgiveness*, 51 PERSONALITY AND INDIVIDUAL DIFFERENCES 267 (2011).

of the contract and her own understanding of what is right or wrong in breach of contract, then she will neither be willing to apologize nor compensate the promisee.

In this case, the normative conflict that emerges is unlikely to be resolved by the parties themselves and will often escalate to a real conflict where the promisee will attempt to redress her own wrong. The promisee that feels aggrieved from breach will behave according to the norm of strong reciprocity. She will retaliate against what she perceives as wrong. This behavior is socially costly and is not in the interest of society itself.

The next chapter studies the behavioral tendency to retaliate to breach of contract in detail. It examines in the existing empirical evidence on costly punishment some of the possible causes for individuals to feel aggrieved and tempted to retaliate. It then studies how those individuals interact with the promissory commitment that is present in any contract, and that is often absent in experiments involving costly punishment. Finally, it studies, in the contractual model developed in the Economic Analysis of Law, how both retaliation and legal remedies can induce socially optimal behavior by the promisor.

Legal remedies can induce performance of contracts and crowd out socially costly acts of retaliation in providing, ex post, relief for victims of breach. There are several compensatory remedies that can be awarded by courts, and they can fulfill that crowding out role in either discouraging breach, or in compensating for some of the harms created by breach, including individual and social harms. The capacity of expectation damages to achieve, concomitantly, both goals of inducing performance by the promisor and in crowding out retaliation by the victim is then subject to experimental investigation in the subsequent empirical chapter.

Chapter 4
Reciprocity and Legal Relief in Breach of Contract

The previous chapter discussed several different reasons why a promisor might fail to perform in situations in which the promisee expects performance. Firstly, contracts are incomplete and fail to specify an agreed course of action in all possible contingencies. Secondly, cognitive biases lead to errors in the assessment of content of the agreement, cognitive dissonance, and selective recall. Thirdly, different theories of the contractual obligation often conflict with each other: While the promisee may expect performance because keeping a promise is the moral thing to do, the promisor in breach may understand that breach is justified when breach is the efficient thing to do.

All these factors are apt to create disagreement between the parties to the contract. Parties will normally try to renegotiate the contract and to solve their dispute privately. Still, apologies and side-payments will not always solve the parties' dispute. If the promisee is convinced that the promisor ought to have performed, then she will not be willing to accept anything less than the value of the promised performance until one considers the costs and uncertainty of litigation. On the other side, if the promisor in breach is convinced she was not obliged to perform in the realized circumstance, then she will not be willing to voluntarily compensate the promisee. She may refuse to offer compensation to the promisee and rather leave her with the only alternative to resort to courts for a remedy for breach.

In case of failure of the private resolution of the dispute, the promisee will feel a sense of grievance; in the absence of public remedy, she will attempt to redress what she perceives as wrong by herself, retaliating against the promisor in breach. This type of behavior, as detailed below, is not in the interest of society itself. While apt to deter breaches of contract, retaliation may overshoot the mark and deter efficient breaches. Most importantly, this type of behavior is socially costly, creating a loss of welfare for the person engaging in it, as well as for the victim.

This chapter studies the elements present in breach of contract that may lead promisees to feel aggrieved from breach of contract and thereby tempted to retaliate. There are different reasons why promisees might feel aggrieved depending on the type of the realized contingency. The question is what it is in breach of contract that

S. Mittlaender, *Equity, Efficiency, and Ethics in Remedies for Breach of Contract*, International Law and Economics, https://doi.org/10.1007/978-3-031-10804-4_4

creates aggrievement leading to retaliation. The chapter focus on the consequences of breach inside the parties' relationship, namely: (i) the social loss of resources (inefficiency), (ii) the unfairness of the resulting outcome (inequality), and (iii) the loss of expected and promised gains endured by the promisee (loss of expectancy).

The chapter reviews the empirical literature that studies private retaliation and punishment and attempts to identify why parties might tend to retaliate to breach of contract. For that, it reviews (i) the possible causes of costly punishment and retaliation in appropriate strategic interactions, (ii) the behavioral effect of retaliation in deterring conduct such as breach, and (iii) its impact on overall social welfare. It then considers, in the traditional model of contractual behavior developed in the Economic Analysis of Law, how both private retaliation and legal damages can induce performance by the promisor. It explains how damages for breach can achieve that very goal without the social losses that private retaliation entails, being therefore a Pareto-superior enforcement mechanism.

In the end, the chapter explains how an award of remedies of breach of contract can achieve the goals of inducing performance by the promisor and of reducing retaliation by the promisee. Under perfectly implemented expectation damages, only efficient breaches are expected to occur, and the crowding out function is necessary to prevent retaliation to efficient but unfair breaches. Under perfectly implemented expectation damages, imperfect rationality, or imperfect information, efficient breaches are expected to be committed in equilibrium, and the need of remedies to crowd out retaliation to breach is even more pervasive. Because of that, damages for breach must still fulfill, in our present societies, both functions to crowd out the human tendency to retaliate to perceived wrong in breach of contract and to provide optimal incentives for performance.

4.1 Introduction

Contractual relations are created by agreement. They are formed, in common law systems, by the giving of promises with consideration and, in civil law systems, by the making of corresponding declarations of will.[1] Not all agreements, however, give rise to a contractual relationship, since the law, as explained in the second chapter, enforces only those agreements that create legal obligations for the parties. Contract law is primarily concerned with *exchanges* and does not ordinarily enforce agreements unless the parties, through the agreement, extract a benefit from the other, such as the immediate payment of a price or the obligation to pay a price in the future.[2]

[1] *See* the discussion *supra* in Chap. 2, Sect. 2.1.

[2] In common law systems, contract law enforces only promises given with consideration, or *bargained-for* promises through which the promisor extracts something in return from the promisee, either in form of a present benefit or a return promise. *See* RESTATEMENT (SECOND) OF CONTRACTS § 3 for the definition of a bargain ("A bargain is an agreement to exchange promises or to exchange a

Contracts, moreover, extrapolate the present moment in entailing a commitment to a future act. Contract law only enforces agreements that relate to the future, and the barter exchange, for example, hence does not create a contractual relationship.[3] Contractual parties commit to take some action in the future, with the aim to implement the parties' desired transaction, and "no question for the law of contracts arises unless the dispute is one over a promise—a commitment as to future behavior."[4]

A *commitment*, in game-theoretical terms, is "an action by one agent before an interaction with other agents that signals to the other agents the intention to perform a particular action later in the interaction."[5] In contracts where both parties incur an obligation to perform in the future, then the type of commitment in question is bilateral.[6] In these, "both agents express that they intend to perform an action under the condition that the other agent commits to perform another action and the commitments become effective if both agents agree on the combination of commitments."[7]

Individuals can commit to a future course of action by signaling their intentions to perform in the future. They may exchange declarations of intentions and announce to the other person that their present intentions are to trade in the future. This often suffices to implement the desired transaction since individuals tend to behave consistently with their previous announcements in order to avoid cognitive dissonance.[8]

---

promise for a performance or to exchange performances"), and § 71 for the definition of a bargained-for promise (a performance or a promise is bargained if "it is sought by the promisor in exchange for his promise and is given by the promisee in exchange for that promise.").

The law, therefore, does not enforce gratuitous promises, or promises for which there was no bargain. *Cf*. FARNSWORTH ON CONTRACTS 53. The function pursued by contract law through the refusal to enforce gratuitous promises is cautionary, to prevent ill-conceived and impulsive gifts. *Cf*. Fuller, *Consideration and Form, op. cit. supra,* at 812 (gratuities do not present a pressing case for legal intervention because there is no reliance and no unjust enrichment). *See* further Richard Posner, *Gratuitous Promises in Economics and Law*, 6 JOURNAL OF LEGAL STUDIES 411, 416–417 (1977) (the general rule that gratuitous promises are not enforceable is economically sound, especially because the administrative costs of enforcement would outweigh the utility gain from enforcement to the promisor); Eric Posner, *Altruism, Status, and Trust in the Law of Gifts and Gratuitous Promises*, 1997 WISCONSIN LAW REVIEW 567 (1997) (considering other motives for the making of gratuitous promises than gift-giving).

[3] *Cf*. FARNSWORTH ON CONTRACTS 4 (in "the transaction of barter, in which the parties simply make a present exchange of, say, apples for oranges, and the present (or 'cash') sale, in which parties make a present exchange of, say, apples for money (...) no promise is given in either of these exchanges [and thus] there is no contract.").

[4] *Id*.

[5] Vincent Buskens & Lambèr Royakkers, *Commitments: A Game-Theoretical and Logical Perspective*, 1 COGNITIVE SCIENCE QUARTERLY 1, 3 (2000).

[6] Bilateral contracts, in legal terms, are agreements in which both parties undertake an obligation to perform in the future. Unilateral contracts, distinctively, entail a commitment from one party to perform in the future, undertaken in exchange for a present act of the other party such as an upfront payment.

[7] Buskens & Royakkers, *Commitments: A Game-Theoretical and Logical Perspective*, *op. cit. supra*, at 5.

[8] *See* the discussion in Chap. 3, Sect. 3.4 *supra*. Stating one's intentions to do something in the future does create commitment since individuals tend to behave consistently in order to avoid *unpleasant*

Telling one's intentions to trade in the future provides a motive for the person to do it when the future date arrives.

However, an individual that solely states her intentions is in fact reserving for herself the right to change her mind. There is nothing wrong in not doing what one truthfully announced as one's intentions at the previous moment.[9] The person might well change her mind because of the realization of a certain event or of a regret contingency. An individual that tells another that she intends to meet another on a certain date, but that later is asked by her boss to work overtime that day, may honestly change her mind. The person commits no wrong when she calls the other one and withdraws from the appointment.[10]

In contrast, the person that promises something to another loses the right to change her mind, since she thereby undertakes an *obligation*.[11] It is then wrong not to do what one promised to the other. Similarly, an individual that makes a declaration of will goes well beyond the one that solely makes a declaration of intentions, since she then in effect becomes bound by it and obliged to perform.

---

cognitive dissonance, following the strand of Psychology that departs from Fritz Heider, *Attitudes and Cognite Organization*, 21 JOURNAL OF PSYCHOLOGY 107 (1946) and LEON FESTINGER, A THEORY OF COGNITIVE DISSONANCE (Stanford University Press, 1957). An alternative explanation is that communication entailed in an agreement creates identification between the individuals who were strangers to each other, but who are not anymore after entering into an agreement. Identification induces individuals to behave more cooperatively or even altruistically towards the other. *See, e.g.*, Roderick Kramer and Marilynn Brewer, *Effects of group identity on resource use in a simulated commons dilemma,* 46 JOURNAL OF PERSONALITY AND SOCIAL PSYCHOLOGY 1044 (1984). Based on such behavioral tendencies, there are thus rational grounds for an individual to rely on a commitment that does not go beyond a statement of intentions or desire and to believe that the person will do what she said she intended to do even in the absence of external enforcement.

[9] If the change of mind and the failure to do what one announced as one's intentions cause a harm to the other person because it induced reasonable reliance by the other, then it is wrong not to compensate the other for the harm endured. It gives rise to a reliance-based obligation, as discussed in Chap. 2, Sect. 2.3 *supra. See* further FRIED, CONTRACT AS PROMISES, *op. cit. supra,* at 9–11. If the other did not make any investment in reliance on the statement of intentions, then there is nothing wrong in not doing what one truthfully announced as one's intentions in the past.

This was already advanced by ADAM SMITH, in LECTURES ON JURISPRUDENCE 87 (R. Meek et al. eds. Oxford, Liberty Fund 1982) ("a bare declaration of will to do such or such a thing cannot produce an obligation. It means no more than that is the present design of the person who makes such a declaration to do so and so; and all that is required of him to make such a declaration lawful is sincerity, that is, that it be really his intention at that time to do as he said. If he should afterwards be induced by circumstances to alter his intention, we could not say that he had violated an obligation … The only thing that can make an obligation in this manner is an open and plain declaration that he desires the person to whom he makes the declaration to have a dependence on what he promises. The words in which we commonly make such a declaration I promise to do so and so.").

[10] If, in the communication of intentions or desires, the party never intended to perform, or never desired the transaction, then the party commits a moral wrong of lying—a wrong that is committed at the time of the utterance. *Cf.* FRIED, CONTRACT AS PROMISE, *op. cit. supra,* at 9 ("When I speak I commit myself to the truth of my utterance, but when I promise I commit myself to *act*, later.").

[11] *Id.* ("Promising is more than just truthfully reporting my present intentions, for I may be free to change my mind, as I am not free to break my promise.").

In entering into a contract, parties incur what is, for many individuals, a *moral* obligation to perform.[12] Promises put a moral charge in the promisor's future conduct, and the promisor is not necessarily free to break the promise whenever a regret contingency materializes, as she is free to reconsider her intentions or desires.[13] Rather than a philosophical theory, this is, arguably, how individuals understand promises. As mentioned by Kaplow and Shavell, the "norm that promises must be kept is widely instilled in members of society and serves a valuable function in channeling behavior in everyday life."[14]

In effect, there is a widely held view by ordinary individuals that there is something wrong in breach of promise and contract, and that breach is, at first sight, an immoral act. Several different empirical studies attest this fact.[15] However, there are different reasons that can lead the promisor to breach, and promisees do not understand all breaches in every possible circumstance as equally wrong. No individual believes that promises and contracts ought to be kept under any possible circumstance and hardship that can materialize.

The question that requires further investigation concerns which elements present in breach of contract are apt to lead promisees to perceive breach as a wrong, thereby feeling aggrieved and consequently tempted to retaliate. The chapter seeks to identify those possible elements in the existing empirical literature on private retaliation and punishment. However, since contracts create obligations for the parties, there is the need to consider how the violation of the norm of keeping promises, or of the norm that *pacta sunt servanda,* interacts with the reasons consistently identified in the experimental literature for the emergence of retaliation.

---

[12] *See, e.g.*, DAVID PARRY, THE SANCTITY OF CONTRACTS IN ENGLISH LAW 1-5 (London: Stevens & Sons, 1959) ("The moral basis of contract"); RESTATEMENT (SECOND) OF CONTRACTS ch. 16, introductory note at 100 (1981); FRIED, CONTRACT AS PROMISE, *op. cit. supra*, at 17. For a careful analysis of the role of *pacta sunt servanda* in the German legal system, *see* WELLER, DIE VERTRAGSTREUE, *op. cit. supra*.

On the immorality of breach in contingencies explicitly foreseen by the agreement as requiring performance, *see* Shavell, *Is Breach of Contract Immoral?*, *op. cit. supra*, at 439 ("The view that there is something wrong with a person's breaking a contract, or, equivalently, that a person ought to meet his or her contractual obligations, is widely recognized"); Shavell, *Why Breach of Contract May Not Be Immoral Given the Incompleteness of Contracts*, *op. cit. supra*, at 1570 ("I presume that if a contract provides explicitly for a contingency, then the moral duty to perform in that contingency is governed by the contract.").

[13] *Cf*. FRIED, CONTRACT AS PROMISES, *op. cit. supra*, at 10–11.

[14] Kaplow & Shavell, *Fairness versus Welfare*, *op. cit. supra*, at 1147.

[15] *See* Wilkinson-Ryan & Baron, *Moral Judgment and Moral Heuristics in Breach of Contract*, *op. cit. supra*, at 406 ("Most people agree that breaking a promise is immoral (…) Our results suggest that people are quite sensitive to the moral dimensions of a breach of contract); Wilkinson-Ryan and Hoffman, *Breach is for Suckers*, *op. cit. supra*, at 1004 ("ordinary people think that breach is morally wrong and believe that contract damages should reflect the ethical culpability of the breaching party"), 1011 (even in single commercial arrangements, individuals "believe that breach is immoral"); Wilkinson-Ryan, *The Commonsense of Contract Formation*, STANFORD LAW REVIEW 1 (forthcoming) ("we also document a series of situations in which misunderstandings have limited practical repercussions, because even parties who believe that legal obligation is about formalities take seriously the moral obligations associated with informal promises and exchanges.").

4.2 Retaliation and Punishment in Experiments

There is presently pervasive and widespread evidence that individuals engage in costly and irrational punishment of others in several different types of social interactions. Evidence of punishing behavior is recurrently observed in public good and prisoners' dilemma games, as well as in dictator and ultimatum games. Individual behavior in these games permits the identification of some of the *possible causes* of retaliatory behavior. Moreover, it shows some of the *possible effects* of retaliation, both in inducing a change in behavior of individuals subject to punishment and in providing net gains or net losses of social welfare. The first subsection reviews the existing evidence and seeks to identify possible causes and effects of retaliation in experimental games.

As explained before, retaliation to breach of contract is different from retaliation observed in those games. Contracts create commitment and establish an obligation to perform: to do what one promised and to keep one's part of the deal. This obligation is recurrently absent in the existing experimental evidence involving costly punishment. There is therefore the need to identify how those elements responsible for the emergence of retaliation in the absence of an obligation are also apt to induce retaliation in its presence, and thus in contractual relationships.

As explained below, they indeed acquire different contours when the individual subject to punishment is also *obliged* to behave in a certain manner because she voluntarily and autonomously agreed and consented to the contract. The second subsection develops this study, which is later included as possible causes of aggrievement and retaliation in the traditional model of contractual behavior adopted in the Economic Analysis of Law, and finally subjects to experimental scrutiny in the next chapter.

4.2.1 *Retaliation in Experimental Games*

Starting perhaps with the studies of Yamagishi and Ostrom, Walker and Gardner, retaliation against those that do not cooperate was always repeatedly and consistently observed in experiments involving prisoners' dilemma and public good games.[16] In these games, individuals can either cooperate and jointly achieve a socially optimal outcome or defect in order to maximize their own individual gains. When the possibility to retaliate and punish is introduced, individuals punish those that do not cooperate but rather defect and free ride on the contribution of others, thereby punishing socially inefficient behavior.[17]

---

[16] *See* Toshio Yamagishi, *The provision of a sanctioning system as a public good*, 51 JOURNAL OF PERSONALITY AND SOCIAL PSYCHOLOGY 110 (1986); Elinor Ostrom, James Walker & Roy Gardner, *Covenants with and without a Sword: Self-Governance is Possible*, 86 AMERICAN POLITICAL SCIENCE REVIEW 404 (1992).

[17] *See*, however, the discussion below on the existence of anti-social punishment, and how individuals also engage, at times, in punishment of those that cooperate.

Retaliation against non-cooperators has been studied at length in *public good games*. In this game, individuals can contribute any share of their endowments to the public good, and each contribution delivers gains of social welfare in being multiplied by a factor larger than one. It is therefore socially optimal to contribute to the public good, since that act delivers net gains of social welfare.

All members of the group, however, benefit equally from each member's individual contribution, and each member receives, in the end, only a fraction of her own contribution. The group is better off if all members contribute, but each member is better off if she does not contribute, retains her endowment for herself, and only shares into the contributions of the others. The individual strictly dominant strategy is not to contribute any amount, but rather to free ride, and this type of behavior is socially undesirable.[18]

The possibility of the members of the group to punish does not alter the equilibrium of the game, which is also under costly punishment not to contribute any amount. Punishment is costly for the individual engaging in it, and each member of the group is better off by not punishing those that do not cooperate and leaving the implementation of punishment for the other members of the group. This is the second-order social dilemma involved in punishment of non-cooperators, and rational individuals must anticipate that other rational individuals will never punish them in case they do not cooperate. Individuals that contribute but do not punish fare better than those that punish. Punishment is therefore not predicted to emerge according to strict rational theory.

Still, punishment is pervasive and individuals consistently engage in it.[19] Among the *causes* of retaliation and punishment of free riders, negative emotions toward defectors are often considered to be the *proximate* cause of that type of behavior.[20] Individuals that contribute positive and sizeable amounts feel angry and annoyed with free riders. Still, as scholars express when advancing emotions as the cause of observed behavior, negative emotions are just the proximate cause; they cannot

---

[18] Individuals provide contributions, in the traditional public good game, halfway between the socially optimal level (the participant's whole endowment) and the individually optimal level (full free riding) in one-shot games or in the first periods of a repeated game (that usually consists of 10 rounds). *Cf.* John Ledyard, *Public Goods: A Survey of Experimental Research*, in THE HANDBOOK OF EXPERIMENTAL ECONOMICS 111, 121 (John Kagel & Alvin Roth eds., 1997). In a more recent meta-analysis of public good games, Zelmer finds a slightly lower average contribution of 37%. *Cf*. Jennifer Zelmer, *Linear Public Goods Experiments: A Meta-Analysis*, 6 EXPERIMENTAL ECONOMICS 299, 306 (2003). Average contributions decline over time, if the game is repeated with the same group members and in the final rounds is usually close to zero.

[19] *Cf.* Ernst Fehr & Simon Gächter, *Cooperation and Punishment in Public Goods Experiments*, 90 AMERICAN ECONOMIC REVIEW 980 (2000); Fehr & Gächter, *Altruistic punishment in humans*, 415 NATURE 137 (2002).

[20] *Cf.* Fehr & Gächter, *Altruistic punishment in humans*, *op.cit. supra*, at 139 ("Free riding may cause strong negative emotions among the cooperators and these emotions, in turn, may trigger their willingness to punish the free riders"); Erte Xiao & Daniel Hauser, *Emotion expression in human punishment behavior*, 102 PROCEEDINGS OF THE NATIONAL ACADEMY OF SCIENCES 7398 (2005); Astrid Hopfensitz & Ernesto Reuben, *The Importance of Emotions for the Effectiveness of Social Punishment*, 119 ECONOMIC JOURNAL 1534 (2009).

be the ultimate cause, since something else is responsible for the arousal of those negative emotions.

The violation of an accepted social norm is proposed as the cause of punishment. Social norms are standards of behavior on how individuals ought to behave in a given situation that are based on beliefs shared by the members of a group, community, or society.[21] The social norm underlying cooperation in social dilemmas is the norm of conditional cooperation. "This norm prescribes cooperation if the other group members also cooperate, whereas the defection of others is a legitimate excuse for individual defection. The norm is violated if an individual defects even though the other group members cooperated."[22] The violation of that norm, or of the belief that individuals ought to cooperate when others cooperate, triggers the arousal of negative emotions that may lead one to retaliate.

In public good and prisoners' dilemma games, deviating behavior is responsible for a loss of social welfare. It is inefficient not to contribute and to free ride in a public good game, just as it is inefficient to defect instead of to cooperate in a prisoners' dilemma. Therefore, the ultimate cause of punishment of those that violate the social norm of conditional cooperation may lie in the loss of welfare that deviating behavior causes. As explained below, punishment of breach of contract may be caused by the social inefficiency of breach, and in this case, it is only expected to emerge when breach is, in the realized circumstances, indeed socially inefficient.

The *behavioral effect* of costly punishment is to induce cooperation and to deter defection and free riding. Differently from strict rational choice predictions, individuals anticipate irrational retaliation and the losses they will suffer by punishment. The possibility of costly punishment largely increases contributions of individuals and leads to the achievement and maintenance of very high or almost full cooperation by the members of the group.[23] It also leads to substantially higher cooperation in prisoners' dilemmas.[24] Other forms of punishment, such as threats of expulsion from the group (ostracism), have also been found to increase contributions to almost 100%.[25]

The *welfare effect* of punishment and retaliation was subject to different experiments in the most recent literature. Punishment has its own social costs. Whenever

---

[21] *See* Ernst Fehr & Urs Fischbacher, *Social Norms and Human Cooperation*, 8 TRENDS IN COGNITIVE SCIENCES 185, 185 (2004).

[22] *Id.* at 186.

[23] *Cf*. Fehr & Gächter, *Cooperation and Punishment in Public Goods Experiments, op. cit. supra;* Fehr & Gächter, *Altruistic punishment in humans, op. cit. supra.* Moreover, when subjects can choose more freely how much to punish, the result is that the less one contributes, the higher the average punishment received. *See* Nikos Nikiforakis & Hans-Theo Normann, *A Comparative Statics Analysis of Punishment in Public-good Experiments*, 11 EXPERIMENTAL ECONOMICS 358, 366 (2009) ("individuals are more severely punished the lower their contribution is compared to that of their peers.").

[24] *See* Dreber et al., *Winners don't Punish, op. cit. supra* (punishment indeed induces quite higher rates of cooperation in prisoners' dilemmas).

[25] *See* Matthias Cinyabuguma, Talbot Page & Louis Putterman, *Cooperation under the Threat of Expulsion in a Public Goods Experiment*, 89 JOURNAL OF PUBLIC ECONOMICS 1421 (2005).

there is defection or free riding and punishment is implemented, the individual retaliating bears the cost of retaliation and its victim suffers the loss from punishment. These are social losses, and they are responsible for a decrease in social welfare, and must be weighed against the welfare gains from higher cooperation in order to assess its net welfare effect.

Experimental evidence that considered both the welfare gains of retaliation in inducing socially desirable behavior and its social costs commonly finds a total net *negative* effect on social welfare in both public good and prisoners' dilemma games.[26]

This negative effect of private and decentralized punishment upon society's welfare is further reinforced by the presence of *anti-social punishment*. Individuals may punish socially undesirable behavior, but they may also punish those that are simply doing better than themselves or that are undertaking actions they personally do not agree with, or personally do not believe are morally required. Hermann, Thöni, and Gächter developed an empirical study in different societies and found that the presence of anti-social punishment is pervasive. Moreover, the higher the rate of anti-social punishment in a society, the lower the increase in cooperation induced by the possibility to punish.[27]

The possibility to punish those that engage in anti-social punishment reduces this type of behavior, but yet again creates second-order inefficiency, and was found not to enhance welfare.[28] Only when punishment is implemented collectively, and when members of the group manage to reach an agreement on whether to punish, is anti-social punishment rarely observed.[29]

In sum, evidence from public good and prisoners' dilemma games shows that costly and irrational punishment is pervasive and that it is most often directed against those that behave in socially undesirable manners, not taking the actions that would

---

[26] *Cf*. Elinor Ostrom, James Walker & Roy Gardner, *Covenants with and without a Sword: Self-Governance is Possible*, 86 AMERICAN POLITICAL SCIENCE REVIEW 404 (1992) (sanctions alone, in the absence of covenants, decrease group earnings because of the costs of sanctioning); Martin Sefton, Robert Shupp & James Walker, *The Effect of Rewards and Sanctions in Provision of Public Goods*, 45 ECONOMIC INQUIRY 671 (2007) (direct costs of sanctioning outweigh the beneficial effect of increased contributions); Martijn Egas & Arno Riedl, *The Economics of Altruistic Punishment and the Maintenance of Cooperation*, 275 PROCEEDINGS OF THE ROYAL SOCIETY BIOLOGICAL SCIENCES 871 (2008) (altruistic punishment leads to an overall loss individual and group welfare); Anna Dreber et al., *Winners don't Punish, op. cit. supra*, (while punishment increased cooperation, it did not increase average payoff). An exception is Simon Gächter, Elke Renner & Martin Sefton, *The Long-Run Benefits of Punishment*, 322 SCIENCE 1510 (2008) (punishment decreased welfare in a public good game repeated 10 times, but increased welfare when the game was repeated 50 times).

[27] *See* Benedikt Herrmann, Christian Thöni & Simon Gächter, *Antisocial Punishment across Societies*, 319 SCIENCE 1362 (2008) (the higher anti-social punishment in a society, the lower the rate of increase in cooperation).

[28] *Cf.* Matthias Cinyabuguma, Talbot Page & Louis Putterman, *Can Second-Order Punishment Deter Perverse Punishment?*, 9 EXPERIMENTAL ECONOMICS 265 (2006).

[29] *Cf.* Nynke van Miltenburg et al., *Implementing punishment and reward in the public goods game: the effect of individual and collective decision rules*, 8 INTERNATIONAL JOURNAL OF THE COMMONS (2014) (noting how reaching an agreement between the members of the group on punishment was scarce).

lead to a maximal welfare (although not always, as in case of anti-social punishment). It has its beneficial effect of inducing cooperation and in creating the associated gains of welfare, but it also has its own costs, given by the losses incurred by the person that punishes and by the person that suffers punishment. Existing evidence attests that the costs of punishment most often outweigh its benefits. Decentralized, private punishment of non-cooperators can hence rarely benefit the group, community, or society.

Moreover, retaliation is not restricted to social dilemmas and not induced only by deviations from a norm of conditional cooperation and by socially inefficient behavior. Perceived unfairness in the behavior of others is also well apt to induce aggrievement and resentment and to lead individuals to retaliate. This type of behavior, or retaliation to perceived unfairness, has also been extensively studied in experiments.

Retaliation to perceived unfairness is observed in the behavior of subjects in *ultimatum games*. In the ultimatum game, a player (the proposer) offers to another player (the responder) a stake in an amount given by the experimenter, and the offer is not negotiable (being therefore an ultimatum).[30] If the responder accepts the offer, each player earns the amount corresponding to offer of the proposer. If the responder rejects the offer, then they both go empty-handed.

Rejections of strictly positive offers in the ultimatum game are a form of costly punishment, since the receiver sacrifices the offered amount (that she would earn) in order to impose a loss on the proposer (equal to the amount the proposer would earn).[31] On average, proposers offer around 40% of the amount at stake and keep 60% to themselves (with a modal offer of 50%).[32]

According to strict rational choice models, the receiver's dominant strategy is to accept any strictly positive offer, irrespective of how low or unfair it is. Preferences are non-satiable, and money is a good, and therefore, earning something is always better than earning nothing. When faced with an unfair division of the stake, however, responders very often reject low, although positive offers, punishing what they perceive as unfair.[33]

This behavior is pervasive across societies and cultures. It is observed among students that are normally used as participants in laboratory experiments, but also among other different types of participants, and occurs when the amount at stake

---

[30] Werner Güth, Rolf Schmittberger & Bernd Schwarze, *An Experimental Analysis of Ultimatum Bargaining*, 3 JOURNAL OF ECONOMIC BEHAVIOR & ORGANIZATION 367 (1982).

[31] Fehr & Gächter, *The Nature of Human Altruism*, *op. cit. supra*, at 786 ("a rejection of a low offer is costly for the responder and it punishes the proposer for the violation of a social norm.").

[32] *Cf*. Werner Güth & Reinhard Tietz, *Ultimatum Bargaining Behavior: A Survey and Comparison of Experimental Results*, 11 JOURNAL OF ECONOMIC PSYCHOLOGY 417 (1990); Colin Camerer & Richard Thaler, *Anomalies: Ultimatums, Dictators and Manners*, 9 JOURNAL OF ECONOMIC PERSPECTIVES 209 (1995); Alvin Roth et al., *Bargaining and Market Behavior in Jerusalem, Ljubljana, Pittsburgh, and Tokyo: An Experimental Study*, 81 AMERICAN ECONOMIC REVIEW 1068 (1991).

[33] *See*, e.g., COLIN CAMERER, BEHAVIORAL GAME THEORY 43–44, 48–55 (Princeton: Princeton University, 2003) (reviewing the existing experimental evidence).

is low but also when it is very high.[34] Although it is present in all countries and continents,[35] and in the most different native tribes and communities from Peru to Mongolia and from Tanzania to Papua New Guinea, it is worth noting that *average* rates of rejection (punishment) vary across those.[36]

The *cause* of punishment in ultimatum games is not the violation of the norm of conditional cooperation, as mentioned above, since the ultimatum game does not involve cooperation. There is no welfare gain from offering a higher share of the endowment. This act is pure redistribution, and redistribution, by itself, does not increase social welfare.

The social norm that is violated, in ultimatum games, by low offers is a norm of fairness. Low offers are perceived by individuals as unfair and induce feelings of aggrievement and negative emotional arousal in the responder, thereby leading the latter to retaliate and punish the proposer.[37]

The *behavioral effect* of retaliation driven by the perceived unfairness is to induce proposers to offer higher, fairer amounts to the responder. A comparison between average offers in ultimatum games with average offers in dictator games shows how the possibility of punishment induces some change in behavior. In dictator games, the responder does not have any possibility to reject the offer and thus to punish perceived unfairness in the proposer's offer. The proposer does not need to fear punishment by the responder. The result is that, instead of an average offer of around 40% of the amount at stake, proposers offer around 28% of the amount when they cannot be punished.[38]

---

[34] *See* Lisa Cameron, *Raising the Stakes in the Ultimatum Game: Experimental Evidence from Indonesia*, 37 ECONOMIC INQUIRY 47 (1999) (endowment equivalent to three months wages); Robert Slonin & Alvin Roth, *Learning in High Stakes Ultimatum Games: An Experiment in the Slovak Republic*, 66 ECONOMETRICA 569 (1998) (endowments ranging from 60 to 1500 Slovenian crowns). With much higher stakes, however, individuals reject offers with a slightly lower probability, and participants are somehow less willing to reject unfair offers.

[35] *See* Hessel Oosterbeek, Randolph Sloof & Gijs van Kuilen, *Cultural Differences in Ultimatum Game Experiments: Evidence from a Meta-Analysis*, 7 EXPERIMENTAL ECONOMICS 171 (2004) (finding no statistically significant difference between continents and countries, with the sole exception of Western U.S.A., where participants rejected offers with a quite lower frequency).

[36] *See* Joseph Heinrich et al., *In Search of Homo Economicus: Behavioral Experiments in 15 Small-Scale Societies*, 91 AMERICAN ECONOMIC REVIEW 73 (2001).

[37] Different models of social preferences consider unfairness, understood as inequality, in the utility of individuals, and predict that individuals that in effect have that type of preference will at times retaliate when faced with inequality. *See* Ernst Fehr & Klaus Schmidt, *A Theory of Fairness, Competition and Cooperation*, 114 QUARTERLY JOURNAL OF ECONOMICS 817 (1999) (modeling disutility from payoff-inequality when individuals compare their earnings with the earnings of each other individual separately) and Gary Bolton & Axel Ockenfels, *ERC: A Theory of Equity, Reciprocity, and Competition*, 90 AMERICAN ECONOMIC REVIEW 166 (2000) (same, but where each individual compares her own payoff with the average payoff of other individuals in a relationship).

[38] *See* Christoph Engel, *Dictator Games: A Meta Study*, 14 EXPERIMENTAL ECONOMICS 583 (2011) (considering 129 different articles and 616 reported or constructed treatments, Engel estimates an average transfer of 28.35% of the pie in calculating a grand mean and 28.3% in implementing a random-effects meta-analysis; the author carefully excluded all studies that gave any kind of power

Still, individuals may not feel obliged to share anything with a stranger. In effect, it is doubtful that there is a social norm prescribing that one ought to share one's own resources with unrelated individuals. In contractual relationships, in contrast, as argued below, fairness is expected to acquire a very different role, for the individuals bound by the contract are not strangers to each other anymore. Moreover, unfairness in breach of contract arises through the commitment of a wrong, the wrong in breaking promises and contracts, and is thus expected to acquire a prominent role in inducing retaliation by the promisee.

The *welfare effect* of retaliation against perceived unfairness is to lower overall social welfare. Whenever the proposer offers an amount perceived as unfair by the responder, and the responder retaliates, both parties lose the entire amount at stake and thereby do not maximize social welfare. While apt to induce fairer offers, retaliation, whenever implemented, decreases total social welfare.

Evidence from ultimatum and dictator games reveals that individuals retaliate against unfairness, because in those games, there is no gain from cooperation to be achieved and no socially inefficient behavior to be punished. Retaliation induces fairer offers, but cannot bring about an overall gain of welfare. Its welfare effect is then solely negative, although it can induce fairer offers.

In general, across 15 different societies studied by Joseph Heinrich and co-authors, estimates of rates of rejection in ultimatum games range from 15 to 60% and deliver substantial variability across societies and across how unfair and unequal the offer was. On average, 56.5% of responders plainly rejected most unfair offers of only 10% of the pie, and the lower and unfair the offer, the higher the rate of rejection.[39] The question that remains concerns whether individuals retaliate to unfair offers because of their expectations or because of the inequality of the result.

Elizabeth Hoffman and co-authors developed different experiments presenting evidence that subject's expectations induce a change in the behavior of individuals. Proposers in ultimatum games offer lower shares when they earn the right to be in that position by a contest (a general knowledge quiz) and hence when one party had an entitlement.[40] Responders, however, did not punish depending on whether the entitlement was earned or not.[41] The authors hence argue that proposers offered on average less when entitled to be a proposer because they anticipate (correctly)

---

to the receiver precisely because of the fact that, in doing so, those experiments come close to ultimatum games).

[39] *See* Joseph Heinrich et al., *Costly Punishment Across Societies*, 312 Science 1767, 1769 (2006).

[40] *See* Elizabeth Hoffman & Matthew Spitzer, *Entitlements, Rights and Fairness: An Experimental Examination of Subjects Concepts of Distributive Justice*, 15 JOURNAL OF LEGAL STUDIES 254 (1985) (reporting substantially lower average offers when the proposer earned the right to be in that position than under random assignment); Elizabeth Hoffman et al., *Preferences, Property Rights, and Anonymity in Bargaining Experiments*, 7 GAMES AND ECONOMIC BEHAVIOR 346 (1994) (similar findings, also reporting lower average offers when the game was presented in a sale context than when presented as a divide context).

[41] Elizabeth Hoffman et al., *Preferences, Property Rights, and Anonymity in Bargaining Experiments*, 7 GAMES AND ECONOMIC BEHAVIOR 346 (1994).

that responders are more willing to accept lower offers (and hence to refrain from punishing) when the proposer was entitled to be in that position.[42]

This evidence thus suggests that entitlements—and the expectations they induce in subjects—lead to a change in behavior. Other studies attest how responders in the ultimatum game are more prone to reject unfair offers when primed with expectations of fairness.[43] Individuals bound by contract are capable of feeling entitled to a certain course of action, and their reactions to perceived unfairness are expected to differ when they feel entitled to the outcome of promised performance than when they do not have such promissory expectations.

Individuals punish deceptive actions, and observed rates of costly punishment were twice as high when the subject had received a previous deceptive message from the other one before than in the absence of a deceptive message.[44] Part of this behavior can be explained by the participants' desire to express their negative feelings and emotions, but the majority of participants still punish and reject unfair offers even when they could express their feelings through a separate channel.[45] The desire to express negative feelings and emotions cannot hence explain, by itself, why subjects punish at a personal cost.

Sanfey and co-authors associated punishment through rejection of unfair offers in ultimatum games with increases in activity in areas of the brain that are traditionally associated with feelings of anger and disgust (the anterior insula).[46] They thereby interpreted their results as providing evidence that anger motivates costly punishment, and their hypothesis received further support in subsequent studies.[47]

---

[42] *Id.* at 362 ("first movers accurately gauged the willingness of second movers to accept lower offers as we shifted treatments eliciting lower offers. It is therefore appropriate to say that in these treatments the self-interests of first movers were served not only in offering less, but also in their expectations that their risks of rejection would not rise significantly.") *See also* Elizabeth Hoffman, Kevin McCabe & Vernon Smith, *On Expectations and the Monetary Stakes in Ultimatum Games*, 25 JOURNAL OF GAME THEORY 289 (1996) (similar findings but with quite higher stakes of 100 dollars).

[43] Alan Sanfey, *Expectations and Social Decision-Making: Biasing Effects of Prior Knowledge on Ultimatum Responses*, 8 MIND & SOCIETY 93 (2009).

[44] Jordi Brandts & Gary Charness, *Truth or Consequence: an Experiment*, 49 MANAGEMENT SCIENCE 116 (2003).

[45] *See* Erte Xiao & Daniel Houser, *Emotion Expression in Human Punishment Behavior*, 102 PROCEEDINGS OF THE NATIONAL ACADEMY OF SCIENCES 7398 (2005) (rates of rejection in ultimatum games were lower when participants responders could express their feelings through other channels).

[46] Alan Sanfey et al., *The Neural Basis of Economical Decision-Making in the Ultimatum Game*, 300 SCIENCE 1755 (2003).

[47] *See* Elise Seip, Wilco van Dijk & Mark Rotteveel, *Anger Motivates Costly Punishment of Unfair Behavior*, 38 MOTIVATION AND EMOTION 578 (2014) (participants experiencing induced anger punished more often in public good and sequential trust games). When investigating whether individuals punish in order to deter future offenses or to impose punishment upon a moral wrong committed, Carlsmith et al. found that punishment was almost exclusively driven by the just desert rationale and not by the deterrence rationale. *See* Kevin Carlsmith, John Darley & Paul Robinson, *Why Do We Punish? Deterrence and Just Deserts as Motives for Punishment*, 83 JOURNAL OF PERSONALITY AND SOCIAL PSYCHOLOGY 284 (2002).

De Quervain and co-authors argue distinctively that punishment is rewarding. They deliver evidence that individuals derive satisfaction from punishment, and that "most people seem to feel bad if they observe that norm violations are not punished, and they seem to feel relief and satisfaction if justice is established."[48] They implemented a trust game followed by the trustor's possibility to engage in costly punishment of those that did not reciprocate trust. Their different treatments distinguish between situations where the trustor could (i) have a desire and opportunity to punish, (ii) have a desire to punish but not the opportunity to do so (because the possibility to punish was symbolic and did not impose material harm), and (iii) not even have desire to punish (because she knew that the decision to punish would be randomly implemented by the computer). In the last two (when the trustor could not effectively punish or could not feel a desire to punish), punishment could not deliver personal satisfaction to the trustor. In those treatments where subjects could desire punishment, brain regions associated with the processing of rewards were activated, delivering evidence that punishment provides "personal *relief* and *satisfaction*" to the punisher.[49]

Singer and co-authors consistently found that men experience increased activation of the reward circuitry of the brain when they saw participants that have played unfairly with them in previous rounds of a prisoners' dilemma receive a painful physical stimuli.[50] Moreover, less equal offers are rejected more often than fairer offers in ultimatum games implemented in several human populations.[51] Claudia Civai, based on this evidence provided by these several studies, recently argued "that rejecting inequality, even when it means sacrificing available resources, could be interpreted as a default response that occurs when there is no other reason to choose otherwise."[52]

---

[48] Dominique de Quervain et al., *The Neural Basis of Altruistic Punishment*, 305 SCIENCE 1254, 1254 (2004).

[49] *Id.* Moreover, the study distinguished between the costly and costless punishment. When punishment is costly, the trustor faced a trade-off between the monetary costs of punishment and the personal satisfaction to be achieved after punishment is implemented, therefore after taking that decision. Dealing with that trade-off requires integrating two distinct cognitive processes, consisting in weighting costs and *anticipated* satisfaction. Their results show that brain regions associated with that integrative operation were activated when punishment was costly, but not when it was costless, presenting evidence that punishing is a goal-directed, rewarding behavior.

[50] Tania Singer et al., *Empathic Neural Responses are Modulated by the Perceived Unfairness of Others*, 439 NATURE 466 (2006).

[51] *See* Joseph Heinrich et al., *Costly Punishment Across Societies*, 312 SCIENCE 1767 (2006).

[52] Claudia Civai, *Rejecting Unfairness: Emotion-driven Reaction or Cognitive Heuristic?*, 7 FRONTIERS IN HUMAN NEUROSCIENCE ARTICLE 126, 3 (2013) ("In conclusion, our findings support an account that considers the rejection of inequality as a cognitive heuristic, a psychological anchor, which is a useful starting point that can be easily adjusted when salient contextual cues enter the environment and influence the decision.") *See* Claudia Civai et al., *Are irrational reactions to unfairness truly emotionally-driven? Dissociated behavioural and emotional responses in the Ultimatum Game task*, 114 COGNITION 89 (2010) (mechanisms different than negative emotions can better explain rejections in the ultimatum game, as, e.g., inequality-aversion); Claudia Civai et al., *Equality versus self-interest in the brain: Differential roles of anterior insula and medial prefrontal cortex*, 62 NEUROIMAGE 102 (2012) (proposing that the default social norm is equal treatment and

4.2.2 *Retaliation to Breach of Contract*

Contractual relationships, as detailed above, involve the norm of keeping promises or the norm that contracts should be kept. It entitles parties to the promised and contracted performance. This *entitlement* is absent in public good and prisoners' dilemma games, as well as in dictator and ultimatum games. Individuals may well expect, in those games, other group members to cooperate and to offer fair shares; there is not, however, any norm that requires others to do exactly what they voluntarily and autonomously undertook to do.

Individuals have expectations to earn something in those games, but they are entitled neither by morality nor by law to receive what they expect. One may expect others to cooperate because of the norm of conditional cooperation or expect others to offer fair shares because of the fairness norm. They may well feel angry and disappointed when the other does not live up to their expectations. Still, these are only expectations, and not *promissory expectations*, for the other never promised and contracted that she would cooperate in the social dilemma and never promised or contracted that she would offer any specific amount in the bargain.

Retaliation to breach of contract, on the other hand, often involves those same elements present in non-contractual relations. Independent of contractual commitment, it is often socially inefficient to break a promise and a contract just as it is socially inefficient to free ride and to defect: Neither is the socially optimal course of conduct. It is also often unfair to breach a contract and to retain all the profits from breach for oneself, just as it is unfair to retain all the amount at stake: Neither is necessarily perceived as a fair act.

While these elements acquire a different character in contracts, as detailed below, they provide reasons and motives for promisees to feel aggrieved and tempted to retaliate against the promisor in breach. Additionally, when individuals are bound to each other by a contractual obligation, then they may feel entitled to receive exactly what they bargained for. This legitimate entitlement that derives its fundament of validity from an autonomous and voluntary promise is absent in the games above. It however provides another possible cause for retaliation to breach of contract.

Firstly, when the promisor breaches a contract, the promisee does not receive what she was entitled to receive. In public good games, it is uncertain what each individual expects to earn in the interaction, and different individuals may expect to earn, when making their contributions, very different amounts. In contractual relations, in contrast, each party can expect to earn exactly what she bargained for. The contractual party thus loses not only expected gains, but also *promised and contracted* gains. The norm that prescribes that one ought to keep promises and ought to respect contracts specifies an action that *ought to* be taken by the promisor

---

that rejection of unfair offers reflects the effort to overcome the default rule of equal treatment in favor of individual benefits); Claudia Civai, Raffaella Rumiati & Aldo Rustichini, *More equal than others: Equity norms as an integration of cognitive heuristics and contextual cues in bargaining games*, 144 ACTA PSYCHOLOGICA 12 (2013) (similar).

because of the promise. The promisee is therefore entitled to receive the promised performance, or, at least, its monetary equivalent.

The promisee that does not receive what she legitimately understands as her entitlement feels harmed, and a person that believes she was unjustly harmed feels, as advanced by Jon Elster, *anger*.[53] The action tendency of a person that feels anger is to cause suffering on the person responsible for it.[54] In other words, she will tend to retaliate and punish the one that created the harm, i.e., the contract-breaker.

The question that remains, in breach of promise and contract, is whether pure *loss of expectancy* is perceived by promisees as a harm and injury, leading the victim to feel anger and to engage in retaliation to an act that causes no more than loss of expectancy. As mentioned by Fuller and Perdue, losing something one does not have, but only would earn from performance of the promise, cannot be immediately equated to a harm.[55] It is rather an empirical question of whether promisees perceived it as a harm capable of inducing retaliation.

Secondly, breach of contract is, at times, socially undesirable from a welfare point of view. Breach can be either socially efficient or inefficient in any given contingency. When the costs of performance are higher than its gains, then performance is socially inefficient and undesirable. In contrast, when the costs of performance are lower than its gains, then performance is socially efficient and desirable and is the action that maximizes the welfare of the group or of the parties to the contract.

Punishment of socially inefficient breach of contract is therefore similar to punishment of defection in a prisoners' dilemma or of free riding in a public good game. It is, however, socially undesirable behavior that does not provide for a maximal welfare only in certain contingencies. If individuals feel aggrieved because the promisor did not consider both parties' interests when making her decision to perform, then the fact that breach was socially inefficient may lead to retaliation in contingencies where performance is socially efficient, but not in those where it is not.

The action of not undertaking the socially optimal course of conduct does not depend on the presence of promissory commitment. Not doing so when one was obliged to perform might be perceived as a different, more serious wrong. It involves disrespect for the other party's interests inside a relationship one voluntarily and autonomously entered into. As argued by Charles Fried, those that are bound by mutual promises stand closer to each other than the member of a community, group, or state: "they have some obligation to share unexpected benefits and losses in the case of an accident in the course of that enterprise."[56] The empirical question that remains is whether individuals retaliate more to inefficient behavior when inside a promissory relationship then in its absence.

---

[53] Jon Elster, *Indeterminacy of Emotional Mechanisms*, in ANALYTICAL SOCIOLOGY AND SOCIAL MECHANISMS 53 (Pierre Demeulenaere ed., Cambridge, Cambridge University 2011).

[54] *Id.* at 57.

[55] *See* Fuller & Perdue, *The Reliance Interest in Contract Damages*, *op. cit. supra*, at 53 ("In actuality the loss which the plaintiff suffers (deprivation of the expectancy) is not a datum of nature but the reflection of a normative order. It appears as a 'loss' only by reference to an unstated ought.").

[56] FRIED, CONTRACT AS PROMISE, *op. cit. supra*, at 72–73.

Thirdly, breach of contract can create inequality in the parties' final earnings and is an act that can be perceived as unfair by the victim. Unfairness in breach of contract, however, is quite different from unfairness in ultimatum and dictator games. In those games, parties never agreed or consented to undertake any specific actions. There is no previous agreement between the involved individuals, as there is in any contractual relationship.

In this respect, it is crucial to note that unfairness in breach of contract concerns *inequality from breach* and not *inequality from performance.* One party may well capture most of the gains from the transaction in the negotiation of the contract, and contract for a price that is much more advantageous for herself than for the other party. If the contract is performed, the resulting distribution of gains from trade will be unequal: One party will capture most of the gains. This is not, however, inequality from *breach.* It is rather inequality from performance, caused by unequal bargaining power, and concerns the questions of what is a fair price and the adequacy of consideration. It is not what is meant by inequality from breach.

Inequality from breach of contract arises only in case one party does not keep her part of the deal, independent of how fair the deal was. It is not defined with respect to a fair distribution of the possible gains from the transaction, but rather only with respect to the realized distribution *after breach.* The wrong in question that may lead to retaliation is breach of contract. In case of performance of the contract, it is not consubstantiated.

There is nothing wrong in performing and in keeping one's part of the deal, and if the implemented outcome is very unequal, then the resulting inequality concerns inequality that the parties consented and agreed to in the negotiation of the price. Inequality from breach, in contrast, does not depend on how the gains from trade are divided through the negotiated price. It depends, on the contrary, on the reasons that lead the promisor to breach.

When the promisor breaches in order to avoid incurring absolute losses from performance, then the promisor earns nothing while the promisee receives nothing, and breach leads to an equal outcome. When faced with a spike in costs of production that would lead to high losses in producing the good promised to the buyer, the seller that does not produce the good and does not deliver it to the promisee earns nothing, avoiding the consubstantiation of inequality by breaching the promise.

In contrast, when the promisor breaches to profit from a higher outside offer, then the promisor earns something by breaching while the promisee does not receive what she was promised and earns, in the absence of damages, nothing. Consequently, the resulting distribution is unequal. In this case, the promisee might understand the action as unfair and feel tempted to retaliate.

Promisees may understand that breaches to profit from a substitutive transaction is wrong because it is, in principle, wrong to profit from one's own wrong. It is not wrong, on the other hand, to profit from a deal, as long as one keeps her word, for there is nothing wrong in buying or selling something for a good and advantageous price. Breaching a promise is, for many individuals, perceived as wrong.[57] Doing so

[57] *See* the empirical literature attesting that individuals perceive breach as wrong *supra* n.66, chap. 2.

to achieve higher profits, in contrast, is *another wrong*. The empirical question that remains is whether promisees retaliate more to inequality from breach of promise than against inequality in the absence of a promise.

4.3 Retaliation in the Contractual Model

Consider the relationship between a promisor (seller) and a promisee (buyer) to a wholly executory contract, i.e., a contract where both parties must perform in the future. The seller must incur costs to deliver performance while the buyer must make the payment of the price. Both parties exchange promises to perform the actions necessary to implement the future transaction and agree on the object, date of delivery, and price. The seller promises to produce and deliver the good to the buyer at the agreed-upon date, and the buyer promises to make the payment of the price at that same date. Both parties thereby undertake an obligation to perform in the future in order to implement the desired, mutually profitable transaction.

Given the necessary lapse of time between the agreement and the time when performance is agreed to take place, the promisor's costs of performance are subject to variations according to the realized state of the world. The analysis focuses on this risk rather than other circumstances that may change. Parties know the possible contingencies and their probabilities of occurrence, but the contract is incomplete and does not condition on all possible contingencies, for any of the reasons discussed in the third chapter.[58]

The promisee promises to pay upon delivery, and her valuation of performance does not depend on the realized state. Therefore, whenever the promisor performs, it is a strictly dominant strategy for the promisee to make payment in order to receive the promised performance, since the promisee necessarily values performance more than the price.[59] Further standard assumptions include the following: Parties are not able to renegotiate the price and face no wealth constraints, information is symmetric, and buyers are indifferent between receiving performance as promised and the monetary equivalent of their valuation of performance. All these assumptions are standard assumptions in models of contractual behavior developed by the Economic Analysis of Law.[60]

The timeline of events is resumed in Fig. 4.1.

---

[58] At the time of negotiating an agreement, parties most often depart from the assumption that the other party will perform and thereby are much more likely to agree on the terms of performance rather than on what would be the consequences of default and breach in possible contingencies. Parties bargain for performance and not for a remedy, and if bargaining for a remedy becomes central, then parties will most often abandon the agreement and look for another more reliable party, for it signals the promisor's unwillingness to perform. *See, e.g.*, Melvin Eisenberg, *The Limits of Cognition and the Limits of Contract*, 47 STANFORD LAW REVIEW 211, 227 (1995).

[59] Otherwise, the promisee would not have entered the contract in the first place, implying that trade was not mutually profitable ex ante.

[60] *Cf.* Kaplow & Shavell, *Fairness versus Welfare*, *op. cit. supra*, at 1118–19, 1130–31.

Date 1	Date 2	Date 3	Date 4
Agreement stage	*Resolution of risk*	*Performance stage*	*Enforcement stage*
Parties meet and exchange promises	Nature draws the contingency, determining the promisor's costs	Promisor decides to perform or breach; Promisee pays in case of performance	Promisee can, it the promisor breaches retaliate, claim damages, or both

Fig. 4.1 Timeline of events

At date 1, parties enter into the contract and thereby undertake obligations to perform at the future date 3 by exchanging promises given with consideration. At date 2, Nature draws the state of the world θ from the compact set Θ and determines the seller's costs of performance, which depend on the costs of production $c(\theta)$ of the good and on the net gains $z(\theta)$ from a substitutive transaction possible only through breach. At date 3, the seller makes the decision to perform or to breach, represented by q_s, with $q_s \in \{0, 1\}$ equal to unit in case of performance. At date 4, and only in case of breach by the seller, the buyer receives damages for breach D and decides to retaliate or not against the seller in breach, represented by $r_b \in \{0, 1\}$, which is equal to unit in case of retaliation.

The different possible contingencies involving either an increase in costs of production $c(\theta)$ or a more profitable outside option $z(\theta)$ distinguish between the "overbidder paradigm" and the "loss-avoidance paradigm," for this distinction is crucial for the perceived unfairness in breach of contract, as explained and detailed below.[61] It serves to distinguish between breaches that *avoid* the creation of inequality (and that can be perceived as fair) from breaches that *create* inequality (and that can be perceived as unfair), respectively.

Moreover, the increase in costs of production or the outside offer can result in costs of performance being lower than the valuation of performance for the promisee, in which case performance is socially efficient, and would still create a gain of social welfare. Alternatively, the increase in costs of performance can be high enough to render performance socially inefficient.

In case of breach by the promisor, the promisee can *react* to the seller's decision by personally retaliating against the promisor in breach and by legally enforcing the contract, thereby claiming the available remedy for breach. Through private retaliation, the promisee must incur costs in order to impose a loss upon the promisor in breach; that is, she can engage in costly punishment of the promisor. In case of expectation damages for breach, legal enforcement of the contract implements a

61 *See* Eisenberg, *Actual and Virtual Specific Performance, The Theory of Efficient Breach, and the Indifference Principle in Contract Law*, *op. cit. supra*, at 997 ("Although commentators typically present the theory of efficient breach in very generalized terms, the theory can only be understood and evaluated in the context of paradigm cases to which it might meaningfully be applied"); Eisenberg, *The Disgorgement Interest in Contract Law*, *op. cit. supra*, at 571 (similar).

transfer of resources from the promisor in breach to the breachee, where the amount transferred depends on the measurement of damages prescribed by the law.

Let U_s and U_b represent the seller and the buyer's utility functions, where

- V is the buyer's valuation of the good or service;
- P is the contract price;
- a is the buyer's level of aggrievement from breach (with its possible causes discussed below);
- β is an individual parameter representing the monetary equivalent of the buyer's experienced aggrievement (how much she would pay to eliminate one unit of aggrievement);
- R is the amount of losses imposed by the promisee upon the promisor at own costs $c(R)$; and
- D is the amount of damages for breach claimed by the promisee and paid by the breacher.

The seller's utility function is then represented by[62]

$$U_s = q_s(P - c(\theta)) + (1 - q_s)(z(\theta) - D - R) \tag{4.1}$$

The seller earns, in case of performance of the contract ($q_s = 1$), the promised price minus the costs of production of the good. In case of breach ($q_s = 0$), the seller earns net gains $z(\theta)$ from any substitutive transaction (if existent) but pays damages for breach D to the buyer and bears the losses R from retaliation.

The buyer's utility function, in turn, is represented by

$$U_b = q_s(V - P) + (1 - q_s)(D - \min\{\beta a(\theta, R, D) - c(R), \beta a(\theta, D)\} \tag{4.2}$$

The buyer earns, in case the seller performs and delivers the good, her valuation of the good minus the price paid for it. In case the seller breaches and does not deliver the good, the buyer earns damages for breach D but bears experienced aggrievement from breach βa that she will attempt to minimize by punishing the seller in breach, as explained below.

---

[62] The model departs from Hart & Moore, *Contracts as Reference Points*, *op. cit. supra*, but relies on fewer assumptions. Moreover, it complements the authors' model in (i) distinguishing the causes of aggrievement in contractual breach and in (ii) endogenizing the effect of remedies for breach, absent in the author's model.

The authors consider "shading" on performance instead of retaliation, both however intimately related, and do not analyze, in their model, how moral understandings interact with the behavioral tendency to retaliate to breach. They rather assume that promisees will shade on performance whenever they do not receive what they felt entitled to, what is determined by the ex ante contract signed by the parties at date 1. Their focus, consonantly, was never to explain the law ("To the extent that the role of the contract is to embody and anchor entitlements, the fact that the contract is legally binding is perhaps of secondary importance. Much of our analysis goes through if the contract is viewed as a nonbinding agreement.") *Id.* at 12.

The seller will rationally decide to perform if and only if her individual gains from performance are higher than her individual gains from breach, or according to the following rule:

$$q_s = 1 \Leftrightarrow U_s(q_s = 1) \geq U_s(q_s = 0)$$

which corresponds, after substituting from Eq. (4.1), to

$$q_s = 1 \Leftrightarrow P - c(\theta) \geq z(\theta) - R - D \tag{4.3}$$

The seller will perform as long as net gains from performance, given by the price P paid by the buyer minus costs of production $c(\theta)$, are larger than net gains from breach, given by the net gains from a substitutive transaction $z(\theta)$ minus losses R from private retaliation and D from the payment of damages.

Private retaliation, just as damages for breach, can induce performance by the seller. They both impose costs on breach, making breach less profitable and performance more attractive. They are therefore different enforcement mechanisms that can both induce performance of the contract, both serving to make promisors keep their word.

Under expectation damages, damages for breach are measured by the promisee's loss of expectancy and given by $D = V - P$. The seller will then perform as long as overall gains from performance are larger than the overall gains from breach, according to the following rule:

$$q_s = 1 \Leftrightarrow P - c(\theta) \geq z(\theta) - R - (V - P)$$

which is given by, after simplifying,

$$q_s = 1 \Leftrightarrow V - c(\theta) - z(\theta) \geq -R \tag{4.4}$$

This corresponds to the well-known result from the literature that states that expectation damages induce breach if and only if breach is socially efficient, but not otherwise (and, conversely, induce performance if and only if performance is socially efficient). The seller will perform, under expectation damages, if and only if overall gains from performance $V - c(\theta) - z(\theta)$ are positive and higher than the losses from retaliation. The model, moreover, explicitly distinguishes between the overbidder and loss-avoidance paradigms and endogenizes the loss from retaliation as capable of deterring breach.

The buyer, on her turn, will decide to retaliate in order to maximize her own utility (or, equivalently, to minimize the utility loss from experienced aggrievement) and will do so according to the following rule:

$$r = 1 \Leftrightarrow \beta a(\theta, D) - \beta a(\theta, R, D) > c(R) \tag{4.5}$$

The buyer will retaliate against the seller in breach if and only if her utility gains from retaliation are higher than her utility loss from retaliating, given by the costs of retaliation $c(R)$. This is consistent with finding that "leaving an unfair act unpunished is associated with higher disutility than bearing the cost of punishing an unfair act."[63] The victim of breach will then, in the absence of a public remedy for breach, attempt to minimize her own experienced aggrievement by private acts of retaliation and will do so only if she has the power and means to do so, captured by the costs of retaliation $c(R)$.

In case it is individually optimal for the promisee to retaliate (to minimize the utility loss from experienced aggrievement), then the buyer bears the costs of retaliation $c(R)$ and possible further remaining aggrievement $\beta a_b(\theta, R, D)$. In the opposite case, where it is not optimal for the promisee to retaliate, given the costs she must incur to do so, then the buyer bears in equilibrium all aggrievement $\beta a_b(\theta, D)$ but incurs no personal cost from retaliation. In this case, the victim of breach must "take the aggrievement back home," and she suffers the associated utility loss without being able to "transfer it back" to the promisor.

Damages for breach are apt to reduce, in Eq. (4.5), retaliation by providing *legal relief* to victims of breach and can therefore perform the function of *crowding out* private retaliation *in substituting for private redress.*[64] Damages thereby provide fundamental gains in social welfare by saving both costs $c(R)$ of retaliation and losses R imposed upon the breacher.

4.4 Aggrievement from Breach and Possible Causes of Retaliation

Until now, aggrievement was a black box, resulting in a utility loss for the promisee in case of breach of contract, and capable of inducing retaliation aimed at offsetting that loss. Disappointed promisees, however, do not retaliate, in reality, indiscriminately against any breach. They retaliate only if they perceive breach as wrong in the realized circumstances, something that can depend on the elements previously discussed: loss of expectancy, the fairness of the result from breach, and its social benefits or costs.

---

[63] *Cf.* Ernst Fehr & Colin Camerer, *Social Neuroeconomics: The Neural Circuitry of a Broken Promise*, 11 Trends in Cognitive Sciences 419, 421 (2007).

[64] This assumes that the promisee is capable, after the occurrence of breach, of anticipating the effect of the legal remedy, and behaving accordingly, thereby not completely driven by her emotions in the heat of the moment. Note that breach is committed at date 3, and that at date 4, the promisee can do nothing to prevent it. The consequences of breach include monetary ones and further non-pecuniary ones such as the creation or avoidance of inefficiency and inequality, being thus different from injuries created, for example, by crimes. Crimes are much more likely to prompt retaliation at the heat of the moment, with prospective legal relief having a smaller role in crowding out retaliation to harm from crime.

Breach of promise is, according to the convention of promises discussed in the second chapter, often understood as *justified* or *excused*. Therefore, even individuals that understand the contractual obligation as a promissory obligation requiring performance of the precisely promised act will not feel aggrieved and tempted to retaliate against any type of breach. Individuals that understand the wrong in breach of contract in a deontological manner will also consider the motives that lead the promisor to breach and the circumstances under which that decision was taken. When the promisee does not understand breach as *wrong* in the realized circumstances, then she will feel neither aggrieved nor tempted to retaliate against an act that was excused by the convention of promises, and that is therefore not immoral.[65]

On the other hand, individuals that understand the moral value of breach depending on its consequences, in a consequentialist fashion, will consider them before assessing the moral value of the concrete breach. The consequences of the act that can consubstantiate the wrong are not restricted to a loss of overall social welfare, in a strict sense, but can, rather, also include the realization of inequality or, perhaps, exclude both of them and be circumscribed only to the loss incurred by the promisee herself.[66]

There can be several other elements responsible for the understanding of breach as wrong and for the arousal of feelings of aggrievement. In this thesis, only those with consequences *inside* the parties' own promissory relation are considered, and other consequences of breach, such the harm that it imposes upon the practice of promising itself, are not considered.[67]

Moreover, even the Holmesian understanding of contractual promises does not exclude that breach of contract is a moral wrong. According to Holmes, "a promise is simply an accepted assurance that a certain event or state of things shall come to pass," and if it does not, "plaintiff's property is sold to satisfy the damages, within certain limits, which the promisee has suffered by the failure." There is, still, something *wrong* in breach *without* compensation for the promisee.[68]

Breach followed by payment of *compensatory* damages is not wrong because it amounts to performance of the contractual obligation. The promisor promises to perform or pay damages, and if she breaches and pays damages, then she performs the contractual obligation, as per Holmes.[69] But breach not followed by compensation for loss created is wrong. Therefore, even under such understanding, there is something wrong in breach, even if the wrong consists only in the causing of loss of expectancy upon the promisee.

---

[65] *See* the discussion *supra* in Chap. 2, Sect. 2.2 (promissory theories of the contractual obligation).

[66] *See* the discussion *supra* in Chap. 3, Sect. 3.4 (disagreement on the negative consequences of breach).

[67] *See* Joseph Raz, *Promises in Morality and Law*, *op. cit. supra,* at 928. This shall not be interpreted as advancing that these other consequences are not relevant, but that they are simply not studied in the present thesis.

[68] *Cf*. HOLMES, THE COMMON LAW, *op. cit. supra*, at 265.

[69] For a recent revitalization of the theory, and its defense, *see* Markovits & Schwartz, *The Myth of Efficient Breach*, *op. cit. supra* (defending the "dual performance hypothesis").

Strict rational choice models of parties' contractual behavior consider that costly retaliation to breach is irrational and a strictly dominated strategy for victims of breach in single interactions.[70] They implicitly or explicitly assume that the moral wrong in breach has no behavioral impact. The hypothesis on human behavior implied by strict rational choice models, which is subject to experimental scrutiny in the next chapter, and that will serve as the null hypothesis against which the following ones can be tested empirically, is stated as follows:

Hypothesis 0: Promisees will not retaliate against breach by the promisor.

$$a_b = 0 \Rightarrow r^* = 0$$

The hypothesis that individuals will not alter their behavior because retaliation is costly and hence irrational does not depend on the realized contingency, on the motives that lead the seller to breach, and on the consequences of the act. The buyer will never, according to strict rational choice theory, engage in individually costly retaliation to breach, if the interaction is not repeated.

4.4.1 Loss of Expected and Promised Gains

Aggrievement from breach of promise can be caused by the loss of expected and *promised* gains from trade and from the fact that the promisee does not receive what she bargained for. Promisees can feel entitled to the promised performance (or, at least, to its monetary equivalent) because of the moral norm that individuals ought to keep promises and that contracts ought to be kept. In case of breach, the promisee does not earn that amount she expected to earn and moreover does not receive what she was entitled to because of the previous promise and contract.

When the promisor makes a promise to the promisee in exchange for a return benefit, then the promisee creates a feeling of entitlement to the promised reward. As noted by Adam Smith, "if one *promises* to give an other five pounds, this naturally creates an expectation that he will receive five pounds from him at the time promised."[71] In case of breach of promise, the promisee suffers a loss of expected and promised gains and is thereby apt to feel aggrieved because of that loss.

This injury is not among the ones more likely to trigger retaliation by its victim, at least when compared to injuries done, for example, by torts or crimes. Still, as argued by Smith, it does require some form of *satisfaction* or a legal remedy that provides compensation for the victim. "The injury done by the breach of a contract is the slightest possible; at least the slightest one can well account to require any satisfaction." In case the promisee cannot recover her expectancy through legal

[70] Unless the interaction between the parties is *infinitely* repeated, and, perhaps, when parties do not know when it will end. This is not the case of the vast majority of trade relations, from building a house to having your car repaired, and is therefore not considered herein.

[71] ADAM SMITH, LECTURES ON JURISPRUDENCE, *op. cit. supra*, at 12.

relief, she may be tempted to redress her own wrong by private means. "Breaches of contracts are in themselves done very quietly and without any open violence. *They may indeed provoke the injured person to revenge*, but do not in themselves produce great disturbance."[72]

If promisees feel aggrieved and injured from loss of expectancy, then they are "provoked to revenge," and thus predicted to retaliate, in the absence of a legal remedy, in *any* case of breach of the promisor. The sole exception would be the case in which the promisee could find a ready-made substitute good in the market for the very same price, thus inevitably realizing the same amount of gains in case of breach or performance (not discussed in this thesis). Whenever this is not available, loss of expectancy occurs in all cases of breach by the promisor, and it does not depend on the circumstances, causes, and motives that lead the promisor to breach, or on the realized contingency. It is, in sum, always present in breach of contract.

This conjecture delivers the first hypothesis on the possible causes of retaliation to breach of contract, subject to empirical examination in the experiment presented in the next chapter:

Hypothesis 1: Promisees will retaliate more often to breach when they do not receive what they were promised, when compared to the situation where no explicit promise was made, independent of the realized contingency.

If loss of expectancy triggers retaliation, then victims shall retaliate more often to breach whenever they do not earn their promised award or its monetary equivalent. This does not depend on whether the promisor breached to avoid losses, to make higher profits from an outside offer, or neither. In any of those cases, the promisee equally loses her expectancy and is expected, under this alternative hypothesis, to be tempted to retaliate in case she loses her expectancy.

4.4.2 Inequality from Breach

Aggrievement from breach of promise can depend upon the inequality created by breach. As discussed above, inequality from breach arises only in case of breach of contract and not in case of performance. It depends on the commitment of perceived wrong *in breach* and not on individual preferences that consider any type of inequality in the outcome.

Inequality in the outcome appears as a determinant of individual utility in models of social preferences that do not consider what one is entitled to earn and to receive. In models of social preferences, individuals derive disutility from the inequality in the realized distribution, without reference to an obligation that entitles individuals to a certain distribution. Extended models consider intentionality of the person that creates inequality, but not entitlements that derive their legitimacy and fundament of validity upon a voluntarily undertaking of an obligation, or *mutual consent*.

[72] *Id*, at 87.

There is by now plenty of evidence that individuals retaliate against unequal outcomes even at a personal cost, even in single, one-shot interactions between complete strangers. Some authors now consider "that rejecting inequality, even when it means sacrificing available resources, could be interpreted as a default response that occurs when there is no other reason to choose otherwise."[73] Individuals retaliate to unequal, intentionally chosen outcomes, punishing the person responsible for it in situations where self-interest alone would require *no* punishment at all. This type of retaliation is not, however, equivalent to retaliation to inequality *from breach* or inequality resulting from *wrongful* behavior.

Inequality from breach abstracts from and does not consider inequality in the original deal or the inequality in the distribution of the gains from the transaction. Individuals bargain for a price and consent to it by agreement. Each party earns something from the transaction, and the total gains from the transaction may well be unfairly distributed, with one party, the one in a better position in the negotiation, capturing most of them. A car dealer that, for example, buys a car for $30,000 and sells it immediately afterward to a buyer that values it at $60,000 for a negotiated price of $59,000 captures the largest share of the gains from trade. This type of inequality, which inquires into the adequacy of consideration, is brought to place only when the contract is performed as agreed, because it is inequality in the original agreement. It is inequality most often caused by unequal bargaining power and is different from the inequality brought about by breach of contract.

Inequality from breach is realized, on the contrary, when the contract is not performed and hence when the parties do not earn what they were entitled to. If the seller performs the contract, in the example above, then there is inequality in the realized outcome of $28,000, created in the result ($29,000, $1000). This type of inequality and unfairness of bargains may well induce further retaliation, but it is not studied in this thesis, which focuses on breach and its consequences. Inequality from breach, in contrast to inequality in the deal that was struck, is realized only in case of breach, while the latter is realized only in case of performance of the unfair deal.

If the seller breaches in order to avoid incurring the costs resulting from an increase in costs of production (e.g., selling the car would require now paying additional late

---

[73] Claudia Civai, *Rejecting Unfairness: Emotion-driven Reaction or Cognitive Heuristic?* 7 FRONTIERS IN HUMAN NEUROSCIENCE art. 126, 3 (2013) ("In conclusion, our findings support an account that considers the rejection of inequality as a cognitive heuristic, a psychological anchor, which is a useful starting point that can be easily adjusted when salient contextual cues enter the environment and influence the decision."). *See* also Claudia Civai et al., *Are Irrational Reactions to Unfairness Truly Emotionally-driven? Dissociated Behavioural and Emotional Responses in the Ultimatum Game Task*, 114 COGNITION 89 (2010) (mechanisms different than negative emotions can better explain rejections in the ultimatum game, e.g., inequality-aversion); Claudia Civai et al., *Equality versus Self-interest in the Brain: Differential Roles of Anterior Insula and Medial Prefrontal Cortex*, 62 NEUROIMAGE 102 (2012) (proposing that the default social norm is equal treatment and that rejection of unfair offers reflects the effort to overcome the default rule of equal treatment in favor of individual benefits); Claudia Civai, Raffaella Rumiati & Aldo Rustichini, *More equal than others: Equity Norms as an Integration of Cognitive Heuristics and Contextual Cues in Bargaining Games*, 144 ACTA PSYCHOLOGICA 12 (2013) (similar).

taxes in total of $40,000), then neither the seller nor the buyer earns anything in case of breach. The good is not delivered, payment is not made, and the inequality from breach in the final outcome (0, 0) is zero. If, in contrast, the seller walks away from the deal because another buyer offered $70,000 for the car, then the inequality from breach in the final outcome ($40.000, 0) is equal to $40,000.

Let π_s resume the profits from the seller and π_b the profits from the buyer. Inequality from breach ($q_s = 0$), in the present model, is then given by

$$\text{Ineq}(q_s = 0) = \max\{\pi_s(q_s = 0) - \pi_b(q_s = 0), 0\}$$

In case of a higher outside offer, or in the overbidder paradigm, the seller's profits from breach are equal to her net gains from the substitutive transaction, and $\pi_s(q_s = 0) = z(\theta)$. The buyer does not receive what she was promised, but also does not make any payment for the seller and earns nothing, with $\pi_b(q_s = 0) = 0$.

In case of an increase in costs of production, or in the loss-avoiding paradigm, the seller's profits from breach are zero. Faced with higher costs of production that render performance individually unprofitable, the seller prefers to not produce the good and to earn nothing, foregoing the opportunity to trade. The buyer, who does not receive the promised performance but also does not make any payment to the seller, also makes zero profits.

Inequality from breach is therefore simply given by

$$\text{Ineq}(q_s = 0) = z(\theta)$$

Therefore, while breaches in the overbidder paradigm create non-contracted inequality, breaches in the loss-avoiding paradigm avoid it. From the point of view of fairness in breach, the first type of breach can be perceived as unfair by the promisee and the second one as fair.

The second hypothesis on the possible causes of retaliation to breach is as follows:

Hypothesis 2: Promisees will retaliate more often against breaches that create inequality than against breaches that avoid the creation of inequality

$$r = 1 \Leftrightarrow (1 - q_s) \cdot z(\theta) > 0$$

The buyer is predicted to retaliate against breaches that create inequality, and thus only in the overbidder paradigm. Breaches that avoid the creation of an unfair distribution, or breaches in the loss paradigm, are not predicted to trigger retaliation under this alternative hypothesis for the causes of retaliation to breach.

4.4.3 Inefficiency from Breach

Aggrievement from breach can, lastly, be caused by the fact that breach is not the socially optimal course of conduct, but rather the action responsible for an overall loss of welfare. Individuals may understand that it is wrong to breach a promise and a contract without considering the consequences of breach upon the interests of both parties, on aggregate. This is especially true when the parties are in a promissory relation, a relationship that implies trust and, arguably, the need to consider how one's actions affect not only one's own interests, but also the interests of the other party.

This is different from the case where parties are not bound to each other by the contractual obligation. In this case, as in public good or prisoners' dilemma games, individuals may well believe that there is a social norm of conditional cooperation and that the promisor ought to perform as long as performance is socially efficient. Individuals are not, however, bound to each because of a voluntary and autonomous promise given with consideration.

In a contractual relation, in contrast, not considering how one's actions affect aggregate outcomes may be perceived as wrong because of the relationship parties consented to enter into. Inefficiency from breach of contract, more strongly than the sole creation of social losses, may be more apt to create aggrievement and to induce retaliation by the promisee. The conjecture is that individuals have additional reasons to retaliate to the loss of welfare when they are bound to each other because they voluntarily and autonomously chose to do so.

The loss of resources caused by the seller's decision is given, in general, by

$$\text{Inef}(q_s = 0) = \max\{\pi_s(q_s = 1) + \pi_b(q_s = 1) - [\pi_s(q_s = 0) + \pi_b(q_s = 0)], 0\}$$

Substituting from each party's profits in case of performance and breach yields

$$\text{Inef}(q_s = 0) = \max\{P - c(\theta) + V - P - z(\theta), 0\},$$

which simplifies to

$$\text{Inef}(q_s = 0) = \max\{V - c(\theta) - z(\theta), 0\}$$

In the loss-avoidance paradigm, total inefficiency from breach is given by $V - c(\theta)$, and is equivalent to the value of the good to the promisee minus its costs of production for the promisor. The price of the contract simply divides those gains between the parties and is irrelevant for the total amount of welfare that the transaction can create. If costs of production are lower than the buyer's valuation of performance, breach is socially inefficient, with the amount of inefficiency given by that difference. If costs of production are higher than the buyer's valuation, breach is socially efficient and inefficiency is zero.

In the overbidder paradigm, similarly, total inefficiency from breach is given by $V - z(\theta)$, and is equivalent to the value of the good for the promisee minus the value of the good to the third party.[74] If the outside offer is lower than the buyer's valuation of performance, breach is socially inefficient, with the amount of inefficiency given by that difference. If the outside offer is higher than the buyer's valuation, breach is socially efficient and inefficiency is zero.

The third hypothesis, which is subject to empirical investigation in the next chapter, is stated as follows.

Hypothesis 3: Promisees will retaliate more often against socially inefficient breaches than against socially efficient breaches

$$r^* = 1 \Leftrightarrow (1 - q_s) \cdot [V - c(\theta) - z(\theta)] > 0$$

As discussed below, if promisees tend to retaliate only to socially inefficient breaches, then under perfectly implemented expectation damages, retaliation would not arise in equilibrium, for expectation damages deter all socially inefficient breaches. Thus, if alternative hypothesis 3 for the causes of retaliation is correct, and all other ones prove to be incorrect, then expectation damages, if perfectly implemented, deter all inefficient breaches and thereby avoid retaliation of promisees.

4.5 Social Welfare and Retaliation to Breach

The impact of the tendency to retaliate to breach upon social welfare depends, ultimately, on the causes of that type of behavior and on the remedy in place. Under perfectly implemented expectation damages or specific performance, the promisee is compensated for her lost expectancy, and retaliation is rarely expected to emerge because there is neither a loss incurred by the promisee, nor the commitment of socially inefficient breaches in equilibrium. There are, however, efficient breaches committed in equilibrium to profit from an outside offer, and they will still trigger retaliation driven by the unfairness of the result. The first section below accordingly discusses the need of legal relief to crowd out retaliation under perfectly compensatory remedies.

Under imperfectly compensatory remedies, imperfect rationality, or imperfect information, inefficient breaches and undercompensatory damages will be implemented in equilibrium, and the need of legal remedies to crowd out retaliation to breach is then pervasive. Promisees that feel aggrieved by the loss they still endure under undercompensatory damages will tend to retaliate, and promisors that anticipate undercompensatory remedies will not perform whenever it is efficient to do so. As discussed in the second section below, under such imperfections, the need

[74] Note that the assumption is that the third party offers a price equivalent to her whole valuation of the good for the seller.

of remedies to crowd out retaliation is then not restricted to unfair breaches, but is rather expected to be pervasive.

Social welfare, in the model, is given by

$$\mathrm{SW} = U_s + U_b$$

It corresponds, after substituting from the parties' utilities in Eqs. (4.1) and (4.2), to

$$\mathrm{SW} = \pi_s + \pi_b - R - c(R) - \min\{\beta a(\theta, R, D) - c(R), \beta a(\theta, D)\}$$

Considering the case where promisees have the means to retaliate, thereby being capable of eliminating experienced aggrievement by transferring it all back to the perceived wrongdoer, then social welfare resumes to

$$\mathrm{SW} = \pi_s + \pi_b - R^* - c\left(R^*\right)$$

In monetary terms, remedies for breach only redistribute, ex post, wealth from the party in breach to the breachee and thereby do not contribute, ex post, to social welfare. They are therefore absent in the total amount of welfare generated by performance or breach. The bare fact that money change hands in a legal suit, after the occurrence of breach, is considered *in itself* of no consequence for social welfare.[75] Their impact upon social welfare occurs through their ex ante effects upon the behavior of parties.

4.5.1 *Social Costs and Benefits of Retaliation under Perfect Legal Enforcement*

Under perfect legal enforcement, expectation damages induce performance if and only if performance is socially efficient, as in Eq. (4.4) above. Retaliation to breach has no role to play in inducing socially efficient performance, since legal damages already completely fulfill that social function. They are therefore not complementary enforcement mechanisms if legal enforcement is perfect, since there is nothing to complement. Moreover, there are no social welfare *gains* from retaliation to breach of contract, but only losses, as explained below.

Breach of contract, however, is predicted to emerge whenever breach is socially efficient. Three different inferences can be made concerning social losses from retaliation to breach under perfect legal enforcement.

[75] *Cf*. Kaplow & Shavell, *Fairness versus Welfare*, *op. cit. supra*, at 998 n.73 ("the bare fact that money may change hands in a lawsuit in certain circumstances, thereby changing how a loss is divided between the two parties, is of no consequence under welfare economics.").

Firstly, promisees that feel aggrieved from loss of expectancy will never have a reason and motive to retaliate to breach under perfectly implemented and compensatory expectation damages, since they are always compensated for the whole loss of expectancy. They can always recover their expectancy through the remedy of expectation damages, and until one considers the costs involved in litigation, the promisee is put in the position she would have been in had the promisor performed.

Secondly, promisees that feel aggrieved from inefficiency from breach will also never have a reason and motive to retaliate to breach, since socially inefficient breaches of contract never arise. The legal remedy of expectation damages, when perfectly implemented, deters all possible socially inefficient breaches.

Thirdly, and in contrast, promisees that feel aggrieved from the unfairness of the outcome of breach have a reason and motive to retaliate whenever the promisor breaches to achieve higher profits from a substitutive transaction. The legal remedy implements an unequal outcome, where the net gains from breach $z(\theta)$, after the payment of expectation damages, are appropriated by the breacher in their entirety.

Therefore, under perfect legal enforcement of contracts, social losses from retaliation to breach of contract arise only because of the unfairness of breach. They are, however, predicted to be real and existent, since, under expectation damages, efficient breaches to profit from an outside offer are in fact encouraged. When they happen, non-contracted inequality is implemented, and the buyer may disagree that the seller is entitled to all those gains. She will feel tempted to retaliate, and the legal remedy of expectation damages does not allow her to recover any of those profits.

The possible behavioral effect of retaliation to breach is then solely to induce performance of contracts in case breach would create an unfair result. Since retaliation can still arise when breach is unfair, it still has a deterrent effect. Promisors are already induced by expectation damages to perform when breach is unfair and socially inefficient. They are not, however, induced to perform when breach is unfair but socially efficient. On the contrary, they are predicted by theory to breach in this type of contingency, pay expectation damages, and retain all profits from the substitutive transaction for themselves, something that can be perceived by the promisee as unfair.

If the seller anticipates that buyers will retaliate, she may perform inefficiently. She could, of course, attempt to buy-off the buyers' aggrievement, and to voluntarily allow the buyer to share in the net profits from breach, in which case the cause of aggrievement and retaliation would disappear. While some sellers, in reality, may do so, many others will not. The law allows them to retain those profits, and, feeling entitled to them, many are unwilling to give to the buyer something the buyer does not have a right to.

The possible welfare effect of retaliation, in deterring unfair but socially efficient breaches, is then negative. Promisors that fear retaliation will refrain from breaching efficiently and will not realize the gains of welfare possible from the substitutive transaction. This effect can, however, be mitigated by the parties' possibility to renegotiate, if that assumption is relaxed. Chapter six of this thesis investigates social welfare under expectation damages, in the absence and presence of renegotiation, in detail.

4.5.2 Social Costs and Benefits of Retaliation under Imperfect Legal Enforcement

Social losses stemming from private retaliation are restricted to unfair breaches only if the legal remedy for breach can perfectly induce socially optimal levels of performance. However, this requires that promisors perfectly anticipate that they will have to pay an amount of damages that perfectly corresponds to the promisee's valuation of the promised performance. Only under such a perfect, highly idealized, and hypothetical legal system would losses from retaliation be necessarily circumscribed to that single case where promisees retaliate because of perceived unfairness of the outcome from breach.

Legal enforcement is, in reality, imperfect for several different reasons. Courts are often unable to measure the loss of expectancy incurred by the promisee accurately and are well known to have great difficulties in assessing the promisee's valuation of the promised performance. It is, in most cases, subjective, and therefore not readily available for courts, which most often award undercompensatory damages. In this case, promisors will not perfectly internalize the negative externality of breach and will breach when breach is not necessarily socially efficient. In reality, damages most often do not compensate the promisee for her whole valuation of performance and are usually undercompensatory for several different reasons.[76]

Firstly, courts often exclude losses that are hard to measure in the amount of damages to be paid. Secondly, the doctrine of foreseeability limits damages to those that could be reasonably foreseen by the promisor. Thirdly, they do not always fully consider the promisee's losses from a delayed gratification. Lastly, they either do not compensate for legal costs or only compensate for some of them, depending on the jurisdiction in question.

Under *undercompensatory damages*, there will be strictly positive levels of socially inefficient breaches in equilibrium, and in this respect, retaliation may have, from the exclusive point of view of inducing performance by the promisor, *positive effects* upon social welfare. Retaliation and damages for breach can then be complementary in inducing performance by the promisor.

Retaliation, as from Eq. (4.4) (reproduced below for convenience), imposes another cost on breach by the promisor and therefore can further induce performance that was not induced by undercompensatory damages. It can, however, achieve that very same goal at the danger of high social costs. Consider the optimal decision of sellers:

$$q_s = 1 \Leftrightarrow P - c(\theta) - z(\theta) \geq -R - D$$

The behavioral effect of retaliation to breach of promise is that the seller, in anticipation of retaliation, is induced to perform by considering her prospective

---

[76] *Cf*. Eisenberg, *Actual and Virtual Specific Performance, the Theory of Efficient Breach, and the Indifference Principle in Contract Law*, *op. cit. supra*, at 990–95; Shavell, *Why Breach of Contract May Not Be Immoral*, *op. cit. supra*, at 1575.

losses. If the promisor anticipates irrational retaliation by the victim of breach, then she will often decide not to breach in the first place.

Retaliation is thereby often not implemented because promisors can anticipate it. Therefore, it could, at first sight, induce optimal levels of performance, just as damages for breach, and without the materialization of the social losses it entails whenever it is implemented. If promisors anticipate it, then they will not breach in the first place, and there will be, consequently, no retaliation. Perhaps even with a crucial advantage of not requiring courts or social investments in the maintenance of courts. There are, however, several problems involved in decentralized private enforcement of promises.

The first problem is that whenever a seller contracts with a buyer that has a very strict understanding of the morality of promises, understanding breach as almost always immoral, then the seller may fear retaliation even when breach is socially efficient and will therefore be induced to perform in situations where performance is socially inefficient. Performing in fear of retaliation when performance is socially inefficient is not, by definition, socially optimal, with its direct negative impact upon social welfare.

The second problem is that sellers, in most interactions, do not know how the buyer they contracted with understands the morality of promissory obligations, or how the buyer will react in case of breach. This is especially true in market interactions without repetition, where parties interact only once and thereby do not learn the "type" of the buyer, thus not gathering information they could use in future interactions. Sellers then can only rely on average expectations of such understandings that they may have built in their daily interactions with many *different* buyers.

Reliance on averages, however, implies that sellers will be at times matched with buyers with a more strict understanding of the morality of promises than the average and at times with buyers with a less strict understanding. Equation (4.4) above, which gives the optimal decision of sellers to perform or breach, is, under uncertainty about the buyer's type, given by

$$q_s = 1 \Leftrightarrow P - c(\theta) \geq z(\theta) - E(R) - D,$$

where $E(R)$ gives only the seller's expected retaliation by buyers, built upon an average that sellers can estimate through their interactions with many other different buyers.

Whenever the seller, in not expecting retaliation in a certain contingency, given her expectation based on averages, breaches a contract with a buyer with a very strict understanding, then retaliation will be implemented. And when it is implemented, the social losses given by $R + c(R)$ are realized, and social welfare is impaired.

Legal enforcement, while requiring costs of maintenance of a judicial system, does not cause this type of loss since whenever damages are awarded, there is just *redistribution of resources*, resulting in no loss in social welfare. Moreover, legal enforcement is not based on compassion for the victim of breach, but is, rather, the same for all citizens, thereby not requiring from sellers an estimation of averages that will not always correspond to the implemented amount.

The ultimate consequence is that sellers are more encouraged to enter into mutually profitable arrangements independent of the distribution of moral understandings on what is right or wrong in breach of contract.

The third problem that arises with decentralized private enforcement of promises is that promisees do not always have the power and means to retaliate against certain types of sellers. Spreading the word in the neighborhood that the mechanic next door, or the usual painter responsible for painting most houses in the block, simply breaches her contracts may lead to serious loss of profits by the contractor in losing clients. The same is not always true with respect to, for example, large firms that have their clientele dispersed and not easily reachable.

This fact acquires higher relevance when the firm enjoys monopoly power in the market. Telling friends, family, and neighbors that the mobile phone company cuts its services and leaves clients without a line whenever its costs rise, even if minimally, may not lead anybody to change company if no other is present and if people need their mobile phones. Even in the presence of some few other companies, if they all behave equally or coordinate, then the disappointed customer can do nothing to retaliate against the company by harming its reputation in the market.[77]

A last and perhaps more serious problem with reliance on private retaliation to induce promisors to perform is that it implies the imposition of the moral understanding of the majority of the population upon others. This may coincide with the legal standard or not. If it does not, then private retaliation will implement an equilibrium that may be more strict than the one intended by the law. It may then override minority rights, or at least the right of a minority to be free from being victim of private, decentralized retaliation as long as they follow the legal standard.

As Atiyah pointed out, "there is therefore a greater danger that morality will overshoot the mark in encouraging too great a degree of respect for the rule that promises must be kept; the law may overshoot the mark also, but given the discretionary and mitigating techniques used by the law, this is less likely to happen."[78] For some, it may be desirable that citizens, through their free actions, implement an equilibrium that reflects the understanding of the majority, even it does not correspond to the one intended by the law—a question open to debate, and not tackled in this thesis.

Perhaps worse, it is often the case that a minority may impose its own moral standards upon the majority if the minority has more *power* than the majority. Guala speaks how "a community, for example, may be prevented from adopting a set of

[77] She could go to customer service and make a complaint or cause a scandal, but that is often very costly and ineffective in imposing a loss to the company. She could further complain in newspapers, in an attempt to reach more potential or existing customers, but this will also prove ineffective unless customers have a decent number of alternatives to choose from. All these options further require the absence of switching costs, since in their presence customers can do nothing to retaliate against abuse of market power by a monopolist.

[78] ATIYAH, PROMISES, MORALS, AND LAW, *op. cit. supra,* at 137.

beneficial strategies, simply because they depart from what is considered 'correct' behavior by an aggressive gang of moralistic punishers."[79]

This does not correspond to the law's ideals that individuals should be free to pursue their own goals as long as one does not harm others.[80] If the majority understands breach of contract in itself as not morally wrong, but is forced to keep promises at all costs simply because a minority understands that breach is fundamentally, and most often morally, wrong and has more power to impose such understanding upon others, than the law's ideals are impaired. Moral norms, just as social norms, have their own limits.[81]

Under present law, promisors are not forced by the law to perform under all costs, as implied by the default remedy of expectation damages that limits the amount of damages to be paid in case of breach to the loss of expectancy. In civil law systems, where the default remedy for breach is specific performance, there are several different circumstances, foreseen by the law, that release the promisor from the obligation to perform. This is intended in the law, where "along with the celebrated freedom to make contracts goes a considerable freedom to break them as well."[82]

4.6 Conclusion

The human tendency to retaliate against perceived wrong, based on the norm of (strong) reciprocity, has been consistently observed in a large body of empirical literature. It is apt to have its own beneficial role in influencing the behavior of the parties to a contract, deterring certain actions such as breach of promise or of contract. Retaliation, however, acquires different contours when individuals are bound by promises they voluntarily and autonomously entered into. While retaliation may, in this context, share many of the characteristics of costly punishment observed in experimental games, it is a form of punishment of what the victim of breach herself might perceive as a wrong.

There are three consequences of breach that are hypothesized to create aggrievement and hence to lead victims to retaliate. They are given by loss of expectancy, inefficiency, and unfairness in the distribution of gains and losses from breach. When the promisee derives disutility from any of those gains and losses, she will retaliate, in the absence of a legal remedy and of compensation, in order to minimize her own loss of utility from experienced aggrievement from breach, imposing a loss upon the promisor in breach even at a personal cost.

Retaliation can induce promisors to perform and hence substitute or complement the legal enforcement of contracts when the former one is absent or ineffective. It

[79] Guala, *Reciprocity: Weak or Strong?*, *op. cit. supra*, at 4.

[80] *See* the "liberal" criticism on the law's strict acceptance of the promissory theory of contracts developed in Chap. 2, Sect. 2.2.

[81] *Cf.* Jeffrey Rachlinski, *The Limits of Social Norms*, 74 CHICAGO-KENT LAW REVIEW 1537 (1999).

[82] FARNSWORTH ON CONTRACTS 730 § 12.1.

has its own beneficial effect in inducing parties to implement agreed exchanges, and possibly gains of social welfare. It can only achieve this, however, imperfectly and subject to several undesirable social consequences.

The main disadvantage of decentralized punishment as an enforcement mechanism is given by the losses that punishment imposes upon the person punishing and upon its victim whenever it is implemented. Decentralized punishment can also deter efficient breaches, for nothing guarantees that victims will retaliate solely against inefficient breaches. Moreover, legal enforcement of contractual promises can achieve those same goals through incentives and ex post *redistribution*. Reliance on private enforcement mechanisms such as retaliation and punishment is hence Pareto-inferior to legal enforcement, especially through expectation damages, since the last achieves the same goal that the second one can achieve without the social loss of resources that private retaliation occasions.

In the presence of perfect legal enforcement, retaliation has only a minor role to generate gains of welfare since expectation damages, just as specific performance, already induce promisors to perform. It is circumscribed, in this case, to retaliation to perceived unfairness in breach of contract and only expected to emerge when breach leads to the realization of non-contracted inequality that the promisee can perceive as unfair. Retaliation is therefore still expected to exist even in our present modern societies where the law, in general, prohibits the use of private punishment by the individuals themselves and compensates the promisee for lost expectancy.

The welfare benefits that retaliation can deliver in inducing promisors to perform are already exhausted by the legal remedy. Retaliation still can, however, deter efficient breaches that promisees may possibly perceive as unfair. Both in deterring socially efficient breaches and in creating a deadweight loss when efficient breach occurs and the victim retaliates, retaliation can only prevent the maximization of social welfare under expectation damages. *Undercompensatory* damages not only fail to create optimal incentives for promisors to perform, but can also fail to eliminate retaliation by those that feel aggrieved by socially inefficient breaches and by the loss of expectancy they endure.

Legal enforcement is surely not, in reality, perfect, and courts are often unable to measure damages accurately and to perfectly assess the promisee's valuation of the promised performance. Undercompensatory damages have in this case two distinct negative effects upon social welfare.

In not deterring all socially inefficient breaches, social welfare is not maximized, as is well known in the Economic Analysis of Law. In not providing satisfactory compensation, they encourage parties to attempt to reduce their own experienced aggrievement from breach privately, through acts of punishment of perceived wrongdoers. In other words, undercompensatory damages do not, firstly, induce socially efficient levels of performance and therefore leave *gains from trade* unrealized. Secondly, they do not effectively crowd out retaliation to breach in leaving losses uncompensated and therefore do not minimize *losses from retaliation*.

While expectation damages are optimal to induce socially optimal performance, they fall short of providing satisfactory relief for victims of breach since they do not fully account for realized inequality between the parties to a promissory relationship.

They limit the losses incurred by promisors, in case of increases in costs of production, but they do not correct for inequality from breach to achieve higher profits from a substitute transaction with a third party. While the experiment presented in the next chapter aims firstly at studying the functions of legal redress to induce performance by the promisor and to reduce retaliation by the promisee, it also inquires into the causes of retaliation to breach. It thereby seeks to identify which of those three elements often present in breach can indeed lead disappointed promisees to retaliate and attempts to specify the circumstances under which breach is most likely to trigger retaliation by the victim. This study can then *inform* the discussion on how damages for breach should be better designed to minimize retaliation while still providing incentives for promisors to perform efficiently, as developed in chapter six.

Chapter 5
Retaliation, Remedies, and Contracts

The present chapter presents the empirical study, firstly, on the behavioral effect of the primary duty to keep promises and contract on the promisor's decision to perform or breach and on the promisee's decision to retaliate or not to breach. With respect to the latter, the experiment further attempts to investigate the circumstances and types of contingencies where promisees in effect are most tempted to retaliate to breach, and it thereby tests the theoretical hypotheses on the causes of retaliation to breach developed in the previous chapter. Secondly, the empirical study focuses on the behavioral effect of the secondary duty to pay damages for breach on the promisor's decision to perform or breach, net of the effect of the moral force of keeping promises, and then on the promisee's decision to retaliate or not to breach.

5.1 Introduction

An award of remedies for breach of contract is justified, on social welfare grounds, because of the exante incentives it creates for parties to behave in socially desirable manners. Promisors anticipate the prospect of the payment of damages—the cost of breach—and change their behavior accordingly, responding rationally to the incentives created by law. Most importantly, by imposing a cost on breach that is equal to the promisee's loss of expectancy, expectation damages are apt to induce

An article related to this chapter was published by Sergio Mittlaender & Vincent Buskens, *Retaliation, Remedies, and Contracts*, 21 AMERICAN LAW & ECONOMICS REVIEW 280 (2019), with the license CC BY.

S. Mittlaender, *Equity, Efficiency, and Ethics in Remedies for Breach of Contract*, International Law and Economics, https://doi.org/10.1007/978-3-031-10804-4_5

promisors to perform when performance is, in any contingency, socially efficient, thereby providing for maximal social welfare.[1]

Economic theories of contract law have, however, largely ignored one specific effect of an award of compensatory damages upon partie's behavior. Among the several incentives created by damages identified in the literature, no reference is made to the effect of compensatory remedies on the victim's tendency to reciprocate to perceived wrong in breach of contract. In the absence of reliance investments, optimal remedies for breach require only that promisors internalize all losses created by breach. They do not need to provide relief for the promisee to redress breach, and economic theories have difficulties providing a justification for compensation for the victim.[2]

For legal scholars, on the contrary, compensation is without doubt the goal pursued by an award of damages for breach.[3] Also, in existing positive law, the goal is to

---

[1] *See* BARTON, *The Economic Basis of Damages for Breach of Contract, op. cit. supra*, at 282; Birmingham, *Breach of Contract, Damage Measures, and Economic Efficiency, op. cit. supra*, at 284, and the detailed discussion *supra* in chap. 2, section 4. Remedies for breach further provide incentives for individuals to enter into mutually profitable contracts, for parties to rely on promises and to take precautions to avoid breach, among others. *See* Shavell, *Damage Measures for Breach of Contract, op. cit. supra* and *The Design of Contracts and Remedies for Breach, op. cit. supra* (introducing incentives for reliance investments); Cooter, *Unity in Torts, Contracts, and Property: The Model of Precaution, op. cit. supra* (introducing incentives for precautions).

[2] See, *e.g.*, Craswell, *Instrumental Theories of Compensation: A Survey, op. cit. supra*, at 1139 ("From the standpoint of modern economics, the analysis is instrumental all the way down, so the concept of compensation does no meaningful work."), and at 1178 ("In short, in economic theories the concept of compensation can be dispensed with entirely, whereas in corrective justice theories that concept is absolutely crucial.").

Steven Shavell mentions two different justifications for why there could be value in compensation for promisees. Firstly, the promisee must earn something through a lawsuit in order to report breach. This, however, does not explain why the promisee is entitled by law to recover all lost expectancy. Secondly, compensation could provide implicit insurance for promisees. This, however, requires that promisees be risk-averse, more risk-averse than promisors, that the risk to be bear is detrimental and monetary, and that insurance markets concomitantly fail. *See* SHAVELL, FOUNDATIONS OF ECONOMICANALYSIS OF LAW, *op. cit. supra* at 311 (in the presence of functioning insurance markets, "the need for damages to compensate the victim is negated, and damages have a role mainly as an incentive device") and the discussion *supra* in chap. 2, section 4.

[3] *See* 2 BLACKSTONE, COMMENTARIES ON THE LAWS OF ENGLAND, *op. cit. supra*, at 226–227 ("upon all contracts or promises ... just as for all infringements of the natural or relative rights of another, the law gives redress by action against the wrongdoer by an action to recover the damage sustained"); 1 SEDGWICK, A TREATISE ON THE MEASURE OF DAMAGES, *op. cit. supra*, at 34 cmt. a ("The general principle undoubtedly at common law, both in actions for breach of contract and ..., is to give compensation for pecuniary injury"); ANSTON, PRINCIPLES OF THE ENGLISH LAW OF CONTRACTS AND OF AGENCY IN ITS RELATION TO CONTRACT, *op. cit. supra*, at 377 ("Damages for breach of contract are by way of compensation"); 3 WILLISTON, THE LAW OF CONTRACTS, *op. cit. supra*, at 2392–2393 ("Compensation is the fundamental principle. In fixing the amount of these damages [for breach of contract], the general purpose of the law is, and should be, to give compensation"); FARNSWORTH ON CONTRACTS 757 ("The basic principle for the measurement of those damages [for breach of contract] is that of compensation based on the injured party's expectation"); Cooter & Eisenberg, *Damages for Breach of Contract, op. cit. supra*, at 1434 ("the

provide compensation, and legal relief aims at placing the victim of breach in the position she would have been in had the promisor performed.[4]

Accordingly, compensation is the fundamental principle in the enforcement of contracts, both in legal theories and in the law.[5] Its goal and function are arguably to *substitute private for public redress*, thereby providing its own contribution to the welfare of society.[6] As argued by Corbin, "[t]here is more than one purpose underlying the rules of law that provide for the giving of damages for breach of contract. One of the ends to be obtained is, without doubt, the keeping of the peace. The party injured by the breach has a sense of grievance. In the absence of a public

---

goal, compensation, and the means, expectation damages, are so ingrained in contract law as to seem self-evident.").

[4] *See* RESTATEMENT (SECOND) OF CONTRACTS, introductory note to chap. 16, at 100 ("The traditional goal of the law of contract remedies has not been compulsion of the promisor to perform his promise but compensation of the promisee for the loss resulting from breach."); U.C.C. § 1–305 cmt. 1 (explaining that the central purpose of contract damages is to provide compensation for disappointed promisees).

[5] At common law, the principle of compensation shaped the legal rule according to which damages must put the promisee in the position she would have been in if the contract had been performed, and thereby the protection of the expectation interest. *See* Robinson v. Harman 1 Exch. 850 at 855 (1848), per Baron Parke ("The rule of the common law is, that where a party sustains a loss by reason of a breach of contract, he is, so far as money can do it, to be placed in the same situation, with respect to damages, as if the contract had been performed."); Wertheim (Sally) v. Chicoutimi Pulp Co. A.C. 301 at 307 (1911), per Lord Atkinson (P.C.) ("And it is the general intention of the law that, in giving damages for breach of contract, the party complaining should, so far as it can be done by money, be placed in the same position as he would have been in if the contract had been performed. (…) That is a ruling principle. It is a just principle.").

The principle and the legal rule it defines are equally found in the American law of contracts. *Cf*. Jaquith v. Hudson, 5 Mich. 123, 133–134 (1858) ("The law, following the dictates of equity and natural justice (…) adopts the principle of just compensation for the loss or injury actually sustained"); Hawkins v. McGee, 84 N.H. 114, 146 A. 641 (1929) ("By 'damages,' as that term is used in the law of contracts, is intended compensation for a breach.").

[6] *Cf*. JHERING, GEIST DES RÖMISCHEN RECHTS, *op. cit. supra*, at 113 ("*Die ersten unausbleiblichen Regungen des verletzten Rechtsgefühls bestehen in der gewaltsamen Reaktion gegen das zugefügte Unrecht, in der Selbsthülfe und Rache; mit Selbsthülfe und Rache hat daher ein jedes Recht begonnen.*") ("The first inevitable impulse of the injured sense of justice consist in a violent reaction against the inflicted wrong, in self-help and revenge; every right thus began with self-help and revenge.") (own transl.); HOLMES, THE COMMON LAW, *op. cit. supra*, 37 ("My aim and purpose has been to show that the various forms of liability known to modern law spring from the common ground of revenge"); WEBER, WIRTSCHAFT UND GESELLSCHAFT, *op. cit. supra*, at 421 ("*Die ökonomische Rationalisierung des Rechts begünstigte die Entstehung der Vorstellung, dass die Sühnehaftung nicht sowohl Abkauf der Rache (die ursprüngliche Auffassung) wie Ersatz des Schadens sei. Nichterfüllung eines Kontrakts konnte nun ebenfalls als sühnepflichtige Schädigung qualifiziert werden.*") ("The economic rationalization of the law favored the rise of the conception that liability for composition was not only buying off of vengeance (the original conception) but also compensation for harm. Non-performance of contract could now be qualified as harm requiring compensation.") (own transl.).

remedy, he would do his best to redress his own wrong. This means private war, with all of the resulting harm that it entails to the interest of other people."[7]

In effect, the human tendency to reciprocate to perceive wrongful and unfair behavior is a well-established type of behavior repeatedly documented in a large body of empirical literature, and often with its own beneficial effect, for it is apt to induce cooperation by the potential victim.[8] In case of contracts, retaliation can possibly deter violations of the moral norm of keeping promises, or of *pacta sunt servanda*, if promisors fear and anticipate acts of retaliation by promisees. It is, however, most often unable to provide a net contribution to welfare, since whenever implemented, retaliation entails costs for the individual retaliating as well as for the victim. As several empirical studies repeatedly identify, its social costs most often outweigh the benefits, and the result is a loss of welfare.[9]

Moreover, in the presence of legal enforcement, retaliation is not necessary to induce promisors to perform, for the prospect of the payment of damages fulfills that very same function. Damages for breach consist in a transfer of resources from the party in breach to the breachee and thus do not create the same loss of resources that

---

[7] 5 CORBIN, A COMPREHENSIVE TREATISE ON THE RULES OF CONTRACT LAW, *op. cit. supra*, at 30–31 § 1002 (complementing with the remark that "[a] second purpose in the giving of damages, however, one that is equally important as the first, is the prevention of similar harms in the future. The fact that damages must be paid tends directly to the prevention of breaches of contract.").

[8] Retaliation and costly punishment induce cooperation in social dilemmas, as observed in the existing literature detailed in the previous chapter. *See, e.g.*, Fehr & Gächter, *Cooperation and Punishment in Public Goods Experiments, op. cit. supra* (costly punishment of free riders leads to almost universal cooperation in a game where defection was rational and maintains cooperation stable in repeated interactions); Fehr & Gächter, *Altruistic Punishment in Humans, op. cit. supra* (similar); Dreber et al., *Winners don't punish, op. cit. supra* (costly punishment more than doubles the amount of cooperation in prisoner's dilemma); Rockenbach & Milinski, *The Efficient Interaction of Indirect Reciprocity and Costly Punishment, op. cit. supra* (interaction between punishment and reputation building further increases cooperation in public good games); Casari & Luini, *Cooperation Under Alternative Punishment Institutions: An Experiment, op. cit supra* (punishment under consensus by members of the group induces higher levels of cooperation than individual punishment). *See also* the detailed discussion in the review of the literature on costly punishment and retaliation presented in Chap. 3, section 2.

[9] *See* Ostrom, Walker & Gardner, *Covenants with and without a Sword: Self-Governance is Possible, op. cit. supra* (sanctions alone decrease group earnings because of the costs of sanctioning); Sefton, Shupp & Walker, *The Effect of Rewards and Sanctions in Provision of Public Goods, op. cit. supra* (direct costs of sanctioning outweigh the beneficial effect of increased contributions); Egas & Riedl, *The Economics of Altruistic Punishment and the Maintenance of Cooperation, op. cit. supra* (costly punishment leads to an overall loss in individual and group welfare); Dreber et al., *Winners don't Punish, op. cit supra* (while punishment increased cooperation, it did not increase average payoff in prisoner's dilemmas). *See*, however, Gächter, Renner & Sefton, *The Long-Run Benefits of Punishment, op. cit. supra* (punishment decrease welfare in a public good game repeated 10 times, but increased welfare when the game was repeated 50 times). Moreover, spiteful anti-social punishment aimed at those that cooperate also exists and is responsible for lower average rates of cooperation. *See* Herrmann, Thöni & Gächter, *Antisocial Punishment across Societies, op. cit. supra* (the higher anti-social punishment in a society, the lower the rate of increase in cooperation).

retaliation creates when they are implemented.[10] Legal relief is thereby well suited to substitute private for public redress efficiently and to induce performance of contracts while crowding out the tendency to retaliate to breach of contract, thereby avoiding the loss of welfare it occasions.[11]

This conjecture has not yet been subject to empirical investigation.[12] The existing literature has not examined whether disappointed promisees in fact retaliate to breach of bargained-for promises responsible for no more than loss of expectancy. Moreover, no experimental evidence exists either for the effect of expectation damages to induce performance if and only if performance is socially efficient, or for the role of legal relief to crowd out retaliation to breach of promises given with consideration.

This chapter seeks to fill in this gap in the literature by developing an experimental study into these two functions of damages for breach, and it attempts to provide empirical evidence for the welfare benefits of legal relief through both channels. To achieve those goals, it investigates, firstly, the function of expectation damages to induce efficient levels of performance. Secondly, it investigates the function of compensatory remedies to crowd out retaliation to breach by the victim. Lastly, it compares the estimated gains of social welfare provided by each of these two functions of damages for breach in order to discuss how far, and under what circumstances, compensation is necessary for the maximization of social welfare.

In order to investigate those questions empirically, the experiment distinguishes between different situations in which the promisor can breach. These take the form of contingencies not covered by the partie's agreement, which is, in the experiment, incomplete and does not condition upon those, as most real-life agreements. The different contingencies distinguish between socially efficient and inefficient breaches and between breaches committed to avoid losses resulting from an increase in costs of production ("unfortunate contingencies," in the "loss-avoidance paradigm") from breaches committed to achieve higher profits from another transaction ("fortunate contingencies," in the "overbidder paradigm").[13]

---

[10] *Cf.* Kaplow & Shavell, *Fairness versus Welfare, op. cit. supra*, at 998 n. 73 ("the bare fact that money may change hands in a lawsuit in certain circumstances, thereby changing how a loss is divided between the two parties, is of no consequence under welfare economics.").

[11] Under expectation damages, breach is predicted to occur whenever it is, in the realized contingency, socially efficient. When it occurs, the victim might feel aggrieved and tempted to retaliate if she is not entitled to a legal remedy. Therefore, even if promisors anticipate the prospect of payment of damages perfectly, and only efficient breaches are committed, the function of legal relief to crowd out retaliation is still necessary for maximal social welfare. Moreover, under imperfect information, imperfect cognitive abilities, or imperfect legal enforcement, breach of contract may arise even it is when not socially efficient (as it in fact happened in the experiment) and is hence expected to be more often committed in reality than in theory. Under any of those imperfections, the need to crowd out retaliation is then even more pervasive.

[12] *See*, however, the discussion in the next section (existing empirical studies on contractual behavior).

[13] The distinction between the "loss-avoidance paradigm" and the "overbidder paradigm" is developed by Melvin Eisenberg, who argues that it is in the context of the second one that the theory of efficient breach is most inaccurate. *Cf.* Eisenberg, *Actual and Virtual Specific Performance, the*

Moreover, both functions of damages for breach operate inside a relationship in which parties are bound to each other by contractual obligation. Damages provide monetary incentives for promisors to perform when the promisor is already committed to perform. This commitment, established by the giving of a promise with consideration, can already induce promisors to perform, independently of the material incentives provided by the legal remedy. At the same time, breach of that commitment provides a reason and motive for the promisee to feel aggrieved and thereby tempted to retaliate. The experiment does not neglect those, but, quite on the contrary, explicitly studies how far promissory commitment, independent of damages for breach, can by itself induce performance by the promisor, and how far breach of promise can trigger retaliation by the promisee.

In sum, the experiment investigates the role of promises given with consideration to (i) induce performance by the promisor and (ii) instigate retaliation to breach by the promise. It then studies the role of expectation damages to (iii) induce efficient performance by the promisor and (iv) crowd out retaliation to breach by the promisee. All these four effects are captured in different types of contingencies that distinguish between the efficiency and inefficiency, and the fairness and unfairness of breach. With that, the experiment provides estimates for the behavioral and welfare effects of expectation damages to induce performance only when performance is socially efficient and of compensatory remedies for breach to crowd out retaliation in circumstances where breach of promise may in fact induce retaliation.

The next section presents the individual contractual behavior examined in the experiment and the related existing literature. The third section explains the design of the experiment and describes the trade game that subjects played in the different treatments, the content of each treatment, predictions from rational choice theory, alternative hypotheses, and the details of the experimental procedure. The fourth section reports the obtained results and the statistical analysis, and the last section concludes.

5.2 Partie's Behavior Under Investigation and Related Literature

The behavior of contractual parties that is subject to investigation involves the promisor's decision to perform and the promisee's decision to retaliate. They can both be influenced by the two duties created by the contractual obligation: the primary duty to perform and to keep one's part of the deal and the secondary duty to pay

---

Theory of Efficient Breach, and the Indifference Principle in Contract Law, op. cit. supra, at 997; Eisenberg, *Disgorgement Interest in Contract Law, op. cit. supra,* at 571 ("In the context of the overbidder Paradigm, the theory of inefficient breach is incorrect for three reasons: (1) it rests upon incorrect factual predicates; (2) it does not have any support in efficiency; and (3) if widely followed, it would lead to inefficiency.") The distinction between "fortunate" and "unfortunate" contingencies is made in ROBERT COOTER & THOMAS ULEN, INTRODUCTION TO LAW AND ECONOMICS 238, 241 (3rd ed., Reading: Addison Wesley Longman 2000).

damages and to compensate the promisee in case of breach. Both duties can influence the behavior of both parties, thus delivering four different effects under empirical scrutiny.[14]

The primary duty to perform arises with the giving of a promise with consideration and creates an obligation for the promisor to undertake the promised act. In establishing that obligation, promissory commitment is apt to induce, by itself, performance by the promisor. In case it is breached, a wrong is committed, which is apt to instigate retaliation by the promisee.

There is evidence that individuals often keep their promises even at a cost for themselves.[15] There is still, however, a wide and unresolved debate on the causes of such behavior, or on why individuals keep promises. Two main explanations put forward in the literature are guilt aversion and moral commitment.

According to the theory of guilt aversion, individuals feel guilt when they let the other individual's expectations down and, in doing so, suffer a loss of utility because of that act.[16] According to the theory of moral commitment, individuals have preferences for keeping promises per se and derive disutility from behaving inconsistently.[17] While there is some evidence for the existence of guilt aversion, there is perhaps, under the current state of the art, more evidence in favor of the commitment explanation.[18]

---

[14] Additionally, the experiment studies the effect of the prospect of retaliation by the promisee upon the promisor's decision to perform. This effect is described with the alternative hypothesis in section 5.3.4.

[15] *See* Gary Charness & Martin Dufwenberg, *Promises and Partnerships*, 74 ECONOMETRICA 1579 (2006); Christoph Vanberg, *Why do People Keep their Promises? An Experimental Test of Two Explanations*, 76 ECONOMETRICA 1467 (2008); Charness & Dufwenberg, *Bare Promises: An Experiment*, 107 ECONOMIC LETTERS 281 (2010); Tore Ellingsen et al., *Testing Guilt Aversion*, 68 GAMES AND ECONOMIC BEHAVIOR 95 (2010); Charness & Dufwenberg, *Participation*, 101 AMERICAN ECONOMIC REVIEW 1213 (2011).

[16] *See* Charness & Dufwenberg, *Promises and Partnerships, op. cit. supra*, at 1580, 1583 (stressing that the motivation for this type of behavior is the individual's beliefs about the beliefs of the other; that is, an individual only experiences guilt if she believes her behavior falls short on the expectation of the other). For the formal model, *see* Pierpaolo Battigalli & Dufwenberg, *Guilt in games*, 97 AMERICAN ECONOMIC REVIEW, PAPERS AND PROCEEDINGS 170 (2007); Battigalli & Dufwenberg, *Dynamic Psychological Games*, 141 JOURNAL OF ECONOMIC THEORY 1 (2009).

[17] *See* Tore Ellingsen & Magnus Johanesson, *Promises, Threats and Fairness*, 114 Economic Journal 397 (2004) for a formal model and initial empirical evidence, and Ying Chen et al., *Selecting Cheap-Talk Equilibria*, 76 Econometrica 117 (2008) for a model of belief-independent costs of inconsistency.

[18] Charness & Dufwenberg, *Promises and Partnerships, op. cit. supra*, presents initial evidence in favor of guilt-aversion. Vanberg, *Why do People Keep their Promises? An Experimental Test of Two Explanations, op. cit. supra*, presents a subsequent study with evidence that favors the commitment explanation. Charness & Dufwenberg, *Bare Promises: An Experiment, op. cit. supra*, presents further results with a modified version of their initial experiment and provides only limited support for both explanations. Ellingsen et al., *Testing Guilt Aversion, op. cit. supra*, presents results concerning the existence of guilt-aversion in different games (dictator game, and two versions of a trust game, with complete and incomplete information) and finds very scarce support for a theory of guilt-aversion. Lastly, Charness & Dufwenberg, *Participation, op. cit. supra*, presents a more

Existing evidence that individuals keep promises relies, however, on a modified version of the trust game and is thus obtained where the promisee incurs real monetary losses in case of breach by the promisor. Existing experimental studies, therefore, do not present evidence that individuals keep promises when breach would cause no more than loss of expectancy, as in case of breach of wholly executory contracts studied in the experiment.

There is pervasive evidence that individuals engage in costly punishment against those that violate a norm of cooperation in social dilemmas, or a fairness norm in bargaining games.[19] Quite remarkably, there is very little evidence on the existence of retaliation to breach of promise, and, similarly to existing evidence of the effect of promises, existing evidence is obtained in games where the promisee suffers material losses because of breach, and not only a loss of expectancy.[20]

In the present study, the question examined experimentally is whether promisees retaliate to breach of promise when no more than the expectation interest is at stake, and why they may do so: because of (i) the loss of expectancy they endure, (ii) the unfairness of the resulting distribution, or (ii) the inefficiency of the result. In distinguishing between different contingencies where breach of promise arises, and where only some lead to an unfair or inefficient result, the experiment inquires into the circumstances where retaliation to breach of promise is most likely to arise.

The secondary duty to pay damages, in turn, arises only if the promised event does not come to pass, and it creates an obligation for the promisor to compensate the promisee. In imposing a monetary cost on breach, expectation damages are apt to induce efficient levels of performance by the promisor. In providing compensation for the promisee, they are apt to crowd out retaliation.

To the author's best knowledge, there is no precise experimental evidence that expectation damages in effect induce performance of contractual promises if performance is socially efficient, and not otherwise.[21] Expectation damages make the

---

recent experimental test and concludes that "since, on balance, both theories capture many but not all aspects of the data, we shall not declare a winner" (at 1234).

19 *See* the discussion *supra* in chapter 4, section 2 for evidence that individuals retaliate in social dilemma games. Punishment in ultimatum games is pervasive across societies and cultures, as attested by Joseph Heinrich et al., *In Seach of Homo Economicus: Behavioral Experiments in 15 Small-Scale Societies*, 91 AMERICAN ECONOMIC REVIEW 73 (2001).

20 *See* Olivier Bochet & Louis Putterman, *Not just babble: Opening the black box of communication in a voluntary contribution experiment*, 53 GAMES AND ECONOMIC BEHAVIOR 309 (2009) (finding evidence of retaliation to breach of promise in a public good game, thus where the individual that promised induced the other to contribute to the public good, and hence to incur a real monetary loss—and not just loss of expectancy—in case of breach).

21 *See* Iris Bohnet, Bruno Frey & Steffen Huck, *More Order with Less Law: On Contract Enforcement, Trust, and Crowding*, 95 AMERICAN POLITICAL SCIENCE REVIEW 131 (2001) (experiment with a trust game that included expectation damages but where breach could never be efficient, and where the promisee could not decide whether to claim damages or not, since the promisor was held liable according to some exogenous probabilities); Ben Depoorter & Stephan Tontrup, *How Law FramesMoral Instuitions: The Expressive Effect of Specific Performance*, 54 ARIZONA LAW REVIEW 673 (2012) (experiment that included, among others, the possibility for parties to claim the equivalent of expectation damages, but with very different research questions).

promisor internalize the negative externality of breach, given by the amount the promisee does not earn because of breach, and are predicted to induce only socially efficient performance. This clear theoretical prediction concerning partie's individual behavior further implies that social welfare will be maximal under expectation damages and is subject to empirical examination.

Expectation damages further provide relief for promisees to redress breach and can thereby provide their own contribution to social welfare by crowding out the victim's tendency to retaliate to breach, in effect fulfilling the function to substitute private for public redress, thereby avoiding a loss of welfare. If promisees perceive breach of contractual promises as a wrong in need of redress, and in effect tend to retaliate against it, then damages for breach are well apt to crowd out retaliation. This requires that legal enforcement of contracts go beyond the imposition of a price on breach and further provide relief for promisees to redress breach, as it in fact does.

Lastly, the experiment investigates whether legal relief to promisees to redress breach has its own beneficial impact upon social welfare not only by inducing efficient performance, but also by reducing welfare losses from retaliation.[22] In order to estimate the welfare gains from inducing promisors to perform, there is the need to subtract from those gains the possible gains that promises themselves deliver, independent of damages, in inducing performance. On the other hand, in order to estimate the welfare gains from reducing retaliation by promisees, there is the need to subtract the gains created by retaliation in deterring breach from the social costs of retaliation, so that the total net effect upon social welfare captures both the benefits and costs of retaliation.[23] By comparing those net estimated social welfare effects, the welfare functions of legal redress are examined. If legal redress indeed provides net gains through both channels, then compensation for breach of promise can be, on social welfare grounds, justified in the law of remedies for breach.

5.3 The Empirical Study

The experiment attempts to investigate the effects of contractual promises, expectation damages, and retaliation to breach on individual behavior in a controlled environment. This approach permits a more careful analysis of causal relationships

[22] This does not imply that social losses from retaliation will be minimal under expectation damages, and while expectation damages provide compensation for all lost expectancy, they do not establish a final equal distribution of gains between the parties. The seller that breaches to profit from an outside transaction retains all extra profits possible only through breach, and inequality persists. The next chapter explores this point in detail, together with the discussion on how damages for breach could be designed to better fulfill the function of crowding out retaliation while maintaining optimal incentives for promisors to perform.

[23] As explained before, retaliation induces cooperation and other forms of socially desirable behavior, but it does so only at a cost, and this is the reason why its net effect upon social welfare must consider both.

between those institutions and individual behavior in a game where subject's decisions and rewards are real and material. It attempts to abstract from, and to control for, all other factors that can influence partie's contractual behavior, with the goal of providing evidence for the effect of the institutions under study, and their interactions, in isolation.[24]

This does not mean that other factors present in real contractual relationships are irrelevant for the behavior of the parties. Trust, custom, commercial good manners, reputation, and several others elements all play their role upon contractual behavior. Empirical research, however, must control for the factors outside the scope of the study in order to investigate the effect of any specific institution upon individual behavior, and this guided the design of the study.

The experimental design attempts to establish such a controlled environment first through the implementation of a control group. It aims at capturing the influence of other factors on partie's behavior, providing estimates of the effect of promises and damages net of those. Moreover, the experiment followed the orthodox procedure in economics, ensuring anonymity, the absence of external communication between subjects, monetary rewards for individual choices (incentive-compatibility), no deception, and the precise same amount of information provided to all subjects.

5.3.1 The Implemented Trade Game

Subjects played, in all treatments, a trade game that resembles the interaction between a seller and buyer. In it, sellers take the role of promisors and buyers of promisees. The seller could produce and deliver one unit of a good to the buyer, who in return makes the payment of its price. The trade game consisted of four different phases or "dates": At date 1, parties met and could enter into an agreement to trade (except in the control group, where parties could not communicate and were then only matched with each other). At date 2, the state of the world, which might imply some unexpected contingency for the seller, was realized, and both parties were informed of it. At date 3, the seller decided to perform or to breach. At date 4, and only in case of breach by the seller, the buyer could retaliate (in the treatments with retaliation) and concomitantly claim damages for breach (only in the treatment with contracts).

After the realization of the state of the world, at date 2, both parties observed the realized state, and the buyer observed the decision of the seller at date 3. Consequently, the seller was always well aware of the consequences of her decision upon her own earnings and upon the earnings of the buyer, as well as of the efficiency and fairness of the result of her decision. The seller knew that the buyer also observed the realized state and her decision to perform or breach and that the buyer could thus

[24] *Cf*. VINCENT BUSKENS, BETWEEN HOBBE'S LEVIATHAN AND SMITH'S INVISIBLE HAND, *op. cit. supra*, as well as CHRISTOPH ENGEL, LEGAL EXPERIMENTS: MISSION IMPOSSIBLE?, *op. cit. supra* (discussing the value and method of experimental studies in the Law).

Date 1	Date 2	Date 3	Date 4
Agreement stage	*Resolution of risk*	*Performance stage*	*Enforcement stage*
Subjects are matched and can enter into an agreement	The state of the world is realized, determining the seller's costs	Seller decides to perform or breach; Buyer pays in case of performance	Buyer decides, in case of breach, to retaliate and to claim damages

Fig. 5.1 Timeline of events[25] Reproduced from Mittlaender & Buskens, *Retaliation, Remedies, and Contracts, op. cit. supra*

take the motives and consequences of breach into consideration before deciding to claim damages and to retaliate (in the treatments including those actions).

The timeline of the game is resumed in Fig. 5.1.

The buyer's valuation of the good was given by $V = 30$ and the price in the agreement was $P = 20$. The buyer's expectancy in the performance of the agreement was hence always equal to 10. The seller's costs of performance, in contrast, depended on her costs of production $c(\theta)$ and on her net gains $z(\theta)$ from breach to profit from a substitutive transaction, where θ_n denotes the realized state of the world, with $n = \{0, 1, 2, 3, 4\}$.

Under the status quo θ_0, the seller's costs of production c_0 were equal to 10, and the seller had no outside option. She thereby earned, just as the buyer, 10 through performance of the agreement. In all other states, either the seller's costs rose by $\Delta c(\theta)$, or the seller was offered an outside option and could breach in order to make net profits of $z(\theta)$[26]

The trade game, depicted in Fig. 5.2, in the absence of any type of enforcement possibility, was as follows:

[25] The buyer could not actively decide to pay or to default on payment, as detailed below, since this would create uncertainty in the seller, who could then decide to breach because of fear of default by the buyer. Since this is not the object of the study, there is the need to control for such effect, and therefore, payment by the buyer was implemented automatically whenever the seller delivered the good to the buyer and automatically *not* implemented whenever the seller decided not to deliver.

[26] Note that the third-party was not, in the experiment, a real person but a mere offer that the seller could accept instead of trading with the buyer. This was reiterated to participants: "This offer is hypothetical and not done by another participant in the lab" (as in the instruction in the experiment). Moreover, it is assumed that the third-party, who "arrives later" than the first buyer, makes an offer corresponding to her whole valuation of the good.

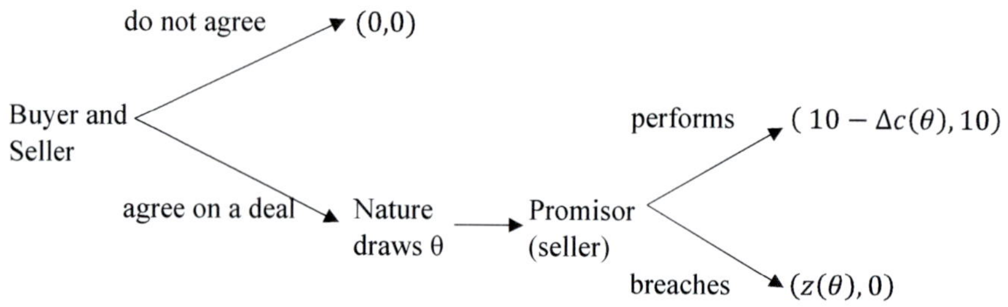

Fig. 5.2 The trade game[27]

There were five different possible contingencies that could be drawn at date 2. The status quo (state 0) was maintained in half of the interactions. In the other half, Nature selected one out of four possible contingencies (states 1 to 4). These included a low and a high increase in costs of production, and an outside price offer that was slightly or considerably higher than the price in the original contract. They thereby distinguish socially efficient from socially inefficient breaches, and breaches committed to achieve higher profits (the ones that create inequality, or unfair breaches) from breaches committed to avoid incurring losses (the ones that avoid inequality, or fair breaches), as resumed in Table 5.1.

More precisely, the contingencies were as follows:

θ_0, the status quo, with $c(\theta_0) = 10$ and no outside offer
θ_1, increase in costs of production by 15 and no outside offer, $c(\theta_1) = 25$
θ_2, outside price of 25 and cost of production remain as in θ_0, $z(\theta_2) = 15$
θ_3, increase in costs of production by 25 and no outside offer, $c(\theta_3) = 35$
θ_4, outside price of 35 and cost of production remain as in θ_0, $z(\theta_4) = 25$

Table 5.1 Variations in the seller's costs of performance across states

Higher costs of production (fair breach)	Higher outside offer (unfair breach)
State 1 (θ_1) *Inefficient breach that is fair (avoids inequality)*	State 2 (θ_2) *Inefficient breach that is unfair (creates inequality)*
State 3 (θ_3) *Efficient breach that is fair (avoids inequality)*	State 4 (θ_4) *Efficient breach that is unfair (creates inequality)*

Reproduced from Mittlaender & Buskens, *Retaliation, Remedies, and Contracts, op. cit. supra*

[27] If either the buyer or the seller do not agree to exchange promises to perform, then they cannot trade and realize any gain from trade or loss. The seller would not incur costs to produce the good if the buyer does not promise to come back to pick it up and pay for it, and the buyer will not come back to pick up the good if the seller does not promise she will produce it. If they both agree to exchange promises, or on a contract, then the game proceeds.

For convenience, the final payoffs of the seller and of the buyer, in each contingency, are all presented below, together with the predictions on the seller's behavior.

5.3.2 Experimental Treatments

The experimental design consisted of three main treatments (trade, promises, and contract), all implemented with and without the possibility of retaliation, and hence in six treatments. In all of them, subjects took the role of a buyer or a seller and played a series of single anonymous trade games. The parameters of the game described above and the different possible contingencies were constant across all treatments, which differed only in the possibility to exchange promises before playing the game and in the possibility to retaliate or to claim damages after the game.

In the *first treatment "trade"* (the control group), subjects played the trade games without any previous communication between them, and hence in the absence of any form of promissory commitment. They were, in each interaction, only randomly allocated with another participant in the opposite role at date 1 and took no decision or action at that moment. They subsequently observed the state of the world at date 2, and at date 3, the seller decided to produce the good and deliver it to the first buyer in exchange for payment of the price or not.

In the *second treatment "promises,"* subjects were matched at date 1 and could enter into an exchange of promises. It stated that "the seller promises to produce the good and trade it with the current buyer, while the buyer promises to pay the price of 20 points to the seller for the good."[28] If the seller and the buyer both promised, then the state of the world was realized at date 2, and the seller decided to keep the promise at date 3. Apart from the promises, all other remaining elements of the game were identical to the control group.

In the *third treatment "contract,"* subjects were matched at date 1 and could enter into a contract. The contract consisted in an exchange of promises with the precise same content as in treatment promises, but also included a clause allowing the buyer to claim damages in case the seller decided "not to deliver the good to the buyer." The amount of damages the buyer was entitled to claim in case of breach was measured by her loss of expectancy, equal to 10. Apart from this clause and the related possibility to claim damages in case of breach, all remaining elements were identical to treatment promises.

Each main treatment was implemented with and without the possibility of retaliation by the buyer. Retaliation was implemented in the traditional form of costly punishment, meaning that the buyer could spend 2 points to deduct 10 points from the earnings of the seller. Each subject played in just one main treatment (trade, promises, or contract), in the presence and absence of the possibility to retaliate (the

---

[28] As in the instructions of the experiment. Their precise contents are all detailed below in Sect. 5.3.5.

Table 5.2 Implemented treatments

Seller's decision to perform	Buyer's decision to retaliate
Treatment trade no commitment, no enforcement	*Treatment trade with retaliation* no commitment, retaliation
Treatment promises promissory commitment, no enforcement	*Treatment promises with retaliation* promissory commitment, retaliation
Treatment contract promissory commitment, expectation damages	*Treatment contract with retaliation* promissory commitment, retaliation, and expectation damages

details of the procedure are presented below). The experimental design is depicted in Table 5.2.

Although subjects actively decided to enter into the exchange of promises, or into the contract, as well as, only in treatment contract, to claim damages for breach, the treatment variables under study are *performance* and *retaliation*.[29] In treatments without retaliation, depicted in the first column of Table 5.2, the focus lies on the effect of promissory commitment (between treatments trade and promises) to induce performance by the promisor and of the material and pecuniary incentives created by expectation damages to induce performance *net* of the effect of promises (between treatments promises and contract). In treatments with retaliation, depicted in the second column, the focus lies on the effect of breach of promise to trigger retaliation by the promisee (between treatments trade and promises) and of expectation damages to crowd it out (between treatments promises and contract).

The function of treatment trade in the experiment is to control for the effect of other factors beyond promissory commitment and damages on the behavior of the parties. For example, the seller may want to keep the promise because of her individual preferences against the inequality that would result from breach. The buyer may, in turn, desire to retaliate to breach because of the resulting inequality, independent of the presence of promissory commitment. With the control group, the estimated *difference* in behavior across treatments excludes those effects, which are captured inside the control group, and can then be attributed solely to the effect of promises and damages for breach.

Considering all treatments, the complete version of the game is described as follows.

[29] All three treatments equally involved a seller and a buyer of a good, who only in treatments "promises" and "contract" can accurately be denoted promisor and promisee (because they entered into the exchange of promises). In the present text, these terms are used interchangeably. In the experiment, differently, parties were always called seller and buyer in all treatments in order to avoid possible demand effects, as explained below in the section that explains the experimental procedure.

Let

$q_s \epsilon \{0, 1\}$ be the decision variable of the seller to produce the good and deliver it to the buyer, equal to unity in case of performance;

$r_b \epsilon \{0, 1\}$ be the decision variable of the buyer to retaliate against the seller by imposing a loss of $R = 10$ at own personal costs $K = 2$, and

$e_b \epsilon \{0, 1\}$ be the decision variable of the buyer to enforce the contract and claim the equivalent of expectation damages, given by $D = V - P = 10$.

The profits of sellers and buyers, represented, respectively, by π_s and π_b, are as follows:

Seller's payoff:

$$\pi_s = q_s(P - c_0 - \Delta c(\theta)) + (1 - q_s) \cdot (z(\theta) - e_b D - r_b R)$$

For the parameters of the game, the seller's payoffs are given by

$$\pi_s = \begin{cases} 20 - 10 - \Delta c(\theta) & \text{if seller performs} \\ z(\theta) - 10e_b - 10r_b & \text{if seller breaches} \end{cases}$$

The seller earns the price of 20 minus costs of production $c_0 = 10$ if she decides to perform, minus possible increases $\Delta c(\theta)$ in those. If she breaches, then she makes net profits $z(\theta)$ from the possible outside transaction ($z(\theta) = 0$ if no outside offer materializes), loses 10 if the buyer decides to claim damages, and loses another 10 if the buyer decides to retaliate.

Buyer's payoff:

$$\pi_b = q_s(V - P) + (1 - q_s) \cdot (-r_b K + e_b D)$$

For the chosen parameters, the buyer's payoffs are given by

$$\pi_b = \begin{cases} 10 & \text{if seller performs} \\ -2r_b + 10e_b & \text{if seller breaches} \end{cases}$$

The buyer always earns her expectancy of 10 in case of performance by the seller. In case of breach, the buyer neither earns nor loses anything in the absence of retaliation and damages. Only her expectancy is at stake in the game. In the treatments that include enforcement possibilities, the buyer incurs the costs of retaliation equal to 2 if she decides to retaliate and earns damages for breach equal to 10 if she decides to enforce the contract. For convenience, the partie's payoffs in each possible contingency, depending on the seller's decision, are resumed in the next section, together with the predictions from strict rational choice.

The complete game-tree takes the following form (Fig. 5.3).

Entering into the agreement was individually profitable for both parties independent of the promisor's individual understanding of the morality of promises and contracts. A promisor that for moral reasons planned to keep promises under

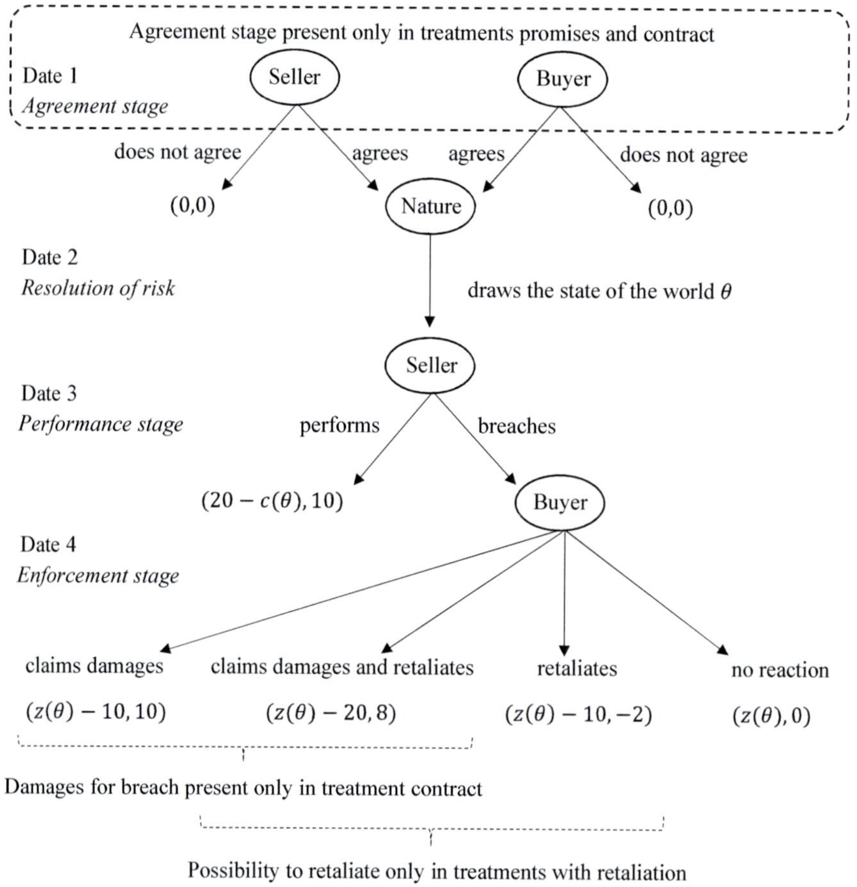

Fig. 5.3 Complete game-tree

all circumstances had an expected utility of 5 by entering into the agreement and accordingly performing in all contingencies:

$$EU(q_s, \theta) \sum_{\theta=0}^{\theta=4} p_\theta \pi_s(q_s = 1) = 0.5 \cdot 10 + 0.125(-5)$$
$$+ 0.125(-15) + 0.125 \cdot 10 \cdot 2 = 5$$

5.3.3 *Strict Rational Choice Predictions*

The payoffs and further consequences of the seller's decision, in each possible contingency, are resumed in Table 5.3. In the absence of retaliation and damages, the seller's decision at date 3 completely determined both partie's earnings, which are depicted in the first and second columns. The seller's individually optimal decision is there denoted with the star.

The seller is predicted to perform, in the absence of damages, only under the status quo (state 0). In all other states, it is individually optimal for the seller not to trade, but rather to breach, since by doing so the seller maximizes her individual gains. The third column summarizes the consequences of breach for the seller herself. These are calculated with respect to the gains or losses that the seller would make through performance and reflect the distinction between gain-seeking and loss-avoiding breaches. Although there is no difference, in economic terms, between breach in states 1 and 2, and between breach in states 3 and 4, the distinction is of relevance for the creation or avoidance of an unequal final distribution between the parties.

The last three columns summarize the consequences of the seller's decision that are, under strict individual self-interest, immaterial for the seller's maximization of profits. The fourth column reports the consequences of the seller's decision for the buyer, given by the buyer's loss of gains from trade, which is equal to 10 in all contingencies. The fifth column reports the consequences of breach for aggregate social welfare and the last column the consequences of breach for the disadvantageous inequality in the final payoffs experienced by the buyer.

In the absence of promises and damages for breach, strict rational choice predictions are clear and univocal. As explained in the following paragraphs, these do not change in the presence of promises nor in the presence of retaliation, but only in

Table 5.3 Payoffs and consequences of the seller's decision in treatments trade and promises (stars indicate equilibrium behavior and outcomes)

	Seller's decision and related payoffs (seller, buyer)		Effect of breach *for the seller*	Effect of breach *for the buyer*	Effect of breach *on social welfare*	Effect of breach *on inequality*
State 0	*Perform* Breach	*(10,10)* (0,0)	Does not earn 10	Does not earn 10	−20	None
State 1	Perform *Breach*	(−5,10) *(0,0)*	Avoids loss of 5	Does not earn 10	−5	Avoids inequality of 15
State 2	Perform *Breach*	(−15,10) *(0,0)*	Gains extra 5	Does not earn 10	−5	Creates inequality of 15
State 3	Perform *Breach*	(−15,10) *(0,0)*	Avoids loss of 15	Does not earn 10	+5	Avoids inequality of 25
State 4	Perform *Breach*	(10,10) *(25,0)*	Gains extra 15	Does not earn 10	+5	Creates inequality of 25

Reproduced from Mittlaender & Buskens, *Retaliation, Remedies, and Contracts, op. cit. supra* the presence of expectation damages. Additionally, the buyer is never predicted to retaliate, either in the absence or in the presence of promises.

Consider first the *seller's decision to keep promises.* According to standard rational choice models, promises, in the absence of an effective enforcement mechanism, are simply "cheap talk" because they do not directly affect payoffs.[30] They cannot induce a change in the behavior of the seller between treatments trade and promises. Sellers are hence predicted not to change their behavior because of a prior promise, but are rather, on the contrary, *predicted to behave equally in treatment trade and in treatment promises*, keeping their promises only under the status quo, and breaking them in all other states.

Rational choice models also do not predict *buyers to retaliate*, since costly punishment is a strictly dominated strategy in single and anonymous interactions. It cannot deliver any material gain to the individual, either present or prospective. The same prediction holds for the buyer's decision to retaliate to breach of promise. The perceived wrong in breach by the seller is irrelevant for self-interested behavior that requires *no* investment in retaliation by the buyer. *Buyers are hence predicted to behave equally in the absence or presence of prior promises*, never retaliating against the seller's decision.[31]

---

[30] The only equilibrium in any game with cheap-talk is a "babbling" equilibrium where communication and promises do not alter individual behavior. *Cf*. Joseph Farrell & Matthew Rabin, *Cheap Talk*, 10 JOURNAL OF ECONOMIC PERSPECTIVES 103, 107–108 (1996) (because of common knowledge of rationality, cheap-talk is ignored and irrelevant in search for equilibria). A player's utterances need not be correlated with her private information or true intentions, such that the other player must ignore the other one's utterances, which are just "babble" and meaningless. The refined argument for talk being cheap is in Robert Aumann, *Nash Equilibria are not Self-Enforcing*, in ECONOMIC DECISION MAKING: GAMES, ECONOMETRICS AND OPTIMISATION 201 (J. Gabszewicz et al. eds, Amsterdam: North-Holland 1990) (communication will not affect the result of a game if the signaler's preferences depend on the other player's strategy choice). *See* Ying Chen et al., *Selecting Cheap-Talk Equilibria*, 76 ECONOMETRICA 117 (2008) ("every cheap-talk game has a degenerate, 'babbling' equilibrium outcome in which the Sender's message contains no information, and, on the equilibrium path, the Receiver's response is equal to her ex ante optimal choice"); Vincent Crawford, *A Survey of Experiments on Communication* via *Cheap Talk*, 78 JOURNAL OF ECONOMIC THEORY 286, 287 (1998) ("When player's preferences are perfectly opposed, such a [cheap-talk] message cannot convey any useful information. Then the only equilibria are 'babbling' equilibria, in which the Sender's message is uninformative and is ignored by the Receiver. This is the grain of truth in the cheap-talk intuition.") For a criticism on the conception of cheap talk, *see* David Sally, *Can I say "bobobo" and mean "There's no such thing as cheap talk"?*, 57 JOURNAL OF ECONOMIC BEHAVIOR AND ORGANIZATION 245 (2005).

[31] Notice that promises, in the present experiment, do *not* consist of information passed by an informed party to an uninformed decision-maker, as in the seminal model of Vincent Crawford and Joel Sobel, *Strategic information transmission*, 50 ECONOMETRICA 1431 (1982). Here, although it is the case that one party makes a decision that affects both player's welfare (to trade or not, or to perform or breach) as in Crawford and Sobel's model, it is this *same* party who made a promise conveying her intention and commitment to trade that must make that decision. Therefore, promises made by the promisor create only a promissory commitment upon the person making the promise and fulfill no role to convey information to the other party that could be relevant for future decision-making (the other party makes no future decision), apart from encouraging the other individual to enter into the agreement in the first place.

The conjunction of both predictions from strict rational choice models delivers the prediction concerning the *seller's decision under retaliation*. Rational sellers must anticipate the buyer's decision not to retaliate, both in treatment trade and promises. Sellers are hence predicted never to alter their behavior because of the possibility of costly punishment. They are predicted to take the very same decisions in treatments *trade, promises, trade with retaliation*, and *promises with retaliation*, never deciding to trade except in state 0, the only case where trade and promise-keeping are individually profitable.

Predictions do change when the agreement is legally enforceable. In the treatment contract, damages for breach do change the equilibrium of the game, as the contract allows buyers to claim damages whenever the seller breaches the contract. In the experiment, this action was a real choice of the participant in the role of a buyer, and one that did not entail any cost for her. The buyer is hence predicted to claim damages whenever the seller breaches, since this maximizes the buyer's earnings. Sellers, accordingly, must anticipate the choice of buyers when making their ex ante optimal decision to perform or breach in the first place.

Table 5.4 resumes the final payoffs of the parties whenever the seller breaches the contract and the buyer claims damages for breach. In case the buyer opts *not* to claim damages, then payoffs are exactly as the ones reported in the previous Table 5.3.

Incentives created by expectation damages induce performance under the status quo but also in states 1 and 2, as reported in the second column of Table 5.4. In the game, expectation damages induce performance if and only if performance is, in the realized contingency, socially efficient. In contingencies where performance is socially inefficient, i.e., in states 3 and 4, expectation damages do not induce performance, but rather give incentives for the seller to breach and pay damages. The prediction is that sellers will perform in states 1 and 2 and will breach in states 3 and 4, when breach and payment of damages are the individual strictly dominant strategy.

Promises, in the present game and experiment, also cannot, according to refined economic theory, *signal* anything meaningful for the other individual about one's true type, morality, or true intentions because they are, first of all, costless. Secondly, even if they were costly utterances, they would further need to be *negatively* correlated with what they would be signaling, otherwise everybody would invest in the signal equally and the signal would then not distinguish between types (such as moral, immoral, and amoral individuals). In precise terms, promises here do not fulfill Spence's critical assumption in his canonical model of signaling (in the labor market). *Cf*. Michael Spence, *Job Market Signaling*, 87 QUARTERLY JOURNAL OF ECONOMICS 355, 358 (1973) ("a signal will not effectively distinguish one applicant from another, unless the costs of signaling are negatively correlated with productive capability.").

Table 5.4 Payoffs and consequences of the seller's decision to breach in treatment contract (stars indicate equilibrium behavior and outcomes)

	Seller's decision and related payoffs (seller, buyer)		Consequence of breach *for the seller*	Consequence of breach *for the buyer*	Consequence of breach *for social welfare*	Consequence of breach *on inequality*
State 0	*Perform* Breach	*(10, 10)* (−10,10)	Loses 20	–	−20	Creates inequality of 20
State 1	*Perform* Breach	*(−5,10)* (−10,10)	Loses 5	–	−5	Increases inequality by 5
State 2	*Perform* Breach	*(10,10)* (5,10)	Loses 5	–	−5	Creates inequality of 5
State 3	Perform *Breach*	(−15,10) *(−10,10)	Avoids losing 5	–	+5	Avoids (disadv.) inequality of 5
State 4	Perform *Breach*	(10,10) *(15,10)*	Earns 5 extra	–	+5	Creates (disadv.) inequality of 5

The buyer, as reported in the fourth column, never suffers any loss in treatment contract, independent of the seller's decision. Expectation damages make the buyer whole and compensate her for lost expectancy, the buyer's sole interest at stake in the game. The fifth column reports the consequences of breach for overall social welfare, and the last column reports the consequences of breach for inequality between the parties. The only contingency where breach of contract followed by the payment of expectation damages still creates disadvantageous inequality (of 5) for the buyer is state 4, as reported in the last column of Table 5.4.

Note that although damages for breach do alter the *equilibrium* of the game, they do not alter in any manner the maximal possible gains of social welfare that parties could realize in any contingency—as well as the overall maximal gains from trade in the game as a whole. That is, the same total social welfare is equally achievable in treatments trade, promise, and contract, with and without retaliation

Table 5.5 resumes the predictions from strict rational choice models for the seller's decision to trade (or perform) and for the buyer's decision to retaliate in all three treatments.

5.3.4 Alternative Hypotheses

The *first hypothesis is that promisors will perform more often in the presence of promissory commitment than in its absence.* According to the design, sellers are hypothesized to perform more often in treatment promises than in treatment trade,

Table 5.5 Predictions from strict rational choice models

	Seller	Buyer
Treatment trade	Perform under the status quo θ_0, refuse to trade in other contingencies	Never retaliate against any type of refusal to trade
Treatment promises	Perform under the status quo θ_0, breach in other contingencies	Never retaliate against any type of breach of promise
Treatment contract	Perform when efficient ($\theta_0, \theta_1, \theta_2$), breach the contract otherwise (θ_3, θ_4)	Never retaliate against any type of breach of contract, always claim damages

where there was no obligation for sellers to take any specific course of action. Except in the status quo, performance is individually costly while breach is the action that maximizes the seller's profits and is hence the strictly dominant strategy for the seller. However, individuals may feel morally obliged to undertake the promised act even when circumstances change and performance becomes individually unprofitable, and hence to keep their promises for moral reasons.

The *second hypothesis is that disappointed promisees will retaliate more often in the presence of promises than in their absence.* In the design, it corresponds to hypothesized higher rates of retaliation in treatment promises than in treatment trade, where the seller, in deciding not to implement the exchange, does not break any promise.[32] Moreover, this effect may depend or not on the type of the realized contingency.

There are three possible causes, distinguished by the different contingencies, for the buyer to retaliate. If loss of expectancy causes retaliation, then buyers are expected to retaliate more often in all contingencies because they equally lost their expectation in all of them. If inefficiency from breach causes retaliation, then buyers are expected to retaliate more often only in the contingencies where breach is inefficient, and hence only in states 1 and 2. If the realization of inequality from breach of promise causes retaliation, then buyers shall retaliate more often only in states 2 and 4, where the seller creates inequality through breach.

The third hypothesis is that expectation damages induce performance when performance is socially efficient and breach when breach is socially efficient. In the design, it corresponds to the inducement of performance only in the contingencies where performance is socially efficient. These are, as detailed above, states 1 and 2, or those in which performance can generate overall gains of welfare. In states 3 and 4, in contrast, expectation damages are predicted to induce breach.

The *fourth hypothesis is that the availability of expectation damages reduces retaliation by the promisee*, in effect fulfilling the function to substitute private for public redress. Promisees are expected to retaliate less often in treatment contract,

[32] Individuals with social preferences may have a tendency to retaliate against the decision of the seller because of the inequality or inefficiency it creates. Between treatments trade and promises, however, inequality and inefficiency are held constant by design and therefore cannot explain any difference in behavior between treatments, and in the same contingency. If buyers retaliate more often against the seller in treatment promises than in treatment trade, then this is caused by the presence of promissory commitment.

Table 5.6 Order of implementation of treatments

Session	Main treatment	Part 1	Part 2	Part 3
1	Trade	Trade	Trade + retaliation	Trade + retaliation
2	Trade	Trade + retaliation	Trade	Trade + retaliation
3	Promises	Promises	Promises + retaliation	Promises + retaliation
4	Promises	Promises + retaliation	Promises	Promises + retaliation
5	Contract	Contract	Contract + retaliation	Contract + retaliation
6	Contract	Contract + retaliation	Contract	Contract + retaliation

where they can claim expectation damages in case of breach, than in treatment promises, where this possibility is absent. If promisees perceive breach of bargained-for promises as a wrong in need of redress, and in effect retaliate more often against breach of promise than mere refusals to trade, as in hypothesis 2, then damages for breach are predicted to crowd out retaliation to breach.

A last and fifth hypothesis is that *promisors will perform more often whenever promisees can retaliate.* This hypothesis relates the impact of retaliation to breach, if existent, upon the seller's behavior and decision to perform. Promisors may well anticipate irrational retaliation and decide to keep promises and contracts in order to avoid possible losses from retalisectation by buyers. Sellers are hypothesized to perform more often in treatments where the buyer has the option to retaliate than in those where the buyer does not have it.

5.3.5 *Experimental Procedure*

There were six experimental sessions, and each session included three parts. Participants were randomly allocated to the role of either buyer or seller at the beginning of the session and kept the same role throughout the whole session. Each subject participated in only one session. In each, subjects played only one of the main three treatments, and in the different parts of the session, that main treatment was implemented with and without retaliation, as described in Table 5.6.

In each part, participants played a series of *eight trade games.* They played four games in which the status quo was maintained and one game where each of the four different contingencies materialized.[33] Sellers received feedback on whether they

[33] The order in which the contingencies materialized was not known to participants but rather pseudo-randomized. It was not simply random only because of the need to have each contingency

were punished or not only at the end of each treatment. With three parts in each session, participants played in total 24 games that were simple, brief, and easily understandable, and each complete session took only about one hour.

After each game, subjects were randomly rematched and played the next game with another subject, and hence, only single interactions were implemented throughout the whole experiment. It is worth emphasizing that only one-shot interactions are analyzed and studied. By abstracting from repetition and other factors, and controlling for its effects upon partie's behavior, the experiment analyzes the relationship between promissory commitment, retaliation, and damages for breach in isolation, developing a *ceteris paribus* analysis. Therefore, prospective gains from cooperation that could be induced by punishment in the form of tit-for-tat or grim-trigger strategies, reputational concerns, signaling, and self-selection all *cannot* explain partie's behavior in the experiment. All such factors are isolated, abstracted from, and kept constant *by design.*

Written instructions were distributed at the beginning of each part, and subjects were not informed about the content of each part until the beginning of that part. For example, subjects in session 1 first played treatment trade without any knowledge of the content of the subsequent parts and only in part 2 received new instructions explaining that they would participate in another part that included the possibility of retaliation. Another treatment with retaliation was implemented in part 3 of each session in order to obtain more observations on the buyer's decision to retaliate, which could only be observed when the seller effectively breached and were expected to be fewer.[34]

In the control group "trade," parties did not have any option to enter into an agreement to trade and therefore were only randomly matched at date 1. Accordingly, in the experiment, subjects in the control group read on the first screen:

> "You have been randomly matched by the computer to another (buyer/seller) with whom you may trade one unit of a good."

In treatment *promises*, subjects read the exact same sentence above, but were also presented with the possibility to agree to enter into an exchange of promises with the following content:

> "In the exchange of promises, the seller promises to produce the good and trade it with the current buyer, while the buyer promises to pay the price of 20 points to the seller for the good."

---

materialize once in each treatment, and a random ordering could lead to a certain contingency never being implemented. This was the reason for the pseudo-randomization of the order of realization of the different states of the world. Subjects were informed that the status quo would occur in half of the eight interactions and that each of the other contingencies would occur in one out of every eight interactions, as in fact implemented.

[34] Regressions considering data collected only in part 1, in part 1 and part 2, and in all three parts are all developed and concomitantly presented in the tables of results, and controls for ordering effects are also included.

In treatment *contract*, the agreement was complemented with a damages clause that "allows the buyer to claim 10 points of compensation in case the seller does not fulfill it."[35]

Both parties were then informed of the realized state in that game. The seller then had to decide whether "to produce the good and deliver it to the buyer," and was always informed of the earnings that she and the buyer would make depending of her decision. The seller was also informed of the possibilities that the buyer would have depending on her decision. With that, subjects did not have to engage in the (very simple) calculations needed in order to make a well-informed decision in each state of the world and also did not have to remember the buyer's possible ex post reactions to their decision.[36]

In all three treatments, sellers equally read:

"Do you want to produce the good and trade it with the original buyer?
If you choose yes, you earn $\langle 20 - c(\theta) \rangle$ points and the buyer earns 10 points."

Since payoffs of not doing so depended on the realized contingency, sellers read in the status quo and in all contingencies involving increases in costs of production (states 0, 1, and 3) that

"If you choose no, you earn 0 points and the buyer earns 0 points."

In contingencies involving an outside option (states 2 and 4), sellers read instead

"If you choose no, you sell the good to the third party and earn $\langle z(\theta) \rangle$ points while the buyer earns 0 points."[37]

In treatment contract, sellers were always informed that if they chose not to deliver the good to the original buyer, then

"in this case, the buyer can claim 10 points of compensation."

In all treatments with retaliation, sellers were informed that if they made that choice, then

"the buyer can spend 2 points to deduct 10 points from your earnings."

---

[35] The only difference in the way both agreements were stated was in how they were called: an exchange of promises in treatment promises and a contract in treatment contract. All the remaining wording was exactly the same. Therefore, in treatment contract, the agreement consisted of: "In the contract, the seller promises to produce the good and trade it with the current buyer, while the buyer promises to pay the price of 20 points to the seller for the good. The contract allows the buyer to claim 10 points of compensation in case the seller does not fulfill it.".

[36] Moreover, subjects had in the written instructions a table with payoffs of both decisions in each state.

[37] Note that the third party was not, in the experiment, a real person but a mere offer that the seller could accept instead of trading with the buyer. This was explicitly explained to participants: "This offer is hypothetical and not done by another participant in the lab" (as in the instruction in the experiment). Moreover, it is assumed that the third party, who "arrives later" than the first buyer, makes an offer corresponding to her whole valuation of the good, in the hope to induce the seller to sell to her instead of to the buyer that "arrived earlier.".

Table 5.7 Initial aggregate findings

	Trade	Trade with retaliation	Promises	Promises retaliation	Contract	Contract with retaliation
Average performance in the status quo (θ_0)	1	1	0.99	1	1	1
N	104	208	96	194	112	230
Proportion of decisions to enter into agreement			0.985	0.98	0.98	0.99
N			400	800	464	928
Proportion of decisions to enforce the contract					0.99	0.98
N					136	220

Adapted from Mittlaender & Buskens, *Retaliation, Remedies, and Contracts, op. cit. supra*

The experiment was implemented in the Experimental Laboratory for Sociology and Economics at Utrecht University between April and May 2013. A total number of 160 participants participated in the experiment. All interactions were anonymous, and participants did not know the identity of other participants they interacted with. The computer program was written with the software z-Tree, and all the implementation of the experiment was fully computerized.[38] Average earnings per participant were of 12 Euros, and each session lasted around one hour. There was no instance of any anomaly and subjects understood the game extremely well, as documented by several types of decision subjects consistently made, as described in the outset of the next section.

5.4 Results

5.4.1 Descriptive Results

Initial aggregate findings, presented in Table 5.7, reveal that subjects understood the game well. Firstly, there were 994 observations of the decision to perform under the status quo in all different treatments, as reported in the first row. In 993 cases, sellers did choose to implement the exchange, to keep the promise, or to fulfill the contract under the status quo (state 0), as always expected.

Secondly, the number of successful agreements is extremely high in all treatments that included them (promises and contract), as reported in the second row. This was predicted since entering into the exchange of promises, enforceable or not, was always profitable even for an individual who planned to keep her word under all

[38] *See* Urs Fischbacher, *z-Tree: Zurich toolbox for ready-made economic experiments*, 10 EXPERIMENTAL ECONOMICS 171 (2007).

Table 5.8 Frequency of breach (treatments without retaliation)

	Characteristics of breach	Trade	Promises	Contract
State 0		0% (*N* = 104)	1% (*N* = 96)	0% (*N* = 112)
State 1	Socially inefficient, avoided inequality	96% (*N* = 26)	96% (*N* = 23)	28% (*N* = 29)
State 2	Socially inefficient, created inequality	88% (*N* = 26)	84% (*N* = 25)	28% (*N*= 29)
State 3	Socially efficient, avoided inequality	100% (*N* = 26)	100% (*N* = 25)	100% (*N* = 28)
State 4	Socially efficient, created inequality	92% (*N* = 26)	96% (*N* = 25)	92% (*N*= 26)
Total *(excluding status quo)*		94% (*N* = 104)	94% (*N* = 98)	61% (*N*= 112)

circumstances. There were 2553 observed instances of participants deciding to enter into the agreement out of a total of 2592 observations of that decision.

Thirdly, there were 356 instances where buyers could claim damages, following breach by the seller, as seen in the last row. In 350 of them, disappointed buyers actively chose to do so, as predicted from theory, since this decision could deliver only benefits for the buyer.

In sum, whenever there were no reasons or arguments for deviations from strictly rational behavior, subjects behaved far and away as predicted in theory. In virtually all instances, (i) sellers chose to perform whenever doing so was individually profitable and circumstances did not change (in 99.89% of the cases), (ii) subjects opted to enter into the mutually profitable agreement (in 98.49% of the cases), and (iii) buyers decided to claim compensation for breach (98.31%).

Observed results concerning the behavior of sellers, or the decision to perform and to keep promises and contracts, in the absence of retaliation, are largely in accordance with the predictions delivered by strict rational choice. Table 5.8 presents the frequency of breach in the three main treatments implemented without retaliation.

The only difference between treatments trade and promises is the presence of promissory commitment, and observed differences in rates of breach between them, in the same contingency, are attributed to the behavioral effect of promises, providing estimates for the test of hypothesis 1. Analogously, the only difference between treatments promises and contract is the availability of damages for breach, and observed differences in rates of breach between those treatments are attributed to the material incentives created by expectation damages, net of the effect of promise-keeping, hence providing estimates for the test of hypothesis 2.

Firstly, there is clearly no difference in observed rates of breach between treatments trade and promises. Descriptive results thus deliver *no evidence that promises induce performance* when performance becomes individually unprofitable and when breach caused no more than loss of expectancy for the promisee. Promissory commitment alone, in states 1 to 4, did not lead sellers to perform, and average rates of breach in those states in treatments trade and promises are virtually identical.

Table 5.9 Frequency of breach (treatments with retaliation)[39]

	Characteristics of breach	Trade	Promises	Contract
State 0		0% ($N = 208$)	0% ($N = 194$)	0% ($N = 230$)
State 1	Socially inefficient, avoided inequality	64% ($N = 52$)	50% ($N = 48$)	5% ($N = 56$)
State 2	Socially inefficient, created inequality	50% ($N = 52$)	49% ($N = 49$)	14% ($N = 57$)
State 3	Socially efficient, avoided inequality	100% ($N = 52$)	96% ($N = 48$)	89% ($N = 57$)
State 4	Socially efficient, created inequality	90% ($N = 52$)	91% ($N = 45$)	84% ($N = 57$)
Total *(excluding status quo)*		76% ($N = 208$)	71% ($N = 190$)	51% ($N= 227$)

Secondly, there is a pronounced difference in observed rates of breach between treatments promises and contract, and *promisors performed, under expectation damages, significantly more often than in absence.* In total, 94% of them breached in the absence of damages while only 61% did so in their presence. Moreover, *expectation damages induced performance only when it was socially efficient, and not otherwise.* These differences, observed only in states 1 and 2, are not only very pronounced but also statistically extremely significant in both cases ($p = 0.000$, Fisher's exact test). Still, expectation damages did not induce all sellers to perform whenever performance was socially efficient. In fact, 28% of them (8 out of 29) behaved irrationally and breached when breach was individually and socially unprofitable.

Table 5.9 presents frequencies of breach in the main treatments implemented with the possibility of retaliation by the buyer. As the comparison of average rates of breach without retaliation, in Table 5.8, with average rates of breach with retaliation reveal, the possibility of irrational retaliation can be a powerful force driving the decision of the seller, inducing sellers to perform, to avoid retaliation, in situations where sellers would not be willing to trade.

Observed frequencies of breach reveal that retaliation induced a change in behavior of the seller in all treatments in states 1 and 2. The possibility of being punished by the other party reduced the frequency of breach by approximately half, providing evidence for hypothesis 5 and for the fact that sellers did change their behavior when faced with the possibility of irrational punishment by the buyer.

In treatment trade, sellers that would virtually never trade in the absence of retaliation (and that rather breached in around 90% of cases) changed their behavior in order to avoid punishment by the buyer and refused to perform much less often when they could suffer losses from retaliation. Similarly, in treatment promises, promisors kept their promises around half of the times when the promisee could retaliate to breach,

[39] Considering only data collected in parts 1 and 2 of the experiment, and excluding all data collected in part 3, rates of breach were quite consistent.

Table 5.10 Frequency of retaliation to breach

	Characteristics of breach	Trade	Promises	Contract
State 0		. ($N = 0$)	. ($N = 0$)	. ($N = 0$)
State 1	Socially inefficient, avoided inequality	36% ($N = 33$)	50% ($N = 24$)	0% ($N = 3$)
State 2	Socially inefficient, created inequality	31% ($N = 26$)	58% ($N = 24$)	12% ($N = 8$)
State 3	Socially efficient, avoided inequality	21% ($N = 52$)	17% ($N = 46$)	20% ($N = 51$)
State 4	Socially efficient, created inequality	29% ($N = 47$)	49% ($N = 41$)	23% ($N = 48$)
Total (*excluding status quo*)		28% ($N = 158$)	40% ($N = 135$)	20% ($N= 110$)

Adapted from Mittlaender & Buskens, *Retaliation, Remedies, and Contracts, op. cit. supra*

remarkably more than in the absence of retaliation, when sellers almost never kept their promises. Retaliation induced a change in behavior of sellers, but the effect of retaliation to breach of promise is not different from the effect of retaliation against a mere refusal to trade, as sellers did not anticipate higher retaliation to breach of promise.

In treatment contract, retaliation further contributed to induce performance by the seller beyond expectation damages. In states 1 and 2, expectation damages already provided incentives for sellers to perform and should have led to full compliance. They however fell short in achieving that goal by 28%, corresponding to observed rates of breach in those states under expectation damages. Retaliation contributed to induce efficient performance beyond that level, decreasing rates of breach from 28 to 5% (state 1) or 14% (state 2), thereby contributing to social welfare in inducing efficient behavior and in deterring inefficient breaches.

Results concerning the buyer's decision to retaliate were in contrast to those concerning the behavior of the seller (at least in the absence of the possibility of retaliation) much less in line with the strict rational choice hypotheses. They reveal that costly punishment of wrongdoers, even if irrational and predicted not to emerge, is a strong behavioral tendency. Table 5.10 presents the frequency of retaliation by disappointed buyers in each treatment and contingency.

Average rates of retaliation should, under strict rational choice hypotheses, be equal to zero in all treatments and in all possible contingencies. Observed rates of retaliation reveal, however, that retaliation is present in all treatments. They are, moreover, much higher when the seller had promised to perform, in some specific contingencies (states 2 and 4). Lastly, they are substantially lower when the buyer is entitled to claim damages for breach.

In effect, individuals engage in costly punishment of sellers that did not implement the exchange in all contingencies already in treatment trade, differently from what strict rational choice models predict. There are different possible reasons for this behavior even in single interactions, and in the absence of any form of agreement and

Table 5.11 Frequency of retaliation to breach and related tests of hypotheses[40]

	Characteristics of breach	Trade	Promises	Fisher's exact	Promises	Contract	Fisher's exact
State 0		. ($N = 0$)	. ($N = 0$)		. ($N = 0$)	. ($N = 0$)	
State 1	inefficient, avoided inequality	36% ($N = 33$)	50% ($N = 24$)	$p =$ 0.416	50% (N= 24)	0% ($N = 3$)	$p =$ 0.230
State 2	inefficient, created inequality	31% ($N = 26$)	58% (N= 24)	$p =$ 0.086	58% ($N = 24$)	12% ($N = 8$)	$p =$ 0.041
State 3	efficient, avoided inequality	21% (N= 52)	17% ($N = 46$)	$p =$ 0.800	17% ($N = 46$)	20% ($N = 51$)	$p =$ 0.800
State 4	efficient, created inequality	30% ($N = 47$)	49% ($N = 41$)	$p =$ 0.082	49% ($N = 41$)	23% ($N = 48$)	$p =$ 0.014
Total		28% ($N = 158$)	40% ($N = 135$)	$p =$ 0.047	40% ($N = 135$)	20% ($N = 110$)	$p =$ 0.001

commitment. Inequality-averse individuals have a reason to retaliate in states 2 and 4, since selling the good to the third party in those states realizes an unequal outcome where the seller earns something while the buyer does not. Individuals that care for social welfare have a reason to retaliate in states 1 and 2, since not implementing the exchange in those states did not maximize welfare. The implemented control group captures those effects, as this was its function by design.

Firstly, individuals retaliate more often to breach of promise than to the seller's mere refusal to trade. The total rate of retaliation, reported in the last row of Table 5.10, is substantially higher in treatment promises (40%) than in treatment trade (28%). Statistical tests for the equality of proportions, reported in the next table, reveal that this difference is significant ($p = 0.047$). It delivers *supporting evidence for hypothesis 2 that breach of promise induced retaliation by the victim.*

However, higher rates of retaliation to breach of promise are restricted to some specific contingencies, revealing that promisees did not punish all breaches equally and did not punish all violations of the moral norm of keeping promises indiscriminately. Punishment of breach of promise depended on the consequences of breach, and the planned design of the experiment allows for that identification. In fact, in state 3, where breach of promise was efficient and fair, buyers did not retaliate more

40 Excluding data from part 3 of the experiment, results are consistent with the exception of the crowding out effect in state 4, which is not significant when excluding half of the observations. The crowding out effect of retaliation in state 2 is still significant, with $p = 0.026$.

often than in treatment trade. When breach joined both desirable consequences of avoiding inefficiency and avoiding inequality, breach of promise was not punished.

In contrast, in states 2 and 4, where breach of promise created an unfair result, breach of promise was punished significantly more (the results of the statistical tests are presented below). These breaches conjoin two different negative elements, the wrong in breaking promises and the unfairness of the resulting outcome. Results reveal that retaliation to breach of promise committed to achieve a higher profit from an outside transaction is more pervasive than sole retaliation to breach or sole retaliation to unfairness.

Secondly, in the presence of damages for breach, observed rates of retaliation to breach of promise were substantially lower (in total, $p = 0.001$). This is observed in all states except for state 3, where retaliation to breach of promise in fact did not emerge, since breach there was not unfair, and did not create any inequality in the final payoffs. These differences rely on fewer observations but are still highly significant ($p = 0.041$ in state 2 and $p = 0.014$ in state 4). There is hence *supporting evidence for hypothesis 4 that compensatory remedies in effect crowd out retaliation to breach.*

Table 5.11 presents results of Fisher's exact test between observed rates of retaliation. The first test, reported in the fifth column, concerns the hypothesis that differences in rates of retaliation between treatments trade and promises are due to the presence of promissory commitment. It provides evidence that individuals retaliate to breach of promise more often than they retaliate to a mere refusal to trade and that this effect occurs only when there was breach of promise and the creation of inequality (in the overbidder paradigm).

The second test, presented in the last column, delivers results of that same test of hypothesis between treatments promises and contract. It reveals that observed differences are statistically significant, and hence due to the effect of expectation damages, thereby providing evidence that damages in fact crowd out retaliation to breach. This effect is, as expected, observed only in those contingencies where breach of promise induced retaliation, revealing how compensation crowds it out in those states.

Compensation seems to be necessary when the promisor breaches in order to profit from an outside transaction, but not when the promisor breaches in order to avoid incurring losses because of a spike in the costs of production. In this case, breach avoided the creation of inequality and can arguably be perceived as the fair thing to do. It did not induce retaliation, and promisees possibly did not perceive it as a wrong in need of redress. It is in the case of outside offers, when the promisor profits from her own wrong, so compensation is necessary to crowd out the observed tendency to reciprocate to perceived wrongful behavior.

5.4.2 Regression Results

The first regression analyzes the effect of promissory commitment, expectation damages, and the possibility of retaliation on the behavior of sellers. That is, interest lies in the determinants of performance and on whether promises, damages, and retaliation can induce sellers to perform. The analysis distinguishes these effects according to the consequences of the seller's decision in terms of inefficiency and inequality.

Since subjects made the same decision multiple times in each session, standard errors are clustered by subject. Moreover, different controls for possible ordering effects due to the treatment having been implemented in later parts of each session are also included in the model. The seller's decision was, in the game, dichotomous: If the seller decided to "produce the good and deliver it to the buyer," then *perform* $= 1$, otherwise *perform* $= 0$.

Accordingly, the parametric model has the following form:

$$\begin{aligned} &Prob(perform|promises, contract, retaliation, inef, ineq) \\ &= \beta_0 + \beta_1 inef + \beta_2 ineq + \beta_3 promises \\ &\quad + \beta_4 promises \cdot inef + \beta_5 promises \cdot ineq \\ &\quad + \beta_6 contract + \beta_7 contract \cdot inef + \beta_8 contract \cdot ineq \\ &\quad + \beta_9 retaliation + \beta_{10} retaliation \cdot inef + \beta_{11} retaliation \cdot ineq + u \end{aligned}$$

where

inef is an indicator for the creation of losses for both parties (inefficiency) as a consequence of the seller's decision, equal to unity only in states 1 and 2;

ineq is an indicator for the creation of inequality in the partie's final earnings as a consequence of the seller's decision, equal to unity only in states 2 and 4;

promises is an indicator for promissory commitment, equal to unity in case both parties agreed to the exchange of promises (present in treatments promises and contract);

contract is an indicator for the possibility of buyers to claim expectation damages to breach promise, equal to unity whenever parties agreed to the enforceable exchange of promises (present in treatment contract);

retaliation is an indicator for the buyer's possibility to retaliate, equal to unity if the observation was collected in a treatment with retaliation.

Regressors for the different treatments are resumed in Table 5.12.

Table 5.12 Regressors

Main treatment	Without retaliation	With retaliation
Trade	Promises = 0 Contract = 0 Retaliation = 0	Promises = 0 Contract = 0 Retaliation = 1
Promises	Promises = 1 Contract = 0 Retaliation = 0	Promises = 1 Contract = 0 Retaliation = 1
Contract	Promises = 1 Contract = 1 Retaliation = 0	Promises = 1 Contract = 1 Retaliation = 1

Different regressions with observations collected only in part 1, in part 1 and part 2, and in all three parts of each session are all reported in the three columns of Table 5.13.

Consider first the isolated impact of inefficiency and inequality. The fact that the seller's decision would lead to an overall loss of resources (being thus inefficient) or to an unequal distribution (being thus "unfair") induced some sellers to trade even in the absence of any form of commitment or enforcement. This reflects the same findings reported in Tables 5.8 and 5.9, where in state 3 (the contingency in which deciding *not* to perform created neither inefficiency nor inequality), sellers in fact never decided to perform (frequency of breach was 100% in the absence of retaliation, and 96% in its presence).

In all other states, sellers at times decided to trade even when doing so was individually unprofitable, thereby avoiding the realization of those negative consequences. The magnitude of the estimated impact of inefficiency and inequality on that decision is quite comparable, and the probability of trade was, on average, around 20% points higher when trade was socially efficient or fair.

Promises, on the other hand, never had any effect upon the seller's decision, as reported in Tables 5.8 and 5.9. Rates of trade in the absence and presence of promises were virtually identical, and regression results confirm that there is *no evidence supporting hypothesis 1* (promises induce trade in the absence of any type of enforcement mechanism). In comparison to other empirical studies that attest the existence of that effect when breach of promise caused a material loss of resources for the promisee, the experiment provides no evidence for the existence of that same effect when breach of promise caused only loss of expectancy.

Damages for breach induced performance by the promisor, and this effect is mostly concentrated when performance was, in the realized contingency, socially efficient. The effect of expectation damages to induce efficient performance is statistically very significant and the strongest one leading to the implementation of the transaction. There is therefore *strong evidence supporting hypothesis 3* (expectation damages induce efficient levels of performance). Promisors were on average around 35% points more likely to perform when performance was socially efficient than when it was not, which can be summed with 10–15% points induced by damages

Table 5.13 Regression results on seller's decision to perform

Dependent variable: Seller's decision to perform	Specification (average marginal effects reported)		
	Probit Part 1	Probit Parts 1,2	Probit Parts 1,2,3
Inefficiency	0.25* (0.14)	0.21** (0.09)	0.18* (0.10)
Inequality	0.17** (0.07)	0.15** (0.06)	0.18*** (0.06)
Promises	0.06 (0.09)	0.04 (0.07)	0.05 (0.06)
Promises and inefficiency	−0.11 (0.08)	−0.04 (0.07)	0.02 (0.07)
Promises and inequality	0.02 (0.09)	−0.01 (0.07)	−0.05 (0.06)
Contract	0.11 (0.08)	0.14** (0.07)	0.12* (0.06)
Contract and inefficiency	0.32** (0.15)	0.39*** (0.12)	0.34*** (0.10)
Contract and inequality	−0.08 (0.08)	−0.09* (0.05)	−0.05 (0.05)
Retaliation	0.15** (0.07)	0.15*** (0.05)	0.14*** (0.05)
Retaliation and inefficiency	0.16 (0.12)	0.15** (0.07)	0.16** (0.08)
Retaliation and inequality	−0.10 (0.06)	−0.05 (0.04)	−0.08 (0.05)
Controls	None	For part 2	For part 2 and part 3
Observations	306	623	939
Pseudo-R^2	0.382	0.433	0.425
χ^2 (degrees of freedom)	120.3 (11)	264.2 (23)	773.7 (41)
p	0	0	0
Number of clusters	80	80	80

Notes: Controls for part 2 include an indicator variable for that part and its interaction with all regressors, controlling for possible general ordering effects as well as for specific ordering effects. *Controls for part 3* are equally defined and further include an indicator variable for part 3 implemented immediately after another part with retaliation, as well as its interaction with all regressors, controlling for possible effects of implementing retaliation immediately after retaliation (vis-à-vis implemented after no retaliation). Stars notation: ***$p < 0.01$, **$p < 0.05$, *$p < 0.1$ (two-sided tests). *All standard errors corrected for clustering by subject.*

independent of efficiency, making promisors on average twice as likely to perform in those circumstances.

Retaliation further induced performance by the promisor, although to a lower extent than damages. There is a general effect of retaliation that does not depend on efficiency or equality, and a specific one, through which retaliation induced higher rates of performance when performance was socially efficient (except when considering only data from part 1). There is hence *support for hypothesis 5* (fear of irrational retaliation induces a change in behavior of sellers).

The second set of regressions analyzes the determinants of retaliatory behavior in contractual relationships. The effect of breach of promise and of expectation damages is again distinguished according to the motives and consequences of breach. The buyer's decision was also dichotomous, and the model used to estimate those effects, separately with data from part 1, parts 1 and 2, and all three parts is the following:

$$\begin{aligned} Prob(retaliate|promises, contract, inef, ineq) &= \beta_0 + \beta_1 inef + \beta_2 ineq \\ &+ \beta_3 promises + \beta_4 promises \cdot inef + \beta_5 promises \cdot ineq + \beta_6 contract \\ &+ \beta_7 contract \cdot inef + \beta_8 contract \cdot ineq + u \end{aligned}$$

where regressors are defined as in Table 5.12.

There is evidence that buyers retaliate more often against sellers that did not undertake the socially optimal course of conduct (the coefficient of inefficiency, considering only data from parts 1 and 2, has a p value of 0.1). There is no evidence that inequality-aversion, by itself, leads to retaliation in the designed trade game (Table 5.14).

The main factor driving retaliatory behavior is unfairness in breach of promise, or breach that created an unequal distribution of gains between the parties. Promisees retaliated substantially more against sellers that profited from their own wrong. There is therefore *supporting evidence for hypothesis 2* (breach of promise induces retaliation by the promisee), restricted however to breaches responsible for an unequal distribution.

Lastly, there is considerable evidence for the effect of compensatory damages to crowd out retaliation to breach by promisees. This effect is found exactly under the same circumstances where promises induced retaliation, namely when breach created inequality. This presents *supporting evidence for hypothesis 4* (damages for breach crowd out retaliation by promisees), although the scope of this effect seems to be restricted to breaches to profit from a higher outside option.

Regression results are hence all consistent with results of the different test of hypotheses implemented in the previous sections. Promises did not induce a change in behavior of sellers, but both expectation damages and the possibility of retaliation by the buyer did so. While the latter lead to rates of breach that were roughly half of those observed in the absence of any enforcement mechanism, expectation damages proved to be much more effective in deterring breaches, and deterred not half of all inefficient breaches, but around three quarters of them.

Table 5.14 Regression results on buyer's decision to retaliate

Dependent variable: Buyer's decision to retaliate	Specification (average marginal effects reported)			
	Probit Part 1	Probit Parts 1, 2	Probit[41] Parts 1, 2, 3	Probit Parts 1, 2, 3
Inefficiency	0.28** (0.14)	0.15 (0.09)	0.10** (0.05)	0.10** (0.05)
Inequality	0.14 (0.11)	0.02 (0.09)	0.04 (0.06)	0.04 (0.06)
Promises	0.02 (0.13)	−0.07 (0.10)	−0.03 (0.07)	−0.03 (0.07)
Promises and inefficiency	−0.16 (0.11)	0.13 (0.09)	0.13** (0.06)	0.14** (0.06)
Promises and inequality	0.35** (0.17)	0.40*** (0.12)	0.20** (0.10)	0.20** (0.09)
Contract (promises and damages)	0.07 (0.17)	0.13 (0.13)	0.00 (0.09)	-0.00 (0.09)
Contract and inefficiency	Not estimable because of lack of variance[42]			−0.24*** (0.08)
Contract and inequality	−0.19** (0.09)	−0.20** (0.09)	−0.20*** (0.07)	−0.18** (0.07)
Controls		For part 2	For part 2 and part 3	For part 2 and part 3
Observations	105	187	392	403
Pseudo-R^2	0.159	0.147	0.171	0.178
χ^2 (degrees of freedom)	29.5 (7)	81.2 (15)	3175 (31)	3311 (32)
p	0.0001	0	0	0
Number of clusters	43	80	80	80

Notes: Controls for part 2 include an indicator variable for that part and its interaction with all regressors, controlling for possible general ordering effects as well as for specific ordering effects. *Controls for part 3* are equally defined and further include an indicator variable for part 3 implemented immediately after another part with retaliation, as well as its interaction with all regressors, controlling for possible effects of implementing retaliation immediately after retaliation (vis-à-vis implemented after no retaliation). Stars notation: ***$p < 0.01$, **$p < 0.05$, *$p < 0.1$ (two-sided tests). *All standard errors corrected for clustering by subject*

Promises, on the other hand, induced a substantial change in the behavior of buyers, and breach of promise lead to rates of retaliation that were around twice as high as the ones observed in the absence of commitment. Additionally, this effect was restricted to those contingencies where the seller breaches to realize higher profits

[41] As seen in the descriptive results, there was one instance where the buyer decided to retaliate to breach in state 2 with data from all three parts. Therefore, it is possible to estimate the effect of damages to crowd out retaliation with all data, but given the few observations for that, the table distinguishes both types of regressions.

[42] As reported in the descriptive results, there was no observation of retaliation to breach, under expectation damages, in states 1 and 2 when not considering data from part 3.

from an outside transaction, profiting from the act of breach. Compensatory remedies such as expectation damages were then capable of substantially reducing those rates, as both tests of hypotheses and regression analyses confirm.

5.4.3 Analysis of Social Welfare

Once established that damages for breach not only induce performance by the promisor, but also reduce retaliation by victims of breach—at least when breach created inequality inside the partie's promissory relationship—the question that arises concerns the gains of social welfare provided by each of these functions of legal relief. Overall social welfare was given by

$$SW(q_s, r_b, \theta) = q_s(V - c(\theta)) + (1 - q_s) \cdot (z(\theta) - r_b R - r_b K)$$

In case of trade, realized social welfare was equal to the value of performance to the buyer minus the costs of production of the seller. In case of breach, it was given by the net gains of trade with the outside party, minus the loss that seller and buyer incur in case of retaliation to breach. For the chosen parameters, it corresponds to

$$SW(q_s, r_b, \theta) = q_s(30 - c(\theta)) + (1 - q_s) \cdot (z(\theta) - 12r_b)$$

Trade was always expected to take place in state 0, independent of promissory commitment or of any type of enforcement mechanism, and is therefore excluded from the analysis. In all other states, sellers were, in the absence of damages, always predicted not to trade with the buyer and to break their promises. This, however, does not mean that the predicted gains from trade were zero, since in states 2 and 4 the seller earns all the gains from trade by selling the good to the outside party, and breach to profit from an outside option does contribute to social welfare.

Expectation damages are predicted to create gains of welfare by inducing performance in states 1 and 2. In those, gains from trade are expected to be foregone in the absence of damages (in treatments trade and promises) and under expectation damages are predicted to be exhausted. This is the predicted contribution of damages to social welfare in inducing performance of contracts.

Table 5.15 presents the expected social welfare in each treatment.

Graph 5.1, where data collected only in parts 1 and 2 of each session is used, presents the realized social welfare depending on the type of commitment and on damages and retaliation

The graph further reveals that retaliation caused heavy losses of welfare. In the absence of promises, it created a loss of almost 0.9 in welfare. In the presence of promises, that loss was more than three times higher, of more than 3. In the presence of damages, it was minimized, and losses from retaliation to *breach* were almost all eliminated, being brought back to levels similar to those observed in treatment trade.

Table 5.15 Expected social welfare in each treatment

Treatment	Trade and promises		Contract	
	Predicted choice	Resulting outcome	Predicted choice	Resulting outcome
Contingency				
State 1 (efficient trade)	Breach	(0, 0)	Performance	(−5, 10)
State 2 (efficient trade)	Breach	(15, 0)	Performance	(10, 10)
State 3 (inefficient trade)	Breach	(0, 0)	Breach	(−10, 10)
State 4 (inefficient trade)	Breach	(25, 0)	Breach	(15, 10)
Total expected social welfare	10		12.5	

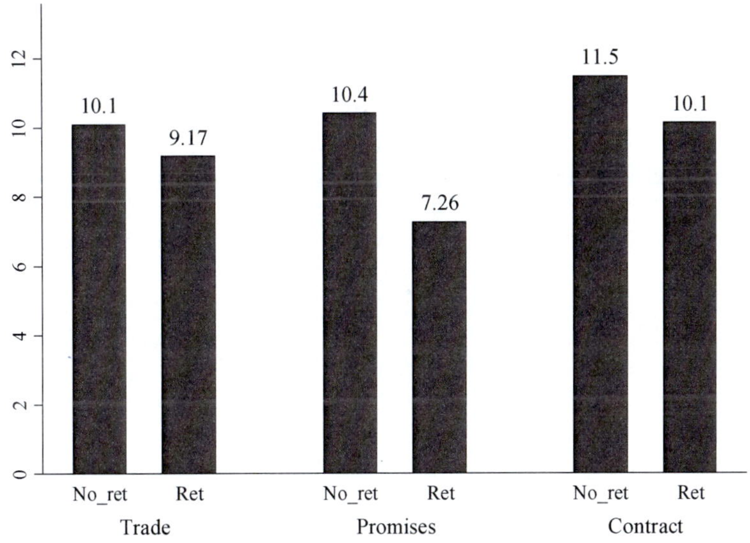

Graph 5.1 Social welfare by treatment

For the investigation of the social welfare function of legal redress, there is the need to consider the possible gains created by retaliation in inducing performance and not only its social costs. Table 5.16 presents those in detail, and separately.

Retaliation did deliver some gains of social welfare by inducing performance by the seller, and thus often leading to trade by itself, without the need for legal enforcement. Sellers traded more often with retaliation than without retaliation, as reported in the descriptive and regression results above. In treatment trade, accordingly, retaliation generated gains from trade of 1.15, but at a social cost of 2.08, thus delivering an overall loss of social welfare of 0.83.

In treatment promises, retaliation was, as described before, more pervasive but did not induce higher rates of performance by the seller than it did in the absence of promises. Retaliation to breach of promise delivered therefore minor gains of only

Table 5.16 Social welfare (SW) generated by promises, damages, and retaliation

Treatment	Without retaliation	With retaliation
Trade	SW = 10.1	SW = 9.17 Gains from trade induced by ret. = 11.25 (net 1.15) Losses from ret. = 2.08 Net welfare effect of retaliation = −0.83
Promises	SW = 10.4	SW = 7.26 Gains from trade induced by ret. = 10.65 (net 0.25) Losses from ret. = 3.39 Net welfare effect of retaliation = −3.14
Contract	SW = 11.5	SW = 11.5 Gains from trade induced by ret. = 11.73 (net 0.23) Losses from ret. = 1.59 Net welfare effect of retaliation = −1.36
Welfare created by damages in	Inducing performance = 1.1	Crowding out retaliation to breach of promise by disappointed promisees = 1.78

0.25 in inducing performance by the seller, and only at a very high social cost of 3.39. It delivered a major net loss of welfare of 3.14.

In treatment contract, retaliation did induce higher rates of performance of contracts than in its absence (and sole presence of damages), but provided by itself a minor gain of social welfare of 0.23. Since the buyer was entitled to compensatory damages, retaliation was lower in treatment contract than in treatment promises and was responsible for social losses of 1.59, considerably lower than the 3.39 observed in treatment promises. Retaliation still caused a loss of welfare, in the presence of compensation, of 1.36, which is, because of the crowding out function of legal redress, much lower than the observed 3.14 in treatment promises.

In conclusion, promises alone provided for almost no gain of welfare. Expectation damages, in inducing socially efficient performance, delivered a net gain of 1.1. In crowding out retaliation, expectation damages avoided a net loss of 1.78. At a minimum, both functions were, in the parameters of the implemented trade game, equally important for the maximization of social welfare. There is evidence that the function of damages to substitute for private redress can be, at times, as under the parameters of the game, even more important than the function of damages to induce socially efficient performance.

5.5 Conclusion

The experimental study provided evidence that contractual parties do not behave exclusively based on their own material self-interest and that deviating behavior is attributable to the behavior of promisees in the presence of the possibility to retaliate. Promisors in fact behaved, in the absence of retaliation, much in line with predictions from rational choice and did not keep their promises whenever doing so was individually unprofitable. They however clearly anticipated the payment of damages for breach when deciding to perform or breach.

Accordingly, obtained results do not provide support for hypothesis 1 (promises induce performance), and there is no evidence for the acceptance of that hypothesis when breach caused no more than loss of expectancy. This result differs from the existing experimental studies on promise-keeping because those studies investigated whether individuals keep their promises when the promisee suffered a real monetary loss from breach. When only the expectation interest is at stake, the moral force of keeping promises was not enough to induce promisors to keep their deals.

In contrast, results deliver strong evidence for hypothesis 3 (expectation damages induce performance if and only if performance is socially efficient). The implemented tests of hypotheses and the obtained regression results favor its acceptance. It is worth noting that expectation damages did not induce all sellers to perform whenever socially efficient, and an estimated 28% behaved irrationally and still breached the contract in those circumstances. The reason underlying that decision lies possibly in their belief that buyers would not claim damages, somehow condoning breach, perhaps because sellers knew buyers did not *really* lose their own money because of breach.

Buyers, in turn, very often behaved irrationally with respect to the predictions derived from strict rational choice theory and did not abstain from costly punishment even in one-shot, single interactions with anonymous counter-parties. Obtained results show that retaliation, in treatment trade, and thus in the absence of promissory commitment and damages for breach, was present when the seller's decision was inefficient.

Sellers anticipated irrational retaliation by the buyer (yet again, differently from the strict rational choice prediction), and rates of trade were substantially higher in the presence of the possibility of ex post retaliation. Sellers anticipated that reaction mostly in contingencies where trade was socially efficient. There is some support for hypothesis 5 (the possibility of irrational retaliation induces a change in behavior of sellers and leads sellers to trade even when unprofitable).

Results present supporting evidence for hypothesis 2 (breach of promises induces higher rates of retaliation), even when controlling for the unfairness and inefficiency of the result, present in treatment trade. Higher rates of retaliation in treatment promises were not driven by inequality-aversion or by a desire to punish behavior that did not maximize social welfare, since these were captured in the control group, and do not explain differences between treatments.

Retaliation to breach of promise was concentrated in situations in which breach created inequality in the final distribution and in which the promisor profited from it. There is no evidence that promisees retaliate against any type of breach of promise, as average retaliation to breach of promise when breach was socially efficient and avoided the creation of inequality (in state 3) was virtually equal to average rates of retaliation in the absence of promise. On the other hand, whenever the promise-breaker profited from her wrong, rates of retaliation were twice as high as in the absence of promissory commitment.

Lastly, the experiment delivers evidence that supports hypothesis 4 (damages for breach crowd out retaliation), and damages for breach do fulfill the function to substitute for private redress and to crowd out retaliation by victims of breach. This effect is concentrated in those situations where breach in fact induced retaliation, in states 2 and 4. As the estimated impact upon social welfare reveals, this function is, at times, neither secondary nor marginal, for its contribution to overall social welfare was more important, in the experiment, than the well-known contribution of damages to induce efficient performance.

Of course, these experimental results do not allow for a generalized conclusion that one function is, in reality, more important than the other. They do allow, however, for the claim that the function of legal relief to substitute for private redress has its own contribution to social welfare and is therefore justified even under strict economic terms. Compensation for victims of breach shall be taken seriously into consideration among the functions of remedies for breach, and, even if only for reasons of social welfare, is in fact fundamental in the law of remedies for breach.

Chapter 6
Implications and Normative Analysis of Remedies for Breach

The sixth chapter studies how expectation and disgorgement damages, as well as specific performance, perform those two functions, and their impact on social welfare. It considers both situations where the promisor can renegotiate with the promisee and where she cannot, and situations where the promisor breaches to avoid incurring losses from those where she breaches to achieve higher profits from a substitutive transaction. Lastly, the chapter assesses, from a normative perspective, recent developments in American, French, German, and English law. Courts and legal scholarship have insisted on the primacy of expectation damages (USA), expanded the scope of specific performance under *astreintes* even upon obligations to do (France), allowed promisees to recover disgorgement damages in cases of breach to make profits, in an extensive interpretation of § 285 I BGB (Germany), and expanded the scope of an award of damages at the common law in awarding, in certain cases, total or partial disgorgement damages (UK).

6.1 Introduction

An award of a remedy for breach of contract can be justified, in economic theory, because of its capacity to alter parties' ex ante behavior and thereby to contribute to the welfare of society. As observed in the experiment, legal redress affects parties' behavior both in its capacity to induce efficient levels of performance and to crowd out the human tendency to retaliate to breach. Moreover, the need of legal redress to suppress retaliation is restricted to those cases where the promisor in breach profits from her own wrong and is hence responsible for an outcome that the promisee can perceive as unfair.

In order to provide a superior contribution to social welfare, remedies for breach should attempt to implement a final distribution of gains and losses that is more likely to be perceived as fair by the parties, and that does not allow the promisor to profit from breach without respect for the interests of the promisee. In doing so, legal

S. Mittlaender, *Equity, Efficiency, and Ethics in Remedies for Breach of Contract*, International Law and Economics, https://doi.org/10.1007/978-3-031-10804-4_6

relief can provide for a higher social welfare, inducing efficient levels of performance by the promisor while and concomitantly being capable of effectively crowding out socially costly forms of retaliation by the promisee.

Promisees tend to retaliate to breach, as observed in the experiment, in situations captured into what Melvin Eisenberg denotes the overbidder paradigm, or those where the promisor profits from breach.[1] Expectation damages do not deter breaches to profit from a more profitable substitutive transaction, but rather encourage them whenever breach is socially efficient, and hence capable of exhausting all possible gains from trade. Legal remedies should *also* implement a fairer distribution of those profits in order to effectively crowd out retaliation by the victim while concomitantly allowing the realization of all possible gains from trade through efficient breaches.

Moreover, retaliation is not an action that only victims of breach can undertake. Certain remedies for breach lead to results that can be perceived as unfair *by the promisor*. Disgorgement damages, for example, allocate all profits from breach to the promisee and prevent the promisor from earning any minor share of those. It is then the promisor who may perceive that result as unfair and be tempted to retaliate, thereby causing a deadweight loss. She may, for example, prefer to perform inefficiently and to forgo the opportunity to breach efficiently if she knows she will not earn any share of its profits. Alternatively, she may breach efficiently but later retaliate in other manners discussed before, for example, attempting to harm the reputation of the promisee, that do not allow her to receive any share of those profits.

This possibility acquires higher relevance when parties renegotiate contracts. Remedies for breach entitle parties either to substitutive or injunctive relief and thereby put either the promisor or the promisee in a better position to renegotiate. Specific performance, in particular, allows the promisee to force the promisor to perform, except for the cases where performance is impossible or impractical, and thus permits the promisee to exploit and extort the promisor that faces hardship and very high unforeseen costs to perform. Retaliation to the perceived unfairness of exploitative renegotiation is expected to be high, just as its social cost, as consistently observed, for example, in experiments involving ultimatum bargaining.[2]

This chapter develops both a positive and a normative analysis of the usual remedies for breach of contract awarded in different legal systems. It analyzes, from a positive perspective, existing remedies according, firstly, to the incentives they provide for promisors to perform efficiently and hence *for the exhaustion of possible gains from trade* in any type of contingency. Secondly, it analyzes how those remedies distribute gains and losses between the parties, being thereby more or less apt to crowd out the individual tendency to retaliate to the perceived unfairness of the result, and hence *for the minimization of social losses from retaliation.* In certain conditions, these coincide and the promisor may opt to retaliate by performing inefficiently, in which case losses from retaliation are those from foregone gains from trade.

[1] *See supra* n.27 (chap. 1), n. 59 (chap. 4), n. 75 (chap. 4), and the accompanying text.

[2] *See* the discussion *supra* in Chap. 4, Sect. 4.2.

From a normative perspective, it argues that remedies shall not allow one of the parties to appropriate all the profits from breach, in case of an unforeseen higher outside offer, because this can lead the other party to retaliate, and in that case, social welfare is not maximized. Moreover, remedies shall not allow promisees to exploit the promisor that faces severe hardship to perform, in an unfortunate contingency, for this would lead the promisor to retaliate, and yet again prevent the maximization of social welfare.

The desirability of different remedies for breach, in the absence of reliance investments, is still largely based, in the Economic Analysis of Law, on the theory of efficient breach.[3] The theory relies on two main assumptions: parties can renegotiate their agreements once economic conditions change without transaction costs, and parties do not make reliance investments. Its conclusion is that, as explained in previous chapters, expectation damages are the best remedy because of their capacity to induce only efficient performance in any possible contingency.

It was, however, an unsound conclusion.[4] The theory, in fact, fails to explain why the law enforces contractual promises through substitutive or injunctive relief or indeed through any specific remedy.[5] Under its assumptions, parties will always bargain around performance once circumstances change, and any legal remedy will induce performance if performance is socially efficient, and not otherwise. One party will either buy performance or sell the right to breach in exchange for a monetary payment, and just mutually beneficial transactions are implemented. Social welfare hence does not depend on the type of the available legal remedy, and the theory lives, as mentioned by Markovits and Schwarz, in a theoretical vacuum.[6]

According to the authors, there are two potential explanations that can rescue the theory from this theoretical vacuum.[7] The first one is to relax the assumption that parties can renegotiate without transaction costs in order to develop an explanation for why these costs are higher under certain remedies, as the authors in fact do.[8] The

---

[3] The original version of the theory stems from Barton, *The Economic Basis of Damages for Breach of Contract, op. cit. supra*, at 277 and Birmingham, *Breach of Contract, Damage Measures, and Economic Efficiency, op. cit. supra*, at 273. The *term* efficient breach theory was introduced by Goetz & Scott in *Liquidated Damages, Penalties and the Just Compensation Principle, op. cit. supra*, at 554.

[4] *See* Eric Posner, *Economic Analysis of Contract Law After Three Decades: Success or Failure?, op. cit. supra*, at 834–836 (the theory's conclusion was "premature.").

[5] *See* Ian Macneil, *Efficient Breach of Contract: Circles in the Sky, op. cit. supra*, at 952 ("It is, therefore, illogical to conclude that either a right to specific performance or a right to expectation damages will lead to such a result [induce performance if and only if performance is socially efficient] in the real world. Whatever 'direction' toward or away from efficiency either of these rules has depends entirely upon the relative transaction costs each will generate.").

[6] *See* Markovits & Schwartz, *The Myth of Efficient Breach, op. cit. supra*, at 1944 ("The theory of efficient breach is vacuous.").

[7] *Id.* at 1945.

[8] This approach is subject to criticism, as mentioned by Ian Macneil ("it is extremely easy to introduce selected transaction costs to show that the model 'proves' what the modeler wants it to prove, while ignoring countless other transaction costs of equal or greater pertinence in the real world—yielding different conclusions.") *Cf.* Macneil, *Efficient Breach of Contract: Circles in the*

second one is to relax the assumption that parties do not make relationship-specific investments that lose value in case the promisor does not perform.[9]

The chapter attempts to explain the advantages and disadvantages of different remedies for breach, in terms of social welfare, *without relaxing any of the assumptions of theory of efficient breach.* Once the remedy's capacity to implement a result that is fair and allows a party neither to capture all gains from breach, nor to exploit the other with a threat of specifically enforcing the contract, then it is possible to justify certain remedies as superior to others, in social welfare terms.

This chapter argues that expectation damages are superior to specific performance, as advanced by the theory of efficient breach, even when parties can renegotiate the contract without transaction costs, although only in the loss-avoidance paradigm. Secondly, it argues that specific performance is superior to expectation damages, in opposition to the theory of efficient breach, again assuming costless renegotiation, but only in the overbidder paradigm. Thirdly, it argues that disgorgement damages can be superior to both of them, especially when they are measured by the hypothetical bargain gains that the promisee foregoes because of breach by the promisor, as recently accepted, under certain circumstances, by the House of Lords, in English law.[10]

Throughout the chapter, two paradigmatic hypothetical cases involving different types of contingencies that can render performance individually and socially unprofitable are considered.

The first case is a variation of the *Murmansk case*, initially proposed by Picker, and later complemented by Canaris.[11] It is the case of an absolute increase in costs of performance and encompasses contingencies that involve an increase in costs of production, just as states 1 and 3 of the experiment from Chap. 5 implemented. It is hence a paradigmatic case of breach to avoid losses, involving an unfortunate contingency:

> Seller enters into a contract with the buyer for the sale of a car for $10,000 at a future date. Before that date, the car is stolen, without fault of the seller. It is subsequently found in the port city of Murmansk, in the extreme northwest part of Russia, above the Arctic Circle. The costs for returning the car to the parties' city are $15,000 (alternative 1) or $25,000 (alternative 2). The buyer values the car at $20,000, and the seller places no value on it.[12]

Sky, *op. cit. supra*, at 962. For the criticism of Markovits and Schwartz's "new defense of the expectation interest" based on that approach, *see* Gregory Klass, *To Perform or Pay Damages*, 98 VIRGINIA LAW REVIEW 143 (2012).

[9] For this approach, *see*, e.g., William Rogerson, *Efficient Reliance and Damage Measures for Breach of Contract*, 15 RAND JOURNAL OF ECONOMICS 39 (1984); Shavell, *The Design of Contracts and Remedies for Breach*, *op. cit. supra*.

[10] *See* the discussion *infra* in Sect. 6.4.

[11] *Cf*. Eduard Picker, *Schuldrechtsreform und Privatautonomie*, 58 JURISTENZEITUNG 1035 (2003); Claus-Wilhelm Canaris, *Die Behandlung nicht zu vertretenden Leistungshindernisse nach § 275 Abs. 2 BGB beim Stückkauf*, 59 JURISTENZEITUNG 214, 216 (2004).

[12] *Cf*. Picker, *Schuldrechtsreform und Privatautonomie*, *op. cit supra*. In the original case, the buyer did not immediately value the car at $20,000 but rather found another person interested in the car and entered into a contract with this third person for the sale of the car for $20,000. It is therefore equivalent to assuming that the buyer values the car at that same amount.

In an economic analysis, the promisee's (in this case, the buyer's) expectancy is $10,000. If costs of performance are $15,000, then performance is still socially efficient because it would lead to an overall gain of $5000. If costs of performance are $25,000, then performance is socially inefficient because it would create social losses of $5000. In case of breach by the seller, neither party earns or loses anything until the legal remedy is considered.

The second case is the analogous version of *Murmansk* where a third party offers a higher price for the car after the promisor had already contracted for its sale to the original buyer. It corresponds to states 2 and 4 of the experiment, where breach was committed in order to achieve higher profits. It is the paradigmatic case of the "double sale" (*Doppelverkauf*) described by Dieter Medicus, referred in what follows simply as the *outside offer* case[13]:

> Another buyer approaches the seller, before the date of delivery, and offers either $15,000 (alternative 1) or $25,000 (alternative 2) for the already promised car, equivalent to her whole valuation of the car. The second buyer is unaware that the seller had contracted for its sale with the first buyer at a previous date. The seller agrees to sell the car to the second buyer.

In an economic analysis, parties' expectancy is again $10,000. Performance of the original contract is socially efficient if the outside offer is $15,000 because it would create overall gains of $20,000 while breach only $15,000. If the outside offer is $25,000, then performance is socially inefficient because it would prevent the realization of further gains of $5000 that are achievable only through breach. The difference lies in the fact that, in case of breach and sale of the car to the third party, and before the legal remedy is considered, the seller earns $15,000 or $25,000 while the buyer earns nothing.

This chapter contrasts injunctive and substitutive remedies for breach, and both expectation and disgorgement damages from a welfare perspective. Section 6.2 studies the welfare consequences of an award of damages, and considers, firstly, the default and common remedy of expectation damages (*exécution par équivalent*, and *Schadensersatz statt der Leistung*). Under it, renegotiation is a moot issue, and results do not change in the presence or absence of renegotiation. It then studies disgorgement damages, reviews the circumstances under which they are awarded in different jurisdictions (including, especially, the claim on the surrogate—*Anspruch auf das stellvertretende Commodus*—in Germany), and then distinguishes the welfare consequences of the remedy in the presence and absence of renegotiation (which is under a disgorgement rule not a moot issue).

More importantly, in the original case, Picker assumed that the costs of returning the car were only $10,000. This was a quite unfortunate choice, as mentioned by Canaris, since with that value, performance or breach followed by the payment of damages would lead to the same result for the seller (and, although not mentioned by Canaris, also to the same social welfare). *See* Claus-Wilhelm Canaris, *Die Behandlung nicht zu vertretenden Leistungshindernisse nach § 275 Abs. 2 BGB beim Stückkauf*, 59 JURISTENZEITUNG 214, 216 (2004) ("*Zweite Abwandlung: höhere Rückführungskosten.*") In order to distinguish the effects of specific performance and damages, the costs of returning the car, or the costs of performing specifically, are assumed in the present version of the example to be either $15,000 or $25,000, and not only $10,000.

13 MEDICUS & LORENZ, SCHULDRECHT I, *op. cit. supra*, at 208 Rn. 432.

Section 6.3 studies specific performance and reviews, firstly, when promisees indeed have that claim in common law and civil law systems (distinguishing between obligations to do and obligations to give). Secondly, it explains the limits for an award of specific performance because they restrict the promisee's possibility to exploit the promisor in the renegotiation, and thereby restrict possible losses of social welfare caused by retaliation. Lastly, it studies the impact of the remedy in the presence and absence of renegotiation.

Section 6.4 summarizes the welfare effects of those remedies and analyzes the recent trends in the enforcement of contracts in four different legal systems. It reviews the insistence on an award of expectation damages in the USA; the expansion of specific performance even to obligations to do in French law, especially after the codification of the *astreinte* in 1992; the availability of specific performance side by side to disgorgement damages, at least in the overbidder paradigm, in German law, after the reform of 2002; and the English expansion of disgorgement damages, both in form of total disgorgement (*Blake's* damages) and in form of hypothetical bargain damages (*Wrotham Park* damages), especially after the decision of the House of Lords in the *Hendrix Experience* case in 2003.

6.2 Damages for Breach

Damages for breach, or substitutive relief, consist of an award of a monetary payment for the victim of breach in lieu of the promised performance. They thereby allow promisors to breach without the need of renegotiation and consent by the promisee. The promisor must solely pay the amount of damages prescribed by the law, and determined by courts, to the disappointed promisee, and damages consequently redistribute wealth between the parties.

Economic theories consider that such redistribution has no consequence for social welfare. Following Kaplow & Shavell, this type of redistribution is *situational*: it refers to the allocation of a particular gain or loss between the disputing parties and not to the overall distribution of income in society as a whole.[14] Since possible gains of welfare from a more equal distribution of income in the whole society are not considered, then situational redistribution based on fairness is of no consequence for social welfare.[15]

---

[14] Kaplow and Shavell, *Fairness versus Welfare, op. cit. supra*, at 998.

[15] Unless one can assume that one of the parties is risk-averse (or, better stated, one is more risk-averse than the other). "But, setting aside these and any other ways that lawsuits may affect individual's well-being, the bare fact that money change hands in a lawsuit in certain circumstances, thereby changing how a loss is divided between the two parties, is of no consequence under welfare economics.") *Id.* at 998, n.73.

As explained in detail in Chap. 4 *supra*, unfairness in *breach* of contract considers exclusively the resulting inequality after breach and not after performance. In other words, it refers to the unfairness of the allocation that results from breach and not to the unfairness in the negotiated distribution of

Welfare economics, however, should be concerned with redistribution in this situational sense because the implementation of a distribution that is perceived as fair by the parties has its own impact on individuals' tendency to retaliate, and consequently on overall social welfare. In other words: as defended by Kaplow and Shavell, welfare economics is not concerned with the fairness of the distribution of gains and losses between the parties per se. But in triggering or suppressing socially costly retaliation, it does have consequences on social welfare, and because of that is taken into account.

Different measurements of damages for breach implement different distributions of gains and losses from breach and are thereby more or less apt to crowd out retaliation and to provide for the maximal well-being of society. There is, in the traditional measures of damages for breach, a strong convergence between the default measurement at common law and at civil law. In effect, both systems, as detailed in what follows, aim at protecting the *expectation* or *positive interest* of the promisee.[16]

6.2.1 The Protection of the Expectation Interest in Common Law and Civil Law Systems

The default and common remedy for breach of contract at common law is an award of expectation damages. The fundamental principle of remedies for breach is compensation, and the goal pursued by award of damages is to compensate the promisee, who ought to be made whole. The law favors expectation damages because they are apt to achieve that purpose and to provide adequate satisfaction to the victim by putting her in the position she would have been in had the promisor performed.[17]

Accordingly, sales contracts are generally enforced by expectation damages. The exceptions that allow the promisee to seek injunctive relief (explained in detail below) include mainly cases where the promised good is unique, such as 18-year-old Pelé's boots from the 1958 World Cup final, or tracts of land, which are also considered unique. Service contracts, even more strictly, are almost never enforced by injunctive

---

gains from trade. The last one refers to a fair deal, inquiries into the adequacy of consideration, and is excluded from the scope of this thesis.

[16] For the concept of the positive interest, *see* Rudolf von Jhering, *Culpa in Contrahendo oder Schadenserstaz bei nichtigen oder nicht zur Perfektion gelangten Verträgen*, in 4 JAHRBÜCHER FÜR DIE DOGMATIK DES HEUTIGEN RÖMISCHEN UND DEUTSCHEN RECHTS 1 (1861). For the translation of the notion into the expectation interest, *see* Fuller and Perdue, *The Reliance Interest in Contract Damages*, *op. cit. supra*, at 54 *et seq.*

The distinction between the positive and negative interest, however, was not "discovered" by Jhering but is already found in Mommsen, as argued by HELGE DEDEK, NEGATIVE HAFTUNG AUS VERTRAG 161 (Tübingen, Mohr Siebeck, 2007) ("*Jhering hingegen gibt dem Kind einen Namen, und dies in besonders einprägsamer und geschickter Weise.*").

[17] *See* RESTATEMENT (SECOND) OF CONTRACTS, § 344 (b) (the promisee's expectation interest is "his interest in having the benefit of his bargain by being put in as good a position as he would have been in had the contract been performed.").

relief, with disappointed promisees entitled only to an award of damages in case of breach.[18]

In civil law systems, specific performance is certainly the default remedy, but a remedy of damages is also available for the disappointed promisee. She may prefer to receive a monetary award instead of insisting on receiving performance as promised, and civil law systems allow, in general, the promisee to seek the remedy she prefers.[19] Moreover, there are several different legal norms and doctrines that bar the promisee from seeking injunctive relief, as described in the next section, in which case the promisee must content herself with a monetary payment in lieu of performance in kind.

For these reasons, as noted by Reinhard Zimmermann, "it is widely recognized among modern comparative lawyers that in the actual practice ... the claim to specific performance does not have anything like the significance attached to it in theory."[20] Quite on the contrary, as mentioned by Ulrich Huber, "the claim for damages for breach has a central position among the remedies of the creditor."[21] The promisee will often prefer to claim damages than to insist on specific performance and will often have no access to specific performance, being then entitled only to an award of damages according to the measure prescribed by the law.

In France, damages for breach, or *dommages et intérêts*, comprise the loss of gain and the loss sustained by the promisee, as foreseen by the *Code Civil*:

> Art. 1149. Damages due to a creditor are, in general, for the loss which he has suffered and the gain which he has been deprived of, subject to the exceptions and modifications below.[22]

Loss sustained is characterized by the fact that "the assets of the obligee, after the event, have diminished in value."[23] Lost gain, on the other hand, is "the increase in the value of his assets of which the obligee is deprived as the result of the failure to perform the contract."[24] Had the promisor performed, then the promisee would have

---

[18] *See*, however, the discussion *infra* in Sect. 6.3 concerning the availability of injunctions in obligations not to do.

[19] However, the promisor often has the *right to cure* in case she delivers defective performance (*Recht zur zweiten Andienung*). The promisee must give her the second chance to perform without defect and, for example, to repair the delivered defective good or to deliver a new good without defect (at the choice of the buyer) before claiming damages for breach, as detailed below.

[20] Reinhard Zimmerman, *Savigny's Legacy: Legal History, Comparative Law, and the Emergence of a European Legal Science*, 112 LAW QUARTERLY REVIEW 576, 591 (1996).

[21] *Cf.* Huber, *Schadensersatz statt der Leistung, op. cit. supra*, at 320 ("*Unter diesen Rechtsbehelfen nimmt der Anspruch auf Schadensersatz die zentrale Position ein*"), 360 ("*Unter den Rechtsbehelfen des Gläubigers ist der Anspruch auf Schadensersatz statt der Leistung praktisch wichtiger als der Anspruch auf Erfüllung in Natur.*") ("under the remedies of the creditors, the claim for damages for breach is effectively more important than the claim for specific performance") (own transl.); ULRICH HUBER, 2 LEISTUNGSSTÖRUNGEN, *op. cit. supra*, at 138.

[22] Own transl. In original: "*Les dommages et intérêts dus au créancier sont, en général, de la perte qu'il a faite et du gain dont il a été privé, sauf les exceptions et modifications ci-après.*"

[23] 4 JEAN CARBONNIER, DROIT CIVIL: LES OBLIGATIONS n°206 (22nd ed., Paris, PUF, 2000).

[24] YVES-MARIE LAITHIER, ÉTUDE COMPARATIVE DES SANCTIONS DE L'INEXÉCUTION DU CONTRAT, n. 106, at 172 (Paris, LGDJ, 2004).

earned what she had bargained for, and the expectation interest is therefore protected by the legal norm.

French law protects the expectation interest in what is known as "equivalent performance" (*exécution par équivalent*). The principle is that of integral or total reparation.[25] Damages are calculated by reference to the benefit that the promisee would derive from performance of the obligation.[26] They are, however, limited to those that were foreseen, or could have been foreseen at the time of the contract,[27] and in general exclude consequential damages.[28]

In Germany, nonperformance is a violation of the promisor's primary duty to perform, and it entitles the promisee to seek different remedies at her choice, including damages for breach, provided that the promisee fix a reasonable time limit for the promisor to perform late, and that the period elapses without performance (BGB § 281 I 1).[29] In case of sales contracts, the seller that does not deliver the good violates the primary duty to deliver (BGB § 433 I 1), and the buyer must then fix a reasonable time limit for the seller to perform. If the seller still does not perform, then the buyer has different options, among which is a claim of damages for breach (*Schadensersatz statt der Leistung*) instead of specific performance, if she prefers (BGB § 281 I 1 combined with § 280 I and III).

In an award of damages, the principle is the natural restitution (*Naturalherstellung*), as explicitly defined by the BGB after the reform of 2002:

---

25 *See* Christian Deschamps, *La Réparation du Préjudice Économique pur en Droit Français*, 50 REVUE INTERNATIONALE DE DROIT COMPARÉ 367, 368 (1998) ("*le principe de réparation intégrale demeure un dogme du droit français.*")

26 YVES-MARIE LAITHIER, ÉTUDE COMPARATIVE DES SANCTIONS DE L'INEXÉCUTION DU CONTRAT, *op. cit. supra*, n°106, at 165.

Cf. BÉNÉDICTE FAUVARD-COSSON & DENIS MAZEAUD, EUROPEAN CONTRACT LAW 293 (Munich, Sellier, 2008) (the positive interest, "translated by Fuller as the expression 'expectation interest' ... correspond exactly to the expression, more familiar to French jurists, of *exécution par équivalent.*").

27 *Cf.* Code Civil Art. 1150 ("*Le débiteur n'est tenu que des dommages et intérêts qui ont été prévus ou qu'on a pu prévoir lors du contrat, lorsque ce n'est point par son dol que l'obligation n'est point exécutée.*").

28 *Cf.* Code Civil Art. 1151 ("*Dans le cas même où l'inexécution de la convention résulte du dol du débiteur, les dommages et intérêts ne doivent comprendre à l'égard de la perte éprouvée par le créancier et du gain dont il a été privé, que ce qui est une suite immédiate et directe de l'inexécution de la convention.*").

29 Which is dispensable in case the promisor decisively and definitively refuses to perform or under special circumstances (BGB § 281 II).

In case of defective performance of a sales contract, the buyer may freely choose between specific performance (*Nacherfüllung*), rescission (*Rücktritt*), reduction of the price (*Minderung*), or damages for breach (*Schadensersatz*) (BGB § 437) but must first fix a reasonable time limit for the promisor to repair the defect or to deliver a replacement (according to § 439 I, the buyer can choose between these two). From the point of view of the seller, this is her "right to cure." *See* Ulrich Schroeter, *Das Recht zur Zweiten Andienung im System des Schuldrechts*, 207 ARCHIV FÜR DIE ZIVILISTISCHE PRAXIS 28 (2007).

> § 249 I. A person who is liable in damages must restore the position that would exist if the circumstance obliging him to pay damages had not occurred. [30]

The promisor in breach must put the victim of breach in the position in which she would have been in case the seller had performed. Damages must hence cover the promisee's interest in the performance of the contract (*Erfüllungsinteresse*, or the *Äquivalenzinteresse* in bilateral contracts) and hence also protect the expectation interest.[31]

6.2.2 *Social Welfare Under Expectation Damages*

Expectation damages are justified, according to economic theories, firstly because of the optimal incentives they create for promisors to perform *without the need of renegotiation*. They allow the promisor to breach without the need to obtain consent from the promisee and hence without the need to renegotiate.[32] They induce efficient performance and, at the same time, encourage efficient breach without transaction costs, and this is one explanation for its superiority with respect to other remedies. As noted above, there is no justification, if renegotiation is costless, for why the law should enforce contracts through an award of expectation damages rather than through other legal remedies, as under the assumptions of the theory of efficient breach.

Secondly, expectation damages redistribute wealth between the parties, compensate the promisee for loss of expectancy, therefore undoing that individual harm endured by the promisee, and are well suited to crowd out retaliation triggered by loss of expectancy. Specific performance, however, also compensates the promisee for lost expectancy and clearly puts the promisee in the position she would have been in had the promisor performed. With respect to retaliation by the promisee, both remedies can achieve the same result.[33]

---

[30] Own transl. In original: "*Wer zum Schadensersatz verpflichtet ist, hat den Zustand herzustellen, der bestehen würde, wenn der zum Ersatz verpflichtende Umstand nicht eingetreten wäre.*"

[31] *See* BASIL MARKESINIS, HANNES UNBERATH & ANGUS JOHNSTON, THE GERMAN LAW OF CONTRACT: A COMPARATIVE TREATISE 442 (2nd. ed., Portland, Hart 2006) ("We can therefore conclude that the aim of the remedy of damages for breach of contract is to protect the expectation interest (*Erfüllungsinteresse*) by the means of a substitutionary relief in money."); MEDICUS & LORENZ, SCHULDRECHT I, *op. cit. supra*, at 165 Rn. 352.

[32] As observed in the experiment, and in the absence of renegotiation, promisors did not perform whenever doing so was socially efficient in the absence of expectation damages, independent of the presence of promissory commitment. They in effect provided gains of welfare that were not foregone in the absence of those incentives.

[33] This of course assumes that promisees are indifferent between receiving performance in kind or its monetary equivalent.

There is, however, another effect of expectation damages that can justify its superiority with respect to specific performance in certain types of contingencies, and that favors specific performance in other types of contingencies: *expectation damages limit the redistribution of wealth between the parties to the promisee's loss of expectancy*. This has positive and negative implications, depending on the type of contingency, for the parties' tendency to retaliate to perceived unfairness in the allocation implemented by expectation damages. In this respect, there is the need to distinguish between the two paradigmatic types of contingencies that may render breach individually unprofitable.

In the loss-avoidance paradigm, exemplified in the *Murmansk* case, the promisor will prefer to breach and pay expectation damages whenever she can save resources by doing so (instead of incurring costs to produce and deliver the good). If the costs of returning the car to Germany were $50,000, then the seller will not bear them but instead breach, pay damages, and make a maximal loss of only $10,000. The seller's losses are thereby always limited by expectation damages to the buyer's lost expectancy, independent of how high the absolute costs of performance are. In the final outcome, the seller loses at most $10,000, and the buyer always earns $10,000.

This amount the promisor in breach must pay to the promisee is *compensatory*. It is not the result of exploitation by the promisee, but rather just remuneration and indemnification. It is hence rather unlikely that the promisor in breach will tend to retaliate because she has to pay expectation damages that in fact compensate the promisee for the loss created by the promisor's own deliberate decision.

In the loss-avoidance paradigm, expectation damages are well apt to contribute to social welfare. Since they induce efficient performance and encourage efficient breaches, there is no social loss from inefficient trade. Since the remedy does not allow the promisee to exploit the promisor in hardship, the distribution implemented by expectation damages is fair, and losses from retaliation are expected to be minor, if existent.

In the overbidder paradigm, in contrast, whenever the seller receives a higher outside offer and it is profitable to breach, pay expectation damages, and retain all profits from breach, then the seller will do so. The promisee receives only expectation damages, and there is disagreement on who should earn the extra gains from breach. Parties never agreed that those extra profits would belong either to the promisor or to the promisee.

In the *outside offer case*, if the third party offers $50,000 for car, then the seller will breach, pay expectation damages of $10,000, and appropriate all the remaining $40,000. Parties never agreed that the seller was entitled to all the profits possible only through breach, and disagreement emerges. Expectation damages do not limit the profits the sellers can appropriate but rather allow her to retain all of them.

This outcome implemented by expectation damages can be easily perceived as unfair by the promisee. Individuals that understand that it is wrong to profit from one's own wrong and individuals that are simply inequality-averse will retaliate and thereby cause a loss of welfare. As observed in the experiment, this is in fact the case, as more than half of promisees retaliated against breaches to profit from an outside offer. Moreover, the higher the profits from breach, the higher the inequality

Table 6.1 Social welfare under expectation damages

	Increase in costs of production	Higher outside offer
Expectation damages	Promisor will breach and pay damages	Promisor will breach, pay damages, and appropriate all remaining profits
	• No inefficient trade • Fair result → no retaliation	• No inefficient trade • Unfair result → promisee retaliates
	Social welfare is maximal	Loss of welfare from retaliation

from breach, and the higher the expected losses from retaliation. Therefore, while expectation damages lead to the exhaustion of possible gains from trade, they will often lead to losses from retaliation by the promisee.

Table 6.1 resumes the welfare effects of expectation damages.

The possibility of renegotiation, under expectation damages, does not alter in any manner these results. It is a moot issue under expectation damages, for there is no reason for the parties to bargain around performance.[34] In case of an increase in costs of production, the buyer cannot extract any amount from the promisor, who will simply breach in order to avoid any higher loss. In case of a higher outside offer, the buyer cannot extract any share of the profits from breach from the seller, since the seller is free to breach as long as she pays expectation damages without the need to obtain the assent of the buyer and does not have incentives to allow the buyer to share in those gains.

6.2.3 *The Protection of the Disgorgement Interest in Common Law and Civil Law Systems*

Disgorgement damages put the *promisor* in breach in a position as good as the one she would have been in if she had performed. It is the mirror image of expectation damages, putting the promisor—and not the promise—in that position.[35] The promisor that earns higher profits through a substitutive transaction must disgorge the profits from breach to the promisee and thereby earns exactly what she would have earned if she had kept the promise. Accordingly, the disgorgement interest can be defined as the "promisee's interest in requiring the promisor to disgorge a gain that was made possible by her breach but did not consist of a benefit conferred on her by the promisee."[36]

In the USA, disgorgement damages are awarded in a very limited number of circumstances. The Restatement does not mention the protection of the disgorgement interest as one of the purposes of an award of damages for breach, and this

[34] *See* Steven Shavell, *Specific Performance versus Damages*, 84 Texas Law Review 831, 843 (2006).

[35] *Cf.* Robert Cooter & Thomas Ulen, Law & Economics 234 (3d ed. 2000).

[36] Eisenberg, *The Disgorgement Interest in Contract Law*, *op. cit. supra*, at 560–561.

omission was arguably deliberate. As noted by Melvin Eisenberg, there are two possible reasons for it. The drafters of the Restatement believed this was dictated either by positive law, or by normative considerations.[37]

Allan Farnsworth, one of its reporters, famously argued in a leading article that while courts do award disgorgement damages in a few categories of disputes, its extension beyond those cases would be undesirable.[38] The Restatement's omission was hence arguably motivated by normative considerations and not by positive law. The main reason advanced by Farnsworth against the expansion of the disgorgement principle was the tenuous causal relationship between the promisor's decision to breach, the realized profits and, especially, the absence of harm created for the promisee when the promisor pays expectation damages.[39]

Farnsworth's *normative* position can be criticized on similar grounds as the criticism developed upon Stephen Smith's assessment of the value and legitimacy of the legal enforcement of contracts and of the protection of the expectation interest.[40] While it is true that when the promisor compensates the promisee for the loss sustained, there is no individual harm, there is still the possible *social* harm that often follows breach of contract. When parties disagree, feel aggrieved, and tempted to retaliate, there is the social harm that retaliation creates for the interest of society and for the overall welfare of society.

From the point of view of *positive* law, promisees do have a cognizable claim on the profits from breach in certain circumstances. Outside the strict domains of contract law, and for example in the law of fiduciary obligations, the fiduciary must disgorge any gains achieved through the use of her position to the beneficiary even when the former does not suffer any loss through that act.[41] When the parties to a contract compete with each other, and one of them has given to the other an exclusive license to sell or produce, then courts will usually consider the gains from breach as evidence of the promisee's lost profits.[42] In these cases, profits from breach, and not lost expectancy, are used as the measure for damages.[43]

These cases, however, require more than breach of contract for the recovery of the profits from breach. They are not purely contractual claims. In case of an outside bidder, and in the absence of those other wrongs such as breach of a fiduciary duty

---

[37] *Id.* at 564.

[38] *See* E. Allan Farnsworth, *Your Loss or My Gain? The Dilemma of the Disgorgement Principle in Breach of Contract*, 94 YALE LAW JOURNAL 1339, 1342–43 (1985).

[39] *Cf.* Steve Thel & Peter Siegelmann, *You do Have to Keep your Promises: A Disgorgement Theory of Contract Remedies*, 52 WILLIAM AND MARY LAW REVIEW 1181 (2011).

[40] *See* the discussion *supra* in Chap. 2, Sect. 2.2.

[41] *See* United States, Snepp v. United States, 445 U.S. 507 (1980); Eisenberg, *The Disgorgement Interest in Contract Law*, *op. cit. supra*, at 563; Ernst Weinrib, *Punishment and Disgorgement as Contract Remedies*, 78 CHICAGO-KENT LAW REVIEW 55, 71 (2003).

[42] *See* John Dawson, *Restitution or Damages?*, 20 OHIO STATE LAW JOURNAL 175, 189 (1959).

[43] *See* Weinrib, *Punishment and Disgorgement as Contract Remedies*, *op. cit. supra*, at 71.

or infringement of a property interest, courts do not award disgorgement damages for disappointed promisees.[44]

English courts have been slowly departing from the strict traditional view that, when measuring damages, courts should be "concerned with the [claimant's] loss and not with the [defendant's] profit, the latter being wholly irrelevant."[45] The House of Lords recently recognized, in *Att-Gen v. Blake*, that "[i]n a suitable case damages for breach of contract may be measured by the benefit gained by the wrongdoer from breach. The defendant must make a reasonable payment in respect of the benefit he has gained."[46]

There are two bases for recovery of profits from breach. The promisee may recover *hypothetical bargain damages* and receive an award of partial disgorgement, discussed in Sect. 6.4.4. In contrast, she may recover all profits and receive an award of *total disgorgement* in exceptional circumstances, discussed herein.

Until *Att-Gen v. Blake* in 2000, cases where courts would deliver an award of disgorgement damages were similar to those in the USA, mainly where the disappointed promisee could enforce a fiduciary obligation or had an interest in property used by the promisor without her permission.[47] In other words, the promisor had to breach the contract and concomitantly (i) infringe a property right or (ii) commit a breach of confidence.[48]

In *Blake*, the defendant entered the British secret service (the MI6) and signed the Official Secrets Act of 1911 requiring him not to disclose any information about the MI6 under his contract. He was, however, a double agent working for the Soviet Union, was caught and imprisoned in England, but later escaped to the Soviet Union. There he wrote a book about the secret service with the insider's information he had, and the Crown brought an action for the profits from the sales of the book.

For an award of disgorgement damages, those strict requirements were partially relaxed in *Blake*. There is still the need to demonstrate the presence of "exceptional circumstances" that justify disgorgement. The House of Lords did not provide a definitive definition of "exceptional circumstances," but the judges provided some relevant factors for that. Chitty mentions: firstly, the moral character of breach, in being "deliberate and cynical"; secondly, whether the claimant had an interest in preventing the breach to earn profits, as the Crown had in protecting the secret service's information; thirdly, an *analogy* with fiduciary obligations, as Blake's obligation not to disclose information was "*akin* to a fiduciary obligation" (since by the time of releasing the book, the information was already public knowledge).[49]

German law recognizes that disappointed promisees may have a claim for disgorgement damages in form of the claim on the surrogate (*Anspruch auf das*

---

[44] *See* FARNSWORTH ON CONTRACTS 824.

[45] *Sotiros Shipping Inc v Samiet Solhot (The Solhot)*, 1 Lloyd's Rep. 605 (CA) (1983), at 608.

[46] *Attorney General v Blake*, UKHL 45 (2000), 1 A.C. 268 (2001), at 283–284.

[47] *Cf.* Joseph Chitty & Hugh Beale, CHITTY ON CONTRACTS 26-045 (31st ed. London, Sweet & Maxwell 2013) [hereinafter CHITTY ON CONTRACTS].

[48] *Cf.* CHITTY ON CONTRACTS, 26-051.

[49] *Cf.* CHITTY ON CONTRACTS, 26-054.

Surrogat, or the claim on the *stellvertretendes commodum*).[50] The BGB allows the promisee to recover any surrogate that the promisor received from a third party when the promised performance becomes either "truly or insuperably" or "untruly or superably" impossible:

> § 285 I. If the debtor, as a result of the circumstance by reason of which he, under § 275 I to III, has no duty to perform, obtains reimbursement or a claim to reimbursement for the object owed, the creditor may demand return of what has been received in reimbursement or an assignment of the claim to reimbursement.[51]

A promisor who is relieved of his obligation to perform because of the impossibility of the performance has to transfer to the promisee whatever she has acquired as a substitute for the object he was obliged to deliver. In case performance is insuperably impossible (BGB § 275 I), factually impossible (BGB § 275 II), or personally unreasonable (BGB § 275 III), then the promisor's primary duty to perform is either excluded (in case of insuperably impossibility) or the promisor can refuse to perform (in the latter two options). In all these cases, the disappointed promisee can require that the promisor in breach disgorge all profits achieved through breach.

The leading casebook example covers the case of the accepted higher outside offer (the *Doppelverkaufs*).[52] When the seller sells the same object that she had promised to the first buyer to another buyer for a higher price, *and transfers it to the second one*, then the delivery of that same object to the first buyer becomes impossible, unless the second buyer is willing to sell it.

The promisee has then a claim to recover the profits from breach achieved by the promisor, according to the prevailing view in the literature, because § 285 I encompasses the case of the "contractual surrogate" or the *commodum ex negotiatione cum re*. The plain wording of § 285 I, however, would not allow for that claim. The profits achieved by the promisor are not achieved by the delivery of the good to the first buyer, but only by the contract with the second buyer. A literal interpretation of the norm would hence bar a claim for disgorgement of those profits.[53] The prevailing opinion in the literature, however, interprets the norm as comprising that case.[54]

---

[50] In Latin, *commodum* means "benefit."

[51] Own transl. In original: "*Erlangt der Schuldner infolge des Umstands, auf Grund dessen er die Leistung nach § 275 Abs. 1 bis 3 nicht zu erbringen braucht, für den geschuldeten Gegenstand einen Ersatz oder einen Ersatzanspruch, so kann der Gläubiger Herausgabe des als Ersatz Empfangenen oder Abtretung des Ersatzanspruchs verlangen.*"

[52] *See* MEDICUS & LORENZ, SCHULDRECHT I, *op. cit. supra*, at 208 Rn. 432.

[53] *Id.* ("*Den Verkaufserlös hat er [der Verkäufer] aber nicht aufgrund dieser Übereinigung [an den ersten Käufer] sondern allein aufgrund des Kaufvertrages mit K2 [der zweite Käufer] erzielt. Nimmt man § 285 beim Wort, hätte der K1 [der erste Käufer] keinen Anspruch auf Herausgabe dieses Erlöses.*").

[54] *See* MEDICUS & LORENZ, SCHULDRECHT I, *op. cit. supra*, at 208 Rn. 432 ("*Die h.M. läßt aber auch einen bloß wirtschaftlichen Zusammenhang genügen ... so daß auch der Erlös, den der Schuldner aus einem Rechtsgeschäft mit der Sache erzielt, von § 285 erfaßt wird.*"); BASIL MARKESINIS, HANNES UNBERATH & ANGUS JOHNSTON, THE GERMAN LAW OF CONTRACT: A COMPARATIVE TREATISE 443 (2nd. ed., Portland, Hart 2006) ("If performance is impossible due to a transaction with a third party the price paid by that third party to the promisor may then be claimed by the promisee. (The issue is controvertial, *see Münchner Kommentar* § 288 Rn. 19).").

The claim from § 285 I is a way to balance unjustly distributed benefits.[55] This was the goal of the norm according to German courts, and later accepted by the BGH.[56] Although it could be interpreted as punishment for the seller's deliberate sale of a good that was already promised to the first buyer, rendering performance impossible and restricting the promisee's possible remedies only to damages for breach, this is not, arguably, the underlying rationale of the norm. Instead, the aim of the norm is often understood be the restoration of fairness between the parties.[57]

6.2.4 Social Welfare Under Disgorgement Damages in the Absence of Renegotiation

Disgorgement damages can deter, in theory and in idealized conditions, and in the absence of renegotiation, efficient breaches of contract. In putting the *promisor* in the position in which she would have been in case of performance, perfect disgorgement makes the promisor *indifferent* between performance and breach.[58] It is then uncertain whether the promisor will prefer to perform, realize the gains from breach, and subsequently transfer them to the promisee, or breach and simply forego them.

There are good reasons to assume that promisors will prefer to breach, sell to the outside bidder and realize those further gains. In doing so, the promisor earns the very same amount she would earn in case of performance, and concomitantly provides a benefit to another person at no cost for herself. If the promisor cares, even if minimally, for the well-being of other persons, then she will prefer to breach efficiently. In this case, disgorgement does not cause a loss of welfare from inefficient trade.

If the promisor so breaches efficiently, then the promisee is entitled, under a disgorgement rule, to all those gains if disgorgement damages apply. The promisor may attempt to convince the promisee to allow her to share in some of those gains from breach, so that both parties profit from the extra surplus from the substitutive transaction, but the promisee has the right to all those gains. She is not obliged to deliver any share to the promisee, and since she is entitled, by law, to those profits, she will not be willing to give any sizeable share of them, after the promisor breached, unless for altruistic reasons.

---

[55] *See* FELIX HARTMANN, DER ANSPRUCH AUF DAS STELLVERTRETENDEN COMMODUM 7.

[56] *Id.*

[57] *Id.* Other legal provisions with that same goal are present, for example, in the German Copyright Law. *See* Christoph Engel & Michael Kurschilgen, *Fairness Ex Ante and Ex Post: Experimentally Testing Ex Post Judicial Intervention into Blockbuster Deals*, 8 JOURNAL OF EMPIRICAL LEGAL STUDIES 682 (2011).

[58] ROBERT COOTER & THOMAS ULEN, LAW & ECONOMICS 234 (3d ed. 2000) ("When disgorgement is perfect, the injurer is indifferent between doing right, on the one hand, or doing wrong and paying disgorgement damages, on the other hand.").

Disgorgement does not undo, ex post, unfairness and inequality in the distribution of the profits from breach, *but only inverts its direction.* In receiving all the gains from the substitute transaction, the promisee is better off than the promisor. This may crowd out retaliation by the promisee, for she then earns those profits, but it leaves the promisor in breach in a worse position than the promisee after the payment of such damages.

It is then that the promisor, obliged to disgorge by a court's order all the profits from the substitute transaction, may perceive the implemented allocation as unfair. Parties never agreed that neither the promisor nor the promisee is entitled to those gains, and the contract is silent about that issue. The promisor may feel entitled to a fair share of those, and will feel aggrieved from the implemented unequal distribution of those, and thereby tempted to retaliate.

This is, however, restricted to the overbidder paradigm, for disgorgement damages coincide with expectation damages in any case where the promisor breaches to avoid losses. In the latter, there are no profits from breach, and the amount to be paid, under disgorgement damages, is limited to the promisee's loss of expectancy.

In the opposite case where the promisor that is indifferent between performance and breach decides to perform inefficiently, disregarding the welfare of the other, then she does not realize all possible gains from trade in that type of contingency. The promisee earns the expected and promised gains, and nothing more, and there is a loss of gains from trade. The outcome is, however, one where each party earns exactly what they bargained for, and it is likely to be perceived as fair.[59]

In sum, if the promisor that is indifferent between performance and breach decides to breach efficiently and must then deliver all gains from breach to the promisee, then she realizes all gains from trade but is likely to retaliate because of the perceived unfairness of the result. If she decides to perform inefficiently, then the extra gains from the substitutive transaction are foregone, and the loss of welfare is restricted to the loss of gains from trade. Table 6.2 resumes the welfare effects of disgorgement damages.

Table 6.2 Social welfare under disgorgement damages in the absence of renegotiation

	Increase in costs of production	Higher outside offer
Disgorgement damages without renegotiation	Promisor will breach and pay damages	Promisor will perform inefficiently or breach efficiently, pay damages and disgorge all profits
	• No inefficient trade • Fair result → No retaliation	• Inefficient trade or • Unfair result → promisor retaliates
	Social welfare is maximal	Loss of welfare either from inefficient trade or retaliation

[59] The promisee, in this case, may be tempted to retaliate, for the seller could have breached and with that action provided the promisee a higher gain for no cost.

6.2.5 Social Welfare Under Disgorgement Damages in the Presence of Renegotiation

Disgorgement damages will deter socially inefficient breaches only if parties cannot renegotiate. In contrast to expectation damages, renegotiation is not a moot issue under a disgorgement rule. Such a rule will encourage the promisor to negotiate with the promisee for a share of the profits from breach in order to realize expectation damages, and thereby to deliver higher gains to the promisee. It is plainly possible to secure efficiency with disgorgement damages just as expectation damages do if parties can renegotiate.[60]

The promisor that receives a higher outside offer will contact the promisee, explain the situation, and bargain for a share of the profits from breach. It is important to note that although the promisee is entitled to all those profits, they are realized only if the promisor breaches, and their realization thus depends on the decision of the promisor. If the promisor performs as promised and delivers the good or service to the promisee, then she commits no wrong and realizes only the originally foreseen and contracted gains. The promisee, in that case, also does not realize any gains beyond those that were originally foreseen and contracted.

The promisee that has an interest in breach will rationally offer a share of those profits for the promisor in order to induce the latter to breach. According to rational choice theory, any share the promisee offers will suffice. The promisor will have incentives to breach efficiently, earning that strictly positive share, and the promisee will appropriate all remaining non-contracted profits.

Both parties have bargaining power in this renegotiation. The gains are only realized if the promisor breaches, but the promisor is only entitled to any share of the gains if the promisee consents. Parties will agree on some distribution of them, and in the absence of any type of asymmetry of information, then they will probably agree on an equal split.

The possible problem with renegotiation under disgorgement damages is that the promisee is entitled *by law* to *all* the profits from breach. The promisee may, because of the legal entitlement, also feel *personally* entitled to all of them, or to a major share and may be unwilling to offer a share that the promisor perceives as minimally fair and acceptable. Moreover, strictly rational promisees must anticipate that rational promisors will accept any minute share in order to breach, and may, in effect, offer no more than such a minor share. If the promisee makes a take-it-or-leave-it offer on that basis, then there is the serious risk that the promisor will punish the promisee.

The situation where parties can bargain around efficient breach in the overbidder paradigm, under disgorgement damages, thus resembles the one in the ultimatum game. The promisee is not endowed with those gains, as in the ultimatum game, for she must induce the promisor to breach in order to receive them. The rationale, however, is similar: the promisee that believes that the promisor is strictly rational must anticipate that any share will do; the promisor that derives disutility from offers

---

[60] *Cf*. Richard Brooks, *The Efficient Performance Hypothesis*, 116 YALE LAW JOURNAL 568 (2006).

perceived as unfair will reject unfair offers and will punish the promise in one of two different manners.

She may punish the promisee that behaves unfairly by *performing inefficiently*. In this case, possible gains from trade are foregone, and social welfare is impaired. In the overbidder paradigm, performing the contract as promised is a form of *retaliation* and *costly punishment* against the promisee that offers unfair amounts to the promisor.[61] The promisor foregoes minor gains (thereby incurring, in economic terms, minor costs) in order to impose a higher loss upon the promisee that treats her unfairly. There is, as detailed in the review of the evidence from hundreds of ultimatum bargaining experiments, a consistent and pronounced tendency of individuals to do so.[62] In this case, it is the promisor who retaliates and who does so by performing, inefficiently. The loss of welfare is therefore a loss arising from inefficient trade *that is a form of retaliation and punishment of perceived unfair offers* in the renegotiation.

The promisor that feels aggrieved from an unfair offer may retaliate in a second manner. She may breach efficiently, earn a minute share of the profits, and deliver most of them to the promisee, thereby being free from legal liability because of the renegotiated agreement. In this case, there is no loss of welfare from inefficient trade but there may be losses from socially costly retaliation in other forms different from performing inefficiently. She may engage, after breaching efficiently, in any of those acts described before, for example, by refusing to transact again in the future with the promisee, by harming the promisee's reputation in the market, etc.[63]

In sum, if the renegotiation is fair, then disgorgement damages, in the presence of renegotiation, will induce efficient breaches and will not lead to retaliation. If the renegotiation breaks down because of perceived unfairness, then the promisor may punish the promisee by performing inefficiently, or by breaching efficiently but later on retaliating against the promisor. Table 6.3 resumes the welfare effects of disgorgement damages under renegotiation.

Table 6.3 Social welfare under disgorgement damages in the presence of renegotiation

	Increase in costs of production	Higher outside offer
Disgorgement damages with renegotiation	Promisor will breach and pay damages	Promisor will breach, pay damages and profits from breach are split (if renegotiation is fair)
	• No inefficient trade • Fair result → No retaliation	• No inefficient trade • Fair result → No retaliation
	Social welfare is maximal	Social welfare is maximal (if renegotiation is fair)

[61] Compare with the definition of retaliation in Chap. 3, Sect. 3.6 *supra*.

[62] *See* the discussion *supra* in Chap. 4, Sect. 4.2.

[63] *See* the discussion *supra* in Chap. 3, Sect. 3.6.

6.3 Specific Performance

Specific performance, or injunctive relief, consists in an order by a court that the promisor must specifically perform the contracted obligation, or face jail, fines, or contempt. Clearly, only an order from a court may not be enough to lead the promisor to perform if no sanction is attached to it. Different legal systems adopt different instruments to implement specific performance.

Among the most commonly used ones, courts will request that the bailiff or sheriff directly seize the thing that the promisor refuses to deliver (in the enforcement of obligations to give) or will impose monetary sanctions on the promisor until she performs (in obligations to do). They have different consequences on the outcome of the parties' renegotiation, and thus also on the fairness of the result, and are reviewed in the next section.

When the promisee has a claim for specific performance, then the promisor is not free to breach whenever breach is individually profitable, as long as she compensates the promisee, for she must obtain the consent of promisee to do so. The promisor must bargain around performance and pay the amount required by the promisee and is only then free to breach without legal consequences.

Specific performance, just as expectation damages, also put the promisee in the position in which she would have been had the promisor performed.[64] In ordering that the promisor perform the contract as promised, courts attempt to implement the same effect as if the contract had been performed.[65] Specific performance thereby undoes loss of expectancy, and crowds out retaliation caused by that type of loss. It will, however, have other consequences and will lead to unfair outcomes in some types of contingencies. The resulting allocation of gains and losses depends crucially on whether parties can renegotiate the contract and on the moment they can do so.

6.3.1 Specific Performance in Common and Civil Law Systems

In common law systems, specific performance may be granted where expectation damages would be inadequate.[66] Courts in equity developed specific relief in order to supply deficiencies of the common law, but the remedy in equity was always "extraordinary" and hence available only when damages did not pass the adequacy test.[67] At this day, and according to the Restatement, substitutive relief is inadequate

---

[64] *See* Farnsworth, *Legal Remedies for Breach of Contract*, *op. cit. supra*, at 1151.

[65] This may require, for example, that the promisor, apart from performing late, also pays damages for the losses incurred by the promisee for not having received performance on time.

[66] RESTATEMENT (SECOND) OF CONTRACTS § 359 (1).

[67] *See* FARNSWORTH ON CONTRACTS 739–743.

when (i) damages cannot be proven with reasonable certainty, (ii) substitute performance cannot be obtained in the market, or (iii) damages cannot be collected from the party in breach.[68]

The critical factor for determining whether an award of damages is adequate is whether the promisee can buy a substitute for the promised performance in the market.[69] If this is possible, then an award of damages is generally considered to be adequate to compensate the promisee. However, the promisee often cannot obtain a substitutive performance in the market, as when the promised good is unique, as works of art or tracts of land are.[70] Equally unique are patents or copyrights, as well as shares of stocks that cannot be bought in the open market.

If damages are inadequate, then the promisee *may* obtain an injunction. In this case, if the promise is to deliver an existing good and to convey property, then the court will order that the promisor delivers the good to the promisee, and order the bailiff to seize it if she does not comply. If the promised thing is a tract of land, the bailiff will evict the promisor from the land and allow the promisee to enter in its possession.

Courts will not order a performance that becomes impossible, impractical, or unlawful. They will also not award those injunctions if performance is personal in nature, as is often the case in service contracts. They will not, for example, order a singer to specifically perform the contract.[71] The promisor that has to *do* something for the promisee cannot be compelled to take the due act.

However, the promisor that has to *refrain from doing something* is subject to an injunction ordering her not to do it. This is the case when, similarly to sales of unique or particular goods, the contracted person possesses special skills or special knowledge of the promisee's business. This was the case in Lumley v. Wagner, where Johana Wagner, niece of Richard Wagner, entered into a contract to sing exclusively in Lumley's theater for three months, but later reneged on the deal by accepting a better offer from a third party. The chancellor mentioned how "it is true that I have

---

68 RESTATEMENT (SECOND) OF CONTRACTS § 360 ("In determining whether the remedy in damages would be adequate, the following circumstances are significant: (a) the difficulty of proving damages with reasonable certainty, (b) the difficulty of procuring a suitable substitute performance by means of money awarded as damages, and (c) the likelihood that an award of damages could not be collected.").

69 *See* FARNSWORTH ON CONTRACTS 748.

70 RESTATEMENT (SECOND) OF CONTRACTS § 360 cmt. b (listing examples of unique performances, such as "Typical examples include heirlooms, family treasures and works of art that induce a strong sentimental attachment. Examples may also be found in contracts of a more commercial character.") and cmt. e ("A specific tract of land has long been regarded as unique and impossible of duplication by the use of any amount of money. Furthermore, the value of land is to some extent speculative. Damages have therefore been regarded as inadequate to enforce a duty to transfer an interest in land.").

71 RESTATEMENT (SECOND) OF CONTRACTS § 367 (1); FARNSWORTH ON CONTRACTS 781 § 12.7 ("A court will not grant specific performance of a contract to provide a service that is personal in nature.").

not the means of compelling her to sing, but she has no cause of complaint if I compel her to abstain from the commission of an act which she has bound herself to do."[72]

Under French law, *obligations to give*, which include contracts to convey property, are generally enforced by specific performance, unless in exceptional cases such as when delivery is impossible. The reason for that, peculiar to French law, lies in the fact that sales contracts already transfer the property of the good. Therefore, the unperformed contractual obligation to give boils down to an obligation to deliver (*obligation de livrer*) and is specifically enforceable whenever the seller refuses to do it.

As in common law systems, if the good is movable, it is apprehended by a seizure and is handed to its rightful owner.[73] If the promised thing is immovable, restitution of possession of the property to the owner is obtained by the eviction and expulsion of the occupier.

In contrast, *obligations to do*, which have as object a work or service, i.e., an act or series of acts, were traditionally understood not to permit specific performance.[74] The fundamental principle is (or, perhaps, "was") that *nemo præcise cogi potest ad factum*, meaning that nobody can be coerced to act. This was so since ancient Roman law, under the *ius commune*.[75]

The reasons underlying the principle are given, from a practical point of view, by the fact that doing so would lead the promisor to usually deliver a performance of poor quality; from a legal point of view, it would require the use of violent means that are contrary to individual liberties.[76] Because of that, the *Code Civil* stipulates that "every obligation to do is resolved by an award of damages" (Art. 1142).

The promisee can, in case of breach of an obligation to do, obtain equivalent performance (*dommages-intérêst*). Alternatively, she can procure substitutive performance at the expense of the promisor, who must then compensate the promisee for the costs of substitutive performance (*Code Civil*, Art. 1144).

Specific performance of obligations to do (and not to do) is further achieved, under French law, through the institute of the *astreinte*. It consists of a penalty imposed by the court on the promisor in breach until she performs, and that is, moreover, increasing over time, thereby making it completely irrational for the promisor not to

---

[72] *Lumley v. Wagner*, 42 Eng. Rep. 687, 693 (Chap. 1852). In most cases, the purpose of the injunction is to prevent the promisor from working for a competitor of the original promisee. *Cf. Shubert Theatrical Co. v. Rath*, 271 F. 827 (2d. Cir. 1921) (where the manager of a theater was granted an injunction against acrobats that later contracted with a rival manager in a rival theater). This requirement is not however absolute. *Cf. Mission Indep. School Dist. v. Diserens*, 188 S.W. 2d 568 (Tex. 1945) (declining to restrict injunctive relief to cases where parties were competitors).

[73] In effect, in France, the disappointed promisee is the owner of the good, for the contract already translated its property.

[74] *See* 2 MARCEL PLANIOL, TRAITÉ ÉLÉMENTAIRE DE DROIT CIVIL 61 (4th ed., Paris, Libraire Générale de Droit & Jurisprudence, 1907).

[75] *See* ZIMMERMANN, THE LAW OF OBLIGATIONS: ROMAN FOUNDATIONS OF THE CIVILIAN TRADITION, *op. cit. supra*, at 810–811.

[76] *See* 2 MARCEL PLANIOL, TRAITÉ ÉLÉMENTAIRE DE DROIT CIVIL, *op. cit. supra*, at 62.

perform, independent of how costly it is, in the realized contingency, to do so. It is, as exposed by Josserand, a very effective system to force the promisor to perform:

> "The astreinte ... tends to overcome the resistance of the debtor of an obligation to do, (and) to exert pressure on the will: because of the escalation that characterizes it, this system is of an efficiency, and of a security foolproof; there is no wealth that is able to withstand such continuous pressure constantly accentuated; the patient's capitulation is fatal; it was because of his resistance, and without exercising violence on his own person: it is his goods that are taken; it is his property, his material resources that are intended."[77]

French courts can impose *astreintes* even without request by the plaintiff.[78] *Astreintes* do not depend on the amount of damages that promisor may have to pay, since they have the aim to compel the promisor to perform, and not to compensate the promisee.[79] Their implications are discussed in Sect. 6.4.2.

Under German law, performance in species is the general remedy for breach of contract, as long as performance is possible.[80] The types of injunctions are not very different from the ones described above, except for the specific enforcement of obligations to do, which is, in fact, different from French law.

In case the promised performance is the delivery of a good, if the promisee insists on performance as promised, requiring *Nacherfüllung*, and the promisor refuses to perform, then the court can request the bailiff or the marshal to (i) take away the moveable good from the promisor by force and give it to the promisee (ZPO § 883 I), or (ii) eject the promisor from the possession of land or ship and put the promisee in its possession (ZPO § 885 I). In case the promised performance involves other actions, then the promisee can obtain an authorization from the court to undertake the actions necessary for performance at the expense of the promisor (ZPO § 887 I). For example, in the *Murmansk* case, the buyer can herself contract for the car to be brought back to Germany and these costs must be borne by the promisor in breach.

---

[77] 2 LOUIS JOSSERAND, COURS DE DROIT CIVIL POSITIF FRANÇAIS n° 594 (1932–1933) ("*L'astreinte est une condamnation pécuniaire qui est prononcée à raison de 'tant' par jour, par semaine, par mois ou par année de retard, et qui tend à vaincre la résistance du débiteur d'une obligation de faire, à exercer une pression sur la volonté: grâce à la progressivité qui le caractérise, ce système est d'une efficience, d'une sûreté à toute épreuve; il n'est pas de fortune qui soit à même de résister à une pression continue et sans cesse accentuée; la capitulation du patient est fatale; on a raison de sa résistance, et cela sans avoir exercé de violence sur sa personne même: c'est à ses biens que l'on s'en prend; c'est sa fortune, ses ressources matérielles que l'on vise.*").

See also MARCEL PLANIOL, TRAITÉ ÉLÉMENTAIRE DE DROIT CIVIL, *op. cit. supra*, at 74 ("*On appelle 'astreinte' une condamnation pécuniaire (...) destinée à obtenir du débiteur l'exécution d'une obligation de faire par la menace d'une peine considérable, susceptible de grossir indéfiniment. Ce qui caractérise l'astreinte est donc l'exagération du chiffre de l'indemnité.*").

[78] *See* Law n. 91-650 of 9 July 1991 (*Loi portant réforme des procédures civiles d'exécution*), *Art 33* ("*Tout juge peut, même d'office, ordonner une astreinte pour assurer l'exécution de sa décision.*"), modified by Law n. 92-644 of 13 July 1992, Art. 3 (JORF 14 July 1992).

[79] *See* Law n. 91-650 of 9 July 1991, Art 34 ("*L'astreinte est indépendante des dommages-intérêts.*") *Astreintes* have some compensatory nature. They provide to the promisee a certain compensation for the recalcitrant promisor's obstruction of the enforcement of the contract.

[80] *See* HANNES UNBERATH, DIE VERTRAGSVERLETZUNG 276 (Tübingen, Mohr Siebeck, 2007) ("*Voraussetzung dafür, den Primäranspruch ungeschmälert bestehen zu lassen, ist, daß der Schuldner genau die Leistung versprochen hat, die noch möglich ist.*").

German law distinguishes between the case where performance can be performed by a third party (*vertretbare Handlung*) and when it is unavailable (ZPO § 887 I). When performance cannot be undertaken by a third party (*unvertretbare Handlung*) and depends on the will of the promisor, then the promisee can obtain from the court the imposition of a fine similar to the *astreinte* (*Zwangsgeld*) upon the promisor in case she refuses to perform (ZPO § 888 I 1).

It has, however, fundamental differences. The fine is not increasing over time and cannot be higher than €25,000 (ZPO § 888 I 2). The law explicitly foresees that "a threat of means of coercion does not take place" (ZPO § 888 II). It is also not applicable in case of service contracts (ZPO § 888 III). Moreover, the amount is not directed to the disappointed promisee, but rather to the state, and hence *Zwangsgeld* has absolutely no compensatory character, being solely an instrument of execution.

6.3.2 *Limits of a Claim to Specific Performance*

As noted above, courts will not award an injunction when performance becomes impossible or impractical, but rather only *rescind* the contract, and put parties in the position they were before the contract was made. These doctrines (at common law) or the legal rules that foresee these limitations (in civil law systems) have an important welfare effect in limiting the amount that the promisor can extract from the promisee or that she can be forced to perform specifically, depending on the will of the promisee. They are thus briefly reviewed in this chapter, before the disadvantages of specific performance, which include the promisee's possibility to exploit the promisor that faces unforeseen hardship to perform, are discussed.

Under German law, the promisor is released from the primary duty to perform mainly in four different cases. These can be divided in the case of insuperable (or "true") impossibility (BGB § 275 I), and in the case of superable (or "untrue") impossibility. The latter comprises the cases of "factual or practical" impossibility (BGB § 275 II), personal unreasonableness (BGB § 275 III), and the case of economical impossibility.

Performance is truly impossible because of physical reasons, as when the promised object is destroyed (e.g., the Ming vase to be delivered next week is struck by a lightning bolt), or by legal reasons, as when supervening law makes performance illegal (e.g., the sale of a chemical compound is later on defined by law as a prohibited drug).[81] Most importantly, perhaps, is the fact that the sale (and delivery) of the promised good to another buyer in good-faith renders performance of the first contract impossible, since the second buyer becomes the proprietor of the good. The consequence is the duty to perform is excluded *ipso jure* and independent of fault by the promisor. The promisee is then only entitled to a claim of damages for breach *or* to a claim at the surrogate, as explained above.

---

[81] *See* MEDICUS & LORENZ, SCHULDRECHT I, *op. cit. supra*, at 196–199, Rn. 413–419.

Performance is only practically impossible when the costs of the promisor to perform stands in gross disproportion to the benefits of the promisee. "Roughly and imprecisely formulated: performance must cost *plainly* more for the promisor than its benefits to the promisee."[82] It therefore does not encompass any case of inefficient performance: it must be substantially inefficient to perform. The promisor is not allowed to refuse to perform in kind simply because the costs of performance exceed the expectation interest of the promisee.[83] The classical case is the case of the promised ring that falls into the bottom of the sea.[84] It is possible to recover the ring with, for example, specialized divers, but this is practically impossible. It is not enough that the costs of performance outweigh the benefits for the promisee, as required by the theory of efficient breach: the latter must substantially outweigh the former.[85]

Performance is economically impossible when an unforeseen risk, which was not allocated to any of the parties to the contract, materializes and makes performance as promised for one of the parties unreasonable.[86] The promisor is, in this case, *not* released from the duty to perform, but is only entitled to claim the revision of the contract (*Vertragsanpassung*) (BGB § 313 I). Only if this is impossible or unreasonable can the promisor withdraw from the contract and rescind it (BGB § 313 III 1).

These different limits to a claim of specific performance work to prevent the promisee, who is, in principle, entitled to require that the promisor perform specifically under very high and unreasonable costs, from *exploiting* the promisor in the renegotiation process in getting more than what she had contracted for. However, given their strictness and restricted scope of application, they only impede such exploitation in extreme or unusual cases. Whenever the promisor's costs of performance are larger than the promisee's benefits from performance, it is not automatically the case that the promisor is released because of impossibility, in any of its forms, or because the promisor is entitled to the restoration of the contractual parity.

---

[82] MEDICUS & LORENZ, SCHULDRECHT I, *op. cit. supra*, at 201, Rn. 424.

[83] *Cf*, e.g., Hector MacQueen, Barbara Dauner-Lieb & Peter Tettinger, *Specific Performance and the Right to Cure*, in THE COMMON EUROPEAN SALES LAW IN CONTEXT: INTERACTIONS WITH ENGLISH AND GERMAN LAW 627 (Gerhard Dannemann & Stefan Vogehauer eds., Oxford, Oxford University, 2013).

[84] According to Canaris, the example was first introduced by Heck, in GRUNDRIß DES SCHULDRECHTS §28, at 5 (1929). *See* Canaris, *Die Reform des Rechts der Leistungsstörungen*, *op. cit. supra*, footnote 25.

[85] *Cf.* Canaris, *Die Reform des Rechts der Leistungsstörungen*, *op. cit. supra*, at 457.

[86] *See* MEDICUS & LORENZ, SCHULDRECHT I, *op. cit. supra*, at 256 Rn. 529 *et. seq.*

6.3.3 Social Welfare Under Specific Performance in the Absence of Renegotiation

Specific performance, from the point of view of optimal incentives to perform, has, in the absence of renegotiation, the well-known disadvantage of inducing performance in contingencies where performance is socially inefficient. It is, however, important to distinguish between absences of communication between the parties at the moment the promisor decides to perform or breach, and absence of communication afterward, when the promisee seeks to enforce her rights. The latter is very rarely (if ever) present, and this distinction is often not fully considered in the existing discussion of the disadvantages of specific performance vis-à-vis damages for breach.

In effect, promisors do not always have the possibility to renegotiate with the promisee, as the promisor might need to make a decision on the spot without the possibility of contacting the promisee.[87] Often, the promisor does not have the information necessary to contact the promisee, and her business might involve deliveries to several hundred different clients, and she may not collect their telephone numbers when closing each and every contract.[88] In these cases, parties cannot renegotiate the contract *at the time the promisor must decide to perform or breach.*

However, ex post, parties can most often renegotiate. When the promisee sues the promisor, parties become embroiled in a legal process, so they meet and can hence always renegotiate. It is mainly only in cases where performance is of value for the promisee by a certain date that parties cannot renegotiate and bargain around performance or breach. The law, in fact, actively encourages parties to settle their disputes privately, and some jurisdictions even mandate that parties attempt to conciliate before being able to proceed with the legal suit, in a prior procedural phase.

Therefore, even when the promisor cannot contact the promisee at the time of deciding to perform or breach efficiently, the promisor knows that she can always renegotiate for a release of the obligation to perform afterward. She will take into consideration, when deciding to perform or breach without the possibility of contacting the promisee at that moment that the promisee will have incentives to renegotiate before asking for an injunction.

Without contact to the promisee at the first moment, the promisor must *anticipate* what the promisee will do after breach. As discussed above, the promisee can, in general, choose between (i) renegotiating with the promisor, (ii) requesting that the promisor perform specifically, or (iii) claiming damages for breach.

The promisor knows that the promisee is *indifferent* between (ii) receiving performance in kind and (iii) its monetary equivalent, and has no rational reason to specifically enforce the contract if she can earn more by (i) bargaining for an amount higher

[87] *See* Steven Shavell, *Specific Performance Versus Damages for Breach of Contract: An Economic Analysis*, 84 TEXAS LAW REVIEW 831, 838 (2006).

[88] For example, a business that delivers custom-made birthday or wedding cakes may not collect the customer's contacts whenever the customer must come to pick up the cake at the agreed date. On the other hand, when the cake must be delivered to the customer's address, then the business will probably have the customer's telephone.

than expectation damages. Whenever breach is efficient, the promisor knows she will save resources by breaching and renegotiating afterward, and that the promisee also has in interest in doing so. There will be, in the absence of problems of information, no inefficient performance.[89]

Consider, for example, the Murmansk case. The buyer values the car at $10,000, and the seller knows that the buyer will prefer an amount higher than $10,000 instead of the car. When the costs of performance are $25,000, then the seller has no reason to perform inefficiently and to incur those costs, since she knows that she will be able to renegotiate afterward and that there is room for a mutually profitable agreement even if only when the promisee sues the promisor.

The result of such renegotiation will lie between the value of the promisee's lost expectancy and what the seller can save by paying that amount plus something more. The promisee thereby earns more than she bargained for and earns more than what she would earn through performance of the contract just because the promisor is, in the realized contingency, in a moment of hardship. The promisor will breach efficiently, but will later be exploited, and will then tend to retaliate to such exploitation.

The possibility of being exploited under specific performance is, however, restricted to the loss-avoidance paradigm. If the seller sells the promised good to another buyer in good faith, performance of the first contract becomes, as explained above, impossible. The buyer cannot then specifically enforce the contract because the seller cannot deliver the promised good.

In this case, the buyer only has a claim of damages for breach. The seller that breached must compensate the promisee for her lost expectancy, since she cannot deliver the good that is with a third party to the first buyer, and can retain for herself all the gains from breach, and the buyer does not receive any share of those.[90] In the absence of renegotiation, there is no loss of gains from trade, but the remaining profits from breach are all appropriated by the seller. The resulting outcome is an unequal one, and the promisee might perceive it as unfair and feel aggrieved from the implemented allocation, being thereby tempted to retaliate. While gains from trade are exhausted, there will be losses from retaliation by the promisee.

Table 6.4 The next table resumes the welfare effects of specific performance without the possibility to renegotiate at the moment of the decision to perform. It does not consider the promisee's possibility to claim the surrogate, peculiar to German law, which is discussed in Sect. 6.4.3.

---

[89] One case in which the promisor might perform inefficiently is when she anticipates that the promisee will use an injunction to punish the promisor that breached for a violation of norm of keeping promises, or that *pacta sunt servanda*. In other words, the promisee may use the legal remedy of specific performance to enforce her own understanding of how individuals ought to behave, i.e., keeping their promises and deals. If the promisor is certain that the promisee will require performance for moral (or perhaps even spiteful) reasons, and is unable to contact the promisee at time of the decision to perform, then she may perform inefficiently. This is, however, an irrational action, for if the promisee can earn more by renegotiation, rational promisees will prefer higher earnings.

[90] In Germany, which combines specific performance with the possibility of a claim on the surrogate in case performance becomes impossible, the result is different, as explained above, and discussed below in Sect. 6.4.3.

Table 6.4 Social welfare under specific performance in the absence of renegotiation at the moment of the decision to perform or breach

	Increase in costs of production	Higher outside offer
Specific performance without renegotiation	Promisor will breach efficiently, bargain for a release and be exploited	Promisor will breach efficiently, pay damages and appropriate all profits
	• No inefficient trade • Unfair result → promisor retaliates	• No inefficient trade • Unfair result → promisee retaliates
	Loss of welfare from retaliation	Loss of welfare from retaliation

6.3.4 Social Welfare Under Specific Performance in the Presence of Renegotiation

When parties can renegotiate at the moment the promisor must decide to perform or breach, the results above change. In case of an increase in costs of production, the promisor will attempt to buy her way out of the contract by offering some side-payment to the promisee. The promisee can force the promisor to perform unless the realized contingency made performance impossible or impractical, or the realized costs of performance allow for a claim on the restoration of the contractual parity. As discussed above, although these in fact limit the scope of specific performance, they do not include all cases of inefficient performance.

The promisee that can require an injunction can force the seller to perform and to incur net losses from performance. Although the promisee is indifferent between performance or expectation damages, she can use her power to specifically enforce the contract and request a higher amount than expectation damages in order to release the seller.

Parties will settle on a side-payment that will allow the promisor to save some of the costs she would incur by performing specifically and will give some windfall gains to the promisee. They may settle, in the *Murmansk* case, when costs of performance are \$25,000, on around \$12,500. The promisee is better off through this renegotiation than through performance, and the promisor equally so. In the final allocation, the promisor loses \$12,500 and the promisee earns that amount.

This result might easily be perceived by the promisor as utterly unfair, for the promisee is using the legal remedy available to her in order to extract more from the promisor than what she bargained for, and is thereby asking in the renegotiation to be put in a better position than she would have been in case of performance. In contrast to the case where parties cannot renegotiate at the moment of deciding to perform or breach, the promisor will feel exploited when attempting to buy her way out of performance and thus *before she decides to perform or breach.*

The exploited promisor will tend to retaliate. She may do so (i) by performing inefficiently, incurring high losses but thereby *preventing* the exploitation, or (ii)

by accepting the negotiated price, saving resources, but later engaging in those other forms of retaliation discussed before. For example, she may, later, after being exploited, attempt to harm the promisee's reputation in the market, refuse ever to transact with her again, etc.

In the first case, there will be social losses from inefficient trade. In the second case, the promisor breaches efficiently and the loss of welfare is restricted to the losses from retaliation. In both cases, the promisor is in fact punishing the promisee that attempts to exploit her, and *specific performance will often lead to a loss of welfare even when parties can renegotiate the contract without transaction costs.*

In case of a higher outside offer, the result is substantially different. Since the profits from breach do not belong, by the contract, to either party, neither the promisor nor the promisee will tend to feel aggrieved or exploited by having to negotiate around them. Promisor and promisee can achieve a higher payoff from breach than from performance as long as they successfully bargain around performance.

Both parties are at arm's length in this negotiation. The promisor can perform and knows that, by doing so, neither party earns any share of those gains. The promisee can require that the promisor specifically perform and knows that both parties will then equally forego those gains. The expected result of renegotiation, in case of a higher outside offer, is hence an equal split of net profits from breach. All possible gains from trade are realized, and the final outcome is a fair one. In the end, there will be no loss of welfare either from inefficient trade or from retaliation.

Table 6.5 resumes those results.

6.4 Normative Analysis

Different remedies for breach, adopted by different legal systems, have different impacts upon overall social welfare both through the incentives they create for promisors to perform, with or without the need to renegotiate, and through the

Table 6.5 Social welfare under specific performance with renegotiation

	Increase in costs of production	Higher outside offer
Specific performance with renegotiation	Promisor will perform inefficiently or bargain for a release, be exploited and retaliate	Promisor will breach, compensate promisee for lost expectancy, and all profits from breach are equally split
	• Inefficient trade or • Unfair result → promisor retaliates	• No inefficient trade • Fair outcome → no retaliation
	Loss of welfare from inefficient trade or from retaliation	Social welfare is maximal

implementation of an allocation that can be perceived as more or less fair by the parties.

Unfair allocations arise, in the absence of renegotiation, because of the distribution of all gains from breach to just one of the parties, leaving the other one with a sense of grievance, and thereby tempted to retaliate. In the presence of renegotiation, unfairness arises either because of exploitative renegotiation or because one party does not give a fair share in the profits from breach to the other one. In both cases, it will often lead to retaliation and to a loss of welfare.

The promisor can punish what she perceives as unfair either by performing inefficiently, or by retaliating ex post. Even when parties can renegotiate without transaction costs, the promisor has reasons to perform, at times, inefficiently, because of the unfairness of the result. The promisee, on the other hand, can only engage in ex post retaliation, since she is the one responsible for the decision to perform.

Table 6.6 resumes the welfare effects of all the remedies for breach of contract studied above in their capacity to *maximize gains from trade* and to *minimize losses from retaliation.*

With these results, an analysis of different recent trends in the USA, France, Germany, and England is undertaken in what follows.

Table 6.6 Social welfare under different remedies for breach of contract

	Increase in costs of production	Higher outside offer
Expectation damages	• No inefficient trade • Fair result → no retaliation	• No inefficient trade • Unfair result → promisee retaliates
	Social welfare is maximal	Loss of welfare from retaliation
Disgorgement damages without renegotiation	• No inefficient trade • Fair result → No retaliation	• Inefficient trade or • Unfair result → promisor retaliates
	Social welfare is maximal	Loss of welfare either from inefficient trade or retaliation
Disgorgement damages with renegotiation	• No inefficient trade • Fair result → No retaliation	• No inefficient trade • Fair result → No retaliation
	Social welfare is maximal	Social welfare is maximal if renegotiation is fair
Specific performance without renegotiation	• No inefficient trade • Unfair result → promisor retaliates	• No inefficient trade • Unfair result → promisee retaliates
	Loss of welfare from inefficient trade or retaliation	Loss of welfare from inefficient trade or retaliation
Specific performance with renegotiation	• Inefficient trade or • Unfair result → promisor retaliates	• No inefficient trade • Fair outcome → no retaliation
	Loss of welfare from inefficient trade, retaliation, or both	Social welfare is maximal

6.4.1 The American Insistence on Expectation Damages

There is a strong resistance, in the USA, against the expansion of disgorgement damages. The Restatement, as argued above, does not mention the protection of that interest, and this was arguably dictated more for normative considerations than by positive law. Up to this day, the instances where American courts award disgorgement damages all involve noncontractual wrongs such as the infringement of a property right or the violation of a fiduciary duty.

In those cases, a claim for disgorgement is not a truly contractual claim. In the absence of those different, additional wrongs, promisees are not entitled to disgorgement of profits, but only to expectation damages that compensate for no more than lost expectancy. Therefore, in the overbidder paradigm, promisees are not entitled to recover profits from the substitutive transaction, possible only through breach, and courts have been very reluctant to allow that.[91]

It is important to note that the promisee can, whenever entitled to recover the profits from breach through disgorgement damages, choose between recovering her lost expectancy and claiming disgorgement damages. She will always prefer expectation damages when they are higher than the profits from breach (and assuming she can prove them), and the promisor thereby internalizes all the losses that the promisee will incur because of breach. The promisor will hence never breach inefficiently, and the promisee will always earn at least her expectancy.

When breach is efficient and can lead to higher profits, however, an award of expectation damages does not maximize welfare. It implements a result that can be perceived by the promisee as unfair in allowing the promisor to retain all profits from breach. Since parties never agreed who would be entitled to those gains, there will often be disagreement. The promisor, not required by law to allow the promisee to share in those profits, is unlikely to offer any share of those to the promisee, who will tend to retaliate. The result will often be social losses in an amount, as estimated in the experiment, possibly quite higher than the gains from trade that expectation damage induce through incentives to perform efficiently.

Allowing promisees to recover those profits, under disgorgement damages, will encourage the promisor to bargain with promisee for a share of those. The promisor can always perform as promised and thereby prevent the promisee from earning those gains. The promisee will always have, if breach is socially efficient, incentives to offer a share to the promisor, and disgorgement can thereby lead to efficient breaches as well as to a fairer distribution of the gains from breach.

Moreover, disgorgement of profits is clearly a moot issue in the loss-avoidance paradigm. In that type of contingency, the promisor will always breach, under a disgorgement rule, whenever breach is socially efficient, without the need to renegotiate and without being exploited by the promisee. In that type of contingency,

---

[91] *Cf.* FARNSWORTH ON CONTRACTS 824 ("Courts have refused to allow recovery for profits that the party in breach has obtained as a result of opportunities that would not have been available but for breach.").

an award of expectation already maximizes social welfare, and there is no reason to change existing law.

The possible disadvantage of disgorgement damages is the unfair allocation of gains when the parties cannot communicate at the time of the decision to perform. The promisor may perform inefficiently or breach efficiently and earn no share of them. In the first case, gains from possible substitutive transactions are foregone. In the second case, losses from retaliation by the promisor may emerge. However, an award of partial disgorgement can overcome these two disadvantages, as explained below (in the discussion of recent developments in English law).

6.4.2 *The French Expansion of Specific Performance with Astreintes*

The *astreinte* is an institute created by courts (a praetorian development), not initially explicitly foreseen in positive law, and only recently codified. After 1972, and especially after the Law from July 9, 1991, they were introduced in French positive law and are now explicitly foreseen in the *Code des Procédures Civiles d'Exécution*, in article L131-1 ("Any judge can, even *ex oficio*, order an *astreinte* to secure the execution of her decision").[92]

The promisee is now free to decide if she prefers the equivalent execution (*exécution par équivalent*, or damages for breach) or forced execution in kind (*exécution forcée en nature*) also of obligations to do.[93] Even obligations to do that have a personal character are now possibly enforced through the use of *astreintes*, unless doing so would conflict with some fundamental rights such as freedom of expression or conscience.[94] The tendency is that, as defended recently, the *astreinte* should be in general applicable even to obligations to do of a personal character.[95]

[92] Own transl. In original: "*Tout juge peut, même d'office, ordonner une astreinte pour assurer l'exécution de sa décision.*" *See* further Law n. 91-650 of 9 July 1991, and Decree n. 92-755 of 31 July 1992 (Articles 51–53).

[93] *See* RÉMY CABRILLAC, DROIT DES OBLIGATIONS 470 (11th ed., Paris, Dalloz, 2014) ("*Le juge peut prévoir une astreinte pour contraindre à l'exécution de toute obligation: donner, faire ou ne pas faire … Les deux seules limites à l'astreinte sont l'impossibilité de l'exécution …, ou l'exécution d'une obligation très personnelle, mettant en jeu la liberté du débiteur.*") In English: "The judge can provide an *astreinte* to compel the performance of any obligation: to give, to do, or not do … The sole two limits to the *astreinte* are the impossibility of performance … or the execution of a very personal obligation putting at stake the freedom of the debtor." (own transl.).

[94] For example, an artisan that promises to fabricate furniture can be coerced to perform. *See.* 3 JACQUES FLOUR, JEAN-LUC AUBERT & ÉRIC SAVAUX, DROIT CIVIL: LES OBLIGATIONS n° 164 (8th ed., Paris, Dalloz, 2013) (*Le Rapport d'Obligation*). *See* also the precedent footnote, and how the *astreinte* is understood to be inapplicable only upon obligations to do of a *very* personal character.

[95] *See* Aubrey Lebois, *Les obligations de faire à caractère personnel*, 47 LA SEMAINE JURIDIQUE EDITION GÉNÉRALE I, at 210 (2008) ("*Malgré la lettre de l'article 1142 du Code civil, il est admis que le créancier peut obtenir l'exécution forcée en nature des obligations contractuelles de faire. Selon la jurisprudence et la doctrine, échappent toutefois à ce principe les obligations à caractère*

Denis Mazeaud recently declared, as a consequence of this development, the death sentence of the Roman principle *nemo præcise cogi potest ad factum*:

> "Aujourd'hui, et depuis des lustres d'ailleurs, il est acquis que l'article 1142 du Code civil est désactivé et que le principe de l'exécution forcée en nature s'applique à toutes les obligations contractuelles inexécutées, qu'elles soient de donner, de faire ou de ne pas faire"[96]

The rationale and economic consequences, as mentioned by Mazeaud, are remarkable:

> "Faut-il s'en féliciter ?
>
> 'Oui!', parce que ce principe illustre à merveille l'idée que le droit est une science profondément humaine et que notre droit des obligations repose sur des principes qui sont dépourvus parfois de rationalité, économique notamment; il est fondé sur des principes qui sont dotés d'une charge symbolique, morale, spirituelle. Ainsi, il est exact que, pas plus que le principe moral, sinon religieux, du respect de la parole donnée dont il constitue «la mise en force», le principe de l'exécution forcée en nature n'est plus performant économiquement, ni plus pertinent, ni plus efficient que l'exécution par équivalent...
>
> Le principe de l'exécution forcée en nature est un signe de résistance du modèle contractuel au diktat de la loi du marché, parce qu'il véhicule d'autres valeurs, morales, sociales, spirituelles, que celles que prône l'analyse économique du droit."[97]

In effect, it is true that the "new" principle that obligations to do, even if of a personal character, can be specifically enforced does not have a sound economic rationale, differently from the ancient Roman principle. In the absence of renegotiation, specific performance leads to losses of welfare in both types of contingencies (as in Table 6.6). In its presence, it maximizes social welfare only in the overbidder paradigm and only in the presence of fair renegotiations.

Specific performance requires only, if the good is already produced, that it can be seized and handed over to the promisee. The promisor does not have, in any obligation to give, to do anything for the promisee apart from delivering the good (*la livraison*). The only loss of welfare, under specific performance, arises in the loss-avoidance paradigm, and is because of the possibility of the promisee to exploit the buyer in the renegotiation.

However, in obligations to do, the good needs to be produced, or the service performed. There is another loss of welfare, in this case, because forcing the promisor

---

personne ... Pour respecter le droit du créancier à l'exécution forcée, il convient d'adopter une conception très restrictive des obligations de faire à caractère personnel et de déterminer, dans chaque cas, si l'exécution en nature est effectivement impossible.").

In English: "Notwithstanding the letter of Article 1142 of the Civil Code, it has been recognized that the obligee may obtain execution in kind of contractual obligations to do. However, according to the jurisprudence and the doctrine, escaping always from this principle obligation of a personal character... In order to comply with the rights of the obligee to obtain enforcement, it is appropriate to adopt an extremely narrow scope for the obligations to do of a personal character and to determine, in each case, whether the specific performance is in fact impossible." (own transl.).

[96] Yves-Marie Laithier & Denis Mazeaud, *La Nature de la Sanction: Satisfaction du Bénéficiaire par des Dommages-intérêts ou Primauté de l'Exécution en Nature?*, 2 REVUE DES CONTRATS 681, 681–682 (2012).

[97] *Id.*

to do something for the promisee, after the relationship breaks down, and aggrievement and animosity is running high, will most likely lead to further aggrievement and stronger retaliation. Beyond that, the promisor is likely to retaliate by delivering a performance of very poor quality, thereby imposing further losses upon the promisor beyond those discussed before.

The application of the *astreinte* was, under the principle previously consecrated in Art. 1142 ("every obligation to do is resolved by damages"), and before its "deactivation," restricted to obligations to give. Its expansion to obligations to do is expected to lead to additional losses of welfare. It can increase aggrievement, obliging the promisor to do something for another perhaps just because the other is being spiteful, and using the legal remedy to punish the promisor that breaches to enforce that "moral, if not religious principle of respect to the word given." If the promisor disagrees that this principle is sacred, is willing to compensate the promisee in order to breach, but is then forced to perform specifically, under the threat of high and increased sanctions, then aggrievement and retaliation may reach another level.

In effect, as explained before, the legal remedy may be used as a way to enforce one's own understanding of the morality of promises. It may be used by a minority to prevent individuals from maximizing welfare, without harming others. Guala speaks how a "a community, for example, may be prevented from adopting a set of beneficial strategies, simply because they depart from what is considered 'correct' behavior by an aggressive gang of moralistic punishers."[98]

It in effect, as Mazeaud and Laithier advance, the principle that one shall be bound by her word no matter what happens has even a religious basis. Josserand, for example, fiercely defended the use of the *astreinte*, writing in the 1930s, and exemplified how the *astreinte* should be applied on the "*obligation qui incombe à la femme mariée d'habiter avec son mari: l'astreinte obligera la fugitive à réintégrer le domicile conjugal, tellement elle rendra ruineuse une indépendance contraire à la loi.*"[99]

One can easily imagine the welfare gains from forcing the "fugitive wife" to reintegrate the conjugal domicile, and how happy and prosperous the marriage would be. She will tend to feel aggrieved and retaliate, for example, by refusing to cooperate with the husband in the future, but is now moreover obliged, because of will of the other, to stay inside the relationship, without any chance to break free. It is not enough to pay the *astreinte*, or to compensate the promisor. The *astreinte* will just increase day after day, until the promisor performs specifically.

---

[98] Francesco Guala, *Reciprocity: Weak or Strong?*, *op. cit. supra*, at 4.

[99] 2 LOUIS JOSSERAND, COURS DE DROIT CIVIL POSITIF FRANÇAIS n. 595 (Sirey, 1932–1933).

6.4.3 *The German Junction of Specific Performance, Expectation, and Disgorgement Damages*

As discussed above, under German law, specific performance is the default remedy for breach, but the promisee is entitled to claim the surrogate if the promisor breached, transferred the good to the outside bidder, and thereby rendered performance in kind impossible. In contingencies involving absolute increases in costs of performance, the promisee can choose between specific performance and expectation damages, subject to the rules described above. In contingencies involving outside offers, the inclusion of disgorgement damages in the remedies available to the promisee presents a combination peculiar to the BGB.

It is a wise solution. The promisor, when deciding to perform or breach in the overbidder paradigm, is thereby encouraged to attempt to negotiate with the promisee. If she does not and sells the good to another buyer, thereby making performance impossible, then she must disgorge all profits to the promisee, who will rationally claim the surrogate. Since she will earn nothing else by doing so, the possibility of the promisee to claim the surrogate encourages negotiation.

If she attempts to renegotiate, then the parties always have incentives to agree on a division of those profits that makes both parties better off, and the outcome is necessarily fairer than the one under expectation damages. In the overbidder paradigm, the outcome implemented by the combination of specific performance and disgorgement damages is the same as under disgorgement damages with renegotiation, as in Table 6.6, which is superior to the one under expectation damages because of the fairness of the result.

The sole disadvantage of that solution, in that paradigm, is that if the promisor cannot contact the promisee at the moment of the decision to perform, then she is indifferent between performance or breach, because she knows that, once she performs, the promisee will claim all the profits from breach. If she performs, then gains from a substitutive transaction are foregone. If she breaches, then the promisee does not need to allow the promisor to share in any of those gains, and the result is unfair, leading promisors to retaliate, and ultimately to a loss of social welfare.

In the loss-avoidance paradigm, however, the disadvantages of specific performance exist. The promisee can exploit the promisor. The different norms that bar an injunction mitigate the problem, for they release the promisor from the obligation to perform, and thereby implement the result that expectation damages implement. That result, in the loss-avoidance paradigm, maximizes welfare.

However, the restrictive requirements adopted by German law, as in § 275 BGB, justified commonly on the basis that the principle is that *pacta sunt servanda*, release the promisor from the duty to perform only in extreme circumstances.[100] These should, in order to provide for a maximal social welfare in that paradigm, and to avoid exploitation and thereby retaliation, be less strict and, perhaps, determined

[100] *See*, e.g., Canaris, *Die Reform des Rechts der Leistungsstörungen*, op. cit. supra, at 499.

more by the fact that performance is more costly for the promisor than its benefits for the promisee than by the principle that *pacta sunt servanda.*

6.4.4 The British Acceptance of Partial Disgorgement (Hypothetical Bargain Damages)

English courts have departed from the plain rejection of disgorgement in contractual cases. Although such recovery is still limited to "exceptional circumstances," promisees can have a truly contractual claim of disgorgement of profits from breach. There are two different bases for recovery of profits, leading to two different measures of disgorgement damages.

In the first case, the promisee has a remedy on the account of profits that encompasses all profits from breach, as explained above. It is, nowadays, in England, not restricted to cases involving a true infringement of a property interest, or a true breach of a fiduciary obligation. Courts require, after *Blake*, only an analogy of that last violation, or a quasi-fiduciary violation where the promisee has interest that is *akin* to a fiduciary one.

In *Blake*, for example, the former secret agent did not have a fiduciary obligation to keep the information secret anymore, since it had fallen into public knowledge. The Crown still had an interest that Blake keep his obligation not to reveal any information about the secret service, even if it had fallen into public knowledge, that is *akin* to a truly confidential obligation. For that, the defendant has to show, mainly, a "legitimate interest in preventing the defendant's profit-making activity and, hence, in depriving him of his profit."[101] *Blake* damages, or total disgorgement, is however still restricted to very limited circumstances.

On another basis for recovery, English courts have allowed recovery of part of the profits from breach on the fundament that, through breach, the promisee lost the value of a bargaining opportunity. She may have a claim on *hypothetical bargain damages* that represent "what the claimant could reasonably have charged for giving permission to the defender to act contrary to his contractual undertaking."[102] It is, simply, a claim on "the value of a bargaining opportunity."[103] They were first awarded in *Wrotham Park*, and are still being developed.[104]

This type of damages does not require infringement of property interests, breach of confidence, or a claim of specific performance. Hypothetical bargain damages, also often denoted *Wrotham Park* damages, or "negotiating damages," are not limited to

---

[101] *Cf.* CHITTY ON CONTRACTS, 26-054.

[102] *Cf.* CHITTY ON CONTRACTS, 26-050.

[103] *Experience Hendrix LLC v. PPX Enterprise Inc and Edward Chaplin*, EWCA Civ 323 (CA) (2003), at 45.

[104] *Wrotham Park Estate Co Ltd v. Parkside Homes Ltd.*, 1 W.L.R. 798 (CH) (1974).

those very exceptional circumstances required by total disgorgement, but their scope of application is still very unclear.[105]

In *Experience Hendrix*, the Court of Appeals used the factors for an award of disgorgement damages for an award of hypothetical bargain damages.[106] These included (i) that the promisor did not do what she promised to do, (ii) that knew she was not doing it, (iii) that she breached deliberately, and (iv) that she was in flagrant contravention to her obligations.[107] Moreover, hypothetical bargain damages are not restricted to cases where the promisee had a claim of specific performance.[108]

In assessing the amount of hypothetical bargain damages, Lord Walker mentioned in the *Pell Frischmann* case that "the court should consider a hypothetical negotiation between a willing buyer (…) and a willing seller (…); both parties to be assumed to act reasonably, so that the fact that one or other would have refused to make a deal is to be ignored."[109]

This is a sound development. It always allows the promisor to breach efficiently and does not induce inefficient performance. Moreover, it implements a fair allocation and thereby is well apt to crowd out retaliation. The outcome of a hypothetical bargain damages claim is expected to be very close to the outcome of the parties' renegotiation under total disgorgement. They will bargain, whenever breach is socially efficient, for mutual gains from breach. Social welfare is expected to be maximized.

The advantage, when compared with disgorgement damages, is to allow the promisor to breach without having to renegotiate with the promisee in order to earn a share of the profits. When only required to disgorge some of those gains, later on, through a lawsuit, efficient breaches will happen in all types of contingencies with certainty. The promisor does not need to negotiate with the promisee for a share of those gains—in that case, parties may not be able to reach an agreement, for example, because of problems of information or moral considerations, and the promisor may perform inefficiently. If she can breach without obtaining consent of the promisee, but being certain that she is entitled to some of the profits from breach, just as the

---

[105] There is, especially, great controversy over whether the promisee's inability to demonstrate an identifiable financial loss is a precondition for the award. For a positive answer, *see WWF-World Wide Fund for Nature v World Wrestling Federation Entertainment Inc.* EWCA Civ 286 (2007), 1. W.L.R. 445 (2008), reiterated in *Abbar v Saudi Economic & Development Co. (SEDCO) Real Estate Ltd.*, EWHC 1414 (CH) (2013), at 226 (rejecting the argument that "the lack of identifiable financial loss was not a precondition to an award of negotiating damages.").

[106] *Experience Hendrix LLC v. PPX Enterprise Inc and Edward Chaplin*, EWCA Civ 323 (2003).

[107] *See* CHITTY ON CONTRACTS, 26-050.

[108] *Cf. Giedo van der Garde BV v. Force India Formula One Team Ltd.*, EWHC 2373 (QB) (2010), at 533 (such an award is not "precluded by any of the following factors: (i) that the claimants advanced no claim for an injunction or specific performance, or the fact that there would have been no prospect of such an order being granted; (ii) the fact that damages are not claimed under Lord Cairns' Act in lieu of an injunction; (iii) the fact that the claim is not based on a breach of a restrictive covenant; and (iv) the fact that the claim is based on breach of contract rather than invasion of property rights.").

[109] CHITTY ON CONTRACTS, 26-053. *See Pell Frischmann Engineering Ltd v. Bow Valley Iran Ltd.*, UKPC 45 (2009), B.L.R. 73 (2010).

promisee is entitled to some of them too, then the result will be efficient breaches and a fairer outcome.

6.5 Conclusion

A comparison of the welfare effects of expectation damages, disgorgement damages, and specific performance, in the presence of renegotiation (even if only after the decision to perform or breach), reveals that both expectation damages and disgorgement damages maximize social welfare only in the loss-avoidance paradigm. Specific performance, in that type of contingency, allows the promisee to exploit the promisor and will lead to retaliation and to lower welfare.

Specific performance and disgorgement damages, when parties can renegotiate, are superior to expectation damages in the overbidder paradigm. They require that the promisor who finds another buyer that values performance more than the original one offer a share of the extra profits from breach to the promisee in order to be released from the obligation to perform specifically, or from the duty to disgorge all those profits.

Optimal remedies for breach should combine elements from both. They should allow the promisor to breach whenever costs of production rise, as long as she pays expectation damages and make the promisee whole, preventing any type of exploitative renegotiation. On the other hand, they should let the promisor breach efficiently as long as the promisee shares in the profits from a substitutive transaction.

At common law, the remedy of expectation damages was the default and common one, but courts in equity developed injunctive relief for certain cases. These always excluded obligations to do, especially when of personal character, and where restricted to obligations to give. In this case, the promised good or the tract of land can simply be seized and handed over to the promisee. Parties are not obliged to stay in a relationship they do not want, and the sole reason for aggrievement and retaliation is given by the unfair allocation of profits from breach. There is no aggrievement from being forced to stay in the relationship, for the promisor does not have to do anything to the promisee beyond transferring the good.

Specific performance of obligations to give, in case of a higher outside offer, performs well. In this case, if the promisor still can make profits from breach, then she will contact the promisee, bargain for a release, and the result is efficient and fair. Specific performance of obligations to give does not lead to losses of welfare in obligations to give, as long as renegotiation is fair. The historical development of injunctive relief is hence well grounded in social welfare terms. The sole disadvantage in when parties cannot renegotiate at the moment of the decision to perform or breach.

In obligations to do, the promisor may also receive a better offer, but is then not obliged to keep her promise and perform for the original buyer. There is no specific performance of obligations to do, expect for obligation not to do. In this case, the promisor is not obliged to perform specifically but only to refrain from accepting the outside offer. The promisee is only entitled to a negative injunction that would prohibit the promisor from accepting the outside offer. If breach is socially efficient, then this rule encourages parties to bargain, so that the promisor will release the promisee in exchange for a share of those profits. It is again a sound historical development of injunctive relief for obligations not to do. The result is fair and efficient, as long as renegotiation does not break down.

In civil law systems, the remedy of specific performance was the default and common one, but the law evolved and came to encompass more and more cases where, in the loss-avoidance paradigm, the promisor is released from the obligation to perform specifically. These include impossibility, impracticability, and change of circumstances. When faced with much higher costs of production, specific performance does not lead to a maximal social welfare, since the promisor may exploit the promisee that faces unexpected hardship, thereby leading to unfairness and retaliation. Those rules that bar injunctions avoid that result and provide for a fairer outcome. It was a sound development to depart from a strict observance of *pacta sunt servanda* in cases where performance becomes much more costly, in absolute terms, and hence only in the loss-avoidance paradigm.

In the overbidder paradigm, at least in German law, the claim on the surrogate avoids the unfairness that would result from letting the promisor appropriate all profits from breach after compensating the promisee for her lost expectancy. The seller that deliberately sells the promised good to somebody else makes performance impossible and would be allowed to retain all profits from breach, since the promisee would then have a claim only of damages for breach that protect the expectation, or positive interest. The combination of both remedies encourages renegotiation, and provides a fairer result. It was a sound development, capable of minimizing aggrievement and retaliation. Its sole disadvantage is that parties may behave unfairly in the renegotiation, and when this one breaks down, then the promisor may retaliate by performing specifically and foregoing the possible further gains from trade, or breaching efficiently but later on retaliating in other manners.

Lastly, the movement toward hypothetical bargain damages, or partial disgorgement, in English law, is very sound. Those damages provide incentives for promisors to perform if and only if performance is socially efficient, and also allow the promisee to share in the profits from breach. Since it is substitutive relief, it does not require renegotiation. If the promisee attempts to exploit the promisor that has a better trading opportunity, offering unfair shares of those profits, or simply insisting on specific performance for moral reasons, then those social welfare gains will *not* be foregone, for the promisor is free to breach, efficiently, knowing that she will profit from it. The promisee, ex post, has a claim on a share of those profits, and her aggrievement can thereby be minimized, crowding out her tendency to retaliate.[110] And this will happen *without any transaction cost*: even if renegotiation is costly, perhaps very costly, under partial disgorgement there is no need to renegotiate in order to breach

[110] Note that the promisee is free to choose to claim expectation damages if these are higher than disgorgement damages, and hence, the promisor does internalize the negative externality of breach. The promisee will only claim the surrogate, or partial disgorgement, if they are higher than expectation damages.

and to implement a fair result. Transaction costs are also minimized. It is therefore a sound movement in social welfare terms.

Chapter 7
Conclusion

The principle of compensation, considered fundamental in the law of remedies for breach of contract both in legal scholarship and in existing law, finds its justification, in promissory and reliance theories, on moral considerations and on the dictates of corrective justice.[1] Economic theories, however, have not addressed the social welfare function that compensation has in providing legal relief for disappointed promisees to redress breach, and accordingly consider compensation as an accessory, secondary, or even disposable principle and purpose in the legal enforcement of contracts.[2] The objective of this thesis was to provide one justification and reason for why compensation is, and should be, fundamental in the law of remedies for breach of contract.

Legal scholars have long since advanced how legal relief aims at "keeping the peace" in substituting private for public redress.[3] Remedies that allow promisees to redress breach are apt to have their own economic justification in effectively crowding out private forms of redress that are socially costly, and thus responsible for a deadweight loss whenever implemented.[4] Compensation, in contrast to private redress, does not cause the same loss of welfare that retaliation causes whenever it is implemented, for it consists only in a transfer of resources from the party in breach

---

[1] *See* n.2, chap. 1, *supra* for scholars that considered compensation as the fundamental principle of the law of remedies from breach, ranging from, at the common law, if not from Blackstone himself, at least from Sedwick and Anston to Farnsworth and Fried, through Williston and Corbin. The First and Second Restatements of Contracts, as well as the U.C.C., adopted the same view. *See* n.3, chap. 1, *supra*, and the discussion in chap. 1 and in Sects. 2.1 and 5.1.

[2] Recall Craswell, *Instrumental Theories of Compensation, op. cit. supra*, at 1178 ("In short, in economic theories the concept of compensation can be dispensed with entirely, whereas in corrective justice theories that concept is absolutely crucial.").

[3] *See* n.29–32, chap. 1, *supra* and the accompanying text (discussing several different ways through which victims of breach may retaliate and punish promise and contract-breakers even in modern legal systems that, in general, prohibit the use of violence by the citizens, as discussed by David Charny, Oliver Hart, and John Moore, among others).

[4] *See supra* Sects. 5.4.1 and 5.4.2 (empirical evidence attesting how an award of damages for breach in fact fulfill those functions in affecting parties' behavior).

S. Mittlaender, *Equity, Efficiency, and Ethics in Remedies for Breach of Contract*, International Law and Economics, https://doi.org/10.1007/978-3-031-10804-4_7

to the disappointed promisee, and hence does not necessarily lower social welfare as acts of private retaliation and punishment do.[5]

While the maintenance and operation of a legal system aimed at providing compensation for promisees requires social resources, certain and secure legal enforcement imposes a cost on the decision to breach that promisors anticipate, and hence create incentives that are predicted, in economic theories, to deter breaches of contract.[6] This is achieved, in case of perfect enforcement, without the need of legal intervention, *ex post*, for the promisor must anticipate that she will have to pay damages to the promisee, or perform specifically, in any case of breach.[7] She will prefer to compensate the promisee whenever she breaches than breach without doing so, be sued and ordered to compensate the victim by courts, thereby having to bear further costs from the legal process.[8]

Compensatory remedies and a well-functioning legal system are hence, in theory, and in the absence of legal imperfections, well apt to create incentives for promisors to perform, and to compensate the promisee in case of breach. Only in case of failures in the legal enforcement must the promisee in fact recur to courts for a final resolution of the dispute and conflict. Compensatory remedies are expected to contribute to the welfare of society both in deterring inefficient breaches and in crowding out retaliation by victims of breach with lower social costs than private forms of redress.

Moreover, remedies for breach affect both parties' contractual behavior in situations where promisors are already committed to perform, and where the promisee is apt to perceive the act of breach of that commitment as a wrong in need of redress. The thesis thereby investigated, firstly, the role of the primary duty to perform and to keep contractual promises on both parties' contractual behavior. It concerns the *first research question*: *how does promissory commitment (the primary duty to perform) affect both parties' contractual behavior?*

The main theories of contract and contract law studied in the second chapter stress how parties, in exchanging promises given with consideration, and thereby by entering into contracts, incur a legal obligation that is, because of its structure, apt to

---

[5] Recall Kaplow & Shavell, *Fairness versus Welfare*, *op. cit. supra*, at 998 n.73 ("the bare fact that money may change hands in a lawsuit in certain circumstances, thereby changing how a loss is divided between the two parties, is of no consequence under welfare economics.").

[6] *See supra* Sect. 2.4.4. Expectation damages, as detailed in there, are predicted to deter only socially inefficient breaches, and to encourage socially efficient ones.

[7] As discussed *supra* in Chap. 6, in case performance becomes impossible or impractical, then the promisee is released from the obligation to perform, and courts will, in general, rescind the contract. In this case, damages are generally not measured by the expectation interest, nor is injunctive relief an available remedy.

[8] In legal systems where each party must bear some of the costs of the legal process, there may be instances where the promisor may breach in anticipation that the promisee will not claim the available legal remedy. If the costs of claiming the legal remedy, for the promisee, are higher than the benefits she will receive from the remedy, then the promisee will not claim the remedy. The promisor, anticipating this, can then behave in opportunistic manners, and breach knowing that she will not bear any cost by doing so. In this case, moreover, remedies will not have the effect of inducing performance by the promisor as predicted in economic theories.

carry normative significance for the parties themselves.[9] According to promissory theories, parties ought to perform contracts since contracts are promises, breach of contract amounts to breach of promise, violates the convention and norm of keeping promises, and is thereby a transgression in need of redress.[10] For reliance theories, differently, parties ought not to cause harm upon those they induce to rely upon their promises, and breach of contract, when capable of causing a real and material harm upon the promisee, is a wrong that justifies legal relief.[11] And for Holmes, who understood the contractual obligation as an obligation to perform or to pay damages, in a disjunctive structure, breach followed by the payment of damages amounts to performance of the obligation, and is hence not wrong. Still, breach *not* followed by the payment of damages is, even under the Holmesian "option theory of contract," a wrong in need of redress.[12]

As further argued in the second chapter, the different theories of the contractual obligation do not provide a definite and univocal answer to the question whether breach of promise and contract is, in any concrete case, wrong or otherwise morally acceptable. Quite on the contrary, they instead often conflict with each other, as for example when the promisor breaches in a certain contingency where breach is socially efficient and, in doing so, violates the moral norm of keeping promises, or the principle that *pacta sunt servanda.* The promisee might perceive breach as wrong because of the violation of the moral norm, in a deontological fashion, while the promisor might perceive it as otherwise morally justified, for example, because of the overall gains of welfare it delivers, in a consequentialist assessment of the morality of the act.

The third chapter discussed how disagreement between parties on whether the promisor should have performed or breached is a pervasive and widespread phenomenon, and how disputes that follow breach might often escalate to a serious and real conflict most often responsible for a loss of social welfare.[13] There are several different possible reasons for why the promisor might fail to perform in a situation where the promisee expects performance.

Contracts are incomplete and do not specify the appropriate course of action that parties should take whenever a contingency that was not explicitly discussed in the parties' agreement, and not integrated in the contract, materializes.[14] Parties may then hold different and conflicting understandings of the morality of the act of breach *in concreto*, considering it as excused or not, in the realized circumstances, by the societal convention of promises.[15] They can further perceive its consequences, including the loss of expectancy, the unfairness of the result, or the inefficiency as capable of justifying breach or not.[16] Moreover, parties are, in that type of assessment,

---

[9] *See supra* Sect. 2.1.

[10] *See supra* Sect. 2.2.

[11] *See supra* Sect. 2.3.

[12] *See supra* Sect. 2.4.

[13] *Supra* Sect. 3.1.

[14] *Supra* Sect. 3.2.

[15] *Supra* Sect. 3.3.

[16] *Supra* Sect. 3.4.

subject to several different cognitive biases that facilitate disagreement, and that can hinder the private settlement of the dispute.[17] In cases where parties are unable to solve their dispute privately, through apologies or renegotiation, and the dispute acquires a normative character, then the final expected product will be, if the victim is not entitled to a public remedy, an act of retaliation based on the norm of strong reciprocity.[18]

The fourth chapter studied the behavioral tendency of individuals to retaliate to what they perceive as wrongful behavior *in the presence of promissory commitment,* but in the absence of compensation, and how breach of promise might provide unique reasons for promisees to feel aggrieved and wronged from the act of breach.[19] As consistently observed in experimental studies, individuals tend to retaliate and to punish those that do not take the socially optimal course of action (as in public good games) and that behave unfairly (as in ultimatum games).[20] This tendency to retaliate has its own social benefits, for it is apt to induce others to cooperate in fear of being punished by the other, just as it is apt to induce others to behave more fairly in different situations.[21] It has, however, its own social costs, since retaliation is costly both for the person implementing it and for the victim. Its costs, as observed in several different recent experimental studies, most often outweigh its benefits of inducing others to cooperate, and costly punishment is rarely apt to improve social welfare.[22]

Retaliation is subsequently endogenized, in the fourth chapter, and in the canonical model of contractual behavior developed in the Economic Analysis of Law, not as mere irrational behavior that cannot be understood in any systematic manner.[23] The victim of breach has a sense of grievance responsible for a loss of utility, and acts of retaliation can minimize that loss in providing to the victim "relief and satisfaction if justice is established."[24] Retaliation is a reaction of an individual who feels wronged from breach derives disutility from that state of affairs and, in having the opportunity to retaliate, will tend to punish breach.[25] The victim will do so if the costs of retaliation are lower than the loss of utility she can offset by "transferring the hurt back to the

---

[17] *Supra* Sect. 3.5.

[18] *Supra* Sect. 3.6.

[19] *Supra* Sect. 4.1.

[20] *Supra* Sect. 4.2.

[21] With respect to the capacity of retaliation and costly punishment to induce cooperation (costly punishment lead to quite higher cooperation in public good games), and to induce fairer behavior (offers in dictator games are substantially lower than offers in ultimatum games, where rejection is a form of costly punishment in the last one), *see* the discussion *supra* in Chap. 4, Sect. 4.2.

[22] *See supra* Sect. 4.3.

[23] *See supra* Sect. 4.4.

[24] Dominique de Quervain et al., *The Neural Basis of Altruistic Punishment, op. cit. supra,* at 1254.

[25] This same idea underlies the model of contractual behavior developed by Oliver Hart and John Moore. The authors "believe that to develop more general and compelling theories of contracts and organizational form it is essential to depart from a world in which Coasian renegotiation always leads to *ex post* efficiency" and to introduce behavioral elements, including retaliation, in the economic model of contractual behavior." Hart & Moore, *Contracts as Reference Points, op. cit. supra,* at 3.

other party."[26] When the victim of breach feels aggrieved, for any of the possible reasons discussed in the chapter, then the victim will, as advanced by Corbin "do his best to redress his own wrong."[27]

Individuals can always, in modern legal systems, resort to courts for a final and definitive resolution of their disputes. The thesis thereby investigated, secondly, the role of the secondary duty to pay damages, or to perform specifically, upon both parties' behavior.[28] It then addressed the *second research question*: *how does the legal remedy (the secondary duty to pay damages for breach) affect both parties' contractual behavior?*

In the presence of legal enforcement, private enforcement and retaliation are not necessary to induce promisors to keep promises, and to deter breaches of contract, for legal remedies fulfill that very same role in imposing a cost on the decision to breach.[29] Retaliation is not efficient to induce optimal levels of performance unless legal systems do not function well and promisors cannot well anticipate the duty to pay damages, and promisees the right to receive them. The victims' tendency to retaliate, moreover, depends on how each individual perceives breach in the each concrete case, possibly depending on the different consequences of the act *in concreto*.[30] Compensatory remedies, in contrast, only redistribute wealth between the parties, ex post, and are determined by the law, and not by courts' compassion to the concrete victim, being hence better anticipated than acts of retaliation.[31]

The experiment presented in Chap. 5 developed an empirical study into four different decisions that promisors and promisees often face in contractual relationships. It analyzed (i) the promisor's decision to keep promises, (ii) the promisee's decision to retaliate to breach of promise, (iii) the promisor's decision to perform contracts under expectation damages, and (iv) the promisee's decision to retaliate when entitled to the legal remedy. The theoretical conjectures and predictions developed in the previous chapters were thereby subject to empirical scrutiny, and the gains of welfare provided by the two functions of legal remedies were, under the parameters of the implemented trade game, further estimated and compared.

In its first part, the experiment investigated the behavioral effect of promissory commitment to induce, per se, and independent of legal remedies, promisors to keep promises, and promisees to retaliate to breach of promise. The first two hypotheses subject to experimental scrutiny hence tackled, from an empirical perspective, the *first research question*, and inquired into the role of the primary duty to perform.

The first hypothesis is that individuals tend to keep promises even when doing so becomes individually unprofitable because of the moral norm of keeping promises.

---

[26] Hart & Moore, *Contracts as Reference Points*, *op. cit. supra*, at 8.

[27] 5 CORBIN, A COMPREHENSIVE TREATISE ON THE RULES OF CONTRACT LAW, *op. cit. supra*, at 30–31 § 1002.

[28] While the focus relied on damages for breach, injunctive relief and the different incentives it provides for promisors and for promisees are discussed in Chaps. 2 and 6.

[29] *Supra* Sect. 4.3.

[30] *Supra* Sect. 4.4.

[31] *Supra* Sect. 4.5.

There was, however, no evidence that promises induced a change in behavior of those that promise in a game where the only interest at stake, for the promisee, was the expectation interest.[32] When parties did not promise anything to each other (and did not have the possibility to communicate with each other in any manner), the vast majority of individuals (94%) decided not to go through with an exchange that was, after the realization of the state of the world, individually unprofitable. Virtually identically, when parties promised to each other they would implement the exchange in the future, almost no promisor kept the promise, and the vast majority of the promises remained unfulfilled (94%).

With respect to the estimated effect of promises on parties' behavior, one word of care is indeed valuable. This piece of empirical evidence shall not be interpreted as providing evidence that "individuals do not keep promises." There are existing experimental studies on whether (and why) individuals keep promises, and they do find evidence for the existence of promise-keeping behavior.[33] They do not, however, study the situation where the expectation interest is the only interest at stake, and where the only loss that the promisee incurs because breach is a loss of expected and promised profits.[34] They also do not implement different contingencies where, in most of them, keeping the promise was individually profitable, and where only in some of them, keeping the promise was, after the realization of the state of the world, individually unprofitable.[35]

The second hypothesis is that promisees tend to retaliate to breach of promise even at a personal cost for themselves, in single and anonymous interactions where reputational concerns, signaling, deterrence, and tit-for-tar or grim-trigger strategies all cannot explain that type of behavior. There was substantial evidence for the existence of pure *retaliation to breach* of promise, or retaliation beyond the levels observed in the absence of promissory commitment. When parties never promised to other to go through with the exchange, average retaliation to a refusal to do so was of 28%, and this behavior can be motivated by several factors such as inequality-aversion, preferences for a maximal social welfare, or even spite. When parties exchanged promises to perform in the future, however, and under the exact same payoffs, this average was of 40%, and this difference is statistically significant ($p = 0.047$) and *not* due to all those factors.

This aggregate result does not, however, shed light on the causes of retaliation to breach, and on the elements present in breach of promise that in fact lead to the

---

[32] Recall that in the experiment, the promisor was the seller, and the promisee the buyer. Herein, those terms are used interchangeably but also recall that in the experiment they were always, in all treatments, simply called seller and buyer, and the decision to perform was the decision to "produce and deliver the good to the buyer.".

[33] *See supra* Sects. 5.1 and 5.2.

[34] *See supra* Sect. 5.2.

[35] Additionally, it is rather a negative result, where no evidence supporting the hypothesis was found. Still, while the implemented voluntary exchanged of promises did not induce a change in the behavior of promisors, it did induce a substantial change in the behavior of promisees, and the implemented method of inducing promissory commitment in the laboratory was arguably salient and capable of inducing a change in behavior of participants.

observed increase in rates of retaliation between those treatments. In the inquiry into the possible causes of retaliation, or into the circumstances where it is most likely to emerge developed in the model of the fourth chapter, three main different reasons for why promisees might feel aggrieved and tempted to retaliate to breach were identified.[36] These involve the violation of the moral norm of keeping promises, the unfairness of the result of breach of promise, and the inefficiency resulting from that act.[37]

In circumstances where breach was *efficient* and *fair*, but was still a violation of the moral norm of keeping promises, breach of promise did not induce disappointed promisees to retaliate, a result that points to the fact that the violation of the norm of keeping promises did not cause retaliation to breach of promise in the experiment.[38] When breach was socially *inefficient* but *fair*, observed rates of retaliation were higher in the presence of promises than in their absence, but this difference is not significant.[39] In contrast, in all contingencies where breach was *unfair* and favored only the promisor in breach, promises induce a substantial increase in rates of retaliation, and often more than half of promisees punished the promise-breaker, and this effect was statistically significant.[40]

The experiment therefore delivers *one piece of empirical evidence* that individuals retaliate to breaches that create unequal and unfair outcomes that deviate from the promised one, and where the promisor in breach profits from her own wrong. It also points to the fact that promisees do not retaliate against all breaches, indiscriminately. They rather consider the consequences of breach and seem to condone breaches that are committed to avoid an unfair and unequal outcome, but not breaches committed to achieve higher profits. This finding in not in line with promissory theories, where breach is, because of the violation of the norm of keeping promises, a moral wrong that does not depend of the efficiency and fairness of the result of breach.

---

[36] *See supra* Sect. 4.4.

[37] *See supra* Sects. 4.4.1, 4.4.2 and 4.4.3.

[38] In the absence of a prior promise, average retaliation was of 21% ($N = 52$), and 17% ($N = 46$) in the presence of promises. This is, however, a negative result, and means firstly that there was no supporting evidence for the explicit hypothesis. However, the promise and the experimental manipulation that failed to produce any change in behavior in state 3 produced substantial changes in other states, and was real and perceived as such by subjects that, in fact, reacted to it in some specific states of the world.

[39] The observed rate of retaliation in the presence of prior promises was of 50% ($N = 24$), and thus higher than the rate of 36% in its absence ($N = 33$), but this difference is not significant ($p = 0.41$). The experiment hence does not provide supporting evidence for retaliation to inefficient breaches, but it does not exclude the possibility that this effect exists, for its size is small. In this case, there is the need of further investigation to be able to ascertain whether the observed difference is due to sampling or is, in effect, an existing effect.

[40] Promisee's tendency to retaliate to breach of promise was, in sum, present when breach was *unfair and inefficient* as well as when breach was *unfair* but *efficient*. In the absence of promises, only 31% ($N = 26$) of subjects retaliated when the act was unfair and inefficient, and only 29% ($N = 47$) retaliated when it was unfair but efficient. When the promisor had promised to go through with the exchange, 58% ($N = 24$) of promisees retaliated to unfair and inefficient breaches ($p = 0.086$), and 49% ($N = 41$) did so against unfair but efficient breaches ($p = 0.082$).

In its second part, the experiment investigated the effect of legal enforcement, in the form of expectation damages, on the behavior of the parties. With respect to the behavior of promisors, the interest lies in the effect of expectation damages to induce performance if performance is socially efficient, and breach if breach is socially efficient, net of the effect of promissory commitment. With respect to the behaviors of promisees, the interest lies in the effect of expectation damages to crowd out retaliation by the promisee, and the conditions in which compensation is most likely to be necessary to achieve the last goal. The third and the fourth hypotheses hence tackled, from an empirical perspective, the *second research question*, and inquired into the secondary duty to pay damages for breach.

The third hypothesis is that expectation damages induce promisors to perform when performance is socially efficient and, moreover, to induce promisors to breach when breach is socially efficient. This is the univocal prediction derived from economic models. And in effect, the legal remedy substantially affected individual behavior and deterred breaches. While promisors almost never kept their promises in the absence of damages, promisors performed quite more often in the presence of expectation damages.[41] More importantly, the experiment provides evidence that while expectation damages induce performance if performance is efficient, they do *not* induce performance when performance is socially inefficient, thereby providing empirical support for the prediction from Economic Analysis of Law *in its entirety*. Whenever breach was socially efficient, rates of breach fell from around 90% in the absence of damages to a much lower 28% in the presence of damages, and these differences are statistically extremely significant ($p = 0.000$ in both cases). In contingencies where breach was socially *inefficient*, in contrast, rates of breach remained virtually unaltered.

The fourth hypothesis, lastly, is that expectation damages crowd out the observed tendency of disappointed promisees to retaliate to breach. The experiment provides supporting evidence for this effect of an award of damages for breach that has not been adequately considered in economic models. Average retaliation fell from 40% in the absence of legal redress to a much lower 20% in its presence, and this difference is highly significant ($p = 0.001$). They fell sharply precisely in those same contingencies where breach of promise in fact induced retaliation by victims of breach.[42] Compensatory remedies, such as expectation damages, in effect crowd out the observed tendency of promisees to retaliate to breach of contractual promises.

---

[41] While average breach in the absence of the availability of expectation damages was 94% ($N = 98$), it was a quite lower 61% ($N = 112$) in their presence.

[42] When breach was *efficient* but *unfair*, retaliation fell from an average of 49% ($N = 41$) in the absence of legal relief to a much lower 23% ($N = 48$) in its presence, reducing average retaliation by more than half, and this difference is statistically significant ($p = 0.014$). When breach was *inefficient and unfair*, average retaliation fell from 50 and 58%, in the absence of damages, to almost zero in the presence of damages, but there are few observations of the decision to retaliate when breach was socially inefficient. The reason being that expectation damages already induced 72% of promisors to perform, in those circumstances, and hence, there were fewer instances of inefficient breach of contract.

The unfairness of the result from breach was, as observed in the experiment, the main factor driving retaliation to breach. And the unfairness of the outcome is not completely eliminated by an award of expectation damages, since they allow the promisor to retain all remaining profits from breach after the payment of expectation damages. Expectation damages, in encouraging efficient breaches, allow the contract-breaker *to profit from her own wrong.*[43]

The sixth chapter developed a study aimed at improving the understanding of the functions of legal relief dispensed to promisees to redress breach that considers the function of remedies to crowd out retaliation. It further developed a *normative analysis* of different existing remedies for breach. It thereby tackled the third research question: *How can remedies for breach be designed to provide optimal incentives for promisors to perform while effectively crowding out retaliation, thereby delivering a superior contribution to social welfare than the one delivered by expectation damages and specific performance?*

As argued in the last chapter of the thesis, different legal remedies implement different distributions of losses and profits from breach and are therefore capable of better or worse crowding out retaliation depending on the fairness of the result they implement. It studied how legal relief could better achieve the goal of crowding out retaliation while still providing incentives for promisors to perform when performance is socially efficient, and to breach otherwise, thereby exhausting all possible gains from trade while minimizing losses from socially costly forms of retaliation.

Firstly, *full disgorgement* can provide for a fairer result for the promisee in entitling her to recover all profits from breach. However, it can only *revert* the direction of the unfairness and of the inequality created by breach.[44] The expected result will often be retaliation by the promisor who is stripped off of any share of those profits. Moreover, in putting the promisor in breach in the position in which she would have been in case she had performed, full disgorgement makes the promisor indifferent between performance and breach and might, if the promisor places no value in the welfare of the promisee, deter efficient breaches.[45] When parties can renegotiate without substantial costs, full disgorgement can minimize or perhaps completely eliminate retaliation by both parties while also inducing efficient breaches. However, when renegotiation fails or is rather a costly or uncertain enterprise, then full disgorgement is not apt to provide for a higher social welfare than expectation damages.[46]

Secondly, *specific performance* can eliminate that type of unfairness that expectation damages cannot only when parties can renegotiate the contract, and moreover only in fortunate contingencies, in case of a higher outside offer. The promisee must then offer a share of the possible profits from breach to the promisor in order to induce the latter to breach efficiently and to realize all possible gains from trade.[47] Injunctive relief may lead, however, to an unfair result whenever the promisor faces

---

[43] *See supra* Sects. 6.2.1 and 6.2.2.

[44] *See supra* Sect. 6.2.3.

[45] *See supra* Sect. 6.2.4.

[46] *See supra* Sect. 6.2.5.

[47] *See supra* Sect. 6.3, especially 6.3.3.

an unfortunate contingency, as in case of unforeseen hardship and much higher costs of production, and must then renegotiate with the promisee in order to be released from the obligation to perform.[48] In this type of contingency, even when parties can renegotiate the contract, the promisee might exploit the promisor by requiring more than what she bargained for in order to release the promisor, and retaliation by exploited promisors is expected to be high.[49]

Thirdly, *partial disgorgement*, or *hypothetical bargain damages*, as recently accepted by the House of Lords, in English law, is a remedy capable of inducing performance if and only if performance is socially efficient because the promisor has incentives to breach, efficiently, both when she can retain all profits from breach, and when she can retain only a share of them.[50] Moreover, they provide a fairer distribution of the profits from breach in allowing both parties to profit from efficient breaches. And even more, they do not require parties to renegotiate in order to realize those further gains from trade, for the promisor knows that she cannot be exploited in the renegotiation just as the promisee knows that she will always earn something from the breach. Hypothetical bargain damages induce performance if and only if performance is socially efficient, and implement a result that is fairer to the interests of both parties without any need to incur costs in renegotiation, being thereby Pareto-superior to expectation damages.

The thesis studied the behavioral tendency to retaliate to perceived wrong in breach of contract in perhaps the hardest context to capture that effect. After all, as discussed in the second chapter, it is not at all clear *why* breach of contract, in a situation where the promisee suffers no more than loss of expectancy, is a wrong in need of redress.[51] Simple answers involving the wrong in breaking promises, or the harm suffered by the promisee do not, by themselves, satisfy. The convention of promises itself foresees excusing conditions that release the promisor from the obligation to perform, but there is no specification, in promissory theories, of what defines those conditions. Moreover, the harm incurred by the promisee is not the only harm created by the act of breach, since breach can create social harms, or harms to the interest of society itself, and to overall social welfare in instigating private punishment, and therefore creating a deadweight loss.

The protection of the reliance interest may present a more pressing case for legal redress than the protection of the expectation interest. In situations where the promisee in fact suffers a real and material harm because of breach by the promisor, aggrievement and retaliation are expected to be much higher. When the promisee

---

[48] *See* the discussion *supra* in Sect. 6.3.2 on the doctrines that release the promisor from the obligation to perform, creating then only the obligation to pay damages and to put the promisee in the same position she was *before* the making of the contract, i.e. by *rescinding* the contract.

[49] *See supra* Sect. 6.3.4.

[50] *See supra* Sect. 6.4.

[51] As mentioned by Fuller and Perdue, losing something one does not have, but that one would only earn by performance of the promise cannot be immediately equated to a harm. *Cf.* Fuller & Perdue, *The Reliance Interest in Contract Damages*, *op. cit. supra*, at 53 ("In actuality the loss which the plaintiff suffers (deprivation of the expectancy) is not a datum of nature but the reflection of a normative order. It appears as a 'loss' only by reference to an unstated ought.").

suffers a *loss of reliance*, she is expected to be substantially more likely to feel aggrieved and tempted to retaliate against the promisor that imposes upon her, in a deliberate act, a real and material harm.[52]

The protection of the restitution interest, much stronger, as advanced by Fuller and Perdue, presents an even more pressing case for legal intervention than the protection of the reliance interest. In situations where the promisee suffers a *loss of an upfront benefit* because of breach by the promisor, and this benefit is not restituted to the promisee, then the promisor in breach profits at the expense of the promisee, who loses the benefit that the promise-breaker appropriates. In case of loss of reliance, the promisee suffers a real loss, but the promisor in breach does not appropriate the same amount that the promisee loses. In case of lost benefit, the promisor acquires a benefit that should be restituted to the promisee, who never agreed to give something to the promisor unless in exchange for a performance.

Yet again, this famous conjecture from Fuller and Perdue has not been subject to empirical investigation, and still lacks a social welfare justification. It can, however, be justified based on the promisee's tendency to retaliate, much more often, to loss of benefit than to loss of reliance or loss of expectancy. This conjecture could be investigated, empirically, in future research, in order to *provide a justification for why contract law does not always allow promisees to recover lost profits, but always allows promisees to recover lost benefits.* Even in case of impossibility and impracticability of performance, courts will rescind the contract, and put the parties in the position they were before the contract was made. The study of retaliation to breach in case of a lost benefit may provide an economic justification, on social welfare grounds, for *why rescission is pervasive, while recovery of lost profits is at times dispensable.*[53]

Apart from the incentives that remedies have on parties' decision to invest in reliance on the promise, and to take precautions, another specific function of legal enforcement of promises was not studied in the thesis. As advanced by Joseph Raz, enforcement remedies "are justified by preventing harm to the contracting parties and protecting the practice of undertaking voluntary obligations from erosion … The distinctive mark of contract law is that the harms it protects against are harms to the practice of undertaking voluntary obligations and harms resulting from its abuse."[54]

---

[52] As noted by Atiyah, "[n]o definitional jugglery can actually equate the position of the party who suffers a diminution of his assets in reliance on a promise, and a person who suffers no such diminution." Atiyah, *Contracts, Promises and the Law of Obligation, op. cit. supra*, at 203.

[53] The obtained experimental evidence already points to the fact that, with respect to the tendency to retaliate, recovery of lost expectancy is dispensable when the promisor breaches to avoid high losses, and an unfair and unequal outcome. It is, however, fundamental when the promisor breaches to achieve higher profits from a substitute transaction, and profits from her own wrong. With respected to the need to induce performance and deter breaches, however, there is still the need to protect the expectation interest in order to induce socially optimal levels of performance, as discussed in Chap. 6.

[54] *Promises in Morality and Law, op. cit supra*, at 938.

The practice of promising, mentioned by Raz, has its own welfare benefits in facilitating trade and exchanges with low costs of negotiation, and without the need to reduce agreements to a written form. Breach is possibly capable, if widespread and disseminated, and encouraged by the default remedy, at the common law, of expectation damages, of eroding the practice and its benefits. This conjecture can be subject to experimental investigation in repeated and dynamic trade games, and the protection of the practice itself, by contract law, as advanced by Raz, may also have its very own justification on social welfare grounds. It also remains as an object for future studies.

The introduction of retaliation in the economic model of contractual behavior, in the absence of remedies for breach and of any type of legal enforcement, as developed by Oliver Hart and John Moore, allowed for insightful new advances in the analysis of the hold-up problem and of the theory of firm.[55] Its introduction, in the economic analysis of remedies for breach of contract, shed light into the function of the legal remedy to crowd out retaliation, and into its social welfare function. It may also, in further future research, provide new insights for the role of punishment in criminal law, and into the value of compensation in tort law.

[55] *See* Oliver Hart, *Hold-Up, Asset Ownership, and Reference Points*, 124 QUARTERLY JOURNAL OF ECONOMICS 267 (2009); Oliver Hart & Bengt Holmström, *A Theory of Firm Scope*, 125 QUARTERLY JOURNAL OF ECONOMICS 483 (2010).

Bibliography

Anscombe, Gertrud, *Modern Moral Philosophy*, 33 PHILOSOPHY 1 (1958).
Anston, William, Principles of the English Law of Contracts and of Agency in its Relation to Contract (Ernst W. Huffcut ed., 8th ed. New York, Banks Law Publishing 1899).
Atiyah, Patrick, *Contracts, Promises and the Law of Obligation*, 94 LAW QUARTERLY REVIEW 193 (1978).
Atiyah, Patrick, THE RISE AND FALL OF FREEDOM OF CONTRACT (Oxford, Clarendon 1979).
Atiyah, Patrick, PROMISES, MORALS AND LAW (Oxford, Clarendon 1981).
Atiyah, Patrick, INTRODUCTION TO THE LAW OF CONTRACTS (Oxford, Clarendon 1989).
Aumann, Robert, *Nash Equilibria are not Self-Enforcing*, in ECONOMIC DECISION MAKING: GAMES, ECONOMETRICS AND OPTIMISATION 201 (J. Gabszewicz et al. eds, Amsterdam, North-Holland 1990).
Axelrod, Robert & William Hamilton, *The Evolution of Cooperation*, 211 SCIENCE 1390 (1981).
Babcock, Linda et al., *Biased Judgments in Fairness Bargaining*, 85 AMERICAN ECONOMIC REVIEW 1337 (1995).
Babcock, Linda & George Loewenstein, *Explaining Bargaining Impasse: The Role of Self-Serving Biases*, 11 JOURNAL OF ECONOMIC PERSPECTIVES 109 (1997).
Barnett, Randy, *The Death of Reliance*, 46 JOURNAL OF LEGAL EDUCATION 518 (1996).
Barton, John, *The Economic Basis of Damages for Breach of Contract*, 1 JOURNAL OF LEGAL STUDIES 277 (1972).
Batson, C. Daniel, Rational Processing or Rationalization? The Effect of Disconfirming Information on a Stated Religious Belief, 32 JOURNAL OF PERSONALITY AND SOCIAL PSYCHOLOGY 176 (1975).
Battigalli, Pierpaolo & Martin Dufwenberg, *Guilt in games*, 97 AMERICAN ECONOMIC REVIEW: PAPERS AND PROCEEDINGS 170 (2007).
Battigalli, Pierpaolo & Martin Dufwenberg, *Dynamic Psychological Games*, 141 JOURNAL OF ECONOMIC THEORY 1 (2009).
Becker, Gary, *The Economic Approach to Human Behavior* (Chicago, University of Chicago 1976).
Benabou, Roland & Jean Tirole, *A Cognitive Theory of Identity*, mimeo (Princeton University, 2006).
Birks, Peter, THE ROMAN LAW OF OBLIGATIONS (Oxford, Oxford University 2014).
Birmingham, Robert, Breach of Contract, Damage Measures, and Economic Efficiency, 24 RUTGERS LAW REVIEW 273 (1969).
Blackstone, William, COMMENTARIES ON THE LAWS OF ENGLAND IN FOUR BOOKS (George Sharswood ed., Philadelphia, J.B. Lippincott 1893) (1765–1769).

S. Mittlaender, *Equity, Efficiency, and Ethics in Remedies for Breach of Contract*, International Law and Economics, https://doi.org/10.1007/978-3-031-10804-4

Bochet, Olivier & Louis Putterman, Not just babble: Opening the black box of communication in a voluntary contribution experiment, 53 GAMES AND ECONOMIC BEHAVIOR 309 (2009).

Bohnet, Iris, Bruno Frey & Steffen Huck, *More Order with Less Law: On Contract Enforcement, Trust, and Crowding*, 95 AMERICAN POLITICAL SCIENCE REVIEW 131 (2001).

Bolton, Gary & Axel Ockenfels, *ERC: A Theory of Equity, Reciprocity, and Competition*, 90 AMERICAN ECONOMIC REVIEW 166 (2000).

Bowles, Samuel & Herbert Gintis, *The Evolution of Strong Reciprocity: Cooperation in Heterogeneous Populations*, 65 THEORETICAL POPULATION BIOLOGY 17 (2004).

Brandts, Jordi & Gary Charness, *Truth or Consequence: an Experiment*, 49 MANAGEMENT SCIENCE 116 (2003).

Brooks, Richard, *The Efficient Performance Hypothesis*, 116 YALE LAW JOURNAL 568 (2006).

Buchanan, James, *The Constitution of Economic Policy*, 77 AMERICAN ECONOMIC REVIEW 243 (1987).

Burris, Christopher, Eddie Harmon-Jones & W. Ryan Tarpley, *"By Faith Alone": Religious Agitation and Cognitive Dissonance*, 19 BASIC AND APPLIED SOCIAL PSYCHOLOGY 17 (1997).

Burton, Steven, Normative Legal Theories: The Case for Pluralism and Balancing, 98 IOWA LAW REVIEW 535 (2013).

Buskens, Vincent & Lambèr Royakkers, *Commitments: A Game-Theoretical and Logical Perspective*, 1 COGNITIVE SCIENCE QUARTERLY 1 (2000).

Buskens, Vincent & Lambèr Royakkers, BETWEEN HOBBES' LEVIATHAN AND SMITH'S INVISIBLE HAND (The Hague, Eleven 2011)

Cabrillac, Rémy, DROIT DES OBLIGATIONS (11th ed., Paris, Dalloz, 2014).

Calabresi, Guido & A. Douglas Melamed, Property Rules, Liability Rules and Inalienability: One View of the Cathedral, 85 HARVARD LAW REVIEW 1089 (1972).

Calamari, John & Joseph Perillo, CONTRACTS (6th ed., St. Paul, West, 2009).

Camerer, Colin, BEHAVIORAL GAME THEORY (Princeton, Princeton University, 2003).

Camerer, Colin & Richard Thaler, *Anomalies: Ultimatums, Dictators and Manners*, 9 JOURNAL OF ECONOMIC PERSPECTIVES 209 (1995).

Cameron, Lisa, Raising the Stakes in the Ultimatum Game: Experimental Evidence from Indonesia, 37 ECONOMIC INQUIRY 47 (1999).

Canaris, Claus-Wilhelm, Die Behandlung nicht zu vertretender Leistungshindernisse nach § 275 Abs. 2 BGB beim Stückkauf, 59 Nr. 5 JURISTENZEITUNG 214 (2004).

Canaris, Claus-Wilhelm, *Die Vertrauenshaftung im Lichte der Rechtsprechung des Bundesgerichtshof*, in 2 GESAMMELTE SCHRIFTEN 795 (Grigoleit & Neuner eds., Berlin, Walter der Gruyter 2012).

Canaris, Claus-Wilhelm, *Zur Bedeutung der Kategorie der „Unmöglichkeit" für das Recht der Leistungsstörungen*, in 3 GESAMMELTE SCHRIFTEN 423 (*id.* 2012).

Canaris, Claus-Wilhelm, *Die Reform des Rechts der Leistungsstörungen*, in 3 GESAMMELTE SCHRIFTEN 451 (*id.* 2012).

Canaris, Claus-Wilhelm, *Das allgemeine Leistungsstörungsrecht in Schuldrechtmodernisierungsgesetz*, in 3 GESAMMELTE SCHRIFTEN 541 (*id.* 2012)

Carbonnier, Jean, DROIT CIVIL: LES OBLIGATIONS (22nd ed., Paris, PUF, 2000).

Carlsmith, Kevin, John Darley & Paul Robinson, *Why Do We Punish? Deterrence and Just Deserts as Motives for Punishment*, 83 JOURNAL OF PERSONALITY AND SOCIAL PSYCHOLOGY 284 (2002).

Casari, Marco & Luigi Luini, *Cooperation Under Alternative Punishment Institutions: An Experiment*, 71 JOURNAL OF ECONOMIC BEHAVIOR AND ORGANIZATION 273 (2009).

Charness, Gary & Martin Dufwenberg, *Promises and Partnerships*, 74 ECONOMETRICA 1579 (2006).

Charness, Gary & Martin Dufwenberg, *Bare Promises: An Experiment*, 107 ECONOMIC LETTERS 281 (2010).

Charness, Gary & Martin Dufwenberg, *Participation*, 101 AMERICAN ECONOMIC REVIEW 1213 (2011).

Charny, David, *Nonlegal Sanctions in Commercial Relationships*, 104 HARVARD LAW REVIEW 373 (1990).
Chen, Ying et al., *Selecting Cheap-Talk Equilibria*, 76 ECONOMETRICA 117 (2008).
Chitty, Joseph & Hugh Beale, CHITTY ON CONTRACTS (31st ed. London, Sweet & Maxwell 2013).
Christensen-Szalanski, Jay, *The Hindsight Bias: A Meta-Analysis*, 48 ORGANIZATIONAL BEHAVIOR AND HUMAN DECISION PROCESSES 147 (1991).
Cinyabuguma, Matthias, Talbot Page & Louis Putterman, *Can Second-Order Punishment Deter Perverse Punishment?*, 9 EXPERIMENTAL ECONOMICS 265 (2006).
Cinyabuguma, Matthias, Talbot Page & Louis Putterman, *Cooperation under the Threat of Expulsion in a Public Goods Experiment*, 89 JOURNAL OF PUBLIC ECONOMICS 1421 (2005).
Civai, Claudia, *Rejecting Unfairness: Emotion-driven Reaction or Cognitive Heuristic?*, 7 FRONTIERS IN HUMAN NEUROSCIENCE ARTICLE 126 (2013).
Civai, Claudia et al., Are irrational reactions to unfairness truly emotionally-driven? Dissociated behavioural and emotional responses in the Ultimatum Game task, 114 COGNITION 89 (2010).
Civai, Claudia et al., *Equality versus self-interest in the brain: Differential roles of anterior insula and medial prefrontal cortex*, 62 NEUROIMAGE 102 (2012).
Civai, Claudia & Raffaella Rumiati & Aldo Rustichini, More equal than others: Equity norms as an integration of cognitive heuristics and contextual cues in bargaining games, 144 ACTA PSYCHOLOGICA 12 (2013).
Coase, Ronald, *The Nature of the Firm*, 4 ECONOMICA 386 (1937).
Coleman, Jules, *Efficiency, Utility and Wealth Maximization*, 8 HOFSTRA LAW REVIEW 509 (1980).
Cooter, Robert, Unity in Torts, Contracts, and Property: The Model of Precaution, 73 CALIFORNIA LAW REVIEW 1 (1985).
Cooter, Robert & Melvin Eisenberg, *Damages for Breach of Contract*, 73 CALIFORNIA LAW REVIEW 1434 (1985).
Cooter, Robert & Thomas Ulen, LAW AND ECONOMICS (3rd ed. Reading, Addison Wesley Longman 2000).
Cooter, Robert & Ariel Porat, *Anti-Insurance*, 31 JOURNAL OF LEGAL STUDIES 203 (2002).
Corbin, Arthur L., A Comprehensive Treatise on the Rules of Contract Law (1st ed. Saint Paul, West Law 1951).
Craswell, Richard, *Instrumental Theories of Compensation: A Survey*, 40 SAN DIEGO LAW REVIEW 1135 (2003).
Crawford, Vincent, *A Survey of Experiments on Communication via Cheap Talk*, 78 JOURNAL OF ECONOMIC THEORY 286 (1998).
Crawford, Vincent & Joel Sobel, *Strategic information transmission,* 50 ECONOMETRICA 1431 (1982).
Dawson, John, *Restitution or Damages?*, 20 OHIO STATE LAW JOURNAL 175 (1959).
Dedek, Helge, Negative Haftung aus Vertrag (Tübingen, Mohr Siebeck, 2007).
Dedek, Helge & Martin Schermaier, *Obligation (Greek and Roman), in* ENCYCLOPEDIA OF ANCIENT HISTORY (Roger Bagnall et. al. eds. Oxford, Wiley & Blackwell 2011).
Depoorter, Ben & Stephan Tontrup, How Law FramesMoral Instuitions: The Expressive Effect of Specific Performance, 54 ARIZONA LAW REVIEW 673 (2012).
Deschamps, Christian, *La Réparation du Préjudice Économique pur en Droit Français*, 50 REVUE INTERNATIONALE DE DROIT COMPARÉ 367 (1998).
Desmet, Pieter, David de Cremer & Eric van Dijk, On the Psychology of Financial Compensations to Restore Fairness Transgressions: When Intentions Determine Value, 95 JOURNAL OF BUSINESS ETHICS 105 (2010)
Desmet, Pieter, David de Cremer & Eric van Dijk, *In Money we Trust? The Use of Financial Compensations to Repair Trust in the Aftermath of Distributive Harm*, 114 ORGANIZATIONAL BEHAVIOR AND HUMAN DECISION PROCESSES 75 (2011).
Desmet, Pieter, David de Cremer & Eric van Dijk, *Trust Recovery Following Voluntary or Forced Financial Compensations in the Trust Game: The Role of Trait Forgiveness*, 51 PERSONALITY AND INDIVIDUAL DIFFERENCES 267 (2011).

Domat, Jean, LES LOIS CIVILES DANS LEUR ORDRE NATUREL, in 1 OUVRES DE JEAN DOMAT 75, (Joseph Remy ed., Paris, Firmin Didot 1828) (1695).

Dreber, Anna et al., *Winners don't punish*, 452 NATURE 348 (2008).

Dworkin, Ronald, *Is Wealth a Value?*, 9 JOURNAL OF LEGAL STUDIES 191 (1980).

Egas, Martijn & Arno Riedl, *The Economics of Altruistic Punishment and the Maintenance of Cooperation*, 275 PROCEEDINGS OF THE ROYAL SOCIETY BIOLOGICAL SCIENCES 871 (2008).

Ehmann, Horst & Holger Sutschet, MODERNISIERTES SCHULDRECHT 125 (München: Vahlen 2012).

Eisenberg, Melvin, *The Limits of Cognition and the Limits of Contract*, 47 STANFORD LAW REVIEW 211 (1995).

Eisenberg, Melvin, *Actual and Virtual Specific Performance, the Theory of Efficient Breach, and the Indifference Principle in Contract Law*, 93 CALIFORNIA LAW REVIEW 975 (2005).

Eisenberg, Melvin, *The Disgorgement Interest in Contract Law,* 105 MICHIGAN LAW REVIEW 559 (2006).

Ellingsen, Tore et al., *Testing Guilt Aversion*, 68 GAMES AND ECONOMIC BEHAVIOR 95 (2010).

Ellingsen, Tore & Magnus Johanesson, *Promises, Threats and Fairness*, 114 ECONOMIC JOURNAL 397 (2004).

Elster, Jon, *Norms of Revenge*, 100 ETHICS 862 (1990).

Elster, Jon, *Indeterminacy of Emotional Mechanisms*, in ANALYTICAL SOCIOLOGY AND SOCIAL MECHANISMS 53 (Pierre Demeulenaere ed., Cambridge, Cambridge University 2011).

Engel, Christoph, *Dictator Games: A Meta Study*, 14 EXPERIMENTAL ECONOMICS 583 (2011)

Engel, Christoph, LEGAL EXPERIMENTS: MISSION IMPOSSIBLE? (The Hague, Eleven 2013)

Engel, Christoph & Michael Kurschilgen, Fairness Ex Ante and Ex Post: Experimentally Testing Ex Post Judicial Intervention into Blockbuster Deals, 8 JOURNAL OF EMPIRICAL LEGAL STUDIES 682 (2011).

Farnsworth, E. Allan, *Legal Remedies for Breach of Contract*, 70 COLUMBIA LAW REVIEW 1145 (1970).

Farnsworth, E. Allan, *Your Loss or My Gain? The Dilemma of the Disgorgement Principle in Breach of Contract*, 94 YALE LAW JOURNAL 1339 (1985).

Farnsworth, E. Allan, CONTRACTS (4th ed. New York, Aspen 2004).

Farrell, Joseph & Matthew Rabin, *Cheap Talk*, 10 JOURNAL OF ECONOMIC PERSPECTIVES 103 (1996).

Fauvard-Cosson, Bénédicte & Denis Mazeaud, EUROPEAN CONTRACT LAW (Munich, Sellier, 2008).

Fehr, Ernst & Urs Fischbacher, *Social Norms and Human Cooperation*, 8 TRENDS IN COGNITIVE SCIENCES 185 (2004).

Fehr, Ernst & Colin Camerer, *Social Neuroeconomics: The Neural Circuitry of a Broken Promise*, 11 TRENDS IN COGNITIVE SCIENCES 419 (2007).

Fehr, Ernst & Simon Gächter, *Cooperation and Punishment in Public Goods Experiments*, 90 AMERICAN ECONOMIC REVIEW 980 (2000).

Fehr, Ernst & Simon Gächter, *Altruistic Punishment in Humans*, 415 NATURE 137 (2002).

Fehr, Ernst & Klaus Schmidt, *A Theory of Fairness, Competition and Cooperation*, 114 QUARTERLY JOURNAL OF ECONOMICS 817 (1999).

Fehr, Ernst, Urs Fischbacher & Simon Gächter, *Strong Reciprocity, Human Cooperation and the Enforcement of Social* Norms, 13 HUMAN NATURE 1 (2002).

Feinberg, Joel, The Moral Limits of the Criminal Law Volume 1: Harm to Others (Oxford, Clarendon 1987).

Feldman, Fred, Actual Utility, the Objection from Impracticality, and the Move to Expected Utility, 129 PHILOSOPHICAL STUDIES 49 (2006).

Fercia, Riccardo, *Le Obbligazzioni Naturali*, in TRATTATTO DELLE OBBLIGAZZIONI 165 (Luigi Garofalo ed. Padova, Wolters Kluwer 2010).

Festinger, Leon, A THEORY OF COGNITIVE DISSONANCE (Stanford, Stanford University Press, 1957).

Festinger, Leon, *Cognitive Dissonance*, 207 SCIENTIFIC AMERICAN 93 (1962).

Festinger, Leon, Henry Riecken & Stanley Schlachter, WHEN PROPHECY FAILS (New York, Harper 1956)
Fischbacher, Urs, z-Tree: Zurich Toolbox for Ready-made Economic Experiments, 10 EXPERIMENTAL ECONOMICS 171 (2007).
Jacques Flour, Jean-Luc Aubert & Éric Savaux, DROIT CIVIL: LES OBLIGATIONS (8th ed., Paris, Dalloz, 2013).
Fried, Charles, CONTRACT AS PROMISE: A THEORY OF CONTRACTUAL OBLIGATION (Cambridge, Harvard University Press 1981).
Friedman, Milton, *The Methodology of Positive Economics*, in ESSAYS IN POSITIVE ECONOMICS 3 (Chicago, University of Chicago Press 1966).
Fuller, Lon, *Consideration and Form*, 41 COLUMBIA LAW REVIEW 799 (1941).
Fuller, Lon & William Perdue, *The Reliance Interest in Contract Damages I*, 46 YALE LAW JOURNAL 52 (1936).
Gächter, Simon, Elke Renner & Martin Sefton, *The Long-Run Benefits of Punishment*, 322 SCIENCE 1510 (2008).
Geest, Gerrit de, *N Problems require N instruments*, 35 INTERNATIONAL REVIEW OF LAW AND ECONOMICS 42 (2013).
Goetz, Charles, Enforcing Promises: An Examination of the Basis of Contract, 89 YALE LAW JOURNAL 1261 (1980).
Goetz, Charles & Robert Scott, Liquidated Damages, Penalties and the Just Compensation Principle: Some Notes on an Enforcement Model and a Theory of Efficient Breach, 77 COLUMBIA LAW REVIEW 554 (1977).
Goetz, Charles & Robert Scott, *The Limits of Expanded Choice: An Analysis of the Interactions Between Express and Implied Contract Terms*, 73 CALIFORNIA LAW REVIEW 261 (1985).
Gordley, James, The Philosophical Origins of Modern Contract Doctrine (Oxford, Clarendon 1991).
Gouldner, Alvin, *The Norm of Reciprocity*, 25 AMERICAN SOCIOLOGICAL REVIEW 161 (1960).
Grossman, Sanford & Oliver Hart, The Costs and Benefits of Ownership: A Theory of Vertical and Lateral Integration, 94 JOURNAL OF POLITICAL ECONOMY 691 (1986).
Gilmore, Grant, THE DEATH OF CONTRACT (1st ed. Columbus, Ohio State University 1974).
Gintis, Herbert, *Strong Reciprocity and Human Sociality*, 206 JOURNAL OF THEORETICAL BIOLOGY 169 (2000).
Gintis, Herbert et al., *Strong Reciprocity and the Roots of Human Morality*, 21 SOCIAL JUSTICE RESEARCH 241 (2008).
Guala, Francesco, Reciprocity: Weak or Strong? What Punishment Experiments do (and do not) Demonstrate, 35 BEHAVIORAL AND BRAIN SCIENCES 1 (2012).
Güth, Werner, Rolf Schmittberger & Bernd Schwarze, *An Experimental Analysis of Ultimatum Bargaining*, 3 JOURNAL OF ECONOMIC BEHAVIOR & ORGANIZATION 367 (1982).
Güth, Werner & Reinhard Tietz, *Ultimatum Bargaining Behavior: A Survey and Comparison of Experimental Results*, 11 JOURNAL OF ECONOMIC PSYCHOLOGY 417 (1990).
Harmon-Jones, Eddie, *A Cognitive Dissonance Theory Perspective on Persuasion*, in THE PERSUASION HANDBOOK: DEVELOPMENTS IN THEORY AND PRACTICE 99 (James Dillard & Michael Pfau eds. Thousand Oaks, Sage 2002).
Hart, Herbert. L. A., *Are There any Natural Rights?*, 64 THE PHILOSOPHICAL REVIEW 175 (1955).
Hart, Oliver, *Hold-Up, Asset Ownership, and Reference Points*, 124 QUARTERLY JOURNAL OF ECONOMICS 267 (2009).
Hart, Oliver & John Moore, *Property Rights and the Nature of the Firm*, 98 JOURNAL OF POLITICAL ECONOMY 1119 (1990).
Hart, Oliver & John Moore, *Contracts as Reference Points*, 73 QUARTERLY JOURNAL OF ECONOMICS 1 (2008).
Hart, Oliver & Bengt Holmström, *A Theory of Firm Scope*, 125 QUARTERLY JOURNAL OF ECONOMICS 483 (2010).
Hartmann, Felix, Der Anspruch auf das Stellvertretenden Commodum (Tübingen, Mohr Siebeck 2007).

Hausman, Daniel & Michael McPherson, *The Philosophical Foundations of Mainstream Normative Economics*, in THE PHILOSOPHY OF ECONOMICS 226 (Daniel Hausman ed., 3rd ed. Cambridge, Cambridge University Press 1984).

Hawkins, Scott & Reid Hastie, Hindsight: Biased judgments of past events after the outcomes are known, 107 PSYCHOLOGICAL BULLETIN 311 (1990).

Heider, Fritz, *Attitudes and Cognite Organization*, 21 JOURNAL OF PSYCHOLOGY 107 (1946) .

Heinrich, Joseph et al., In Seach of Homo Economicus: Behavioral Experiments in 15 Small-Scale Societies, 91 AMERICAN ECONOMIC REVIEW 73 (2001).

Henrich, Joseph et al., *Costly Punishment Across Human Societies*, 312 SCIENCE 1767 (2006).

Hermalin, Benjamin, Avery Katz & Richard Craswell, *Contract Law*, in HANDBOOK OF LAW AND ECONOMICS 3 (A. Mitchell Polinsky & Steven Shavell eds. Amsterdam, North Holland 2006).

Herrmann, Benedikt, Christian Thöni & Simon Gächter, *Antisocial Punishment across Societies*, 319 SCIENCE 1362 (2008) .

Hoffman, Elizabeth & Matthew Spitzer, Entitlements, Rights and Fairness: An Experimental Examination of Subjects Concepts of Distributive Justice, 15 JOURNAL OF LEGAL STUDIES 254 (1985).

Hoffman, Elizabeth et al., *Preferences, Property Rights, and Anonymity in Bargaining Experiments*, 7 GAMES AND ECONOMIC BEHAVIOR 346 (1994).

Hoffman, Elizabeth, Kevin McCabe & Vernon Smith, *On Expectations and the Monetary Stakes in Ultimatum Games*, 25 JOURNAL OF GAME THEORY 289 (1996).

Hoffrage, Ulrich, Ralph Hertwig & Gerd Gigerenzer, *Hindsight Bias: A By-Product of Knowledge Updating?*, 26 JOURNAL OF EXPERIMENTAL PSYCHOLOGY: LEARNING, MEMORY AND COGNITION 566 (2000).

Holmes, Oliver Wendell, THE COMMON LAW (Paulo Pereira & Diego Beltran eds., Toronto, Typographical Society 2011) (1881).

Holmes, Oliver Wendell, *The Path of the Law*, 10 HARVARD LAW REVIEW 457 (1897).

Hopfensitz, Astrid & Ernesto Reuben, *The Importance of Emotions for the Effectiveness of Social Punishment*, 119 ECONOMIC JOURNAL 1534 (2009).

Huber, Ulrich, LEISTUNGSSTÖRUNGEN (Tübingen, Mohr Siebeck 1999).

Huber, Ulrich, *Schadensersatz statt der Leistung*, 210 ARCHIV FÜR DIE ZIVILISTISCHE PRAXIS 319 (2010).

Jackson, Frank, Decision-theoretic Consequentialism and the Nearest and Dearest Objection, 101 ETHICS 461 (1991).

Jhering, Rudolph von, GEIST DES RÖMISCHEN RECHTS (Leipzig, Breitkopf und Härtel 1852).

Jhering, Rudolph von, *Culpa in Contrahendo oder Schadenserstaz bei nichtigen oder nicht zur Perfektion gelangten Verträgen*, 4 JAHRBÜCHER FÜR DIE DOGMATIK DES HEUTIGEN RÖMISCHEN UND DEUTSCHEN RECHTS 1 (1861).

Josserand, Louis, COURS DE DROIT CIVIL POSITIF FRANÇAIS (Paris, Sirey 1932–1933).

Kahn-Freund, Otto, LABOUR AND THE LAW (Paul Davies & Mark Freedland eds., 3rd. ed. London, Stevens & Sons 1983).

Kaplow, Louis & Steven Shavell, Why the Legal System is Less Efficient than the Income Tax in Redistributing Income, 23 JOURNAL OF LEGAL STUDIES 667 (1994).

Kaplow, Louis & Steven Shavell, *Fairness versus Welfare*, 114 HARVARD LAW REVIEW 961 (2001).

Klass, Gregory, *To Perform or Pay Damages*, 98 VIRGINIA LAW REVIEW 143 (2012).

Kramer, Roderick & Marilynn Brewer, *Effects of group identity on resource use in a simulated commons dilemma*, 46 JOURNAL OF PERSONALITY AND SOCIAL PSYCHOLOGY 1044 (1984).

Kraus, Jody, *The Correspondence of Contract and Promise*, 109 COLUMBIA LAW REVIEW 1603, 1606 (2009).

Kronman, Anthony, *Wealth Maximization as a Normative Principle*, 9 JOURNAL OF LEGAL STUDIES 227 (1980).

Laithier, Yves-Marie, Étude Comparative des Sanctions de l'Inexécution du Contrat (Paris, LGDJ, 2004).

Laithier, Yves-Marie & Denis Mazeaud, La Nature de la Sanction: Satisfaction du Bénéficiaire par des Dommages-intérêts ou Primauté de l'Exécution en Nature?, 2 REVUE DES CONTRATS 681 (2012).
Lebois, Aubrey, *Les obligations de faire à caractère personnel*, 47 LA SEMAINE JURIDIQUE EDITION GÉNÉRALE I (2008).
Ledyard, John, *Public Goods: A Survey of Experimental Research*, in THE HANDBOOK OF EXPERIMENTAL ECONOMICS (John Kagel & Alvin Roth eds., 1997).
MacCormick, Neil, *Voluntary Obligations and Normative Powers*, 46 PROCEEDINGS OF THE ARISTOTELIAN SOCIETY supp. 59 (1972).
Macneil, Ian, *Efficient Breach of Contract: Circles in the Sky*, 68 VIRGINIA LAW REVIEW 947 (1982).
MacQueen, Hector, Barbara Dauner-Lieb & Peter Tettinger, *Specific Performance and the Right to Cure*, in THE COMMON EUROPEAN SALES LAW IN CONTEXT: INTERACTIONS WITH ENGLISH AND GERMAN LAW 627 (Gerhard Dannemann & Stefan Vogehauer eds., Oxford, Oxford University 2013).
Markesinis, Basil, Hannes Unberath & Angus Johnston, THE GERMAN LAW OF CONTRACT: A COMPARATIVE TREATISE (2nd. ed., Portland, Hart 2006).
Markovits, Daniel, *Making and Keeping Contracts*, 92 VANDERBILT LAW REVIEW 1325 (2006).
Markovits, Daniel & Alan Schwartz, The Myth of Efficient Breach: New Defenses of the Expectation Interest, 97 VIRGINIA LAW REVIEW 1939 (2011).
Markovits, Daniel & Alan Schwartz, *The Expectation Interest and the Promissory Basis of Contract*, 45 SUFFOLK LAW REVIEW 799 (2012).
Mas-Colell, Andreu, Michael Whinston & Jerry Green, MICROECONOMIC THEORY (New York, Oxford University 1995).
Maskin, Eric & Jean Tirole, *Unforeseen Contingencies and Incomplete Contracts*, 66 REVIEW OF ECONOMIC STUDIES 83 (1999).
Mazeaud, Henry, Léon Mazeaud & Jean Mazeaud, LEÇONS DE DROIT CIVIL (3rd ed., Paris, Montchrestien 1966) (1955).
Medicus, Dieter, SCHULDRECHT II: BESONDERER TEIL (14th. ed, Munich, Beck 2007).
Medicus, Dieter & Stephan Lorenz, SCHULDRECHT I: ALLGEMEINER TEIL (18th ed. Munich, Beck 2008).
Messick, David & Keith Sentis, *Fairness and Preference*, 15 JOURNAL OF EXPERIMENTAL SOCIAL PSYCHOLOGY 418 (1979).
Mill, Stuart, ON LIBERTY (Oxford, Oxford University 1859).
Miltenburg, Nynke van et al., Implementing punishment and reward in the public goods game: the effect of individual and collective decision rules, 8 INTERNATIONAL JOURNAL OF THE COMMONS (2014).
Mittlaender, Sergio & Vincent Buskens, *Retaliation, Remedies, and Contracts*, 21 AMERICAN LAW & ECONOMICS REVIEW 280 (2019).
Mittlaender, Sergio, *Morality, Compensation, and the Contractual Obligation*, 16 JOURNAL OF EMPIRICAL LEGAL STUDIES 119 (2019).
Murphy, Liam, *The Practice of Promise and Contract* (forthcoming in PHILOSOPHICAL FOUNDATIONS OF CONTRACT LAW, Gregory Klass et al. eds. 2014).
Nikiforakis, Nikos et al., *Normative Conflict & Feuds: The Limits of Self-Enforcement*, 96 JOURNAL OF PUBLIC ECONOMICS 797 (2012).
Nikiforakis, Nikos & Hans-Theo Normann, *A Comparative Statics Analysis of Punishment in Public-good Experiments*, 11 EXPERIMENTAL ECONOMICS 358 (2009).
Ohtsuki, Hisashi, Yoh Iwasa & Martin Novak, Indirect Reciprocity Provides a Narrow Margin of Efficiency for Costly Punishment, 457 NATURE 79 (2009).
Oosterbeek, Hessel, Randolph Sloof & Gijs van Kuilen, *Cultural Differences in Ultimatum Game Experiments: Evidence from a Meta-Analysis*, 7 EXPERIMENTAL ECONOMICS 171 (2004).
Ostrom, Elinor, James Walker & Roy Gardner, *Covenants with and without a Sword: Self-Governance is Possible*, 86 AMERICAN POLITICAL SCIENCE REVIEW 404 (1992).

Parisi, Francesco, *The Genesis of Liability in Ancient* Law, 3 AMERICAN LAW AND ECONOMICS REVIEW (2001).

Parry, David, THE SANCTITY OF CONTRACTS IN ENGLISH LAW (London, Stevens & Sons 1959).

Perillo, Joseph, Misreading Oliver Wendell Holmes on Efficient Breach and Tortious Interference, 68 FORDHAM LAW REVIEW 1085, 1092–1093 (2000).

Pettit, Philip, *Consequentialism,* in A COMPANION TO ETHICS 230 (Peter Singer ed. Oxford, Blackwell 1991).

Picker, Eduard, *Schuldrechtsreform und Privatautonomie*, 58 JURISTENZEITUNG 1035 (2003)

Planiol, Marcel, TRAITÉ ÉLÉMENTAIRE DE DROIT CIVIL (4th ed., Paris, Libraire Générale de Droit & Jurisprudence 1907).

Posner, Eric, Altruism, Status, and Trust in the Law of Gifts and Gratuitous Promises, 1997 WISCONSIN LAW REVIEW 567 (1997).

Posner, Eric, Altruism, *Economic Analysis of Contract Law After Three Decades: Success or Failure?*, 112 YALE LAW JOURNAL 829 (2003).

Posner, Richard, ECONOMIC ANALYSIS OF LAW 57 (1st ed. Boston, Little, Brown 1972).

Posner, Richard, *Gratuitous Promises in Economics and Law*, 6 JOURNAL OF LEGAL STUDIES 411 (1977).

Posner, Richard, *Utilitarianism, Economics, and Legal Theory*, 8 JOURNAL OF LEGAL STUDIES 103 (1979).

Posner, Richard, *Retribution and Related Concepts of Punishment*, 9 JOURNAL OF LEGAL STUDIES 71 (1980).

Posner, Richard, *The Value of Wealth: A Comment on Dworkin and Kronman*, 9 JOURNAL OF LEGAL STUDIES 243 (1980).

Posner, Richard, *Wealth Maximization Revisited*, 2 JOURNAL OF LAW, ETHICS AND PUBLIC CHOICE 85 (1985).

Posner, Richard, *Let us Never Blame a Contract Breaker*, 107 MICHIGAN LAW REVIEW 1349 (2009).

Pothier, Robert-Joseph, TRAITÉ DES OBLIGATIONS, in 1 OUVRES DE R.-J. POTHIER 1 (Ainé Dupin org., Bruxelles, J. P. Jonker 1761) (1831).

Pufendorf, Samuel, DE JURE NATURAE ET GENTIUM (Londini Scanorum 1688).

de Quervain, Dominique et al., *The Neural Basis of Altruistic Punishment*, 305 SCIENCE 1254 (2004).

Rabin, Matthew, *Moral Preferences, Moral Constraints, and Self-Serving Biases*, mimeo (University of California at Berkeley).

Rachlinski, Jeffrey, *The Limits of Social Norms*, 74 CHICAGO-KENT LAW REVIEW 1537 (1999).

Radin, Max, *Fundamental Concepts of the Roman Law*, 12 CALIFORNIA LAW REVIEW 481 (1924).

Rawls, John, *Two Concepts of Rules*, 64 THE PHILOSOPHICAL REVIEW 3 (1955).

Rawls, John, A THEORY OF JUSTICE (1st ed. Cambridge, Harvard University Press 1971).

Raz, Joseph, *Promises and Obligations*, in LAW, MORALITY AND SOCIETY: ESSAYS IN HONOUR OF H. L. A. HART 210 (Peter Hacker & Joseph Raz eds. Oxford, Oxford University 1977).

Raz, Joseph, *Authority and Consent*, 67 VIRGINIA LAW REVIEW 103 (1981).

Raz, Joseph, *Promises in Morality and Law*, 95 HARVARD LAW REVIEW 916 (1982).

Raz, Joseph, THE MORALITY OF FREEDOM (Oxford, Clarendon 1986).

Raz, Joseph, *The Problem of Authority: Revising the Service Conception*, 90 MINNESOTA LAW REVIEW 1003 (2006).

Riehm, Thomas, DER GRUNDSATZ DER NATURALERFÜLLUNG (Tübingen, Mohr Siebeck 2015).

Rockenbach, Bettina & Manfred Milinski, The Efficient Interaction of Indirect Reciprocity and Costly Punishment, 444 NATURE 718 (2006).

Rogerson, William, Efficient Reliance and Damage Measures for Breach of Contract, 15 RAND JOURNAL OF ECONOMICS 39 (1984).

Roth, Alvin et al., Bargaining and Market Behavior in Jerusalem, Ljubljana, Pittsburgh, and Tokyo: An Experimental Study, 81 AMERICAN ECONOMIC REVIEW 1068 (1991).

Rousseau, Denise, Psychological Contract in Organizations: Understanding Written and Unwritten Agreements (London, Sage 1995).

Sally, David, *Can I say "bobobo" and mean "There's no such thing as cheap talk"?*, 57 JOURNAL OF ECONOMIC BEHAVIOR AND ORGANIZATION 245 (2005).
Sanfey, Alan et al., The Neural Basis of Economical Decision-Making in the Ultimatum Game, 300 SCIENCE 1755 (2003).
Sanfey, Alan, Expectations and Social Decision-Making: Biasing Effects of Prior Knowledge on Ultimatum Responses, 8 MIND & SOCIETY 93 (2009).
Savigny, Friedrich Carl von, PANDEKTENVORLESUNG 1824/25 (Horst Hammen org. Frankfurt, Klostermann 1993) (1824–1825).
Savigny, Friedrich Carl von, SYSTEM DES HEUTIGEN RÖMISCHEN RECHTS (Berlin, Veit 1840).
Scanlon, Thomas, *Promises and Practices*, 19 PHILOSOPHY & PUBLIC AFFAIRS 199 (1990).
Schlesinger, Rudolf et al., COMPARATIVE LAW (6th ed. New York, Thomson Reuters 1998).
Schroeter, Ulrich, *Das Recht zur Zweiten Andienung im System des Schuldrechts*, 207 ARCHIV FÜR DIE ZIVILISTISCHE PRAXIS 28 (2007).
Scott, Robert, *The Death of Contract Law*, 54 UNIVERSITY OF TORONTO LAW JOURNAL 369 (2004).
Scott, Robert & George Triantis, *Embedded Options and the Case Against Compensation in Contract Law*, 104 COLUMBIA LAW REVIEW 1428 (2004).
Sedgwick, Theodore, A TREATISE ON THE MEASURE OF DAMAGES (Arthur Sedgwick & G. Willet van Nest eds., 7th ed. New York, Baker, Voorhuis 1880) (1847).
Sefton, Martin, Robert Shupp & James Walker, *The Effect of Rewards and Sanctions in Provision of Public Goods*, 45 ECONOMIC INQUIRY 671 (2007).
Seip, Elise, Wilco van Dijk & Mark Rotteveel, *Anger Motivates Costly Punishment of Unfair Behavior*, 38 MOTIVATION AND EMOTION 578 (2014).
Shavell, Steven, *Damage Measures for Breach of Contract*, 11 BELL JOURNAL OF ECONOMICS 466 (1980)
Shavell, Steven, *The Design of Contracts and Remedies for Breach*, 99 QUARTERLY JOURNAL OF ECONOMICS 121 (1984)
Shavell, Steven, FOUNDATIONS OF ECONOMIC ANALYSIS OF LAW (Cambridge, Harvard University Press 2004).
Shavell, Steven, *Specific Performance versus Damages*, 84 TEXAS LAW REVIEW 831 (2006).
Shavell, Steven, *Is Breach of Contract Immoral?*, 56 EMORY LAW JOURNAL 439 (2006).
Shavell, Steven, *Why Breach of Contract may not be Immoral given the Incompleteness of Contracts*, 107 MICHIGAN LAW REVIEW 1569 (2009).
Sherman, David & Geoffrey Cohen, *The Psychology of Self-defense: Self-affirmation theory*, 38 ADVANCES IN EXPERIMENTAL SOCIAL PSYCHOLOGY 183 (2006).
Shiffrin, Seana, *The Divergence between Contract and Promise*, 120 HARVARD LAW REVIEW 708 (2007).
Shiffrin, Seana, *Could Breach of Contract be Immoral?*, 107 MICHIGAN LAW REVIEW 1551 (2009).
Shiffrin, Seana, *Harm and its Moral Significance*, 18 LEGAL THEORY 357 (2012).
Simon, Herbert, A Formal Theory of the Employment Relationship, 19 ECONOMETRICA 293 (1951).
Simon, Herbert, *A Behavioral Model of Rational Choice*, 69 QUARTERLY JOURNAL OF ECONOMICS 99 (1955).
Simon, Herbert, THE SCIENCES OF THE ARTIFICIAL (Cambridge MA, MIT Press 1981).
Singer, Tania et al., Empathic Neural Responses are Modulated by the Perceived Unfairness of Others, 439 NATURE 466 (2006).
Slonin, Robert & Alvin Roth, Learning in High Stakes Ultimatum Games: An Experiment in the Slovak Republic, 66 ECONOMETRICA 569 (1998).
Smith, Adam, LECTURES ON JURISPRUDENCE (R. Meek et al. eds., Oxford, Liberty Fund 1982)
Smith, Stephen, CONTRACT THEORY (Oxford, Clarendon 2003).
Spence, Michael, *Job Market Signaling*, 87 QUARTERLY JOURNAL OF ECONOMICS 355 (1973).
Steele, Claude, *The Psychology of Self-affirmation: Sustaining the Integrity of the Self*, 21 ADVANCES IN EXPERIMENTAL SOCIAL PSYCHOLOGY 261 (1988).
Sugden, Robert, Rational Choice: A Survey of Contributions from Economics and Philosophy, 101 ECONOMIC JOURNAL 751 (1991).

Variable Geometry Turbine Technology for Marine Gas Turbines

Jie Gao · Qun Zheng · Feng Lin · Chen Liang ·
Yu Liu

Variable Geometry Turbine Technology for Marine Gas Turbines

国防工業出版社
National Defense Industry Press

Springer

Jie Gao
College of Power and Energy Engineering
Harbin Engineering University
Harbin, Heilongjiang, China

Qun Zheng
College of Power and Energy Engineering
Harbin Engineering University
Harbin, Heilongjiang, China

Feng Lin
Harbin Marine Boiler and Turbine Research Institute
Harbin, Heilongjiang, China

Chen Liang
Harbin Marine Boiler and Turbine Research Institute
Harbin, Heilongjiang, China

Yu Liu
Harbin Marine Boiler and Turbine Research Institute
Harbin, Heilongjiang, China

ISBN 978-981-19-6951-5 ISBN 978-981-19-6952-2 (eBook)
https://doi.org/10.1007/978-981-19-6952-2

Jointly published with National Defense Industry Press
The print edition is not for sale in China (Mainland). Customers from China (Mainland) please order the print book from: National Defense Industry Press.
ISBN of the Co-Publisher's edition: 978-7-118-10313-7

This Springer imprint is published by the registered company Springer Nature Singapore Pte Ltd.
The registered company address is: 152 Beach Road, #21-01/04 Gateway East, Singapore 189721, Singapore

Preface

As the main propulsion power unit of large- and medium-sized surface warships, gas turbines have become the development trend of navies worldwide. The use of variable geometry turbine technology can improve the acceleration and deceleration characteristics and low working condition performance of gas turbine units and significantly improve the maneuverability of ships. For example, the high-powered WR-21 marine intercooler regenerative gas turbine developed by the US Navy and Rolls-Royce has adopted variable geometry turbine technology, which reduces its annual fuel consumption by approximately 30%~40% compared with the simple-cycle, LM2500 gas turbine, and has become the symbol of a new generation of marine gas turbines.

The variable geometry turbine is an innovative technology for gas turbines. Although the use of variable geometry turbines can meet the very demanding performance requirements for marine gas turbines, their design is challenging. The aerodynamic efficiency levels under low working conditions, full-load power output ability and precise control, maintainability and reliability of variable vanes in a high-temperature and high-pressure environment determine the success or failure of variable geometry turbine gas turbines. However, the core technology of gas turbines is still monopolized and strictly blocked by a few countries in Europe and America, preventing China from improving its design level through technology introduction.

The No. 703 Research Institute of China State Shipbuilding Corporation Limited and Harbin Engineering University are the first domestic units to engage in the design and research of marine gas turbines. For this book, our team has been working on the design technology of variable geometry turbines for marine gas turbines since the National Tenth Five-Year Plan. Following the principles from simple to complex, our team gradually carried out systematic and in-depth investigations of the flow mechanisms and characteristics of variable geometry turbines, aerodynamic design methods, variable vane turning design methods, the structural design technology of the variable vane system and the aerodynamic characteristics and reliability test technology of variable geometry turbines. This book is the collation and summary of the results of these investigations. Our goal was to comprehensively explore the development of the design theory and engineering design technology of high-performance, variable geometry turbines for marine gas turbines in China.

The book is divided into six chapters.

Chapter 1, the overview, introduces the application, typical models, and working characteristics of marine gas turbines and explains the working principle, structural form, typical model applications and aerodynamic structural design features and design requirements of variable geometry turbines. Chapter 2 introduces in detail the internal complicated flow mechanism of the variable vane, variable vane stage and multistage variable geometry turbine and discusses the flow, power and efficiency characteristics of the variable geometry turbine. Chapter 3 investigates the selection rules of low-dimensional, aerodynamic design parameters of the variable geometry turbine, analyzes the aerodynamic performance of turbine blades suitable for variable geometry work and discusses the three-dimensional, aerodynamic design method of high endwall angle variable geometry turbine blades. Chapter 4 analyzes the endwall structure of variable vanes and the selection criteria and laws of parameters, discusses new methods for controlling the endwall loss of variable vanes and proposes two turning design concepts and methods: the high endwall angle variable vane turning design based on the stepped spherical endwall and the full, three-dimensional turning design of high endwall angle variable vanes for the high endwall angle variable geometry turbine. Chapter 5 systematically introduces the structural design technology of the variable vane system for variable geometry turbines, including the detailed structural design of the variable vane and the design of the turning control system of the variable vane. Chapter 6 discusses the variable geometry turbine aerodynamic characteristics and reliability test technology in four aspects: the variable vane linear cascade aerodynamic performance, variable vane sector cascade aerodynamic performance and transition state characteristics, variable vane turbine stage aerodynamic performance and full-ring variable vane thermal environment structure verification.

The authors of this book are affiliated with Harbin Engineering University and No. 703 Research Institute of China State Shipbuilding Corporation Limited. Chapter 1 was written by Jie Gao of Harbin Engineering University and Feng Lin and Yu Liu of No. 703 Research Institute of China State Shipbuilding Corporation Limited. Chapter 2 was written by Jie Gao of Harbin Engineering University. Chapters 3 and 4 were written by Jie Gao and Qun Zheng of Harbin Engineering University. Chapters 5 and 6 were written by Feng Lin, Chen Liang and Yu Liu of No. 703 Research Institute of China State Shipbuilding Corporation Limited. Jie Gao is responsible for drafting the entire book.

We have been engaged in the research of turbine aerodynamic structural design and test technology of marine gas turbines for many years. During this period, the book has received the support of many teachers, leaders and peer experts. Part of this book is a culmination of the exchange and cooperation with peer experts, to whom we sincerely express our gratitude for their support. The content of this book refers to the degree thesis of certain graduate students of the author's university and the scientific research or summary report of certain technical personnel of the research institute. The following individuals are recognized: Yongming Feng, Qiyan Lin, Shengqi Yin, Guozhi Sun, Xiaoxu Jing, Dong Li, Endong Zhou, Pengfei Liu, Fukun Cao, Yufeng Du, Fusheng Meng, Weiliang Fu, Shenghua Bai, Xiying Niu, Lin Wang and so on. The excellent work on the thesis and scientific research report has enriched the content of this book. Xuezheng Liu, Guojun Ma, Yufeng Du, Fukun Cao and others have performed much work in data collection and collation, formula and image processing and text editing. We appreciate their contributions.

We are grateful for the funding received from national defense basic research projects, navy pre-research projects, National Natural Science Foundation of China projects (51779051, 51979052, and 51406039), the Fundamental Research Funds for the Central Universities of China and projects entrusted by research institutes.

We are also grateful for the National Defense Science and Technology Book Publishing Fund, which supported the publication of this book.

This book can help readers understand the technological progress of gas turbine variable geometry turbine aerodynamics, structural design and testing, and the essence of variable geometry turbine design technology. This book can provide a reference for researchers and engineering technicians in the fields of gas turbines or aeroengines in power engineering and engineering thermophysics and aerospace propulsion theory and engineering.

We ask the readers to critique and correct any unintended errors, omissions and shortcomings in the content of this book.

Harbin, China
March 2020

Jie Gao
Qun Zheng
Feng Lin
Chen Liang
Yu Liu

Brief Introduction

This book discusses the design requirements of variable geometry turbines for marine gas turbines. Additionally, it systematically and comprehensively introduces the flow mechanism and characteristics of variable geometry turbines, aerodynamic design methods, variable vanc turning design methods, the structural design technology of the variable vane system and the aerodynamic characteristics and reliability test technology of variable geometry turbines.

This book can serve as a reference for scientific research in gas turbines and related fields for not only technical personnel, university teachers, etc., but also graduate students at higher education institutions.

Contents

Chapter 1
Introduction

Abstract This chapter provides an overview of marine gas turbines, marine gas turbine variable geometry turbines, and variable geometry turbine design features and requirements. The development of modern advanced marine gas turbines must meet the military needs of ship power and the special requirements of the marine working environment. The variable geometry turbine is a technical method for effectively improving the acceleration and deceleration characteristics and low working condition performance of marine gas turbines.

1.1 Introduction to the Marine Gas Turbine

1.1.1 Marine Gas Turbine Power Unit

Gas turbines are a new generation of marine power plants that emerged after steam turbines and diesel engines. The most prominent advantage of gas turbines for ships is their light weight; they are much lighter than high-speed diesel engines with the same power. Another excellent advantage of gas turbines is their large power per unit volume, which enables ships to reach higher speeds. Additionally, gas turbines are very suitable for use as ship power equipment due to their fast start, low vibration, combustible multiple liquid fuels, high reliability, and good maneuverability. Based on its own advantages, the use of ship power units has evolved from the early combined use of steam turbine and gas turbine (COSAG) to the alternative use of diesel engine or gas turbine (CODOG; refer to Fig. 1.1) (diesel engines for cruise power, and gas turbines for acceleration power) to the alternative use of gas turbine or gas turbine (COGOG). Presently, the trend of large and medium-sized surface ship power plant gas turbines has become increasingly obvious, and their application has become an important indicator of naval modernization.

However, the gas turbine power plant has some shortcomings: first, the gas turbine power host cannot be reversed and must be especially equipped with reversing mechanism or controllable-pitch propeller. In recent years, reversing gas turbine technology has also been utilized to achieve direct reversal. In addition, the gas turbine power plant is operated under part-load conditions for more than 90% of its life cycle.

J. Gao et al., *Variable Geometry Turbine Technology for Marine Gas Turbines*,
https://doi.org/10.1007/978-981-19-6952-2_1

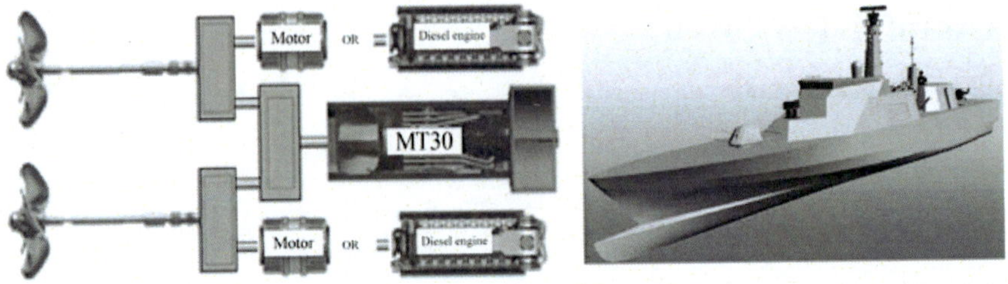

Fig. 1.1 Application of MT30 gas turbine on marine

Due to changes in thermal parameters during off-design point operation, the fuel consumption rate under part-load conditions sharply increases, and the efficiency is low. Therefore, to effectively solve the two major contradictions between the ship's requirements for high power during wartime and the requirements for high economy under cruise conditions, large and medium-sized surface ships usually prefer to use gas turbines as combined power units of afterburner units instead of single model power units.

In general, gas turbines have been recognized as the most comprehensive marine power plant. In warships with a displacement of more than several thousand tons, gas turbines will exhibit a good development trend and maintain the existing advantages of marine power plants. Presently, approximately three-quarters of the large and medium-sized surface ships worldwide use gas turbine power units. The various methods utilized for the ship loading situation of gas turbines varies by country: The United States uses the LM2500 gas turbine as the basic type and adopts the use of combined gas turbine and gas turbine (COGAG); the current British ship power plant uses the COGOG method; and countries such as Germany, France, and Japan use CODOG due to their large base of diesel engines. Presently, most of the power units of the surface ships of the Chinese navy are still dominated by medium- and high-speed diesel engines, and only a small number of surface ships use gas turbines. As the Chinese navy moves into the open sea, numerous modern surface ships with high endurance and good maneuverability powered by gas turbines will be needed in the future.

1.1.2 Introduction to a Typical Marine Gas Turbine

Due to the difficulty of manufacturing marine gas turbines, few manufacturers worldwide can design and produce marine gas turbines. The main manufacturers of marine gas turbines are the American company GE (products include LM1600 and LM2500 series), the British company Rolls-Royce (products include WR-21 and MT30) and Ukraine Dawning Company (products include GT25000). The United States, the United Kingdom and other countries have very advanced aero engine development systems. The development of marine gas turbines is based on aeronautical modified gas turbines, while Ukraine mainly adopts the technical approach of the specialized design of marine gas turbines. China's specialized design and aeronautical modified marine gas turbines have also entered a golden period of rapid development.

1. GT25000 gas turbine

The GT25000 gas turbine is a new generation of marine/industrial, split-shaft gas turbines from the Ukraine Dawning Company. The gas generator has a high- and low-pressure two-shaft structure: the low-pressure axial compressor is a 9-stage compressor driven by a 1-stage, low-pressure turbine; the high-pressure axial compressor is also a 9-stage compressor driven by a 1-stage, high-pressure turbine. The combustion chamber is a cannular counterflow type with 16 flame tubes, 16 fuel injection nozzles and 2 igniters. The power turbine is a 4-stage, reaction-type, axial turbine that drives the output shaft. The gas turbine can be used for natural gas booster stations, mechanical drives, power stations and ship main power; it is currently the preferred power source for large and medium-sized ship gas turbines in the Chinese navy.

2. LM2500 series gas turbine

The LM2500 gas turbine, which is the most successful marine gas turbine developed by GE in the United States, is modified from the TF39/CF6-6 aviation turbofan engine. This gas turbine retains the core engine of the original aero engine and removes the low-pressure fan, and simultaneously, the original low-pressure turbine was changed to a power turbine. This modification method inherits the working reliability of the tens of millions of operating hours accumulated by the aero engine series to the greatest extent, which makes the LM2500 gas turbine establish a good international reputation in a relatively short period.

The LM2500 marine gas turbine has been developed since 1967. In 1970, the first production type, LM2500, was put into operation and trial use. Its output power is 16.54 MW, and its efficiency is 36%. For more than 40 years, the LM2500 marine gas turbine has been serially improved (refer to Fig. 1.2). By means of advanced technology, such as adding a zero stage in front of the low-pressure compressor, using new materials and new cooling structures in the high-pressure turbine and aerodynamically redesigning blade profiles, many typical models have been developed and derived, such as LM2500 +, LM2500 + G4 and other performance-improving marine gas turbines, forming a series of gas turbine power development spectra.

3. WR-21 gas turbine

The WR-21 gas turbine is based on the RB211 and Trent aero engines of the British Rolls-Royce Company and was developed by introducing intercooling and recuperation technology to a simple cycle engine. More specifically, the low-pressure compressor, high-pressure compressor and low-pressure turbine of the WR-21 gas turbine are modified from the RB211-535E engine; the high-pressure turbine is derived from the RB211-524G/H engine; the power turbine is derived from the low-pressure turbine of the Trent (variable area guide vanes are added); and the combustion chamber is modified from the Spey ship gas turbine and Tay aero engine.

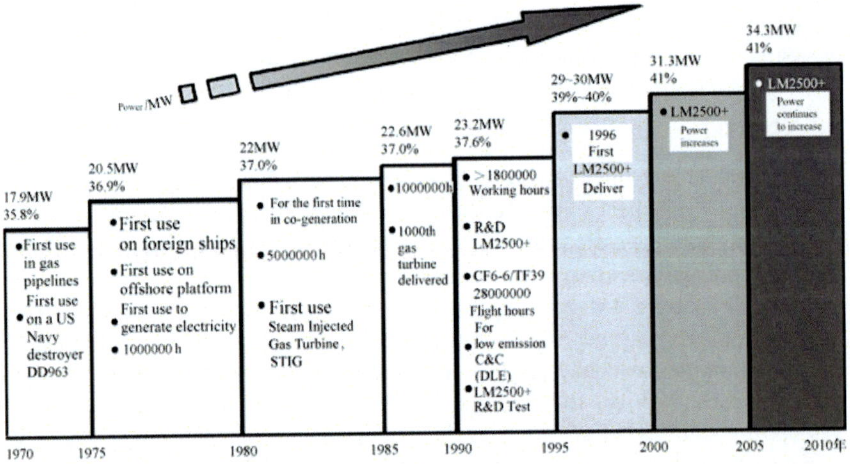

Fig. 1.2 Continuous improvement in LM2500 gas turbine products

In the typical US Navy ship operating mode, due to the use of intercooling and recuperation cycles and variable geometry power turbine technology, the WR-21 gas turbine has a high efficiency of 42% at the rated operating conditions. At 1/3 the rated load, the efficiency (approximately 41.16%) is near the level of medium- and high-speed diesel engines, which is particularly suitable for the requirements of ships. In general, the WR-21 gas turbine has excellent performance in the entire operating range, and the efficient and compact regenerator gives it low exhaust noise and infrared characteristics, which is the symbol of the new generation of marine gas turbines.

The WR-21 gas turbine is now installed in the integrated electric propulsion system of the British Type 45 destroyer and the "Queen Elizabeth" aircraft carrier. Although the WR-21 gas turbine was sought by many national navies during its development, when it was officially launched, it did not receive the expected enthusiastic response due to its complicated structure and doubtful reliability. In recent years, the operation performance of the Type 45 destroyer has confirmed this finding.

4. MT30 gas turbine

The MT30 gas turbine (refer to Fig. 1.3) is a simple-cycle gas turbine for three-shaft ships that is improved from the Trent 800 aviation turbofan engine of the British company Rolls-Royce. The MT30 has an 8-stage, variable geometry, low-pressure compressor: the high-pressure compressor is a 6-stage compressor, and the power turbine is a 4-stage compressor. The rated power can reach 36 MW, and the thermal efficiency can reach 39.8%.

To ensure high reliability, efficiency and maintainability, the MT30 gas turbine was designed as follows: the necessary marine coating was added to adapt to a salt spray environment and fuels with high sulfur content; the original aero engine parts are retained to the greatest extent (80% common parts of the Trent 800 engine); the

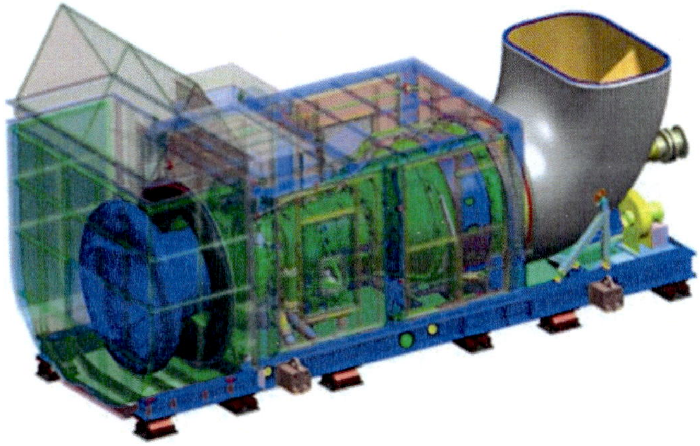

Fig. 1.3 MT30 compact box body structure

hot-end parts are designed to be overhauled at an interval of 12,000 h; and the life of the whole machine is 24,000 h.

The MT30 marine gas turbine was developed in June 2000, and prototype testing began in 2002. The DDG-1000 destroyer was first put into service in 2012 and was installed in the British Navy "Queen Elizabeth" class aircraft carrier for testing in 2013. Due to its excellent characteristics, the MT30 marine gas turbine has been installed in the US Navy's warships and has combined with the WR-21 in the form of a power generation module to form the comprehensive electric propulsion system of the new British aircraft carrier. Today, the MT30 marine gas turbine is recognized by the industry as the most advanced, high-power, marine gas turbine in the world.

1.1.3 Working Characteristics of the Marine Gas Turbine

The working environment and working characteristics of marine gas turbines are very different from those of aero engines. The development of modern advanced marine gas turbines must meet the military needs of ship power and the special requirements of the marine working environment. The design methods, design specifications and design experience of aviation turbofan/turbojet engines and industrial heavy-duty gas turbines cannot be simply copied. Their main working characteristics are presented as follows:

(1) High salt and high humidity deteriorate the working environment of marine gas turbines, which results in higher requirements in the design of marine gas turbines;
(2) Only the aero-engine bears the impact load and maneuvering load (generally less than 10 g) when an aircraft is landing, while the marine gas turbine is

subject to the vast impact caused by underwater explosion (more than 15 g after vibration reduction);

(3) The operating range of aero-engines is lower than the operating range of 0–100% for marine gas turbines, and marine gas turbines are operated under low operating conditions during more than 90% of their lifespan. In addition, the wartime mobility of a ship's requirements also leads to frequent changes in its working conditions, and a wide range of working conditions make it very sensitive to changes in the working characteristics;
(4) The working time of the aero-engine's full-load working conditions is generally only approximately 10 min, while the continuous operation time of full-load working conditions of marine gas turbines is generally not less than 12 h. The long-term, high-load operation makes marine gas turbines more demanding for working stability;
(5) Modern advanced marine gas turbines usually adopt advanced and complicated cycle methods, such as intercooling and recuperation cycles. Intercoolers and regenerators will generate greater aerodynamic and thermal inertia, which requires higher design requirements for components;
(6) Marine gas turbines usually burn diesel oils. Compared with high-quality aviation kerosene, diesel oil has poor combustion organization ability and an uneven temperature distribution at the outlet of the combustion chamber, which easily forms hot spots, and there are many impurities in diesel oils. Small combustion particles are corrosive, and the deposits formed by adhesion on the surface of the turbine blades will also cause local cooling failure and ablation, which will substantially impact the stability of the turbine cooling and thermal protection structure;
(7) Marine gas turbines work under the atmospheric characteristics of sea level, where the air density is high, the pressure is high, and the aerodynamic load is large, which requires a longer repair life;
(8) Marine gas turbines generally have an axial-flow, compact box-body structure. The inlet of the compressor is radially inhaled through the inlet volute, and the power turbine is radially exhausted through the exhaust volute. The large turning angle change in the airflow direction results in special requirements for the aerodynamic and structural design of compressors and turbines.

The poor working conditions of marine gas turbines complicates the design of marine gas turbines. Therefore, it is necessary to develop and produce marine gas turbines under the working conditions of ships so that ships can achieve good technical and tactical performance.

1.2 Introduction to the Variable Geometry Turbine Technology for the Marine Gas Turbine

1.2.1 Principles of a Variable Geometry Turbine

The working characteristics of marine gas turbines under full-load working conditions make the adoption of effective technical methods to improve their part load performance the focus of research on marine power gas turbine technology. To improve the high efficiency, stability and fast maneuverability of marine gas turbines in low working conditions, the use of variable geometry turbine technology has become an important consideration. The main reason is that under part-load conditions, the closing of the vane turning angle reduces the throat area of guide vanes, thereby reducing the flow capacity and flow rate of turbines and the turbine output power without reducing the turbine inlet gas temperature. At this time, since the initial gas temperature of the gas turbine is still high, the efficiency of the gas turbine can be maintained at a high level, and the economy is higher than that of the fixed geometry gas turbine.

In general, the variable geometry turbine has the following advantages: (1) It can improve the economy of part-load conditions; (2) It can change the flow capacity of the turbine, expand the freedom of selecting the working point of the gas generator, and ensure that the unit has a sufficient surge margin in all working states; (3) It can improve the acceleration of the unit (refer to Fig. 1.4), which is extremely important for the wartime power requirements; and (4) It can improve the starting characteristics of the unit. In addition, the variable geometry turbine has the advantage of improving the braking capacity of the unit. Recently, a study by Haglind from the Technical University of Denmark pointed out that variable geometry turbine technology can also significantly improve the part load performance of a ship's combined cycle.

In general, the use of variable geometry turbine technology can effectively control turbine flow changes, thereby adjusting and optimizing the matching relationship among various components of marine gas turbines, effectively improving the acceleration and deceleration characteristics of the entire unit and the performance in low working conditions. As shown in Fig. 1.5, under low working conditions, the variable vanes are generally closed to reduce the gas mass flow and output power, while during starting and acceleration conditions, the variable vanes are opened to increase the surge margin and output power.

1.2.2 Structure of a Variable Geometry Turbine

The structure of the variable geometry turbine is diverse, and its ultimate goal is to control the turbine mass flow by changing the throat area of the guide vane.

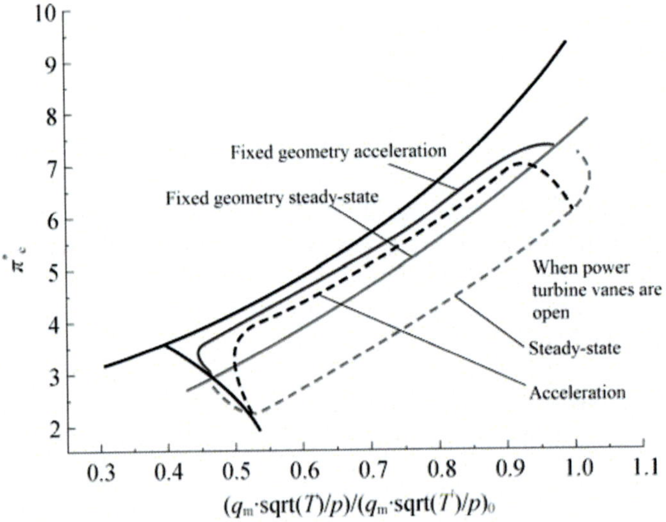

Fig. 1.4 Acceleration characteristics of gas turbines with variable geometry

Fig. 1.5 Schematic of the vane turning angle variation

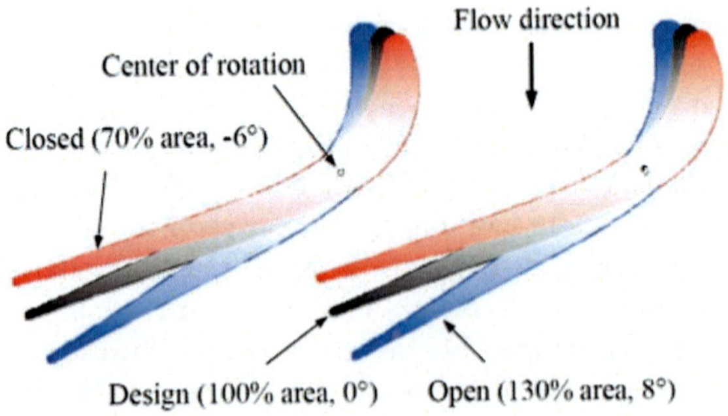

Advanced Western countries carried out theoretical research and experimental verification research on the feasibility of gas turbine variable geometry turbine technology as early as the 1950s and 1960s and gradually determined the variable geometry turbine technology scheme with variable vane installation angles, as shown in Fig. 1.6. Changing the guide vane installation angle requires a corresponding adjustment mechanism. The variable vane turning mechanism often requires flexible and reliable rotation to ensure accuracy during vane turning. The guide vane turning mechanism has different forms and arrangements on different units. Figure 1.6 shows a basic variable vane turning mechanism. The drive shaft at the top of the guide vane extends from the end of the guide vane to the top. The surface of the casing is connected to the guide vane transmission belt, and the purpose of controlling the turning of the guide vane and then adjusting the characteristics of the gas turbine is achieved by controlling the circumferential movement of the transmission belt. The

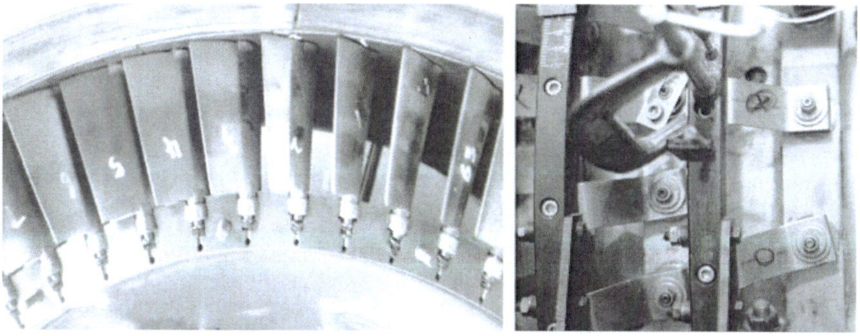

Fig. 1.6 Variable vane and its turning mechanism for variable geometry turbines

turning angle change of the guide vane can be displayed on the turning angle scale of the guide vane drive belt, which can realize precise control.

With the continuous development of variable geometry turbine technology, turbine aerodynamic adjustment technology has also attracted increasing attention from aero-engine researchers Because it can deflect and change the mainstream by injecting a controlled air flow near the trailing edge of the blade pressure surface. The turning angle and mass flows in the turbine blade channel ultimately change the working state of the turbines. Rolls-Royce was the first company to try to change the turbine mass flow by the aerodynamic adjustment method. They introduced a secondary jet in the turbine endwall and changed the incident position of the secondary jet. The experiment showed that this method can achieve effective adjustment of the gas mass flow, but due to the research limitations at the time, the aerodynamic adjustment causes a significant drop in efficiency. In general, the structure of the aerodynamic adjustment is simpler than that of the geometric adjustment. The jet can use the original cooling structure and air system inside the turbine vane of the aero engine, so major changes to the existing structure of the turbine are not necessary, and the thrust-to-weight ratio and life of the engine will not be affected. However, the aerodynamic adjustment method is limited by factors such as the ratio of the total pressure at the inlet of the jet hole to the total pressure at the inlet of the turbine blade, the relative flow rate of the jet and the turbine efficiency. Therefore, at the current level of technology, although this method can be applied to the low-pressure turbines of aeroengines, the application to marine gas turbines is difficult.

1.2.3 Influence of Variable Geometry of Different Types of Turbines on Gas Turbine Performance

Modern mid-range power marine gas turbines generally have a three-shaft structure, and their turbine components include high-pressure turbines, low-pressure turbines, and power turbines. The variable geometry of different types of turbines has different effects on the performance characteristics of gas turbines. According to Qiu Chao and Song Huafen's theoretical simplified calculations, in a simple cycle unit, either a high-pressure turbine, low-pressure turbine, or power turbine with variable geometry has minimal effect on the economics of the gas turbine power system but will affect the compressor's balanced operation line. The variable geometry of the low-pressure turbine has a greater influence on the balanced operation line of the low-pressure compressor; the variable geometry of the high-pressure turbine and low-pressure turbine has a greater influence on the balanced operation line of the high-pressure compressor; and the variable geometry of the power turbine has a certain impact on the balanced operation line of the low-pressure compressor but has minimal effect on the balanced operation line of the high-pressure compressor.

Since turbines are hot-end components, many technical difficulties are often encountered in changing their geometric structure. For example, variable geometry technology has high requirements for materials and processing, which will increase the cost and complexity of the entire gas turbine power unit and have consequences of reduced unit safety. Based on this finding, modern marine gas turbines mainly use variable geometry power turbine technology.

1.2.4 Introduction to a Typical Marine Variable Geometry Turbine

1. LM1600 variable geometry turbine

The structure of the LM1600 variable geometry power turbine, which is shown in Fig. 1.7, has 2-stage axial flow, a design speed of 7900 r/min and an intake air temperature of 743 °C. The fixed structure of the power turbine includes a transition section casing, a turbine casing and an exhaust section casing. The installation angle of the first-stage guide vane is turned by an electronic adjustment system, which can improve the maneuverability of the marine gas turbine. The design of the partition on the inner diameter of the second-stage guide vane is unique. The partition is designed as two 180° bolted halves and is positioned on the inner diameter of the guide with three sliding flanges. Therefore, the spacing between the baffle and the rotor is only determined by its temperature and the radial extension of the rotor. The result is to reduce the working distance between it and the rotor, thereby reducing the leakage through the grate seal on its inner diameter, which is conducive to improving the turbine efficiency.

2. GT25000 improved variable geometry turbine

The variable geometry power turbine is a 4-stage reaction-type axial turbine that converts the gas energy discharged from the gas generator into mechanical energy and drives the load output through the speed reducer. The turbine is composed of a large radial expansion casing of power turbines, inner shroud, guide vanes, power turbine rotors and support ring and is characterized by a constant-diameter flow and

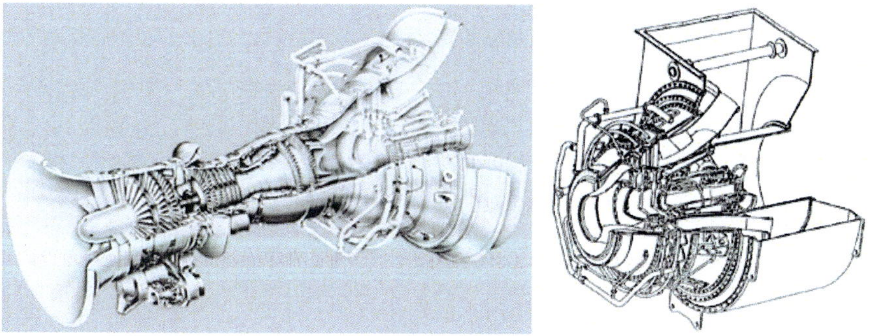

Fig. 1.7 LM1600 gas turbine and its power turbine structure

cantilever structure. As shown in Fig. 1.8, the design speed is 3270 r/min, and the vane turning angle range is −6° to +8°.

3. WR-21 variable geometry turbine

The variable geometry power turbine is a newly designed, 5-stage, shrouded turbine based on the British Rolls-Royce Trent 700 and Trent 800 designs, as shown in Fig. 1.9. The first stage has variable inlet guide vanes; the inlet temperature is 852 °C; the second to fifth stages are very similar to the Trent series; and the design speed is 3600 r/min. The variable vane is assisted by a ring gear structure and actuated by the oil hydraulic pressure to ensure that all variable vanes have the same throat area. Each variable vane can be separately removed. The variable vane is closed to the minimum at 40% or below 40% power and opened to the maximum at 100% or above 100%

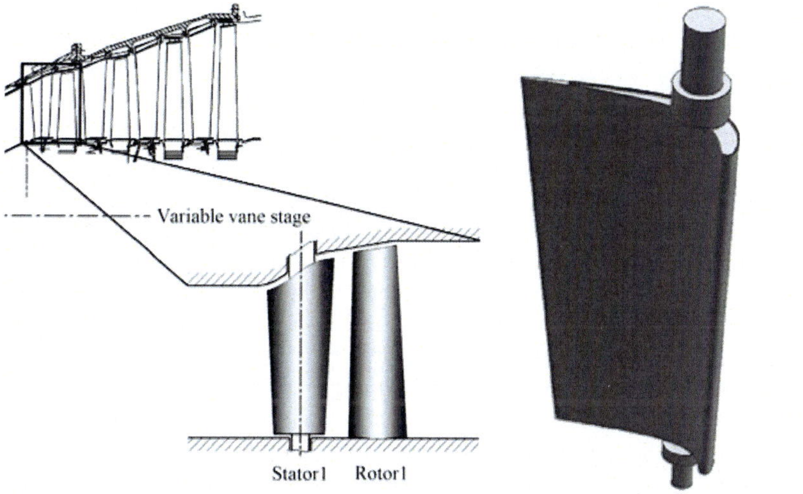

Fig. 1.8 GT25000 improved power turbine and its variable vane structure

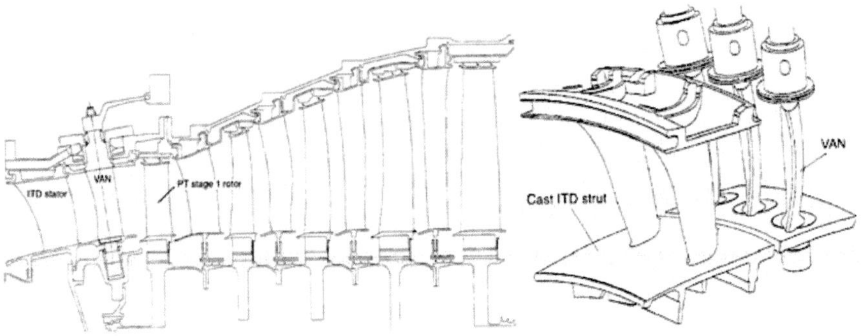

Fig. 1.9 WR-21 power turbine meridional profile and variable vane structure

power. Stage 1 works with impulse turbines at 40% power and with 100% reaction turbines at full power. The design point of the power turbine is selected at 67% power so that the fuel efficiency at low output power and full-power requirements are simultaneously considered.

1.3 Variable Geometry Turbine Design Features and Requirements

1.3.1 Problems with Variable Geometry Turbines

The variable geometry turbine is an innovative technology of gas turbines and a technical means to effectively improve the acceleration and deceleration characteristics of gas turbines and the performance under low working conditions. The use of variable geometry turbines can certainly meet the very demanding performance requirements for marine gas turbines. However, to realize the free rotation of the variable vanes of the variable geometry turbine, a certain clearance gap must be left at the end of the variable vanes, and a turning shaft must be installed. This approach will cause additional losses in the end regions of the guide vanes. Although every effort is made to reduce the additional losses caused by variable geometry in the aerodynamic and structural design, the efficiency of the design operating point of the variable geometry turbine is always lower than that of the fixed geometry turbine. The efficiency is reduced by approximately 2%. At the NASA Lewis Research Center, Moffitt et al. performed early experimental research on the influence of a ±30% change in the turning angle of the guide vane on a single-stage rotating turbine. Their research findings pointed out that when the variable guide vane is opened, the efficiency reduction is 1.5%, and when it is closed, the efficiency reduction reaches 5.5%. Recently, the calculation and analysis of the variable geometry turbine flow field of modern marine gas turbines by Feng Yongming et al. from Harbin Engineering University also pointed out that the closure of the variable guide vane significantly reduces the efficiency of the entire variable geometry turbine by 1–5%. It can be seen that regardless of whether the variable guide vane is opened or closed, the turbine efficiency is significantly reduced, which partly offsets the gas turbine cycle benefits obtained by the variable geometry of turbines. In addition, the use of variable geometry has also created problems such as a more complicated structure and adjustment of gas turbines and reduced safety of gas turbines. For example, the rapid throttling caused by variable geometry often causes the danger of gas flow oscillation, and the variable geometry of turbine blades will expand the blade resonance range. In addition, the use of variable geometry also increases the complexity of the unit's control system.

1.3.2 Aerodynamic and Structural Design Features of Variable Geometry Turbines

The aerodynamic efficiency of variable geometry turbines under low working conditions, full-load power output capability, and precise control, maintainability, and reliability of variable guide vanes in high-temperature and high-pressure environments are the keys to the success of marine gas turbines using variable geometry turbines. Therefore, the engineering design of the variable geometry turbine has the following two characteristics:

(1) In the aerodynamic design of the variable geometry turbine, in addition to meeting the various requirements of the conventional blade modeling, the special influence factors of the guide vane turning on the guide vane and blade must also be considered so that the variable geometry turbine maintains good aerodynamic performance in a wide range of working conditions (such as 30–100%).

① Turbine design operating point and design parameter selection: For the WR-21 marine gas turbine, the power turbine design point is selected at 67% power to optimize the low working condition efficiency and meet full-load requirements, which provides a realistic reference for the choice of design conditions of variable geometry turbines. To improve the performance of the variable geometry turbine in all operating conditions, the initial design parameters of the turbine, such as turbine stage enthalpy drop distribution and reaction degree, also need to be carefully considered.

② Variable guide vane end clearance design: Modern marine gas turbine power turbines are generally designed for large endwall angle turbine casings. There are two types of clearance design options for spherical endwalls and conventional cylindrical endwalls. For spherical endwalls, consideration is required to better integrate the spherical endwall part into a large endwall angle turbine casing. For the cylindrical endwall, the complex unsteady leakage flow problem caused by the change in the gap clearance shape and clearance size at the leading and trailing edges of the vane end needs to be considered. Vane-end gap clearance control methods, such as tip cavities and winglets, can be considered.

③ Choice of blade profile incidence angle: The turning of the variable guide vane will have an impact on the incidence angle of attack of the turbine vane and blade. Generally, the impact on the guide vane is relatively small, with a greater impact on the blade. It is necessary to consider that the incidence angle is better in the design state; the incidence angle in the off-design state is appropriate; and the design incidence angle can be used as a negative value to reduce the negative impacts caused by the large positive incidence angle of the variable vane by vane closing.

④ The choice of vane profile geometry and endwall parameters: Considering the impact of blade incidence angle caused by the turning of the guide vane, generally the blade load can adopt the form of aft-loaded distribution. In addition, the larger radius of the leading edge of the blade can be selected to weaken the sensitivity of the blade profile to the change in the incidence angle. To address the problem of the separation area of the leading edge of the downstream rotor blade caused by the turning of the variable vane, contouring of the hub endwall based on unsteady effects can also be discussed to reduce the leading-edge separation of the rotor blade.

(2) In the mechanical design of the guide vane turning mechanism of the variable geometry turbine, in addition to meeting the requirements of flexible and reliable turning of the variable guide vane and accurate positioning to a specific position, the influence of the flow field characteristics of the guide vane on the design of the guide vane turning mechanism must also be considered so that the guide vane turning mechanism can completely and reliably work in harsh environments.

① Guide vane turning mechanism and sealing form: Generally, the gas temperature before the inlet of the variable geometry turbine exceeds 1000 K, and the variable geometry turbine components will be deformed under high temperature and high-pressure effects, resulting in high temperature gas leakage, obstruction of the guide vane turning mechanism, and the inability of the guide vanes to be accurately positioned. To ensure that the turning mechanism is reliable under all working conditions, the temperature difference and thermal expansion problems must be solved. In the design of the vane turning mechanism, if the rotating ring and the rotating lever of the guide vane are directly linked, a large rotational torque is needed, which will cause difficulties in specific operations, making the position accuracy difficult to guarantee. Therefore, careful design of the guide vane turning mechanism is needed. In addition, to effectively control the radial clearance at the vane end, in certain turbine designs, cooling measures such as the WR-21 variable geometry turbine are adopted.

② Choice of the position of the turning shaft: In the design of the variable guide vane, the guide vane turning shaft should be located upstream of the position of the pressure acting point on the guide vane so that when the guide vane rotary actuator loses control, the aerodynamic force will turn the guide vane to a more open position, which produces a lower gas turbine temperature and load rather than a reverse process. The turning shaft should be located near the trailing edge of the guide vane so that when the guide vane rotates, the amount of swing of the trailing edge of the guide vane is small. The axial distance between the vane and the blade undergoes minimal change to weaken the gas flow oscillation caused by the variable guide vane.

1.3.3 General Requirements for Variable Geometry Turbine Design

As mentioned in Sect. 1.2.3, marine gas turbines are mainly using variable geometry power turbine technology, so the engineering design of marine gas turbine variable geometry turbines should meet not only the design requirements based on the variable geometry reliable work described in Sect. 1.3.2 but also the general design requirements of marine gas turbines for power turbines. The main requirements are described as follows:

1. High efficiency

In the design of aerodynamic performance, there is no essential difference between the design of the power turbine and the design of the gas generator turbine, and the design system can be shared. The difference is that the power turbine is generally multistage; the stage load is low; and the blades do not need to be cooled. Therefore, a higher aerodynamic efficiency can be designed based on the direction and tireless efforts of the designers. The wheel efficiency is usually in the range of approximately 0.9–0.93.

2. Long life

Because the gas generator of marine gas turbines adopts "integral hoisting" and "replacement repair" for maintenance and use, the power turbine is usually designed to have a long life due to the decrease in operating temperature and pressure; a life greater than 100,000 h is generally required. In this way, the continuous, long-term use of the power turbine is feasible, which is beneficial to the maintenance method for replacing the gas generator, so that the gas turbine power plant achieves a high utilization rate.

3. Versatility

Based on the long-life design requirements of the power turbine, it is expected to have a certain versatility in the design of the power turbine, that is, it is suitable for multiple gas generators and multiple uses to reduce costs.

4. High reliability

The power turbine is generally connected to the ship's shafting and propeller through the reduction gearbox, and the total speed ratio is generally at least approximately 10. Under the marine environment and combat conditions, wind waves and underwater explosions place special requirements on the reliability of the power turbine structure.

Therefore, in structural design, it is necessary to overcome the problems of structural strength, oxidation resistance, corrosion resistance, long life, and axial force balance design caused by working stress, temperature difference, materials, use environment and other factors.

1.4 Summary

This chapter provides an overview of marine gas turbines, marine gas turbine variable geometry turbines, and variable geometry turbine design features and requirements.

The trend of large and medium-sized surface ship power plant gas turbines has become increasingly obvious, and its application has become an important sign of naval modernization. The development of modern advanced marine gas turbines must meet the military needs of ship power and the special requirements of the marine working environment.

The variable geometry turbine is an innovative technology of gas turbines and a technical method for effectively improving the acceleration and deceleration characteristics and low working condition performance of marine gas turbines. The variable geometry turbine can also significantly improve the part load performance of a ship's combined cycle. Presently, the variable geometry power turbine technology scheme with variable guide vane turning angle is mainly employed.

The aerodynamic and structural design of variable geometry turbines is challenging. The low working condition aerodynamic efficiency, full-load power output capability, and precise control, maintainability, and reliability of variable guide vanes under high temperature and high-pressure environments are the keys to the success of marine gas turbines with variable geometry turbine technology.

Chapter 2
Flow Mechanisms and Characteristics of Variable Geometry Turbine

Abstract This chapter provides an overview of marine gas turbines, marine gas turbine variable geometry turbines, and variable geometry turbine design features and requirements. The development of modern advanced marine gas turbines must meet the military needs of ship power and the special requirements of the marine working environment. The variable geometry turbine is a technical method for effectively improving the acceleration and deceleration characteristics and low working condition performance of marine gas turbines.

2.1 Variable Vane-End Part Clearance Leakage Flow Characteristics and Loss Mechanisms

2.1.1 Variable Vane-End Part Clearance Leakage Flow Fields

The endwall structure of the variable vane determines the existence of part clearance and the resulting gap clearance leakage flow. Figures 2.1 and 2.2 show the typical variable vane structure and its static pressure coefficient distribution near the vane tip. Figure 2.2 shows that the load distribution near the tip of the vane tends to be an "aft-loaded" distribution and that the turning shaft is located near the maximum load position, which effectively blocks the part gap leakage flow of variable vanes.

The existence of the part gap causes not only gap leakage flow but also interference between the leakage vortex and the passage vortex, which changes the flow field structure and loss distribution in the endwall area of the variable vane. The distribution of the gap leakage flow streamlines at the tip of the variable vane is shown in Fig. 2.3. The gap leakage flow is divided into two parts by the turning shaft. Both parts of the leakage flow experience the blocking effect of the cavity structure, thereby reducing the gap leakage flow. As the leakage flow at the endwall clearance develops downstream, the leakage flow on the front side of the turning shaft does not roll up to form a leakage vortex but is attracted by the passage vortex and becomes a part of it. The leakage vortex core is mainly composed of leakage streamlines near the tip of the vane on the rear side of the turning shaft, and other gap leakage fluid surrounds the leakage vortex core to form an endwall leakage vortex.

J. Gao et al., *Variable Geometry Turbine Technology for Marine Gas Turbines*,
https://doi.org/10.1007/978-981-19-6952-2_2

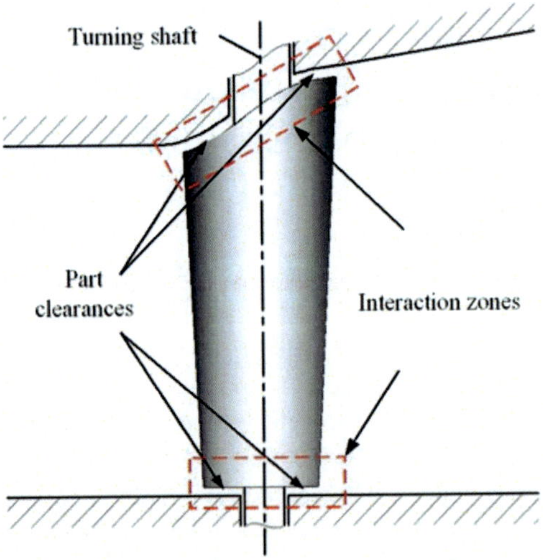

Fig. 2.1 Variable vane structure

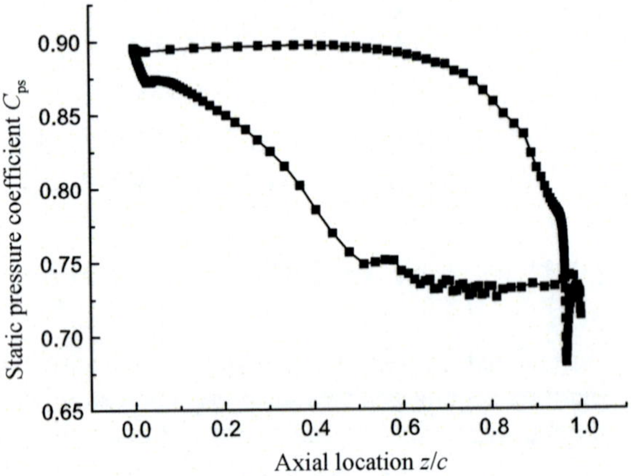

Fig. 2.2 Variable vane near-tip profile static pressure coefficient distribution

The above analysis can also be confirmed from the development of the leakage loss of the variable vane tip gap in Fig. 2.4. As shown in Fig. 2.4, on the front side of the turning shaft, the near-gap suction side loss strength is relatively small, but the scale is large, which is mainly caused by the passage vortex formed in advance. At this time, the gap leakage vortex is relatively weak and is basically not visible in Fig. 2.4. As the flow develops downstream, at the rear side of the turning shaft, part of the mainstream fluid is driven by a large lateral pressure difference to form a gap leakage vortex and becomes stronger as the flow develops downstream, but the scale is smaller. Note that the root of the variable vane also undergoes the same gap leakage vortex formation process, which is not repeated here.

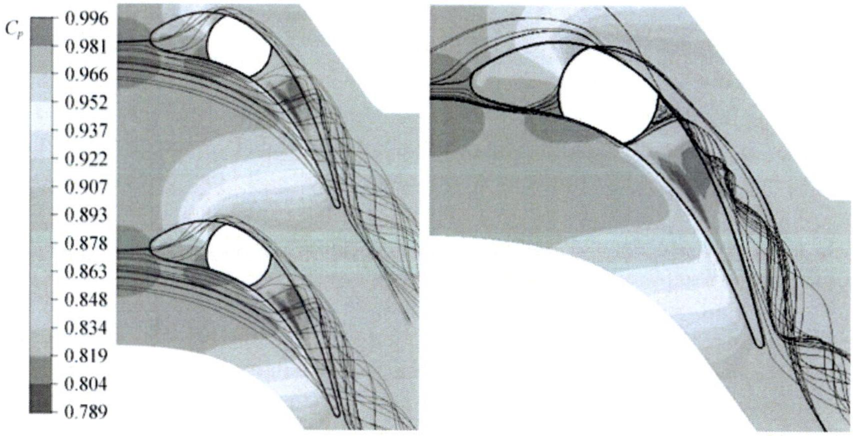

Fig. 2.3 Leakage streamlines and static pressure coefficient distribution at the tip of variable vanes

Fig. 2.4 Variable vane tip clearance leakage loss development

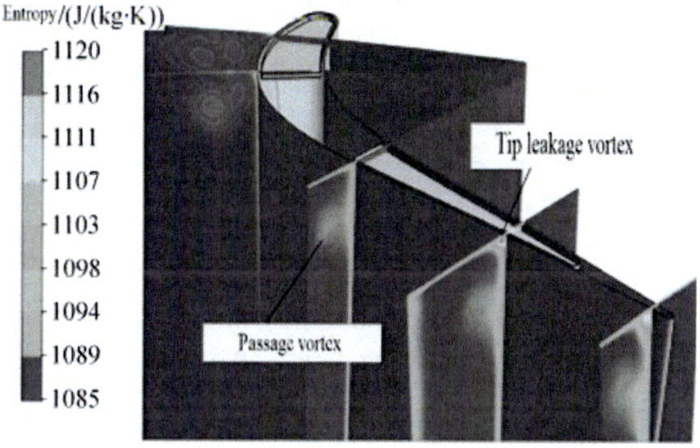

2.1.2 *Evolution of Variable Vane Flow Fields Under Multiple Working Conditions*

The turning of variable vanes of the variable geometry turbine changes the area of the vane throat, which causes the blade rows of the variable geometry turbine to run under off-design conditions. Figure 2.5 shows the distribution of the static pressure coefficient of the midspan variable vane profile at different turning angles. At a zero turning angle, the lowest pressure point of the variable guide vane is at approximately 75% of the axial chord length, and the variable vane belongs to the "aft-loaded" profile. As the variable vane closes, the variable vane channel converges, the degree of gas flow expansion in the rear section of the variable vane channel increases, and the aft-loaded degree of the vane heightens. When the variable vane is opened, the expansion and acceleration ability of the gas flow in the rear section of the vane channel is weakened, and the vane gradually changes from aft-loaded to front-loaded. Simultaneously, the area surrounded by the vane static pressure distribution line is smaller, indicating that the vane load decreases, and the reaction degree of the variable vane stage increases at this time.

The effect of the variable vane turning angle on the load distribution near the tip of the vane is shown in Fig. 2.6. The impact is completely different from that of the inlet incidence angle on the vane load distribution, and compared with Fig. 2.5, the endwall gap leakage flow has a very obvious effect on the load size and load distribution of the vane, especially in the second half of the vane tip pressure side. The static pressure is greatly reduced, which is mainly attributed to the acceleration of the endwall gap leakage flow into the vane-end gap. In addition, due to the effect of the flow around the endwall turning shaft, the static pressure rapidly decreases and then increases in the vicinity of the turning shaft on the tip suction side of the vane. However, the presence of the turning shaft has minimal effect on the static pressure distribution on the vane pressure side. In general, the flows at the endwall of the variable vane are caused by the superposition of the part gap leakage flow and the flow effect around the turning shaft and have obvious unsteady characteristics.

The above analysis can also be confirmed from the midspan-section Mach number distribution of the variable vanes of variable geometry turbines at different vane turning angles, as shown in Fig. 2.7. When the variable vane is closed, the vane gradually enters the high subsonic flow from the medium subsonic flow, the vane trailing edge blockage increases, and the variable vane incidence angle of attack tends to be positive. When the variable vane is opened, the vane trailing edge blockage is reduced, and the variable vane's incidence angle of attack tends to be negative. At this time, at the variable vane's pressure surface, a flow separation vortex zone is formed, as shown in Fig. 2.8.

Since the variable vane adopts an "aft-loaded" vane profile, it has good adaptability to the incoming incidence angle of attack. Although a flow separation zone appears when the variable vane is opened, the flow separation zone basically exhibits two-dimensional separation characteristics. It can be inferred that at this time, the variable vanes of the variable geometry turbine incur relatively small off-design incidence losses.

2.1.3 Effect of Part Clearance on Aerodynamic Loss Characteristics of Variable Vanes

Figure 2.9 shows the static pressure coefficient distribution of the casing endwall of the variable vane under two gap clearance heights. The "+" in the figure represents the position of the pressure sensor. As previously mentioned, the combined effect of the leakage flow at the end of the variable vane and the flow around the turning shaft makes the local flow fields extremely complicated. A distinct low-pressure area is visible in the trailing edge area of the suction side of the vane tip gap, which extends from the vane front side to the trailing edge, and the low-pressure zone can be divided into two parts: the influencing area of the flow around the turning shaft and

Fig. 2.5 Midspan vane profile static pressure coefficient distribution at different vane turning angles

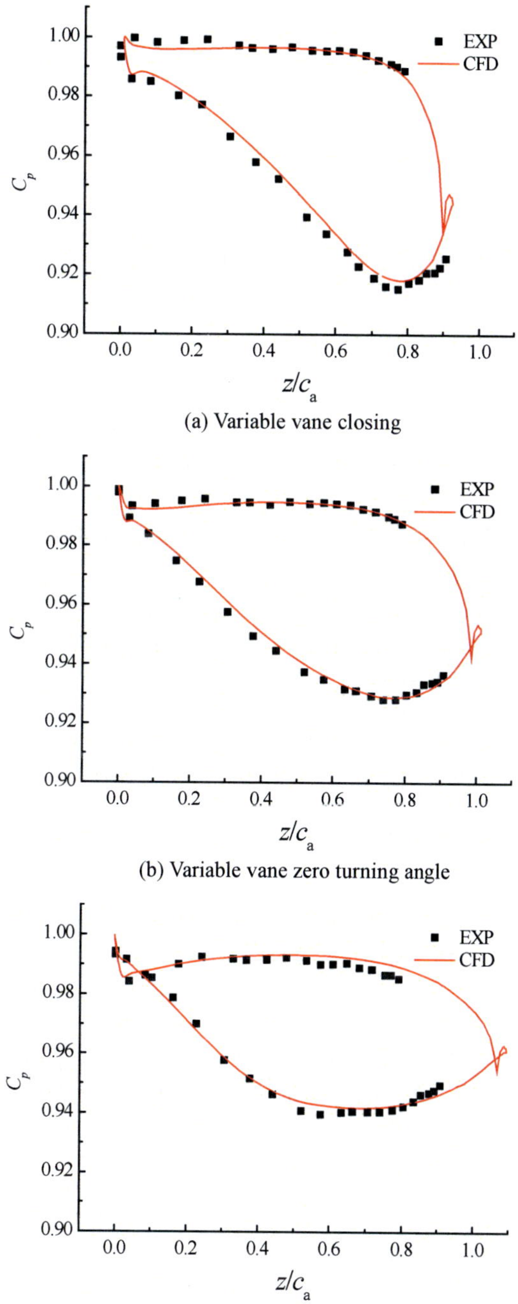

(a) Variable vane closing

(b) Variable vane zero turning angle

(c) Variable vane opening

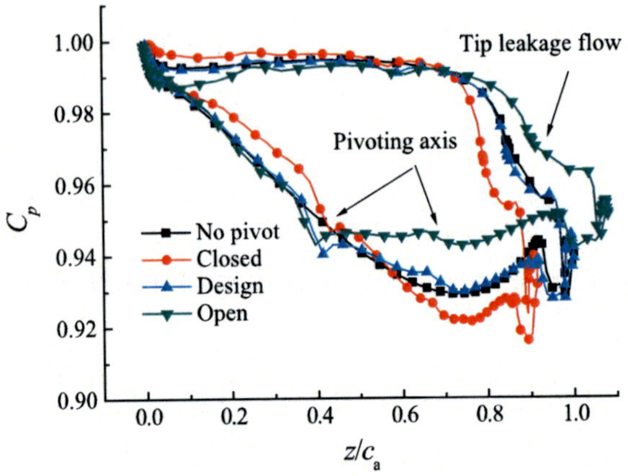

Fig. 2.6 Effects of vane turning angle and turning shaft on near tip vane loading distribution

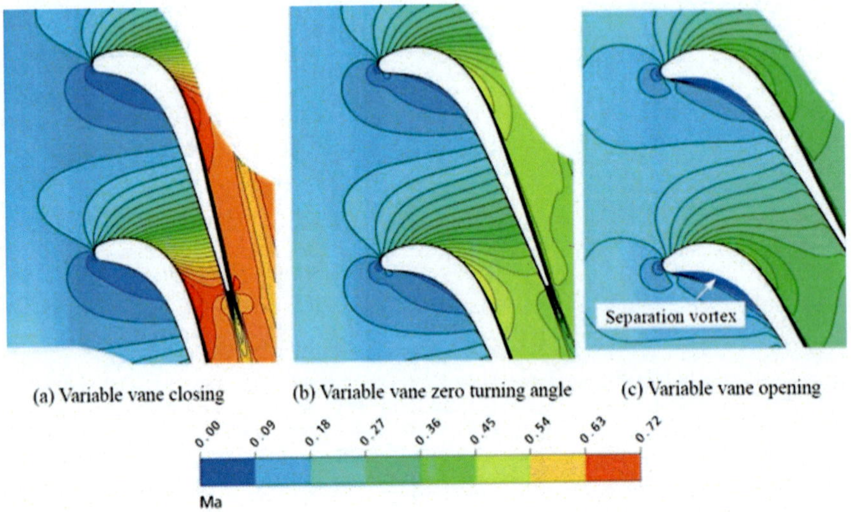

Fig. 2.7 Mach number distribution of the middle section of variable vanes at different turning angles

the influencing area of the leakage flow at the trailing edge of the vane. In general, under the influence of the large variable vane-end gap clearance height, the range of this low-pressure area is large.

To reveal the mechanism of the gap leakage loss at the end of the variable guide vane of variable geometry turbines, the development of the internal flow loss of the variable vane at a zero turning angle along the flow direction is shown in Fig. 2.10. At different vane-end gap clearance heights, the total pressure loss remains the same before the variable vane leading edge. At approximately 15% axial chord length, the

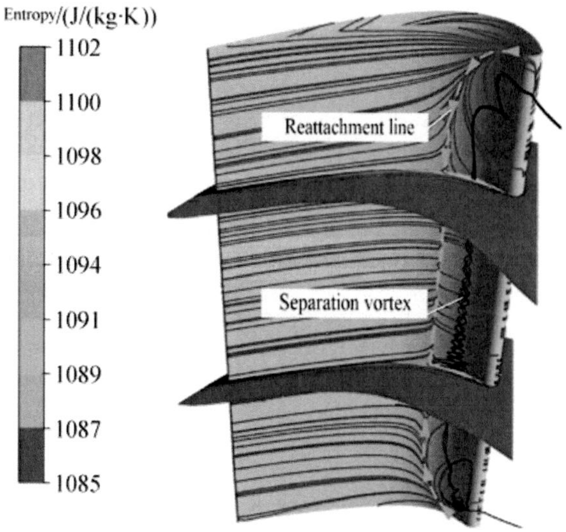

Fig. 2.8 Vane pressure surface separation zone structure when the variable vane is opened

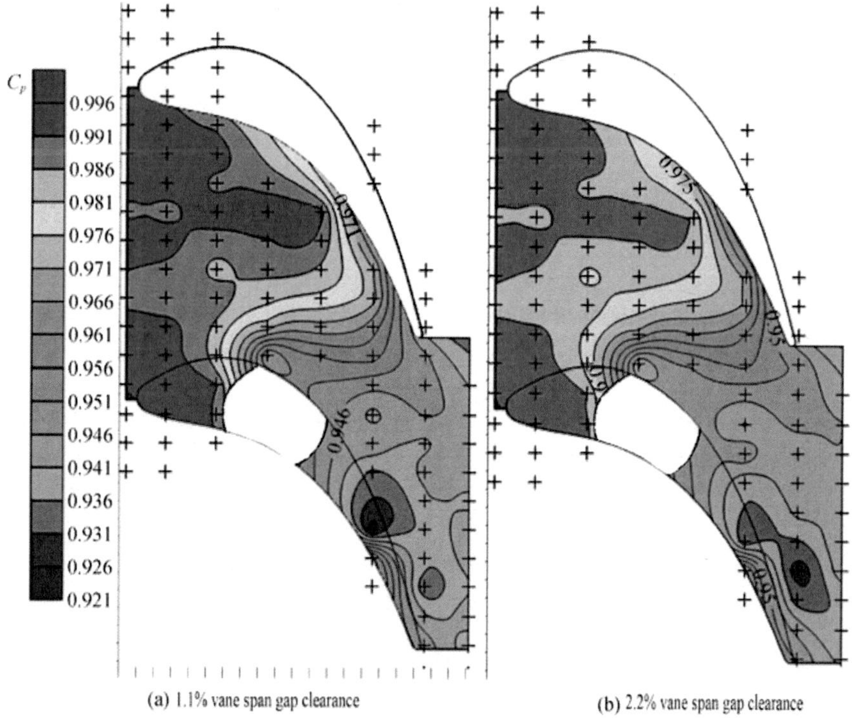

Fig. 2.9 Variable vane casing endwall static pressure coefficient distribution

total pressure loss at a 2.2% gap clearance begins to exceed the 1.1% clearance case. The increasing speed of the total pressure loss coefficient along the flow direction remains approximately unchanged until the position downstream of the turning shaft. However, from the downstream of the turning shaft to the trailing edge area of the vane, the total pressure loss sharply increases. To clearly explain the interference between the flow around the turning shaft and the leakage flow at the rear side of the vane tip, a hypothetical shaftless calculation case is also given. By comparing the two cases of with a shaft and without a shaft, the total pressure loss coefficient in the shafted case is slightly lower than that in the shaftless case upstream of the variable vane turning shaft, which is attributed to the local gap leakage field changes. However, in the region downstream of the turning shaft, due to the mutual interference between the two types of flows, the total pressure loss coefficient in the shaft calculation case substantially increases.

Figure 2.11 shows the distribution of the test total pressure loss coefficient at the variable vane outlet at a zero turning angle. The total pressure loss is mainly generated in the area where the leakage vortex is located and the wake area behind the trailing edge of the vane. Moreover, the highest total pressure loss coefficient is just in the center of the leakage vortex, which means that the leakage vortex has a key role in the generation of aerodynamic losses downstream of the variable vane. In addition, the existence of passage vortices is hardly visible in this figure, which is mainly attributed to the sparse measurement points. However, overall, the gap leakage loss at a 2.2% clearance gap is significantly greater than that at a 1.1% clearance gap. The above analysis can also be confirmed from the spanwise distribution of the pitch-averaged total pressure loss coefficient in Fig. 2.12.

Figure 2.13 shows the spanwise test and calculation for the total pressure loss coefficient distributions at the variable vane outlet at a zero turning angle. The measurement data is derived from the position of the 40% axial chord length downstream of the vane trailing edge. As shown in Fig. 2.13, the test and calculation results differ, the deviation in the mainstream area is within 1.5°, and the maximum measurement

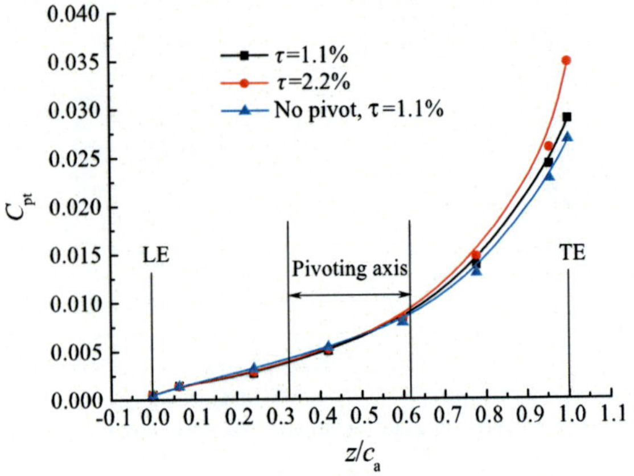

Fig. 2.10 Streamwise development of variable vane flow losses at zero vane turning angles

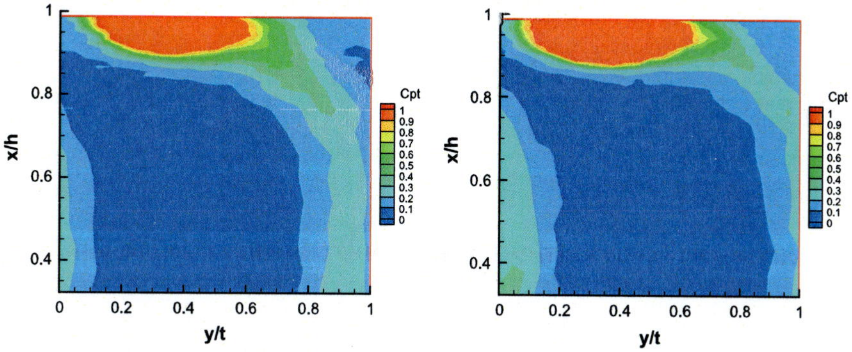

(a) 1.1% vane span gap clearance

(b) 2.2% vane span gap clearance

Fig. 2.11 Variable vane outlet total pressure loss distribution

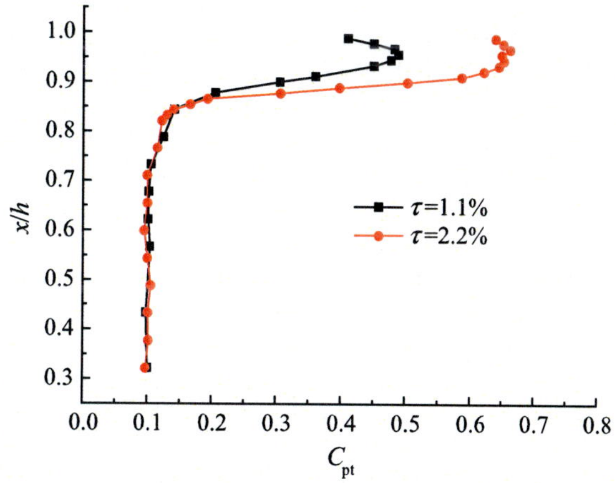

Fig. 2.12 Spanwise test total pressure loss distribution at the variable vane outlet at a zero vane turning angle

deviation in the gap area is approximately 4°. These results are mainly attributed to the fully developed entrance boundary layer of the test cascade, which makes the incoming flow nonuniform, and the inconsistent boundaries caused by an incorrect setting of the inlet during calculation. In the mainstream area of the variable vane, with an increase in the endwall gap clearance height, the outflow angle of the variable vane remains almost unchanged and the phenomenon of underdeflection of the gas flow is significantly enhanced, which, to a certain extent, deteriorates the good matching of the endwall flow between the blade rows of variable geometry turbines.

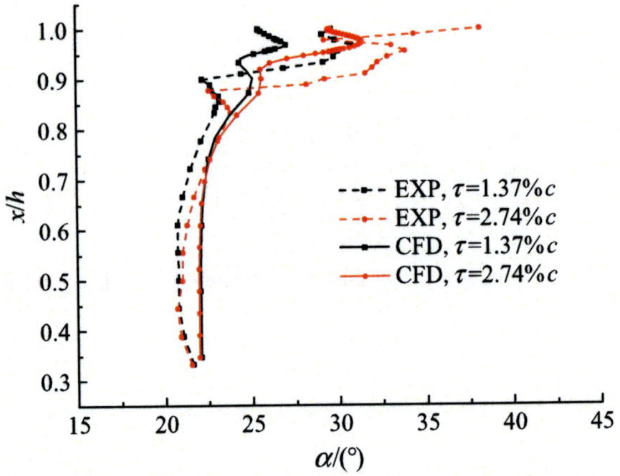

Fig. 2.13 Spanwise test outflow angle distribution at the variable vane outlet at a zero vane turning angle

2.2 Flow Interaction Mechanism and Loss Characteristics in Variable Vane Turbine Stage Endwall Regions

2.2.1 Three-dimensional Flow Field Structure and Loss Characteristics

The variable vane turning not only causes the vane to have an incidence angle of flow but also has a significant effect on the downstream rotor blade flow field. Figure 2.14 shows the distribution of the midspan static pressure coefficient of the rotor blade profile at different turning angles. At a zero turning angle, the rotor blade load distribution tends to be "uniformly loaded" (refer to Fig. 2.15b). As the variable vane closes, the rotor blade's incidence angle of attack tends to be more positive, the forward stagnation point moves toward the blade pressure surface, the lateral pressure difference at the front of the rotor blade increases, and the working state of the rotor blade changes from uniformly loaded to front loaded. Along the suction surface of the rotor blade, a slender flow separation vortex area is formed (refer to Fig. 2.15a). When the variable vane is opened, the inlet incidence angle of attack of the rotor blade changes to a negative angle of attack, the front stagnation point moves toward the suction surface, the lateral pressure difference at the front of the rotor blade decreases, and the rotor blade works in the aft-loaded state, which is conducive to suppressing the development of secondary flows in the rotor blade channel. However, at this time, a large-scale flow separation area is formed along the pressure surface of the rotor blade (refer to Fig. 2.15c).

Figure 2.16 shows the distribution of the limiting streamlines on the surface of the rotor blade when the variable vane is closed and opened. The separation area on the suction side of the rotor blade when the variable vane is closed is generated by the upward spiral movement of the separation bubble induced by the inlet incidence angle of attack near the rotor hub endwall. This area exhibits obvious three-dimensional

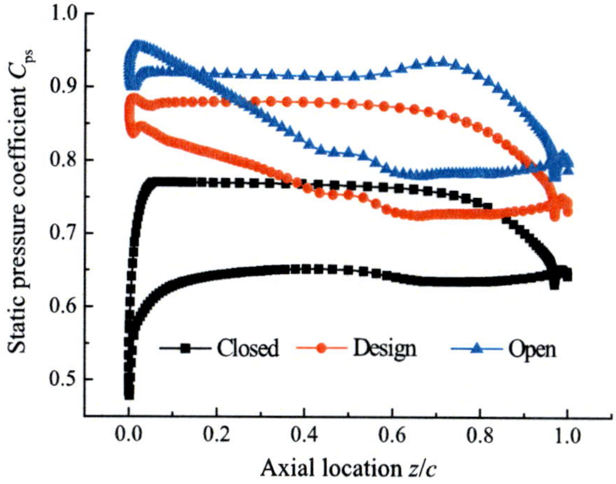

Fig. 2.14 Midspan rotor blade static pressure coefficient distribution at different vane turning angles

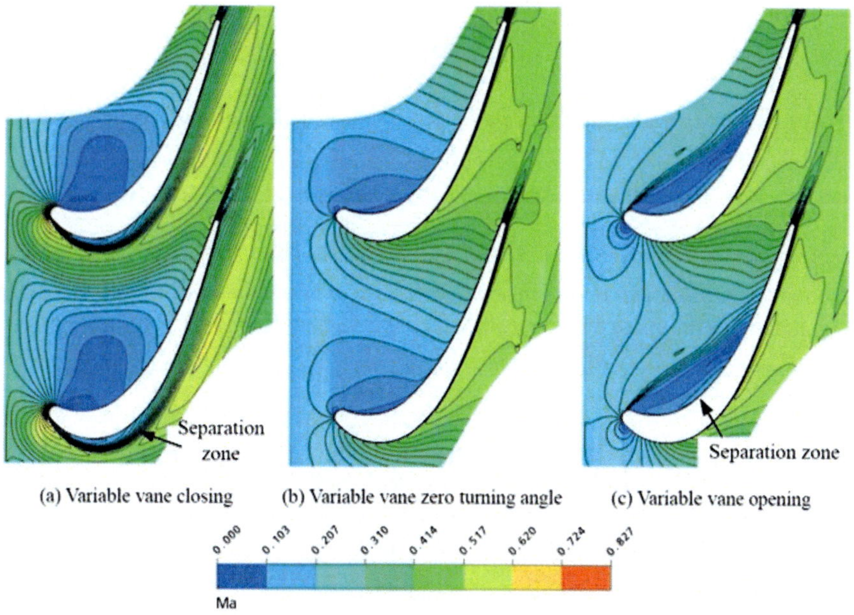

Fig. 2.15 Variable vane stage rotor blade midspan section Mach number distribution at different vane turning angles

separation characteristics. In addition, the increase in blade load when the variable vane is closed also enhances the leakage flow at the tip of the rotor blade. When the variable vane is opened, a closed three-dimensional separation vortex is generated at the hub endwall of the rotor blade pressure side and performs a counterclockwise

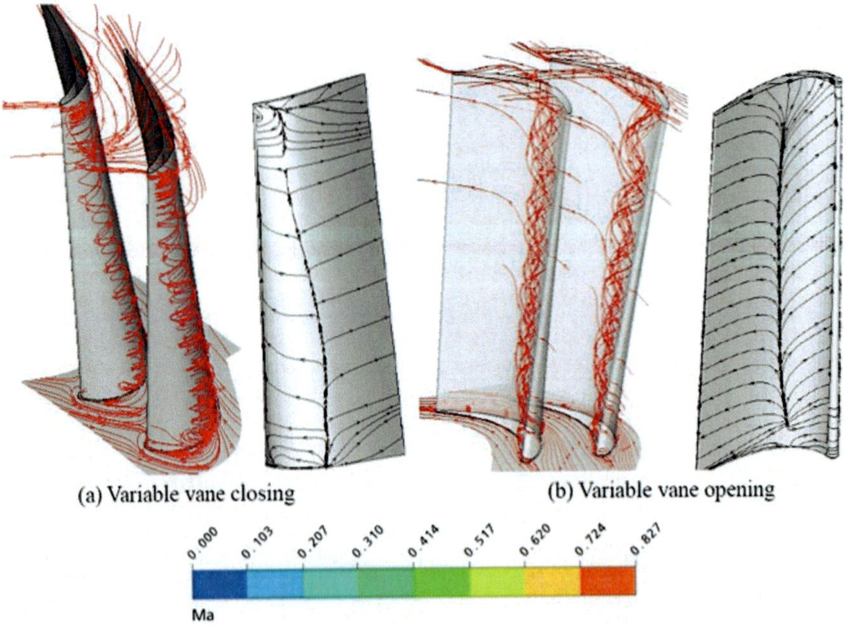

Fig. 2.16 Rotor blade surface limiting streamline distribution when the variable vane is closed and opened

spiral upward movement. The overall three-dimensional separation characteristics are weak.

The above analysis reveals that whether it is operating under a large positive angle of attack or a large negative angle of attack, flow separation of the leading edge of the variable vane stage rotor blade has occurred. However, the position and mechanism of the two types of flow separations are completely different, and the size of the induced loss is also different. Figure 2.17 shows the entropy distribution at the rotor blade outlet of the variable vane stage for different vane turning angles. When the variable vane is closed, the rotor blade outlet loss is mainly caused by the secondary flow at the rotor blade hub and the leakage vortex at the tip, and the loss intensity becomes significantly larger. When the variable vane is opened, the loss at the rotor blade outlet is slightly reduced, but the difference is not large.

2.2.2 *Unsteady Flow Interaction Mechanisms*

Unlike traditional fixed geometry guide vanes, the variable vane flow loss is mainly caused by secondary flows such as gap leakage vortices and passage vortices in the upper and lower endwall areas. The unsteady influence of the variable vane on the downstream rotor blades has the effects of wakes, potential flows and the interference

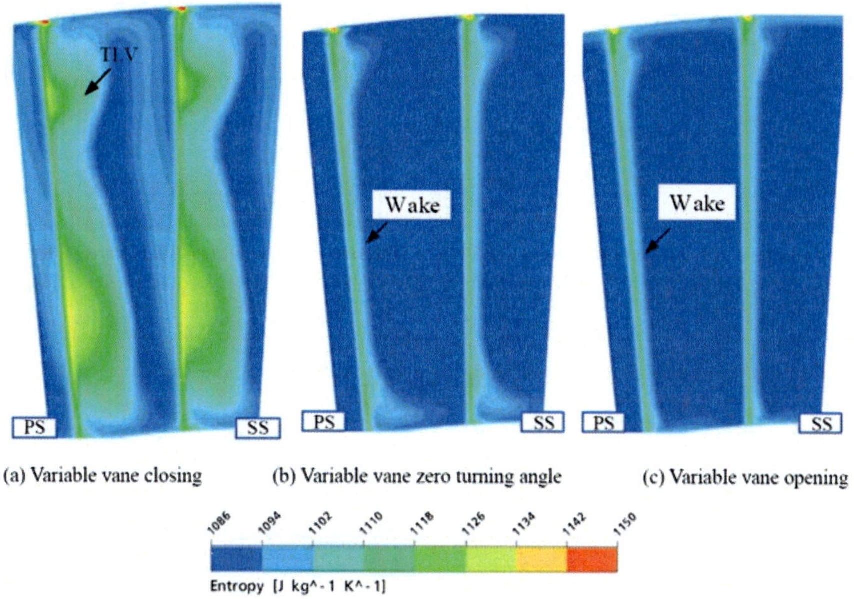

Fig. 2.17 Variable vane stage rotor blade outlet entropy distribution at different vane turning angles

of the leakage vortex and passage vortex. The unsteady pulsation of the pressure and other parameters in the vane passage is caused by rotor–stator flow interaction and unsteady vortex effects. To further reveal the characteristics of the transient flow field inside the variable geometry turbine, this section discusses its internal flow interference mechanism.

Figure 2.18 shows the entropy increase distribution at the variable vane outlet at different times. The main losses at the vane outlet are the leakage vortex and passage vortex losses in the upper and lower endwall regions. Since the cross-sectional display position is not perpendicular to the vane trailing edge outlet section, the vane wake loss area is not obvious, and only a high loss area from the upper passage vortex to the lower passage vortex area is observed. This area contains the entropy increases caused by both the fluid separation of the vane suction surface and the vane wake. Within a period of time, the range and location of the loss zone of the upper endwall leakage vortex are basically unchanged, and the entropy increase caused by the upper endwall leakage vortex has a tendency to decrease with time. The entropy increases at $2T/4$ is significantly higher than that at $0T/4$; a high-loss core is visible again at $3T/4$; and the intensity of leakage vortex A is basically unchanged. The upper endwall passage vortex also shows a tendency to decrease and then increase. The changes in the vortex system of the lower endwall are also basically the same. The passage vortex of the lower endwall begins to decrease from $0T/4$, is almost invisible at $2T/4$, and reappears at $3T/4$.

The position change range of the high-entropy zone caused by the vortex is not very large, but the range of the loss zone is significantly changed, which is closely

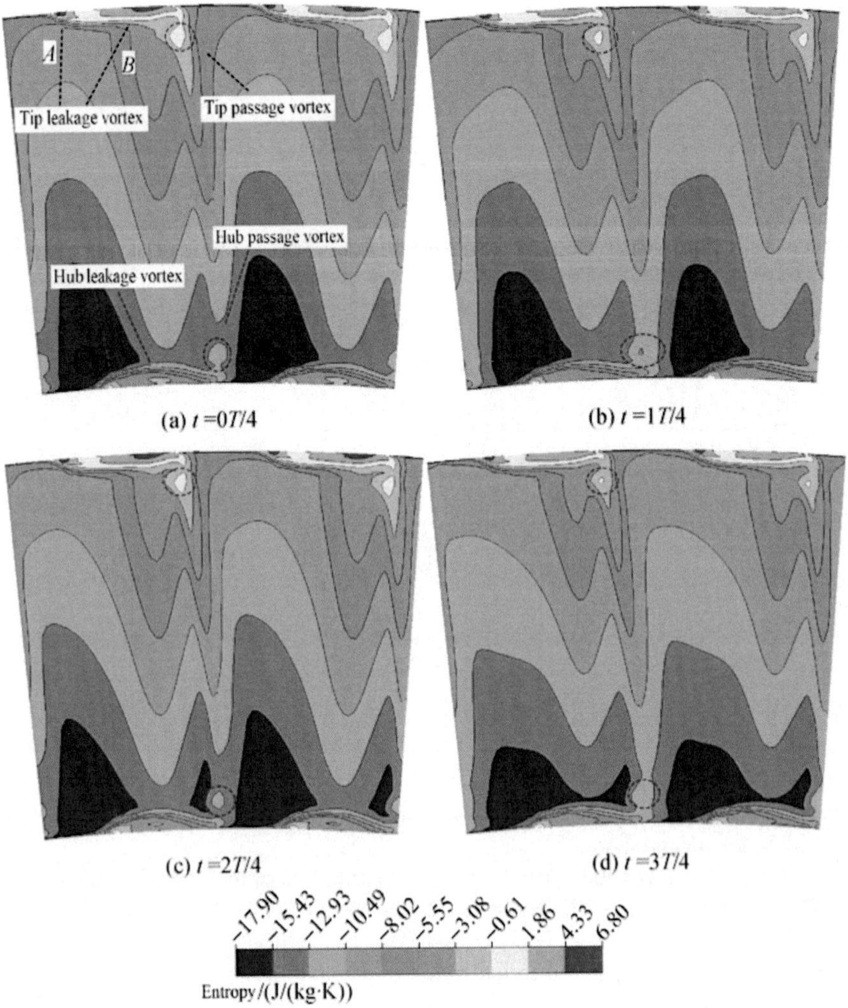

Fig. 2.18 Entropy-increase distribution at the variable vane outlet at different times

related to the instantaneous relative position of the vane and blade. Under unsteady flow conditions, the pressure distribution in the turbine passage is variable. As the rotor blade rotates, the pressure at the throat of the vane will be affected by the interference effect of the leading edge of the downstream rotor blade. Flow turbulence at the leading edge of the rotor blade causes local pressure changes; it periodically passes the position of the vane throat, thus changing the local pressures, and therefore affects the pressure gradient on the suction surface of the vane. When the low-pressure region on the suction surface of the leading edge of the blade passes near the outlet of the vane, a reverse pressure gradient is formed at the outlet of the suction surface of the vane, resulting in an increase in flow losses. However, the enhancement of the reverse pressure gradient will weaken the vortex, resulting in a smaller endwall leakage loss core.

Figure 2.19 shows the distribution of entropy increase at the variable vane stage rotor blade inlet at different times. The four typical moments are connected in an unsteady period, which is equivalent to the process of moving the rotor blade through a guide vane pitch. First, observe the entropy increase distribution at time $0T/4$. The flow loss at the inlet of the rotor blade is mainly affected by the upstream vane trailing edge wake and the leakage vortex at the upper and lower endwalls. The passage vortex and the wake interfere with each other, and their influence range is small. At this moment, when the root area of the leading edge of the rotor blade rotates near the leakage vortex of the lower endwall, the left side of the leading-edge projection Line B is the main body of the leakage vortex, and area A on the right is the high loss area of the wake root, which contains part of the leakage flow and the lower endwall passage vortex. Thus, the high entropy area is larger than the upper endwall passage vortex, and the upstream vane wake is a complete area. From $0T/4$ to $2T/4$, the root of the rotor blade leading edge cuts the wake flow. The range of the wake area becomes slender, and the wake is almost divided into two parts at $3T/4$: the upper part and the lower part. The wake area recovers at $0T/4$, and the rotor–stator interaction makes the upstream vane wake show unsteady characteristics, periodically cut by the blade and developing into the downstream rotor blade passage. In general, the change in the vane leakage vortices is related to the relative position of the vane and blade. From $0T/4$ to $1T/4$, the root of the leading edge of the rotor blade sweeps through the lower endwall leakage vortex, causing the leakage vortex to stretch in the circumferential direction, flatten in the radial direction, and then return to an approximately circular shape. This finding indicates that the instantaneous effect of the leading edge of the rotor blade on the upstream guide vane shedding vortices is different. In the interaction between the variable vane and the rotor blade, it is necessary to thoroughly analyze the influence of the vane outlet vortices on the flow of the downstream rotor blade endwall zone.

Figure 2.20 shows the radial vorticity distribution at the 5% blade span section of the variable vane stage rotor blade at different times. The radial components of the wake and the passage vortex on this section are more obvious, which avoids the effects of the variable vane gap leakage vortex. In the figure, we can completely observe the propagation and evolution of the vane wake in the rotor blade passage, as well as the influence on the rotor blade passage vortex and rotor blade outlet flow. The region of negative vorticity near the suction surface of the rotor blade in Fig. 2.20 is the radial component range of the rotor blade hub endwall passage vortex. According to the analysis of the four typical moments in the figure, when the upstream wake propagates in the rotor blade passage, the upstream wake shape changes by the pressure gradient, velocity gradient, etc., and continuously interacts with the lower endwall passage vortex of the rotor blade. The wake moves from front to back along the flow direction rather than simultaneously acting on the entire passage vortex. Therefore, only the unsteady influence of the upstream variable vane wake on the local area of the downstream rotor blade passage vortex is analyzed here.

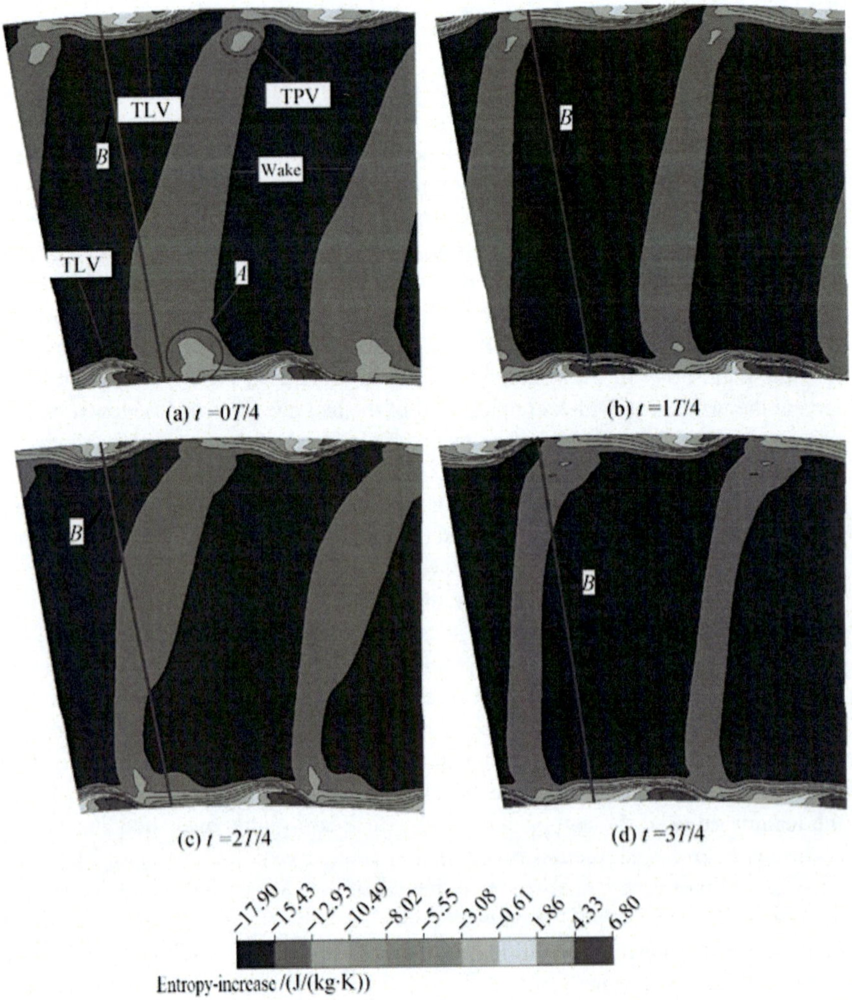

Fig. 2.19 Entropy-increase distribution at the variable vane stage rotor blade inlet at different times

Researchers know that the vane wake contains a positive–negative radial vorticity pair, and the rotor blade passage vortex is a negative radial vorticity. As shown in Fig. 2.20, at 0*T*/4, the positive vorticity wake is located in front of the negative vorticity wake and has just entered the rotor blade flow passage entrance. Simultaneously, there are two positive and negative vorticity clusters in the middle of the rotor blade passage. The positive vorticity wake at the inlet of the rotor blade extends to the pressure surface of the rotor blade, which enhances the positive vorticity of the adjoining layer of the pressure surface at the rotor leading edge, while the trailing edge with the negative wake vorticity is cut by the leading edge of the rotor blade. The positive vortex cluster that entered earlier sweeps across the suction surface of

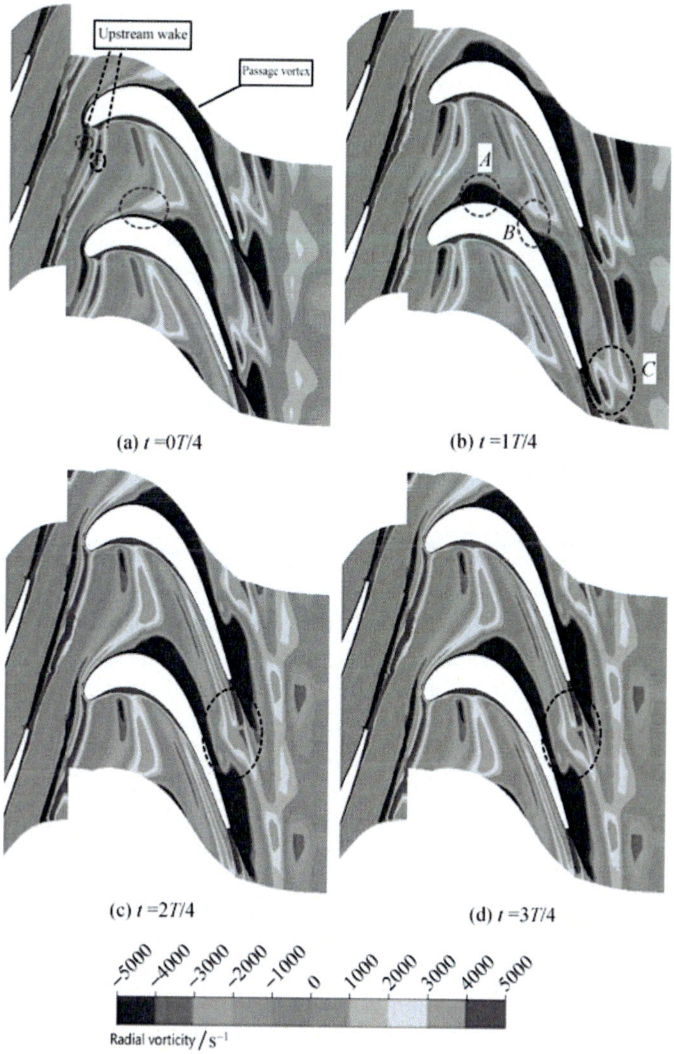

Fig. 2.20 Radial vorticity distribution at 5% rotor blade span of the variable vane stage at different times

the rotor blade and begins to interact with the passage vortex. Since the positive and negative vortices are opposite, they cancel each other, so that the radial vorticity of the hub passage vortex in the dotted coil decreases. At $1T/4$, the wake that just entered the rotor blade passage moves downstream, and the negative wake vortex cluster near the suction surface of the rotor blade merges with the passage vortex of the same negative vorticity and disappears, increasing the scale of the suction surface passage vortex at area A. This scenario is distinctly different from $0T/4$. Simultaneously, the positive vorticity wake in the middle of the rotor blade passage is stretched, and the contacting passage vortices are further cancelled. A distinct falling positive vorticity cluster is visible in area C at the rotor blade outlet. At $2T/4$ and $3T/4$, the wake at the entrance develops toward the middle of the flow passage. Due to the low velocity of the blade boundary layer, the speed in the middle of the flow passage is high, and the wake exhibits tensile fracture under the action of the viscous force on the suction surface wall of the rotor blade. The phenomenon that at $0T/4$, the wake of the middle of the passage periodically sweeps over the front half of the suction surface and cancels each other with the passage vortex is obviously unsteady. At $3T/4$, the positive vorticity wake of the vane near the pressure surface of the rotor blade enters the wake of the rotor blade at its exit, and the positive wake vortex cluster at the suction surface of the rotor blade continues downstream to cut the passage vortex. The result of this motion is that a positive–negative vortex cluster is generated at the outlet of the rotor blade. The negative vortex cluster is offset by the positive vortex cluster of the vane wake and passage vortex, is squeezed and then falls off by two positive vorticity clusters of the rotor blade wake and vane wake at the trailing edge of the rotor blade. This flow condition is observed at the exit of the rotor blade at $1T/4$.

Figure 2.21 shows the radial vorticity distribution of the 95% blade span cross-section of the variable vane stage rotor blade at different times. The figure shows the positive and negative wake vorticity clusters at the trailing edge of the vane. The positive vorticity extending from the middle of the vane is the vane gap leakage vortex. There is a negative vorticity cluster between the leakage vortex and the positive vorticity wake. Negative vortex fluid is induced by the vane leakage vortex. The rear high vorticity area in the suction surface of the rotor blade is the leakage vortex at the tip of the rotor blade. In area A at $0T/4$, the part of the vortex cluster with the opposite rotation direction between the leakage vortex at the blade tip and the suction surface is part of the passage vortex on the upper endwall of the rotor blade. Similar to the propagation process of the vane wake in the rotor blade passage, the vane leakage vortex, induced vortex and wake enter the rotor blade flow passage in a positive–negative law from front to back. At this cross-sectional position, the strength of the vane gap leakage vortex and induced vortex is greater than that of the vane wake, so the change in the flow field of the rotor blade is mainly caused by the vane leakage vortex and induced vortex. At $0T/4$, the tip of the vane leakage vortex just touches the pressure surface of the leading edge of the rotor blade. At this moment, the induced vortex end of the negative vorticity flows to the suction surface at the leading edge of the rotor blade. In the following moments, the vane leakage vortex and the induced vortex are cut by the rotor blade leading edge and then enter the rotor blade flow passage, which is supplemented and restored by the negative vortex of the subsequent induced vortex, and therefore, the unsteady nature of the leakage vortex of the rotor blade is weak. In addition, the flow velocity at the suction surface of the rotor blade is faster, elongating the leakage vortex and induced vortex of the vane. In area B at $1T/4$, the leakage vortex of the vane gradually merges into the wake of the rotor blade, and the induced vortex, supplements the rotor blade. On the other hand, the induced vortex is cancelled by the forward and backward positive vortices in the flow passage and is almost invisible at the outlet of the rotor blade.

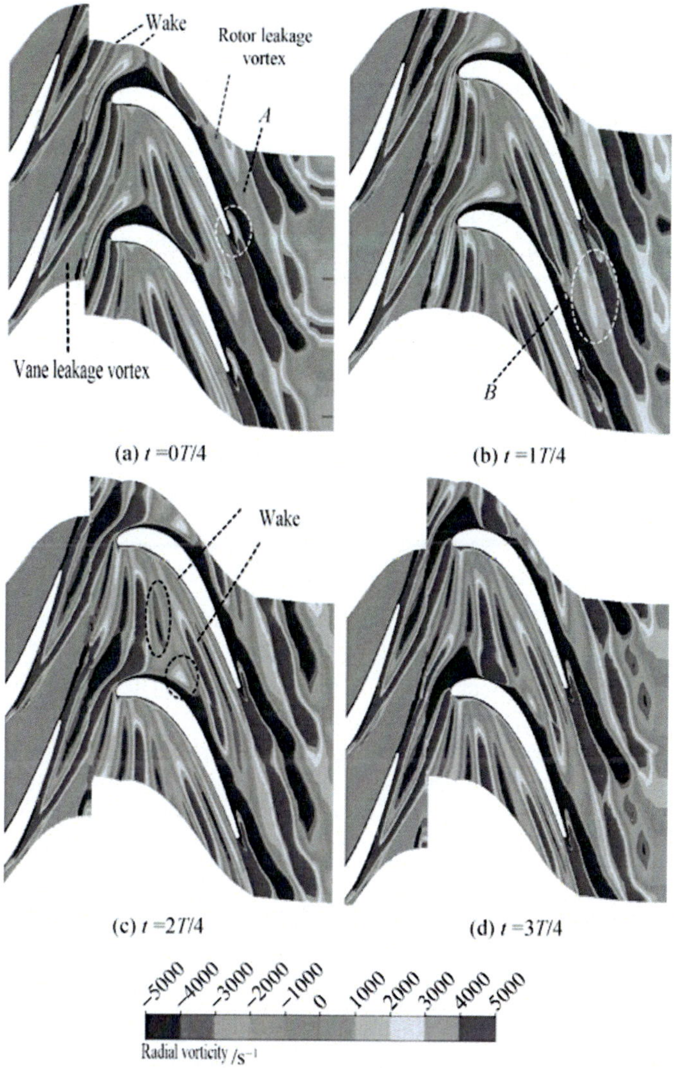

Fig. 2.21 Radial vorticity distribution at 95% rotor blade span of the variable vane stage at different times

Figure 2.22 shows the limiting streamlines and entropy distribution at the suction surface of the variable vane stage rotor blades. The separation line of the upper and lower endwall passage vortices gathers to the blade middle span. At $0T/4$, the lower endwall passage vortex, upper endwall passage vortex, and tip leakage vortex accounts for approximately 32.3%, 21.6%, and 4.4%, respectively, of the trailing edge height. At other times, the data have small oscillations but exhibit minimal change. Although the passage vortex accounts for minimal change in the entire blade span at each moment, as shown by the marked area in Fig. 2.22, the entropy near the rotor blade surface increases, and the passage vortex limiting streamline rises toward the midspan location. This phenomenon is caused by the development of the leading edge of the rotor blade to the vicinity of the trailing edge during the entire unsteady period, which changes in a volatile manner. Combined with the above analysis, the rotor blade passage vortex is affected by the upstream variable vane wake and leakage vortex. This effect is propagated from front to back, causing the passage vortex to exhibit an unsteady effect. However, the unsteady effect has been weakened before the rotor blade exit, which is caused by the mixing of the vane wake and the leakage vortex with the main flow and wall boundary layer in the rotor blade flow passage. Thus, the radial range of the passage vortex exhibits a very small change.

2.3 Multistage Variable Geometry Turbine Flow Field and Aerodynamic Characteristics Analysis

2.3.1 Internal Flow Field Evolution Characteristics of a Multistage Variable Geometry Turbine

The distribution of the Mach number of the middle section of the multistage variable geometry turbine at different turning angles is shown in Fig. 2.23. As shown in Fig. 2.23b, the gas flow matches the blade rows, and no incidence angle of attack occurs. When the variable vane is closed (Fig. 2.23a), the matching between the incoming flow and the vane becomes poor, resulting in a positive incidence flow at the inlet of the vane, which causes increased leakage in some gap areas and stronger secondary flows. A similar phenomenon is observed in the flow path of the rotor blade, and an elongated separation area is visible on the suction side of the blade. Overall, it can be speculated that the incidence angle of attack-induced losses rapidly increase, which deteriorates the turbine aerodynamic efficiency. Similarly, when the variable vane is open (Fig. 2.23c), at the vane and blade inlets, a negative incidence angle of attack is produced. A wide separation zone is observed near the pressure side of the rotor blade passage. In addition, as shown in Fig. 2.23, under the above three vane turning angles, as the flow develops downstream, the influence of the vane geometry on the aerodynamic performance of the downstream blade row gradually weakens.

Figure 2.24 shows the change in the relative inflow angle of the turbine blades at each stage with two negative turning angles of the multistage variable geometry turbine. These trends show that as the turbine power and variable vane are closed, the relative inflow angle β_1 of the variable vane stage rotor blade is reduced by approximately 3° at the root and by 5°–10° along the upper half of the blade span, although the variable vane is only further closed by 1°. These reductions substantially affect the flow characteristics in the entire upper half of the blade span. For the analyzed marine variable geometry turbines, the vanes at all stages basically adopt

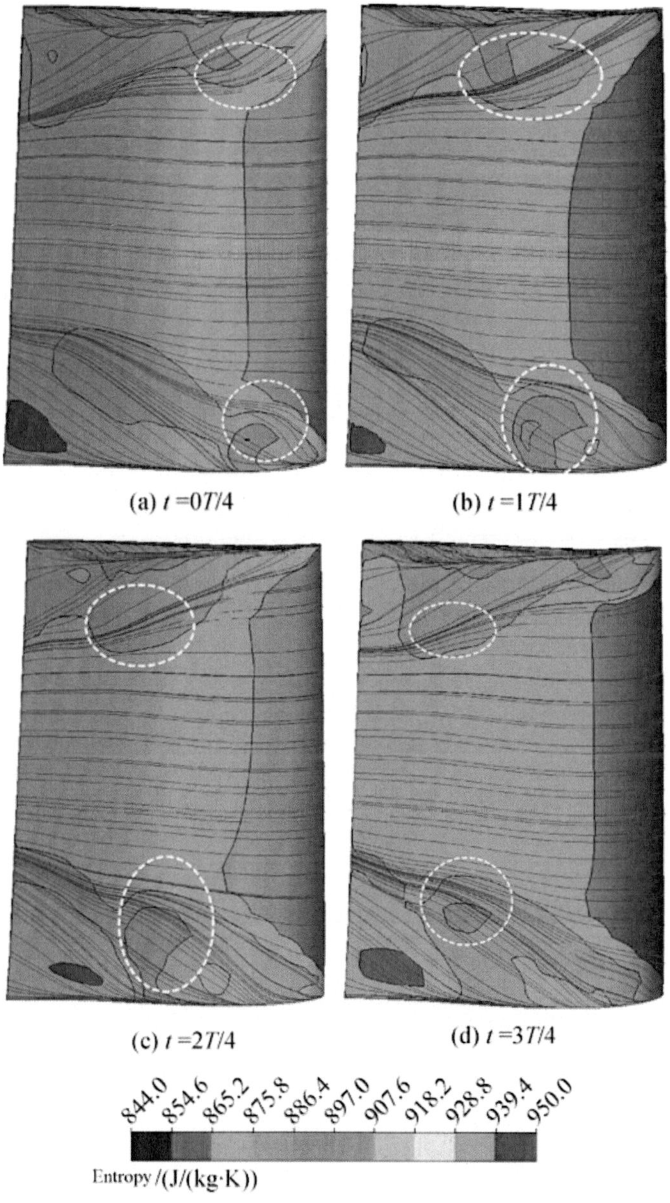

Fig. 2.22 Rotor blade surface limiting streamlines and entropy distribution for variable vane turbine stages

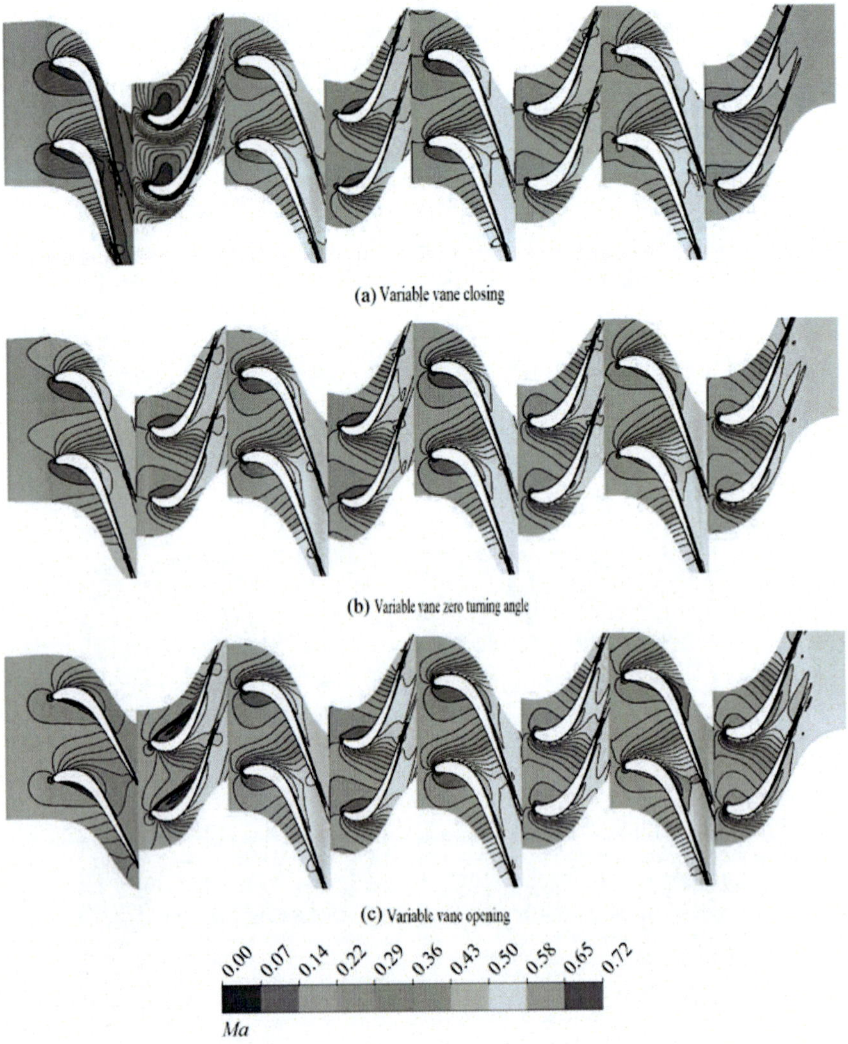

Fig. 2.23 Mach number distribution of the middle section of the multistage variable geometry turbine at different vane turning angles

the design of the aft-loaded profile, and the geometric leading edge with a large fillet radius is also applied, which is not sensitive to the change in the inflow incidence angle of attack. Therefore, the change in the inflow incidence angle of attack of the other three-stage rotor blades is not substantial; in contrast, the change in the relative inflow angle β_1 of the fourth-stage rotor blade is larger, and the change in the lower half of the blade span is more obvious.

Figure 2.25 shows the change in the relative inflow angle of the rotor blade of each stage of the multistage variable geometry turbine at two positive turning angles.

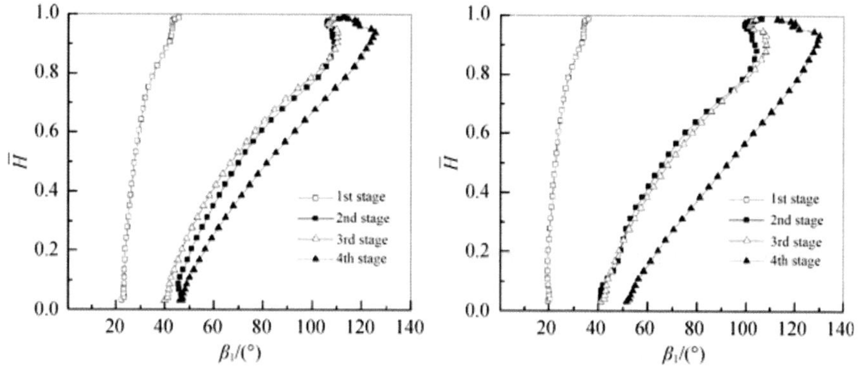

(a) –5° turning angle (b) –6° turning angle

Fig. 2.24 Variation in the relative rotor inflow angle of each stage of the multistage variable geometry turbine at two negative turning angles

When the variable vane is further opened by +4°, the variable vane stage rotor blade inlet flow angle β_1 accordingly increases, the tip increases by approximately 10°, and the roots undergo further changes, increasing by approximately 22°. However, the changes in the other three stages is not obvious. Therefore, with the exception of the variable vane stage, the structure of the entire turbine flow field will only slightly change. Generally, as the negative incidence angle of attack of the gas flow increases, the flow loss of the turbine blade will not significantly increase. For the analyzed marine variable geometry turbine, when the variable vane is opened from +4° to +8°, the efficiency of the entire variable geometry turbine decreases by only approximately 0.5%.

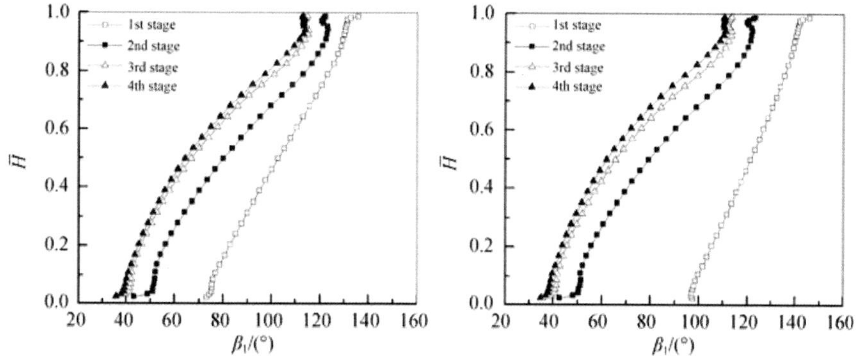

(a) +4° turning angle (b) +8° turning angle

Fig. 2.25 Variation in the relative rotor inflow angle of each stage of the multistage variable geometry turbine at two positive turning angles

2.3.2 *Effect of Vane Turning on the Aerodynamic Parameters of Turbines*

Figure 2.26 shows the variation in the radial distribution of the relative inlet flow angle β_1 of each stage of the four-stage variable geometry turbine with the turning of the variable vane. When the variable vane gradually opens from a fixed geometry, the relative inlet flow angle β_1 of the first-stage rotor blade accordingly increases, and the root undergoes further changes (when the variable vane is at a +8° turning position, the root increases nearly 50°, and the tip increases by nearly 30°), but the changes in the other three stages are not obvious. When the variable vane is gradually closed from the fixed geometry, the β_1 of the first stage correspondingly decreases, and greater changes in the tip occur (when the variable vane is at a −6° turning position, the root decreases by nearly 30°, and the tip decreases by nearly 50°), but β_1 of the other three stages slowly increase. After closing to the −6° turning position, β_1 of the third and fourth stages rapidly increases with the largest change in the middle location, and β_1 of the second stage only significantly increases in the upper half of the blade span.

Figure 2.27 shows the variation in the radial distribution of the absolute outflow angle α_2 of each stage of the four-stage variable geometry turbine blade with the turning of the variable vane. When the variable vane is gradually closed from a fixed geometry, the absolute outflow angle α_2 at the lower half of the first-stage rotor blade span will accordingly increase However, only when the variable vane is at the −9° turning angle is α_2 in the upper half of the blade span significantly reduced, so that the gas flow is underdeflected in the upper half and overdeflected in the lower half. The gas flow angle α_2 of the rotor blades of the second to fourth stages in the radial direction gradually increases as a whole. After the −6° turning position, the increase is more significant. When the variable vanes gradually open from a fixed geometry, the gas flow angle α_2 of the rotor blades at all stages in the radial direction decreases as a whole.

Whether the variable vanes are opened or closed, the variable geometry turbine will operate under off-design conditions, and the turbine efficiency will decrease with the turning of variable vanes. However, the overall performance of turbines will vary with the variable vanes. The change rule indicating that the turbine overall performance varies with the turning of vanes differs when it is turned on and off. The distribution of the inlet flow angle of each blade row at different turning angles is shown in Fig. 2.28. As the variable vane closes, the inlet flow angle of the variable vane stage rotor blades significantly decreases, and the turbine rotor blades run at a large positive incidence angle of attack. However, the gas flow angle at the inlet of the vanes and rotor blades of other stages gradually increases, tending to flow toward a large negative incidence angle of attack, and the fourth stage most obviously increases. When the variable vane is opened, the inlet flow angle of the variable vane stage rotor blade is significantly increased, and the turbine rotor blade operates at a large negative incidence angle of attack. At this time, the blades of other stages operate at a large positive incidence angle.

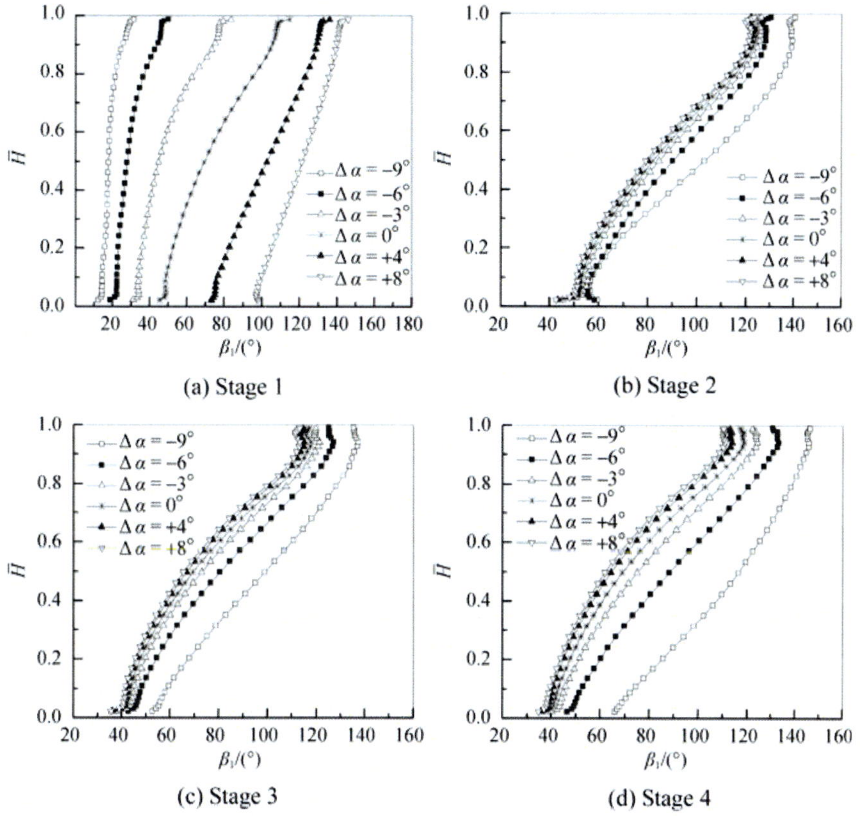

Fig. 2.26 Variation in the radial distribution of the relative rotor inflow angle of each stage of the multistage variable geometry turbine with vane turning

2.3.3 *Effect of Vane Turning on the Overall Parameters of Turbines*

Figure 2.29 shows the change rule of the radial distribution of the reaction of the various stages of the multistage variable geometry turbine with the turning of the vane. When the variable vane is closed, the thermal reaction of the first stage decreases in the entire radial direction. A lower reaction occurs at the hub than at the tip, and there is a negative reaction at the −9° turning position. While the vane is open, the change is reversed, and overall, the first stage exhibits the largest change. When the variable vane is closed from +8° to −6°, the changes in other stages are not obvious. When the variable vane is further closed, the middle and lower parts of the second stage are reduced, and the middle and upper parts of the third and fourth stages are reduced. The mutual interference among the turbine stages will obviously affect the flow of other stages, thereby changing the operation of the entire turbine components. Therefore, the change in the flow characteristics of the variable vane

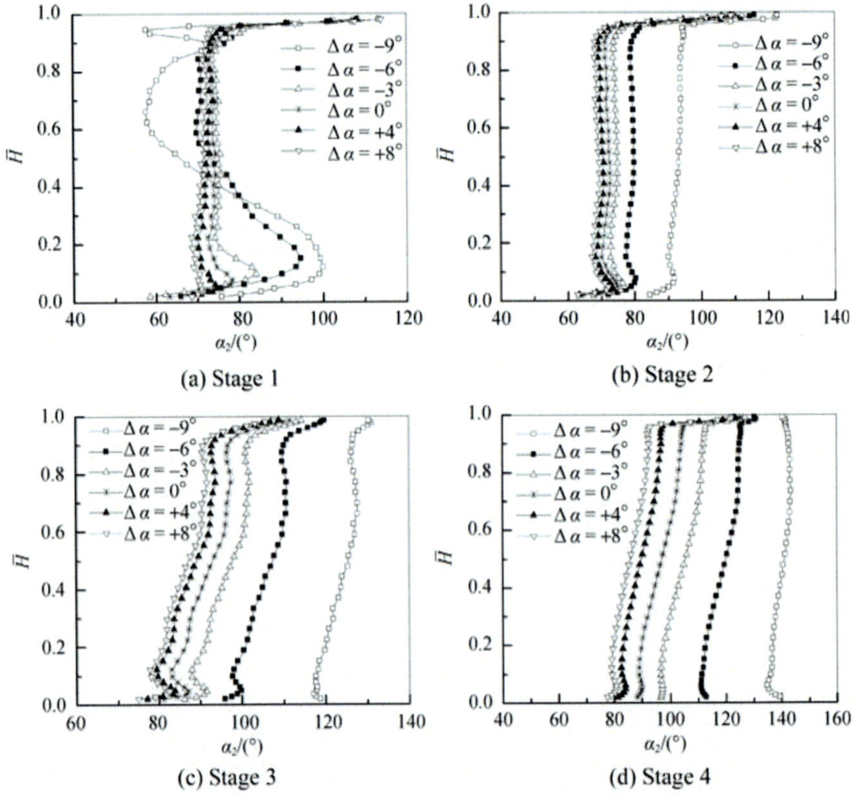

Fig. 2.27 Variation in the radial distribution of the relative rotor outflow angle of each stage of the multistage variable geometry turbine with vane turning

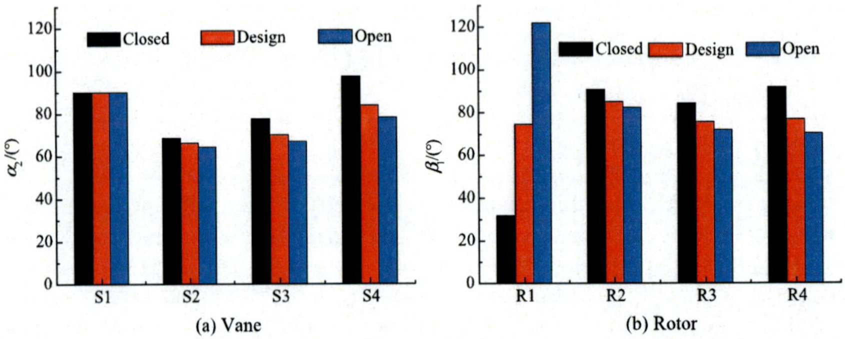

Fig. 2.28 Changes in each blade inflow angle with vane turning for multistage variable geometry turbines

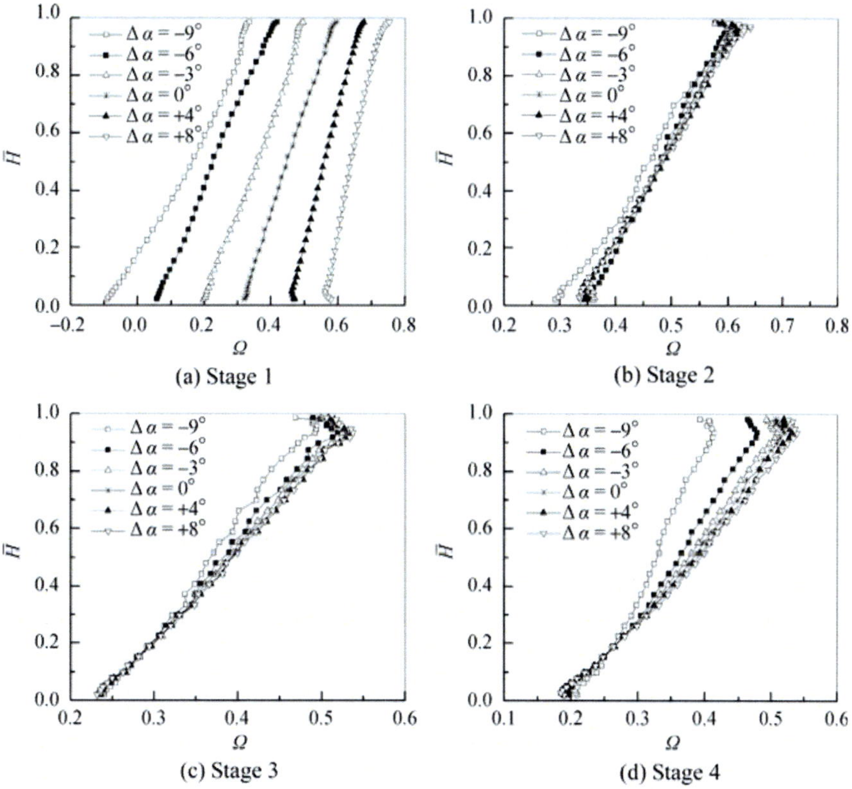

Fig. 2.29 Variation in the radial distribution of each stage reaction of the multistage variable geometry turbine with vane turning

stage will largely determine the aerodynamic characteristics of the entire variable geometry turbine.

Regardless of whether the variable vane is opened or closed, the parameters between the turbine blade rows change significantly, and the turbine stage reaction also changes accordingly. As shown in Fig. 2.30, the closing of the variable vane significantly decreases the reaction of the variable vane stage, while the opening of the variable vane significantly increases the stage reaction, which can also be obtained from the above analysis. As shown in Fig. 2.30, the turning of the variable vane has a relatively minimal effect on the other stages. Nevertheless, the power and efficiency of variable geometry turbines at all stages have significantly changed, as shown in Fig. 2.31. Although the closing of the variable vane significantly increases the output power of the variable vane stage, the power of the other three stages is significantly reduced. Overall, the closing of the variable vane reduces the turbine output power, and vice versa. As shown in Fig. 2.31b, the closing of the variable vane significantly reduces the efficiency of the variable vane stage, while the negative effect of the variable vane on other stages gradually weakens. Even the efficiency of the final stage has been improved, mainly because the output power of the turbine stage is significantly reduced at this time, which improves the turbine throughflow. The opening of the variable vane has a similar effect on all stages of the turbine. In conjunction with Figs. 2.28 and 2.31, the turning of the variable vane has a greater influence on the flow performance of the first stage in the four-stage power turbine and a lesser influence on the latter three stages.

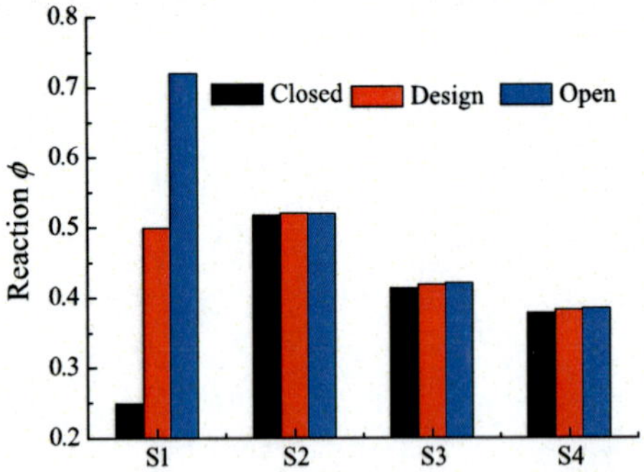

Fig. 2.30 Variation in each stage reaction of the multistage variable geometry turbine with vane turning

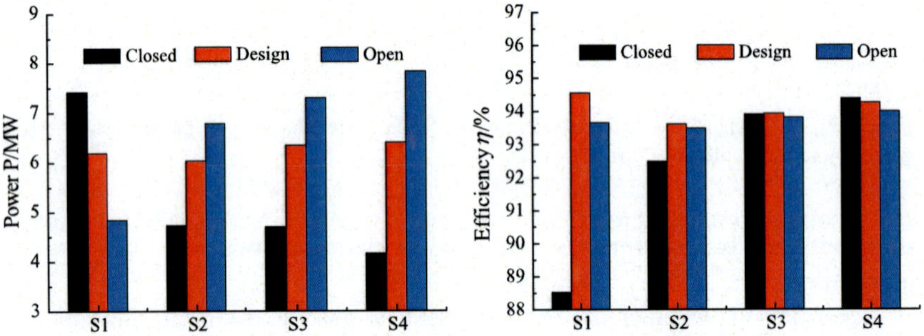

(a) Power (b) Efficiency

Fig. 2.31 Variation in each stage power and efficiency of multistage variable geometry turbine with vane turning

2.4 Flow, Power and Efficiency Characteristics of a Variable Geometry Turbine

2.4.1 Flow Characteristics

Figure 2.32 shows the typical flow characteristics curve of the variable geometry turbines. Under two typical operating conditions, the increase in the reduced flow rate is proportional to the increase in the flow area, or as the variable vane opens, the reduced flow rate gradually increases. However, with the opening of the variable vane, although the flow area is further increased, the flow rate of the turbine is gradually reduced due to the restriction of the downstream rotor blade throat area. Correspondingly, as the variable vane closes, the reduced flow rate gradually decreases as the flow area decreases. Figure 2.32 also shows that with an increase in the expansion ratio and the reduced flow rate, the variable geometry turbine quickly enters the choked condition.

2.4.2 Power Characteristics

Figure 2.33 shows a typical power characteristics curve of variable geometry turbines. As the variable vane opens, the turbine's power performance rapidly increases, which is mainly related to the scenario in which the turbine flow rate increases with the opening of the variable vane. Moreover, when the variable vane is further opened from the +4° turning position, the turbine power is not significantly improved, mainly because the flow capacity of the turbine is limited by the variable vane stage rotor

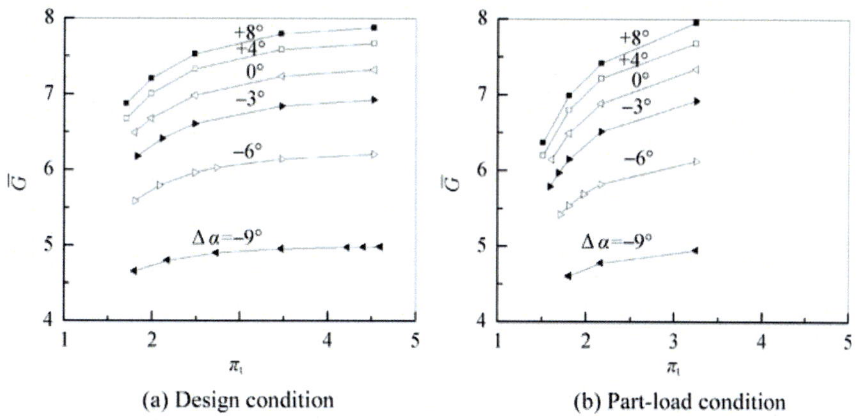

Fig. 2.32 Flow characteristics of a multistage variable geometry turbine

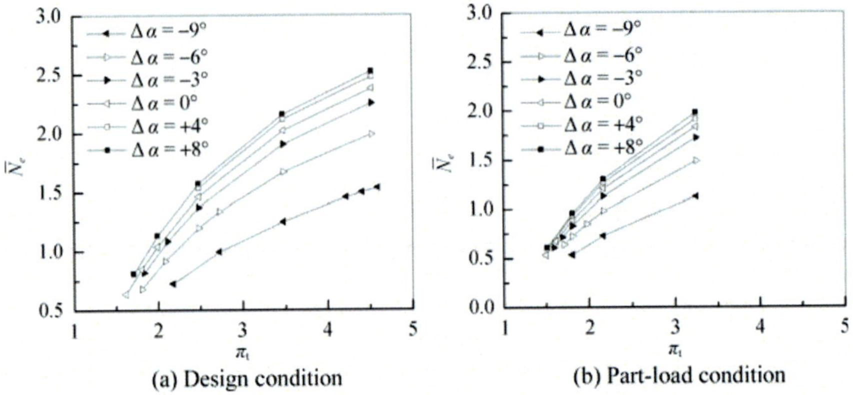

Fig. 2.33 Power characteristics of a multistage variable geometry turbine

blade throat area. The overall trend reveals that the power characteristics of the variable geometry turbines are consistent with the change in flow characteristics.

2.4.3 Efficiency Characteristics

Figure 2.34 shows the typical efficiency characteristics curve of variable geometry turbines. In the smaller turning range of the variable vane, that is, when the turning angle $\Delta\alpha$ takes a value of $-3°$ to $+4°$, there is no obvious change in the efficiency characteristics of the variable geometry turbine, mainly because the geometries of the leading edge of turbine vanes and blades are not sensitive to the change in the incidence angle of attack. Furthermore, typical high-performance blade profiles, both aft-loaded and uniformly loaded, and a small change in the incidence angle of attack will not cause a significant increase in the internal flow loss of the entire turbine. However, when the variable vane is further closed from the $-3°$ turning position, the efficiency of the variable geometry turbine is significantly reduced at all operating rotational speeds, especially at lower operating speeds, because the entire turbine runs away from the design incidence angle of attack condition, resulting in a sharp drop in turbine efficiency and working power. When the variable vane is further opened from the $+4°$ turning position, although the efficiency of the variable geometry turbine also decreases, the trend of decrease is small. During the actual operation of the variable geometry turbine, the turning of the variable vane will inevitably increase the gap clearance loss of the turbine, causing a decrease in turbine efficiency. Therefore, whether the variable vane is opened or closed, the aerodynamic efficiency of the multistage variable geometry turbine decreases with the turning of the variable vane, but the degree of efficiency reduction varies. As shown in the figure, the reduction caused by the opening of variable vanes is smaller than the reduction caused by the closing of variable vanes.

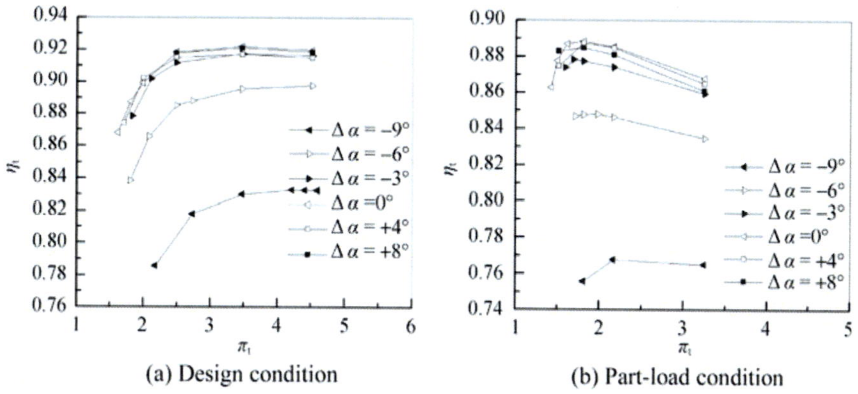

Fig. 2.34 Efficiency characteristics of multistage variable geometry turbine

2.4.4 *General Characteristics*

Figure 2.35 shows the general change curve of the variable geometry turbine expansion ratio, reduced flow rate and efficiency with different variable-vane turning angles. When the variable vane is closed from a fixed geometry to a −9° turning position, the entire variable geometry turbine is operating in the low-efficiency region. However, when the variable vane is opened from a fixed geometry, the high-efficiency operating area in the turbine general characteristics curve is relatively slowly reduced.

In summary, when discussing the feasibility of the variable geometry turbine design, the quantitative impact of the reduction in turbine efficiency on the benefits of using variable geometry turbines for the entire engine unit must be considered, and the mechanical mechanism that controls the turning of the variable vane must be high. It can be seen that the design of the variable geometry turbine is very difficult. In addition, considering the organic matching with the whole unit, the selection of the turning angle of the variable vane not only depends on the variable geometry turbine mass flow to meet the power change requirements but also must consider its matching with the gas generator. On the other hand, the selection is also limited by the adaptability of the variable vane stage rotor blade's incidence angle of attack, especially the variable vane stage rotor blade's ability to resist separation flow with the positive incidence angle of attack, and the variable vane's turning strength requirements and blade profile limits.

2.5 Summary

This chapter mainly analyzes the leakage flow characteristics and loss mechanism of the vane-end gap clearance, the flow interference mechanism and loss characteristics of the variable vane stage endwall zone, the multistage variable geometry turbine

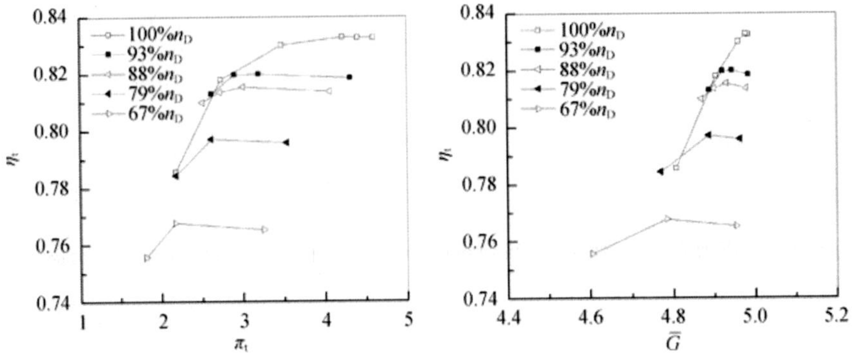

(a) -9° turning angle

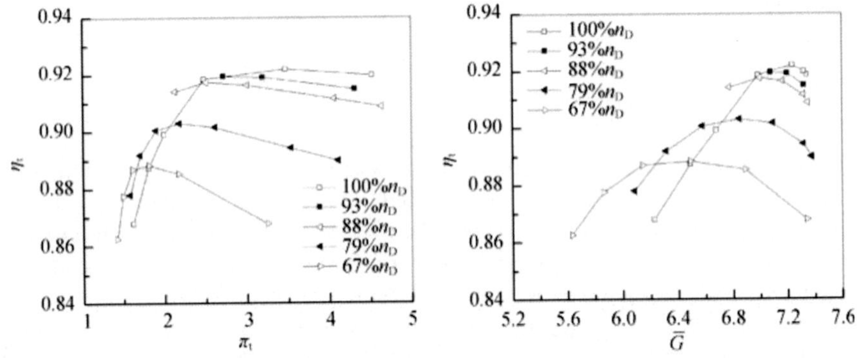

(b) 0° turning angle

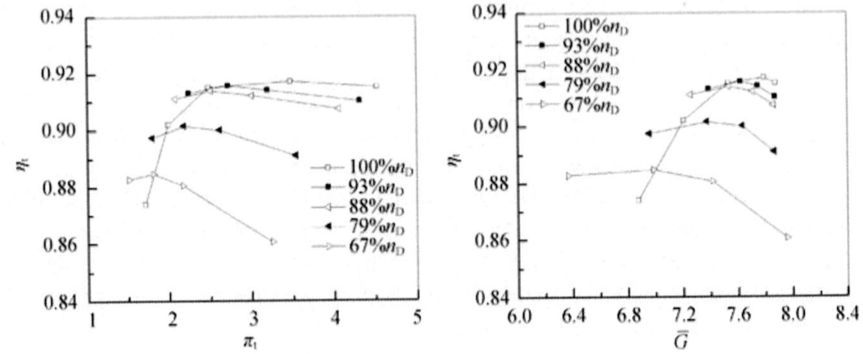

(c) +8° turning angle

Fig. 2.35 General characteristics of multistage variable geometry turbine flow field and corresponding aerodynamic characteristics analysis, and the variable geometry turbine flow, power and efficiency characteristics.

The variable geometry of the turbine introduces a part clearance at the vane end and causes interference of the leakage vortex and passage vortex, thereby changing the flow field structure and loss distribution in the endwall area of the vane. The leakage vortex core of the variable vane is mainly composed of the leakage streamline on the rear side of the turning shaft, which is obviously different from the leakage vortex core of the conventional rotor blade.

The turning of the variable vane changes its own throat area and load distribution, which causes not only its own off-design incidence angle of attack flow but also a large incidence-angle separation flow near the leading edge of the rotor blade. However, the location and mechanism of the rotor blade flow separation caused by the opening or closing of variable vanes are completely different, and the size of the loss also differs. In particular, the large separation flow on the suction side of the rotor blade caused by the variable vane closing is caused by the spiral upward movement of the separation bubble near the endwall of the turbine, showing strong three-dimensional separation characteristics, which deteriorates the aerodynamic performance of the variable geometry turbine.

The turning of variable vanes changes their throat area, leading to the redistribution of the inlet flow angle of each blade row and an enthalpy drop between the turbine stages and the degree of reaction, thereby deteriorating the aerodynamic performance of the variable geometry turbine at various levels. However, the change in the overall performance of the turbine with the turning of the variable vane differs between the time a vane is opened and the time a vane is closed, that is, the reduction caused by the opening of the variable vane is smaller than the reduction caused by the closing of the variable vane. Nevertheless, the turning of the vane as a whole has the most obvious effect on the variable vane stage of the multistage variable geometry turbine.

Chapter 3
Aerodynamic Design Method for a Variable Geometry Turbine

Abstract This chapter mainly summarizes the selection and optimization of low-dimensional, aerodynamic design parameters of variable geometry turbines, the aerodynamic performance of turbine blade profiles suitable for variable geometry work, and the three-dimensional, aerodynamic design method of variable geometry turbines with large meridional expansion. The wide operating condition design of variable geometry turbines requires careful selection of low-dimensional aerodynamic design parameters. The variable vane design can be given priority in the adoption of a high, new, "aft-loaded" profile with small turning angles. The variable geometry turbine inversion design can be employed to reduce the endwall loss of the variable vane for large expansion flow channels.

3.1 Selection Rule and Optimization of Low-Dimensional Aerodynamic Design Parameters for a Variable Geometry Turbine

The aerodynamic design of turbines needs to be continuously improved from one dimension to three dimensions. The calculation results of the one-dimensional parameters are the basis of the three-dimensional design. Although the design itself can be directly optimized in a high-dimensional space, it often benefits from a wealth of design experience and depends on the accurate calculation results of the three-dimensional flow fields. Therefore, in the absence of the design basis, the gains by the improvement are often outweighed and even cause the failure of the entire aerodynamic design. In the design of low-dimensional space, the basic theory and design experience of the turbine elementary stage must be increased. However, if the essence of the internal flow of the turbine and the design theory basis are fully understood, the design optimization of the final high-dimensional space will serve as a key link in the success of turbine aerodynamic design. Therefore, this section investigates the selection rule for the low-dimensional design variables of a variable geometry turbine.

J. Gao et al., *Variable Geometry Turbine Technology for Marine Gas Turbines*,
https://doi.org/10.1007/978-981-19-6952-2_3

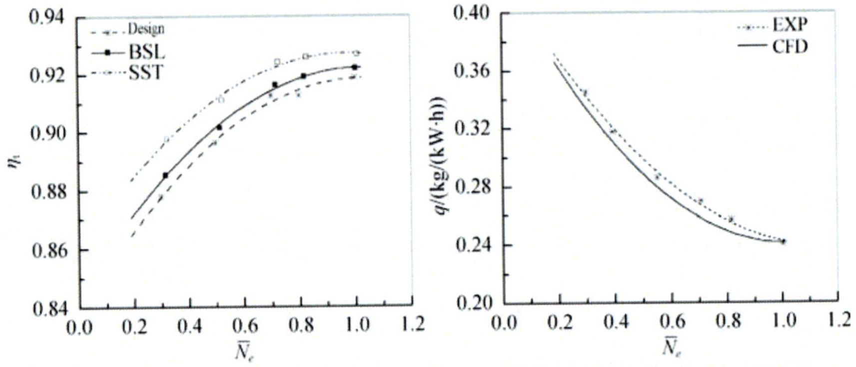

(a) Turbine efficiency changes with power

(b) Comparison between unit fuel consumption characteristics and experiments

Fig. 3.1 Turbine overall performance and unit fuel consumption rate characteristics

3.1.1 *Aerodynamic Characteristics for a Variable Geometry Turbine*

The operating range of marine gas turbines is wide, and the cruising operating point is approximately 30% of the operating conditions. As shown in Fig. 3.1, under cruise conditions, the turbine efficiency under low conditions is reduced by 3–5% compared with that under the design conditions, and the fuel consumption of the unit significantly increases. Thus, the efficient operation of turbines under wide operating conditions a key issue that needs urgent attention. The aerodynamic design of a fixed geometry turbine is often based on various parameters at specific operating conditions to complete the transition from a low-dimensional design to a high-dimensional design. Due to different operating characteristics, turbines with variable geometry usually need to work under a wide range of variable and stable operating conditions. It is not realistic to design variable geometry turbines using conventional turbine design methods. Therefore, the rational selection of variable geometry turbine design parameters from multiple dimensions is important to improve the variable working condition capability of variable geometry turbines.

3.1.2 *Variation Law of Low-Dimensional Aerodynamic Design Parameters with the Turning of Variable Vanes*

1. Design condition point

In the aerodynamic design of a conventional fixed geometry turbine, a series of design parameters, such as total temperature and total pressure at the turbine inlet, mass flow rate, and power, are generally given. Next, a suitable throughflow scheme is selected, and the key aerodynamic parameters and blade profile parameters are selected. Based on this approach, the basic modeling of the turbine blade according to the calculation results is completed. However, gas turbine power turbines often need a stable operation under multiple operating conditions and for an extensive period during their lifetime. The initial design of a conventional turbine does not consider the problem of efficient and stable operation under multiple operating conditions. Therefore, the performance of the power turbine will be acceptable under design conditions. However, the flow rate of the intake and exhaust systems will be mismatched under off-design conditions, in which the incidence angle of attack of each blade row increases, and overall, the turbine efficiency decreases. Therefore, in view of the characteristics of variable geometry turbines that need to stably operate under different operating conditions, this section uses a one-dimensional average-diameter method to reasonably select the design operating point in a low-dimensional space to ensure that the turbine adequately operates under different operating conditions.

This subsection relies on the five operating condition points of the four-stage power turbine as the design basis. In the low-dimensional space, the low-dimensional model with different operating conditions as the design point is analyzed under variable operating conditions. This subsection mainly examines the corresponding relationship among the changes in rotational speed, expansion ratio and total-static efficiency. Figure 3.2 shows the corresponding relationship among efficiency, rotation speed, and expansion ratio when different operating conditions are selected as the design point. According to Fig. 3.2a, when the design point is selected at 30% operating conditions, the turbine design-point performance is excellent, but at off-design operation points, such as that for an increased rotational speed of 100.86 r/(min • $K^{-0.5}$), the performance substantially deteriorates. Similarly, when the design point is selected at 100% working conditions, the turbine performance at the design point is ideal and the total-static efficiency is 87.8%, while at off-design points, such as 30% working conditions, the total-static efficiency drops to 79.5%. At each design rotational speed, when the rotational speed is slightly increased, the efficiency will be improved. However, when the rotational speed exceeds a certain range, the efficiency will show a downward trend because a high rotational speed means that the turbine blade is flowing at a negative incidence angle of attack, and a low rotational speed means that the turbine blade is flowing at a positive incidence angle of attack. Many researchers suggest that the aerodynamic performance of turbine blades against incoming flow at negative incidence angles of attack is much better than that at positive incidence angles of attack. Therefore, when the design point at a low rotational speed is selected, the efficiency drop at the extreme low rotational speed can be greatly avoided. It can be ensured that the turbine is at a negative incidence angle of attack at most off-design points when running at a relatively high rotational speed. It is beneficial for improving the aerodynamic characteristics of turbines with variable geometry in wide operating conditions. An analysis and summary of the data revealed that when the design condition point is selected as the 50% working condition, the overall fluctuation of the efficiency is the lowest and that the relatively high efficiency stability characteristics at the off-design rotational speeds can be maintained.

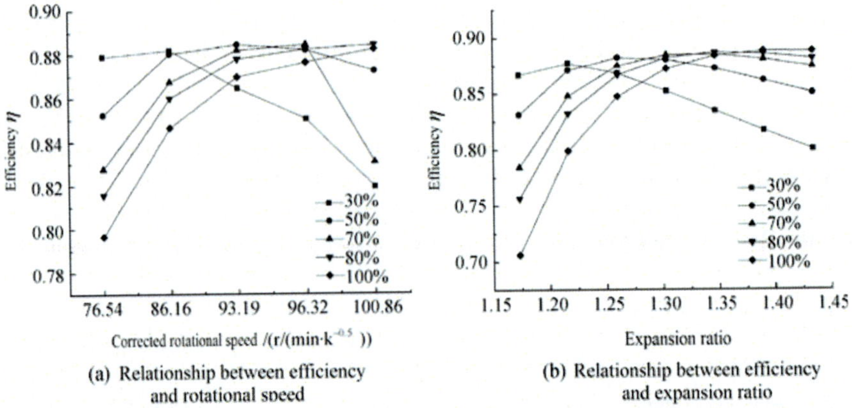

Fig. 3.2 Correspondence among efficiency, rotational speed and expansion ratio when different working conditions are selected as design point

Subsequently, further analysis is performed to determine under which working conditions is the design point the least sensitive to changes in the expansion ratio. Figure 3.2b shows the curve of efficiency versus expansion ratio when using different operating conditions as the design point. When the design point is selected as the 30% working condition, as the expansion ratio increases, the efficiency slightly rises and then shows a sharp downward trend, and the efficiency drops by at most 10%. When the design point is selected as the 100% working condition, with an increase in the expansion ratio, the efficiency shows an upward trend, but at the lowest expansion ratio, the efficiency is only 71.2%. When the design condition is selected as the 50% working condition, the change in the overall efficiency with the expansion ratio is basically stable, and the efficiency amplitude at the off-design point is lower and performs best.

In summary, when the 50% operating conditions are selected as the design operating condition, the efficiency is ensured to be higher under the design operating condition, and the relative efficiency stability can be maintained under off-design operating conditions. Both design and off-design operating conditions are considered. In addition, a relatively good wide operating performance is achieved. Therefore, when redesigning the variable geometry turbine, this method can be selected to choose a reasonable design operating point.

2. Loading coefficient and flow coefficient

In the low-dimensional, aerodynamic design space of turbines, determining the main parameters of the turbine elementary-stage, velocity triangle is the key to a successful design. Therefore, this section mainly discusses the selection rules of certain dimensionless design parameters that describe the velocity triangle, such as the loading coefficient and flow coefficient. Through the multioperating condition, aerodynamic calculation of the four-stage power turbine, the changing rules of three dimensionless design parameters—loading coefficient, flow coefficient and reaction degree—under different working conditions are analyzed, which can provide ideas for selecting low-dimensional design parameters for the wide working condition design research of variable geometry turbines.

The loading coefficient is defined as the ratio of the flange work to the square of the circumferential velocity, which is usually applied to characterize the power of the turbine. If the loading coefficient is too small, it will yield an excessive number of turbine stages or radial dimensions that are too large, causing a series of problems, such as excessive turbine blade mass. If the loading coefficient is too large, the streamwise direction of the flow passage will deviate from the axial direction, which is undesirable for the final stage of a single-stage or multistage turbine, and excessive kinetic energy losses will occur. If the loading coefficient is too large, the torque of the turbine blade must be large. Based on the premise of a certain axial velocity, a greater gas flow turning angle will be produced, resulting in a more severe secondary flow in the endwall zone, thereby reducing the overall power turbine efficacy. Figure 3.3 shows a change diagram of the loading coefficient and flow coefficient of the power turbine at various stages. Under the same operating conditions, the loading coefficient of the first to fourth stages of the power turbine decreases in sequence, as shown in Fig. 3.3a, and the first stage, which is the variable vane stage, has the largest torque. As the operating conditions decrease, the loading coefficient of the first three stages shows an upward trend, and only the fourth stage shows a downward trend. The change in operating conditions makes the first-stage loading coefficient of the power turbine undergo the most significant changes. Therefore, when the variable geometry turbine is redesigned, the selection of the loading coefficient in the low-dimensional space can be appropriately reduced to prevent an excessively large loading coefficient in the first-stage vane under low operating conditions and an increase in the flow loss in the endwall zone.

The flow coefficient is used to describe the flow capacity of the turbine, which is defined as the ratio of the axial component of the turbine elementary stage's absolute

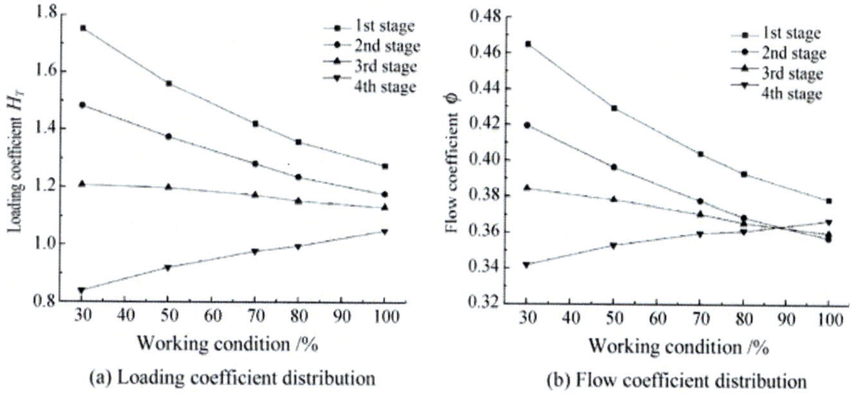

Fig. 3.3 Distributions of loading coefficient and flow coefficient of power turbines under various working conditions

velocity to that of the circumferential velocity. Generally, when other conditions, such as the mass flow rate and rotational speed, are fixed, a smaller flow coefficient generally leads to a lower inlet velocity and a larger corresponding turbine blade turning angle. Therefore, a change in incoming flow has a more obvious impact on the flow coefficient, and it is easy to cause a change in the attack angle. With a relative increase in the meridional channel height, the friction area of the turbine blade profile will increase, which may cause strength and other problems. When the flow coefficient is too large, the blade inlet velocity increases, the flow area of the blade is reduced under the same conditions, the height of the corresponding meridional flow channel naturally decreases, the flow range of the endwall zone expands, and the secondary flow effect is enhanced. Generally, the turning angle of the turbine blade corresponding to the large flow coefficient is generally small, the inlet velocity is high, and the blade is less sensitive to the incoming flow.

Figure 3.3b shows the distribution of power turbine flow coefficients at different stages under different operating conditions. Figure 3.3b shows that the overall change trend of the flow coefficient is similar to the change in the loading coefficient. As the operating conditions decrease, the flow coefficients of the first three stages of the power turbine increase, and the fourth stage presents a downward trend. The difference is that under the design conditions, the flow coefficient of the fourth stage of the power turbine is only lower than that of the first stage, and the second stage is the smallest. Therefore, when redesigning the variable geometry turbine, a relatively small flow coefficient should be selected to reduce the secondary flow loss in the turbine endwall zone, thereby improving the turbine performance under low operating conditions.

The selection rules of the reaction degree and its radial distribution of variable geometry turbines and the aerodynamic parameters at different radial positions are shown in Sect. 3.2.3; therefore, they will not be repeated here.

3.1.3 Optimization of Low-Dimensional Aerodynamic Design Parameters for a Variable Geometry Turbine

In this section, through the above meticulous research on the selection rules of the low-dimensional design parameters of turbines, combined with the design experience, the first stage of the original power turbine is subjected to wide-condition modification design and verification. The profiles at 1, 50 and 99% of the first-stage vanes of the original power turbine are extracted and modified, and then the three-dimensional vanes are generated by the stacking method of the center of gravity consistent with the original vane profile, as shown in Fig. 3.4. According to the design parameter selection rules obtained in Sect. 3.1.2, first, the true chord length of the vane is shortened, while the axial chord length is basically unchanged to move the profile load backward. Second, the deflection angle of the vane trailing edge is adjusted to reduce the incidence angle of attack at the rotor blade inlet under low operating conditions. As the vane height increases, the angle of deflection angle adjustment decreases. Simultaneously, the thicknesses of the profiles at 50 and 99% vane spans are increased, and the thicknesses of the first half of the pressure side and suction side are increased. When it is close to the trailing edge, the thicknesses is slightly smaller than the original vane profile, which moves the maximum load position of the optimized vane profile backward. Compared with the original vane profile, the profile at 99% vane span has an increased curvature and thickness on the pressure and suction sides of the middle of the vane profile to ensure that the mass flow rates of the vane and blade are matched. Since the chord length of the vane profile decreases and the axial chord length is basically unchanged, the outlet flow angle of the first-stage vane increases. Therefore, to avoid mismatch with the downstream rotor blades, attention should be given to controlling the amount of modification of the chord length. According to the above analysis, under low operating conditions, the positive incidence angle of attack at the turbine inlet near the tip of the blade is large, and the positive incidence angle of attack at the turbine inlet near the blade root is small. However, if you rashly increase the deflection angle at the vane tip and trailing edge, it will misalign the flow matching between two turbine stages. Therefore, by increasing the deflection angle of the trailing edge of the root of the variable geometry turbine vanes and enabling its gradual decrease as the vane height increases, the turbine aerodynamic performance at low operating conditions can be improved.

Figure 3.5a shows the radial variation in the outflow angle of the variable vane. At less than approximately 50% vane span, the outflow angle of the optimized profile is greater than the original profile at the same vane span, the optimized profile outflow angle continuously increases with a decrease in the vane height, and the change amplitude of the original vane profile outflow angle is small. Simultaneously, near the root of the vane, the gas flow angles suddenly drop, and the overall change trend is similar. When the vane span is higher than approximately 50%, the overall trend of the optimized and original vane profiles is similar to the increase in the vane span. However, the gas flow angle of the optimized vane profile is smaller than that of the original vane profile at the same position. Figure 3.5b shows the radial variation in the inlet flow angle of the rotor blade downstream of the variable vane. At less than approximately 60% vane span, the blade profile outflow angle for the optimized case is greater than the original case at the same blade span. The outflow angle change range for the optimized case is smaller than that of the original case. As the operating conditions decrease, the relative outflow angle substantially. At this time, the increase in the relative outflow angle can reduce the positive attack angle in the range of less than 60% of the blade span, thus improving the aerodynamic performance of the turbine blade under wide operating conditions. In the blade span range of more than 60%, the turbine blade outflow angle for the optimized case is smaller than that of the original case for the same blade span. The outflow angle for the optimized case varies similarly to the original case. The outflow angle slowly increases near the tip of the blade, the transition is gentle, and there is no sudden change. The three-dimensional flow field inside the power turbine under multiple operating conditions shows that the rotor blade is at a positive incidence angle of attack near the tip of the blade

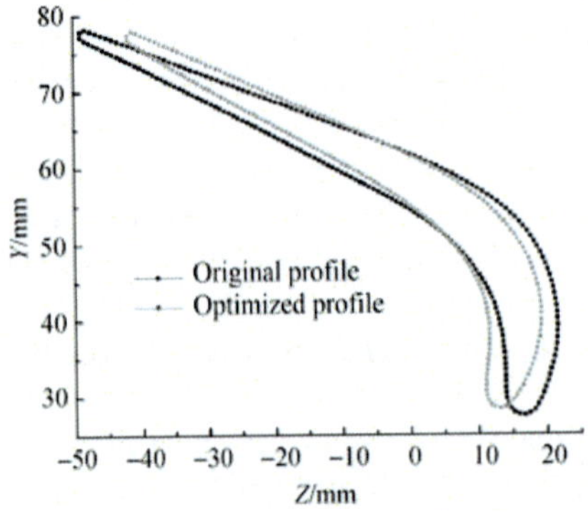

(a) 1% span

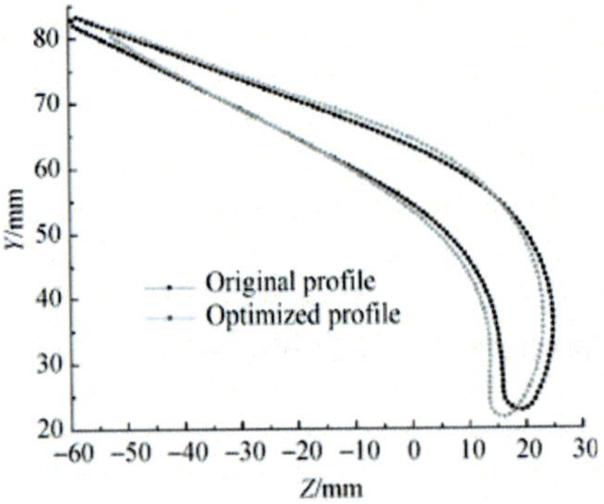

(b) 50% span

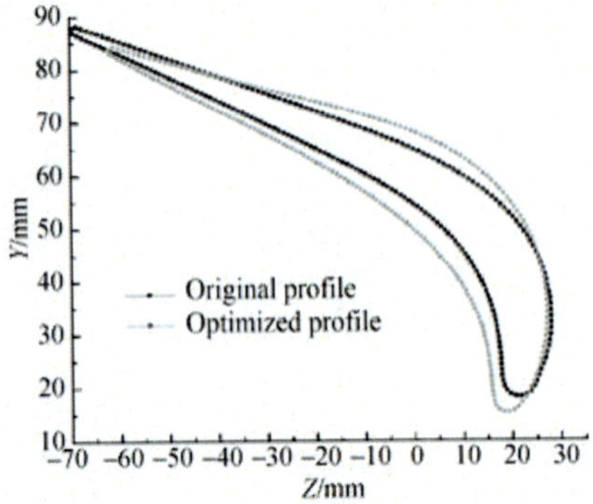

(c) 99% span

Fig. 3.4 Optimization results of low-dimensional design parameters of variable geometry turbines

and that the optimized case is slightly larger than the original case at the relative blade outflow angle near the tip gap, thereby improving the flow conditions inside the variable geometry turbine.

Figure 3.6 shows a comparison of the spanwise distribution of the total pressure loss coefficient at the variable vane outlet. Within the range of less than 80% vane span, the total pressure loss coefficient of the optimized vane profile is less than the original case, and as the vane height decreases, the degree of control of the total pressure loss gradually increases. In the range of 80–95% vane span, the total pressure loss coefficient of the optimized vane profile is slightly lower than that of the original case. In the range of 95% vane span to vane tip, the total pressure loss coefficient of the optimized vane profile is slightly higher than that of the original case. In general, the optimized vane profile is significantly better than the original case in controlling flow losses, and the flow is optimized to a certain extent.

Table 3.1 shows the optimization results of low-dimensional design parameters of variable geometry turbines under five operating conditions. For different operating conditions, the efficiency of the modified turbine is improved compared with the original turbine. The efficiency is increased by 0.43% under the 50% working

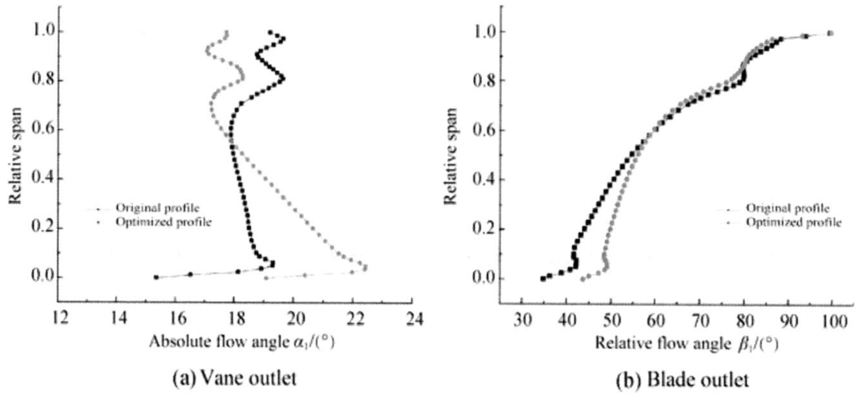

Fig. 3.5 Vane outflow and blade inflow angles of variable geometry turbines

Fig. 3.6 Spanwise total pressure loss coefficient distribution at the variable vane outlet

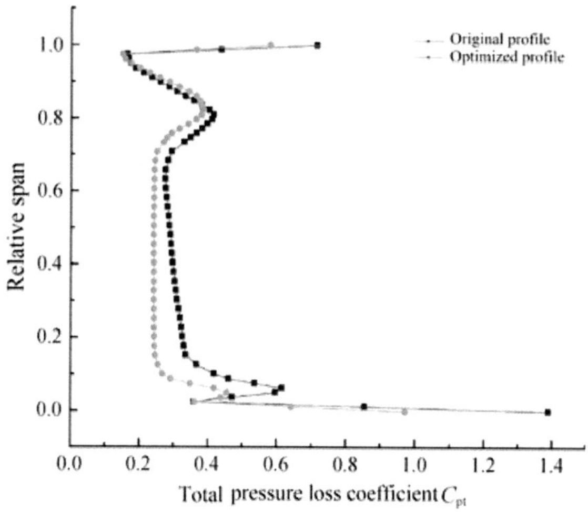

condition, and the efficiency is improved by a minimum of 0.33% under the 100% working condition. Simultaneously, the flow deviation of the modified turbine is approximately 1% compared with the original turbine, which has a small impact on the matching performance of the subsequent multistage turbine. Thus far, an original variable geometry turbine with low sensitivity to changes in incoming flow conditions and a certain wide operating performance has been designed.

Table 3.1 Optimization results of low-dimensional design parameters of variable geometry turbines

Working condition (%)	Original turbine efficiency (%)	Modified turbine efficiency (%)	Efficiency increase (%)	Original turbine mass flow (Ratio to design result)	Modified turbine mass flow (Ratio to design result)	Mass flow deviation (%)
30	92.6315	93.0082	0.41	0.64	0.64	0.92
50	93.0934	93.4951	0.43	0.77	0.78	1.02
70	93.4124	93.7796	0.39	0.87	0.88	1.07
80	93.5396	93.8845	0.37	0.92	0.93	1.23
100	93.7074	94.0123	0.33	1.00	1.01	1.31

3.2 Investigation of the Aerodynamic Performance of the Turbine Blade Profile Suitable for Variable Geometry Operation

A characteristic of the variable geometry turbine is that the first-stage vanes of the turbine will rotate with a change in working conditions. Therefore, the requirement for the first-stage vanes of the variable geometry turbine is that it can still have good aerodynamics when the inlet incidence angle of attack changes. Note that the aft-loaded profile has good adaptability to the incidence angle of attack compared with profiles that exhibit other load distributions. Therefore, the aft-loaded profile is widely employed in the aerodynamic design of variable geometry turbine vanes and blades.

3.2.1 *Variable Geometry Turbine Blade Profile Characteristics*

Figure 3.7 shows the B2B flow path of a turbine blade profile, which is intended to be geometrically analyzed. Due to the determination of the camberline in the profile, the chord length b, pitch t, turning angle θ, and angle φ between the chord and the pitch line have been determined. This blade profile adopts a 90° gas intake, so the angle between the inlet flow angle and the pitch line is 90°. The quantitative geometric relationship of Eq. 3.1 is expressed as follows:

$$\frac{x}{\sin \alpha} = \frac{t}{\sin c} \Rightarrow x = \frac{t \sin \alpha}{\sin c} \tag{3.1}$$

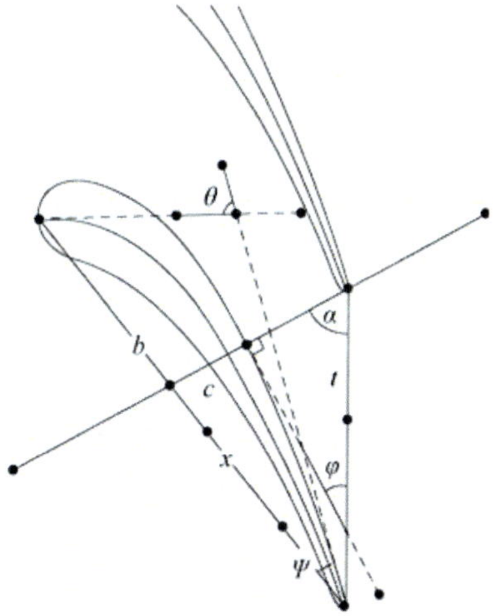

Fig. 3.7 Typical turbine vane profile B2B flow path

Therefore, the decrease in α can make the blade profile load move backward; φ is the angle between the tangent line and the pitch line at the lowest static pressure on the suction surface; and increasing φ can make the load move backward, that is, the larger the angle of the second half of the camberline in the blade profile, the more backward the load will be. The following part analyzes five examples with the same geometric inlet and outlet angles, the same maximum thickness, and the same pitch.

As shown in Fig. 3.8, an analysis of the relationship between the camberline angle distribution at the 50−100% position of the turbine blade profile and the static pressure distribution on the blade surface reveals that the larger the absolute camberline angle is, the larger the distance that the load moves backward. This finding is consistent with the above theoretical analysis.

Two main geometric factors affect the blade profile: the profile camberline and profile thickness distribution. Therefore, the thickness distribution of the blade profile has a great influence on its load distribution, which is analyzed below. The blade profile is simplified into a triangle, as shown in Fig. 3.9. For a turning angle of 0°, as shown by the thick line in Fig. 3.9, suppose that the maximum thickness position is located at p along the chord and that the maximum load position is located at q along the chord. At this time, the position of the throat of the profile is located at p. As the turning angle θ increases, the position of the throat gradually moves backward. Here, since the chord length is defined as t, the quantitative relationship between Eqs. 3.2 and 3.3 is obtained.

$$q = p + \frac{t \sin\theta}{b}, q \leq 1 \tag{3.2}$$

$$p \leq 1 - \frac{t \sin\theta}{b} \tag{3.3}$$

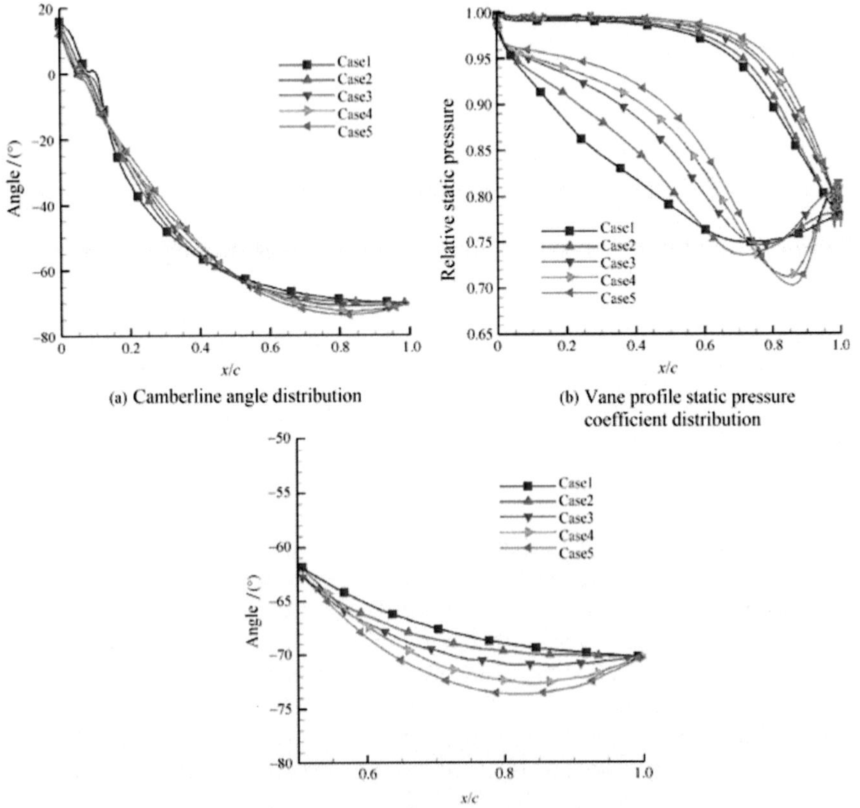

(a) Camberline angle distribution

(b) Vane profile static pressure coefficient distribution

(c) Camberline angle distribution at the 50%~100% axial chord position

Fig. 3.8 Turbine vane profile surface static pressure coefficient and camberline angle distributions

Fig. 3.9 Simplified distribution of the maximum vane thickness

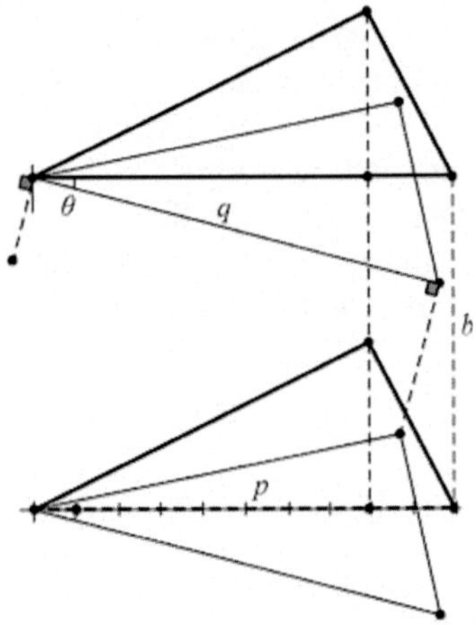

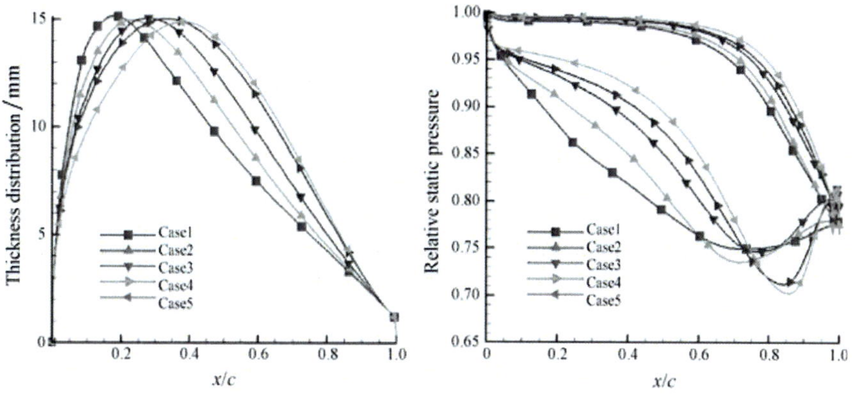

Fig. 3.10 Correlation between turbine vane thickness distribution and surface static pressure

Therefore, when $p = 1 - t\sin\theta/b$, the load can reach the maximum. For a blade profile with $t/b = 0.58$ and a turning angle of 83°, $p_{max} = 0.427$. The following part will verify and analyze the surface static pressure distribution of blades with the same geometric inlet angle, geometric outlet angle and pitch but different thickness distributions.

Figure 3.10 shows the comparison of the surface static pressure distributions for five cases with the same geometrical inlet angles, geometric outlet angles and pitches and different thickness distributions. The maximum thickness of case 1 is 20%, and its maximum load position is 75%; the maximum thickness of case 2 is 23%, and its maximum load position is 70%; the maximum thickness of case 3 is 32%, and its maximum load position is 80%; the maximum thickness position of case 4 is 37%, and its maximum load position is 85%; the maximum thickness position of case 5 is 40%, and its maximum thickness position is 87%. Figure 3.10 shows that within a certain range, with the maximum thickness position moving backward, the lowest static pressure position of the blade suction surface, that is, the maximum load position of the surface static pressure distribution, also moves backward. This finding verifies the above description of the relationship between the maximum thickness position and the maximum load position.

3.2.2 *Effect of Loading Distribution on Turbine Endwall Leakage Flow*

Another significant feature of the variable geometry turbine compared with the fixed geometry turbine is that there will be a certain gap clearance at the tip and bottom of the vanes because its first-stage vanes need to rotate. The existence of the gap clearance has a great influence on the flow in the turbine vanes and the efficiency of the turbine stage. Analysis of the effect of load backward movement on the vane gap clearance flow can provide the necessary reference for the design of variable geometry turbine vanes.

Figure 3.11 shows the two load distributions of the turbine blade profile. The suction surface pressure of the aft-loaded blade profile is higher than that of the original blade profile before 65% of the axial chord and lower than that of the original blade profile between 65 and 90% of the axial chords. After 90% of the axial chord, the suction surface pressure of the aft-loaded blade profile is again higher than that of the original blade profile. The suction pressure surface of the aftloaded blade profile is not much different than that of the original blade profile at the first 50% of the axial chord; after 50% of the axial chord, it is higher than that of the original blade profile; after 90% of the axial chord, it is not much different than that of the original blade profile. Therefore, the lateral pressure gradient at the first 60% of the axial chord is smaller, and the lateral pressure gradient at the latter 40% of the axial chord is larger. Therefore, before 60% of the axial chord, the lateral secondary flow of the aft-loaded blade profile is smaller than that of the original blade profile, which can effectively reduce the lateral secondary flow loss. In addition, the forward pressure gradient of the suction surface of the aft-loaded blade profile is smaller than that of the original blade profile before reaching the lowest pressure point. Downstream of the lowest pressure point, the reverse pressure gradient of the suction surface of the aft-loaded profile is larger than that of the original blade profile. On the pressure surface of the turbine profile, at the first 50% axial chord, the downward pressure gradient of the suction surface of the aft-loaded blade profile is slightly reduced compared with that of the original blade profile, and after 50% axial chord, the forward pressure gradient is slightly increased. On the entire pressure surface, a forward pressure gradient is observed, and the pressure surface boundary layer may always maintain a laminar flow state under the action of the pressure gradient. The reverse pressure gradient of the suction surface of the aft-loaded blade profile is smaller than that of the original blade profile, which can effectively reduce the turbulent zone length. Analysis of the load distribution characteristics of the original and aft-loaded blade profiles indicates that the pressure gradient in the aft-loaded blade profile flow passage is smaller than that in the original blade profile flow passage before reaching the lowest point of the suction surface but sharply expands after the lowest pressure point, causing the pressure gradient to be larger than that in the original blade profile. Because the lateral pressure gradient in the first half of the blade profile is relatively small, the aft-loaded profile can effectively reduce the lateral secondary flows, while the pressure gradient in the second half of it increases, making the gas rapidly expand and accelerate, which is also beneficial for the reduction in aerodynamic losses of the turbine blade profile boundary layer.

Figures 3.12 and 3.13 show the static pressure distribution of the turbine root and tip profile. Figure 3.12 shows a dense static pressure contour along the pressure surface at the pressure surface side, which indicates a large pressure gradient and that the nearby fluid is squeezed to the pressure gradient. Within the gap, the pressure sharply expands, and the pressure sharply drops. The static pressure contour distribution of the aft-loaded profile is not as dense as that of the original profile; it extends to a larger range upstream and downstream with a greater backward position. This

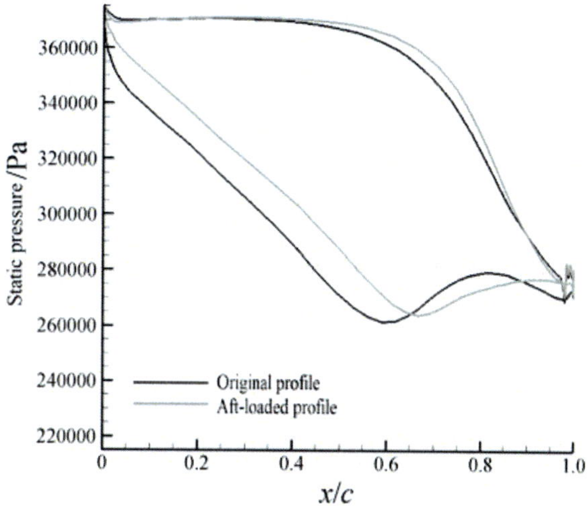

Fig. 3.11 Two load distributions of turbine vane profiles

finding shows that the fluid expansion of the aft-loaded blade profile is not as severe as that of the original blade profile but has a larger expansion range. At the suction surface side, there is also a low-pressure area near the throat of the two profiles. The low-pressure area of the aft-loaded profile has a larger range, and the static pressure contours are more densely distributed. The fluid expands again when it flows out of the gap clearance due to the interaction between the leakage flow and the secondary flow when the fluids flow out of the gap clearance, resulting in fluid separation. From the profile throat to the outlet section, the existence of the reverse pressure gradient will have a greater impact on this fluid separation. The aft-loaded profile will have a smaller degree of separation than the original profile due to the short reverse pressure gradient. In addition, due to the effect of inertial force, the flow of fluid in the gap clearance in the first half of the profile flows from the suction surface into the gap clearance and then out of the suction surface. At the aft of the blade profile, the fluid flows from the pressure surface to the suction surface, which means that at the aft of the blade profile, the pressure gradient has more influence on the flow than the inertial force. The aft-loaded blade profile has a lower maximum load, so its pressure gradient will have less influence on the flow than the original blade profile. Similar phenomena are shown in Fig. 3.13 and will not be repeated here.

Figure 3.14 shows the comparison curve of the spanwise distribution of the blade outflow angle under different load distributions. Compared with the outflow angle of the original and aft-loaded blades without gap clearance, the outflow angle of the aft-loaded blade is smaller at a 0–60% blade span, and the outflow angle of the two is equivalent at a 60–100% blade span. Therefore, it is valuable to analyze the outflow angle of blades with gaps at a 60–100% blade span. An analysis of the outflow angle curves of the blades with and without gap clearances indicates that the presence of the gap clearance significantly changes the blade outflow angle, especially the outflow angle at both endwalls, which is significantly increased due to gap leakages. The gap clearance causes the gas flow near the endwall to underdeflect, the outflow angle to

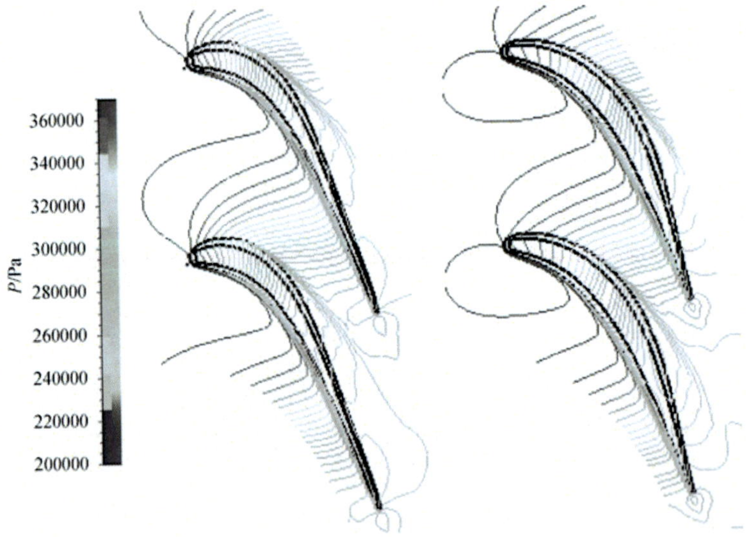

(a) Baseline (b) Aft-loaded vane profile

Fig. 3.12 Turbine hub vane profile static pressure distribution

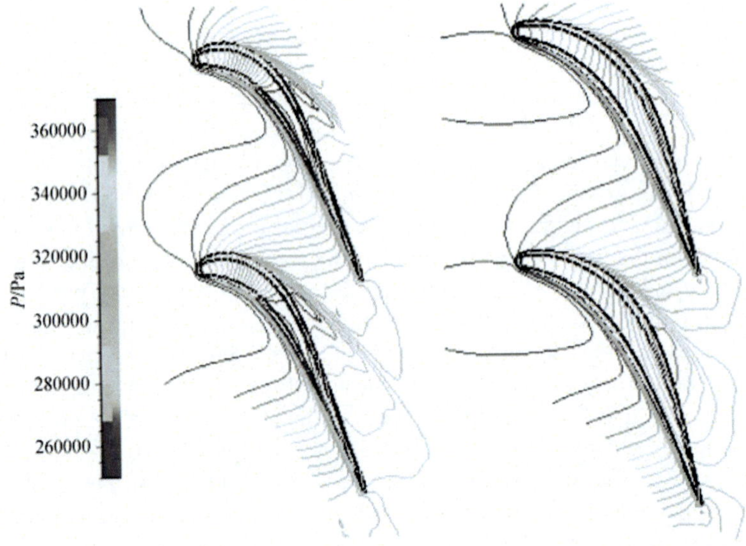

(a) Baseline (b) Aft-loaded vane profile

Fig. 3.13 Turbine casing vane profile static pressure distribution

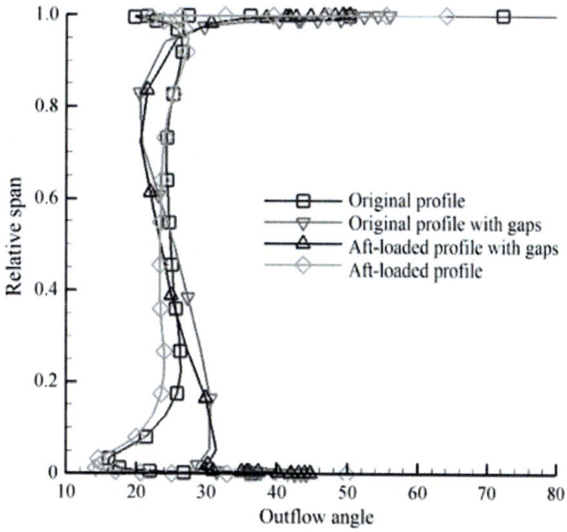

Fig. 3.14 Comparison of spanwise vane outflow angle distributions under different load distributions

increase, and the change in the outflow angle at the root to be greater than that at the tip. Because the fluid velocity at the root of the blade is lower than that at the tip, the inertial force at the root of the blade is smaller than that at the tip of the blade.

An analysis of the outlet flow angle distribution of the original and aft-loaded profiles shown in Fig. 3.14 reveal that the outflow angle of the aft-loaded profile is greater than that of the original profile at a 80–100% blade span, which shows that the ratio of the inertial force to the pressure difference of the aft-loaded blade is smaller than that of the original blade. For the outflow angle distribution at 0–10% span at the root of the blade, the aft-loaded profile without gap clearance is smaller than the original profile, but the outflow angle of the aft-loaded profile with gap clearance is larger than that of the original profile, which shows that the outflow angle of the root aft-loaded blade undergoes greater changes. The root inertial force has a smaller influence on the outflow angle, and the pressure difference has a more obvious influence on the outflow angle.

Figure 3.15 shows a comparison of the internal loss development of the blade under different load distributions. Three sections are obtained at the axial positions of 25, 50 and 95% of the original blade and the blade with the load backward. The left side and right side of the figure shows the suction surface and pressure surface, respectively. Observation of the total pressure loss development of the blade with the blade chord length clearly indicates the development of the loss. As the flow develops downstream, the total pressure loss near the tip and root of the suction surface the range formed by the contour of the total pressure loss also increase, and the maximum total pressure loss in the blade flow passage also develops toward the center of the flow passage. The total pressure loss of the tip gap and the bottom gap of the original blade is greater than that of the aft-loaded blade at 50% of the axial chord. The total pressure loss of the original blade is also greater than that of the aft-loaded blade at 100% of the axial chord. This finding shows that the aft-loaded blade effectively reduces the total pressure loss at the gap clearance, and especially for the total pressure loss in the first half of the blade, the aft-loaded blade profile is significantly smaller than that of the original blade profile. A comparison of the total pressure loss at the tip gap of the blade with the total pressure loss at the bottom gap shows that the total pressure loss at the bottom gap is greater than that at the tip gap, because the velocity of the bottom fluid is slower due to centrifugal force effects. The boundary layer at the bottom is thicker than at the tip, which causes greater pressure loss.

As shown in Fig. 3.16, the existence of the gap clearance increases the total pressure loss to a large extent. However, a comparison of cases of the original blade profile with and without gap clearances and cases of the aft-loaded blade profiles with and without gap clearances indicates that the presence of gaps has a smaller effect on the aft-loaded blade profile. A comparison of the two cases with gap clearance indicates that the total pressure loss of the original blade and aft-loaded blade before 40% of the axial chord is very similar. However, after 40% of the axial chord, the total pressure loss of the original blade starts to rapidly rise, while that of the aft-loaded blade occurs at 60% of the axial chord, and the difference between the total pressure losses of the original and aft-loaded blade profiles decreases. However, the total pressure loss of the aft-loaded blade is always smaller than that of the original blade.

(a) Baseline (b) Aft-loaded vane profile

Fig. 3.15 Comparison of vane internal loss development under different load distributions

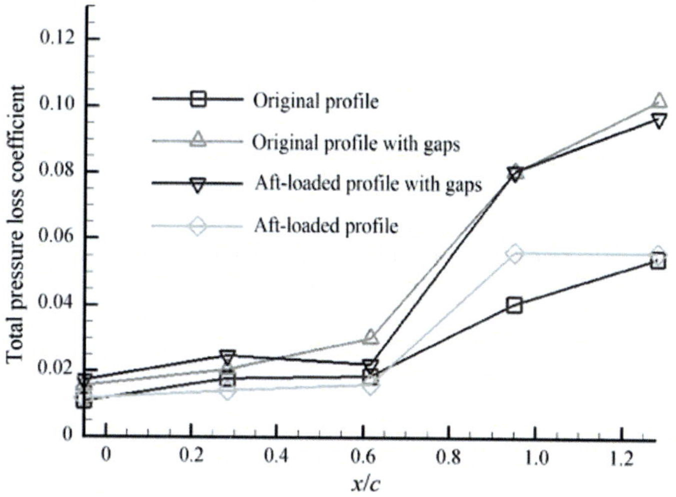

Fig. 3.16 Comparison of loss development in turbine blade flow channels

3.2.3 *Variable Geometry Characteristics for Turbine Blade Profiles*

The turbine blade rotates around its center of rotation, which satisfies the calculation formula for the turning angle shown in Fig. 3.17a, and the change in its turning position is shown in Fig. 3.17b. The 0° scheme is the reference model, and the turning center is at the (0, 0) position in the *z*-*y* coordinate system. This model obtains other rotation turning calculation models by rotating around the turning axis. After the vane rotates around the turning axis, the absolute coordinates change. The formula for calculating the coordinates after rotation is shown in Eqs. 3.4 and 3.5:

$$x_2 = R\cos\beta = R\cos(\alpha+\gamma) = R\cos\alpha\cos\gamma - R\sin\alpha\sin\gamma \tag{3.4}$$

$$y_2 = R\sin\beta = R\sin(\alpha+\gamma) = R\sin\alpha\cos\gamma + R\cos\alpha\sin\gamma \tag{3.5}$$

$$\sin\gamma = \frac{y_1}{R} \tag{3.6}$$

$$\cos\gamma = \frac{x_1}{R} \tag{3.7}$$

$$\begin{cases} x_2 = x_1\cos\alpha - y_1\sin\alpha \\ y_2 = x_1\sin\alpha + y_1\cos\alpha \end{cases} \tag{3.8}$$

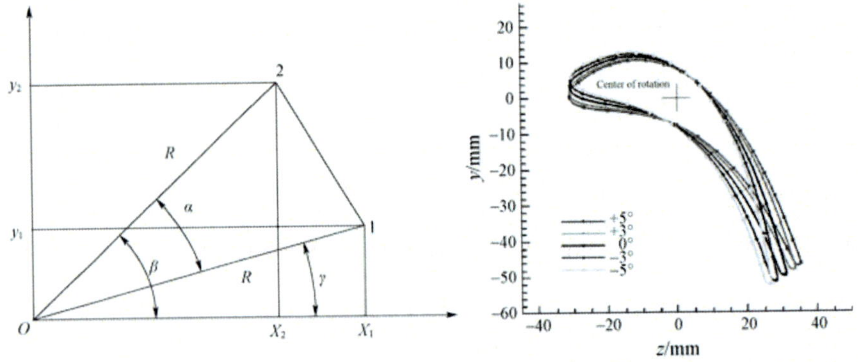

(a) Calculation formula of vane turning (b) Change in the turning position of variable vanes

Fig. 3.17 Schematic of variable vane turning

The cross-sectional schematic of the blades in the radial direction at five turning angles is shown in Fig. 3.17b. The direction of turning of the vane throat area is defined as a positive direction or counterclockwise direction, as shown in the scheme of +5° and +3°. The direction of decrease for the vane throat area is defined as a negative direction, which is the clockwise direction, as shown in the scheme of −3° and −5°.

Table 3.2 provides a comparison of the leakage flow rate, leakage mass rate ratio and total pressure recovery coefficient at the 10% axial chord downstream of the blade outlet (i.e., 110% axial chord position) of each cascade turning scheme. As the turning angle gradually increases from −5° and −3° to +3° and +5°, respectively, the increase in throat area changes with the turning angle, as shown in Fig. 3.18a. The increase in throat area is basically linear. When the turning angle is −5° and −3°, compared with the 0° scheme, the throat area changes by −9.58 and −5.7%, respectively. When the turning angle is +3° and +5°, the throat area is changed by +5.56 and +9.18%, respectively, which causes the cascade outlet mass flowrate to continuously increase from negative to positive, as shown in Fig. 3.18b, because the throat area of the turbine cascade gradually expands.

During the turning of the variable vane, the mass flow of the leakage flow out of the suction surface through the gap clearance changes within a small range, and the leakage rate also tends to decrease, as shown in Fig. 3.18c. In addition, from scheme I to scheme V, the absolute leakage flow rate decreases by approximately 0.6%, and the relative change in the leakage rate decreases by approximately 36%. Because the turbine cascade passage is convergent, the high-temperature and high-pressure gas fully expands in the passage, the positive direction of the turbine vane will increase the throat area, and the degree of blockage at the trailing edge of the turbine cascade will be relieved. If the variable vane rotates in the opposite direction, the area of the throat of the passage is reduced, and the degree of choking of the trailing edge of the cascade will further deteriorate, resulting in greater losses. Therefore, the coefficient of total pressure recovery at the 10% axial chord position downstream of the cascade

Table 3.2 Comparison of leakage mass flow rate and total recovery coefficients for five schemes

Schemes	I (−5° turning angle)	II (−3° turning angle)	III (0° turning angle)	IV (+3° turning angle)	V (+5° turning angle)
Turbine mass flowrate (kg/s)	0.296	0.316	0.367	0.402	0.427
Leakage mass flow rate (kg/s)	0.00348	0.00341	0.00348	0.00324	0.00322
Gap leakage mass rate ratio (%)	1.180	1.172	0.947	0.807	0.755
Total pressure recovery coefficient	0.979	0.980	0.982	0.985	0.987

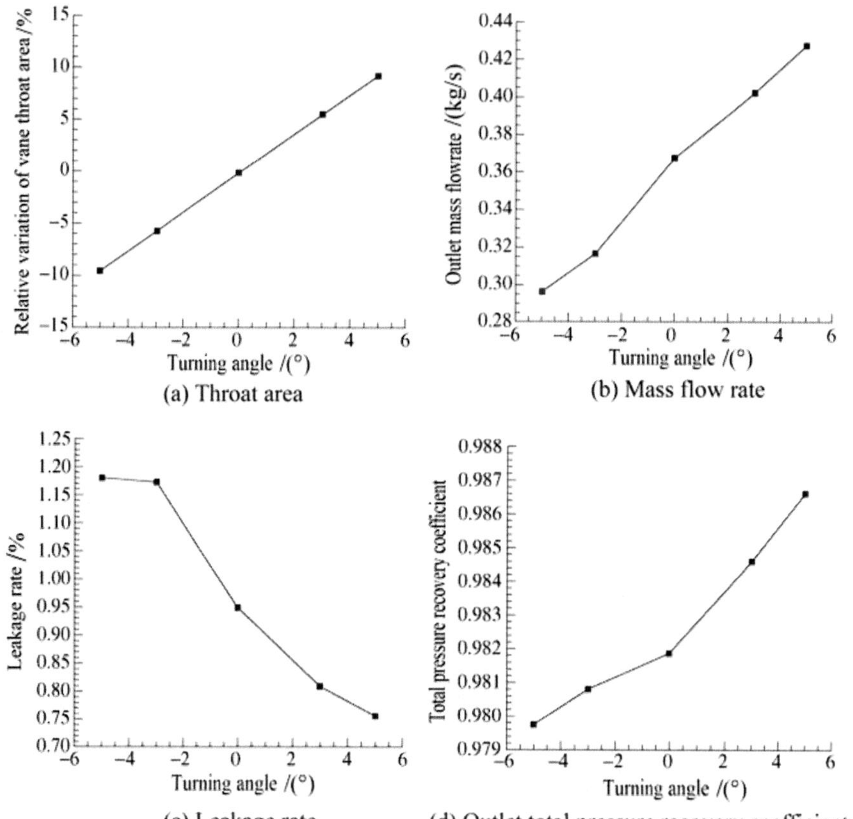

(a) Throat area (b) Mass flow rate

(c) Leakage rate (d) Outlet total pressure recovery coefficient

Fig. 3.18 Variation in the vane throat area, mass flow rate, leakage rate and total pressure recovery coefficient with vane turning outlet is shown in Fig. 3.18d. If the vane rotates in the forward direction (0 to + 5°), the first derivative of the total pressure recovery coefficient, that is, the slope, is significantly greater than the slope of the total pressure recovery coefficient during the reverse rotation of the vane (0 to −5°).

3.3 Three-Dimensional Aerodynamic Design Method for a High Endwall Angle Variable Geometry Turbine

3.3.1 Three-Dimensional Pressure Controlled Vortex Design for a Conventional Turbine

The turbine efficiency is closely related to the flow performance of the throughflow section, which depends on the aerodynamic characteristics of the cascade. Therefore, how to better design the turbine cascade and reduce the loss of vanes and blades has become a hot spot in research on high-performance turbines. Generally, the energy loss in the cascade can be divided into two types: profile loss and endwall loss. Endwall loss can be subdivided into secondary flow loss and gap clearance leakage loss. Profile loss is mainly related to the flow pattern of the boundary layer on the blade surface and whether there is flow separation, while the endwall loss is mainly related to the secondary flow near the endwall, including the growth of the endwall surface boundary layer and various vortex separations. These two parts of the losses are largely affected by the three-dimensional pressure field in the cascade, and the reduction in the flow loss in the turbine cascade can be attributed to the redistribution of the blade surface pressure. These findings suggest that if the pressure distribution in the cascade passage can be changed, a new pressure balance can be established in the cascade passage, and the corresponding passage vortex development and other secondary flow losses will be affected. Based on this information, a pressure-controlled vortex design method that can integrate stream surface changes and pressure control is proposed and a high-performance turbine cascade design framework is established. Based on this design method, the first-stage redesign of a low-pressure turbine was carried out, and numerical simulation was performed to verify the performance of the newly designed turbine stage.

The proposed three-dimensional, pressure-controlled, vortex design framework is shown in Fig. 3.19. The three-dimensional pressure control mainly regulates the pressure gradient in the radial, axial and circumferential directions to form a favorable pressure gradient in the abovementioned area and obtains a redistribution of the blade surface pressure to establish a new pressure balance in the cascade passage.

Using this design idea, the three-dimensional pressure field in the cascade can be changed, and the pressure gradients in all directions can be reasonably matched so that each section is in the best flow state, and the separation and thickening of the boundary layer can be effectively controlled, thus reducing the profile losses. The pressure-controlled vortex purposely changes the distribution of the main flow

Fig. 3.19 Three-dimensional, pressure-controlled vortex design framework

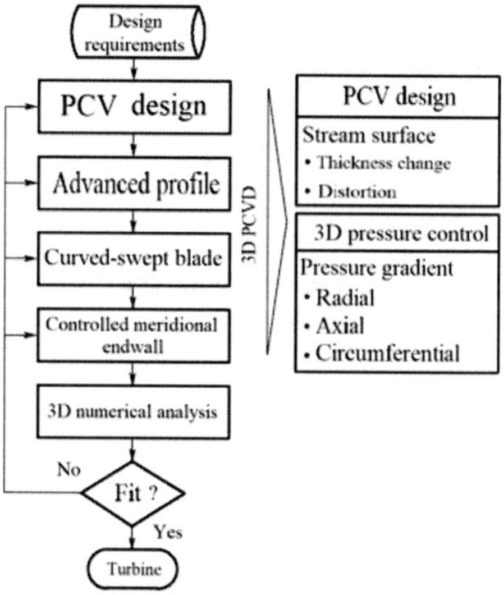

along the blade span, and from the perspective of secondary flow generation, the flow patterns of the endwall and the boundary layer of the blade surface are reasonably organized. By changing the thickness of the stream surface, its deflection is utilized to suppress the development of the blade surface and endwall boundary layer, thereby reducing the flow loss of the cascade. Although the pressure-controlled vortex design is based on the one-dimensional and two-dimensional throughflow design, the influence on the three-dimensional flow is also obvious. If combined with comprehensive optimization methods such as advanced blade profiles, curved-twisted joint modeling and controlled meridional endwall contouring, the turbine efficiency can be further improved, which is very beneficial to the design of high-performance turbines. After the turbine design is completed, it needs to be verified by numerical simulation or experiments. By comparing the isentropic efficiency, mass flow rate and power of the original turbine, it is determined whether the design requirements are met and whether the flow field meets the design expectations. In addition, the efficiency of the turbine designed by the mature, quasi-three-dimensional method is already high, but it still cannot meet people's pursuit of higher performance turbines. The aerodynamic design considering viscous effects is difficult to achieve in the short term. There are still many theoretical problems that have not been effectively resolved. Therefore, the turbine performance can only be improved by perfecting existing design methods. Therefore, the three-dimensional, pressure-controlled vortex design can be considered a design idea in the transition stage from nonviscous design to viscous design.

The original turbine is the first stage of a gas turbine power turbine. Due to the relatively large load of the original turbine, relatively small diameter-to-span ratio, and relatively large meridional expansion angle, the three-dimensional effect of the internal flow of the turbine stage is strong, and the turbine stage itself is very efficient.

Therefore, many scholars use curved and swept blades, forward swept wide-chord blades, local modification of the cascade, meridional endwall contouring, etc., to improve the design of this type of turbine however, they have failed to achieve the desired results. To further improve the turbine aerodynamic performance, this section attempts to redesign the original turbine vanes and blades by adopting a three-dimensional pressure-controlled vortex design to reduce adverse factors in the flow process, thereby improving the turbine efficiency. In addition, to ensure the turbine power and blade strength, the original turbine cascade meridional flow passage, axial chord length of the cascade, maximum blade thickness, number of blades, blade stacking line, etc., do not change.

Figure 3.20 shows the changes in axial velocity and mass flow in the turbine stage of the pressure-controlled vortex design. This change is still reflected between the vane and the blade. With the pressure-controlled vortex design, the design law of equal mass flow is still applied at the inlet and outlet in the turbine stage. At this time, $\rho A c_z$ remains constant along the blade span. Since the area A increases with increasing radius, the axial velocity c_z in the turbine stage is gradually reduced from the blade root to the blade tip. Therefore, the density ρ will increase with increasing radius. In the pressure-controlled vortex design turbine stage, although the axial velocity c_z gradually decreases from the blade root to the blade tip, ρ also increases with increasing radius, but the reduction rate of c_z is greater than the rate of increase of ρ. Thus, the mass flow rate ρAcz will gradually decrease from the blade root to the blade tip. The flow capacity at the blade root will be greater than that at the tip, that is, $\rho_h A_h c_{z,h} > \rho_t A_t c_{z,t}$. The figure shows that relative to the axial velocity distribution for the equal mass flow design, the axial velocity of the pressure-controlled vortex design decreases at the upper end of the blade and increases at the lower end of the blade, thereby ensuring continuous flows.

Figure 3.21 shows the redistribution of static pressure in the axial gap between the vane and the blade in the radial direction before and after the pressure-controlled

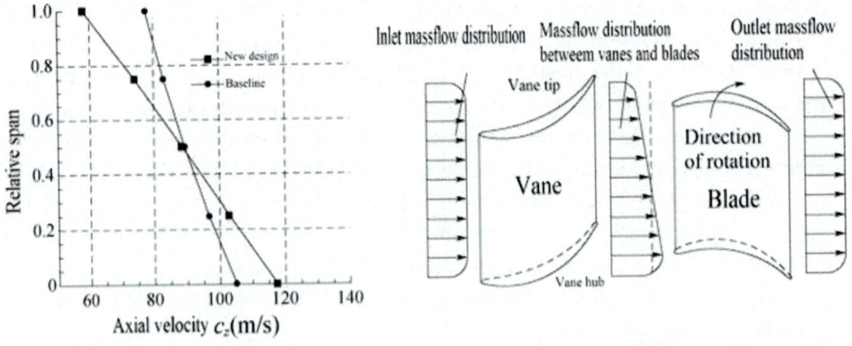

(a) Change in axial velocity in front of the blade

(b) Spanwise redistribution of mass flow corresponding to the axial velocity

Fig. 3.20 Axial velocity and mass flow changes for pressure-controlled, vortex design turbine stages vortex design. The static pressure in the upper endwall area at the vane outlet is reduced, and the tip load of the vane is increased. The static pressure in the lower endwall area at the vane outlet is increased, and the root load of the vane decreases. The pressure-controlled vortex design significantly changes the rule of the vane outlet pressure along the vane span and ultimately makes the vane outlet have a smaller radial pressure gradient, which can be regarded as an important feature of the pressure-controlled vortex design. The overall effect of the pressure-controlled vortex design is to provide a favorable pressure distribution between the vanes and the blades to ensure that the gas flow parameters at the outlet of the vanes tend are uniform. Although the conventional controlled vortex design method can also affect the radial pressure gradient, the range of change is very limited and cannot be significantly changed as demonstrated in the pressure-controlled vortex design. It can be seen intuitively inferred from Fig. 3.21 that the improvement in the radial pressure gradient not only causes redistribution of the load of the vanes and blades but also decreases the pressure gradient along the streamwise direction. Furthermore, the changes in the vane load will affect the circumferential pressure gradient. Until now, the pressure-controlled vortex design has only controlled the radial pressure gradient, while the three-dimensional, pressure-controlled vortex design mentioned above can control the pressure gradient in the radial, axial and circumferential directions. Comprehensive optimization methods, such as advanced blade profile technology, curved-swept blades and controlled meridional endwalls, are needed to further control the pressure. Since advanced blade profile technology can only change the axial and circumferential pressure gradient in the turbine stage, it does not have a substantial impact on the radial pressure gradient and the change in the stream surface along the blade span. The flow field is relatively simple. The blade profile technology, which is relatively easy to understand, has achieved many relatively successful experiences. Therefore, in this section, advanced blade profile technology is selected to redesign the turbine cascade. This section intends to proceed from the perspective of positive problem analysis and to introduce some advanced results of the blade profile for reference in the turbine vane design. By combining the aft-loaded blade profile with the pressure-controlled vortex design, the pressure gradient in the radial, axial and circumferential directions inside the turbine cascade flow passage can be effectively controlled, thereby weakening the secondary flow intensity.

In the research in this subsection, the blade profiles at 0, 25, 50, 75 and 100% blade spans were selected for the parametric design of vanes and blades. Figure 3.22 shows the comparison of the three-dimensional geometric shapes of the vane and blade before and after the three-dimensional, pressure-controlled vortex design. The original vane is the leading edge of gravity stacking, and the blade is the center of gravity stacking. The newly designed blade stacking rule is the same as that in the original design. The figure shows that the newly designed vanes have the characteristics of reverse twist. Compared with the original design, the tip turning angle of the vane decreases, and the root turning angle increases, which tends to press the mainstream toward the root. The newly designed blades undergo relatively small changes. With the exception of a slight reduction in the degree of twisting, the other geometric parameters are basically unchanged. The three-dimensional,

Fig. 3.21 Static pressure distribution before and after the rotor blades

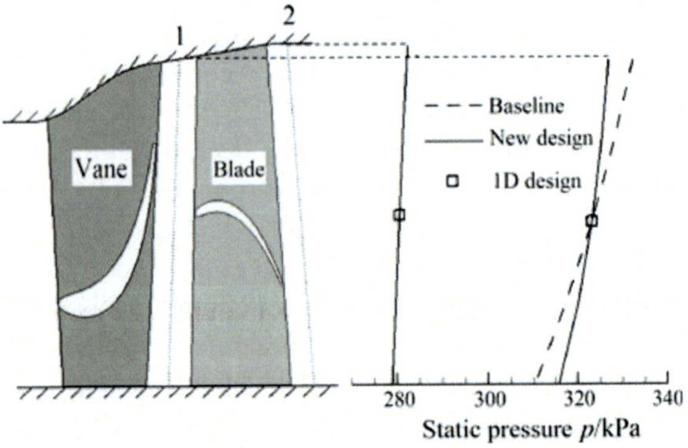

pressure-controlled vortex design is mainly aimed at vane modification. In addition, compared with the original design vane, the thickness of the leading edge of the newly designed vane is slightly increased, which can improve the incidence angle of attack characteristics and has a minimal effect on the blade profile loss. The newly designed vane trailing edge curvature decreases at the root and increases at the tip. In addition, the vane of the three-dimensional, pressure-controlled vortex design appropriately shortens the vane chord length, effectively increases the vane's aspect ratio, and is beneficial for reducing the blade profile loss and secondary flow loss. The newly designed blade profile appears relatively smooth; the thickness is basically the same as the original design; and the change in the blade curvature along the blade span is not obvious.

Table 3.3 shows the overall performance parameters of the turbines before and after the three-dimensional, pressure-controlled vortex design. The turbine performance after the three-dimensional, pressure-controlled vortex design is significantly improved. The turbine isentropic efficiency increases from 92.51 to 93.27%. Compared with the original turbine, the efficiency of the newly designed turbine has

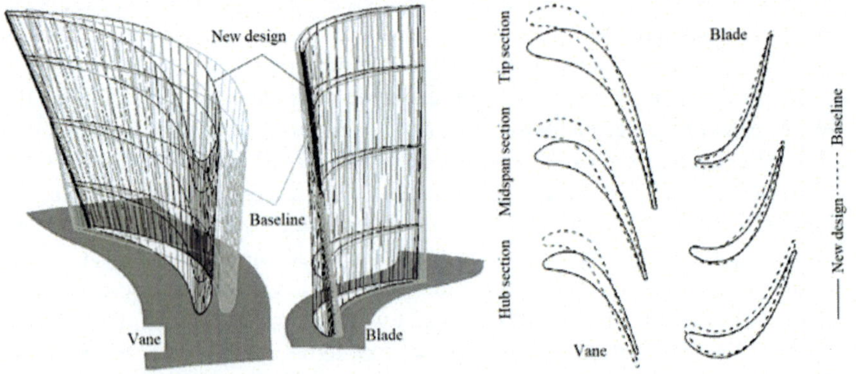

Fig. 3.22 Baseline and newly designed blade shape and its blade cross-sections

Table 3.3 Comparison of pressure-controlled vortex design results

	Baseline	New design	Increment (%)
Mass flow G/(−)	1	1.0010	0.104
Total pressure ratio π^*/(−)	1	1.0009	0.09
Isentropic efficiency η/(−)	1	1.0083	0.832
Static pressure ratio π/(−)	1	1.0000	0
Power P/(−)	1	1.0062	0.617
Torque M/(−)	1	1.0061	0.613
Thrust F/(−)	1	0.9916	−0.835

increased by 0.832%, while the mass flow rate and total pressure ratio remain at the same level as the original design. In addition, other performance parameters, such as torque and output power, have also increased accordingly, with an increase of 0.61%. Similar to the pressure-controlled vortex design, the axial thrust generated by the rotor of the turbine stage for the three-dimensional, pressure-controlled vortex design also decreases by approximately 0.84%.

Figure 3.23 shows the spanwise distribution of the relative flow angle at the vane and blade outlet. The numerical calculation results show agreement with the design results within a considerable range, but there is a significant difference at the endwall zone of the cascade. This difference is mainly caused by the accumulation of the boundary layer of the endwall in the corner area of the suction surface. This additional boundary layer deposited in the corner area of the suction surface forces the main flow to deflect from the suction surface toward the adjacent pressure surface. This deflection causes the actual outlet flow angle to increase, a reduction in the flow turning angle and a decrease in the output power. Affected by the large meridional expansion casing endwall, the deviation between the calculated result and the design result of the flow angle at the tip of the vane is significantly larger than that at the root, and the maximum deviation is in the range of approximately 2° ~ 3°. The spanwise change in the flow angle of the blade is consistent with the original design, which is very beneficial to the multistage turbine design and multistage turbine modular design and will not change the matching characteristics of the original turbine in a multistage environment. In addition, as shown in Fig. 3.23, the original turbine uses a conventional, controlled vortex design method. If the effect of the large meridional expansion and endwall secondary flow on the outlet flow angle is disregarded, the outlet flow angle of the original turbine vane will not change along the blade span, and the original design vane can be regarded as adopting the design law of equal α angle.

Figure 3.24 compares the static pressure distribution on the blade surface at 10, 50 and 90% blade spans for the original and newly designed vanes. The position of the lowest pressure point on the suction surface of the newly designed vane shifts from 50 to 55% of the axial chord length to 75–80% of the axial chord length, and the load

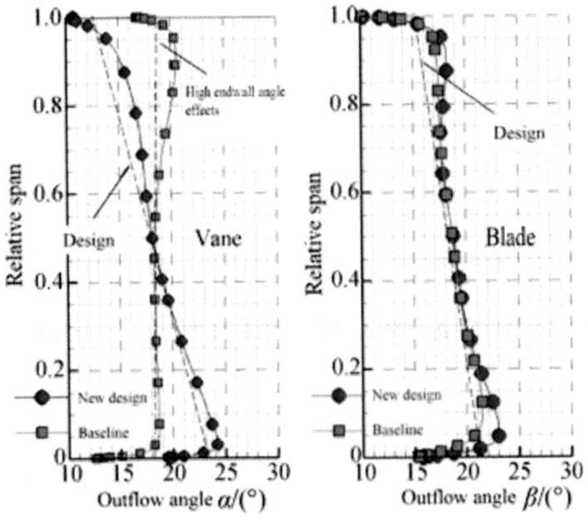

Fig. 3.23 Spanwise vane and blade outflow angle distributions

obviously moves backward. Relative to the original design, the newly designed vane suction surface experiences a significant increase in the forward pressure gradient section, which is beneficial to the attachment of the boundary layer, and effectively controls the degree of tailings edge diffusion. The static pressure corresponding to the pressure surface is always maintained at a high level and as far as possible to the outlet of the cascade, which produces a more aft-loaded load distribution, and the acceleration of the gas pressure on the pressure surface is mainly concentrated within 20% of the relative chord length near the trailing edge. In general, the maximum load occurs in the area of the second half of the cascade. In the area of the front half of the cascade, the pressure difference between the pressure surface and the suction surface is small. The aft-loaded design of the vane is very successful. The figure shows that at 50% of the axial chord length of the suction surface of the vane tip of the original and new design, there is an unavoidable pressure surge, which causes the static pressure in the middle of the cascade to rise due to the relatively large expansion angle of the outer endwall of the passage. Because the meridional passage expands sharply in the streamwise direction, part of the gas flow does not have time to expand, so the pressure increases after the gas flow enters the vane. The shape of the meridional passage has a great influence on the three-dimensional flow fields, which will cause a significant change in the lateral pressure gradient near the endwall area. The position of the original design vane throat is just in this pressure recovery area, which easily separates the boundary layer or makes the boundary layer transition early, which substantially affects the performance of the turbine blade. Therefore, in the turbine design process, the meridional expansion of the flow passage should be avoided as much as possible. For the newly designed vane, due to the increased convergence of the cascade, the load has significantly shifted, effectively offsetting the pressure recovery zone caused by the expansion of the meridional passage. Although the pressure at the tip section is still rising, the new design vanes ensure that the cascade has sufficient expansion capacity. Thus, the pressure at the lowest pressure point of the suction surface is sufficiently low.

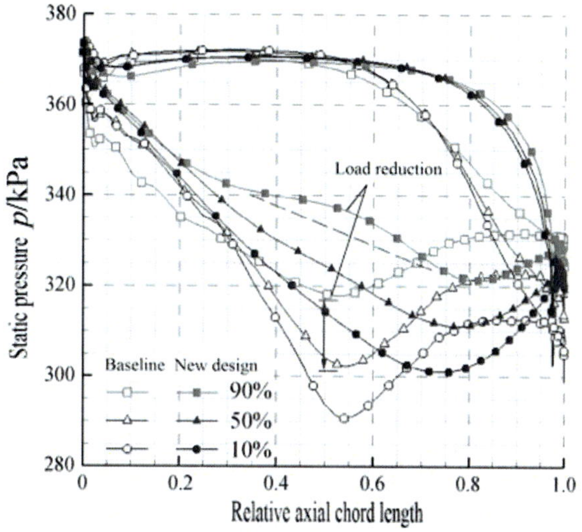

Fig. 3.24 Baseline and newly designed variable vane surface, static pressure distributions at different spans

The three-dimensional pressure control effect of the three-dimensional, pressure-controlled vortex design is obvious. As shown in Fig. 3.24, due to the redistribution of the vane load, the outlet static pressure at the tip of the newly designed vane decreases, and the static pressure at the root outlet increases, reducing the radial pressure gradient in the axial gap, which provides relatively uniform pressure fields. The backward movement of the load causes the suction surface of the newly designed vane in the direction of the streamwise direction between 50 and 80% of the axial chord length to fall within a favorable pressure gradient, which can effectively delay the transition of the boundary layer. Compared with the original design, the pressure on the suction surface of the newly designed vane increases before the vane throat, and the pressure decreases after the vane throat. Thus, a favorable streamwise pressure gradient is formed before and after the vane cascade, which creates an advantage for reducing the blade profile loss. Simultaneously, the pressure at the lowest pressure point on the suction surface of the newly designed vane increases at the blade root, middle and tip cross-sectional positions. Therefore, the lateral pressure gradient at the throat position in the cascade passage decreases, and the lateral pressure gradient at the front of the cascade increases. The reduction in the abovementioned lateral pressure gradient reduces the transmission of the low-energy fluids in the endwall boundary layer to the suction surface and the development of secondary flow in the blade channel. Based on the above analysis, the effect of the three-dimensional, pressure-controlled vortex design can control not only the radial pressure gradient in the axial gap between the vane and the blade but also the pressure distribution in the streamwise direction and the circumferential direction in the cascade passage to reduce the profile losses and to control the secondary flows.

Figure 3.25 compares the pressure distribution on the rotor blade surface of the original design and new design. Affected by the newly designed vane, the average static pressure at the tip of the newly designed rotor blade has decreased, and the average static pressure at the root has increased. The decrease in the average static pressure at the inlet of the blade tip causes a decrease in the load at the leading edge of the blade tip and a decrease in the lateral pressure gradient in the channel at the leading edge of the tip, which is beneficial for controlling the early development of the secondary flow and tip clearance leakage flow. The increase in the static pressure at the root inlet increases the overall load of the blade root to some extent, and the power output ability at the blade root is enhanced. On the whole, the axial load of the newly designed rotor blade is more backward than the original design in the spanwise direction of the entire blade, and the pressure at the lowest pressure point on the suction surface is also significantly reduced. The position of the lowest pressure point on the suction surface moves backward from 65 to 82% of the axial chord length, which increases the length of the forward pressure gradient section of the suction surface, thereby effectively weakening the degree of pressure expansion at the trailing edge of the rotor blade. In addition, there are small fluctuations in the static pressure distribution in the second half of the suction surface of the original rotor blade Thus, the pressure at the outlet edge of the trailing edge remains basically unchanged, which indicates unstable flow of the gas flow and the possibility of local separation of the gas flow. The new design of the blade not only effectively eliminates the unstable flow in this area but also enables more uniform acceleration of the suction surface acceleration section and smoother diffusion in the diffuser section.

Figure 3.26 shows the limiting streamline map of the pressure surface of the blade before and after the three-dimensional pressure control vortex design. In the upper half of the front edge of the rotor blade pressure surface in the original design, a separation bubble appears, showing a negative incidence angle of attack flow. Flow separation occurs at approximately 5% of the axial position and is attached to approximately 15% of the axial chord position. Due to the small size of the separation bubble, the effect on the aerodynamic performance of the turbine is small. With the

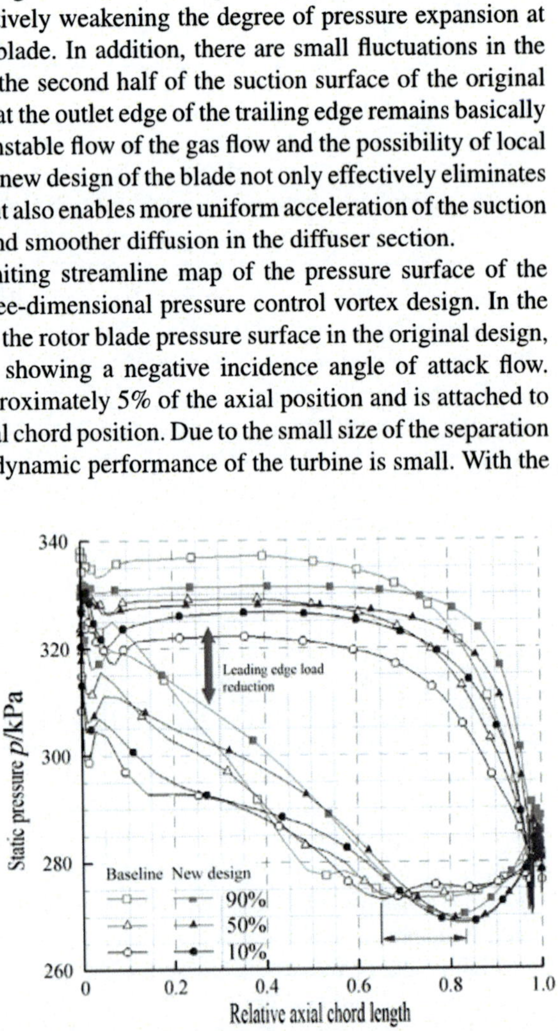

Fig. 3.25 Baseline and newly designed rotor blade surface, static pressure distributions at different spans

redesign of the three-dimensional, pressure-controlled vortex, the flow separation on the pressure surface is effectively controlled, and the incidence angle of attack is reduced, as indicated by the limiting streamline on the blade surface. The surface flow pattern on the pressure surface also exhibits a large change from the original design. With the exception of the leading-edge separation bubble and the streamlines near the endwalls of the cascade deflecting toward the endwall, the streamline on the pressure surface is basically parallel to the upper and lower endwalls. In addition to the deflection of the streamline near the lower endwall toward the endwall, the remaining streamlines are significantly shifted toward the tip of the blade, and the deflection amplitude of the streamline near the lower endwall is significantly reduced, which means that the radial flow of the blade surface is opposite to the traditional secondary flow. The limiting streamline on the blade surface also characterizes the radial movement of the boundary layer along the pressure surface from the root to the tip caused by the three-dimensional, pressure-controlled vortex design. This radial motion can not only eliminate the boundary layer accumulation in the corner of the lower endwall of the pressure surface but also reduce the lateral secondary flow of the lower endwall from the blade pressure surface to the suction surface.

The velocity triangle on the right of Fig. 3.26 illustrates the positive effect of the three-dimensional, pressure-controlled vortex design on the matching performance of the vane and blade. Since the original turbine is a large meridional expansion design, the tip flow area sharply increases along the streamwise direction. Thus, the shrinkage of the vane cascade flow channel is not enough to compensate for the expansion of the meridional flow channel, resulting in an increase in the mass flow rate through the tip of the vane. The outlet axial velocity c_z sharply increases, and the incident direction of the relative velocity ω into the downstream rotor blades will slide to the suction surface side of the rotor blades, resulting in a negative incidence angle of attack flow of the downstream rotor blades. In this case, one of the most direct and effective ways to improve the tip incidence angle characteristics of the blade is to reduce the axial velocity c_z at the outlet of the vane. The three-dimensional, pressure-controlled vortex design reduces the axial velocity c_z by reducing the percentage of flow in the tip area of the turbine stage. The three-dimensional, pressure-controlled vortex design not only further enhances the shrinkage of the cascade flow channel and

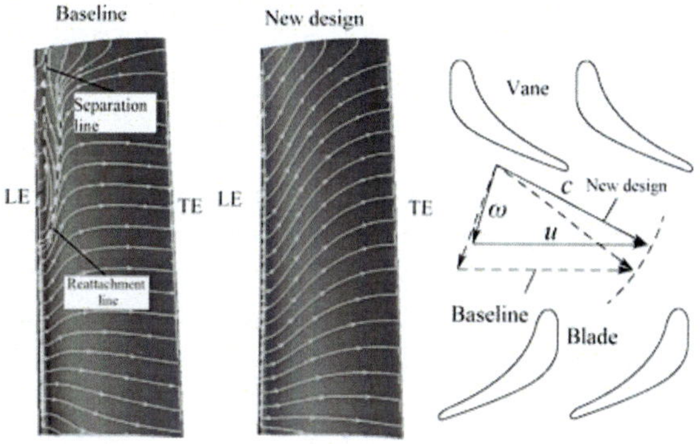

Fig. 3.26 Blade pressure surface limiting streamline and velocity triangle in the casing region

offsets the negative effects caused by the expansion of a part of the meridional flow channel but also increases the relative flow angle at the rotor blade inlet, eliminating the adverse gas flow impact of the rotor blade. In summary, the three-dimensional, pressure-controlled vortex design improves not only the flow characteristics of the large meridional expansion turbine but also the matching characteristics of the vanes and blades of the large meridional expansion turbine.

Figure 3.27 shows the limiting streamline spectrum of the suction surface of the vane and blade. This figure also shows the flow characteristics of the blade surface of the three-dimensional, pressure-controlled vortex design. When the fluid flows through the vane with the expanded endwall, due to the inertial effect of the gas flow movement in the streamwise direction, the gas flow cannot immediately fill the entire tip area of the cascade. Once the gas flow enters the cascade passage, the suction side boundary layer at the tip of the vane rapidly thickens, a large-scale separation, as shown in Fig. 3.27, is formed on the tip, and the energy loss at the tip of the vane sharply increases. In addition, due to the effect of the three-dimensional, pressure-controlled vortex design, the movement trend of the low-energy fluid from the root to the tip on the suction surface of the vane and blade is obviously reduced. In contrast, the movement trend of the low-energy fluids on the suction surface from the tip to the root is enhanced. The inclination of the streamline and the three-dimensional separation line in Fig. 3.27 clearly illustrate these points. The vortex scale of the lower endwall channel of the newly designed blade has been weakened, while the probability of the upper endwall passage vortex being fully developed is significantly increased. However, the change in the vortex size of the vane tip channel is not obvious compared with the original design, mainly because the three-dimensional pressure-controlled vortex design improves the expansion characteristics of the vane tip and weakens the diffuse flow of the vane tip. Figure 3.27 also shows the entropy distribution at the exit section near the trailing edge of the blade. The loss range near the upper endwall of the original design vane is significantly larger than that near the lower endwall because the large meridional expansion of the upper endwall causes rapid growth of the endwall boundary layer grow, accumulating a large amount of low-energy fluids and forming a larger-scale passage vortex, resulting in additional flow loss. The exit section of the near-blade trailing edge can also be regarded as a wake occurrence area. Due to the effect of the three-dimensional, pressure-controlled vortex design, the newly designed vane has a strong trailing edge tilt feature. Therefore, the trailing edge is not distributed along the radial direction but is inclined. The newly designed vane tip loss area is slightly wider than that of the original design, but the entropy at the core loss area is slightly reduced compared with that of the original design. With the exception for the tip area of the vane, the wake width and strength at the trailing edge in the remaining areas are significantly smaller than those of the original design. A comparison of the entropy distribution at the lower endwall of the suction surface of the cascade reveals that the loss area at the corner of the suction surface of the newly designed cascade is reduced and that the low-energy fluids near the lower endwall are also significantly reduced.

According to the entropy distribution at the outlet section of the trailing edge of the blade, the largest source of the rotor blade profile loss is caused by the tip gap leakage

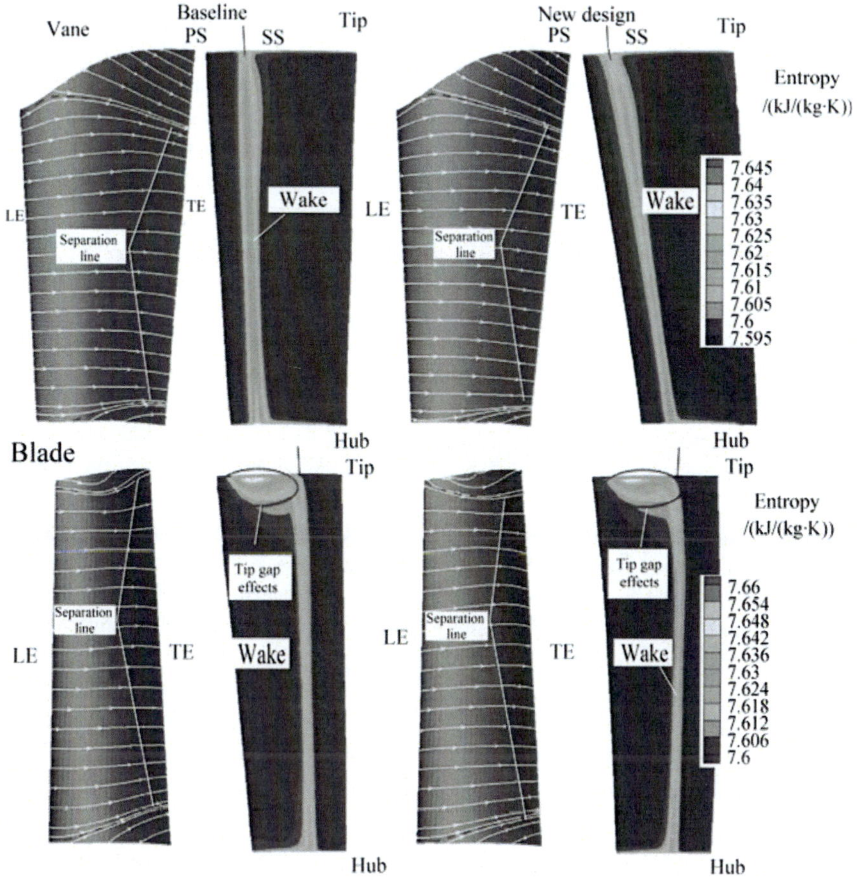

Fig. 3.27 Blade suction surface limiting streamline and its outlet entropy distribution

flow and the loss area occupies 0.6 pitch width and extends to the 18% blade span due to the relatively large tip blade reaction (the original turbine is approximately 0.6) and tip gap size (1 mm). Generally, the reaction at the tip of the turbine stage is reduced, and the leakage loss of the rotor blade gap must be reduced; however, this is not the case. As shown in Fig. 3.27, before and after the three-dimensional, pressure-controlled vortex design, the loss area occupied by the gap at the tip of the blade is almost unchanged in the direction of the blade span and pitch, and the corresponding maximum loss does not change. Therefore, it can be inferred that the pressure-controlled vortex design does not have a good control effect on the leakage loss of the turbine blade with large meridional expansion, which also shows that the large meridional expansion has a greater impact on the leakage flow of the turbine blade tip.

Figure 3.28 shows the distribution of the circumferential average total pressure loss coefficient C_p of the vane and blade and the turbine-stage isentropic efficiency

η along the blade span. For the vane, due to the lower outlet flow angle of the upper half of the blade and the increase in the installation angle, the gas flow turning angle at the tip of the cascade, the power output ability, and the loss accordingly increase. As the outlet flow angle of the lower half of the blade increases and the installation angle decreases, the turning angle of the gas flow decreases, the power output ability increases, and the loss of fluid flowing through the root of the guide blade decreases. Since the newly designed vane adopts some aft-loaded blade design rules, the vane profile loss is further reduced, which decreases the range of performance deterioration caused by the increase in the tip, that is, 50% deterioration for the original is reduced to 20% deterioration. However, the reduction in the profile loss is still insufficient to offset the increase in the loss caused by the increase in load in the tip area. The total pressure loss coefficient of the newly designed blade decreases along the entire blade span. The pressure-controlled vortex design has a very positive role in improving the flow of the rotor blade. Although the geometrical changes of the blade cascade are not as large as those of the vanes, the effect of reducing the flow loss of the blades is obvious.

Figure 3.28 also compares the radial distribution of the isentropic efficiency of the original turbines and the newly designed turbines. The turbine isentropic efficiency distribution is similar to the vane total pressure loss. The improvement in turbine stage efficiency comes at the expense of the aerodynamic performance at the tip of the vanes. Notably, the total gain is substantially greater than the loss, and ultimately, the turbine efficiency is greatly improved. The efficiency of the newly designed turbine is greatly improved from the blade root to 82% of the blade span. In general, the performance of the newly designed turbine in both vanes and blades has been improved, and the increase in turbine efficiency fully affirms the feasibility

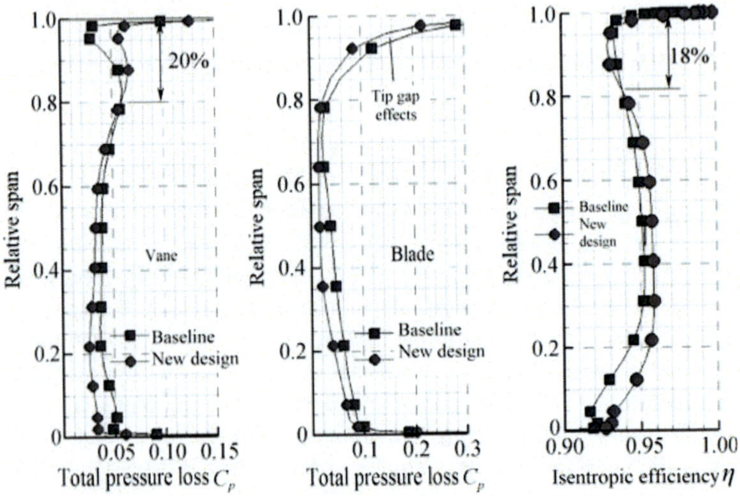

Fig. 3.28 Effects of three-dimensional, pressure-controlled vortex design on the spanwise distribution of total pressure loss and isentropic efficiency

of the three-dimensional, pressure-controlled vortex design. A comparison of the distribution of the relative total pressure loss along the blade span between the vane and the blade indicates that although the performance of the three-dimensional pressure control has improved the vane, the improvement of the turbine performance is mainly derived from the turbine blade. Since the isentropic efficiency of the original turbine is already very high, the potential for improving the turbine efficiency from the perspective of reducing the blade profile loss is also limited.

3.3.2 Endwall Flow Characteristics for a High Endwall Angle Turbine

With continuous improvement in turbine blade design technology, turbine blade design is developing along the direction of high efficiency and high load. The high blade row load produces a large turning angle of the blade, and the high turning angle profile design produces high profile losses. By increasing the turbine meridional channel expansion angle, the profile rotation angle can be effectively reduced, which causes the variable geometry turbine to have large expansion channel characteristics. However, this characteristic of the large expansion channel causes strong secondary flows to form near the endwall of the flow channel, thereby increasing the flow losses. At this stage, evaluating the method for reducing the flow loss of the endwall zone of the large meridional expansion, variable geometry turbine is important.

Figures 3.29 and 3.30 show the endwall-region, secondary flow vortex structure of a typical, large meridional expansion, fixed geometry turbine, and Fig. 3.31 shows the local enlarged fine flow structure at the blade tip. The passage vortex structure in the endwall zone is clearly visible in Fig. 3.29, and the passage vortex under the endwall with a large expansion angle is stronger and tends to develop toward the middle of the blade. This flow phenomenon is clearly visible in Fig. 3.30. There is a flow separation line from the leading edge to the trailing edge of the blade not far from the upper and lower endwalls of the suction surface of the vane. These two lines indicate that the separation line is formed when the vane passage vortex reaches the suction surface. Judging from the exit positions of the two separation lines at the trailing edge of the blade, the scale of the upper passage vortex is larger than that of the lower passage vortex. This result is attributed to the radial pressure gradient formed by the annular vane and the notion that the upper endwall uses a meridional endwall modeling technology that combines a concave curvature (first half of the vane) and a convex curvature (second half of the vane). The modeling technology causes a radial positive pressure gradient, which causes the low-energy fluids in the boundary layer to migrate toward the middle of the blade span over a larger range. The limit streamlines of the pressure surface shown in Fig. 3.30b point to the endwall surfaces of the casing and hub near the upper endwall surface and lower endwall surface, respectively, which are caused by the horseshoe vortex formed by the separation of the incoming boundary layer.

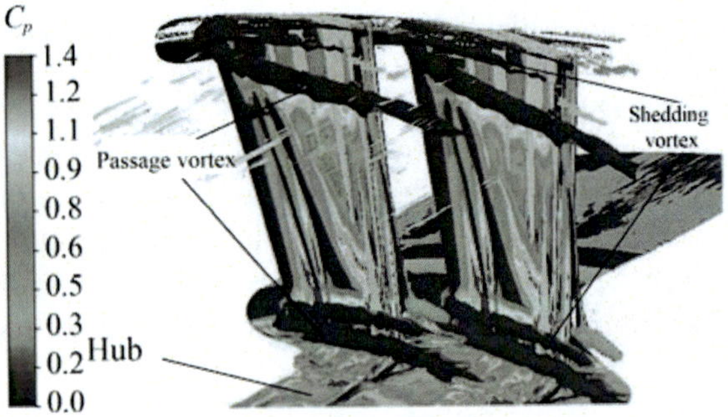

Fig. 3.29 Secondary flow vortex structure in the endwall region of high endwall angle turbines

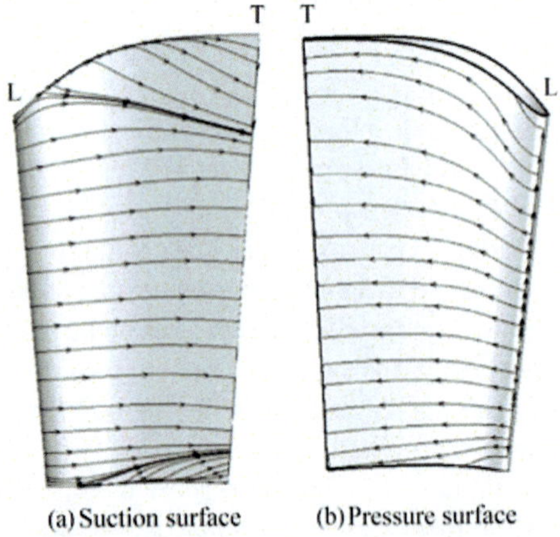

Fig. 3.30 Variable vane surface limiting surfaces

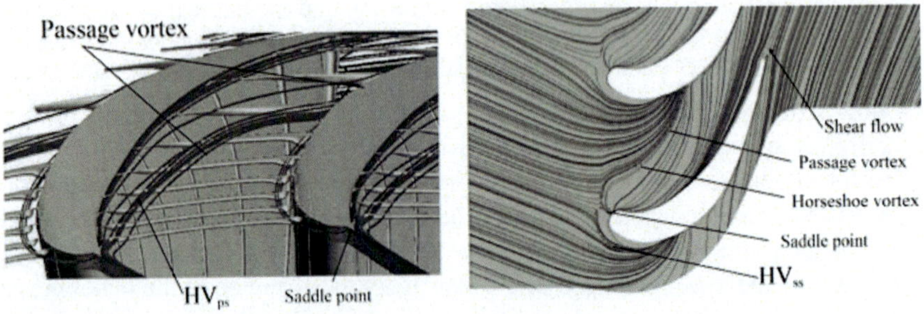

Fig. 3.31 Secondary flow structure of high endwall angle turbine casing endwall

According to Figs. 3.30 and 3.31, the vortex structure at the endwall of the large meridional expansion turbine starts at the stagnation point of the leading edge of the blade, and at 20% of the axial chord length of the blade pressure side, the horseshoe vortex pressure surface branches begin to separate. Under the effect of the lateral pressure gradient of the blade channel, the vortex laterally penetrates the channel and connects with the shedding vortex on the pressure surface and reaches the suction surface at 65% of the axial chord length. The horseshoe vortex on the suction surface is reintegrated into the suction surface again at the leading edge of the suction surface due to the lateral pressure difference effects. The passage vortex of the lower endwall has the same principle as the upper endwall and will not be repeated here. In addition, combining Figs. 3.29, 3.30 and 3.31, it can be inferred that the large meridional expansion endwall structure causes the turbine endwall zone flow loss to significantly increase.

3.3.3 Orthogonal Design for a High Endwall Angle Turbine

The orthogonal design of the turbine blade is an innovative design. Presently, there is still a considerable lack of research and engineering applications in related fields in China. However, the orthogonalized turbine design is creatively employed in Rollo-Royce's Trent series aero engines and MT30 marine gas turbines. Based on this finding, this section attempts to orthogonalize the design of the existing large meridional expansion variable geometry turbine blade and analyze its aerodynamic performance.

In marine gas turbines, a transition section structure and low-pressure turbine exist at the variable geometry power turbine inlet. Based on the original transition section of the turbine, this section increases the average radius and reduces the axial length of the low-pressure turbine upstream of the power turbine and transition section to achieve the compact transition section design of modern marine gas turbines. On this basis, the orthogonal design of the variable vane of variable geometry power turbines is carried out. To raise the front transition section of the variable geometry power turbine, the power turbine is axially shifted by 220 mm, and the transition section is shortened, as shown in Fig. 3.32. Due to the increase in the expansion angle of the shortened transition section, the flow separation is further strengthened, which will inevitably cause serious flow losses in the transition section. Figure 3.33 shows the static pressure coefficient distribution of the upper endwall of the front transition section of the turbine. When the original design transition section is utilized, the axial position increases from the inlet to 30% of the relative chord length, and the static pressure coefficient rapidly increases from 30% to the outlet location. The static pressure coefficient of the upper endwall slowly increases, which reduces the diffusion effect of the second half of the original design flow channel. When the compact transition section is adopted, the static pressure coefficient in the new flow channel is greater than the original flow channel from the inlet to the 20% axial chord length. At this downstream location, although the static pressure coefficient is smaller than the original flow channel, the growth trend shows that the slope of the static pressure coefficient in the new flow channel is larger, but the increase is more stable, which helps improve the flow state of the upper endwall.

To understand the impact of the compact transition section on the performance of the downstream variable geometry power turbine, it is necessary to analyze the characteristics of the parameter changes at the outlet of the compact transition section.

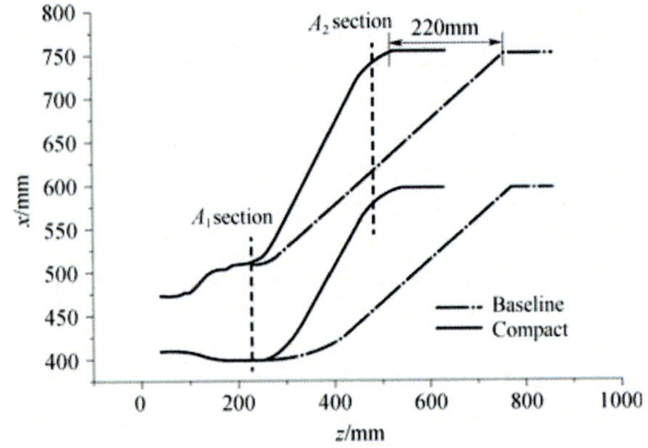

Fig. 3.32 Comparison of the meridional profile of intermediate turbine ducts

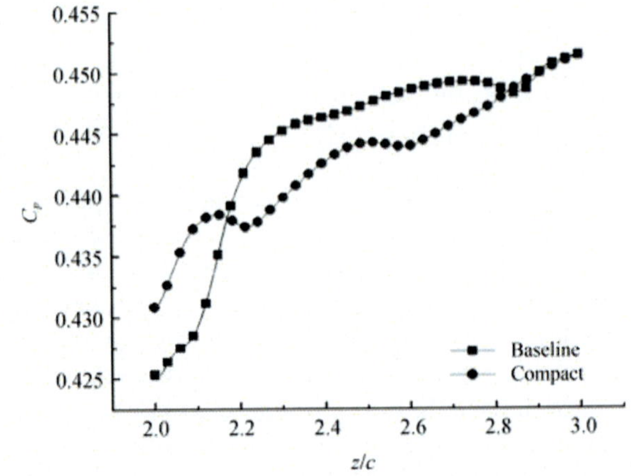

Fig. 3.33 Static pressure coefficient distribution of the casing endwall for intermediate turbine ducts

Figure 3.34 shows the radial distribution of the outlet flow angle before and after the transition section is raised. By comparison, we discover that from the hub to 20% of the span, the outlet flow angle of the compact transition section has decreased. From 20% of the span to the upper endwall, the outlet flow angle of the new flow channel has small fluctuations, which can reduce the loss caused by gas flow mixing. Therefore, raising the transition section is helpful to improve the gas intake condition of the power turbine and to reduce the mixing loss. Simultaneously, the flow angle at the upper endwall is increased, which helps reduce the blade tip clearance loss of the next stage. It can be speculated that further optimization of the transition section has the potential to improve the overall aerodynamic performance of turbines.

Figure 3.35 shows the distribution of entropy increase at the exit of the front transition section of the turbine. In the original design flow channel, there is an obvious entropy increase zone in the middle of the exit of the transition section, that is, the passage vortex. There is a distinct drop-off vortex at the upper endwall. With the compact transition section, the flow channel is raised, the entropy at the upper

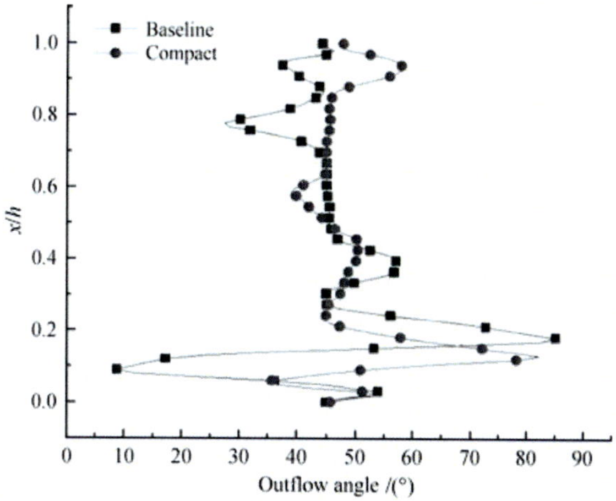

Fig. 3.34 Spanwise outflow angle distributions for intermediate turbine ducts

endwall of the outlet increases, and the shedding vortex disappears. The larger area of entropy increase in the middle part decreases. The shedding vortex at the outlet of the compact transition section is concentrated at the lower endwall. From the perspective of the entropy increase, the use of a compact transition section increases the overall loss at the outlet, but the loss of the passage vortex is reduced. Through design optimization, the flow separation loss can be further reduced.

Based on the impact of the compact design of the transition section on the downstream variable geometry turbine, the orthogonal design of variable vanes is discussed. Figure 3.36 shows the definition of the orthogonalization parameters of the turbine blades. In this section, the orthogonal design of the blades is carried out on the basis of the original design. The original design blade model is parameterized and stacked along the leading-edge line of the vane. The Bezier mode modifies

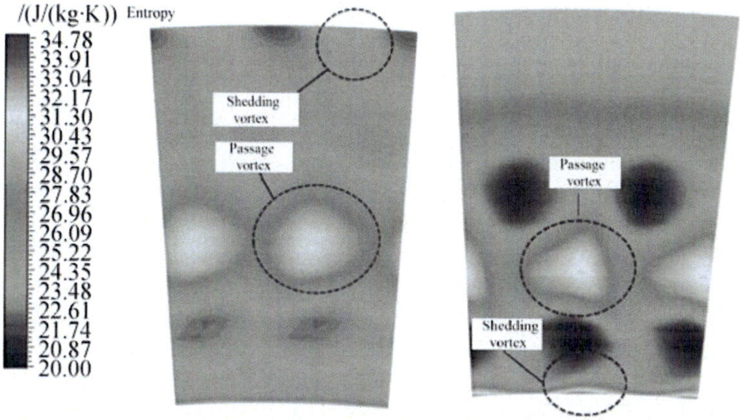

Fig. 3.35 Outlet entropy increase distributions for intermediate turbine ducts

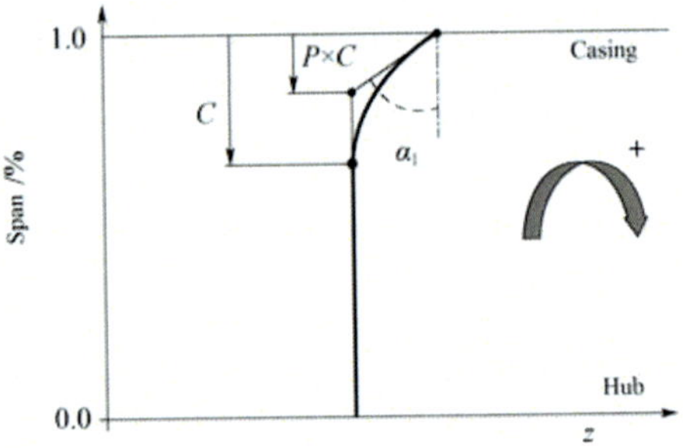

Fig. 3.36 Definition of turbine blade orthogonalization parameter

tangential swept stacking lines, that is, the coefficient C is set to 0.3 to ensure that the blade profile changes 30% in the spanwise direction, and P is set to 0.5 to ensure that the curved arc is smooth, which is conducive to improving the flow performance. The orthogonalization of the endwall zone is realized by adjusting the angle of α_1 to $\alpha_1 = 90°$ to carry out the design calculation of the original and orthogonalized blade profiles.

Figure 3.37 shows the three-dimensional geometric comparison of the original design and the final orthogonal design of variable vanes. Figure 3.38 shows the static pressure distribution on the upper endwall of the variable vane of the variable geometry turbine. The pressure distribution on the suction surface and pressure surface of the orthogonal blade endwall is well optimized compared with the original blade profile. In the original design blade, a relatively large separation vortex and a small separation vortex are formed on the suction surface not far from the blade leading edge. Due to the existence of these large passage vortex low-energy fluids, at the suction surface of the original blade profile, a large adverse pressure gradient is formed at a very early stage. Orthogonal turbine blades have a smooth flow of high-energy fluid at this position. Downstream of the suction surface, the original profile has an obvious passage vortex with higher fluid energy at the trailing edge and its rear part, forming an adverse pressure gradient. At the trailing edge of the orthogonal turbine suction surface, there is only one small passage vortex, and the fluid energy of the trailing edge of the orthogonal turbine and its rear part are low. Thus, the suction surface of the orthogonal turbine forms a positive pressure gradient with smooth flows. Simultaneously, on the pressure surface, the pressure at the leading edge of the orthogonalized blade profile is significantly increased, which reduces the losses caused by the adverse pressure gradient at the pressure surface and promotes reasonable flow at the upper endwall.

Figure 3.39 shows an increase in the entropy distribution at the variable vane outlet of the variable geometry turbine. At the vane outlet, there are two obvious passage vortices. Compared with the original blade and orthogonal design blade, the passage vortex of the orthogonal turbine is closer to the relative blade spans of 20% and 80%, and the strength of the passage vortex is reduced. The entropy increase at the exit indicates that the entropy increase of the shedding vortex significantly decreases,

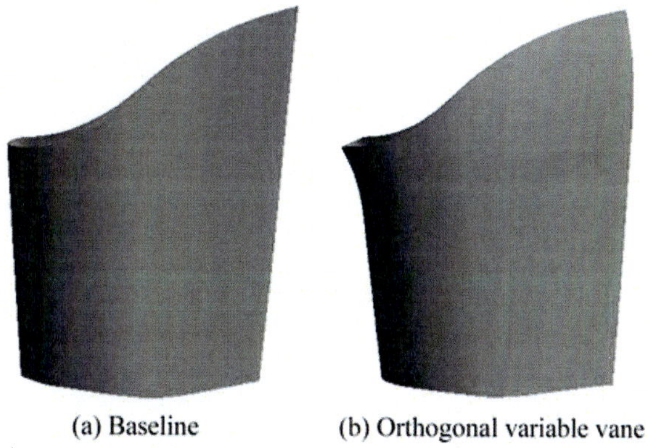

Fig. 3.37 Variable geometry turbine vane comparison

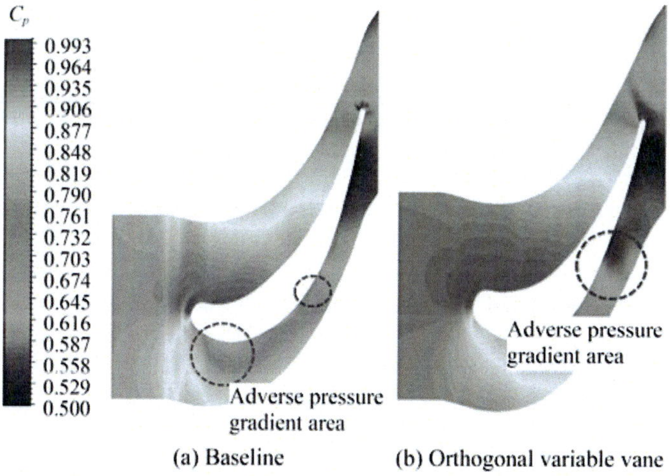

Fig. 3.38 Static pressure distributions of the variable geometry turbine vane casing

showing that the orthogonal design can effectively reduce the aerodynamic loss in the endwall zone.

3.3.4 Exploration of the Reversing Design Method for a Variable Geometry Turbine

To reduce the additional loss caused by the endwall clearance of the variable vane of the large meridional expansion turbine, thereby improving the turbine efficiency, this section proposes the concept of using a variable geometry turbine and an upstream low-pressure turbine reversal design to fully utilize the upstream outlet gas flow

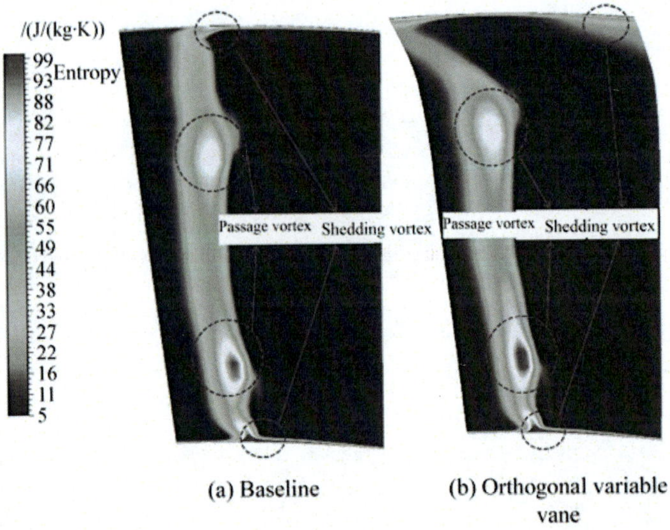

Fig. 3.39 Increase in entropy distribution at the variable geometry turbine vane outlet

prerotation and to reduce not only the variable vane profile turning angle but also the variable vane aerodynamic losses.

Based on the turbine elementary-stage velocity triangle theory, the change in the turning angle before and after turbine reversal is analyzed, as shown in Fig. 3.40. Before reversal, $\alpha = 4.5°$, $\gamma = 52.2°$, $\delta = 10°$, $\beta = \delta_2 + \gamma = 62.2°$, and $a = \alpha + \beta = 66.7°$. After reversal, $\delta_2 = 10°$, $\beta = \delta_2 + \gamma = 62.2°$, and $a = \beta\text{-}\alpha = 57.7°$, where δ_1 and δ_2 are the inlet structure angle and outlet structure angle, respectively; γ is the installation angle; α and β are the inflow angle and outflow angle, respectively; and a is the turning angle.

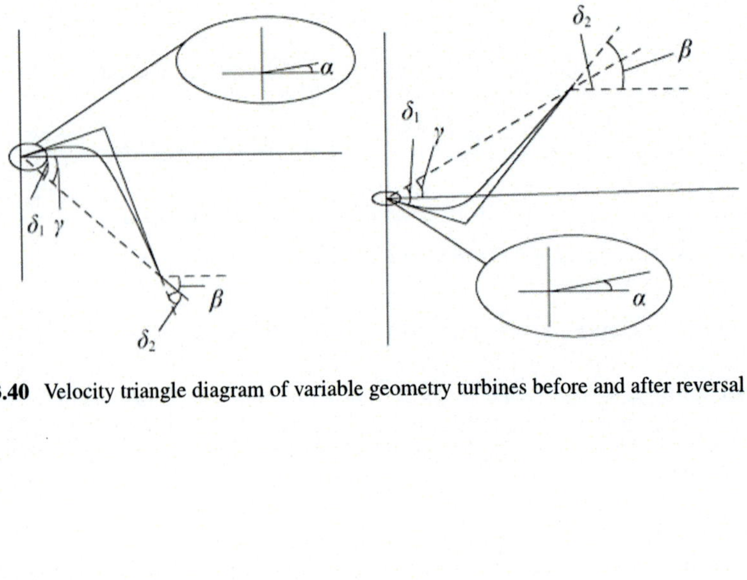

Fig. 3.40 Velocity triangle diagram of variable geometry turbines before and after reversal

After theoretical analysis of the velocity triangle, the turning angle of the blade profile after reversal is smaller than that before reversal, which proves that the efficiency of the turbine after reversal is higher than that before reversal and verifies the feasibility of the variable geometry turbine for reversal design.

3.3.5 Analysis of Refined Flow Organization and Design for a Variable Geometry Turbine

After decades of development, traditional marine gas turbine aerodynamic design technology based on conventional blade modeling and three-dimensional stacking has become relatively mature, and the turbine design capability and design level have been significantly improved. However, with the increasing power requirements of large surface ships, traditional turbine design technology has had difficulty meeting the future high-power, high-efficiency marine gas turbine requirements for further improvement in turbine performance. Therefore, it is necessary to conduct in-depth systematic research on the flow details and flow characteristics that are disregarded in the traditional design system, such as the influence of the asymmetrical blade shroud structure, the blade root rim sealing structure, the structure of the transition section and the structure of the outlet asymmetric exhaust volute. On this basis, the refined flow organization inside the variable geometry turbine must be deliberately explored to add new degrees of freedom to the variable geometry turbine aerodynamic design, to improve the variable geometry turbine design method, and to achieve further improvement of the turbine design capability. Presently, for the variable geometry turbine aerodynamic design, the main turbine refined flow organization and design technology are mainly developed for the following aspects: full, three-dimensional, coupled design of turbine blade endwalls, fine optimization of the nonaxisymmetric blade shroud structure, fine design optimization of blade root rim seals, integrated design of the transition section and variable geometry turbine, integrated design of the exhaust turbine and variable geometry turbine, etc. Due to space limitations, readers who are interested can refer to relevant journal/conference papers published by the authors.

3.4 Summary

This chapter mainly summarizes the selection and optimization of low-dimensional, aerodynamic design parameters of variable geometry turbines, the aerodynamic performance of turbine blade profiles suitable for variable geometry work, and the three-dimensional aerodynamic design method of variable geometry turbines with large meridional expansion.

The wide operating condition design of variable geometry turbines involves careful selection of low-dimensional aerodynamic design parameters. Specifically, for the variable geometry power turbines investigated in this chapter, the design operating point should be selected at 50% operating conditions, which considers the requirements for turbine design and off-design operating conditions. The loading and flow coefficients are selected as relatively small values, and a relatively large value is set for the degree of reaction, which can improve the secondary flow in the variable geometry turbine endwall zone and avoid negative reactions at the root of the blade under low operating conditions.

The backward movement of the turbine blade profile load causes the total pressure loss of the blade to decrease in the first half and to increase in the second half. The total pressure loss at the outlet position is reduced. Therefore, the variable vane design can be given priority to adopt a high, new, "aft-loaded" profile with small turning angles, such as strength and good adaptability to a wide range of angles.

Marine gas turbine power turbines with variable geometry are generally designed for large expansion flow channels. The secondary flow in the endwall zone is relatively violent, and the loss in the endwall zone is large. In view of the unique flow loss characteristics in the endwall zone, an orthogonal design concept suitable for large meridional expansion turbine blades is proposed. It is confirmed that the variable geometry turbine inversion design can be employed to reduce the endwall loss of the variable vane. The refined flow organization and design technology of variable geometry turbines are proposed.

Chapter 4
Variable Vane Turning Design Method for a Variable Geometry Turbine

Abstract After a turbine is converted from fixed geometry to variable geometry, a gap clearance must be created at the end of the guide vane, and a turning shaft must be provided to ensure the free rotation of the vane, which will cause additional losses in the endwall region of the vane and a decrease in turbine aerodynamic efficiency. This chapter focuses on the selection criteria and rule of a variable vane-endwall structure and its parameters, new methods for controlling variable vane-endwall losses, a high endwall angle variable vane turning design based on a stepped spherical endwall, and the proposal and validation of a full, three-dimensional, turning design concept for a high endwall angle variable vane. Additionally, a variable vane turning angle adjustment method and law for variable geometry turbines are summarized.

4.1 Selection Criteria and Rule of the Variable Vane Endwall Structure and Its Parameters

After a turbine is converted from fixed geometry to variable geometry, a gap clearance must be provided at the end of the guide vane, and a turning shaft must be installed to ensure the free rotation of the vane, which will cause additional loss in the endwall region of the vane and a decrease in turbine aerodynamic efficiency. Therefore, it is necessary to investigate the variable vane-endwall turning structure and its parameter selection to minimize the negative impact of the vane turning design on the aerodynamic performance of variable geometry turbines. For this reason, this section analyzes and discusses the parameters of the turning shaft near the turbine endwall clearance region, vane-endwall structures, etc.

J. Gao et al., *Variable Geometry Turbine Technology for Marine Gas Turbines*,
https://doi.org/10.1007/978-981-19-6952-2_4

4.1.1 *Effect of Parameters of the Turning Shaft Near the Turbine Endwall Clearance Region on Turbine Performance*

1. Diameter of turning shaft

Based on the basic characteristics of the variable vane, when the turning shaft is installed at 20% of the chord length, the lower endwall area is affected by the turning shaft with the same size of the upper and lower endwall turning shafts. This effect is attributed to the shorter chord length of the vane root section than that of the vane tip section. To analyze the maximum possible impact of the change in the size of the turning shaft, this section focuses on the impact of the area at the lower end of the vane. Figure 4.1 shows the vane structure with the variation in turning shaft diameter. Four schemes of turning shaft diameters are detailed, among which the shaftless scheme is utilized as a control scheme.

The endwall clearance leakage flowrate of the variable vane with varying diameter of the turning shaft is obtained by numerical calculation. As shown in Table 4.1, the upper and lower endwall clearance leakage decreases as the shaft diameter increases. Compared with the change in the upper endwall gap leakage flow rate, the lower endwall gap leakage flow rate is more sensitive to whether the turning shaft is installed. With an increase in the diameter of the turning shaft, the relative change in the gap leakage flow rate of the lower endwall also increases. Therefore, it can be speculated that the influence of the diameter change of the turning shaft is also

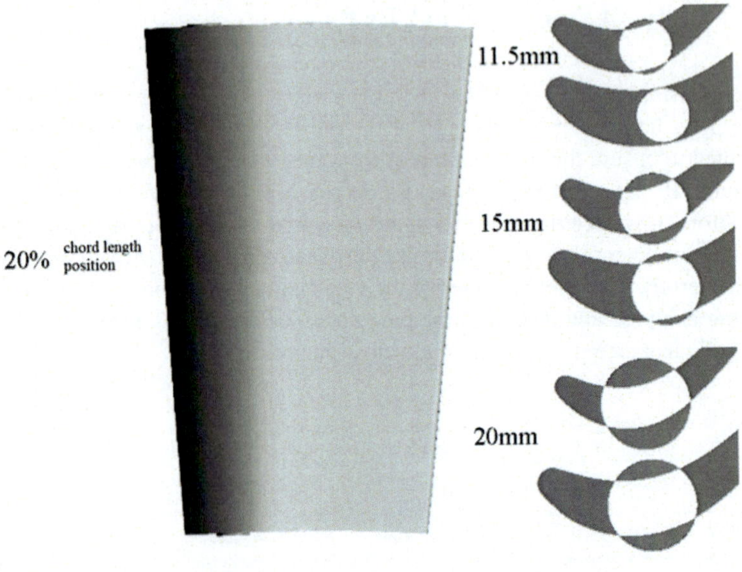

Fig. 4.1 Variable vane structure with varying diameters of the turning shaft

Table 4.1 Summary of the gap clearance leakage flow rate of variable vanes with varying diameters of the turning shaft

	Hub endwall gap clearance leakage flowrate (kg/s)	Casing endwall gap clearance leakage flowrate (kg/s)
No shaft	0.0183	0.0207
$D = 11.5$ mm	0.0159	0.0191
$D = 15.0$ mm	0.0149	0.0181
$D = 20.0$ mm	0.0138	0.0170

affected by the installation position of the turning shaft and the ratio of the turning shaft diameter to the chord length of the vane-endwall.

Figure 4.2 shows the static pressure distribution at the 1% vane span cross-section of the variable vanes with different turning shaft diameters. The reference line in the figure indicates that as the diameter of the turning shaft of variable vanes increases, the phenomenon of backward load is more obvious. Thus, as the diameter of the turning shaft increases, the effect of the mixing zone behind the turning shaft on the static pressure at the endwall of the vane increases. The increase in the diameter of the turning shaft causes more leakage fluids to flow downstream against the suction surface, and the phenomenon of load shift downstream caused by mixing with the mainstream is more obvious. In addition, a low-pressure area appears at the position of the turning shaft in Fig. 4.2, and as the diameter of the turning shaft increases, the range of the low-pressure area gradually increases. A clear low-pressure area already exists, as shown in Fig. 4.2d.

The development of the total pressure loss at the endwall area of the vane with different diameters of the turning shaft is shown in Fig. 4.3. When the turning shaft is installed at 20% of the chord length, the change in the diameter of the turning shaft further affects the loss core position and the size of each cross-section of the endwall loss along the flow direction. As the diameter of the vane turning shaft increases, within 30–50% of the chord length, the position of the loss core moves backward, the distance from the suction surface decreases, the loss of the core decreases, and the size of the area occupied by the endwall loss decreases. However, at the outlet, the leakage vortex has completely developed, and the distribution of the total pressure loss coefficient at its endwall undergoes minimal changes. As the diameter of the turning shaft increases, the position of the leakage vortex continues to move backward. The turning shaft causes the size of the leakage vortex to decrease in the downstream part of the region, and the endwall gap clearance leakage vortex is suppressed. However, after the leakage vortex at the exit of the variable vane is fully developed, the size change of the turning shaft has minimal effect on the position and size of the leakage vortex.

Figure 4.4 shows the spanwise distribution of the total pressure loss at the vane outlet with different diameters of the turning shaft. When the turning shaft is installed at the position of 20% of the chord length, as the diameter of the turning shaft increases, the mass-averaged total pressure loss coefficient at the vane outlet is

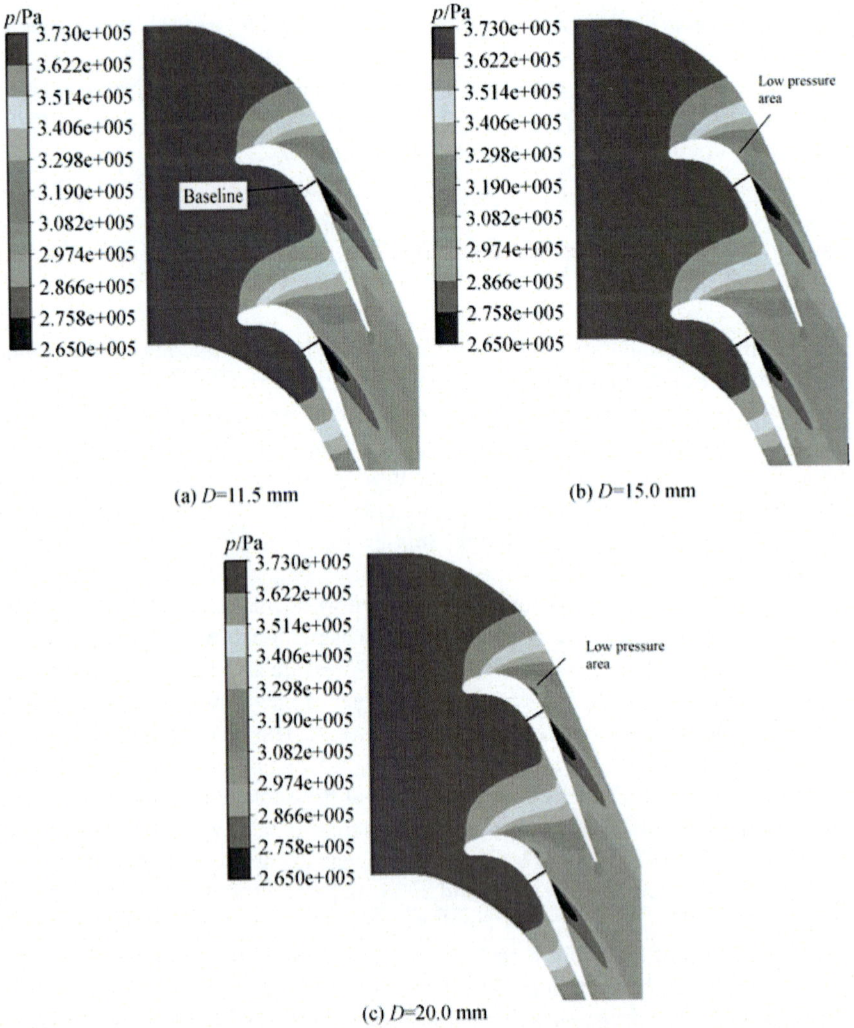

Fig. 4.2 Static pressure distribution at 1% span for variable vanes with different turning shaft diameters

significantly reduced in the leakage flow areas of the upper and lower endwalls, with basically no change in the mainstream area.

2. Installation position of the turning shaft

Figure 4.5 shows a schematic of the vane structure with the change in the turning shaft installation position. There are five kinds of turning shaft installation position change schemes, of which the shaftless scheme is the control scheme. Table 4.2 shows the amount of clearance leakage at the endwall of the vanes at different installation positions of the turning shaft. The clearance leakage at the upper and lower endwalls

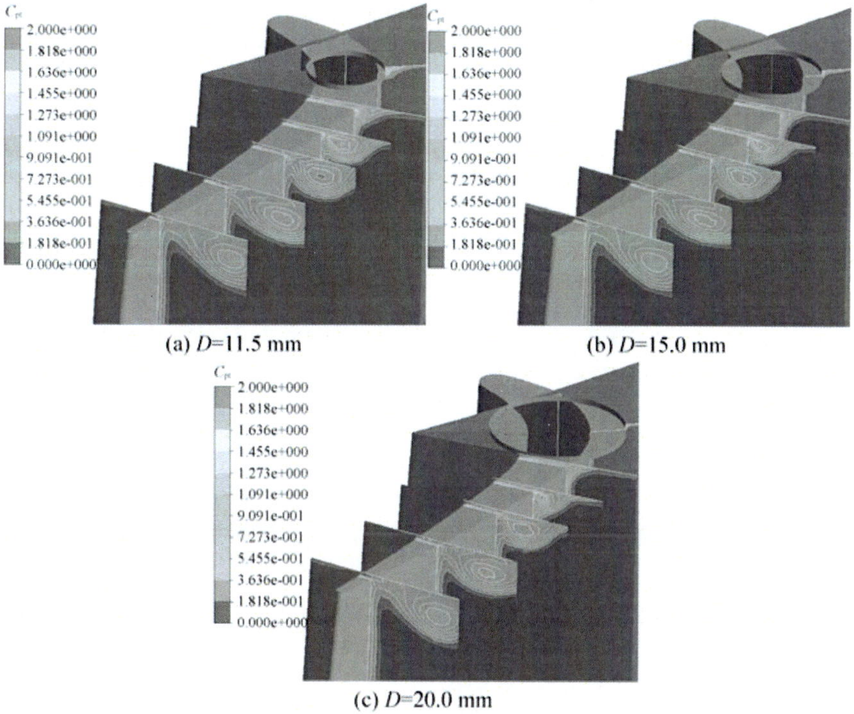

Fig. 4.3 Streamwise development of the total pressure loss in the hub endwall regions of variable vanes

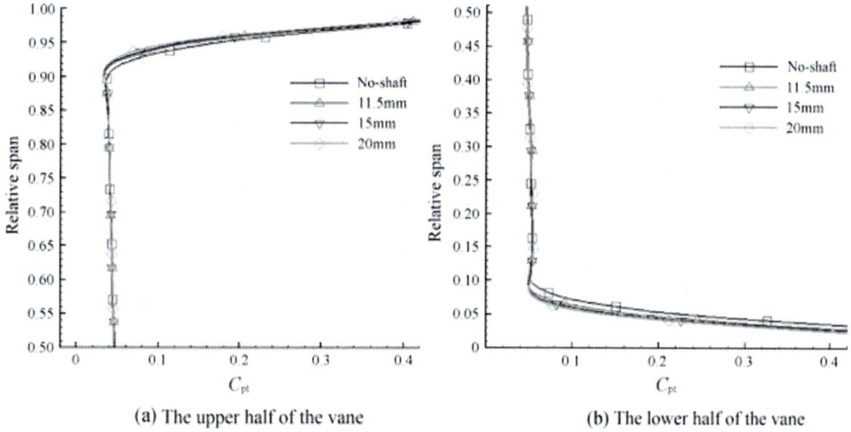

Fig. 4.4 Spanwise total pressure loss distribution at the variable vane outlet

decreases and then increases as the turning shaft moves backward. When the turning shaft is installed at 50% of the chord length, the leakage reduction is most obvious.

Figure 4.6 shows the static pressure distribution at the 98% vane span cross-section of the variable vane with different turning shaft installation positions. A comparison of Fig. 4.6a and c shows that when the turning shaft is installed at 50% of the chord length, the low-pressure area caused by the leakage of the endwall gap is obviously broken in the area of the turning shaft. Two low-pressure areas are formed in front of and behind the turning shaft. The pressure in the low-pressure area in front of the shaft is lower than that behind the turning shaft, and the pressure in the low-pressure area behind the shaft slightly increases. When the turning shaft is installed at 70% of the chord length, the leakage vortex is far from the turning shaft. The turning shaft reduces the range of the low-pressure area, but the impact is small. When the turning

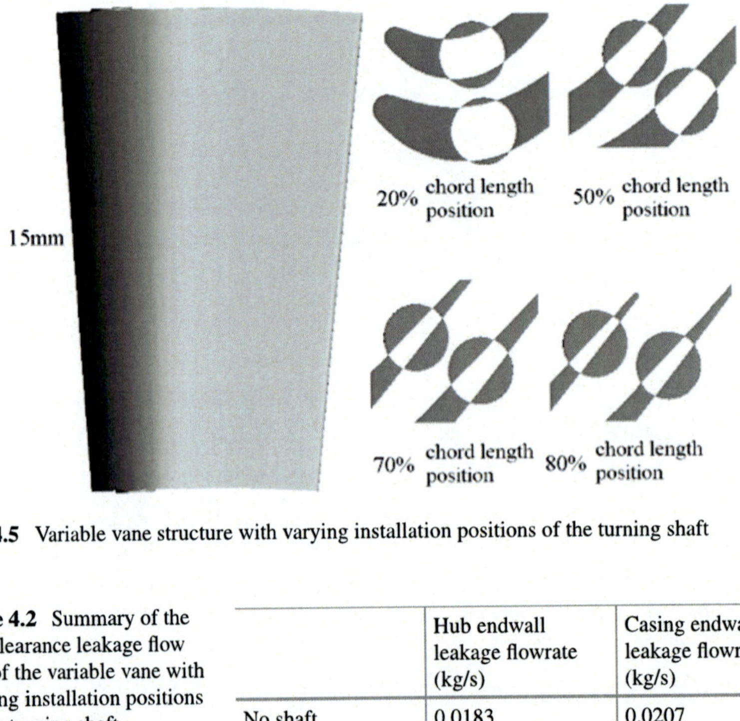

Fig. 4.5 Variable vane structure with varying installation positions of the turning shaft

Table 4.2 Summary of the gap clearance leakage flow rate of the variable vane with varying installation positions of the turning shaft

	Hub endwall leakage flowrate (kg/s)	Casing endwall leakage flowrate (kg/s)
No shaft	0.0183	0.0207
20% of the axial chord	0.0149	0.0181
50% of the axial chord	0.0147	0.0177
70% of the axial chord	0.0149	0.0179
80% of the axial chord	0.0155	0.0182

shaft is installed at 20% of the chord length, the position of the low-pressure zone caused by the turning shaft moves backward, and the minimum pressure near the suction surface decreases.

Figure 4.7 shows a distribution diagram of the total pressure loss coefficient of the various streamwise cross-sections of the upper endwall area of the vane passage

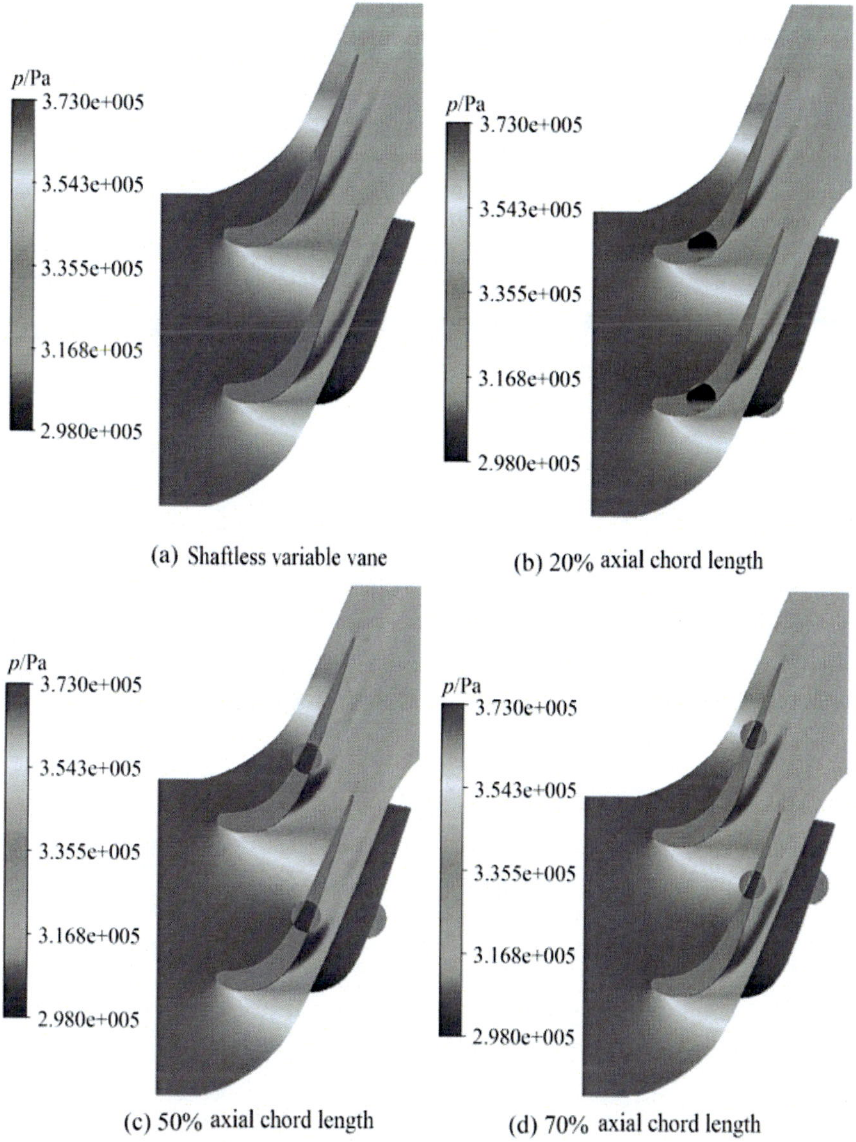

Fig. 4.6 Static pressure distribution at 98% of the span for variable vanes with varying installation positions of the turning shaft

at different installation positions of the turning shaft. When the turning shaft is installed at 20% of the chord length and 50% of the chord length, the total pressure loss changes greatly along the streamwise direction, especially at the cross-section before and after the position of the turning shaft. In addition, at 70% of the chord length, the endwall loss core is far from the suction surface, and the turning shaft has no obvious effect on the loss distribution of the front and back sections.

Figure 4.8 shows the spanwise distribution of the total pressure loss at the variable vane outlet for different installation positions of the turning shaft. As the position of the turning shaft moves backward, the total pressure loss coefficient exhibits minimal change in the midspan region; only in the area below 1% of the vane span and above 90% of the vane span does it have a great influence on the suppression of the leakage vortex by the turning shaft. In addition, due to the suppression effect of the turning shaft on the leakage flow of the gap clearance, the total pressure loss caused by the interaction of the endwall vortices is reduced. When the turning shaft is installed at the positions of 20 and 50% of the chord length, the loss reduction is the largest, while the turning shaft is installed at the positions of 70 and 80% of the chord length, respectively, and the loss reduction is very small. This finding further shows that the

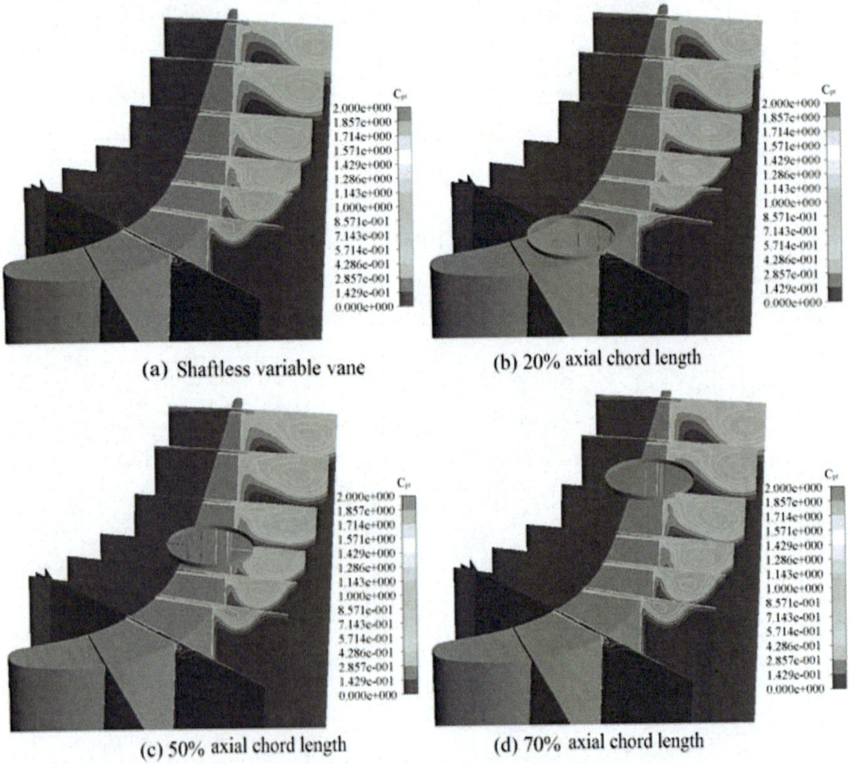

(a) Shaftless variable vane (b) 20% axial chord length

(c) 50% axial chord length (d) 70% axial chord length

Fig. 4.7 Streamwise development of the total pressure loss in the casing endwall regions of variable vanes

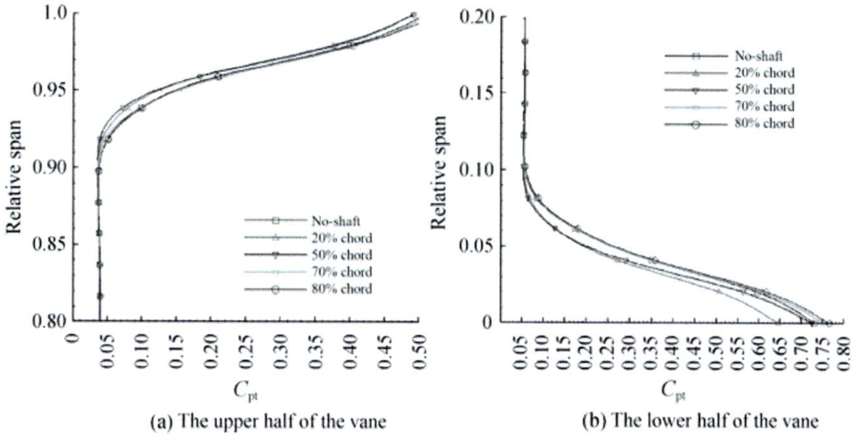

Fig. 4.8 Spanwise total pressure loss distribution at the variable vane outlet

development of the leakage vortex at different positions in the flow channel affects the suppression effect of the turning shaft at the corresponding position on the leakage vortex. If the turning shaft is installed at a position where the leakage vortex does not deviate from the suction surface, the endwall loss is greatly reduced. In addition, compared with the loss at the vane tip area, the loss at the root of the vane is further reduced, and the maximum reduction amplitude of the flow loss is nearly 0.1.

In general, the total pressure loss at the outlet of the variable vane with different rotation parameters of the endwall gap is shown in Table 4.3. As the diameter of the turning shaft increases, the expansion ratio decreases, and the amount of decrease and the outlet total pressure loss coefficient gradually decreases. As the installation position of the turning shaft moves backward, the expansion ratio increases. When the turning shaft is installed at 70% of the chord length, the expansion ratio undergoes minimal changes, and the outlet total pressure loss coefficient decreases and then increases. When the turning shaft is installed at 50% of the chord length, the loss is minimal; when it is installed at 80% of the chord length, the total pressure loss coefficient is similar to that of the shaftless vane.

4.1.2 Clearance and Performance Characteristics for Cylindrical and Spherical Endwall Variable Vanes

1. Cylindrical endwall

In this section, the variable design of the vanes of a typical marine power turbine is carried out by numerical calculation. Figure 4.9a shows the meridional flow channel of the cylindrical endwall. The positioning pattern of variable vanes are shown in Fig. 4.9b. The numerical calculation is performed after changing the installation

Table 4.3 Summary of the total pressure loss coefficient at the variable vane outlet

Schemes		Expansion ratio	Outlet total pressure loss
Shaftless vane		1.183	0.088
Turning shaft diameter change	$D = 11.5$ mm	1.179	0.084
	$D = 15.0$ mm	1.177	0.082
	$D = 20.0$ mm	1.177	0.080
Turning shaft installation position change	20% of the axial chord	1.177	0.082
	50% of the axial chord	1.180	0.081
	70% of the axial chord	1.182	0.085
	80% of the axial chord	1.182	0.087

angle of the vane cascade. To change the vane turning angle, one must select the position of the vane turning shaft. In this section, from the aspect of strength, the turning shaft is installed at the vane end where the vane thickness is large. As shown in Fig. 4.9b, the position of the shaft is (45, 18). Figure 4.10 shows the cross-sectional positions of the tip of the vane after rotating around the turning shaft. To rotate the entire vane around the turning shaft, it is necessary to perform the rotation for each vane cross-section. The selection of the turning shaft has been explained above. Since the variable vane turning shaft is perpendicular to the turbine rotor shaft, the turning point of each vane cross-section can be determined, and therefore, the vane rotation only needs to rotate each section around the turning point of vanes.

Before performing the numerical calculation of vane variable geometry, in the case of the original installation angle of the variable vane of 0°, the tip clearance of the variable vane is set to 0.8 mm considering the effect of thermal stress and the sufficient rotation space to meet the vane requirements. As previously mentioned, when the variable geometry turbine with a cylindrical endwall rotates the variable

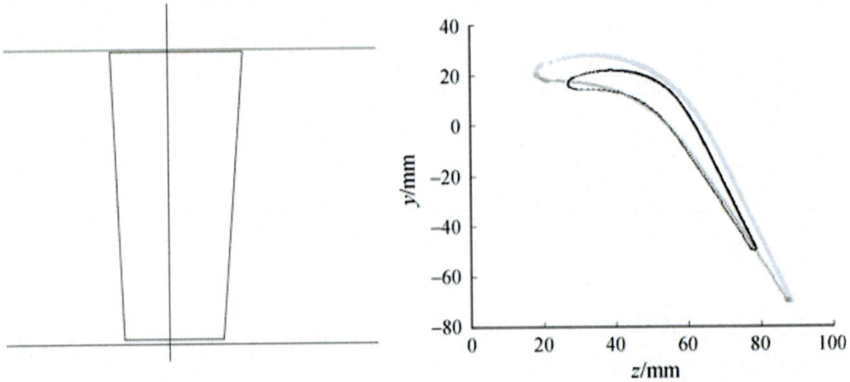

(a) Meridional flowpath (b) Endwall vane profile

Fig. 4.9 Meridional flow path and endwall vane profile for variable vanes with a cylindrical endwall

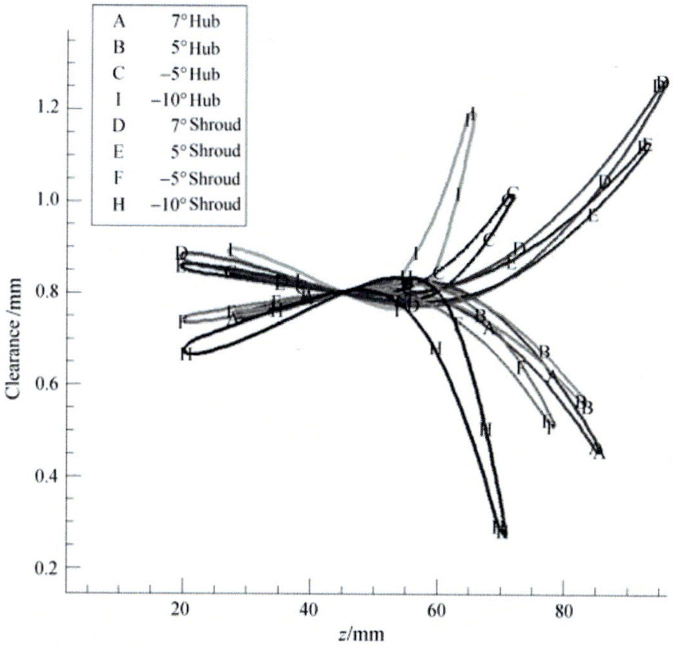

Fig. 4.10 Vane-endwall gap clearance height variation with the turning angle

vane, the gap clearance distribution at the vane end changes with the change in the turning angle, which is clearly shown in Fig. 4.10. The vane-end gap clearance is distributed along the vane profile with different vane turning angles. In Fig. 4.10, the two curves corresponding to each letter are the pressure surface and suction surface of the vane profile. When the variable vane rotates toward +5° and +7°, the gap clearances of the root of the leading and trailing edges of the vane are gradually reduced, and the decrease in the root clearance at the trailing edge of vanes is greater than that at the leading edge of the vanes, that is, the root gap clearance at the trailing edge is smaller than that at the leading edge. The tip clearance at the leading and trailing edges of the vane increases, and the increase in the tip clearance at the trailing edge of the vane is greater than that at the leading edge. When the variable vane rotates to −5° and −10°, the root gap of the leading and trailing edges of the vane is gradually increased, and the increase at the trailing edge is larger than that at the leading edge, which means that the gap clearance at the trailing edge of the vane is larger than that at the leading edge, the tip gap clearance at the leading and trailing edges of the vane are decreasing, and the endwall-gap clearance at the trailing edge is smaller than that at the leading edge.

Table 4.4 shows that as the turning angle changes from +7° to −10°, the mass flow rate of the variable vane gradually decreases, which indicates that the turning of the vane toward +7° is open and that toward −10° is closed. Table 4.4 shows that in the variable geometry turbine, when the vane turning angle is at +5°, the efficiency

Table 4.4 Comparison between calculation results and main parameters of variable geometry turbines

Turning angle	Isentropic efficiency	Mass flow (Ratio to design result)	Power (Ratio to design result)	Total recovery coefficient
+7°	0.9093	1.1403	0.9255	0.9255
+5°	0.9195	1.1067	1.0692	0.9260
0°	0.9139	1.0000	1.0000	0.9080
−5°	0.8966	0.8300	0.8419	0.9025
−10°	0.8043	0.5681	0.5121	0.8408

of the vane is the highest, followed by the angle of 0°, and the efficiency of the turning angle of −10° is the lowest. According to the trend of the efficiency change with the turning angle, when the vane is changing from 0° to +7°, the efficiency exhibits a small increase and then a decrease; when the turning angle changes from 0° to −10°, the efficiency is always in a state of decrease, as shown in Table 4.4. The efficiency at the turning angle of −10° is 11% lower than that at the 0° turning angle, while the efficiency at the +7° turning angle is 0.4% lower than that at the 0° turning angle. Therefore, it can be concluded that a large turning angle of vanes has a relatively small impact on the efficiency, while a small turning angle of vanes has a great impact on the efficiency. The following reasons are given:

If the vane is opened, it will cause the position of the vane throat to change, the peak pressure of the vane back surface to shift and increase, resulting in increased loss; and the negative incidence angle of attack of the rotor blade to substantially increase. Although the loss caused by the negative incidence angle of attack loss is significantly lower than that caused by the positive incidence angle of attack, a larger negative incidence angle of attack can still cause greater loss. In addition, the large opening of the vane leads to a relatively reduced degree of choking at the trailing edge of the vane, a decrease in the relative Mach number at the rotor blade inlet, and an increase in the reaction degree of the turbine stage. These factors are beneficial to the improvement in turbine efficiency. A comprehensive analysis shows that when the vane is opened to a larger extent, the efficiency will slowly decrease for variable geometry turbines.

For the closing of the vane, the vane flow channel is convergent, and the gas excessively expands in the channel; the trailing edge is more choked; the rotor blade increases toward the positive incidence angle of attack; the rotor blade inlet velocity is higher; and the root gas flow decelerates and may start to separate from the root surface. Examining the area of the vane from another perspective, the turbine reaction degree rapidly decreases, and even a negative reaction degree appears at the root of the rotor blade. All of the above factors have caused a substantial increase in aerodynamic loss.

Figures 4.11, 4.12 and 4.13 show the surface static pressure distributions at the tip of the vane (99% of the vane span) near the tip gap and at the bottom of the vane (1% of the vane span) near the root gap at different turning angles. This finding reflects the effect of the nonuniform gap clearance on its static pressure distribution. First, as indicated by the static pressure distribution at the 0° turning angle in Fig. 4.11, at the vane root (1% of the vane span), the static pressures on the pressure surface and the suction surface rapidly decrease in the first 50% of the axial chord section, and the pressure has a gentle area at 50–70% of the axial chord for the vane pressure surface and a weak adverse pressure gradient, followed by a pressure drop area. The suction surface does not experience a gentle area after 50% of the axial chord length and directly reaches a more obvious adverse pressure gradient section. Among them, the pressure in the front half of the vane pressure surface rapidly drops, mainly because the gap clearance structure at the vane root endwall causes the fluid at the endwall pressure surface to leak into the gap clearance. The static pressure distribution law at the tip of the vane (99% of the vane span) is the same as that at the root. The pressure surface undergoes a process of gradually descending, while the static pressure of the suction surface undergoes a process of falling and then rising. The difference is that the gentle area at the vane pressure surface is wider, while the adverse pressure gradient at the vane suction surface is gentler.

Figure 4.12 reflects the change in the static pressure distribution when the turning angle is increased to +5°. A comparison with the static pressure distribution at a 0° turning angle, the static pressure on the pressure surface of the vane end (99% vane span) does not experience a gentle area; instead, it directly drops, and the change law of the suction surface is similar to that at the 0° turning angle. At the root of the vane (1% of the vane span), the pressure surface still undergoes a process of gradual

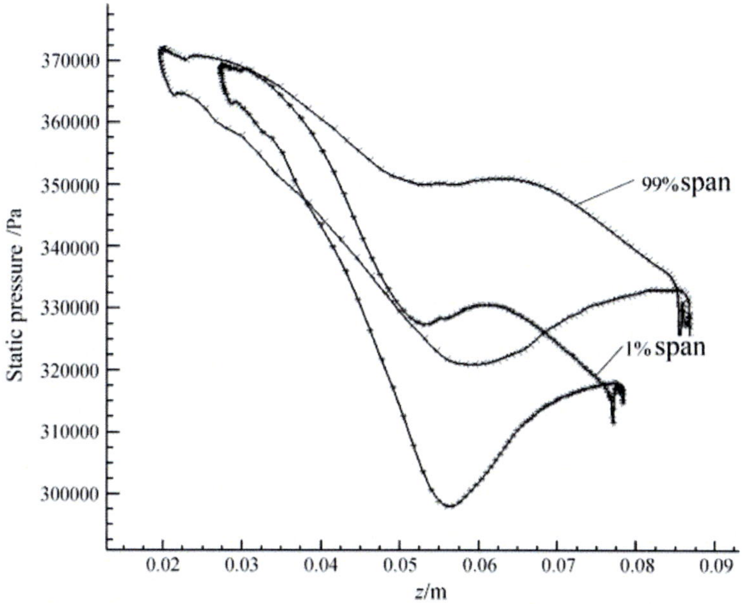

Fig. 4.11 Static pressure distribution at 1 and 99% vane spans at a 0° turning angle

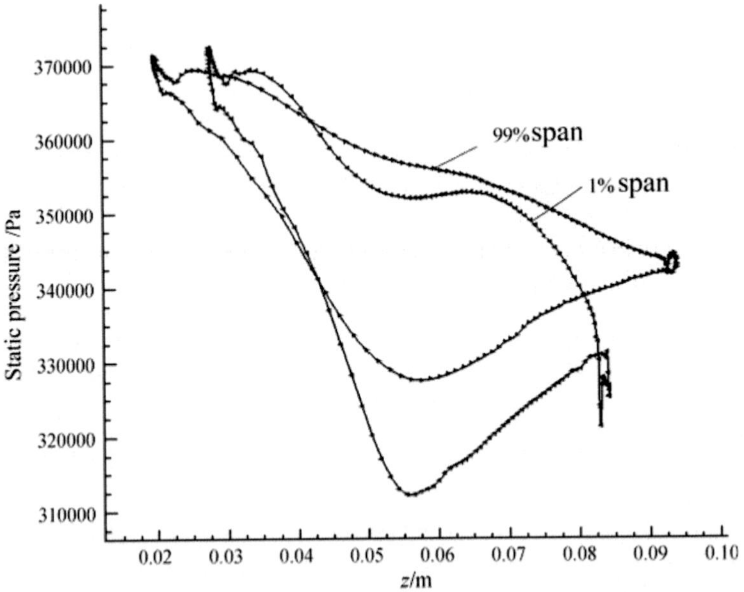

Fig. 4.12 Static pressure distribution at 1 and 99% of the vane span at a +5° turning angle

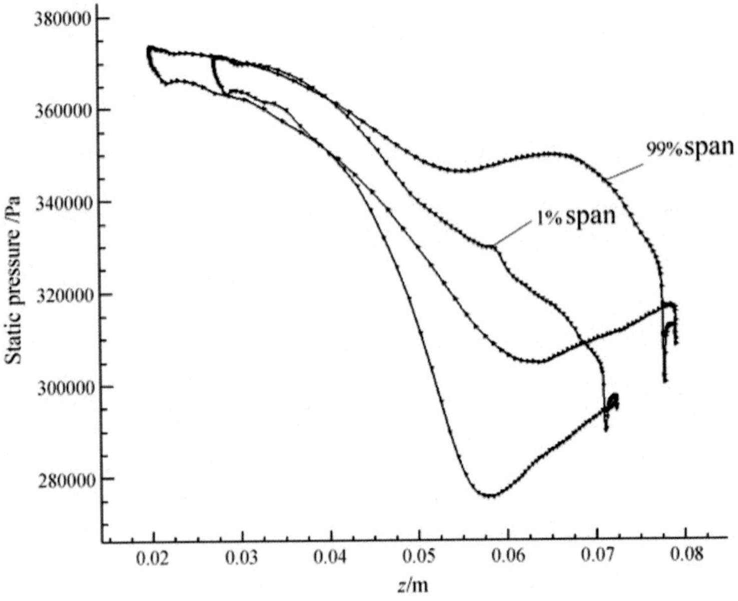

Fig. 4.13 Static pressure distribution at 1 and 99% of the vane span at a −5° turning angle

descent, while the change law of the suction surface is the same as that at the 0° turning angle. The area surrounded by the static pressure distribution line reveals that the root load of the vane significantly increases after a turning angle of +5° and that the load is mainly located at the rear part of the vane.

Figure 4.13 reflects the change in the static pressure distribution when the turning angle is nearly −5°. The distribution law of the pressure at the vane tip pressure surface is the same as that at the 0° turning angle, that is, it gently declines. The trend at the vane suction surface has not changed. On the pressure surface of the vane root, the same distribution law as that of the vane tip pressure surface shown in Fig. 4.12 appears, and the trend at the vane suction surface has not changed.

Since the gap clearance at a turning angle of 0° is uniform, the effect of the shape of the nonuniform gap clearance on the endwall flow of the variable vane can be obtained by a comparison with the static pressure distribution at a turning angle of 0°. The gap clearance height is the main factor affecting the vane pressure distribution trend. As shown in Fig. 4.10, at the vane root for the −5° turning angle, the gap clearance gradually increases after 50% of the axial chord length. Additionally, at the vane tip for the −5° turning angle, the gap clearance gradually increases after 50% of the chord length. Precisely because of the continuous increase in the endwall gap, the development of the endwall leakage flow is not effectively suppressed, and the fluid on the vane pressure surface continues to flow into the gap, leading to the disappearance of the gentle zone in the static pressure distribution trend of the vane pressure surface.

Therefore, the above analysis reveals that the existence of the vane-end gap clearance affects the static pressure distribution in the vicinity and that the influence of the gap clearance on the local flow field is also reflected from the side. In addition, the vane leakage loss causes the pressure in the front half of the endwall pressure surface to rapidly drop, and the nonuniform gap clearance will affect the static pressure distribution trend of the vane end. The gradual increase in the gap clearance will cause the static pressure of the vane pressure surface to more rapidly drop in the axial direction, thus reflecting the trend of increasing gap clearances to accelerate leakage and to increase gap leakage loss.

As indicated by the total pressure coefficient in Fig. 4.14, the total pressure loss coefficient at the tip and bottom of the variable vane is relatively large, mainly due to the gap clearance structure of the variable vane. To prevent the variable vane from being jammed by the casing when rotating, a sufficiently large gap is provided at the end of the variable vane, and the existence of the gap causes a large vane-end leakage loss. The main areas of gap clearance leakage are concentrated both below the 18% vane span and above the 80% vane span. In addition, when the variable vanes are at +7° and +5°, the total pressure loss coefficient at both endwalls is the smallest. When the turning angle is 10°, the total pressure loss at the vane-endwalls increases, while the total pressure loss at 50% of the vane span is the smallest at a 0° vane turning angle. When the vane is at a positive turning angle, the total pressure loss at the midspan slightly increases. When the turning angle becomes positive, the total pressure loss at the midspan significantly increases. Therefore, the turning of the variable vane affects not only the total pressure loss at the vane midspan but also

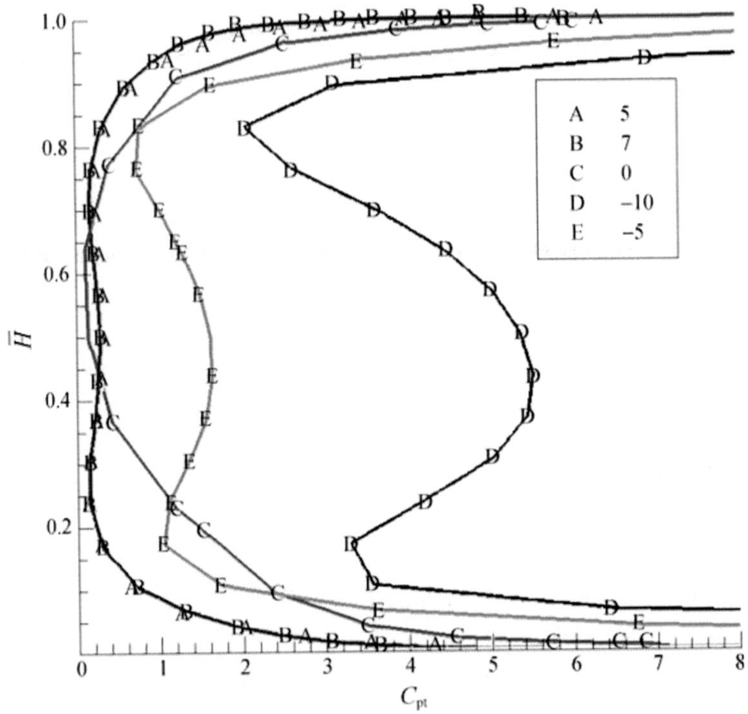

Fig. 4.14 Spanwise total pressure loss coefficient distribution at the variable vane outlet for variable geometry turbines with a cylindrical endwall

that at the vane endwalls. Furthermore, when the vane is closed, the total pressure loss of the variable vane is increased more significantly than when it is opened.

2. Spherical endwall

As previously mentioned, due to the effects of the endwall structure of the cylindrical variable geometry turbine, when the variable vane is installed, there is a requirement for the selection of the endwall gap, that is, to ensure that the vane is not blocked by the casing when rotating. To address this problem, this section modifies the endwall structure of the turbine and compares the performance of the variable geometry turbine before and after modification. In addition, this section adopts the same variable geometry scheme as the cylindrical endwall turbine for the modified spherical endwall turbine and compares the aerodynamic characteristics of different endwall turbines and the local flow field at different turning angles.

The design idea of the endwall at the variable vane in the variable geometry turbine is to transform the traditional cylindrical endwall into a spherical endwall. The purpose of the spherical endwall clearance design is described as follows: In most cylindrical variable geometry turbine vanes, the gap clearance height at the vane end is changing. Therefore, when the vane turning angle is too large, the vane and the endwall of the casing will be stuck. To avoid the occurrence of such phenomena, the gap clearance height of the cylindrical endwall case will generally be correspondingly increased during the design process to avoid the phenomenon of jamming, which will increase the vane-end leakage loss. The spherical endwall designed in this section can ensure that the vane-end gap clearance remains unchanged during rotation. In the vane design, only the effect of thermal stress on the gap clearance needs to be considered, disregarding the effect of vane rotation factors.

The specific design process is presented as follows:

1. Required parameters: variable vane profile data (vane tip section profile data and vane bottom profile data) and meridional flow channel data (shroud profile data and hub profile data).
2. Modification steps:

1) Determining the turning shaft: as shown in Fig. 4.15, the Z_2 line is the variable vane turning shaft. Point O is the intersection of the turbine rotor and vane turning shaft.

Specific requirements:

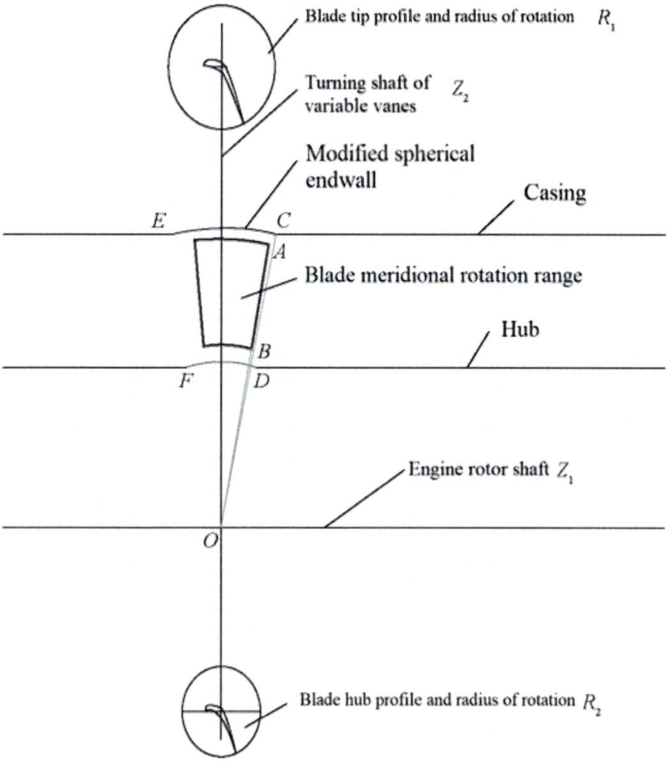

Fig. 4.15 Schematic of the transformation of the cylindrical endwall into a spherical endwall

(1) The turning shaft of the vane should pass through the tip section and bottom section of the vane;
(2) The turning shaft of the vane passes through the rotor shaft.

2) Determining the turning radius of the vane (that is, the turning range of the variable vane)

Using the vane turning shaft position and vane tip cross-section data, the maximum radius from the vane shape data point to the vane turning shaft can be calculated as the vane turning radius. As shown in the figure, the tip R_1 line contains the vane-end section profile, and the vane meridional scheme turning range is drawn on the meridional channel surface according to the vane tip and bottom section heights. The positions of points *A* and *B* are the positions of the largest area formed on the meridional surface when the vane upper and lower endwalls rotate.

3) Determining the radius *R* of the spherical endwall.

The position and radius of the spherical endwall through the positions of points *O*, *A*, and *B* are determined. The *OA* extension and shroud line are connected to *C* and the *OB* and hub line are connected to *D*, with *O* as the center and *OC* and *OD* as the radii. The shroud, hub lines at *E* and *F*, and arcs *CE* and *DF* are intersected to form the modified spherical endwall.

To investigate the influence of the endwall and gap clearance on the aerodynamic efficiency of the turbine, this section uses four different schemes to conduct a comparative study. The four schemes consist of a 0.5 mm gap on the spherical endwall, a 0.8 mm gap on the spherical endwall, a 0.5 mm gap on the cylindrical endwall, and a 0.8 mm gap on the cylindrical endwall.

For the schemes analyzed in this section, as shown in Table 4.5, the efficiency of the variable vanes with different meridional channels with the same gap clearance and the aerodynamic performance of different gap vanes with the same meridional channel are compared: With the same vane-end clearance, the efficiency for the spherical endwall case is slightly higher than that for the cylindrical endwall case; with the same turbine endwall, the efficiency for the small gap case is higher than that for the large gap case; the maximum effect of the endwall change on the efficiency is 0.12%, and the maximum effect of the gap clearance change on the efficiency is 0.67%. Therefore, the change in the vane-end gap is the main factor affecting the turbine efficiency change.

To analyze the effect of different endwalls on the overall performance of the variable geometry turbine, this section performs variable geometry treatments on

Table 4.5 Comparison of isentropic efficiency for different schemes

Schemes	Efficiency (%)
Spherical endwall (0.5 mm)	92.114
Spherical endwall (0.8 mm)	91.448
Cylindrical endwall (0.5 mm)	92.083
Cylindrical endwall (0.8 mm)	91.394

the spherical endwall turbine according to the above findings. Since the endwall clearance of the spherical endwall vanes does not change with the turning angle, a spherical clearance height of 0.5 mm is selected in the current investigation.

Table 4.6 shows the efficiency distribution for the spherical endwall cases for different vane turning angles. When the vane is at a turning angle of 0°, its efficiency is the highest. When the vane rotates toward −10° and +7°, the efficiency decreases, but when the vane rotates forward, the rate of efficiency decrease is significantly higher than that when the vane rotates backward. From the mass flow point of view, the vane is at the highest efficiency when it is operating at the design flow rate. Both the large flow rate and small flow rate will reduce the turbine efficiency, and the small flow rate will have a greater impact on the efficiency drop.

As shown in Fig. 4.16, through the modified design of the endwall, the variable geometry turbine flow has been improved at all turning angles. In Fig. 4.17, a comparison of the efficiency distribution of the variable geometry turbines between the spherical endwall and the cylindrical endwall shows that the spherical endwall increases the efficiency of the variable geometry turbine at all turning angles, but the degree of improvement is different. At a 0° turning angle, the efficiency is increased by 0.72%, while at a −10° turning angle, the efficiency is increased by 0.53%. At a +7° turning angle, the efficiency is increased by 0.69%, which shows that the use of spherical endwalls and narrowing the gap can effectively improve the variable geometry turbine multiturning angle aerodynamic performance. In addition, in the efficiency curve of the cylinder endwall, when the turning angle ranges from 0° to +5°, the efficiency shows an upward trend, while in the spherical endwall, the efficiency shows a downward trend, indicating that the trend of the gap clearance change in the cylinder endwall may help improve the efficiency.

In Fig. 4.18, when the turning angle is +7°, +5°, and 0°, the total pressure loss at the outlet of the vanes on the spherical endwall is mainly concentrated below 20 and 90%. When the turning angle is −5° and −10°, the total pressure loss at the outlet of the variable vane significantly increases, and at a turning angle of −10°, the loss at the bottom of the vane is higher than that at the tip of the vane. As shown in Fig 4.18, when the variable vane is at a +7° turning angle, the total pressure loss coefficient at the 20−80% vane span is approximately 0.3, and at a 0° turning angle, the midspan total pressure loss reaches 0.8. When the turning angle is −5° and −10°, the total

Table 4.6 Overall parameters of variable geometry turbines with spherical endwalls

Turning angle	Efficiency	Mass flow (Ratio to design value)	Power (Ratio to design value)	Total pressure recovery coefficient
+7°	0.9163	1.1443	1.0789	0.9383
+5°	0.9198	1.1112	1.0645	0.9309
0°	0.9211	1.0000	1.0000	0.9242
−5°	0.9037	0.8304	0.8424	0.9118
−10°	0.80975	0.5644	0.5215	0.8633

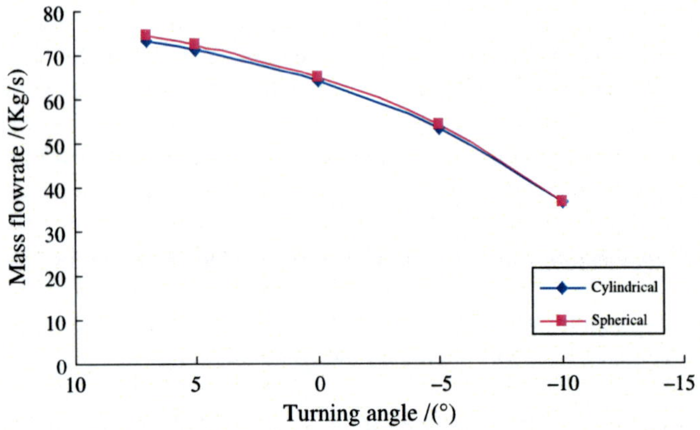

Fig. 4.16 Comparison of the mass flow rate at different turning angles for variable vanes with different endwalls

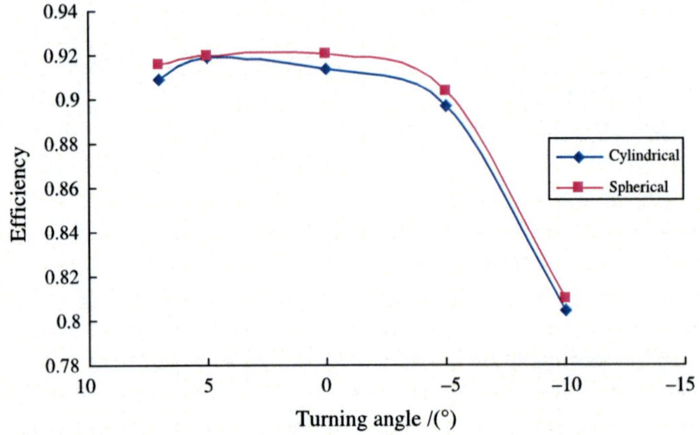

Fig. 4.17 Comparison of the efficiency at different turning angles for variable vanes with different endwalls

outlet pressure loss at the middle location of the vane sharply increases, reaching 1.5 and 4.5, respectively.

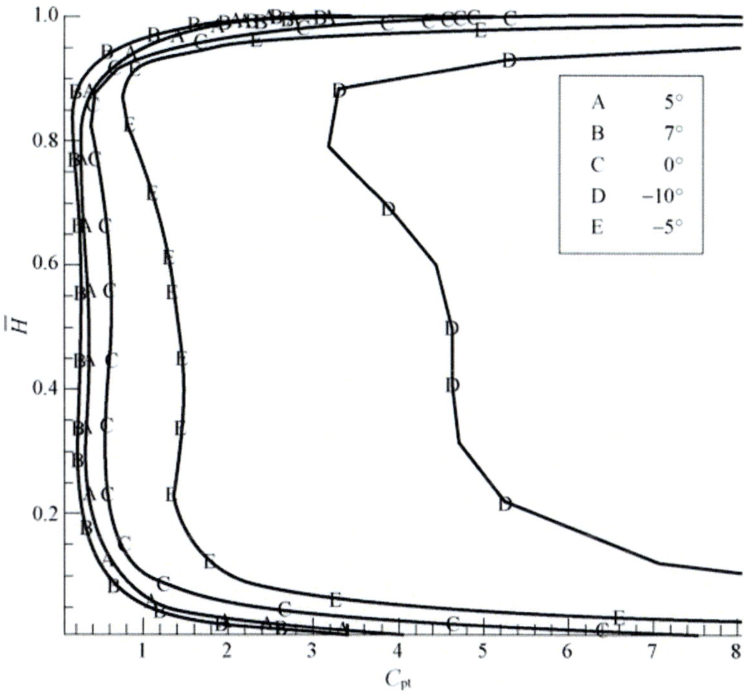

Fig. 4.18 Spherical endwall vane outlet total pressure loss distribution along the spanwise direction

4.2 Investigation of a New Method for Controlling Variable Vane Endwall Loss

4.2.1 Variable Vane-End Slotting/Winglet Technology

1. Vane-end slotting technology

The vane tip groove structure can effectively suppress gap clearance leakage and leakage loss, which has been confirmed by numerous studies. Therefore, the vane-end groove structure should also be utilized to control the variable vane-end gap leakage loss. To verify the effectiveness of the vane-end groove technology, Fig. 4.19 shows the research scheme of the variable vane-end groove, in which the flat-tip scheme without the turning shaft and the flat-tip scheme with the turning shaft are employed for comparison.

According to the above analysis, the position of the turning shaft of the variable vane has a great influence on the flow fields of the variable vane. For different vanes, the load in the endwall zone and the distribution position of the high leakage zone are different. Generally, the turning shaft is arranged at 20–50% of the chord length. In the calculation model in this section, the position of the turning shaft is at 50%

(a) No shaft, flat tip (b) With shaft, flat tip (c) With shaft, cavity tip

Fig. 4.19 Research scheme for vane tip cavities

of the axial chord length of the cascade. For the selection of the diameter of the turning shaft, generally, the larger the diameter of the turning shaft is, the larger the proportion of the turning shaft in the gap clearance, and the smaller the leakage area. However, as the diameter of the turning shaft continues to increase, the axial pressure gradient in the area behind the shaft increases, and a highly loaded area appears behind the shaft. In addition, considering the actual structure of the vane, the turning shaft should be assembled with other complicated components. In summary, the diameter of the turning shaft is 21 mm. In this section, the depth of the vane-end groove is set to 2 mm, and the thickness between the groove sidewall and the vane surface is set to 1.5 mm. Considering the actual machining process, note that rounding treatment is performed at the junction of the groove and the turning shaft to meet the requirements of the machining process.

Table 4.7 shows the gap leakage flow rate and total pressure recovery coefficient for different schemes. The end of scheme B does not have a shaft; it is flat-tipped, and the gap clearance is 0.3 mm. Compared with the end of scheme A, the total pressure recovery coefficient is somewhat decreasing. The drop is mainly attributed to the effect of the gap clearance leakage flow loss. Comparing scheme C with the shaft and scheme B without the shaft for the flat tips, the relative gap flow leakage rate is reduced by 19.81%, and the total pressure recovery coefficient is increased, indicating that the presence of the turning shaft can reduce the gap clearance leakage flow. The turning shaft makes the endwall gap clearance leakage flow area smaller; the circular flow caused by the turning shaft and the backflow vortex behind the turning shaft increase the turbulence of the downstream flow; and the resistance to suppress the leakage flow at the vane end accordingly increases. Comparing scheme D with grooves at the end of the shaft and scheme B with flat tips at the end of the shaft, the relative gap leakage rate is decreased by 21.98%, and the total pressure recovery coefficient is increased to a certain extent, which shows that the simultaneous existence of the turning shaft and vane-end groove can better suppress the vane-end gap leakage.

Figure 4.20 shows the static pressure distribution in the middle section of the gap clearance for different vane-end structures. The static pressure distribution in the gap clearance at 99.85% of the vane span is shown for three schemes. As the

Table 4.7 Gap leakage mass flow rate and total pressure recovery coefficient for different schemes

	Outlet mass flow rate (kg/s)	Gap leakage mass flow rate (kg/s)	Relative gap leakage ratio (%)	Total pressure recovery coefficient (%)
A: No gap	0.3673	–	–	98.77
B: No shaft, flat tip	0.3676	0.0046	1.27	98.03
C: With shaft, flat tip	0.3671	0.0037	1.02	98.10
D: With shaft, cavity tip	0.3669	0.0036	0.99	98.19

turbine vane cascade channels gradually shrink, along the streamwise direction, the vane pressure gradually decreases, the change trend and pressure distribution on the pressure surface side are basically the same, and the static pressure on the suction surface side greatly changes. Since the fluid quickly flows into the gap clearance at the small gap on the vane pressure surface, the pressure gradient between the pressure surface and the gap clearance greatly changes, as shown in the enlarged view. For scheme B, in which the vane adopts flat tips, after 50% of the axial chord length, there is a lower pressure area near the pressure surface because the endwall fluid directly flows through the gap clearance through the pressure surface. At this time, the fluid has high kinetic energy. According to the Bernoulli equation, the fluid accelerates in the narrow gap clearance, and the static pressure decreases; it decelerates when entering the vane suction side, and the static pressure increases. Under the action of the transverse pressure gradient, the fluid in the gap clearance flows out of the vane suction surface. Next, the fluid shifts to the middle of the vane span, and the distribution of the low-pressure zone is mainly concentrated in the middle and downstream areas of the vane. In scheme C, the fluid static pressure behind the turning shaft is increased compared with the same position in scheme B. In scheme D, the vane end is grooved. Compared with scheme C and scheme B, the static pressure of the groove is significantly increased, the distribution range of the low-pressure area downstream of the vane gradually decreases, and the low-pressure area gradually spreads out.

To analyze the gap clearance leakage flow pattern at the outlet of the cascade, the entropy distribution at 10% of the axial cross-section of the cascade outlet is investigated, as shown in Fig. 4.21. Different vane-end shapes have a great influence on the vane flow fields and performances. The source of the loss at the vane end is mainly caused by the dissipation of the leakage vortex and the interaction of the passage vortex. Due to the existence of the vane-end turning shaft and the vane-end grooves, the high-entropy zone at the core of the vane-end leakage vortex is significantly reduced in scheme D compared with scheme C and scheme B. Since the rotation directions of the leakage vortex and the passage vortex are opposite, changes in the shape of the leakage vortex will inevitably affect the formation and development of the passage vortex. In addition, the passage vortex in schemes B and

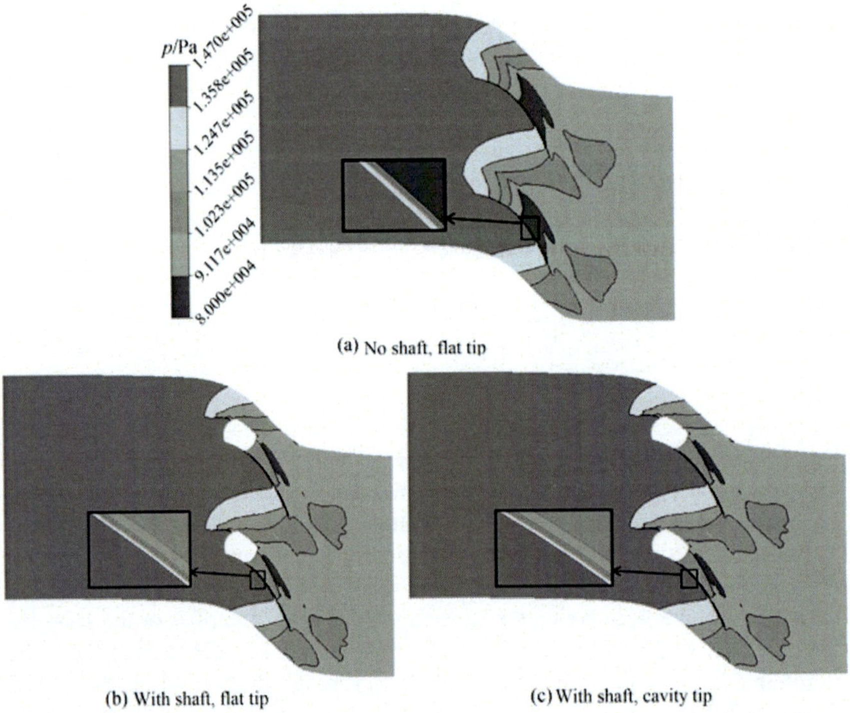

Fig. 4.20 Static pressure distribution in the middle section of the gap for different vane-end clearance structures

C does not produce a clear core area, while the passage vortex in scheme D clearly indicates a high-entropy core area, which shows that the vane-end groove structure does not show obvious advantages in the formation of the passage vortex. Compared with scheme C and scheme B, scheme D has many low-energy fluid clusters near the groove in front of the turning shaft. This part of the fluid will eventually be completely sucked by the passage vortex, and these low-energy fluid clusters are the main reason for passage vortex enhancement.

Figure 4.22 shows the entropy distribution of the variable vane at different axial chord lengths. The mass-averaged entropy of scheme D is greater than that of schemes C and B because the existence of the turning shaft and grooves complicates the endwall zone flow. Compared with scheme B without a turning shaft, the flow process additionally increases the effects of the cylindrical flow around the turning shaft and numerous vortices in the vane-end groove. These are important reasons for the increase in resistance during the leakage flow process, which also increases the irreversible degree of the flow process. The mass-averaged entropy of each section of scheme B gradually increases along the flow direction, while the entropy difference of scheme C at 20% of the axial chord length and 50% of the axial chord length is very small. However, the mass-averaged entropy of scheme C is much larger than

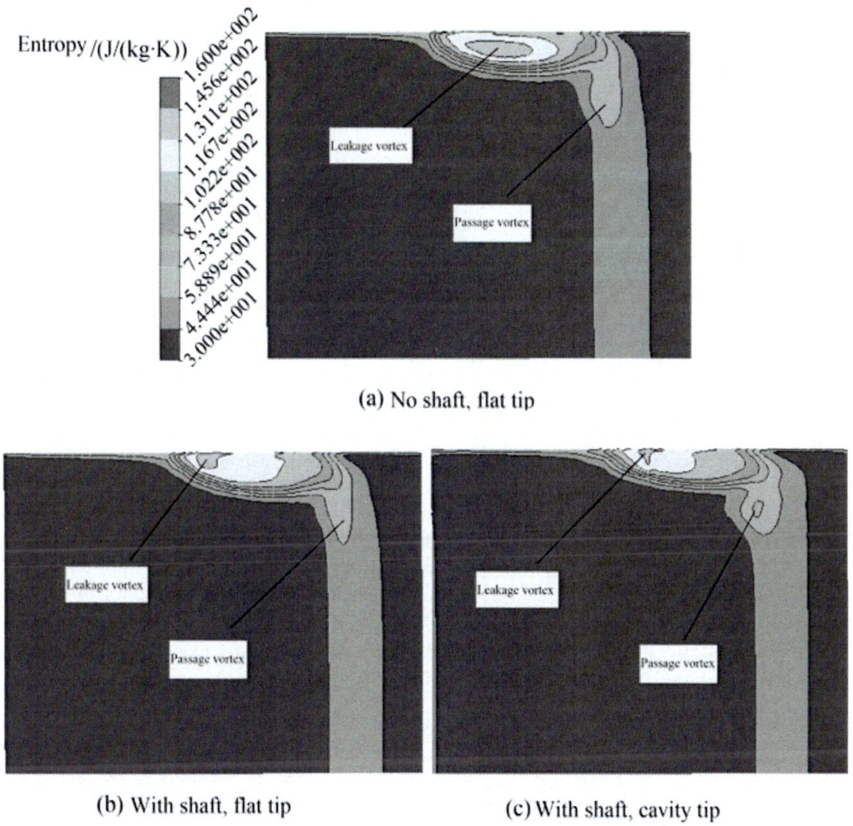

Fig. 4.21 Entropy distribution at 10% of the axial chord section of the variable vane for different vane-end structures

that of scheme B. Thus, the presence of the turning shaft affects not only the entropy distribution of each section after the turning shaft but also the entropy distribution of each section before the turning shaft. In addition, the distribution of the mass-averaged entropy of each section of scheme D is slightly increased compared with scheme C, indicating that the increase in entropy caused by the addition of grooves is not obvious.

2. Vane-end winglet technology

The vane-end winglet technology can effectively suppress the vane-end gap clearance leakage and leakage loss. This section discusses the feasibility of its application to the end of the variable vane through numerical calculations. Figure 4.23 shows the research scheme of the variable vane-end winglet structure, and the flat tip scheme is employed as a baseline. The width of the winglet is uniformly distributed along the vane-end profile. To ensure that the vane tip surface can completely include the end of the turning shaft, a width of 5 mm is initially given. In addition, the winglet

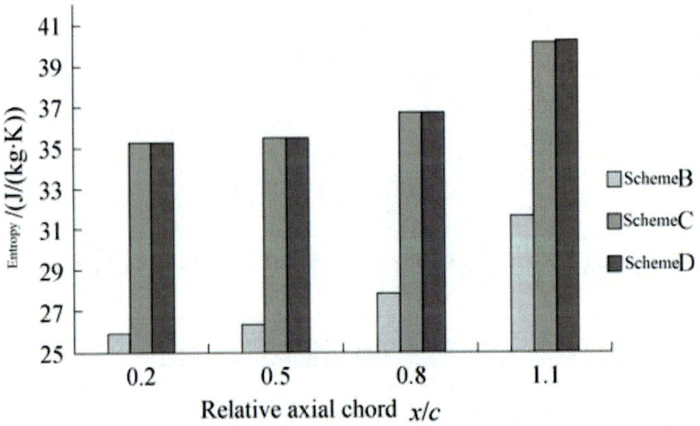

Fig. 4.22 Entropy distribution at vane cross-sections of different axial chord lengths

and vane are rounded in a 45° direction. The extended winglet structure parameter is relatively small relative to the cascade pitch and does not affect the actual installation.

The end structure of the variable vane contributes to the end part of the gap clearance and the resulting gap clearance leakage flow. Figure 4.24 shows the endwall streamlines and the casing dimensionless static pressure distribution for the variable vane with winglets at the vane end and baseline vanes at a zero turning angle. The presence of the turning shaft reduces the circumferential leakage area and thereby has a certain role in blocking the gap clearance leakage. In addition, the turning shaft divides the gap clearance leakage flow into two parts: the gap clearance leakage flow on the front side of the turning shaft is weak, which is mainly attributed to the small lateral pressure gradient; on the rear side of the turning shaft, the lateral pressure gradient is large, strengthening the gap clearance leakage flow. The rear side of the turning shaft is the main area of vane-end gap clearance leakage.

The streamline and static pressure distribution of the vane end in Fig. 4.24 shows a low-speed recirculation area along the flow direction behind the turning shaft.

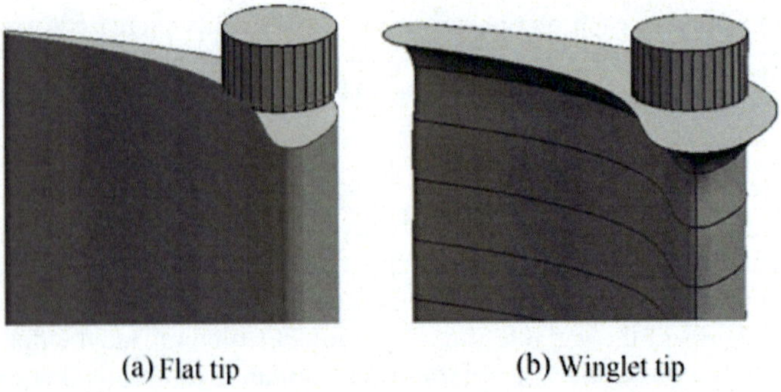

Fig. 4.23 Investigated variable vane-end winglet structure

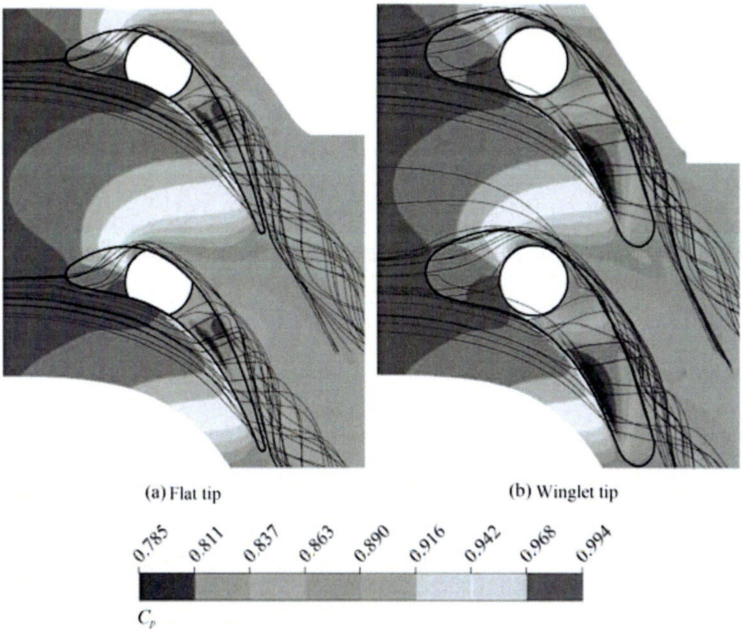

Fig. 4.24 Vane-end streamlines and casing dimensionless static pressure distribution

Considering that the direction of the streamline near the turning shaft is oblique to the main leakage flow, it can be speculated that there is a relatively obvious interference between the flow effect around the turning shaft and the gap clearance leakage flow. Subsequently, the leakage flow flows out of the vane-end gap, the gap leakage vortex core is formed, and the leakage flow on the front side of the turning shaft forms a leakage vortex around the leakage vortex core. A comparison of Fig. 4.24a and b reveals that the vane end with winglets moves the low-pressure area on the rear side of the turning shaft toward the vane trailing edge and that the vane end with winglets also increases the low-pressure area. However, the static pressure on the pressure side of the gap clearance decreases, while the pressure on the vane suction side significantly increases, and the overall lateral pressure gradient at the vane end is reduced. This finding can be confirmed by the effect of the tip winglet in Fig. 4.25 on the vane-end load distribution.

Figure 4.25 also shows that the effect of the flow around the turning shaft has a significant effect on the load distribution at the vane end. Especially on the suction side of the near gap, near the front side of the turning shaft, the pressure at the vane end sharply decreases due to the influence of the gas flow around the turning shaft. During the process of rotating around the turning shaft, the pressure at the vane end also slightly fluctuates. On the rear side of the shaft, the pressure at the vane end suddenly decreases due to the presence of the low-speed recirculation zone. The winglets on the vane end smooth the static pressure change on the pressure side and the suction side of the gap clearance near the vane end, significantly reducing

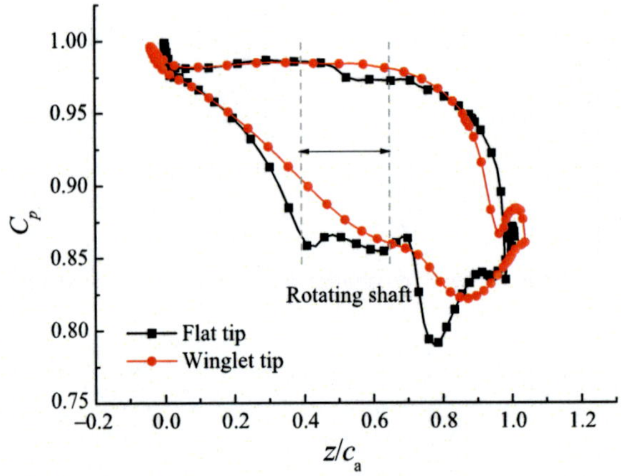

Fig. 4.25 Effects of winglet tip on near-tip load distribution

the effect of the flow around the turning shaft, and the load on the vane end is also significantly reduced, which reduces the gap leakage driving force and gap clearance leakage flow to a certain extent.

The above analysis can also be confirmed from the comparative distribution of the Mach number at the 70% axial chord cross-section of the two vane-end structures, as shown in Fig. 4.26, where the right side is the vane suction side. As shown in Fig. 4.26, because the winglet structure at the vane end significantly reduces the load at the near vane end, the leakage jet velocity in the gap clearance also decreases, and the range of the low velocity region where the leakage vortex on the suction side of the gap exist is also significantly reduced.

As clearly shown in the entropy-increase profile in the variable vane cascade in Fig. 4.27, in the fourth section, that is, the area before the front side of the turning shaft, there is no obvious change in the range and peak of the loss area caused by the gap clearance leakage. However, downstream, the gap leakage loss has been significantly reduced, especially in the last two cross-sectional areas.

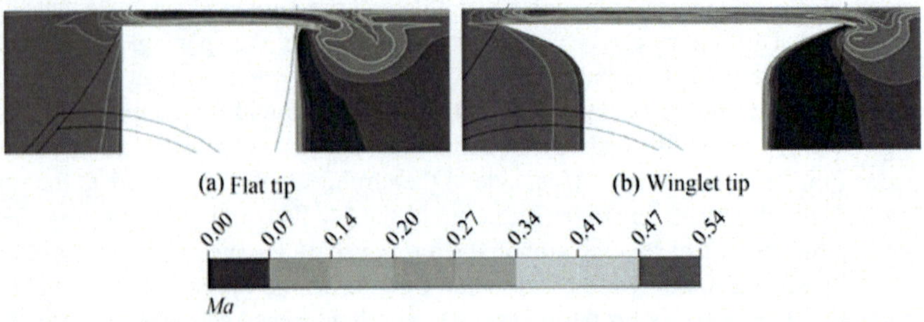

Fig. 4.26 Mach number distribution at the 70% axial chord cross-section

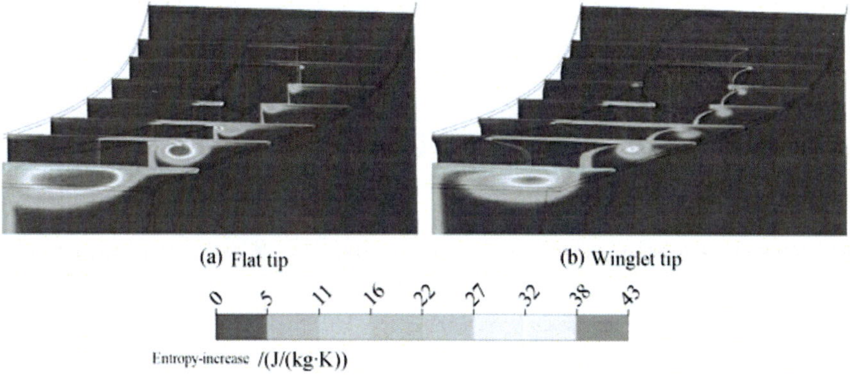

Fig. 4.27 Entropy-increase contour inside the variable vane cascade

The turning of variable vanes changes the vane throat area, which not only changes the vane load distribution and its size for variable geometry turbines but also has an important impact on the turbine vane cascade channel loss and matching with the downstream blade rows. Figure 4.28 shows a comparison of the total pressure loss coefficient of the variable vane cascade for different turning angles. The closing of the variable vane significantly increases channel loss, while the opening of the variable vane reduces channel loss. In addition, the vane-end winglets reduce the loss of the vane channel at all turning angles.

Figure 4.29 shows the pitchwise-averaged outflow angle distribution along the vane span for the two variable vane-end structures at different turning angles. As pointed out in previous research results, the closing of the variable vanes reduces the outlet angle, while the opening of the variable vanes increases the outlet angle, which satisfies the requirements of gas turbine variable geometry turbine regulation.

Fig. 4.28 Comparison of the variable vane total pressure loss coefficient at different vane turning angles

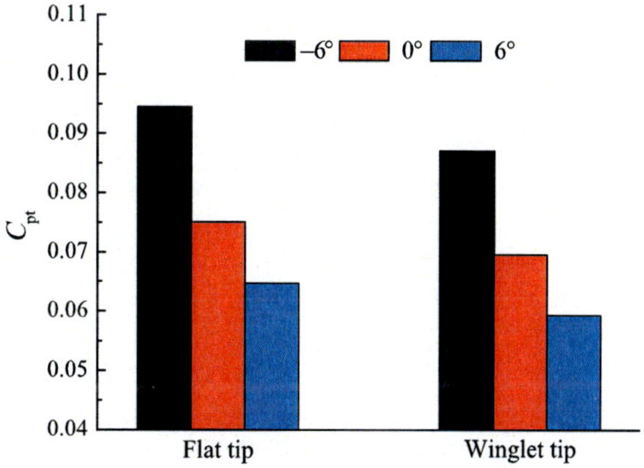

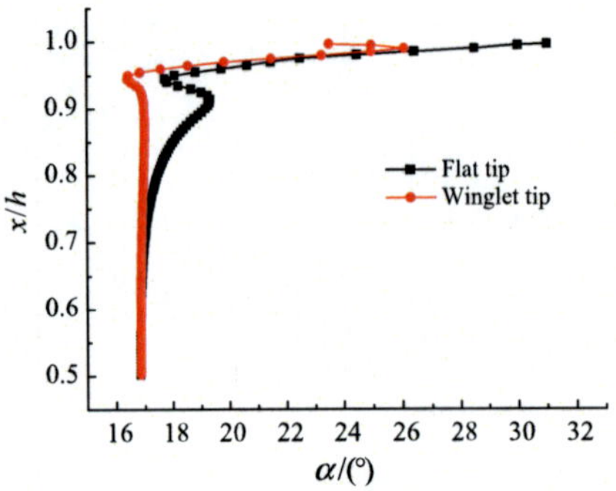

(a) -6° turning angle

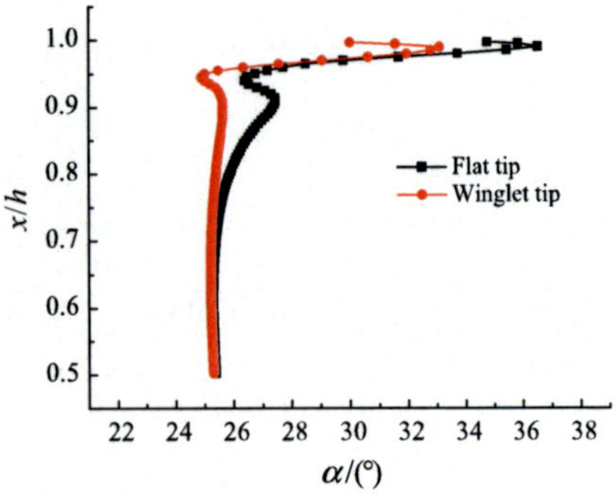

(b) 0° turning angle

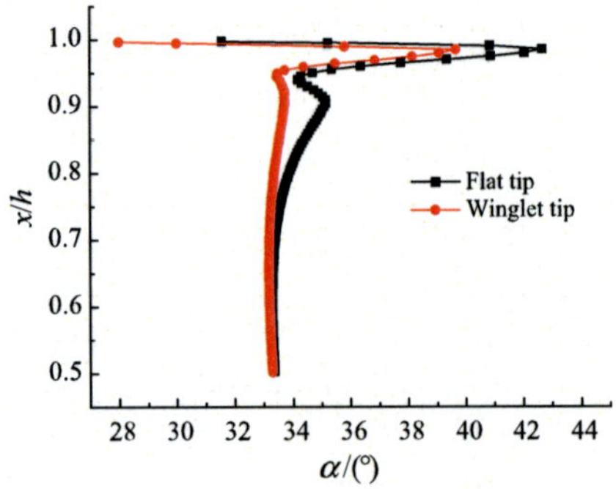

(c) +6° turning angle

Fig. 4.29 Pitch-averaged spanwise outflow angle distribution at different vane turning angles

Figure 4.29 shows that the winglet at the vane end significantly reduces the under-deflection of the gas flow at the end of the vane at all turning angles, especially at a −6° turning angle.

Note that the rear gap of the variable vane turning shaft is the main area of the vane-end gap leakage. Marine gas turbines are operated under partial load conditions for more than 90% of their lifetime, which means that the variable vanes will be operated in a turn-down state or closed state for a long time, which further makes the partial gap downstream of the turning shaft become the main gap leakage area. To further reduce the gap clearance leakage flow at the end of the variable vane, this subsection attempts to provide a groove structure on the base of the vane-end winglet to further increase the leakage flow resistance and to reduce the gap leakage driving force, thereby significantly reducing gap leakage loss. The preliminary design of the variable vane-end groove-winglet structure for variable geometry turbines is shown in Fig. 4.30. A groove structure is provided on the front and back sides of the variable vane turning shaft, wherein the width and depth of the groove shoulder wall are 1.4 and 1.8 mm, respectively.

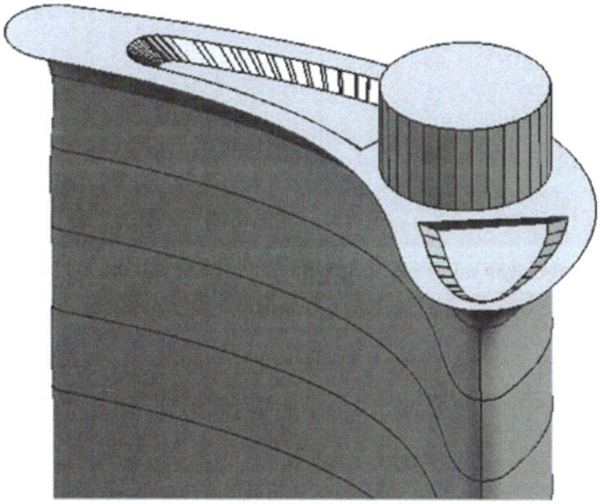

Fig. 4.30 Variable vane-end cavity-winglet structure

Figure 4.31 shows the distribution of the pitchwise-averaged total pressure loss coefficient along the vane span for different vane-end structures, where the gap clearance height is 1 mm. Based on the winglet structure, the vane-end groove-winglet structure is assumed to further reduce the vane-end gap leakage loss.

Figure 4.32 shows the change curve of the total pressure loss coefficient of the variable vane for different vane-end structures with the gap clearance. At vane-end gaps of 1 and 2 mm, the vane-end winglet structure and groove-winglet structure reduce the total pressure loss coefficient at the variable vane outlet, the loss of the groove-winglet structure is reduced, and the maximum pressure loss coefficient of the variable vane is reduced by a maximum of 8.9%. However, the control effect of the two structures on the channel loss with different gap clearance heights differs. As shown in Fig. 4.32, the vane-end winglet structure increases the sensitivity of the variable

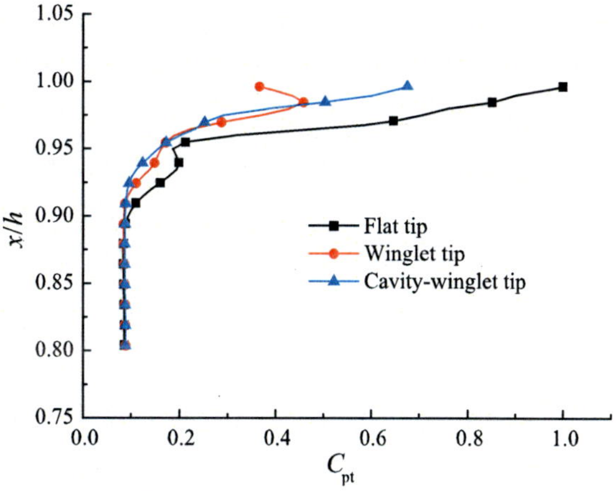

Fig. 4.31 Spanwise total pressure loss distribution for different vane-end structures

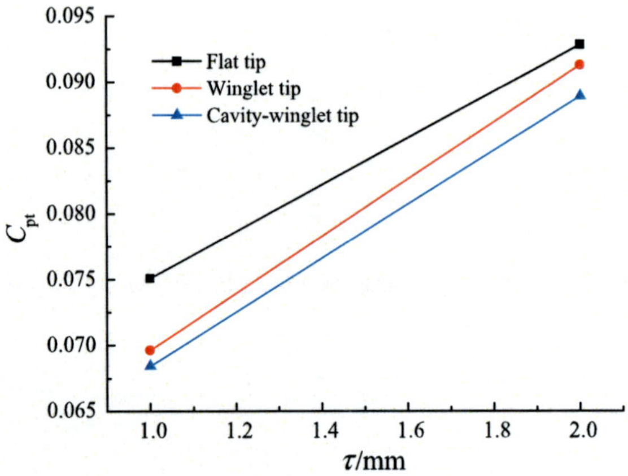

Fig. 4.32 Total pressure loss coefficient variation with the gap clearance height for different vane-end structures

vane performance to gap clearance changes. The vane-end winglet combined with the groove structure reduces the sensitivity to vane-end gap changes, and the sensitivity of the variable vane performance to the gap clearance change is comparable to that of the baseline.

4.2.2 Variable Vane-End Modification Technology for a High Endwall Angle Turbine

The power turbine of modern marine gas turbines is generally a large meridional expansion structure, especially in the vane casing. Figure 4.33 shows the variable vane-end position at −6° and 8° turning angles. When the variable vane is closed (−6°), on the front side of the tip of the suction side of the vane, the end of the turning shaft protrudes from the casing; on the rear side of the tip of the vane, the end of the turning shaft is slightly recessed. For most of the tip of the pressure side of the vane, the end of the turning shaft almost sinks into the inside of the casing, forming a large depression (not shown in the figure). Both protrusions and depressions interfere with the flow in the endwall zone and become more obvious with an increase in the vane turning angle, thereby worsening the endwall flows. Similarly, when the variable vane is opened (8°), a protrusion is formed on the tip of the pressure side of the variable vane, and a depression is formed on the tip of the suction side, which also significantly interferes with the gas flow in the endwall zone. Therefore, it can be speculated that for the large meridional expansion variable geometry turbine, whether the variable vane is opened or closed, the end of the turning shaft has a significant interference with the flow in the endwall zone, producing a strong secondary flow. In addition, for large meridional expansion variable geometry turbines, it is generally necessary to give a larger gap clearance at the end of the variable vane, which will inevitably produce a stronger leakage flow, thereby complicating the endwall zone flow.

To carry out the turning design of vanes for variable geometry turbines, we should fully understand the problem of the position change of the end of the vane: when the vane is at a −6° turning angle, the problem of improving the depression on the pressure side of the turning shaft will improve the performance of the corresponding turbine stage at a −6° turning angle. However, when the vane is at a turning angle of + 6°, the situation where the pressure side of the turning shaft protrudes from the casing will be more serious. Similarly, when the vane is at a +6° turning angle, improving the problem of the suction side of the turning shaft sinking into the casing will cause the suction side of the turning shaft at a −6 degree turning angle to sink deeper into the casing. Therefore, the problem of the relative change in the end position of the variable geometry turbine variable vane during the turning of vanes should be understood, and then the mutual interference mechanism of the variable vane-end gap flow and associated losses is clarified. Based on this approach, the relatively effective vane turning design method for large meridional expansion variable geometry turbines can be obtained.

Figure 4.34 shows the entropy increase distribution along the axial section of the vane at different turning angles. At the three turning angles, there is no obvious loss change on the pressure side vane tip, while the suction side has different loss areas. Among them, the transverse pressure gradient at the front end of the variable vane turning shaft is small, the flow velocity is low, the entropy increase is basically unchanged, and the loss is small. Simultaneously, the development of the fluid along the axial direction gradually increases. Considering the existence of the gap clearance behind the turning shaft with the increase in the lateral driving force behind the vane turning shaft, the three cases show a relatively sharp leakage vortex core loss area.

When the turning angle of the vane is −6°s, although the position of the pressure side shaft end is recessed relative to the shaft hole, there is no obvious loss change. Simultaneously, a small-scale vortex system is generated at the shaft end of the suction side, and the strength and scale of the vortex system are relatively

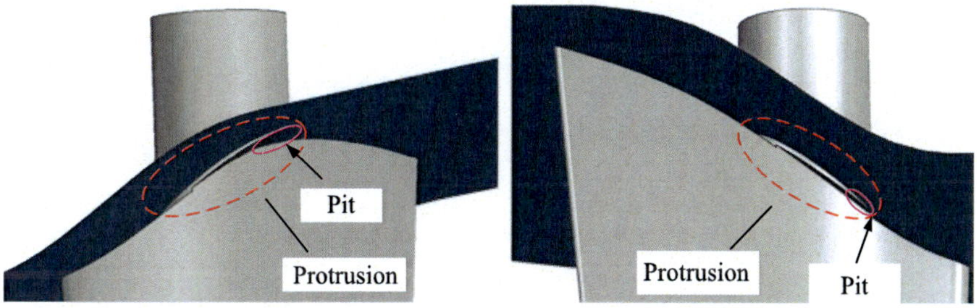

Fig. 4.33 Variable vane-end position at −6° and 8° turning angles

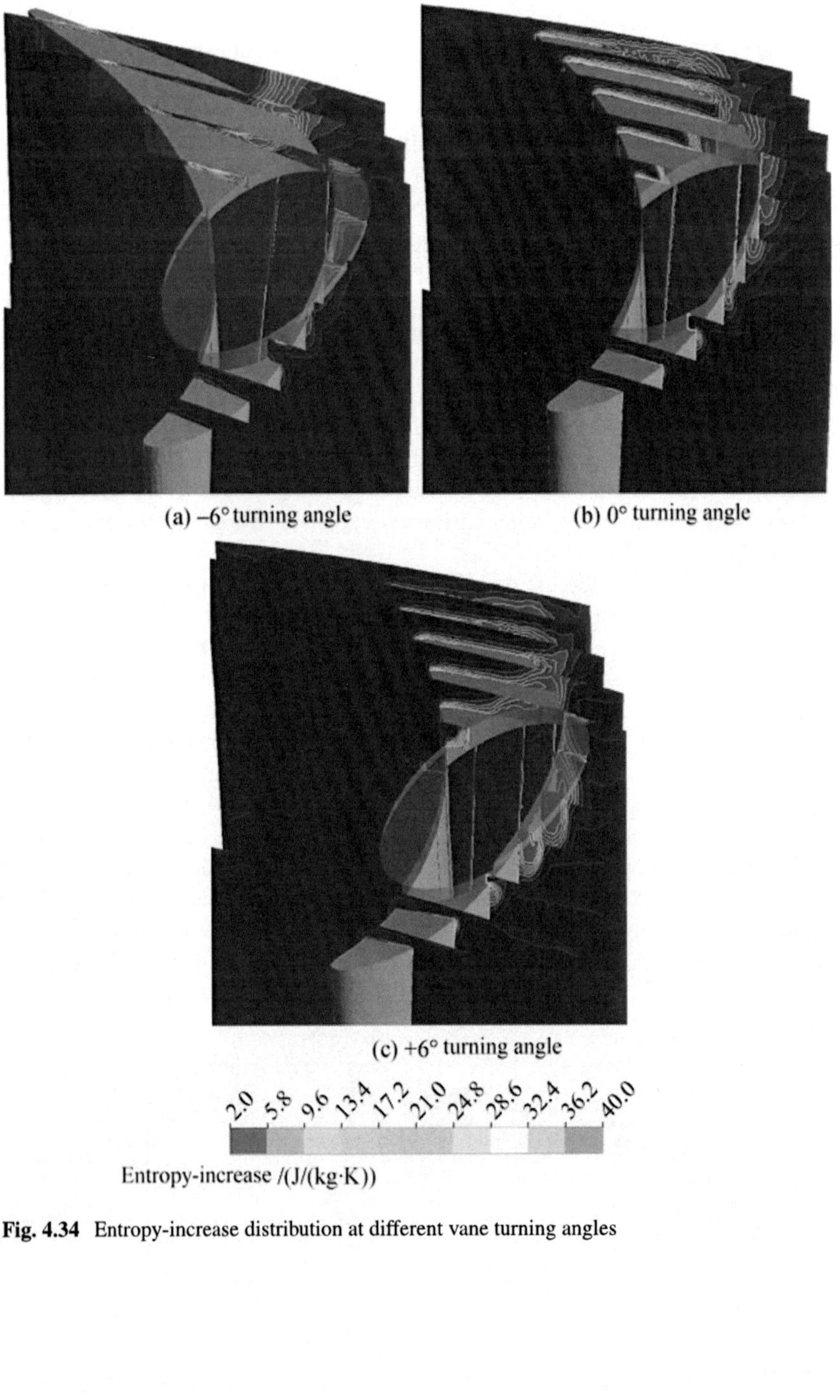

Fig. 4.34 Entropy-increase distribution at different vane turning angles

small. Observing the rear side of the vane turning shaft, the low-energy fluid on the pressure side endwall zone, under the action of the lateral pressure gradient, evolves into a vane-end gap clearance leakage vortex. With the development along the flow direction, the scale and strength of the vortex system gradually strengthen, forming a concentrated area of endwall zone losses.

When the vane turning angle is 0°s, the pressure side vane tip entropy-increase area is basically unchanged, and the loss is small. Although there is no bulge or depression in the relative shaft hole position at a 0° turning angle, a small-scale vortex system still appears at the front end of the suction side of the vane. As the flow develops downstream, the vortex system gradually strengthens when passing the vane turning shaft and develops into a passage vortex. On the rear side of the vane turning shaft, the driving of the lateral pressure gradient causes the fluid to form a strong gap leakage vortex core at the gap clearance. As the flow develops downstream, it gradually merges into the passage vortex formed on the vane suction side. Compared with the case of a −6° turning angle, the leakage vortex behind the turning shaft of the vane has a smaller scale and intensity.

When the vane turning angle is +6°s, the pressure side shaft end is convex relative to the shaft hole position, but no obvious loss occurs. However, on the suction side of the vane, a vortex system with a smaller scale is formed from the leading edge. When the vortex system develops into the area of the shaft end groove, the vortex system gradually increases in size and develops into an area with increased loss. At this time, the gap leakage vortex formed on the rear side of the vane turning shaft is smaller in scale and strength than that in cases of the other two turning angles.

Based on the analysis of the flow field at the end of the variable vane, the effect of the end structure of the vane on the flow loss at different turning angles varies, and regarding the effect of the flow loss at the end of the turning shaft of the variable vane, the suction side is larger than the pressure side, and the groove is larger than the protrusion. For this reason, this section intends to redesign the end of the turning shaft of the vane. Figure 4.35 shows the design method of the variable geometry turbine vane shaft end, that is, the center of the elliptical section of the original turning shaft is rotated clockwise so that the lower surface of the suction side shaft end moves downward, and the pressure side turning shaft surface remains unchanged to reduce the size of the groove formed at the vane shaft end at the positive turning angles. The turning angles are 1, 2, 3 and 4°s, which are denoted as the +1 axis scheme, +2 axis scheme, etc. The shaft end design method of this vane is selected to reduce the depth of the vane shaft end into the casing at a +6° turning angle. However, this shaft end design method will also cause the suction side shaft end to protrude from the casing when the vane is at a 0° turning angle, as shown on the right side of Fig. 4.35, which will also cause a larger protrusion of the vane shaft end pressure side at a −6° turning angle. However, this design method can reduce the loss caused by the shaft end under multiturning angle conditions.

To verify the advantages and disadvantages of this variable geometry turbine variable vane turning design method, the flow field changes and loss distribution in the endwall zone are carefully analyzed here to determine the relatively optimal variable vane turning design method. Note that because the modification scheme in

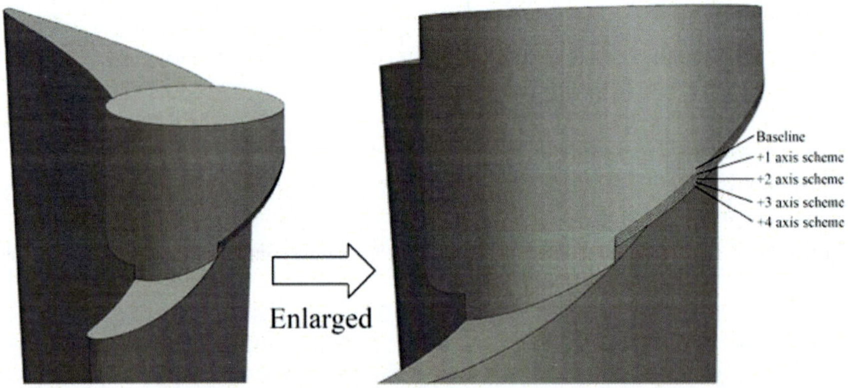

(a) Shaft-end design method

(b) +3 shaft scheme at 0° turning angle

Fig. 4.35 Variable geometry turbine vane shaft-end design method and +3 shaft scheme at a 0° turning angle

this section is for the groove state at the end of the turning shaft at a +6° turning angle, to verify the feasibility of the above scheme, the change in the end flow field at the +6° vane turning angle is analyzed. Figure 4.36 shows the distribution of entropy increase of different schemes at a +6° turning angle. Compared with the groove on the suction side of the shaft end, the peak entropy-increase area of the four newly proposed schemes is smaller than and different from the original shaft end scheme. The entropy increase of different cross-sections has a lower scale, which has a certain effect on the loss control of the shaft end flow. The wake evolution trend of the vanes under the modified schemes is similar, but the control of the wake scale is better than that of the original shaft end scheme. The change trend of the flow field at the shaft end of different vanes is carefully observed. As the depth of the groove on the vane suction side shaft gradually becomes shallower, the flow loss gradually decreases, and the flow field at the shaft end of the +3 axis scheme is the most ideal.

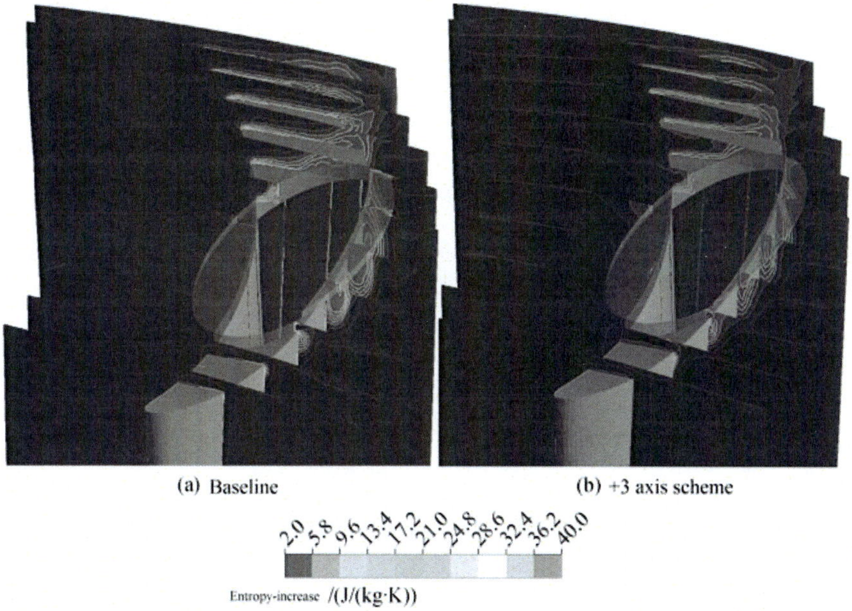

Fig. 4.36 Entropy-increase distribution at +6° turning angle for different shaft-end schemes

Figure 4.37 shows the distribution of the mass-averaged total pressure loss coefficient along the axial direction above the position of 70% of the vane span at the turning angle of +6°s for the five schemes. After passing the front end of the turning shaft, the total pressure loss of the four new schemes begins to decrease compared with the original scheme. After developing along the flow direction, the losses of the four schemes are lower than those of the original scheme. Among them, the change trend of the total pressure loss of the +3 axis scheme and +4 axis scheme is similar, and therefore, the suction side of the turning shaft of the vane has a relatively shallow depth relative to the groove. At this time, the flow field structure will not be affected by the shape of the groove on the suction side.

Table 4.8 shows the efficiency and flow changes of the five schemes at different turning angles. As previously predicted, the efficiency of the four newly proposed shaft end schemes is lower than that of the original shaft scheme at a turning angle of 0°s, but the efficiency drop is not high because the position of the shaft end of the pressure side of the vane relative to the shaft hole of the casing is a protrusion and no longer a tight fit. In the case of a + 6° turning angle, the efficiency of the newly proposed four shaft end schemes has been improved to a certain extent, with a maximum increase of 0.29%. In the case of a −6° turning angle, the efficiency of the new shaft end scheme does not cause a significant drop in efficiency because the end of the turning shaft protrudes further from the casing. Only in the +4 shaft scheme was the drop in degree greater than other schemes. Therefore, the calculation results of different schemes confirm the above analysis, that is, when the position of

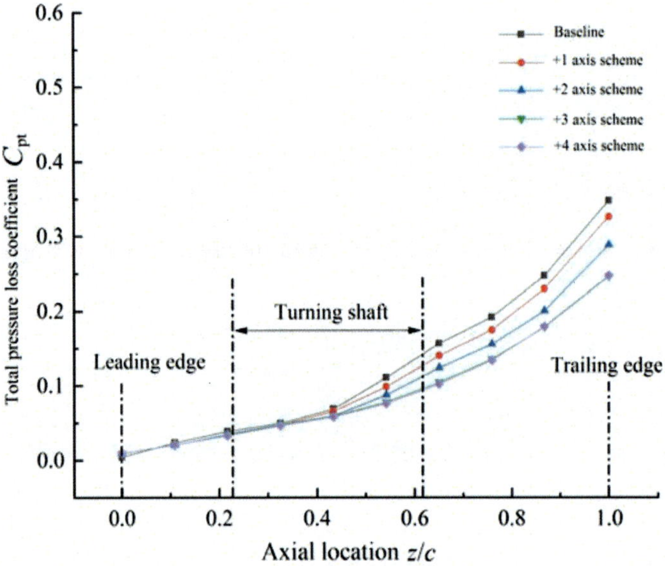

Fig. 4.37 Streamwise distribution of the total pressure loss coefficient at +6° turning angle for different schemes

the vane shaft end relative to the casing shaft hole is a groove, it is more likely to deteriorate the endwall zone flow of the variable geometry turbine.

Regarding the influence of the vane turning angle on the flow, as shown in Table 4.6, at the +6° turning angle, the new shaft end scheme increases the mass flow of the vane because the depth of the suction side shaft end groove gradually reduces,

Table 4.8 Variable geometry turbine efficiency and mass flow changes for different shaft-end improvement schemes

	−6° turning angle		0° turning angle		+6° turning angle	
	Efficiency (%)	Mass flow (−)	Efficiency (%)	Mass flow (−)	Efficiency (%)	Mass flow (−)
Original shaft scheme	88.6886	0.7790	91.5926	1.0000	91.9568	1.1297
+1 shaft scheme	88.6797	0.7785	91.5869	0.9997	91.9628	1.1303
+2 shaft scheme	88.6707	0.7780	91.5843	0.9995	91.9927	1.1315
+3 shaft scheme	88.6691	0.7779	91.5814	0.9992	92.2142	1.1318
+4 shaft scheme	88.5661	0.7773	91.5595	0.9987	92.2248	1.1319

and the low-speed recirculation zone reduces. In addition, at turning angles of 0°s and −6°s, the mass flow rate of the new shaft end scheme is slightly lower than that of the baseline because the relative height of the pressure side shaft end protrusion increases, creating a flow recirculation zone, which hinders the gas flow. For the five schemes, the flow change at five vane turning angles is relatively small, and the maximum mass flow change is 0.21% of the baseline scheme, thereby ensuring the flow matching between two variable geometry turbine stages.

Combining the flow characteristics and loss distribution of the five schemes, the newly proposed vane turning design method effectively improve the wide operating characteristics of the variable geometry turbine. Among the schemes, the overall performance of the +3 axis scheme is the best, and the efficiency is improved by 0.29% at a +6° turning angle. The efficiency is basically unchanged compared with the original shaft end scheme at 0° and −6° turning angles. A certain degree of optimization of the suction side groove at the end of the vane turning shaft is indispensable for the turning design of the vane. The +3 axis scheme has the best performance among the five schemes currently investigated.

4.2.3 Variable Vane-End Casing Treatment Technology

Based on an in-depth understanding of the turbine tip leakage flow structure and the mechanism of its loss, different types of measures are employed to control the mixing loss caused by the vane-end leakage flow. In addition to the variable vane-end treatment techniques, there is also casing endwall modeling technology. Figure 4.38 shows three casing endwall modeling structures, of which Fig. 4.38a shows the baseline casing endwall structure and Fig. 4.38b shows the casing step structure when the rear step structure exists. The front step is arranged at a position of 15% of the axial chord length upstream of the leading edge of the vane, and the rear step is arranged at a position of 25% of the axial chord length downstream of the vane trailing edge. On this basis, the rear step surface is replaced with a smooth slope to smoothly introduce the gas flow in the groove into the mainstream, thereby forming the grooved casing structure shown in Fig. 4.38c. In Fig. 4.38d, the front and rear steps are replaced by arcs to obtain a smoother endwall. Due to space limitations, refer to the literature for specific flow field results and overall performance.

The physical mechanism of the casing endwall modeling to reduce the gap leakage is also reflected in the mechanism of reducing the deflection angle of the rear side

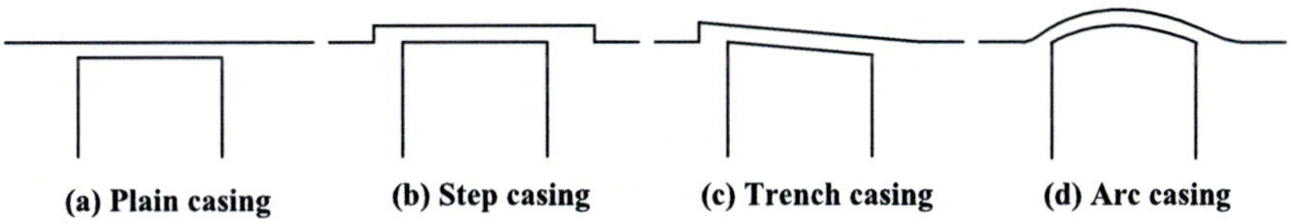

Fig. 4.38 Investigated casing endwall structure (left: Leading edge)

of the step for the different casing structures shown in Fig. 4.39. The figure shows velocity triangles at the vane inlet, the middle position between the front step and the vane leading edge, and the rotor blade outlet. The area used to calculate the speed triangle is located in the range of 5% of the vane span near the casing side. According to the analysis in the above subsections, due to the influence of the lateral pressure gradient toward the suction surface in the rotor channel, many helical lateral secondary flows occur behind the front steps. The deflection angle of the spiral lateral separation flow in the groove casing is greater than that of the step casing and arc casing, which means that there is a stronger separation vortex behind the step in the groove casing. This vortex has the greatest plugging effect on the downstream direct leakage flow, but the direct leakage flow in the arc casing is the weakest. In addition, the indirect leakage flow at the rear part of the vane end can also be qualitatively analyzed from the figure. Due to the pressure fields in the rotor channel, the spiral separation flow at the rear side of the step means that the fluid at the rear side of the step performs work in advance, which reduces the work performed near the tip of the blade, thereby reducing the blade tip leakage loss of variable geometry turbines.

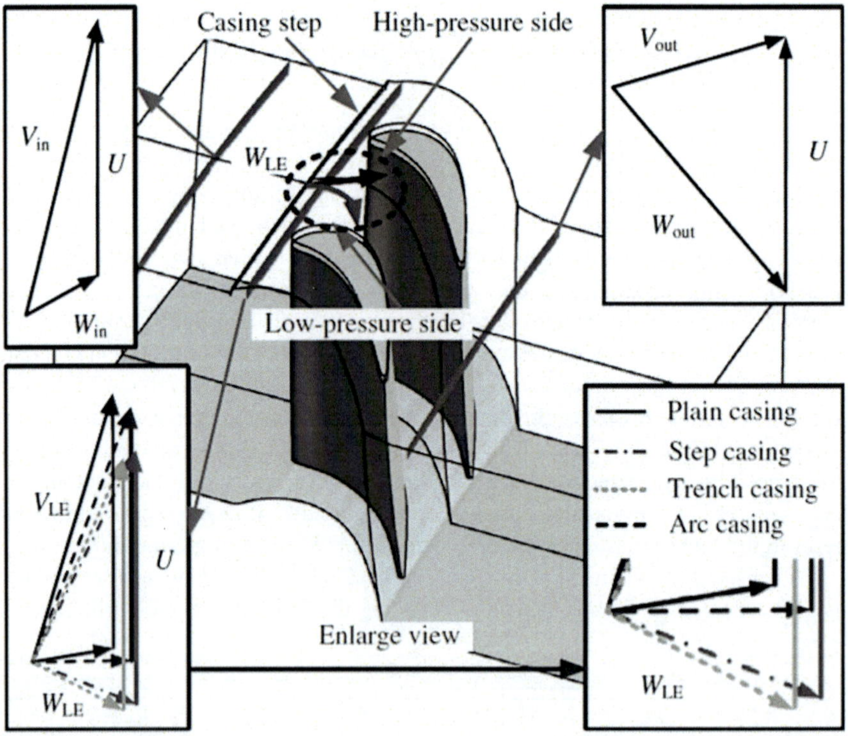

Fig. 4.39 Schematic of the mechanism for reducing the deflection angle downstream of the step for different casing endwall structures

(a) Spherical endwall

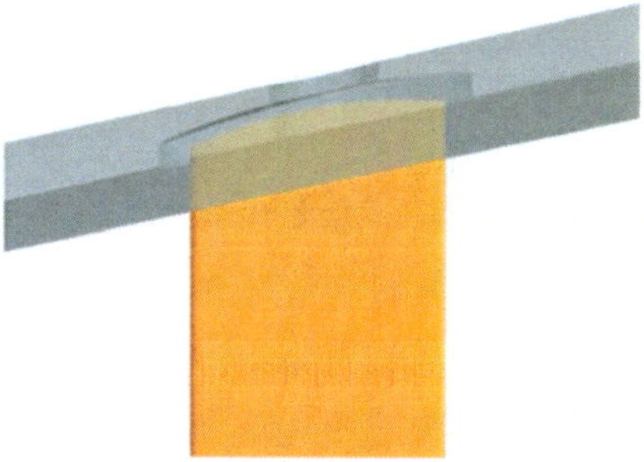

(b) Casing-shaped groove

Fig. 4.40 Application of casing treatment in the design of a variable vane-end structure

Because of the effectiveness of the vane-end casing treatment technology, it has been applied in the actual variable vane turning design of variable geometry turbines. For details, refer to the design work of the Shenyang Aero Engine Research Institute, as shown in Fig. 4.40. The vanes are designed with spherical endwalls, and grooves are designed on the casing to increase the gas flow resistance, to form a gas vortex and to reduce the additional loss caused by the change in the vane installation angle.

4.3 High Endwall Angle Variable Vane Turning Design Based on a Stepped Spherical Endwall

4.3.1 Variable Vane-End Clearance Chordwise Distribution at Different Vane Turning Angles

Figure 4.41 shows a typical variable vane structure with a large expansion angle endwall. When the variable vane rotates, the vane-end gap clearance becomes nonuniform, and different nonuniform gap clearances form at different turning angles.

Figure 4.42 shows the chordwise distribution of the vane-end gap clearance at the two extreme positions of the vane closing and opening (the vane throat area is reduced or increased by 30%), where the turning angles are $-6°$ and $+8°$. Based on actual engineering experience, to ensure that the vanes can smoothly rotate under actual operating conditions, the thermal gap clearance at the end of the vanes should be at least 0.5 mm, and the thermal gap is evenly distributed in the chordwise direction at a zero turning angle. As shown in Fig. 4.41a, at a $-6°$ turning angle position, the hub clearance slightly increases at most gap clearance positions. However, the change in the casing gap clearance is the most obvious: on the front side of the vane, the gap clearance increases, and on the rear side of the vane, the gap clearance quickly decreases. At the $+8°$ turning angle position shown in Fig. 4.41b, the hub clearance is slightly reduced at most gap clearance positions, while the change in the casing

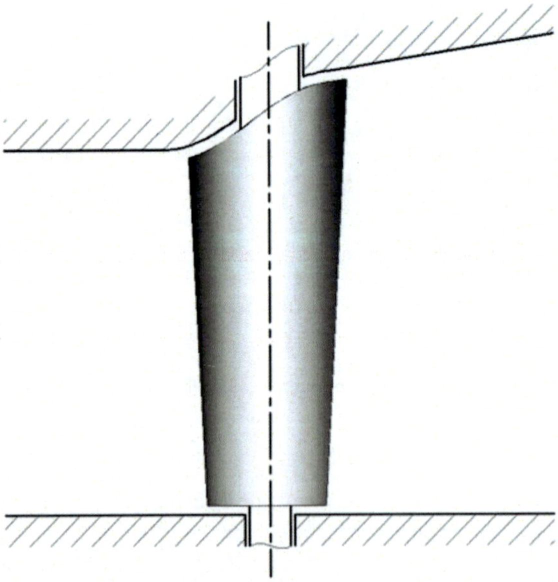

Fig. 4.41 Typical variable-vane structure with high endwall angle

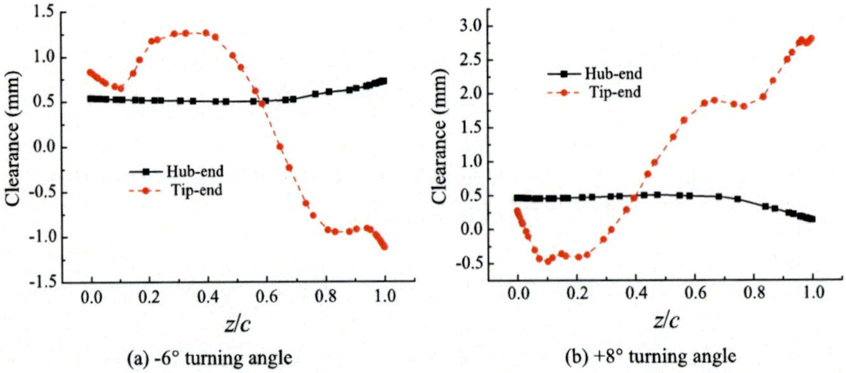

Fig. 4.42 Chordwise distribution of high endwall angle, variable-vane-endwall gap clearances at different vane turning angles

gap clearance is also significant. It can be inferred that to ensure that the thermal gap clearance in all positions at different turning angles has at least a 0.5 mm safety gap, the original design thermal gap is at least 2.1 mm, and this larger gap clearance will naturally cause more leakage loss at the end of the vane, which substantially deteriorates the aerodynamic performance of variable geometry turbines. Therefore, the direct application of the traditional variable vane turning design method for variable geometry turbines to the large meridional expansion turbine is difficult.

4.3.2 Proposal of the Stepped Spherical Endwall Modeling Method

Based on a distinct understanding of the endwall flow and structural characteristics of the variable vane with a large expansion angle and the control of the vane-end gap clearance leakage flow, the stepped spherical endwall modeling method was proposed. The main purpose of the method is to avoid the problem of the gap clearance height change caused by the traditional variable vane turning design.

Figure 4.43 shows a schematic of the stepped spherical endwall modeling method for variable geometry turbines. In the variable geometry design of the large meridional expansion turbine, four key factors are considered: (1) The endwall of the vane casing is a spherical structure, and the center of the spherical surface is located on the axis of rotation of the gas turbine to ensure that the gap clearance remains unchanged when the vane rotates; (2) Steps are introduced upstream and downstream of the spherical endwall of the casing/hub to match the original S-shaped endwall profile to the greatest extent to ensure minimal changes and to reduce the vane-end gap clearance leakage loss. In addition, the spherical surface endwall must include the range of movement of the leading edge and trailing edge of the vane at all turning angles; (3) The vane and its turning axis are meridional forward to further match the original S-shaped endwall profile, and the vane is forward inclined, that is, the orthogonal design is simultaneously carried out to reduce the secondary flow loss in the endwall area with a large expansion angle. Note that the minimum axial gap between the variable vane and the downstream rotor blade must be maintained; and (4) The design of the vane-end groove is adopted to further reduce leakage loss in the endwall zone.

The newly designed variable geometry turbine stage, which is based on the abovementioned stepped spherical endwall modeling method for variable geometry turbines, is shown in Fig. 4.44. The turning shaft has a meridional tilt of 3°, and the diameters of the turning shaft at the casing end and hub end are 28 and 20 mm, respectively. Note that in the variable geometry design of the large meridional expansion turbine, the vane profile remains unchanged. For the vane-end groove structure, the width of the partition wall of the groove is 0.77 mm, and the depth of the groove is 1 mm.

4.3.3 Design Results and Analysis

The most obvious difference in the flow fields between the variable geometry vane and the fixed geometry vane is the flow interference between the endwall gap leakage area and the endwall passage vortex. Figure 4.45 shows the structure of the flow field at the leading edge of the variable vane. There is a relatively obvious recirculation area in the leading edge of the vane, which is mainly attributed to the flow separation caused by the adverse pressure gradient in the casing area. Based on the author's

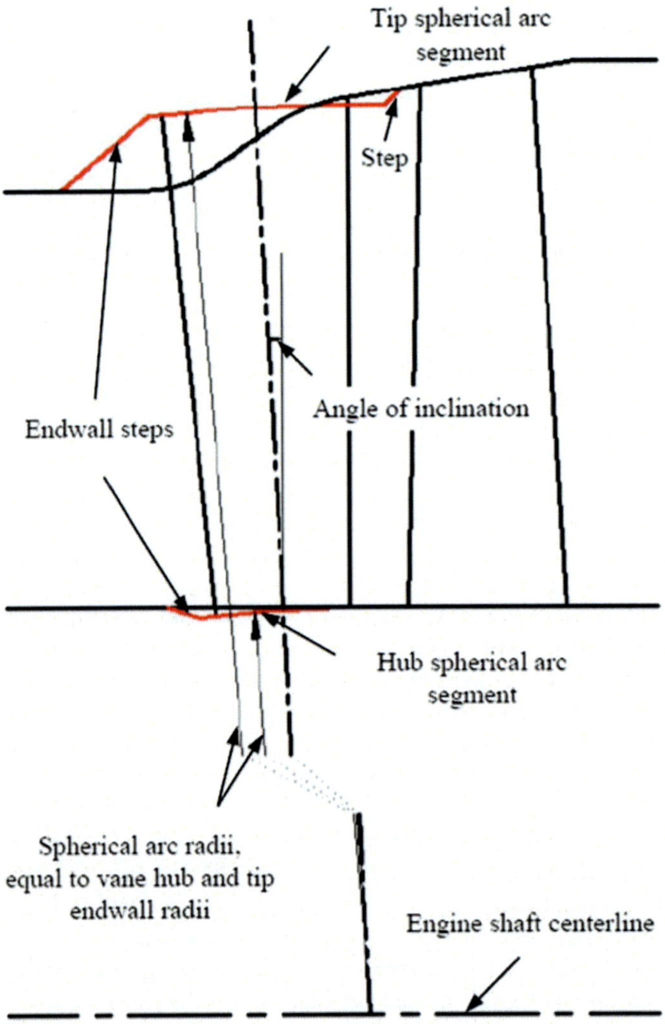

Fig. 4.43 Proposed stepped spherical endwall contouring method

previous research work, it can be speculated that this obvious recirculation zone causes a blocking effect on the direct gap clearance leakage flow through the gap clearance along the streamwise direction, thus reducing the vane-end gap leakage loss to some extent. However, note that the recirculation area is relatively large, causing additional separation losses. Therefore, the current structure of the endwall of the casing needs to be further optimized.

Figure 4.46 shows a comparison of the distribution of limiting streamlines on the suction side of the gap clearance between fixed-geometry turbine vanes and the variable-geometry turbine vane. For variable vanes, the secondary flow is weakened to some extent due to the introduction of vane-end gap clearance leakage flows. The

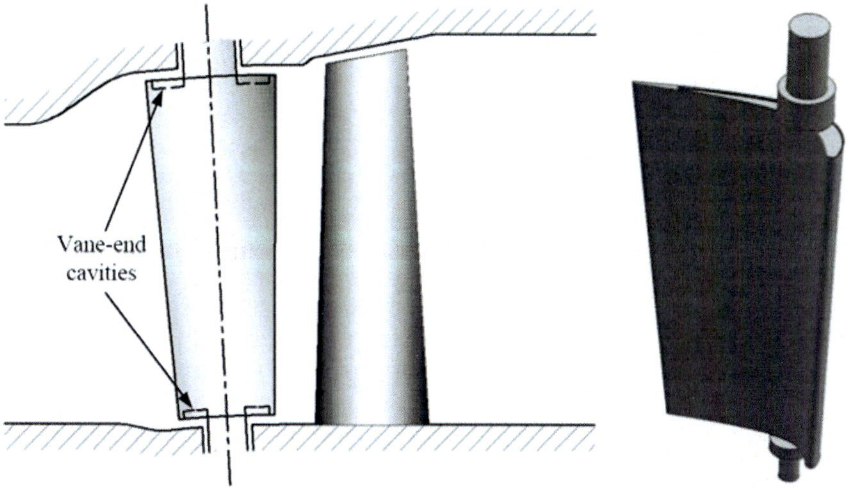

Fig. 4.44 Newly designed variable geometry turbine stage

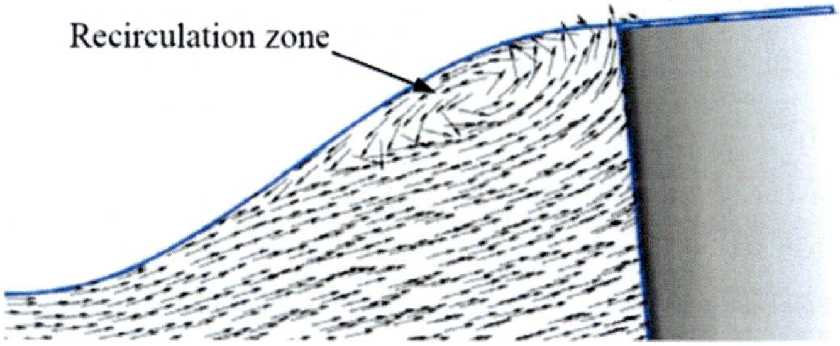

Fig. 4.45 Variable vane leading edge flow field structure

separation line tends to be closer to the tip of the vane, which means that the span range of the influence of vortex interference is significantly reduced. Nonetheless, as shown in Fig. 4.47, due to the presence of vane-end gap clearance leakage flow, the loss in the endwall zone significantly increases. This finding can also be confirmed from Fig. 4.48a. Figure 4.48a also shows that at a zero turning angle, the secondary flow loss at the end of the vane is significantly reduced, which is mainly attributed to the mutual interference between the secondary flow of the hub endwall and the gap clearance leakage flow. The vane profile flow loss in the vane midspan area is also significantly reduced.

A comparison of Fig. 4.48a and b indicates that the variable vane also affects the downstream rotor blade flow field and that the leakage loss of the rotor blade tip gap has significantly increased, which is attributed to the effects of unfavorable inlet conditions. In addition, the secondary flow in the endwall zone of the rotor hub slightly increases. As the flow develops downstream, the influence of the vane turning

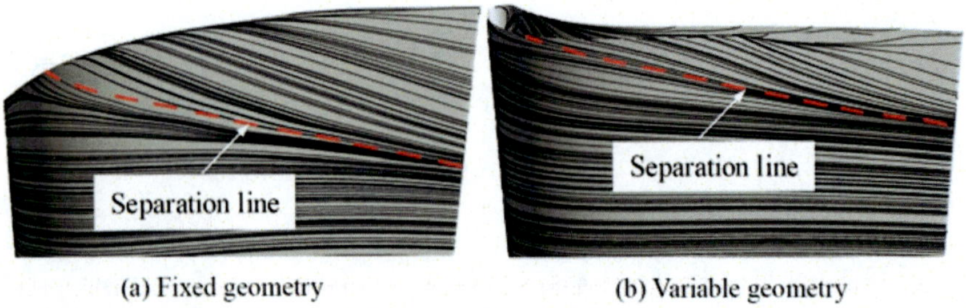

Fig. 4.46 Comparison of near-tip suction side limiting streamline of fixed and variable geometry vanes

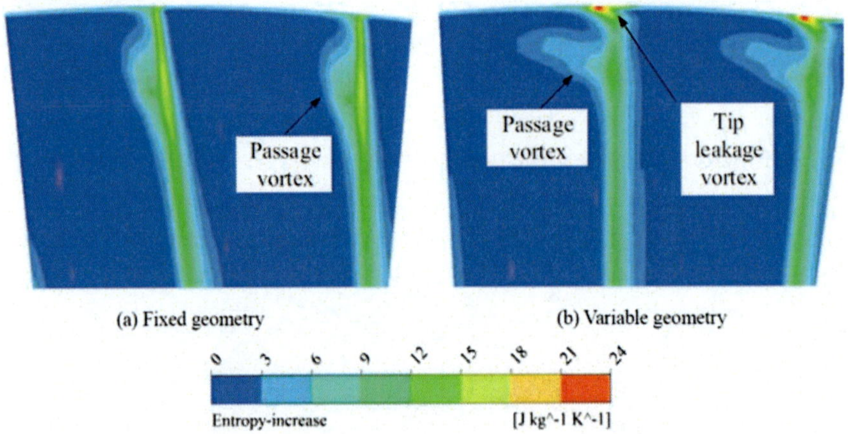

Fig. 4.47 Comparison of fixed and variable geometry vane outlet entropy-increase distribution

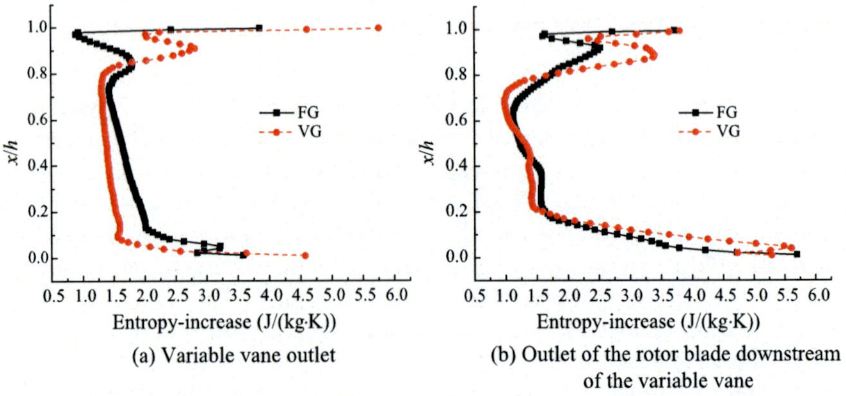

Fig. 4.48 Comparison of spanwise entropy-increase distribution for fixed and variable geometry turbine blade rows

on the variable vane is significantly greater than its impact on the downstream rotor blade, that is, the effect of the vane variable gradually weakens as the flow develops downstream.

The above analysis can also be confirmed from Figs. 4.49, 4.50 and 4.51. As the flow of the channel develops downstream, the difference between the Mach number distribution of the fixed geometry turbine and the variable geometry turbine gradually narrows, and there is no difference in the Mach number distribution of the last-stage rotor blade and the load distribution of the rotor blade.

Table 4.9 gives a comparison of the design-condition overall performance of fixed geometry and variable geometry turbines. The data are obtained from numerical calculations, and the impact of the interface between two blade rows on the loss estimation has also been considered. Compared with the fixed geometry turbine, under the premise that the turbine inlet flow rate remains unchanged, although the efficiency of the variable vane stage turbine is reduced by 0.3%, the overall efficiency and total entropy increase of the four-stage turbine are basically unchanged. Thus, the overall turbine efficiency is not sensitive to changes in efficiency caused by a single blade row, although the theoretical analysis suggests that this effect is linear. Notably, when the fluid propagates between two different turbine stages, the flow will be mixed and the flow incidence of attack impact will be smoothed out, but the entropy caused by the flow mixing will not disappear. However, due to the positive effect of the vane forward, it accelerates the flow in the mainstream area, thus reducing the blade

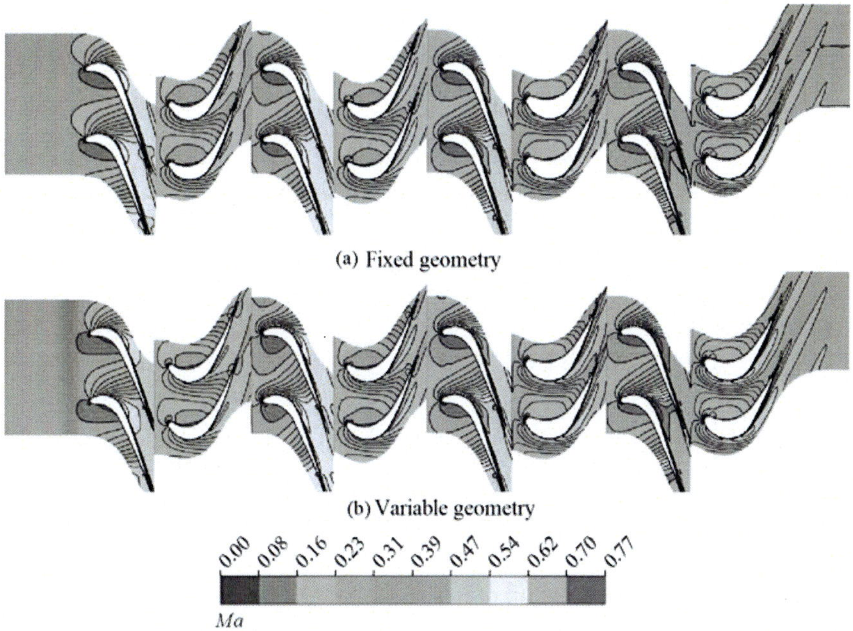

Fig. 4.49 Comparison of the Mach number distribution at 5% of the blade span for four-stage fixed geometry and variable geometry turbines

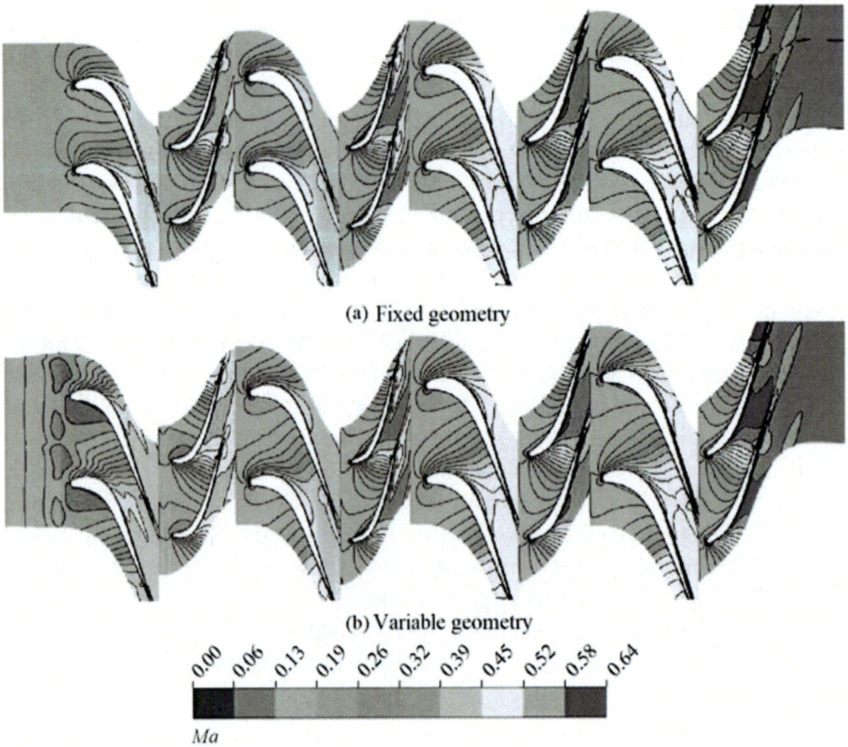

Fig. 4.50 Comparison of the Mach number distribution at 95% of the blade span for four-stage, fixed geometry and variable geometry turbines

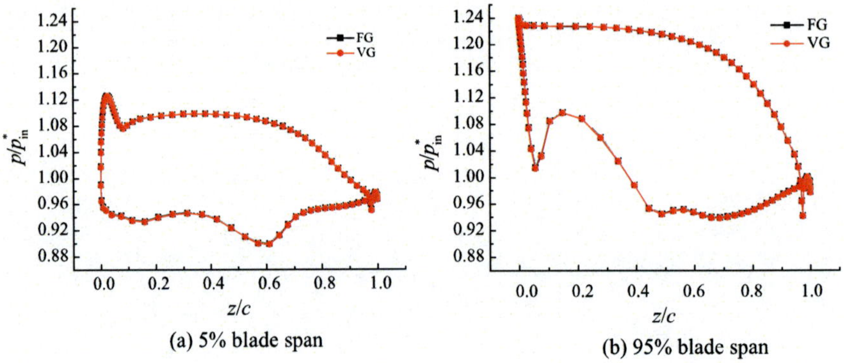

Fig. 4.51 Comparison of the last-stage rotor blade load distribution for fixed and variable geometry turbines

loss, so that the total blade loss remains basically unchanged. The current numerical calculation results also confirm that the stepped spherical endwall modeling method can be employed for variable geometry design of large meridional expansion turbines.

Figure 4.52 shows the aerodynamic characteristics at equal design speeds for fixed and variable geometry turbines. At a specific pressure ratio, the turbine isentropic efficiency decreases as the vane turning angle changes from zero to open or closed. With the design pressure ratio, as the vanes open, the newly designed variable vanes have a less effect on the turbine performance, and the efficiency is only reduced by 0.3%; however, it has a greater impact on the turbine mass flow rate, and the mass flow rate is increased by 7.7%. As the vane closes, the variable geometry has a significant impact on turbine performance. Specifically, at the design pressure ratio, the 14% reduction in turbine flow rate and 2% reduction in turbine efficiency simultaneously occur. In addition, the decrease in turbine efficiency caused by vane closing is much greater than the opening of the vane, which is mainly attributed to the influence of the inlet incidence of attack caused by vane turning.

Table 4.9 Comparison of design-point overall performance for fixed and variable geometry turbines

Parameters	Turbine mass flow rate (–)	Variable vane stage efficiency (%)	Four-stage turbine efficiency (%)	Total entropy-increase (excluding the influence of interface calculation) (J/kg·K)
Fixed geometry	1	94.9	94.78	19.59
Variable geometry	1.00085	94.6	94.77	19.72
Increment	0.00085	−0.3	−0.01	0.13

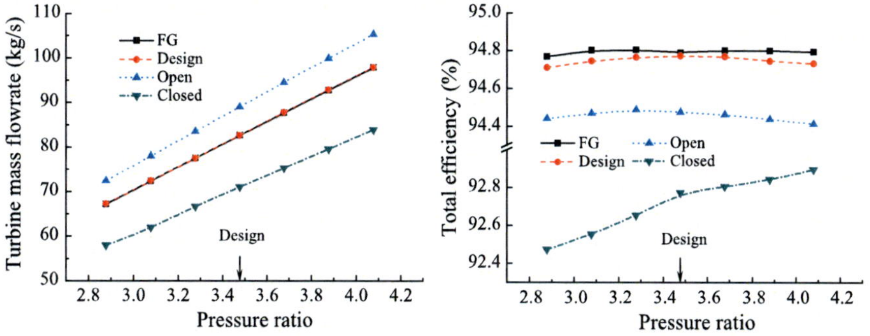

Fig. 4.52 Aerodynamic characteristics at design speeds for fixed and variable geometry turbines

4.4 Proposal and Validation of Full Three-Dimensional Turning Design Concept for a High Endwall Angle Variable Vane

4.4.1 Proposal of the Vane Turning Design Concept

The research object in this section is a turbine with a vane casing expansion angle of approximately 27°. Because the turbine has a large expansion angle casing, a large endwall gap clearance needs to be given to ensure its free rotation. To reduce the gap clearance leakage loss at the end of the variable vane, this section proposes a method to reduce the number of vanes by using a highly loaded design, to increase the diameter of the disc-shaped crown (that is, the diameter of the shaft at the gap position) and to reduce the total circumferential leakage area, combined with the vane for aft-loaded modification to reduce the secondary flow loss due to the highly loaded design. Generally, this method reduces the endwall loss caused by the vane turning. Scholars worldwide have not been involved in research to reduce the gap clearance leakage area, and there have been no studies on the structure of the variable vane disk crown. To verify the performance of the modified variable geometry turbine, this subsection is aimed at three different turbines: fixed geometry turbines, traditional variable geometry turbines with only turning shafts, and variable geometry turbines with disc crowns and combined aft-loaded vane profiles. Numerical simulations were conducted to compare the performance of the three turbines in detail, and on this basis, the aerodynamic characteristics of the variable vanes with disc-shaped crowns and aft-loaded vanes were investigated.

4.4.2 Scheme Design Validation

Since the diameter of the disk crown in the vane-end area is limited by the consistency of the vane, if the disk crown is added to the original vane, it will cause structural interference between two turbine disk crowns. Therefore, this section uses a highly loaded design to avoid this kind of interference and to narrow the limits of vane consistency on the disc-shaped crown. When selecting the calculation schemes, if only the highly loaded design is carried out without changing the vane profile, the negative effects caused by the highly loaded design cannot be eliminated; thus, the design purpose cannot be achieved. Therefore, this subsection uses a variable geometry turbine with a disc-shaped crown combined with an aft-loaded vane profile to perform a comparison with the original vane profile variable geometry turbine and to better illustrate the performance of the newly designed turbine.

This section performs numerical calculation and analysis of the original fixed geometry turbine, the variable geometry turbine with the original vane profile and only the turning shaft, and the variable geometry turbine with reduced vane number and combined aft-loaded vane profile, as shown in Fig. 4.53. The turbines are described as follows: (1) Fixed geometry turbine: the number of vanes is 64, and there is no gap at both vane-ends; (2) Variable geometry turbine with only the turning shaft (using the original vane profile turbine): the turning shaft is located at 50% of the chord length; the diameter of the turning shaft at the tip of the vane is 28 mm; the diameter of the turning shaft at the root of the vane is 20 mm; the number of vanes is 64; the vane-tip clearance is 2.1 mm; and the vane root gap clearance is 0.9 mm; (3) Variable geometry turbine with disc-shaped crown (adopting newly-designed aft-loaded profiles): the turning shaft is located at 50% of the chord length; the diameter of the disc-shaped crown at the vane tip is 92.2 mm; the diameter of the disc-shaped crown at the root of the vane is 73.7 mm; the number of vanes is 52; the vane-tip clearance is 2.1 mm; and the root gap clearance is 0.9 mm. In the calculation of the three turbine vanes, the rotor blade tip gap clearance is 0.5 mm, and the number of blades of the three gas turbine power turbine models is 76.

Figure 4.54 shows a schematic of the vane profile of the newly designed variable vane. In general, the newly designed variable vane throat moves backward so that the load of the vane profile moves backward to achieve the purpose of aft-loaded vane design for variable geometry turbines.

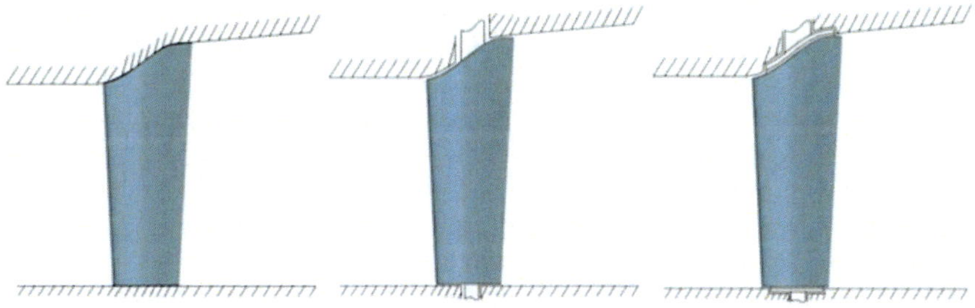

(a) Fixed geometry, FG (b) Traditional shaft structure, ZVG (c) Disc-shroud shaft-end structure, GVG

Fig. 4.53 Three variable geometry turbine variable vane structures

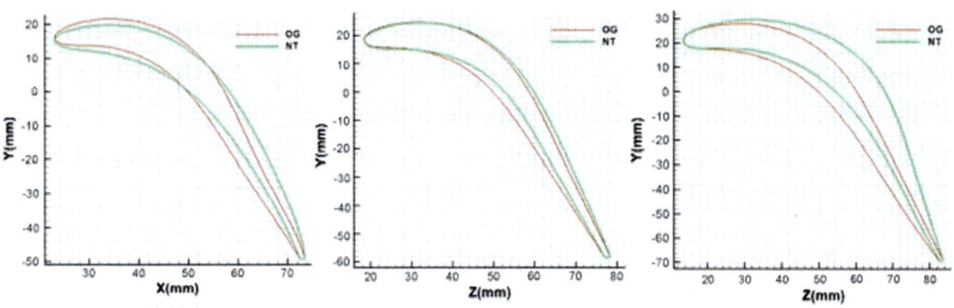

(a) Hub (b) Midspan (c) Tip

Fig. 4.54 Schematic of the new design variable vane profile

4.4.3 Design Results and Analysis

Figure 4.55 shows a comparison of the load distribution of the three variable geometry turbines with variable vanes. At a 5% vane span, the load distribution of the fixed geometry turbine is similar to that of the variable geometry turbine with only the turning shaft at 5% of the vane span. Compared with the other two turbines, the variable geometry turbine with a disc-shaped crown moves the maximum load position backward, and the degree of expansion of the re-exit section of the gas flow is significantly increased. As the maximum load position is moved backward, the axial and radial adverse pressure gradient segments near the vane trailing edge are shortened, thereby reducing the adverse pressure gradient. It can be seen that the turbine gas flow in the tip part of the turbine combined with the retrofitting measures of the vane is optimized. At 50% of the vane span, the load distribution of the three turbines is relatively similar, although the maximum load position of the variable geometry turbine with a disc-shaped crown also moves backward, but its degree of backward movement is greater than that of the vane-end and vane tip. The range of the backpressure gradient in the second half is smaller than that of the other two types of turbine vanes; thus, the length and variation range of the adverse pressure gradient of the turbine vane profiles are optimized. Compared with the other two turbines, the variable geometry turbine with a disc-shaped crown at 95% of the vane span exhibits a significant aft-loaded pattern. There is an adverse pressure gradient in the second half of the profile. However, compared with the other two turbines, while the adverse pressure gradient is gentler, the forward pressure gradient of the first half of the profile is similar to the other two turbines, and the flow is relatively gentle, reducing the endwall flow loss. Therefore, the maximum load of the fixed geometry turbine and variable geometry turbine with only the turning shaft are concentrated in the middle region of the turbine vane, while the maximum load position of the variable geometry turbine with the disc crown moves to the rear side. This finding is attributed to the aft-loaded design modification of the variable geometry turbine vane, which shifts the load distribution of the vane, thereby achieving the aerodynamic optimization of the vane for variable geometry turbines.

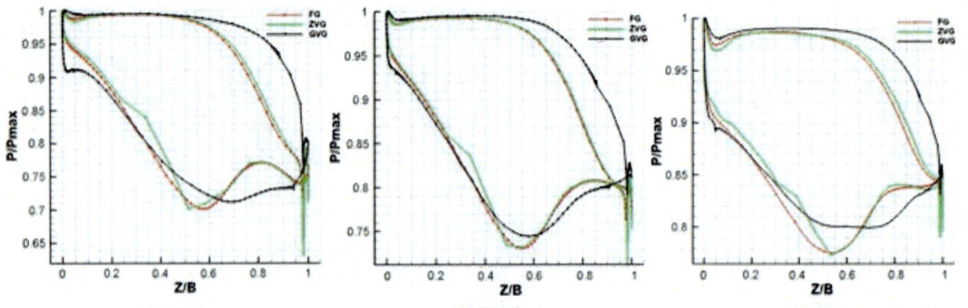

Fig. 4.55 Load distribution profile comparison for three variable geometry turbines with variable vanes

Figure 4.56 shows a comparison of the outlet entropy distribution of three variable geometry turbine variable vanes. There are many reasons for the loss in the cascade flow path: the leakage loss at both ends of the variable vane, the vane profile loss on the vane surface, and the flow loss caused by the passage vortex composed of the branch of the horseshoe vortex at the leading edge of the vane and the secondary flow of the endwall. As shown in Fig. 4.56a, the meridional expansion produces a strong passage vortex to the flow channel, which is far from the casing. Thus, in this turbine design, there should be a balance point between the meridional expansion and the vane loss. The analysis in Fig. 4.56 reveals that the original turbine has already applied this balance point in the design to achieve the best balance between the loss and the meridional expansion. In addition, there is no gap clearance at the end of the fixed geometry turbine vane, the outlet loss is less, and the passage vortex in the mainstream area constitutes the main entropy-increase area. However, due to the existence of the gap clearance, the vanes of the variable geometry turbine with only the turning shaft mainly contain the leakage vortex of the upper and lower gaps and the passage vortex of the upper and lower endwalls. Among them, the relatively large size of the vane-end gap of the variable geometry turbine with only the turning shaft produces a strong gap leakage vortex at the upper and lower endwall regions, and the range of the gap leakage vortex at the upper endwall region has been extended to the upper endwall passage vortex region, showing the trend of integration.

In this section, the disc-shaped crown is used to reduce the circumferential leakage area of the vanes, thereby reducing the gap clearance leakage loss of the endwall zone. However, the highly loaded design will enhance the gap leakage driving force, which will increase the gap leakage loss. Balancing the relationship between the

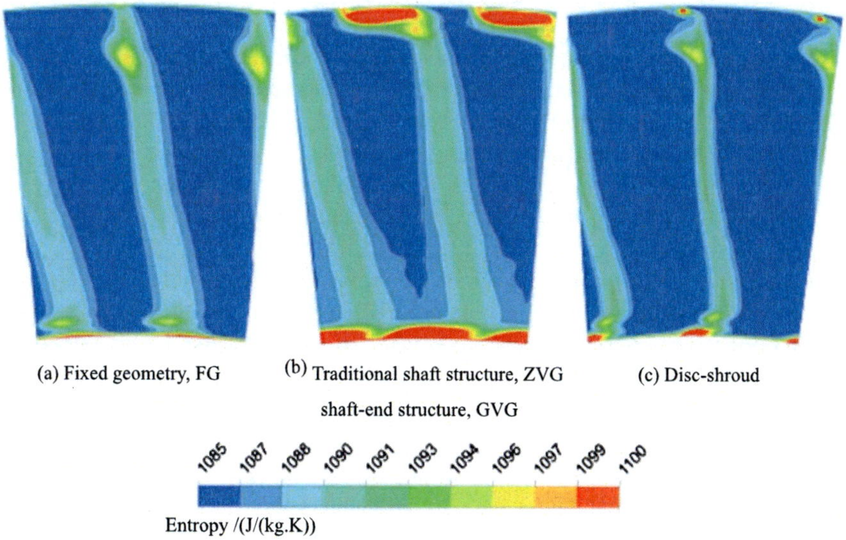

Fig. 4.56 Outlet entropy distributions for three variable geometry turbine variable vanes

two is particularly important. The comparison between Fig. 4.56b and c show that the gap clearance leakage vortex in Fig. 4.56c is significantly reduced compared with Fig. 4.56b. The subsection utilizes the combined highly loaded design of the aft-loaded vane profile to effectively reduce the gap clearance leakage loss, thereby solving the above problems. The gap clearance leakage vortex at the lower endwall merges with the passage vortex at the lower endwall to form a stronger leakage vortex. Since the mutual interference between the gap leakage vortex and the passage vortex can only be employed with an appropriate gap clearance, the gap clearance leakage flow under a large gap will significantly affect the performance of the turbine. According to the outlet entropy distribution of variable geometry turbines with disc-shaped crowns, because the presence of disc-shaped crowns significantly inhibits the gap clearance leakage loss, the intensity of the leakage vortex in the upper and lower endwall areas has become very weak, and the passage vortex in the adjacent area can no longer be affected. As indicated by Fig. 4.56, due to the use of aft-loaded design modification measures, the passage vortex does not significantly increase, which shows that the aft-loaded vane profile successfully suppresses the secondary flow caused by the highly loaded design, significantly improving the aerodynamic performance of variable geometry turbines.

Figure 4.57 provides a comparison of the distribution of the total pressure loss along the vane span of the variable vanes of the three variable geometry turbines. There is not much difference in the vane span range of 10~90% between the fixed geometry turbine and the variable geometry turbine with a disc crown. The total pressure loss coefficients of the three turbines have a very obvious drop near the 80% vane span to the 95% vane span. Among them, the fixed geometry turbine has decreased by 0.03~0.04, and the variable geometry turbine with the turning shaft has decreased by 0.02~0.03, with the variable geometry turbine of the disc-shaped crown dropping by approximately 0.02. From 10 to 90% of the vane span, the total pressure loss coefficients of the three vanes are similar. The total pressure loss coefficient of the variable geometry turbine with a disc crown in this range is slightly lower than that of the other two turbines. From the 10% vane span to the vane root, the total pressure loss coefficients of the three turbine vanes decreased again. Among them, the fixed geometry turbine has a very obvious drop of approximately 0.05. The downward trend of the variable geometry turbine with the disc-shaped crown is not very obvious. Based on the overall parameters, the total outlet pressure loss coefficient of the original fixed geometry turbine is 0.186, the total outlet pressure loss coefficient of the variable geometry turbine with the turning shaft is 0.384, and the total outlet pressure loss coefficient of the variable geometry turbine with the disc crown is 0.172, which clearly shows that the performance of the variable geometry turbine has been greatly improved with the disc crown effects. Therefore, in both vane ends, the design optimization of the variable geometry turbine with a disc-shaped crown is beneficial for suppressing the endwall gap clearance leakage flow and for significantly reducing the endwall secondary flow loss. Additionally, the use of aft-loaded vanes reduces the midspan flow loss. In general, the performance of the variable geometry turbine with a disc crown is stronger than the variable geometry turbine with only the turning shaft.

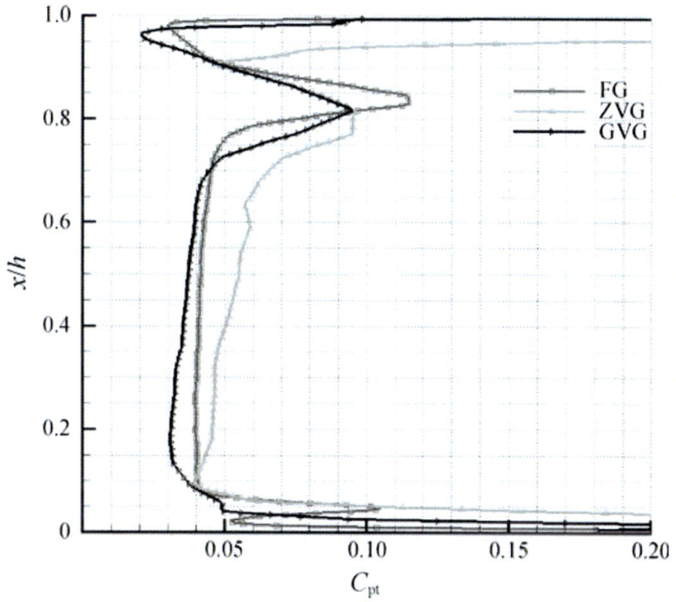

Fig. 4.57 Comparison of total outlet pressure loss coefficients for three variable geometry turbine variable vanes

Table 4.10 shows a comparison of the design-condition aerodynamic performance of three variable geometry turbines. In the case of minimal change in the mass flow rate, the efficiency of the variable geometry turbine with a disc crown is slightly less than that of the fixed geometry turbine. Compared with a variable geometry turbine with only a turning shaft, its efficiency is increased by 3.14%. This result shows that with the large gap clearance scale, adding a disc-shaped crown at the end of the vane can significantly improve the aerodynamic efficiency of the turbine. A comparison of the flow parameters of the three turbines reveals that under the condition that the total mass flow rate is similar, the gap clearance leakage of the variable geometry turbine with a disc crown is reduced by 98.2% compared with the variable geometry turbine with only the turning shaft, which shows that the variable geometry turbine with a disc-shaped crown has a greater degree of suppression of the leakage flow of the vane-end gap than the variable geometry turbine with only a turning shaft. In addition, the power of the variable-geometry turbine with a disc-shaped crown is slightly larger than that of the fixed-geometry turbine, and the variable geometry turbine with only the turning shaft is increased by 2.6%. Therefore, in general, a variable geometry turbine with a disc-shaped crown is superior in aerodynamic performance to a variable geometry turbine with only a turning shaft.

Figure 4.58 shows the variable operating characteristics of the newly designed variable geometry turbine. As the expansion ratio increases, the turbine's outlet mass flow shows an increasing trend, the five characteristic curves increase with the vane turning angle, and there is an upward trend. The flow characteristics of

Table 4.10 Design-point aerodynamic performance comparison of three variable geometry turbines

Turbine type	Fixed geometry	Traditional shaft structure	Disc-shroud shaft-end structure
Outlet mass flow rate (−)	1	1.0005	1.0004
Efficiency (%)	94.33	91.15	94.29
Gap leakage mass flow rate (kg/s)	–	3.4	0.06
Power (−)	1	0.9752	1.0010

the fixed geometry turbine and the variable geometry turbine with a disc crown at a turning angle of 0° basically coincide. In addition, during the forward rotation of the vane (0 to +4°), the mass flow rate is increased by approximately 9.8%. During the continuous rotation of the vane (+4° to +6°), the mass flow rate is further increased by approximately 3.8%. Similarly, during the reverse rotation of the vane (0° to −4°), the mass flow rate is reduced by approximately 13.04%, while the vane continues to rotate in the reverse direction (−4° to −6°), and the mass flow rate is further reduced by approximately 9.8%. As the turning angle gradually changes from −6° and −4° to +4° and +6°, the throat area in the cascade channel continuously increases, resulting in an increase in the outlet mass flow. Thus, the change in turning angle produces changes in the turbine mass flow. As shown in Fig. 4.58, the efficiency of each turbine characteristic line rises and then decreases with an increase in the expansion ratio. The variable geometry turbine with a 0° turning angle is slightly higher than the characteristic curve of the fixed geometry turbine. An analysis of the efficiency characteristics curve reveals that the aerodynamic performance of the variable geometry turbine is better under the design condition, while at low expansion ratios, the efficiency of the variable geometry turbine with a smaller turning angle is similar to that of the fixed geometry turbine, which indicates that under low working conditions, the turbine power can be controlled by reducing the turning angle, and its efficiency will not be reduced. At a high expansion ratio, the efficiency characteristics curve of the variable geometry turbine with an increased turning angle is significantly higher than that of the fixed geometry turbine, which indicates that under high operating conditions, by increasing the vane turning angle, the turbine mass flow rate can be effectively controlled and the aerodynamic efficiency can be improved. In general, the proposed new type of large meridional expansion variable geometry turbine with a disk crown has better aerodynamic performance under all operating conditions.

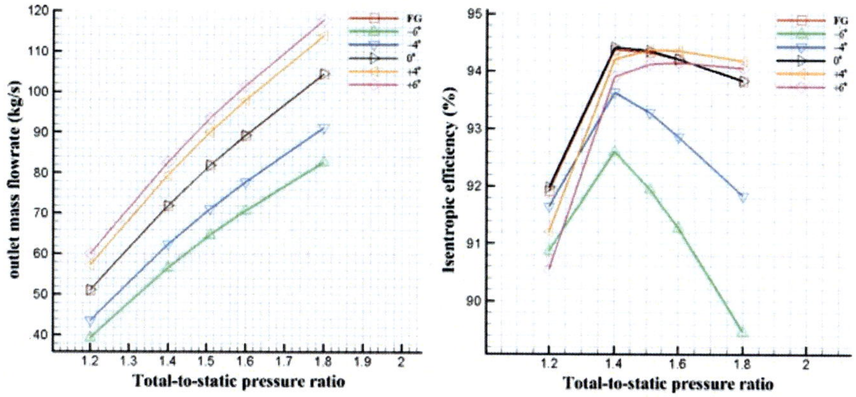

(a) Mass flowrate (b) Efficiency

Fig. 4.58 Off-design characteristics of newly designed variable geometry turbines

4.5 Variable Vane Turning Angle Adjustment Method and Law for a Variable Geometry Turbine

Gas turbines with variable geometry power turbine technology can adjust the installation angle of the variable vanes of the power turbine as the operating conditions change, thereby redistributing the enthalpy drop between the gas generator turbine and the power turbine, and can ensure that the entire unit runs according to the required common working line as the working conditions change. A theoretical analysis reveals that for an entire gas turbine unit, under certain environmental conditions, the aerodynamic parameters of the gas generator have only two independent variables, such as a given gas initial temperature and low-pressure compressor rotational speed, according to the gas turbine shaft power balance condition. One can determine the gas turbine aerodynamic parameters, such as the temperature and pressure at the power turbine inlet, air mass flow rate at the low-pressure compressor inlet, and specific fuel consumption. The rotational speed, efficiency and power of the power turbine can be determined according to the expansion ratio, the reduced mass flow of the power turbine and the general characteristics curve and by introducing the external characteristics, that is, the relationship between power and rotational speed, the balance operating point of the given gas initial temperature and the matching low-pressure compressor rotational speed can be further determined. Selecting different initial gas temperatures can draw a balanced working line, especially the relationship curve between the fuel consumption rate and power. On this basis, from the fuel consumption rate envelopes of different variable vane turning angles, the variation law of the turning angle and the power with the minimum fuel consumption rate can be determined. Similarly, the law of the turning angle of the variable vane of the variable geometry power turbine for the starting process, acceleration process, ensuring surge margin, etc., can be given.

4.5.1 Simple Cycle Gas Turbine

The dual-shaft gas generator has high component efficiency and thermal efficiency under off-design conditions and strong load adaptability, which is particularly suitable for marine gas turbines. Three-shaft gas turbines with dual-shaft gas generators and power turbines are widely utilized in marine gas turbines. For example, the simple cycle gas turbines MT30 and GT25000 and the WR-21 gas turbine use three key technologies of intercooling recuperation and variable geometry power turbines. Three-shaft gas turbines have the best characteristics compared with split-shaft gas turbines or single-shaft gas turbines. The typical marine gas turbines discussed in this subsection adopt a simple cycle and three-shaft structure layout. If further development is carried out, key technologies such as intercooling, recuperation and variable geometry power turbines can be employed. This section discusses the effect of using variable vanes on the position of the common operating point and the trend of the common working line of the entire simple cycle gas turbine unit.

Figure 4.59a shows the effect of variable vanes on the position of the common working point of the entire unit. When the variable vane is closed, the flow area of the power turbine is reduced, the exhaust back pressure of the gas generator turbine is relatively increased, and its expansion ratio is relatively reduced. Thus, the unit enthalpy drop in the gas generator turbine is relatively reduced. In this way, the power of the gas generator turbine is reduced, and the compressor cannot be driven at the original rotational speed. The rotational speed of the gas generator inevitably decreases; the gas mass flow rate is reduced; and the compressor boost ratio is reduced. The effective output power of the unit is correspondingly reduced, and the common operating point moves to the surge boundary, changing from the original point *A* to point *B*. For a certain compressor rotational speed, the gas temperature in front of the gas generator turbine increases, and the fuel consumption rate of the gas generator decreases. If the variable vane is opened, the opposite situation occurs. At this time, due to the increase in the flow area of the power turbine, the exhaust gas back pressure of the gas generator is relatively reduced, the turbine expansion ratio is relatively increased, and the enthalpy drop is also increased. Thus, the rotation speed of the gas generator rotor increases, and the effective output power of the unit accordingly increases. The position of the common working point changes from the original point A to point C, and the common working point is far from the surge boundary. For a certain compressor rotational speed, the gas temperature before the gas generator turbine drops, and the fuel consumption rate of the gas generator increases.

Figure 4.59b shows the influence of variable vanes on the common working line of the entire unit. The dotted line *AE* is the common working line of the unit without variable vanes. If the surge boundary of the compressor has the shape of"2″ shown in the figure, the work cannot be performed at point *E* because at point *E*, it has entered the surge boundary, the compressor must be deflated at point *F*, or the variable vane of the compressor should be used to avoid engine surge. The thick black line in the figure is the common working line of the power turbine unit with variable vanes.

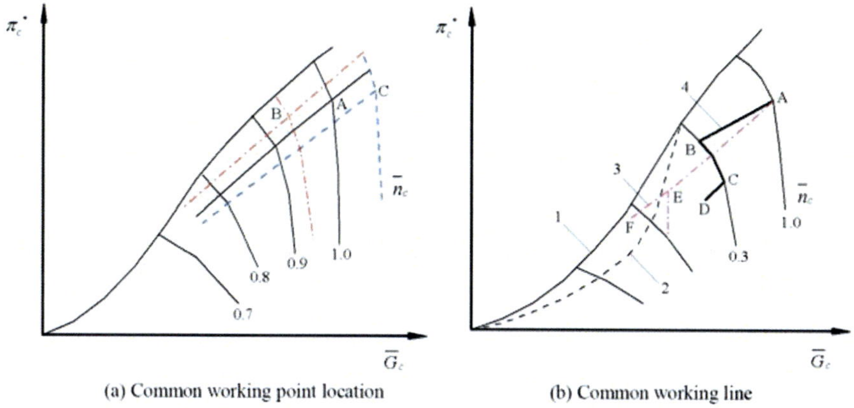

Fig. 4.59 Effect of the variable vane on the common working point location and common working line

Point *D* corresponds to the idle (idle) operating condition, and there is a large margin from the surge boundary line. In slow-moving conditions, the compressor does not need to deflate due to the opening of variable vanes.

The common working line with variable vanes shown in Fig. 4.59b indicate that points *D* and *E* of the idle mode correspond to a higher rotational speed and a lower gas initial temperature before the turbine. This line is also far from the surge boundary, which is beneficial to the acceleration of the unit. When the unit is running at point *D*, as long as the variable vane is quickly closed and the fuel flow rate is increased, a large output power can be quickly obtained.

According to the envelope of the fuel consumption rate of different variable vane turning angles, Fig. 4.60 determines the variation law of the turning angle and power with the minimum fuel consumption rate. Under the design condition and overloaded operation, the variable vane turning angle is at a fixed geometrical zero rotation position. As indicated by point *A*, under 80% working conditions, the variable vane is selected to be $-3°$; as indicated by Point *B* and point *C*, under 50% working conditions and 30% working conditions, the variable vane is selected to be $-6°$; between 50% working conditions and 80% working conditions, the turning angle of the variable vane should be between $-3°$ and $-6°$. For a more accurate determination of the changing law of the turning angle of the variable vane, it is necessary to use a smaller angle interval for numerical verification.

As shown in Fig. 4.60, the fuel consumption rate of the entire unit at low operating conditions has not decreased much. One main reason is that although the variable vane is small, the variable geometry power turbine can be operated at a high inlet total temperature, and the cycle efficiency of the entire unit is improved, but the drop in turbine efficiency will inevitably partially offset the increase in cycle efficiency. Especially when the variable vane is further closed, such as when the variable vane is close to the $-9°$ position, the increase in the cycle efficiency of the entire unit is completely offset by the excessive decrease in turbine efficiency. When the variable

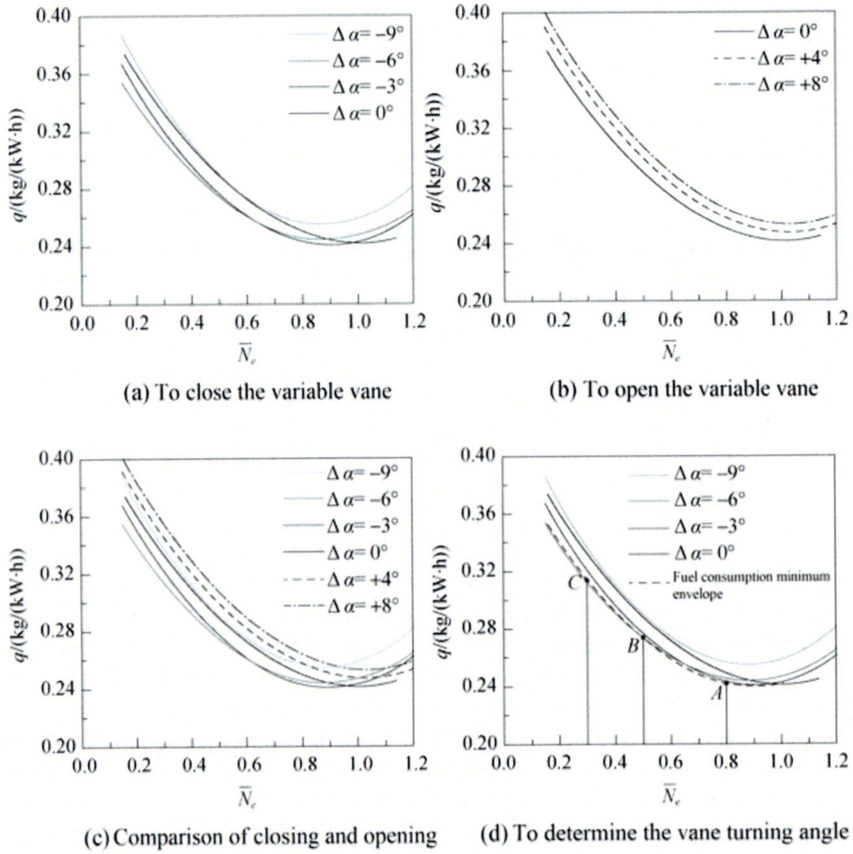

Fig. 4.60 Relationship between the fuel consumption rate of the variable geometry power turbine unit and the change in the variable vane turning angle

vane is opened, the efficiency of the turbine is also reduced at a larger negative incidence angle of attack. On the other hand, due to the small decrease in the total temperature at the turbine inlet, the cycle efficiency of the entire unit is also reduced. Therefore, the opening of variable vanes will also sacrifice the recycling benefits produced by the variable vane.

According to the change rule of the turning angle of the variable vane, Fig. 4.61 qualitatively shows the variable operating performance of the variable geometry power turbine and the fuel consumption characteristics of the variable geometry power turbine for the entire unit. After the variable geometry power turbine is adopted, the fuel consumption curve of the entire unit becomes relatively flat. At low operating conditions, the maximum fuel consumption can be reduced by 3–8%. However, the efficiency characteristics curve of the power turbine also shows that,

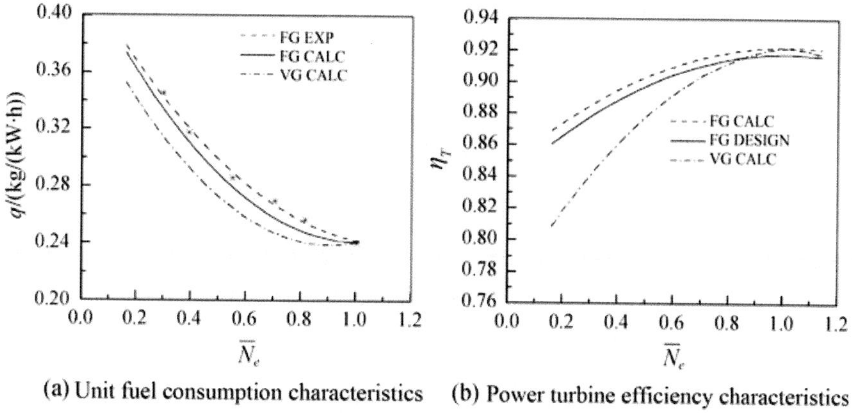

Fig. 4.61 Effects of variable vane on unit performance and efficiency changes of variable geometry power turbines

compared with the fixed geometry power turbine, the efficiency of the variable geometry power turbine is reduced by approximately 4% when the engine is in a low operating condition. Previous experimental research also shows that under the design condition, the radial gap clearance and leakage loss at both ends of the variable vane are relatively large, which reduces the efficiency of the variable geometry turbine to lower than the efficiency of the fixed geometry turbine by approximately 2%. In addition, under off-design conditions, the efficiency of variable geometry power turbines is more significantly reduced. In summary, the use of the variable geometry power turbine technology alone cannot significantly improve the economy of the simple cycle unit at low operating conditions. The variable geometry turbine technology can only show greater advantages when combined with advanced intercooling and recuperation cycle technologies. Nevertheless, the use of variable geometry turbine technology provides a feasible method for marine gas turbines to stabilize under low operating conditions and to achieve reliable and stable operation of gas turbines under all operating conditions.

4.5.2 Complex Cycle Gas Turbine

In gas turbine installations, compared with the simple cycle, the regenerative cycle makes the unit have a heat exchanger referred to as the regenerator. The high-temperature exhaust gas discharged from the turbines is used by this heat exchanger to heat the lower-temperature compressor air, thereby increasing the temperature of the compressed air when it enters the combustion chamber. If the outlet temperature of the combustion chamber is constant, the fuel supply can be reduced. After the variable geometry power turbine technology is adopted for the simple cycle unit, since the drop in turbine efficiency and the gap clearance leakage loss will offset part of the cycle revenue at low operating conditions, the use of regenerative cycle technology can improve the efficiency of the unit under low operating conditions more effectively than the variable geometry power turbine technology.

Figure 4.62 shows the effect of the presence or absence of variable vanes on the fuel consumption characteristics of simple cycle and regenerative cycle units. Using variable geometry power turbine technology, due to the operation at a higher total turbine inlet temperature, the turbine exhaust gas temperature will significantly increase. Therefore, the combination of the variable geometry power turbine technology and the regenerative cycle will further increase the thermal efficiency of the entire unit by improving the regenerative efficiency under low operating conditions. In addition, based on the intercooling recuperation cycle and variable geometry turbine technology, the WR-21 marine gas turbine fuel consumption curve is flat in most power ranges. Compared with the simple cycle LM2500 gas turbine, the total operating fuel consumption of the WR-21 gas turbine can be reduced by approximately 30%, corresponding to the US Navy's specified conditions with an atmospheric temperature of up to 38 °C. Under 30−100% operating conditions, the fuel consumption rate drops to 0.2224−0.2336 kg/kW · h (Fig. 4.63), which is significantly lower than that of the Solar5650 gas turbine.

Under ISO conditions, at 30–100% operating conditions, the fuel consumption rate of WR-21 is correspondingly 0.204–0.208 kg/kW · h, while for the newly launched MT30 gas turbine, although it only uses a simple cycle, its fuel consumption rate is only between 0.212 and 0.290 kg/kW · h. Especially under the design condition, the power of the MT30 gas turbine is up to 36 MW, and the thermal efficiency exceeds 40%. As can be further seen from Fig. 4.63, compared with the WR-21 marine gas turbine, regardless of whether the simple cycle gas turbine uses variable geometry power turbine technology, its fuel consumption level is much higher than that of the WR-21 gas turbine. Therefore, further development of simple cycle

Fig. 4.62 Effect of variable vane on the fuel consumption characteristics of simple cycle and recuperative cycle units

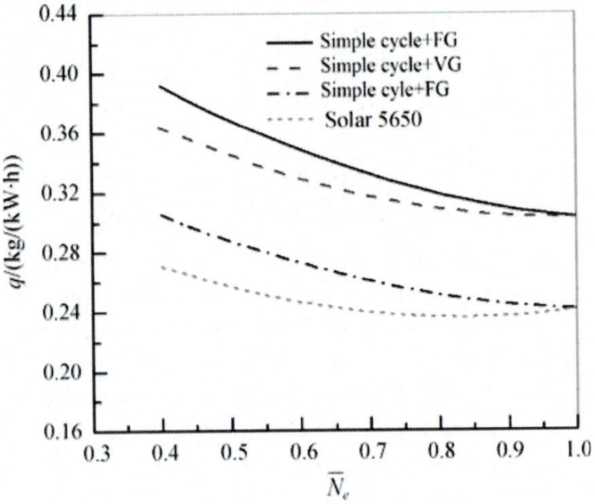

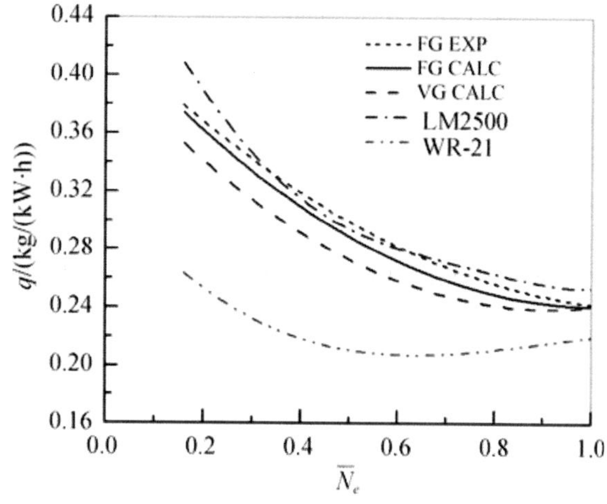

Fig. 4.63 Comparison of fuel consumption characteristics of WR21, LM2500 and typical marine gas turbines

marine gas turbines also needs to consider organic cooperation with intercooling and recuperation cycle technology.

4.6 Summary

This chapter focuses on the selection criteria and rule of the variable vane-endwall structure and its parameters. New methods for controlling variable vane-endwall losses, a high endwall angle variable vane turning design based on a stepped spherical endwall, the proposal and validation of full three-dimensional turning design concept for the high endwall angle variable vane, and a variable vane turning angle adjustment method and law for variable geometry turbine are summarized.

Variable vane-end gap position turning shaft parameters, including diameter and installation position, have a very important influence on the development and evolution of vane-end gap clearance leakage flow. The diameter of the turning shaft should be as large as possible to reduce the circumferential leakage area of the vane-end gap, and the shaft installation position should be arranged at the position where the vane-end profile load is the largest to block the gap clearance leakage flow caused by the lateral pressure difference. The variable geometry turbine adopts the form of a cylindrical endwall, and the vane-end gap clearance changes as the vane rotates, resulting in a nonuniform gap clearance contour. Especially for the large meridional expansion variable geometry turbine, the nonuniform change in the gap clearance is particularly obvious, but the spherical endwall can make the vane-end gap remain constant and minimal when the vane rotates, thereby improving the turbine aerodynamic performance.

The application of the vane-end groove/winglet technology in the variable vane can effectively reduce the leakage loss of the vane-end gap, and combined with the casing treatment technology, it can further improve the endwall zone flow and performance of the variable geometry turbine. For variable vanes with large expansion angle endwalls, pits or protrusions appear on the turning shaft end when the variable vanes rotate substantially deteriorates the flow field and turbine performance in the endwall zone. Based on the recognition of the difference in the loss caused by the pits and protrusions at the end of the variable vanes, variable vane-end modification technology for high endwall angle turbines was proposed, and the design technology was verified here.

Based on the understanding of the endwall flow and structural characteristics of the large meridional expansion variable-geometry turbine, a stepped spherical endwall modeling method is proposed to maintain a uniform and minimum gap, and an appropriate gap flow channel is improved to reorganize the endwall flow. The designed four-stage variable geometry turbine has the same computational efficiency as the fixed geometry turbine at a zero turning angle. A highly loaded design of vanes is proposed to reduce the number of vanes; simultaneously, the diameter of the turning shaft at the gap clearance is increased to reduce the gap leakage area as much as possible; and a three-dimensional redistribution of the vane load is carried out. Therefore, the method can reduce the total endwall load and shift the maximum load location backward, thereby suppressing the increased vane-end secondary flow loss caused by the highly loaded design. The designed single-stage variable geometry turbine has a slightly higher calculation efficiency than the fixed geometry turbine at a zero turning angle.

This chapter also qualitatively analyzes the influence law of variable geometry power turbine technology on the performance of the entire marine gas turbine unit and determines the change law of the variable vane turning angle of the minimum extreme value of the gas turbine fuel consumption rate. The study pointed out that for simple cycle gas turbine units, the use of variable geometry turbine technology cannot significantly reduce its fuel consumption rate, and the organic cooperation of advanced intercooling and recuperation technology with variable geometry turbines will be able to fully utilize their respective technical advantages. Under low working conditions, the fuel consumption rate of the entire unit is significantly reduced due to the improved heat recovery efficiency.

Chapter 5
Structural Design Technology of a Variable Vane System for Variable Geometry Turbines

Abstract This chapter provides an overview of the overall structural design of the variable vane system, detailed structural design of the variable vane, design of the vane turning control system, and evaluation of dynamic characteristics. The turbine variable vane structural design should be designed according to the design characteristics of high-temperature components, and the overall structural design should be based on the marine gas turbine power turbine structure.

5.1 Design of the Overall Structural Scheme of a Variable Vane System

The turbine variable vane structural design should be designed according to the design characteristics of high-temperature components, and the overall structural design should be based on the marine gas turbine power turbine structure. According to the overall requirements and turbine aerodynamic calculation results, the structural type of the turbine variable vane mechanism is selected, and the overall structural design scheme of the turbine variable vanes is formulated. The design structure of a typical marine gas turbine power turbine is shown in Fig. 5.1. From the perspective of assembly structure and function, the turbine is composed of four major parts: the power turbine rotor, variable geometry turbine stage (that is, variable vane stage), 2–5 stage stators, and power turbine support ring.

The front of the power turbine is connected to the corresponding flange of the upstream low-pressure turbine support ring through the front flange of the variable geometry turbine stage casing, and the rear is connected with the reduction gearbox through the coupling of the output end of the power turbine rotor. The adoption of variable geometry turbine technology can improve the gas turbine's maneuverability and gas turbine efficiency under part load conditions and simultaneously provide full preparation for the future development of high-performance complex cycle gas turbines. Stop assembly is adopted for positioning, between the marine gas turbine variable geometry turbine stage casing front, rear flanges and low-pressure turbine support ring, between 2 and 5 stage stator flanges, and between 2 and 5 stage stators

J. Gao et al., *Variable Geometry Turbine Technology for Marine Gas Turbines*,
https://doi.org/10.1007/978-981-19-6952-2_5

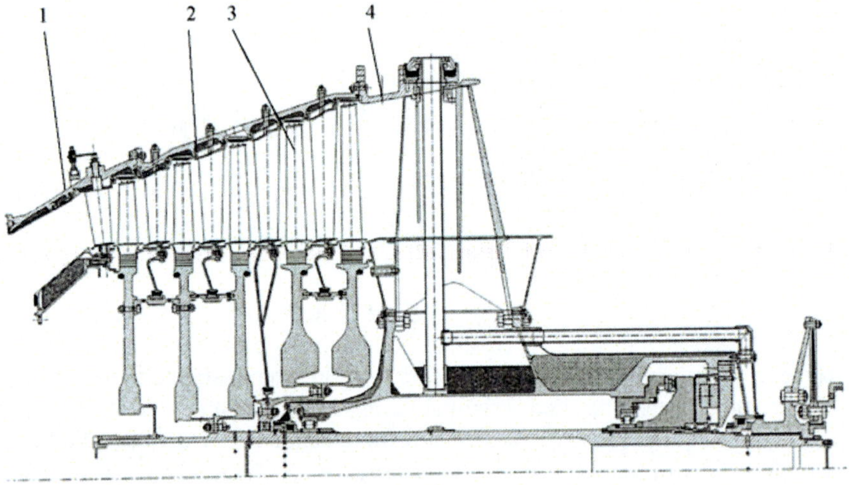

Fig. 5.1 Overall structure of the variable geometry power turbine. 1—Variable geometry turbine, 2—2 ~ 5 stage vane, 3—Power turbine rotor, 4—Power turbine support ring

and the power turbine support ring flanges. The flow section is composed of a 1-stage variable vane, a 4-stage variable vane group and a 5-stage turbine rotor blade. A honeycomb seal structure is utilized between each stage rotor blade tip and the casing. An air seal tooth seal structure is employed between all stages of partitions and rotors, between each stage of rotor blades and stator vane flanges, and between each stage of rotor blades and partitions.

5.2 Detailed Structural Design of a Variable Vane System

The variable geometry turbine stage is mainly composed of a variable vane, vane turning control system, variable geometry turbine stage casing, variable vane support structure and sealing structure. Since variable geometry turbine vanes can be rotated, a certain safety gap clearance must be reserved between the end surfaces of variable vanes and the endwall surfaces. Therefore, the focus of variable geometry turbine structural designs is to ensure that the advantages of variable geometry are not offset by too much reduction in turbine aerodynamic efficiency.

During the operation of the gas turbine, the variable vane turning angle is controlled by the vane turning control system to achieve the best coordination among the various components. The design scheme of the variable geometry turbine stage structure is shown in Fig. 5.2. The design points of the variable vane structural design are listed as follows:

(1) The turning mechanism of the variable vane of the variable geometry turbine adopts an integrated steering ring linkage to control the rotation of all vanes;

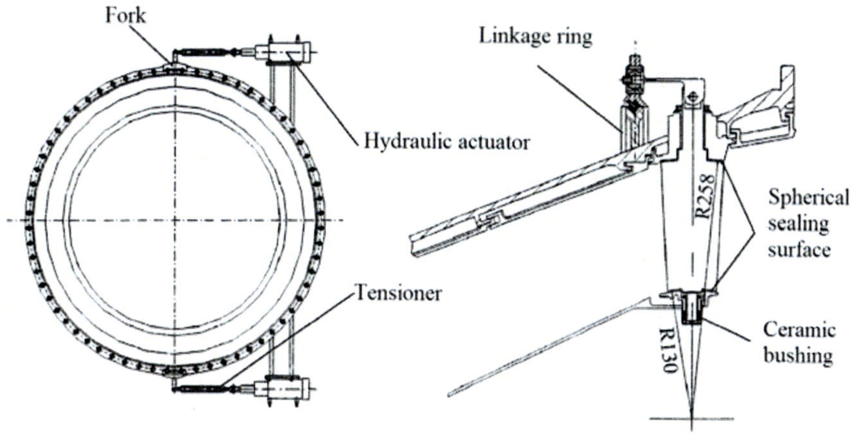

Fig. 5.2 Variable geometry turbine stage structures

(2) The sealing structure adopts a ball-type seal to minimize the gap leakage loss;
(3) Flexible graphite bushings are used for the rotating bearings to prevent the bearing from becoming stuck due to temperature changes.

5.2.1 Design of Variable Vane-End Gap Clearances

According to the analysis of the influence of the turbine vane structure on the aerodynamic performance of the variable geometry turbine, the vane-end structure is an important factor affecting the aerodynamic loss. The change law of the variable vane-end clearance loss gradually increases with a change in the turning angle; that is, it increases as the throat is closed or opened. To minimize the increase in the gap leakage loss caused by a change in the turning angle, the tip of the vane and the matching casing are designed as a concentric spherical structure. This design can reduce the increase in the gap clearance loss caused by a change in the turning angle. The variable vane structure is shown in Fig. 5.3.

To investigate the effect of the endwall and gap clearance on the variable geometry turbine efficiency, four different schemes were selected for a comparative study: 0.5 mm clearance of the spherical endwall, 0.8 mm clearance of the spherical endwall, 0.5 mm clearance of the cylindrical endwall and 0.8 mm clearance of the cylindrical endwall. Through a comparative analysis, it can be seen that under design conditions, the efficiency of the turbine with the spherical endwall structure is better than the variable geometry turbine with the ordinary endwall structure. Note that the variable vane with the spherical endwall structure only needs to consider the thermal expansion gap during the gap clearance design and does not need to consider the gap clearance change caused by the change in the vane turning angle. Thus, the smaller vane-end gap clearance can be reserved during the structural design of variable geometry turbines.

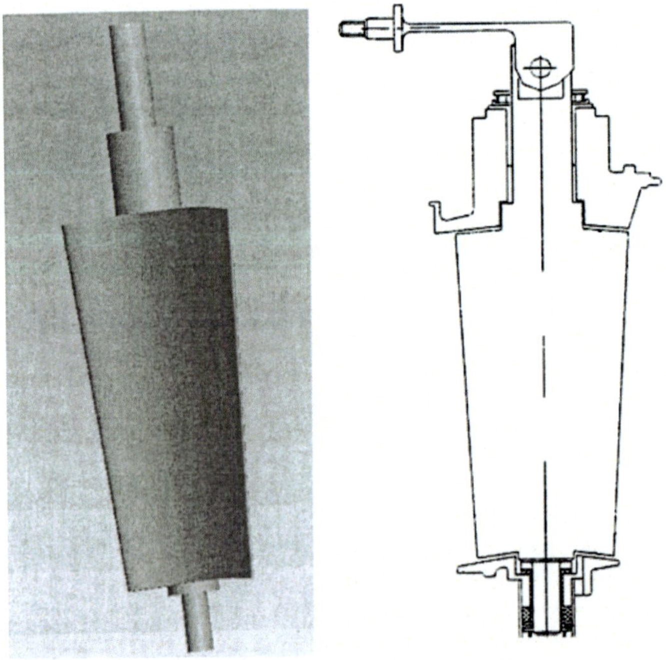

Fig. 5.3 Variable vane with spherical seal endwall

5.2.2 *Design of the Variable Vane Rotating Bearing and Seal*

The turning shaft of the variable vane adopts a cylindrical design; it is mounted on two bushes made of flexible graphite (refer to Fig. 5.4), which avoids the phenomenon of bearing jamming due to temperature changes of the turning shaft and bearing sleeve in all cases. In addition, the use of a flexible graphite sleeve can also reduce the gap clearance between the turning shaft and the sleeve, and simultaneously, it has a sealing role, thereby reducing gas leakage and improving the aerodynamic performance of the variable geometry turbine.

5.2.3 *Variable Geometry Turbine Casing Design*

The variable geometry turbine casing (refer to Fig. 5.5) is mainly used to support the variable vanes and to bear the aerodynamic load and axial force of the variable vanes. The inner hook of the casing is used to hang the front and rear outer casings and guard rings, and aluminum silicate fiber felt is added between the casing and the casing and guard rings to prevent heat. A spherical guard plate is installed above the variable vane, and the matching place of the floating ring and the variable vane

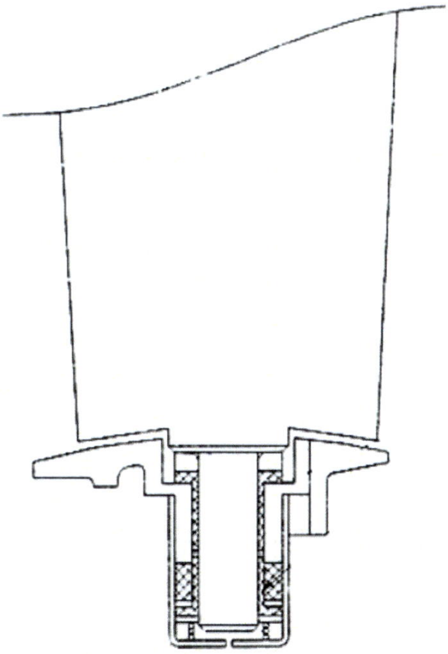

Fig. 5.4 Design scheme of the variable vane rotating bearing

is also designed as a spherical surface to ensure cooperation between the variable vane and the casing. In addition, aluminum silicate fiber quilt is added between the adapter tube and the inner cover to prevent heat. This quilt is connected between the front end of the adapter cylinder and the low-pressure turbine support ring, and the connection cylinder, inner casing and floating ring are connected by a bolt.

5.2.4 *Design of Variable Vane Shaft and Casing Hole*

The variable vane not only needs to be able to flexibly rotate but also to ensure a reliable seal with the casing, and a Teflon bushing is used between the upper journal of the vane and the casing. The coaxiality of the upper and lower journals of the variable vane with an inner ring is 0.02; the cooperation between the upper journal and the bushing can be 14H7/g6; the hole of the bushing and the casing is 17H7/h6; and the width of the boss of the casing installation vane and the size of the transfer boss of the vane body and journal can be determined by optimization. The specific structure is shown in Fig. 5.6.

The lower shaft of the variable vane adopts a cylindrical design. Due to the higher temperature of the lower turning shaft, the turning shaft is mounted on a bush made of flexible graphite (refer to Fig. 5.7), which avoids the phenomenon of bearing jamming due to temperature changes of the turning shaft and bearing bush in all cases. The use of flexible graphite bushings ensures that the gap clearance between

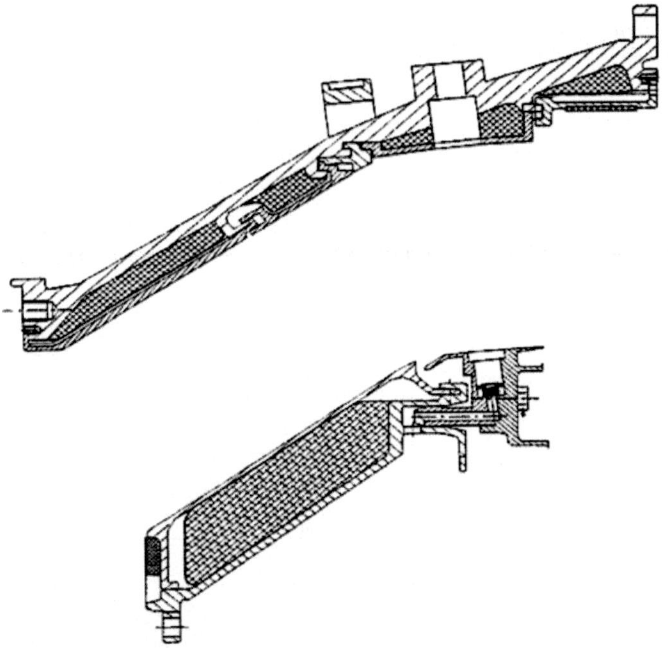

Fig. 5.5 Variable geometry turbine casing

Fig. 5.6 Variable vane tip shaft associated structure

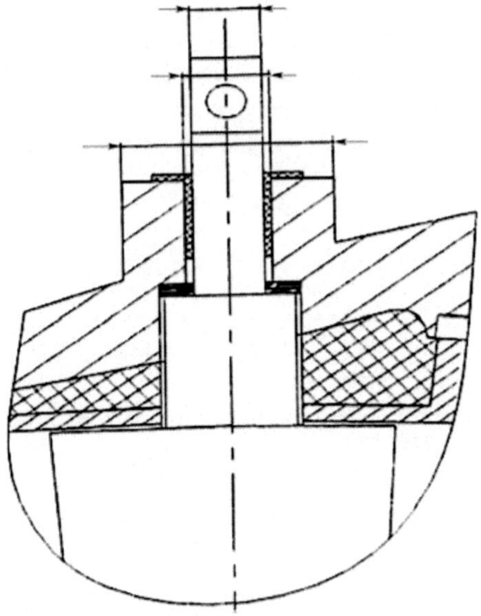

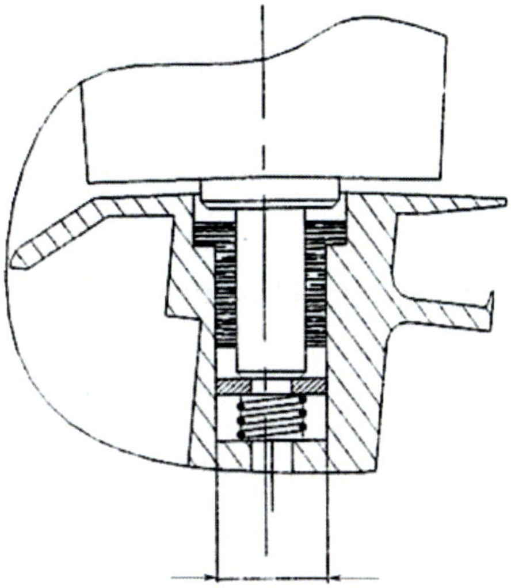

Fig. 5.7 Variable vane hub shaft associated structure

the turning shaft and the bushings is small, thereby having a sealing role and reducing the gas leakage.

5.2.5 *Variable Vane Material Properties*

The actual working conditions of the variable vanes are presented as follows: high temperature gas flow, temperatures up to 1100 K, large temperature difference, uneven vane thickness leading to thermal stresses, aerodynamic force generated when the gas flows through the vane, vibrations caused by pulsation load, etc. Therefore, to reduce the vane-end gap clearance, the selected material must have a small expansion coefficient, and to meet other working conditions, the selected material must also have certain characteristics, such as high temperature resistance, corrosion resistance, low thermal stress, and high rigidity. In this design, the variable vane material was selected as the K452 cast superalloy.

The K452 cast superalloy is a cast nickel-based superalloy with excellent corrosion resistance. It has a smaller expansion coefficient than similar alloys, has high rigidity and toughness, and does not contain precious metals. It is inexpensive and has good casting performance. Its performance characteristics are shown in Tables 5.1, 5.2 and 5.3.

Table 5.1 K452 alloy expansion coefficient table

Temperature (°C)	Room temperature	300	400	500	600	700	800	900
Expansion coefficient ($\times 10^{-6}$/°C)	12.5	13.1	13.4	13.7	14.1	14.6	15.1	15.8

Table 5.2 K452 Alloy thermal conductivity table

Temperature (°C)	Room temperature	300	400	500	600	700	800	900
Thermal conductivity (w/m °C)	8.75	14.1	16	17.8	19.6	21.2	22.8	24.2

Table 5.3 K452 alloy tensile properties

Temperature (°C)	Room temperature	600	700	800	850	900	950	1000
σ (b/MPa)	830	910	930	810	665	540	355	280

5.3 Design and Dynamic Characteristics Evaluation of a Variable Vane Turning Control System

5.3.1 Design of Rocker Arm and Its Components

The rocker arm assembly is an important device connecting the vane turning mechanism and variable vane. The torsional moment of the variable vane is applied through the rocker arm assembly. There are many ways to connect the rocker arm assembly to the vane journal and linkage ring. In this design, the rocker arm assembly with articulated bearing is utilized, as shown in Fig. 5.8. This structure relies on the spherical pair (inclination angle of the radial joint bearing) to compensate for the change in the displacement angle. For the selection of radial joint bearings, please refer to GB304.4 and GB304.7. The joint method of the joint bearing and rocker arm is the nut connection.

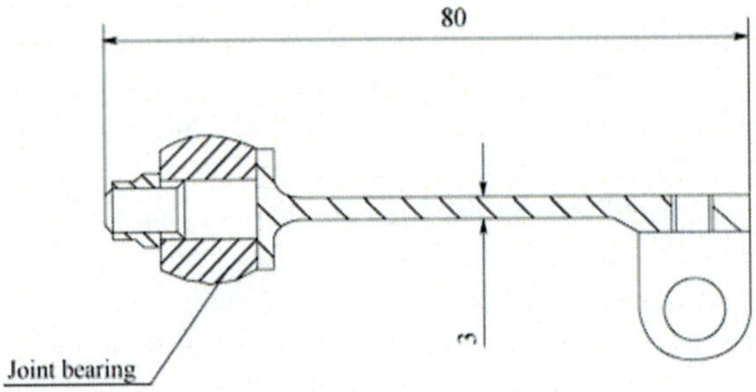

Fig. 5.8 Rocker arm assembly with articulated bearing

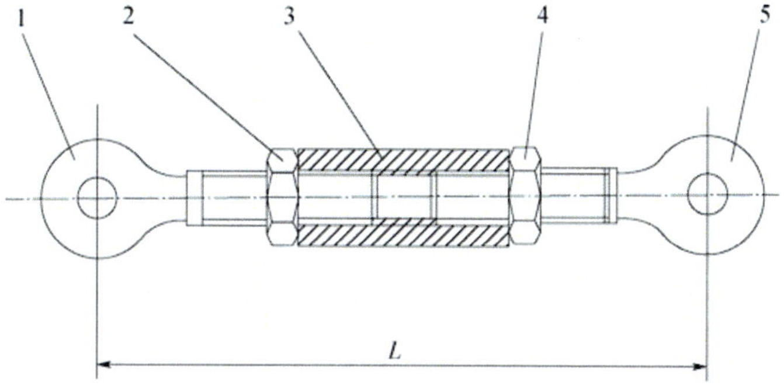

Fig. 5.9 Interlocking rod assembly. 1—Left-hand thread integral rod end joint bearing, 2—Left-hand nut, 3—Interlocking rod, 4—Right-hand nut, 5—Right-hand thread integral rod end joint bearing

5.3.2 Design of Linkage Rods and Their Components

The function of the linkage rod is to connect the linkage ring with the actuating cylinder. The linkage rod is an adjustment device to ensure that the variable vanes are in the initial and end positions. The structure of the linkage rod assembly is shown in Fig. 5.9.

In the structure shown in Fig. 5.9, the threads that form the two ends of the linkage rod adopt a left and right structure to adjust the design position of the connection point of the linkage ring and the actuating cylinder, and its length and the position of the joint bearing hole are determined according to the orientation of the connected actuator or linkage lug. The matching length of the rod end of the joint bearing and the linkage rod is not less than 1.5 times the nominal diameter of the thread.

The type and size of the integral rod end joint bearings of variable geometry turbine variable vanes are selected according to the GB304.2 and GB9161 standard series and refer to the specific stress conditions of the structure (radial and axial loads) and the maximum tilt angle that the structure may appear to select.

5.3.3 Design and Calculation of the Variable Vane Turning Mechanism

The turning mechanism consists of the following parts: hydraulic actuator, shift fork, linkage ring, tensioner and rocker arm. The elastic device is driven by the movement of the hydraulic actuating cylinder. The elastic device is connected to the shift fork, and the left and right shift forks tighten the upper and lower half rings of the linkage ring. The linking ring drives the turning shaft of the variable vane through the turning arm with a self-aligning ball bearing. A schematic of the vane turning mechanism is shown in Fig. 5.10. The reaction force and displacement of the aerodynamic torque

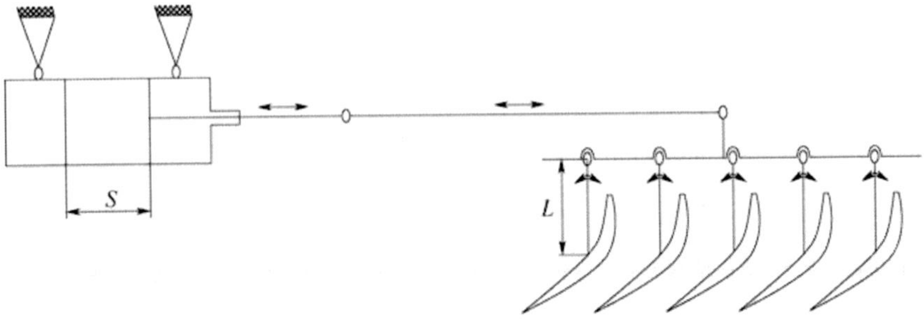

Fig. 5.10 Schematic of the rotating structure

on the piston of the actuating cylinder are obtained through calculation, and a suitable hydraulic actuating cylinder is selected according to the needs of the operator.

1. The reaction force and displacement of the aerodynamic torque on the piston

The reaction force of various stages of the aerodynamic moment acting on the piston rod is:

$$F = \sum_{i=1}^{n} (M_i L_{Bi}/L_D L_{Ai})(R_{A1}/R_{B1}) \tag{5.1}$$

The displacement of the piston rod (any position within the stroke range) is:

$$S = 2[L_D L_{A1}(\sin\alpha_1 - \sin\alpha)/L_{B2}](R_{A1}/R_{A2}) \tag{5.2}$$

The maximum stroke displacement of the piston rod is:

$$S_{MAX} = 2L_{A1}(\sin\alpha_1 - \sin\alpha)(R_{A1}/R_{A2}) \tag{5.3}$$

In the formula, M_i is half of the aerodynamic torque of each variable vane stage (counted by two actuating cylinders). This torque is given by the aerodynamic calculation according to the vane torque at the maximum aerodynamic load of the engine, Nm;

L_{Ai} length of the rocker arm at all stages, mm;
L_{Bi} length of crank follower rod at all stages, mm;
L_D lever length, mm;
R_{Ai} height from the connection point of each stage control ring and linkage to the axis of the engine, mm;
R_{Bi} height from the connection point between the rocker arm and the control ring at all stages to the axis of the engine, mm;
α angle of change of the rocker arm, (°);
α_i angle between the rocker arm of each stage at the maximum working position and the axis of the engine (initial position) (°).

2. Vane torsional moment estimation

As the gas passes through the turbine stage, the static pressure increases, which also changes its axial velocity. The force generated by this process can be estimated by applying the principle of conservation of momentum to the gas in a control body.

$$F_A + P_2A_2 + mV_{a2}^2 = P_1A_1 + mV_{a1} \quad (5.4)$$

$$F_A = P_1A_1 + mV_{a1} - mV_{a2}^2 - P_2A_2 \quad (5.5)$$

In the formula:

F_A—axial force acting on the gas in the body through the vane, N;
P_1—static pressure at the entrance of the vane, Pa;
P_2—static pressure at the outlet of the vane, Pa;
A_1—projection area at the vane control body inlet, mm^2;
A_2—projection area at the vane control body outlet, mm^2;
m—mass flow through each turbine blade, kg/s;
V_{a1}—axial velocity at turbine blade control body inlet, mm/s;
V_{a2}—axial velocity at turbine blade control body outlet, mm/s.

5.3.4 *Evaluation of the Dynamic Characteristics of the Variable Vane Turning Mechanism*

The precise control of variable geometry turbine variable vanes in high-temperature and high-pressure environments is the key to the success of variable geometry turbine technology. Therefore, after the structural design of the variable vane system is completed, its dynamic characteristics need to be evaluated. However, a feasible method for the vane dynamic characteristics evaluation of variable geometry turbines is still lacking. Therefore, to successfully apply turbine variable geometry technology to marine gas turbines, a simulation evaluation method for the dynamic characteristics of the variable vane turning mechanism and research on the evaluation methods of dynamic influencing factors, such as mechanism motion accuracy, blocking force, and structural strength, are urgently needed. The process of the dynamic simulation method of a typical kinematic mechanism is also needed.

5.4 Summary

This chapter provides an overview of the overall structural design of the variable vane system, the detailed structural design of the variable vane, the design of the vane turning control system, and the evaluation of dynamic characteristics.

The precise control, maintainability and reliability of the variable vanes under high-temperature and high-pressure environments are key to the success of marine gas turbines with variable geometry turbines. In the structural design of the vane turning mechanism, in addition to meeting the requirements of flexible, reliable and stable turning of the variable vanes and accurate positioning to a specific position, the influence of the flow field characteristics of the vanes on the design of the vane turning mechanism must also be considered so that the vane turning mechanism can completely and reliably work in harsh environments.

Chapter 6
Aerodynamic Characteristics and Reliability Test Technology for a Variable Geometry Turbine

Abstract This chapter mainly summarizes the aerodynamic performance test of the variable vane linear cascade, aerodynamic performance and transient characteristics test of the variable vane sector cascade, variable vane turbine-stage aerodynamic performance test, and thermal environment structure validation test for a full-loop variable vane. The aerodynamic and structural design of variable geometry turbines is challenging. In the development process of variable geometry turbines, it is necessary to carry out experiments in terms of aerodynamics, structural design and reliability to ensure the high efficiency, high reliability and maintainability of variable geometry turbines under wide operating conditions.

6.1 Aerodynamic Performance Test of a Variable Vane Linear Cascade

To investigate the effect of the variable vane-end groove structure on the endwall performance of the variable geometry turbine, based on the variable vane linear cascade aerodynamic performance test, the static pressure distribution at the midspan and endwall of vanes and the total pressure loss coefficient distribution at the turbine outlet at different vane turning angles are measured. The flow loss characteristics of the variable vane-end gap leakage are also analyzed. The control effect of the vane-end groove on the vane-end clearance leakage flow is examined by comparing the aerodynamic performance difference of the variable vane with and without the end groove structure.

6.1.1 Experimental Device and Test

1. Test device

This test is mainly conducted to evaluate the aerodynamic performance of a variable vane linear cascade at low Mach numbers. Therefore, the low mass flow and high-pressure ratio continuous air source of Harbin Engineering University, which has

J. Gao et al., *Variable Geometry Turbine Technology for Marine Gas Turbines*,
https://doi.org/10.1007/978-981-19-6952-2_6

a flow rate of 4.2 kg/s and a pressure ratio of 2, is employed. The motor power is 560 kW.

The low-speed linear cascade wind tunnel that was used in the test is shown in Fig. 6.1. Stable air flow is generated by a continuous air source with a small flow rate and a high-pressure ratio and then passes through a ventilation pipe to reach the low-speed wind tunnel. When the air flow passes through the wind tunnel, in the stabilizing section, the air flow becomes high-quality air with stable pressure and velocity. The contraction process of the contraction section enables the airflow cross-section to conform to the size of the turbine cascade and then guides the flow through the straight section of the turbine cascade, thereby obtaining the airflow of the axial intake required by the turbine cascade.

2. Variable vane linear cascade

The variable vane linear cascade test is mainly composed of 5 variable vanes (refer to Fig. 6.2a) and upper and lower endwalls. As shown in Fig. 6.2, two sets of cascade test pieces with or without the groove structure on the vane tip are designed and processed (refer to Fig. 6.2b). The test vane is a straight vane structure with a vane pitch of 60 mm and a vane height of 88 mm. A turning shaft is provided at the maximum thickness of the vane; the diameter of the turning shaft is 20 mm; and the height of the turning shaft is 29 mm. The vane tip gap clearance is 2 mm. A disc is connected to the lower end of the vane, and the diameter of the disc is 82 mm. The groove depth of turbine vanes with grooves on the tip is 2 mm. Because the parameters of the turbine cascade under variable vane turning angle conditions must be measured while measuring the parameters, the turning angle of the turbine cascade must be changed. Therefore, this problem is solved by installing an angle scale and vane turning device on the upper endwall of the turbine cascade, as shown in Fig. 6.2c.

Fig. 6.1 Low-speed linear cascade aerodynamic test bench

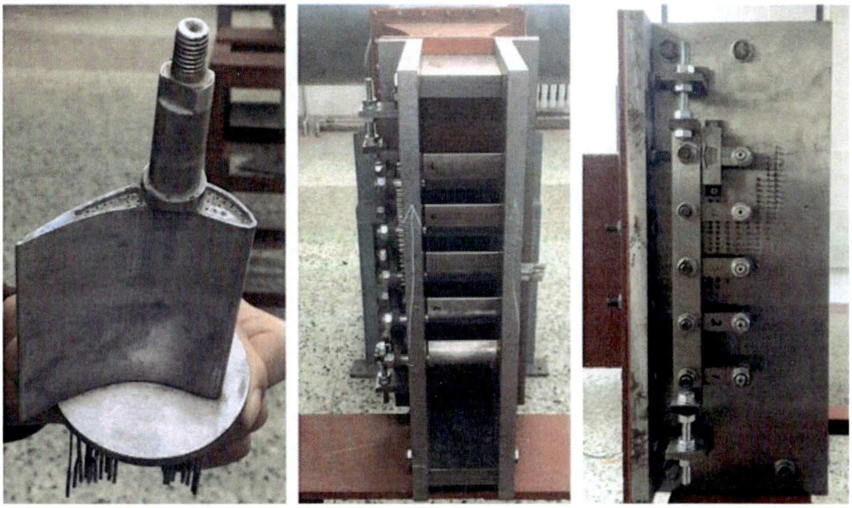

(a) Variable vane (b) Variable cascade (c) Vane turning mechanism

Fig. 6.2 Variable linear cascade test piece

6.1.2 Test Measurement Plan

1. Test scheme

In this test, a steady-state pressure measurement system is utilized for pressure measurement. The variable geometry turbine is measured at an inlet of 90°, a gap clearance of 2 mm and turning angles of −6°, 0° and +6° for the static pressure distribution of the midspan vane profile, the static pressure distribution of the endwall, the total pressure loss and the outflow angle at the vane outlet for the vanes with and without grooves on the tip. The main measurement parameters are described below.

1) Measurement of inlet and outlet parameters of the cascade

To measure the total pressure and total temperature at the inlet of the variable geometry turbine linear cascade and the total pressure, static pressure and velocity distribution along the spanwise direction at the cascade outlet, this experiment uses a three-dimensional coordinate frame. Therefore, a rectangular distribution is applied in the selection of measurement points, as shown in Fig. 6.3. The outlet measurement point distribution is a rectangular measurement area with 24 columns in the axial direction and 25 columns in the circumferential direction. To obtain better measurement results, 1.5 times the width of the flow channel in the circumferential direction is selected to completely cover the measurement flow channel. In addition, the measuring point is encrypted in the vane-end gap clearance area. The total pressure probe, thermocouple and several static pressure measuring holes upstream of the turbine cascade are set to measure the total pressure, total temperature and static pressure before the cascade. Measurement of the flow parameters at the outlet of the cascade is

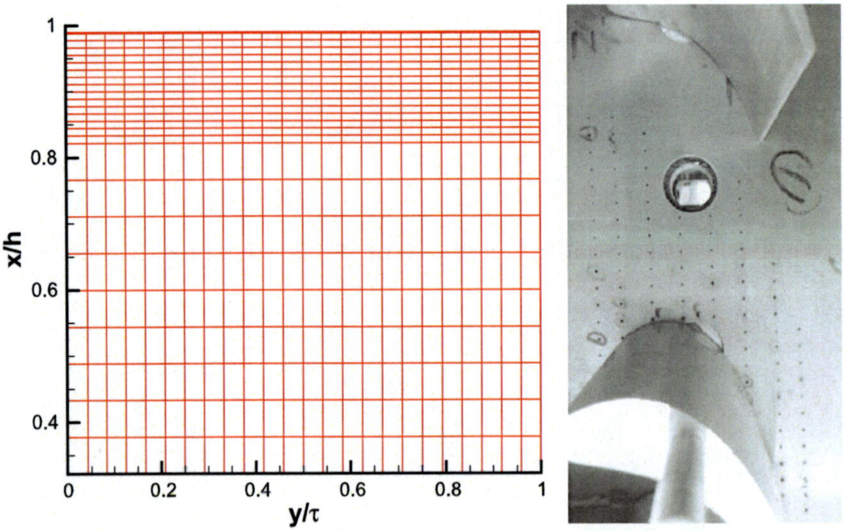

Fig. 6.3 Distributions of cascade outlet measurement and endwall measurement points

performed by means of a five-hole aerodynamic probe and a three-dimensional, automatic positioning coordinate frame system.

The variable cascade outlet measurement adopts an L-shaped, conical head-shaped, five-hole probe with a probe diameter of 1.6 mm. During the cascade test, the five-hole probe is installed on a five-degree-of-freedom coordinate frame driven by a motor. Using the motor, movement in the axial, span and pitch directions and pressure and airflow data measurements can be achieved.

Three types of measurements of three-dimensional flow fields are obtained with a five-hole probe: countermeasurement, semicountermeasurement and noncountermeasurement. This test uses a noncounter measurement method. The steps of the noncountermeasurement is to directly put the probe of the five-hole aerodynamic probe into the measurement flow fields and to ensure that the probe's aerodynamic center direction is consistent with the axial direction of the airflow. Next, according to the pressures of the five pressure measuring holes and the three-dimensional, nonopposed calibration curve of the probe, the pitch angle α and yaw angle β are obtained. According to α and β, the total pressure and static pressure are then obtained through the probe characteristics curve and calculation formula. The magnitude and direction of the measured air velocity are obtained. An advantage of this measurement method is that the measurement operation is simple with a short measurement time, while the disadvantage of this measurement method is that the workload of probe calibration and data processing is greatly increased compared with the first two methods. Generally, this method can obtain better measurement accuracy when the variation range of α and β is $\pm$ 30° during probe calibration.

2) Measurement of pressure distribution on vane surface profile

To measure the pressure distribution of the middle section of the vane profile, the measurement of the profile pressure is carried out by drilling holes in the measuring section and by radially guiding the pressure from the inside of the vane to the pressure sensor. The pressure channel is led out from the bottom end of the vane.

3) Pressure distribution at the vane gap clearance endwall

The pressure distribution at the vane gap clearance endwall is measured. There are 6 columns of measurement points at the endwall (16 measurement points in the first column, 15 points in the second column, 7 points in the third column, 7 points in the fourth column, 17 points in the fifth column, and 16 points in the sixth column), as shown in Fig. 6.3. The pressure measurement at the vane endwall is carried out by using the cross-section punching at the measurement endwall to introduce airflow pressure to the pressure sensor.

Note that during the cascade test, various factors cause errors in the test results. The purpose of analyzing and studying the measurement errors is to determine the causes of the errors and to try to avoid or reduce the factors that cause the errors and improve the measurement accuracy. Second, through the analysis and research of the measurement error, the size and variation rule of the measurement error are obtained, the measurement result is corrected, and the reliability of the measurement is judged. The errors in the test can generally be summarized as instrument error, use error, environmental error, method error, etc. The error accuracy of the main measuring instruments in this cascade test is described as follows: the angular positioning error of the five-hole probe during the cascade test is less than 0.1°; the positioning error of the measurement point is less than 0.5 mm; and the uncertainty in the measurement velocity and total pressure is less than 1%.

2. Experimental scheme

1) Installation of test equipment

(1) On the basis of the test wind tunnel that is selected, the voltage stabilizing section, contraction section and variable geometry turbine cascade are installed;
(2) The automatic positioning coordinate frame system is installed next to the turbine cascade, and the coordinate frame position is adjusted;
(3) The thermocouple and total pressure probe are installed in the voltage stabilizing box; the five-hole probe is installed in the coordinate frame; and the probe and static pressure hole are connected to the sensor with a plastic gasket hose.

2) Check of relevant test equipment

(1) The test air source is checked to ensure normal operation of the air source and to determine whether it can reach the specified wind speed and flow rate;
(2) The ventilation pipe is checked to ensure that it is sealed to prevent air leakage and greater damage at high wind speeds;

(3) The voltage stabilizing section, contracting section and fan-shaped straight section are checked to ensure that they are completely fixed and to determine whether there is any air leakage;
(4) The variable geometry turbine cascade checked to determine whether it is fixed;
(5) Each measuring point is checked to ensure that they are sealed or connected to the sensor, and the thermocouple, total pressure probe and five-hole probe checked to ensure that they are connected to the sensor;
(6) The pressure sensor display is checked to determine whether it is correct;
(7) The program used is checked to ensure that it is correctly written;
(8) The five-hole probe is checked to ensure that it is correctly placed and to determine whether the probe is facing the incoming flow.

3) Opening of the measurement system and sensor data cabinet and starting of the fan

The display result of each sensor was checked to ensure that it was within the normal range, and then the fan was immediately started. For the specific operation, refer to the start-up process in the relevant operating procedures of the test bench.

(1) The circulating water supply pump was turned on, and the water supply pressure was checked to confirm a normal pressure value;
(2) The air source oil circulation system was turned on, and the oil system was checked to ensure normal operation of the system and that the oil system is free of leakage;
(3) The fan control system was debugged to confirm normal operation of the system.

After the fan is started, the working conditions of the flow field are confirmed, and the sensor is checked to ensure normal operation. Afterward, the fan is controlled to change the air flow rate, and the total pressure at the inlet of the cascade is monitored.

4) Measuring various parameters

(1) The coordinate frame is controlled so that the five-hole probe reaches the initial measuring point;
(2) The five-hole probe calibration procedure is run to calibrate the direction of the five-hole probe;
(3) The measuring point program is run to obtain the total pressure, static pressure, velocity and direction parameters of each measuring point at the outlet of the cascade and the total pressure and total temperature at the inlet;
(4) After the measuring point program is completed, the measured data is saved, and the measuring program is closed;
(5) The five-hole probe is moved back to the initial measuring point;
(6) The static pressure measurement program is run to measure the pressure of the profile surface at the vane midspan and save it;
(7) The measurement program is closed.

First, the turbine variable cascade with no groove at the tip of the vane is installed, the mass flow rate of the air flow is changed, and the above processes are separately repeated. Next, the variable geometry turbine cascade with grooves is replaced, and the total pressure, static pressure, velocity and direction parameters of each measuring point of the variable geometry turbine cascade with grooves, as well as the inlet total pressure and total temperature, are measured.

6.1.3 Typical Experimental Results

The main measurement results of this test include the pressure distribution of the variable cascade profile for different vane turning angles, the static pressure distribution of the casing endwall for different turning angles with or without a tip groove structure, the outlet total pressure loss distribution and the outlet airflow angle along the spanwise direction. Some representative results are shown in Figs. 6.4, 6.5, 6.6 and 6.7. Due to space limitations, a detailed discussion of the results will not be repeated. Interested readers can refer to the relevant parts of Chaps. 2, 3 and 4.

6.2 Aerodynamic Performance and Transient Characteristics Test of a Variable Vane Sector Cascade

To investigate the variable vane-end flow performance and the performance characteristics of the transition state generated by the turning of the vanes, experiments on the aerodynamic performance and transient characteristics of the variable vane sector cascades are needed. According to the test requirements, the turbine variable vane

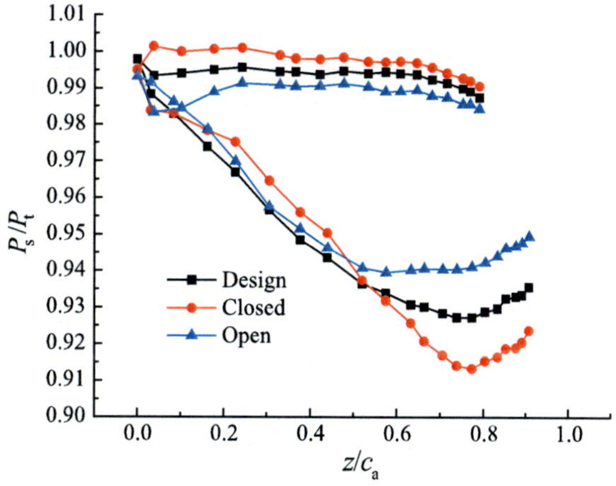

Fig. 6.4 Variable cascade surface pressure distributions at different vane turning angles

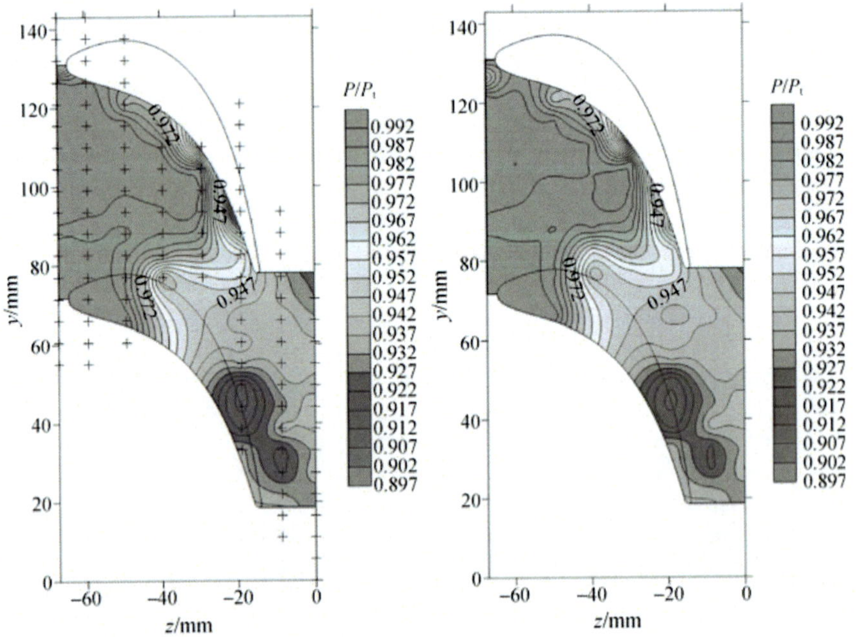

Fig. 6.5 Variable cascade casing endwall static pressure distribution at a −6° turning angle

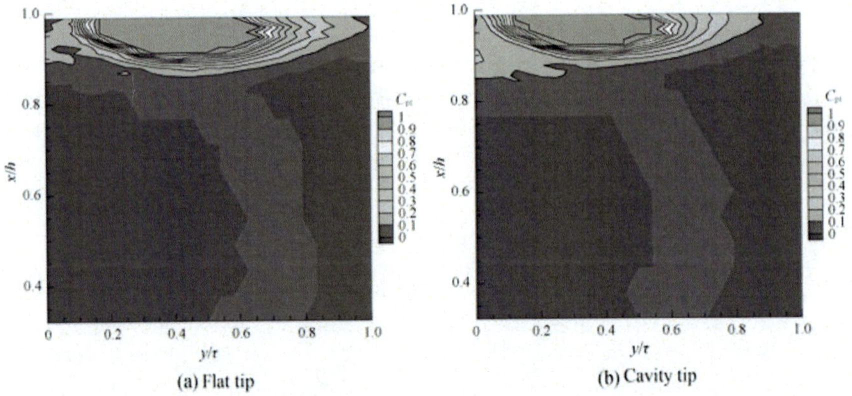

Fig. 6.6 Variable cascade outlet total pressure loss distribution at a −6° turning angle

sector cascade test piece is designed and manufactured, and the aerodynamic performance and transient characteristics test of the variable vane sector cascade under the condition of three outlet Mach numbers and five vane turning angles are completed on the wind tunnel test bench. According to similarity theory, when the test cascade flow is in the self-modeling zone, the model cascade must be geometrically similar to the actual cascade, and the inlet Mach number must be equal to the vane cascade.

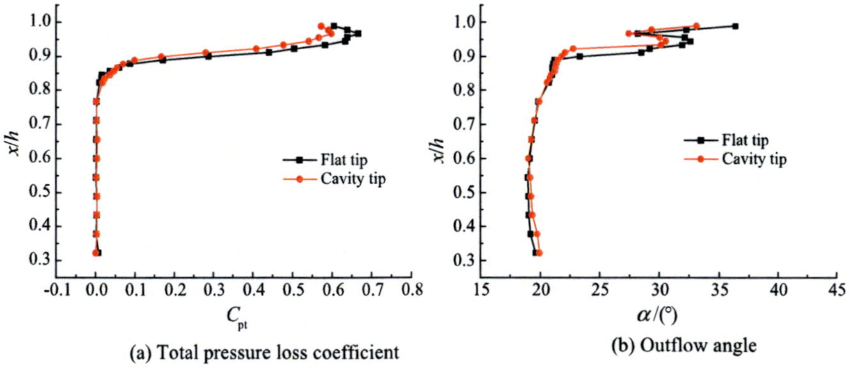

Fig. 6.7 Variable cascade outlet total pressure loss coefficient and outflow angle distribution along the spanwise direction at a −6° turning angle

6.2.1 Test and Measurement System

1. Test bench

The test is completed on the subsonic sector cascade test rig of the 703 Research Institute of the China Shipbuilding Corporation. The test rig has a large mass flow, high-pressure head, coolable air source conditions, stable air volume, and small pressure fluctuations, which can meet the requirements of various working conditions for the aerodynamic performance test of turbine cascades. Figures 6.8 and 6.9 show the sector cascade test system and its on-site diagram, respectively.

2. Measurement method

The measurement of the aerodynamic parameters of the flow field behind the variable sector cascade is performed with a five-hole ball-head probe. The five-hole probe

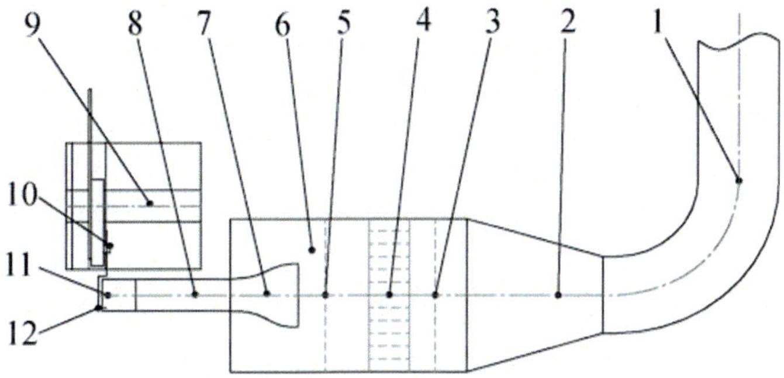

Fig. 6.8 Schematic of the sector cascade test system. 1-Intake pipe, 2-Expansion section, 3-Filter screen, 4-Rectifier grid, 5-Rectifier screen, 6-Stabilizer tube, 7-Contraction section, 8-Transition section, 9-Probe coordinate frame, 10-Probe moving mechanism, 11-Test cascade, 12-Measurement probe

Fig. 6.9 Site view of the sector cascade wind tunnel

is the most basic and most commonly utilized instrument for measuring the time-averaged characteristic parameters of airflow (referring to the magnitude and direction of the flow velocity, total pressure and static pressure). Because this measuring method has the advantages of a simple measuring principle, convenient use, probes that are not easily damaged, and convenient maintenance, it is still one of the main methods for measuring the three-dimensional, time-averaged flow field. In this test, the measurement of the airflow parameters at the outlet of the cascade is performed with a five-hole probe. When measuring the airflow parameters at the outlet of the cascade, the five-hole probe needs to be moved in the radial and circumferential directions of the vane. During the cascade measurement, the probe can be accurately positioned, and the probe must be clamped so that it does not shake in the airflow to ensure the accuracy of the measurement data. The probe motion control coordinate frame that is employed can achieve a circumferential motion range greater than ±30°, a radial motion ranges up to 300 mm, and a probe angle direction control range of 360°, which can meet the requirements of measuring the movement of the cascade exit cross-section in the test. The test of the total pressure in front of the grids is completed by the total pressure test device shown in Fig. 6.9. The total pressure probe is fixed in the stabilizer tube and transition section. The total pressure hole is facing the main channel. The total pressure probe can measure the total pressure in front of the sector cascade.

3. Measuring sensor

In this test, the air pressure of all pressure probes and the static pressure holes on the surface of the vane are collected using the four-channel motion control and

320-channel switching pressure collection cabinet shown in Fig. 6.9. The cabinet can simultaneously control 4-axis movement. Through the on and off feature of the solenoid valve, each sensor of the 16-channel, digital pressure sensor array can be switched to collect 20 on-site gas pressure signals in turn. Through this switching, the number of on-site signals collected by the pressure can reach 16 channels × 20 times = 320 channels. The core pressure sensor of the measurement system is a gauge pressure-type digital pressure sensor array and an absolute pressure-type atmospheric pressure sensor. The 3217 high-precision, intelligent, 16-channel digital pressure sensor array produced by ScaniValve in the United States was selected for the test. The main performance indicators of the sensor array are the range of 30 PSI and an accuracy of 0.05%. The atmospheric pressure sensor is a Setra 278 from the American Sitter Company; the measuring range is 0.8–1.1 bar; and the accuracy is 0.3%. The dynamic pressure sensor is an XTL-140M-2BARA produced by American Kulite Company, with a KEA-B-1B high-frequency signal amplifier (bandwidth of 0–40 kHz); the range is 0–2 Bar; and the working mode is absolute pressure.

4. Measurement and control system

The control room monitoring and test console of this variable vane sector cascade, aerodynamic performance and transition state characteristics test are shown in Fig. 6.10, and the main program of the sector cascade test is shown in Fig. 6.11.

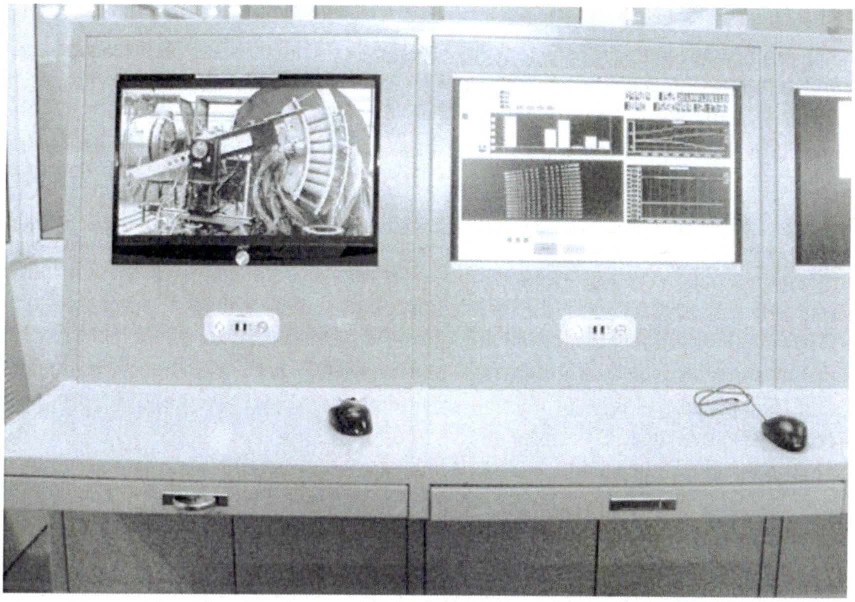

Fig. 6.10 Monitoring and test console of the test control room

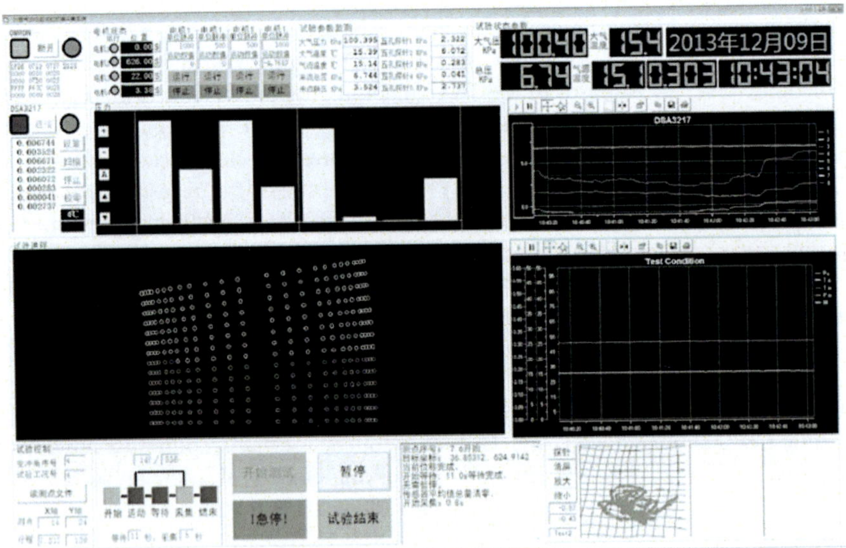

Fig. 6.11 Main program of the sector cascade test

6.2.2 *Variable Vane Sector Cascade Design*

The profile data of the experimental cascade are provided by the 703 Research Institute. After processing, the original data for numerical calculation and vane processing are generated, as shown in Fig. 6.12.

The design of the test model is processed according to the meridional profile provided by the 703 Research Institute, as shown in Fig. 6.13. The test cascade is a sector cascade; the Mach number range measured at the same time is relatively large; and the Mach number is high. Therefore, the test vane is composed of all-metal materials with high strength and is not easy to deform, which ensures that the test vane cascade has good dimensional accuracy under various working conditions. First, the three-dimensional modeling of the experimental vane model is carried out in UG software and then processed one time with a high-precision CNC machine tool. The processed vane profile has high dimensional accuracy, and the processing error does not exceed 0.05 mm.

The surface of the vane after three-dimensional, numerical control processing only needs to be simply polished to assemble the test vane. The upper and lower annular surfaces of the test cascade are completed by mechanical processing according to the design dimensions and drawings. The processing of the test transition section is composed of aluminum alloy casting, as shown in Fig. 6.14. The experimental cascade vane variable turning angle adjustment and turning angle dynamic adjustment mechanisms are shown in Figs. 6.15 and 6.16, respectively.

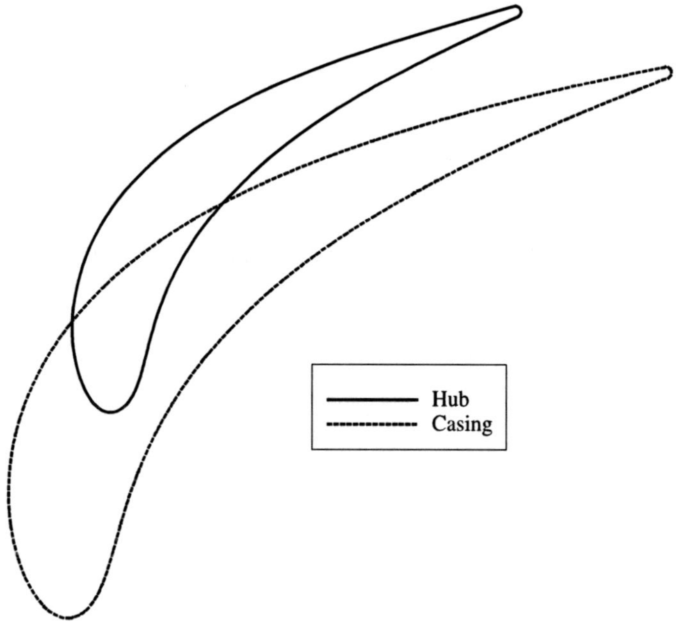

Fig. 6.12 Vane root/tip reference planar profile of the variable sector cascade

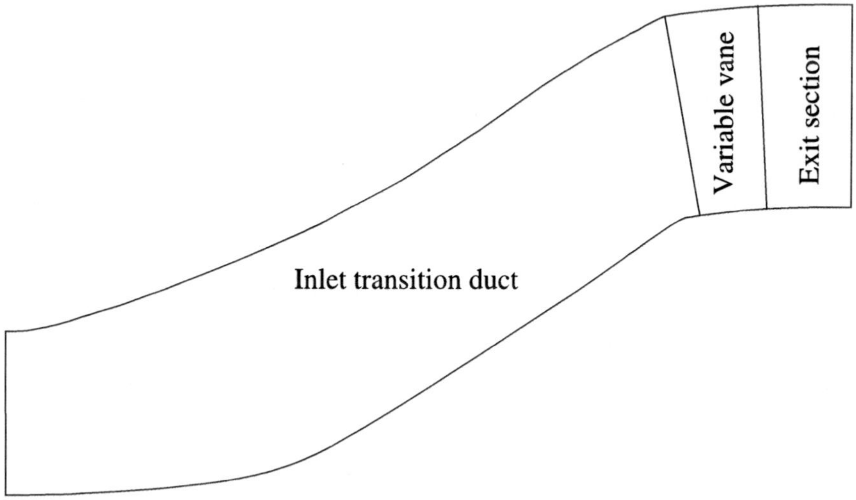

Fig. 6.13 Sector test cascade and meridional profile for the cascade

Fig. 6.14 Processing diagram of the sector test cascade

Fig. 6.15 Variable turning angle adjustment mechanism for the experimental vane cascade

6.2.3 Test Methods and Processes

1. Experimental method

According to the test requirements, for each geometric change of the test cascade, the parameters of the flow field behind the cascade under the three outlet Mach number conditions of 0.3, 0.5 and 0.6 must be measured. Note that the inlet pressures corresponding to these three outlet Mach number conditions need to be calculated and determined.

Fig. 6.16 Turning angle dynamic adjustment mechanism of the experimental cascades

The location of the measurement cross-section has an impact on the measurement results of the flow fields. If the cross-section is too close to the cascade, the development of the wake will not be sufficient. If the wake area is too narrow, the density of the circumferential measurement points will increase. However, when the gas flows out of the ends of the upper and lower endwalls of the test cascade, it will be scattered into the atmosphere. To reduce the influence of this scattered flow on the flow field at the measurement location, it should not be too close to the ends of the upper and lower endwalls of the test cascade. The cross-section of the cascade outlet flow field measurement in this test is selected to be approximately 50 mm downstream from the cascade outlet (equivalent to an axial chord length at the vane root) and approximately 30 mm from the end of the upper and lower endwalls of the test cascade.

The number and distribution of measuring points of the cascade outlet flow field have a great influence on the accuracy of measurement and the capturing ability of the flow field structure. In general, the denser the distribution of measuring points is, the better the parameter distribution of the flow field and the flow structure in the flow field can be measured. However, the increase in the number of measuring points will directly cause an increase in the test time, which will increase the test costs. In this test, according to the requirements of the preanalysis of the cascade flow field structure and test time, the arrangement of measuring points with uniform distribution in the circumferential direction and encryption near the upper and lower ends of the radial direction is adopted.

The circumferential stroke is the pitch of a test cascade. Based on 64 test cascade vanes, the corresponding center angle of a cascade pitch is 5.625° (360°/64 pieces), and 10 measurement points are evenly arranged in the circumferential direction. The angular stroke of each measuring point is 0.5625°, which can used to measure the cascade wake.

The radial size at the exit of the test cascade is 144 mm. Due to the limitation of the probe size and probe structure, the effective radial stroke that the actual probe can measure is 138 mm. Four small-distance measuring points are arranged near the upper and lower endwalls, and the distance of the measuring points is 2 mm, which can adequately measure the parameter changes at the near-endwall. There are three measuring points with a spacing of 4 mm, two measuring points with a spacing of 6 mm, and three measuring points with a spacing of 10 mm. The distance between the two measuring points at the vane midspan is 18 mm, which is a total of 24 measuring points, and the total stroke is 138 mm.

2. Experimental process

Since the five-hole probe is used for the flow field interventional measurement, the change in the position of the five-hole probe will have a certain effect on the flow field, so it is necessary to wait for a delay after the movement of the probe stops and then start to measure the parameters within a certain time. Next, the mathematical parameters of the measurement stage are mathematically averaged to reduce the influence of flow field fluctuations and accidental measurement errors. Before the test, according to the dynamic test analysis of the influence of the movement of the probe on the flow fields, a delay waiting time of 11 s is selected, and the continuous measurement time is 5 s. The initial test operation shows that an appropriate delay waiting time needs to be selected in the test.

During the test, the following test procedures were carried out:

(1) The installation angle of the cascade was determined;
(2) By adjusting the inlet pressure, the outlet Mach number conditions required by the test are achieved;
(3) The flow field parameters at the outlet of the working cascade with the installation angle are measured;
(4) After the exit section measurement is completed, step "2" is repeated to enter the next exit Mach number working condition and to continue the test;
(5) After tests of all three exit Mach number working conditions are completed, the cascade test measurement at an installation angle is completed, step "1" is repeated, the installation angle of the cascade is changed to the next measurement angle condition, and gradual measurements are continued;
(6) After all the installation angle conditions are tested, the test is completed.

As a control test, a gap-free experimental test with the design installation angle is carried out, that is, the upper and lower gaps of the cascade with the design installation angle are filled with gypsum to form a gap-free cascade test state, and the same three-exit Mach number condition measurement of the flow field at the exit cross section is carried out.

6.2.4 Typical Experimental Results

The flow field of the inlet rectification section before the transition section of the test piece is tested for the parameter distribution along the radial direction. The measurement results show that the thickness of the inlet boundary layer is limited to 10% near the endwall, as shown in Fig. 6.17.

Figures 6.18, 6.19 and 6.20 give typical test results for variable vane sector cascades. The test results show the typical structure of the cascade outlet flow field: the wake area and the upper and lower passage vortices. The flat gap leakage vortex structure at the roots and tips of vanes can are also clearly visible. Due to space limitations, the discussion of the results will not be repeated.

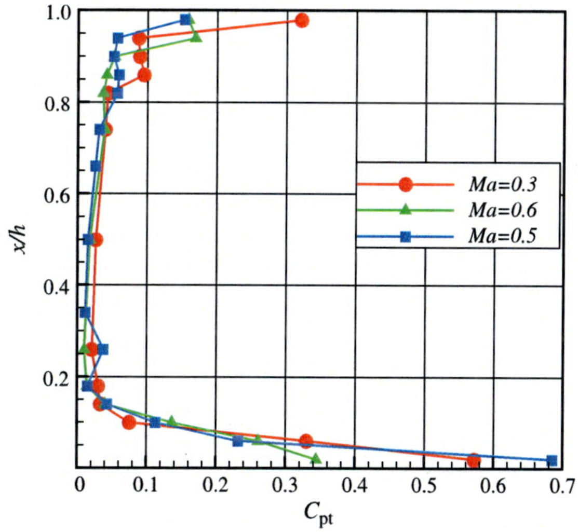

Fig. 6.17 Spanwise inflow parameter distribution of the variable sector cascade

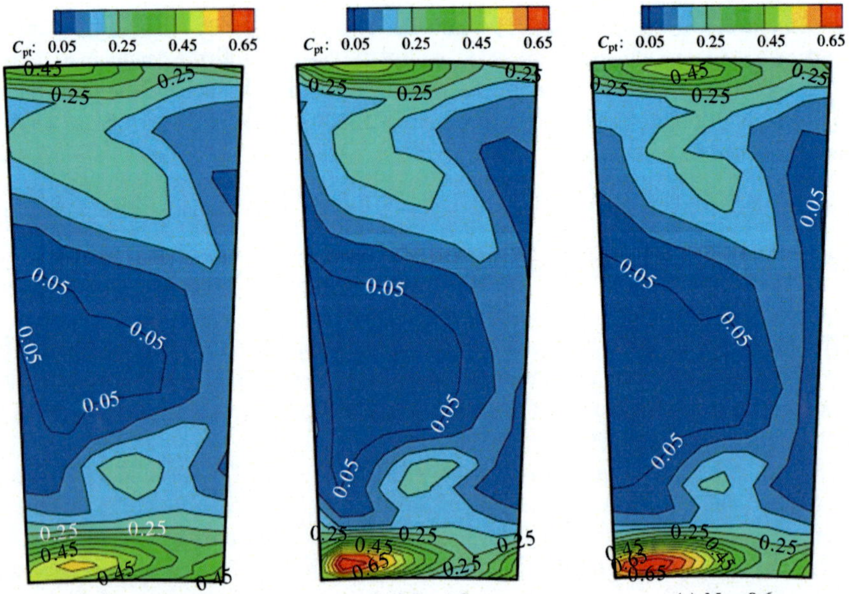

(a) *Ma* =0.3 (b) *Ma* =0.5 (c) *Ma* =0.6

Fig. 6.18 Variable sector cascade outlet total pressure loss distributions

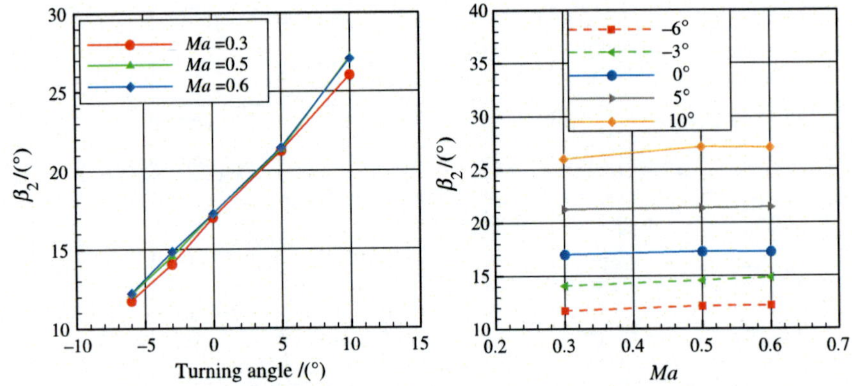

(a) Vane turning angle (b) Outlet Mach number

Fig. 6.19 Variable sector cascade outflow angle distributions

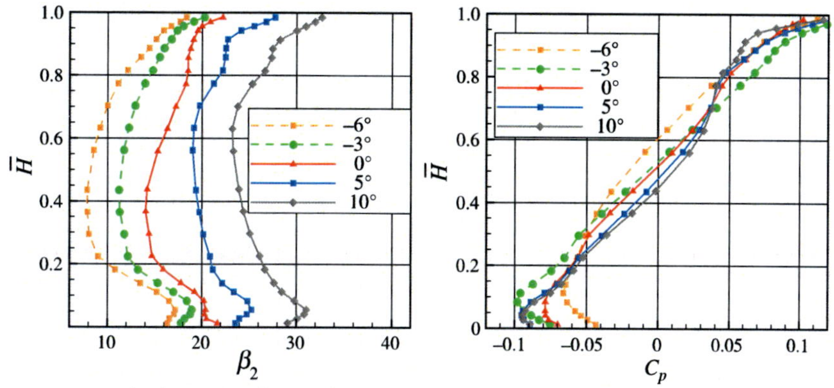

(a) Average outflow angle (b) Static pressure coefficient

Fig. 6.20 Variable sector cascade outflow angle and static pressure coefficient distribution along the spanwise direction at Mach number of 0.3

6.3 Aerodynamic Performance Test of the Variable Vane Turbine Stage

When a turbine is operated at high temperature, high pressure and high rotational speed, the flow of gas in the turbine is a complicated, unsteady, viscous, three-dimensional complex flow. Usually, the designed turbine must be tested for aerodynamic performance on the turbine tester. The test turbine may be a single-stage turbine, a multistage turbine, a full-size turbine, or a model turbine. Due to the limitation of the compressor air source and the power absorption of the hydraulic dynamometer, it is currently difficult to conduct a full-temperature and full-pressure test of the turbine, and only the aerodynamic simulation test can be carried out. The theoretical basis is a similar theory. In this section, through the aerodynamic performance test of the variable vane turbine stage, the aerodynamic performance curve of the variable geometry model turbine stage is obtained, the turbine aerodynamic performance test verification is completed, and the turbine aerodynamic characteristics of the variable vane under different vane turning angle conditions are analyzed.

6.3.1 Turbine Stage Test Device and Test Piece

1. Test device

The turbine performance test rig is a model turbine test rig that heats compressed air to drive a turbine test piece. The compressed air is provided by the air source, and after being heated by the heating system, the model test turbine is driven to perform the

Fig. 6.21 Physical picture of the turbine test bench

turbine aerodynamic performance test. The system of the supertransonic counterrotating turbine test bench includes the following components: (1) Test bench body; (2) Compressed gas source system (including air supply pipeline and control valve); (3) Fuel and heating system; (4) Lubricating oil system; (5) Circulating cooling water system; (6) Electrical control system; (7) Conventional test instruments; and (8) Data acquisition and analysis system. The main body of the test bench includes test pieces, couplings, reducers, eddy current dynamometers, intake and exhaust volutes, corresponding supports, small platforms, large platforms, etc. Photos of the variable geometry turbine performance test rig are shown in Fig. 6.21.

2. Test piece

1) Structural design

The entire model turbine test piece is composed of an air intake casing, a test casing, an intermediate casing, a turbine rotor assembly, an exhaust casing, a bearing housing, etc., as shown in Fig. 6.22. The working blade adopts an integral blade disc structure; the impeller disc and turbine shaft are centered by a small interference fit of the cylindrical surface; the nut is compressed; and the straight tooth involute spline transmits the twist. The rotation direction of the rotor of the test piece is counterclockwise when viewed in the direction of airflow; the rotor adopts a cantilever support method of 0-1-1; a cylindrical roller bearing is arranged at the front; and two ball bearings are arranged at the rear, which is a rigid support structure. Because the aerodynamic axial force received by the rotor is within the bearing load range, the setting of a balanced axial force system is omitted. The front and rear bearings share a chamber and are installed on a bearing seat, which is conducive to ensuring the coaxiality of the front and rear bearing seats and to reducing the vibration of the test piece. The cooling method of spraying lubricating oil on the bearing is adopted; the bearing seat is equipped with an oil inlet and return system, a ventilated sealing structure, and an oil blocking and sealing structure to prevent oil leakage. Torque is transmitted between the rotor of the test piece and the test equipment through a floating shaft.

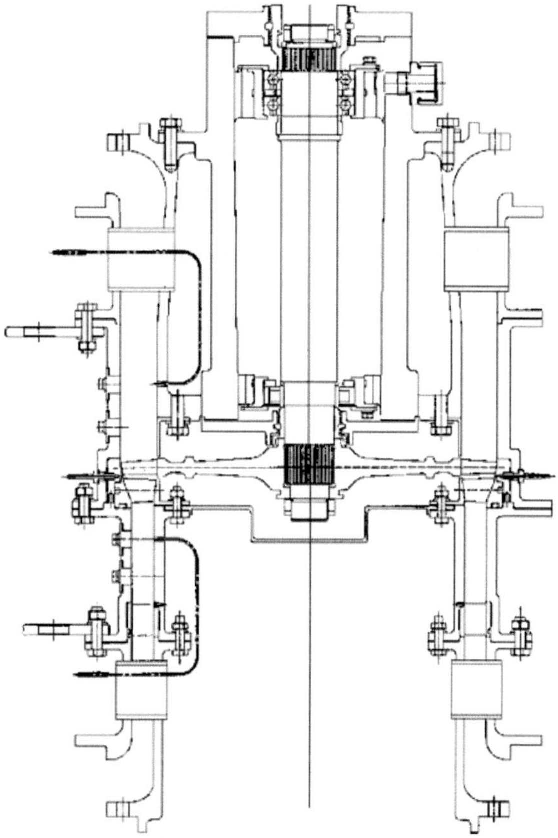

Fig. 6.22 Variable geometry turbine test piece structures

According to the function and assembly requirements of each component of the test piece, it is divided into three major components, namely, the intake section assembly, exhaust section assembly and turbine rotor assembly:

(1) The intake section assembly consists of the outer intake casing, inner intake casing, transition section assembly, first-stage vane and front section of the intermediate casing. The transition section assembly is formed by welding the support plate and fairing to the outer casing of the transition section and the inner casing of the transition section. The mounting surface is processed in the assembly to ensure the assembly requirements. The outer and inner casings of the intake, the first-stage vane and the front section of the intermediate casing are installed on the transition section assembly through centering of the straight face, axial positioning of the end face and bolt tightening.
(2) The exhaust section assembly consists of the rear section of the intermediate casing, the internal and external casings of the exhaust, the bearing housing and the secondary vane. The exhaust inner and outer casings are welded into a component through the support plate. The rear section of the middle casing

Table 6.1 Material selection and technological analysis of newly processed parts

Part name	Material	Processing technology	Technology feasibility
Variable vane	2A70	Forging, CNC milling vane technology	Mature and stable
Vane disk	1Cr11Ni2W2MoV	Forging, CNC milling vane technology	Mature and stable
Casing	20A	Forging, conventional machining	Mature and stable
Turbine shaft	40CrNiMoA	Forging, conventional machining	Mature and stable

and the outer casing of the exhaust are centered by the straight mouth, the axial positioning of the end face and the bolt tightening. The secondary vane and bearing seat are centered on the straight face; the end face is axially positioned; and the bolts are tightened and fixed on the exhaust inner casing.

(3) The turbine rotor assembly consists of the turbine shaft, working blade disk, front grate ring, adapter sleeve teeth, etc. Among them, the working blade disk is connected to the turbine shaft through a straight-tooth involute spline; the front grate ring seal strict grate tooth structure is changed to a stepped form, which lengthens the axial length of the grate tooth and enhances the sealing effect; and a sealing grate structure is added to the adapter sleeve so that it can seal the oil cavity while transmitting torsion, reducing the number of parts.

According to factors such as the working conditions of the parts and the applicable process forming methods, materials are reasonably selected, and inexpensive and mature materials are employed. The material selection and process analysis of the main parts of the variable geometry turbine test piece are shown in Table 6.1.

2) Calculation of axial force strength and vibration

The axial force of the variable vane stage variable geometry turbine rotor consists of two parts: the rotor blade axial force and disc cavity axial force. Both parts need to be separately calculated and confirmed. Only the temperature load and centrifugal load are considered in the strength calculation of the working blade disk. Because the aerodynamic load is small, this calculation is not considered. Because the working blade disk has the characteristics of cyclic symmetry, the finite element calculation intercepts the cyclic symmetry section that contains a completed blade and imposes cyclic symmetry constraints on it. The strength calculation of the working blade disk in the maximum speed state, including the design state and overrotation state, needs to be separately calculated and confirmed. In general, the strength is determined based on the above calculation results, regardless of whether the strength of the blade disk is sufficient.

The model turbine test piece rotor is mainly composed of a turbine shaft, an impeller disk, and a grate ring. The entire rotor adopts a cantilever support method of 0-1-1; the front fulcrum adopts a roller bearing; and the rear fulcrum adopts 2 angular

Table 6.2 Turbine disk evaluation criteria

Frequency order	Margin requirement (%)
1	≧15
2–4	≧18

contact ball bearings. According to the requirements of the turbine disk frequency margin evaluation standard (refer to Table 6.2), the vibration characteristics of the rotor are analyzed. The natural frequency of the working blade disk and the frequency margin of the working blade disk are confirmed by calculation. The critical rotational speed and margin of the rotor also need to be calculated and confirmed, including the front support stiffness of the rotor and the rear support stiffness, to ensure that the margin of the critical speed of the rotor meets the requirements of the design criteria.

6.3.2 Turbine Stage Performance Test

1. Variable geometry turbine test arrangement

1) Arrangement of measuring points

A schematic of the test section of the model turbine is shown in Fig. 6.23. Table 6.3 shows the main aerodynamic parameters (obtained by three-dimensional viscosity calculation) of each section in the test design state for test reference.

2) Various cross-sectional dimensions and probe arrangement and requirements

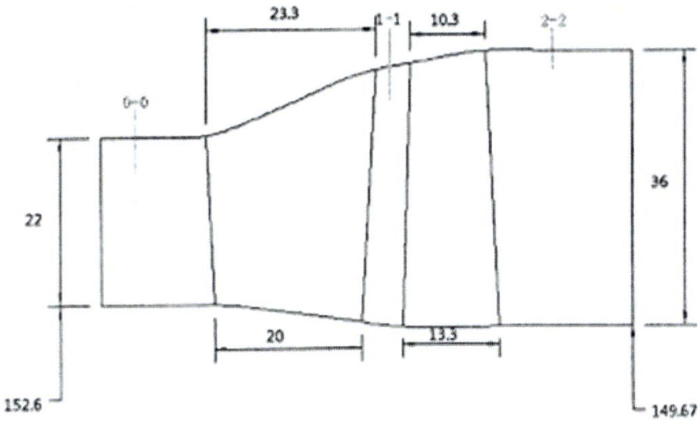

Fig. 6.23 Schematic of the model turbine test section

Table 6.3 Sectional parameters of turbine design points

Section	Before the vane	After the vane	After the rotor
Section code	0–0	1–1	2–2
Total pressure (MPa)	0.2	0.194	0.103
Total temperature (K)	300	300	252.9
Absolute flow Mach number at midspan	0.310	0.8	0.3
Absolute outflow angle α (°)	25	−71	−3

Notice The flow direction is the angle between the gas flow and the axis, and the flow parameters in front of the outlet struts are the parameters without considering the rectifying cascade

(1) 0–0 section

The measuring points of the inlet channel are arranged along the radial torque. There are 3 total pressure tubes, each with 3 points of static pressure. There are 2 total temperature tubes, each with 2 points of static pressure. The inner wall and outer wall each have 3 points of static pressure. The axial position of the static pressure measurement point is identical to that of the total pressure measurement point. The inlet is axial air intake, and the direction of air flow is not affected by state changes. The inlet Mach number is determined by the inlet flow channel area and the flow rate of the model turbine.

(2) Section 1–1

The outlet section of the turbine vane is arranged with 3 points of static pressure on the outer wall, and 3 points of static pressure are distributed in the circumferential distribution.

(3) Section 2–2

The measuring points of the turbine outlet channel are arranged in the radial direction according to an equal ring surface. There are 3 total pressure pipes, each with 3 points of static pressure. There is 1 total temperature tube, each with 3 points of static pressure and 1 point of platinum resistance. There is 1 total pressure pipe, each with 3 points of static pressure. The outer wall has 3 points of static pressure, and the inner wall has 4 points of static pressure. The axial position is identical to that of the outlet total temperature and the total pressure measuring points.

2. Test measurement parameters and data collection

1) Test system overview

The test system is designed based on the supertransonic, contra-rotating turbine test rig of the external unit. The test stand is a comprehensive test stand that can measure the performance of the turbine; it can be utilized as a single-rotor turbine or dual-rotor turbine. The test stand can be rotated in the same or reverse direction. In addition, the test stand can be used for single-stage turbine aerodynamic tests or multiple-stage turbine tests, in addition to sector cascade and flow function tests.

Aimed at the test bench, the test system of the hardware adopts effective test methods, and the accurate measurement of the test parameters is achieved with minimal effect on the test status. By measuring the relevant parameters of the test piece, such as temperature and pressure, real-time performance parameters, such as power and flow, are obtained. Among them, the power measurement is calculated by measuring the rotational speed and torque of the test piece. The torque measurement uses both direct measurement and noncontact measurement to accurately measure the torque of the test piece. In terms of software, the graphical programming language LabVIEW is selected for programming, and DMA parallel processing technology is adopted. The test system achieves high speed, high precision and high stability of the test and provides a very broad platform for future dynamic measurement and test upgrades.

The operation process of the test system is described as follows: the sensor converts the test signal to an electrical signal or a frequency signal, passes it to the signal acquisition module after signal conditioning, and then performs real-time display, calculation and storage of the signal. The collection process of the test system is shown in Fig. 6.24.

2) Test system hardware

(1) Parameter measurement

The test bench is mainly used to test the performance of the turbine. Through the measurement of the test parameters, such as temperature, pressure, pressure difference, rotational speed and torque, the performance parameters, such as the flow rate, efficiency and expansion ratio of the test piece, are obtained. In addition, the test system is equipped with two vibration monitoring points to monitor the vibration of the test in real time to ensure the safety of the test. The specific parameter measurement characteristics are shown in Table 6.4.

Using this test piece as an example, the corresponding sensor conditions are shown in Table 6.5.

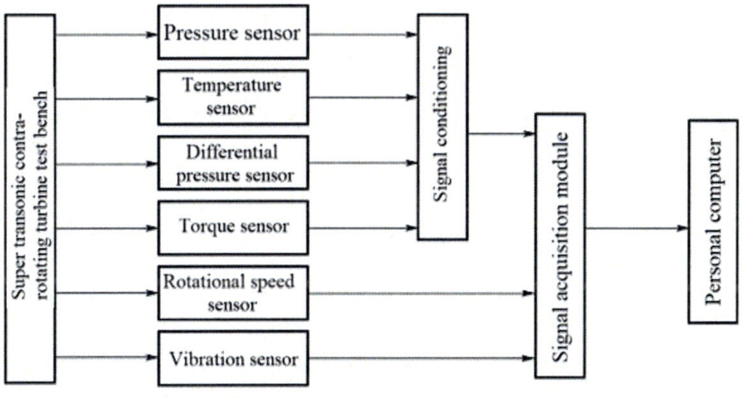

Fig. 6.24 Flow chart of the measurement system

Table 6.4 Parameter measurement characteristics table

Measurement parameters	Measuring instruments	Measuring range	Model	Accuracy
Temperature	Thermocouple	Setting	E type	±0.5 °C
	Thermal resistance	−50 to 50 °C	Pt100	±0.5 °C
	Thermal resistance	−100 to 50 °C	Pt100	±0.5 °C
Pressure	Pressure sensor	0–6 bar	8472.77.5717	0.3%
Differential pressure	Digital differential pressure sensor	0–180 kPa (adjustable)	CL-yB-2A	0.1%F S
Rotational speed	Hall gear sensor	0–25,000 r/min[a]	YM12-01BRT	±1 r/min
	Noncontact speed measurement	0–25,000 r/min	ORT-803	±1 r/min
Torque	Eddy current dynamometer	0–450 kw	PB-WC-450	±0.1%
	Noncontact torque measurement	−1000 to 1000 n m	ORT-803	±0.3%
Vibration	Vibration sensor	0–20 g	LC0105	<1%

[a]Corresponding to the rotational speed range after deceleration, the gearbox reduction ratio is set to 6.931

Table 6.5 Sensor distribution table in the test piece

Section	0–0	1–1	2–2	Total
Total pressure	3 (2 points/branch)		3 (3 points/branch)	15 points
Total temperature	3 (2 points/branch)		1 (3 points/branch) + 1 platinum resistance	10 points
Static pressure	6 points	3 points	7 points	16 points
Total pressure direction			1 (3 points/branch)	3 points

(2) Collection hardware

The data acquisition of this test system is completed by two PCI-1747U acquisition modules and one USB-4750 acquisition module of Advantec. The main parameters of PCI-1747U are listed as follows: L6 high resolution; 250 KS/s sampling rate; automatic calibration function; 64 single-ended or 32 differential analog input or combined input mode; unipolar/bipolar input range; 1 K sampling FIFO universal PCI bus for AI; bus master DMA data transmission; and Board ID switch. USB-4750 is an isolated digital I/0 module with a USB bus. The main features of the 32-channel isolation and protection digital I/0 USB module are listed as follows: compatibility with USB1.1/2.0; bus power supply; 16-channel isolation protection DI and 16-channel isolation protection D0 channel; high voltage isolation protection (2500 Vdc); input channel supporting 5–40 Vdc isolation protection; interrupt handling; timer/counter; suitable for DIN rail installation; and locking USB cable for tight connection. The platform for data collection and real-time processing is a personal computer. The specific configuration is an Intel Celeron E1400 processor, clocked at 2 GHz, 1 GB memory, and 160 GB hard drive.

(3) Test system software

The test software system is written in the graphical language LabVIEW, taking advantage of the graphical and modularity of LabVIEW and combining DMA high-speed processing technology and TDMS binary high-speed storage technology to achieve real-time display, calculation and storage of data. After the physical parameters of the test piece are connected to the computer, the performance parameters of the test piece are displayed, calculated and stored in real time.

(4) Test monitoring operation parameters

The test monitoring operating parameters are shown in Table 6.6.

3. Test process and test procedures

The running status of the test piece and test equipment are checked, including checking whether the water supply system, oil supply system, mechanical operation of the test piece, control system, test system, emergency oil supply system, emergency water supply system, emergency master switch, etc., are properly working. In addition, to keep the turbine expansion ratio unchanged, the load of the dynamometer was adjusted, the turbine's relative reduced rotational speed design was 0.5, 0.6, 0.7, 0.8, 0.9, 1.0, and 1.05, and the relative reduced rotational speed error was kept within ±0.01. After the turbine working state is stabilized, each parameter is sampled and measured, and the sampling time of each state point is approximately 30 s. In this

Table 6.6 Test monitoring operation parameters

Turbine bearing oil return temperature	<70 °C	Regulation: <110 °C
Oil supply temperature	<50 °C	Regulation: 35–50 °C
Transmission oil return temperature	<70 °C	Regulation: <100 °C
Test turbine vibration	Acceleration < 2 g	Regulation: <5 g
Gearbox vibration	Acceleration < 2 g	Regulation: <5 g
Eddy current dynamometer cooling water pressure	0–0.05 MPa (Gauge pressure)	
Cooling water return temperature	<60 °C	
Turbine test overrotation protection speed	<8000 r/min	
Power failure emergency oil supply system	Normal	
Power failure emergency gas shut down system	Normal	

way, the status points at other expansion ratios and different reduced rotational speeds are obtained, measured and recorded.

After stopping, the inlet guide vane is replaced, and the previous work after installation is repeated, including checking equipment and measuring. The test console and test monitoring platform are displayed on separate screens. The control and test personnel strictly followed the test requirements and monitored the test data to ensure test safety. Requirements: bearing temperature is less than 120 °C; turbine oil return temperature is less than 100 °C; dynamometer return water temperature is less than 60 °C; vibration G is less than 5 g; and rotational speed is less than 8000 r/min.

After the test was completed, it was normally stopped according to the test regulations. For details, please refer to the operation manual and specifications of the turbine test stand.

4. Data processing methods

The power of the turbine is transferred to the gearbox through the noncontact torque measurement sensor, where the gearbox transmission ratio is 6.931, and then consumed by the dynamometer, disregarding the mechanical loss of the turbine's bearings. There are many losses, such as bearings and couplings; thus, the mechanical loss test is carried out for this test piece. The test is defined as follows:

The rotational speed of the noncontact torque measuring sensor and dynamometer are n_{sensor} and $n_{\text{dynamometer}}$, respectively; the torque is $M_{T,\text{sensor}}$ and $M_{T,\text{dynamometer}}$, respectively; and the power is N_{sensor} and $N_{\text{dynamometer}}$, respectively. Therefore,

$$N_{\text{sensor}} = M_{T,\text{sensor}} n_{\text{sensor}} \pi / 30{,}000 \tag{6.1}$$

$$N_{\text{dynamometer}} = M_{T,\text{dynamometer}} n_{\text{dynamometer}} \pi / 30{,}000 \tag{6.2}$$

Mechanical efficiency is defined as:

$$\eta_{\text{mechanical}} = N_{\text{dynamometer}} / N_{\text{sensor}} \tag{6.3}$$

Based on past experience, a mechanical efficiency of 0.97 is applied.

The arithmetic averaging method is used to process each section parameter. Taking the inlet total pressure of the turbine as an example, the inlet has a total of 3 probes. Each probe measures the pressure at 2 positions in the radial direction, and a total of 6 measuring points are obtained. The inlet total cross-section pressure is:

$$P_0^* = \frac{\sum_{i=1}^{\sigma} P_{0i}^*}{\sigma} \tag{6.4}$$

5. Test error analysis

1) Flow formula (orifice plate flowmeter)

$$G = a\varepsilon \frac{\pi}{4} d^2 \sqrt{2\rho_1 \Delta P} \tag{6.5}$$

$$\rho_1 = P_1/(29.27gT_1) \tag{6.6}$$

$$G = a\varepsilon\frac{\pi}{4}d^2\sqrt{2\rho_1 \Delta P P_1/(29.27gT_1)} = K\sqrt{\frac{\Delta P P_1}{T_1}} \tag{6.7}$$

Relative mass flow error:

$$\frac{dG}{G} = \frac{1}{2}\left(\left|\frac{\partial \Delta P}{\Delta P}\right| + \left|\frac{\partial P_1}{P_1}\right| + \left|\frac{\partial T_1}{T_1}\right|\right) \tag{6.8}$$

$$\frac{dG}{G} = \frac{1}{2}\sqrt{0.05\%^2 + 0.05\%^2 + 0.17\%^2} = 0.092\% \tag{6.9}$$

The pressure difference adopts a piston-type pressure gauge, and the accuracy reaches 0.05%. The gas source temperature is 300 K; the temperature sensor measurement error is ± 0.5 K; and $|\partial T_1/T_1|$=0.17%.

2) Expansion ratio

$$\pi_{\mathrm{t,exp}} = P^*_{\mathrm{in}}/P^*_{\mathrm{out}} \tag{6.10}$$

Relative error of expansion ratio:

$$\frac{d\pi_{\mathrm{t,exp}}}{\pi_{\mathrm{t,exp}}} = \left[\left|\frac{1}{P^*_{\mathrm{out}}}\partial P^*_{\mathrm{in}}\right| + \left|P^*_{\mathrm{in}}\frac{1}{(P^*_{\mathrm{out}})^2}\partial P^*_{\mathrm{out}}\right|\right]/\pi_{\mathrm{t,exp}} = \left|\frac{\partial P^*_{\mathrm{in}}}{P^*_{\mathrm{in}}}\right| + \left|\frac{\partial P^*_{\mathrm{out}}}{P^*_{\mathrm{out}}}\right| \tag{6.11}$$

$$\frac{d\pi_{\mathrm{t,exp}}}{\pi_{\mathrm{t,exp}}} = \sqrt{0.2\%^2 + 0.2\%^2} = 0.28\% \tag{6.12}$$

3) Turbine power

$$N = \frac{2\pi n}{60}M_t \tag{6.13}$$

Turbine power error: if the turbine rotational speed is 10000 r/min, the dynamometer speed is approximately 1440 r/min.

$$\frac{dN}{N} = \left|\frac{\partial n}{n}\right| + \left|\frac{\partial M_t}{M_t}\right| \approx \sqrt{0.1\%^2 + \left|\frac{\pm 1}{1440}\right|^2} \approx 0.12\% \tag{6.14}$$

4) Turbine efficiency

$$\eta^*_T = \frac{N_{\mathrm{exp}}/(\eta_{\mathrm{mechanical}})}{G_{\mathrm{exp}}\frac{k}{k-1}RT_{t0,\mathrm{exp}}(1 - 1/\pi^{0.286}_{t,\mathrm{exp}})} \tag{6.15}$$

Turbine efficiency error:

$$\left|\frac{d\eta_T^*}{\eta_T^*}\right| = \left|\frac{\partial N}{N}\right| + \left|\frac{\partial G}{G}\right| + \left|\frac{\partial T_{\text{in}}^*}{T_{\text{in}}^*}\right| + \left|\frac{0.286\pi_{\text{t,exp}}^{-0.286}}{1-\pi_{\text{t,exp}}^{-0.286}}\frac{\partial \pi_{\text{t,exp}}}{\pi_{\text{t,exp}}}\right| \tag{6.16}$$

The inlet temperature is 300 K; the measurement error of the temperature sensor is ±0.5 K; and $|\partial T_{\text{in}}^*/T_{\text{in}}^*|$=0.17%. The turbine efficiency is approximately 0.90; the expansion ratio is approximately 1.914; and the turbine efficiency error percentage is:

$$d\eta_T^* = \pm 0.90\sqrt{(0.12\%^2 + 0.092\%^2 + 0.17\%^2 + 1.4^2 * 0.28\%^2)} \approx \pm 0.5\% \tag{6.17}$$

The percentage of turbine efficiency error is ±0.5%.

6.3.3 Typical Experimental Results

Some variable vane turbine-stage aerodynamic performance tests are shown in Figs. 6.25, 6.26 and 6.27. Due to space limitations, the discussion of the results will not be repeated.

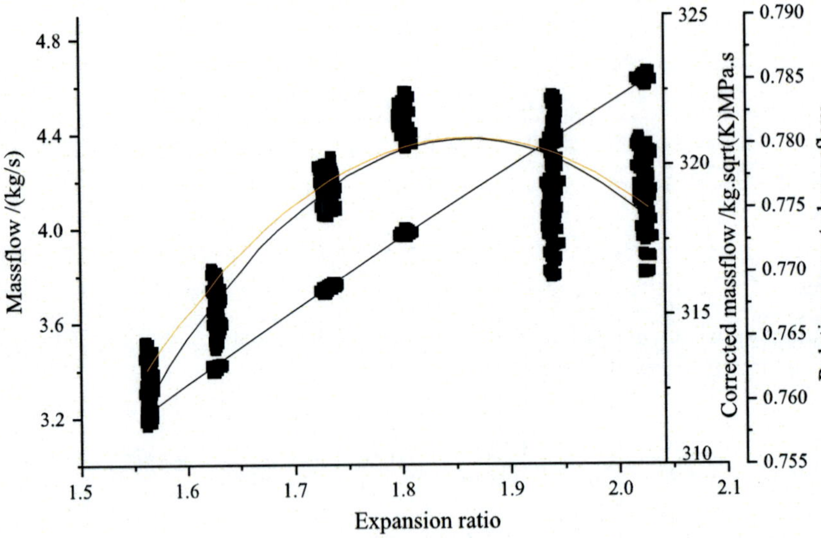

Fig. 6.25 Test flow rate at relative rotational speed $n = 0.6$ at a $-5°$ turning angle

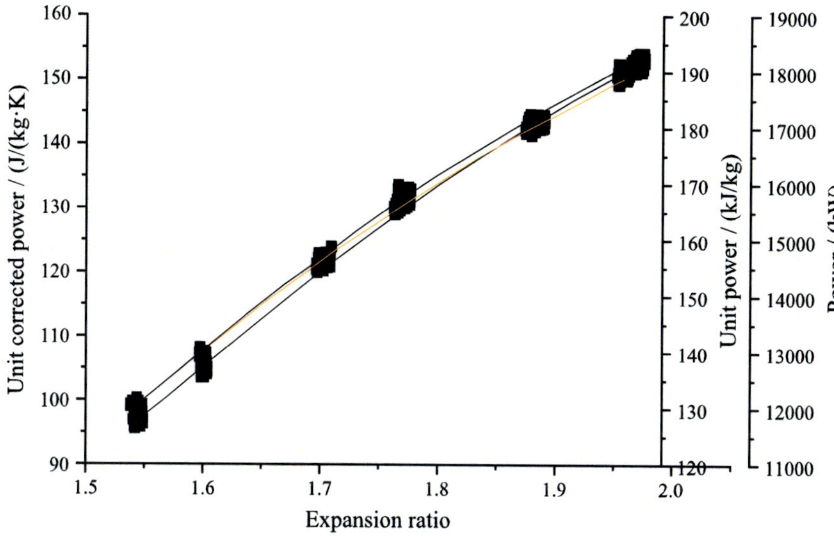

Fig. 6.26 Power at relative rotational speed $n = 1.0$ at a 0° turning angle

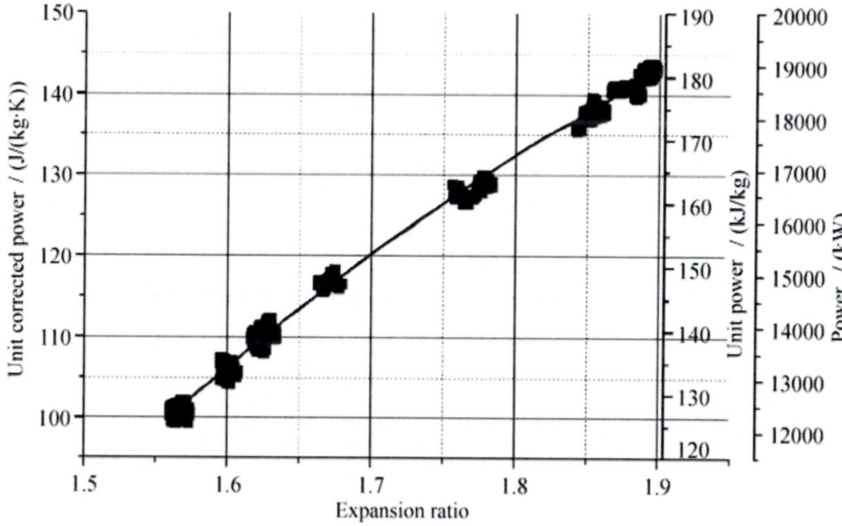

Fig. 6.27 Power at relative rotational speed $n = 1.05$ at a +2° turning angle

6.4 Thermal Environment Structure Validation Test for a Full-Loop Variable Vane

The variable geometry turbine (whole ring) structure verification component is composed of casing components, variable vanes, guard plates, linkage devices, flexible graphite gaskets and bushes, cooling air systems, control system devices, etc. The linkage and control system work together to adjust and control the turning angle of the variable vane. A cooling air system is utilized to measure the amount of air leakage at the tip of the variable vane. The gas temperature in the flow part of the whole device is approximately 800 °C, and the external wall temperature is approximately 400 °C. The purpose of the test is to verify the reliability of the overall structure of the variable geometry turbine.

6.4.1 Thermal Environment Experimental Device and Test

1. Design and processing of the cooling water jacket of the transfer section of the test device

The material of the cooling water jacket is 304 stainless steel; the outer wall thickness is 10 mm; and the inner wall thickness is 4 mm. The cooling air pipe is connected through the inner and outer walls. The water supply pipe is connected to a high-pressure hose. The connection between the transfer section and the test piece is sealed with a graphite spiral gasket. The structure of the cooling water jacket is shown in Fig. 6.28.

2. Commissioning of measurement and control components of hydraulic pump station

The variable geometry turbine test piece applies a tangential force to the rotating ring through the hydraulic transmission device and then drives the variable vane to rotate through the linkage device. In the experimental study, the restoration of the hydraulic pump station measurement and control components and the adjustment of the hydraulic stroke are completed under cold conditions. Figures 6.29 and 6.30 show the hydraulic transmission systems employed in the test. During the test, the force transferred to the transmission ring was adjusted by adjusting the outlet pressure of the hydraulic pump, and the relative position of the pointer on the piston and the stroke switch was adjusted to match the stroke of the piston rod with the required displacement of the variable geometry vane.

Figure 6.31 shows the variable vane turning angle measuring device of variable geometry turbines. The dial is coincident with the center of the turning shaft of the variable vane, and the dial is fixed on the turning shaft of the variable vane. During the test, the variable vanes are required to change between $-10°$ and $+10°$. Therefore, by adjusting the piston rod stroke and the relative position of the pointer during the debugging process, the variable vane displacement meets the specific requirements of the test.

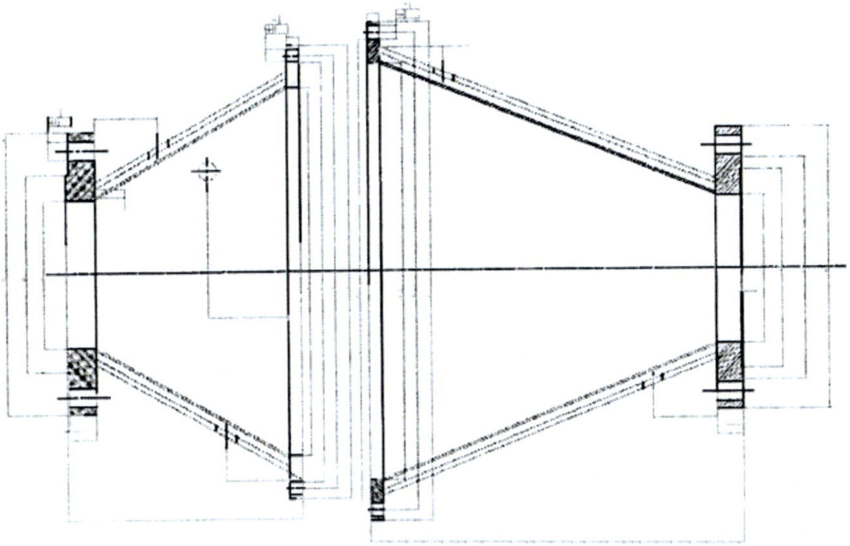

Fig. 6.28 Structure diagram of the cooling water jacket in the transition section

Fig. 6.29 Hydraulic pump

3. Introduction of test equipment

The variable geometry turbine structure verification test is completed at the Harbin Engineering University Chemical Regeneration Test Bench. The test system is shown in Fig. 6.32. The test bench mainly includes the air source, voltage stabilizing tank, combustion chamber, test section, air preheater, fuel pipeline, gas pipeline, cooling air pipeline and cooling water pipeline.

Fig. 6.30 Hydraulic cylinder

Fig. 6.31 Variable vane turning angle measuring device

According to the working substance classification, the test bench is composed of four parts: a gas system, cooling air system, fuel oil system and cooling water system. The gas system is provided with a three-stage, centrifugal air compressor as the air source to provide the compressed air required for the test. The flow adjustment range of the air compressor unit is 1.5–2.7 kg/s, and the rated working pressure ratio is 10. Compressed air enters the combustion chamber through the surge tank to produce high-temperature gas and is fed to the test section of variable geometry turbines.

1) Test bench air system

The air source system in the test is composed of the pipeline system of the three-stage centrifugal air compressor unit of the China Shouli Company (refer to Fig. 6.33). During the test, the outlet pressure setting value of the air compressor unit can be

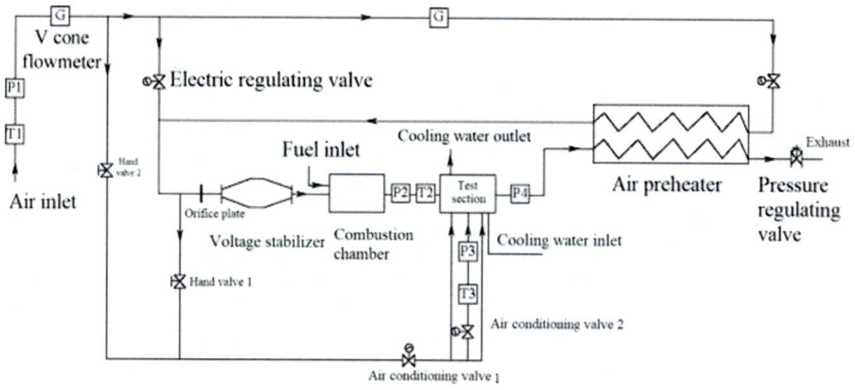

Fig. 6.32 Test bench system diagram

adjusted to ensure that the inlet pressure of the test piece meets the test requirements, a high-temperature regulating valve is set in the exhaust line to adjust the gas flow, and an air-gas heat exchanger (refer to Fig. 6.34) is installed in the test system to ensure that the cold air temperature meets the test requirements.

2) Oil supply combustion system

The fuel supply system pumps diesel out of the oil tank, first, through the low-pressure oil filter, valve and fuel flow meter, second, through the high-pressure oil filter and fuel supply valve, and last, into the test combustion chamber. There is an oil return circuit behind the oil pump, and the oil supply pressure can be electrically adjusted by the oil return valve and oil supply valve.

The fuel for starting ignition is directly supplied from the fuel tank located in the chemical recuperation laboratory. After passing through the low-pressure oil filter and electromagnetic valve, the fuel enters the starting nozzle of the test combustion

Fig. 6.33 Test bench air compressor unit

Fig. 6.34 Air preheater

chamber. The combustion chamber uses a typical marine gas turbine recirculation combustion chamber. The combustion chamber and combustion section of the fuel supply system are shown in Figs. 6.35 and 6.36, respectively.

3) Measuring equipment

The test parameters to be monitored for variable geometry turbine structure tests include gas flow, gas temperature, gas pressure, cold air temperature, and cold air flow. The gas flow rate is an indirect measurement quantity that needs to be calculated according to Formulas 6.18:

$$G_a = K\sqrt{\frac{P}{RT}\Delta P} \tag{6.18}$$

Fig. 6.35 Combustion chamber oil supply system

Fig. 6.36 Combustion section

The verified instruments include an air inlet pressure sensor, a temperature sensor, and a flowmeter differential pressure transmitter. The pressure sensor, temperature sensor and differential pressure transmitter are verified by the Heilongjiang Provincial Institute of Metrology. The pressure sensor verification accuracy is level 2; the temperature sensor accuracy is ±1.5%; and the differential pressure transmitter accuracy is level 0.5.

The measurement of gas temperature and gas pressure is arranged on the measurement section before the transition section of the variable geometry turbine cascade test piece, as shown in Figs. 6.37 and 6.38. The temperature sensor adopts the thermocouple (accuracy of 0.5%) produced by the Shanghai No. 3 Instrument Factory, and the cold air flow is measured by the precession flowmeter (accuracy 1%). All measurement parameters can be collected and recorded by the computer in real time.

Fig. 6.37 Location of gas temperature and pressure measurement

Fig. 6.38 Cooling air temperature and pressure measurement locations

4) Introduction of test piece

The variable geometry turbine (whole ring) structure verification part is composed of casing components, variable vanes, guard plates, linkage devices, flexible graphite gaskets and bushings, cooling air systems, control systems, etc. The gas temperature of the flow part of the whole device is approximately 800 °C, and the temperature of the external wall is approximately 400 °C. The components will be deformed under the action of high temperature, resulting in high-temperature gas leakage or blocking of the rotating parts. The purpose of the test is to test the reliability of the sealing structure and turning mechanism of the turbine variable vane structure under high-temperature and high-pressure conditions (Fig. 6.39).

Fig. 6.39 Test piece system installation drawing

6.4.2 Test Steps and Methods

1. Check before the test

    (1) External inspection of the variable geometry turbine variable vane test piece and the maintenance site were carried out. There should be no irrelevant objects in the test site;
    (2) The connection between the test piece and the test bench was checked to ensure that it is firm and leak-free;
    (3) The variable vane turning control system and the cooling fan of the pumping station were turned on to ensure normal operation of the vane turning under cold conditions;
    (4) The cooling water system was turned on, and the water jacket of the test piece was checked to ensure normal operation;
    (5) The working status of other pipelines and valves are checked;
    (6) The working state of the data collection system (including leakage measurement flow meter, gas intake flow measurement device, pressure test instrument, etc.) was checked;
    (7) The fixation of the variable geometry turbine variable vane test piece on the base and the bolt connection were checked to confirm that they are fully tightened.

2. Test system startup sequence

    (1) The variable vane water jacket cooling water device was started, and the valve was opened to the fully open position;
    (2) To start the variable vane turning control system, press the oil pump start button-oil pump start-press the oil cylinder work button-the oil cylinder piston rod starts to work-press the cooler button-the cooler starts to work;
    (3) The air compressor system was turned on, and cold blowing of the variable vane test piece was performed for 1–5 min;
    (4) The gas generating system was turned on by slowly raising the working conditions, and the data are recorded as needed.

3. End of the test

    (1) The ignition oil solenoid valve is closed;
    (2) The variable vane control system is turned off: the cooler stop button is pressed to stop the cooler. The oil cylinder stops working after the oil cylinder stop working button is pressed. The oil pump stop button is pressed to stop the oil pump;
    (3) To cold blow the test pipeline system, wait until the pipeline system temperature drops below 100 °C, and then shut down the air compressor unit;
    (4) The cooling water system is turned off.

6.4.3 Test Results and Analysis

1. Test record

The variable geometry turbine structure verification test is completed 5 times; the test working pressure is approximately 0.4 MPa; and the initial gas mass flow rate is 2.0 kg/s. When each test is started, the fuel mass flow is adjusted to increase the gas temperature to 500, 600, and 700 °C, and it is stabilized at each temperature point for 30 min. The gas temperature is raised to approximately 800 °C, and the number of reciprocating movements of the guide vane turning mechanism is recorded until shut down.

Figures 6.40, 6.41 and 6.42 show the working conditions of the combustion system, variable vanes and test pieces during the test. After each test is stopped and cooled, the variable vanes are randomly selected for rotation to check whether there is a bite due to thermal stresses. The first test can normally work at 500, 600, and 700 °C. When the temperature is approximately 800 °C, the outlet pressure of the hydraulic pump is appropriately increased, and the connection bolt between the piston rod and the transmission rod will break. The test is temporarily suspended but will continue after maintenance until the reliability test requirements are met. Table 6.7 shows the sample table format of the test record.

Fig. 6.40 Combustion state during the test

Fig. 6.41 Rotating mechanism control and recording system

Fig. 6.42 Surface oxidation of the test piece after the test

Table 6.7 Results of a test record

Recording time	Date			
Total temperature (°C)	500	600	700	800
Test time (min)	20	20	20	150
Start and stop time	9:30–9:50	9:50–10:10	10:10–10:30	10:30–13:00
Inlet gas flow rate (kg/s)	2	1.96	1.9	1.86
Inlet gas total-pressure (MPa)	0.4	0.4	0.4	0.4
Number of reciprocating motions of rotating mechanism	55	55	55	410
Variable vane deflection angle	−10° to 10°	−10° to 10°	−10° to 10°	−10° to 10°

2. Abnormal test conditions and their treatment

In addition to the breakage of the connecting bolt during the test, the overheating phenomenon of the cooling water occurs in the first test. The uneven distribution of the flow rate of the joint water supply of the cooling water jacket of the connecting section and the other water-cooling equipment of the test bench causes local overheating. The opening of the spray water cooler and the cooling water valve of the measuring section are adjusted on the test site, and then the cooling water flow distribution is distributed to eliminate the local overheating phenomenon. After the gas temperature is raised to approximately 800 °C, there are occasional sparks near the variable geometry turbine test section during the test. After careful observation on site, the gap clearance between the transmission ring and the test piece decreases after the temperature is increased, and occasionally, friction is produced. Because this situation does not affect the variable geometry turbine test piece, it is not addressed in the test.

3. Test piece disassembly inspection

After the test, the turbine variable vane test piece is decomposed and inspected, and the key matching dimensions are retested. After inspection, the inner and outer surfaces of the turbine variable vane casing are in good condition, and there are no friction marks at the tip and root of the variable vane (refer to Figs. 6.43 and 6.44). In addition, the ceramic turning shaft and ceramic bushing have no wear marks. The flexible graphite shaft sleeve and flexible graphite gasket are in good condition. There are slight wear marks on the joint bearing. The overall condition of the test piece is good.

4. Test conclusion

(1) Under the control system, the variable vanes of variable geometry turbines reciprocate more than 2600 times in total. The turbine variable vanes rotate flexibly under high-temperature and high-pressure conditions without jamming;
(2) The test piece has no gas leakages;

Fig. 6.43 Variable vane state before the test

Fig. 6.44 Variable vane state after the test

(3) The design accuracy of the stroke switch of the test hydraulic control system is ±0.2 mm, and the reduced deflection angle error of the variable vane is 0.2°;
(4) The test results show that the design of the overall structure and sealing structure of variable geometry turbines is reliable.

6.5 Summary

This chapter mainly summarizes the aerodynamic performance test of the variable vane linear cascade, aerodynamic performance and transient characteristics test of the variable vane sector cascade, variable vane turbine-stage aerodynamic performance test, and thermal environment structure validation test for full-loop variable vanes.

The aerodynamic and structural design of variable geometry turbines is very difficult. In the development process of variable geometry turbines, it is necessary to carry out experiments in aerodynamics, structural design and reliability to ensure the high efficiency, high reliability and maintainability under the wide operating conditions of variable geometry turbines.

Bibliography

1. Cox JC, Hutchinson D, Oswald JI (1995) The westinghouse/Rolls-Royce WR-21 gas turbine variable area power turbine design. ASME Paper 95-GT-54
2. Deng QF, Zheng Q, Liu CL et al (2011) Pressure controlled vortex design of 1.5-stage turbine based on the method of controlling axial velocity variation. Acta Aeronautica et Astronautica Sinica 323(12):2182–2193
3. Feng YM, Liu SL (2005) Numercal investigation on three-dimensional viscous flow of a variable-geometry power turbine for marine gas turbine. J Harbin Eng University 26(5):580–585
4. Feng YM, Liu SL, Liu M et al (2003) Within a multistage environment numerical analysis of the 3-D viscous flow through the turbine cascades at large incidence. Turbine Technol 45(6):347–352
5. Feng YM, Liu SL, Liu M et al (2005) Three-dimensional numerical simulation of the flow characteristics at a large incidence of the variable-geometry power turbine of a marine gas gas turbine. J Eng for Therm Energy and Power 20(5):459–463
6. Feng YM, Huang QJ, Liu SL et al (2005) Numerical investigation on the throughflow characteristiscs of a variable-geometry power turbine for marine gas turbine. Gas Turbine Technol 18(2):37–42
7. Gao J, Zheng Q (2013) Effect of squealer tip geometry on rotor blade aerodynamic performance. Acta Aeronautica et Astronautica Sinica 34(2):218–226
8. Gao J, Zheng Q, Yue GQ et al (2015) Variable geometry design of a high endwall angle power turbine for marine gas turbines. ASME Paper GT2015-43173
9. Gao J, Wang FK, Fu WL et al (2017) Experimental investigation of effects of tip cavity on tip clearance flow in a variable-geometry turbine cascade. ASCE J Aerospace Eng 30(1):04016069.1-04016069.9
10. Gao J, Huo DC, Song YK et al (2020) Numerical investigation on aerodynamic characteristics of variable geometry turbine vane cascade for marine gas turbines. ASME Paper GT2020-14853
11. Gao J, Zheng Q, Yue GQ (2012) Reduction of tip clearance losses in an unshrouded turbine by rotor-casing contouring. AIAA J Propulsion and Power 28(5):936–945
12. Gao J, Zheng Q, Liu PF et al (2016) Aerodynamic performance of a variable geometry turbine cascade using a vane-end winglet. Acta Aeronautica et Astronautica Sinica 37(12):3615–3624
13. Gao J, Zheng Q, Zhao XD et al (2017) Analysis of flow field and loss characteristics of high endwall angle variable-geometry power turbine. J Mech Eng 53(10):193–200
14. Gao J, Wei M, Liu PF et al (2018) Improved clearance designs to minimize aerodynamic losses in a variable geometry turbine vane cascade. Proc IMechE Part C: J Mech Eng Sci 232(17):3085–3101
15. Gao J, Zheng Q, Yue GQ et al (2018) Advances in variable geometry turbine aerodynamic technology for gas turbines. SCIENTIA SINICA Technologica 48(11):1141–1150

J. Gao et al., *Variable Geometry Turbine Technology for Marine Gas Turbines*,
https://doi.org/10.1007/978-981-19-6952-2

16. Gao J, Fu WL, Wang FK et al (2018) Experimental and numerical investigations of tip clearance flow and loss in a variable geometry turbine cascade. Proc IMechE Part A: J Power and Energy 232(2):157–169
17. Gao J, Yue GQ, Zheng Q (2020) Aerodynamic design and flow mechanism of marine gas turbine power turbine. Science Press, Beijing
18. Haglind F (2011) Variable geometry gas turbines for improving the part-load performance of marine combined cycles—combined cycle performance. Appl Therm Eng 31(4):467–476
19. Hu SY (1996) Variable geometry turbine and its design features. Aeroengine 3:21–26
20. Li XT (2017) Aeroderivative gas turbine design and test technology. Aviation Industry Press, Beijing
21. Lin QY, Zheng Q, Yue GQ (2007) Analysis of secondary flow vortex structure and losses in turbine cascades. J Aerospace Power 22(9):1518–1525
22. Liu SL, Feng YM, Liu M et al (2005) The flow field structure of the power-turbine variable-area nozzle stage of a marine gas turbine. J Eng Therm Energy and Power 20(2):120–124
23. Liu PF, Gao J, Niu XY et al (2017) Design and optimization of end zone of large meridional expansion adjustable blades on variable geometry turbine. J Aerospace Power 32(3):558–567
24. McCarthy SJ, Scott I (2002) The WR-21 intercooled recuperated gas turbine engine: operation and integration into the royal navy type 45 destroyer power system. ASME Paper GT2002–30266
25. Meng FS, Gao J, Zheng Q et al (2019) Numerical study of flow-heat transfer and end-zone positive tangential curve technology of large meridional expansion turbine. J Propulsion Technol 40(6):1247–1255
26. Moffitt TP, Whitney WJ, Schum HJ (1969) Performance of a single-stage turbine as affected by variable stator area. AIAA Paper 69–525
27. Ning YZ, Zhang L, Lao XL (2017) Reliability test research of variable geometry turbine. Sci Technol Innov Herald 28:96–98
28. Niu XY, Liang C, Jing XM et al (2016) Experimental investigation of variable geometry turbine annular cascade for marine gas turbines. ASME Paper GT2016-56726
29. Pearson D, Newman S (2011) The development and application of the Rolls-Royce MT30 marine gas turbine. ASME Paper GT2011-45484
30. Qiu C, Song HF (2010) Calculation and analysis of the performance of a variable geometry gas turbine. J Eng for Therm Energy and Power 25(4):377–380
31. Sun GZ, Yue GQ, Gao J et al (2017) Research on the impact of variable geometry cascade by tip slotting. J Eng Thermophys 38(2):242–245
32. Tan SW, Yue GQ, Sun GZ et al (2014) Research on flow interaction mechanism in endwall region for variable geometry turbine stages. In: 2014 annular conference of thermomechanics aerodynamics and fluid machinery of Chinese society of engineering thermophysics
33. Tooke RW, Bricknell D (2003) Propulsion systems and the MT30 marine gas turbine—the quest for power. ASME Paper GT2003-38951
34. Wen B Q, Wang B, Lu XC (2013) In: Handbook of metal materials. 2nd edn. Beijing, Electronic Industry Press
35. Weng SL, Wang YH, Song HF et al (2015) Advanced gas turbine engines. Shanghai Jiao Tong University Press, Shanghai
36. Wu S (2018) Prospect of gas turbine used as warship power plant. Modern Manuf Technol Equipm 12:204–206
37. Yang LS, Zheng PY, Nie HG et al (2013) Technology development approach discussion of high power and high efficiency marine gas turbine derived from aeroengine. Aeroengine 39(6):74–78
38. Yu HL, Feng XM (2017) Concise mechanical design manual for mechanical engineer[M]. Mechanical Industry Press, Beijing
39. Yue GQ, Li D, Zheng Q (2011) Numerical study on the influence of variable geometry turbine turning shaft structure on the flow field of variable vanes. In: 2011 annular conference of thermomechanics aerodynamics and fluid machinery of Chinese society of engineering thermophysics

40. Yue GQ, Yin SQ, Zheng Q (2009) Numerical simulation of flow fields of variable geometry turbine with spherical endwalls or nonuniform clearance. ASME Paper GT2009-59737
41. Yue GQ, Jing XX, Zhang Y et al (2012) Aft-loaded design for turbine blades. In: 2012 annular conference of thermomechanics aerodynamics and fluid machinery of Chinese society of engineering thermophysics
42. Zhao W, Li DB, Fu YS et al (2017) Research on design of variable geometry turbine guide blade and adjustment mechanism. In: Proceedings of the academic conference of the liaoning aerospace society power professional committee 2017 (20th)
43. Zou ZP, Wang ST, Liu HX et al (2014) Axial turbine aerodynamics for aero-engines: flow analysis and aerodynamic design. Shanghai Jiao Tong University Press, Shanghai